# american
# political patterns

conflict and consensus

# american
# political patterns
## conflict and consensus

### third edition

University of Tennessee **Dan Nimmo**
University of Tennessee **Thomas D. Ungs**

**little, brown and company   boston**

Library of Congress Catalog Card No. 72-9497

First Printing

Published simultaneously in Canada by Little, Brown & Company (Canada) Limited

Printed in the United States of America

COVER PHOTOGRAPHS

Front: Top, Ken Heinen, *The Washington Star-News*.
Bottom, Editorial Photocolor Archives.
Back: Top, Fred Ward, Black Star.
Bottom, Burt Glinn, © 1969 Magnum.

# preface

In the early 1960s the authors first discussed a textbook that would provide a different departure for the study of American government. We wanted to give students and teachers alike a book describing American politics and institutions by incorporating the most important findings and insights currently available from the various behavioral sciences. We sought to achieve this aim within a coherent interpretative framework and urge that underlying the discrete, seemingly unrelated events of our times consistent patterns in the way Americans handle social disputes do exist. Anyone provided with an organizing framework, we felt, could better understand both the expected and unexpected in American politics, not only during undergraduate days but throughout life as an active citizen.

Subsequent to those early discussions and our joint writing efforts, two editions of *American Political Patterns* have appeared. The response to those editions, plus the appearance of several works offering alternative interpretations, has encouraged our conviction that there was then and remains now a demand for the text we envisioned. Contemporary students are increasingly responsive to material that integrates and interprets what we know rather than inundating them under the guise of being "comprehensive," preaching to them under the guise of presenting a "point of view," or overloading them with theories about democracy that are far removed from their everyday lives.

The same spirit that motivated our earlier editions has been our guide in preparing this major revision. We have retained our basic view that it is useful to explain politics as a process by which people regulate conflicts in a society. But, reacting positively to countless students and instructors who have learned and taught from the earlier editions, we have made important changes in this version. The most apparent change to those familiar with earlier editions will be the markedly clarified language. In the interest of the student, we have tightened considerably the introductory chapter that describes our overall approach to politics. We have integrated the basic theme of conflict regulation even more carefully into our discussion, especially in Parts Three and Four. And, we have endeavored to assist the student by utilizing chapter titles, headings, and subheadings far more descriptive of the content. Finally, we have emphasized through italicized type those key points throughout the discussion that the student should keep in mind as he moves through the text.

As with the first two editions of *American Political Patterns,* we have woven the discussion of such significant matters as civil liberties and federalism into those portions of the text where they are most appropriate. But we have expanded our treatment of both topics. Thus, the theory underlying civil liberties in a democracy we discuss in Chapter Three; we treat the constitutional aspects of that topic in Chapter Four; the legal opportunities and restraints surrounding civil liberties we consider in discussing the potential for participating in politics in Chapter Five; the dimensions of organized civil action, including disobedience, we treat in Chapter Ten; and the judicial dimensions of civil liberties is one focus of Chapter Fifteen. Similarly we have described federalism in American government in separate chapters dealing with constitutional development, political participation, voting, political parties, and policy formulation.

We know of no way to achieve a consistent and well-integrated teaching tool short of a deliberate effort to link each chapter closely with every other chapter. The product of this linkage is a textbook that must be taught to achieve full effectiveness, but which can provide the essentials for applying our framework even if the student should read through it without the advantage of detailed discussions with the instructor. As with previous editions the authors do not claim this treatment of American government is either definitive or exhaustive. We strongly suggest that students interested in learning more about a topic read works specifically devoted to those matters that we introduce within our interpretative framework. To facilitate this effort we have provided again at the end of every chapter a bibliographical note citing the major works available in paperback editions.

In preparing this revision we have benefited from the advice and suggestions of many persons who were kind enough to comment upon the earlier editions after they had read, studied, or taught them. We are especially obligated to the comments of students who have possessed both the interest and willingness to talk with us or write us about our efforts. In addition we wish to acknowledge the several individuals who read the text very carefully and prepared in-depth commentaries, especially Allan Sindler who provided valuable critiques of both substance and style. We also wish to thank each of the following for critical comments on earlier editions: Norman P. Barth of Sacramento City College, Philip F. Beach of Fresno State College, Dale M. Garvey of Kansas State Teachers College, Thomas A. Henderson of Georgia State University, Frederick A. Klein of the University of Wisconsin at Milwaukee, Sheilah R. Koeppen of the University of Minnesota, Karen E. Lindenberg of Eastern Michigan University, Jerry Rankin of Bradley University, David P. Flint of Moorhead State College, and Robert B. Kennon of Sacramento Community College.

Our colleagues at various institutions have been especially helpful in various ways in providing assistance in the preparation of this volume. A special acknowledgment is due Rondal Downing who endeavored to make the Research Center at the University of Missouri-Columbia a place of healthy skepticism concerning the current orthodoxies of our discipline. Roger Durand and Greg Casey broke from tradition and experimented with the text's approach in their classes. Dean Yarwood volunteered observations on many matters. Thanks are due particularly to two colleagues, Michael Mansfield and James Combs, who demonstrate that the interests of political scientists need not be confined to strictly conventional matters.

Many people at Little, Brown and Company have been closely involved in preparing this edition. We wish particularly to acknowledge the roles played by Donald Hammonds, Basil Dandison, David Lynch (who kept the project going at a critical period), Elizabeth Bates, and Barbara Levitt. We are also grateful for the assistance of the late Gene Farmer and Marina Finkelstein.

# contents

# american
# political patterns
## conflict and consensus

# political conflict, community, and consensus in america

American government is our subject, but we have our own way of looking at it. We feel strongly that marshaling facts is no way to explain what goes on in our government. Facts are useful only when gathered to form a whole perspective that shows what all of politics is about and shows how the facts of political life fit together. We want you to see that despite the piled-up, seemingly unrelated events in our lives, really consistent patterns in human political activity can be uncovered if we know how to look for them. The student who can spot these patterns has a tool for interpreting, understanding, and evaluating what has happened in American politics and what may happen. In this book we want to give you such a tool.

Any account of American government rests upon assumptions.

We believe in making these assumptions explicit and so we begin by outlining our way of studying politics and the perspective we build throughout the book. We explain how we understand the key ideas and premises in our definition of politics: *politics is the way in which people regulate social conflict within a community.* The American community has a distinctively pluralist character and we will see how pluralist communities promote social conflict. The two primary ways of regulating conflict are representing social disputes and resolving those disputes. Each consists of recognizably patterned political activity, which we will introduce and then spell out in detail. We will describe distinctive American ways of thinking about politics, especially how much agreement, or consensus, they reach on their political values and institutions, what the popular image of politics is, and whether people must share specific values in order to have a democracy. These are the ideas that we think underlie American political patterns: conflict, community, and consensus.

# chapter 1

# political patterns: an introduction

The world of global politics includes more than one hundred independent national governments that draw up rules of conduct for nearly four billion human beings. Innumerable smaller political units, distinct in form and practice, operate below the national level. America alone has a multitude of jurisdictions which overlap more often than not: the federal government, state governments, counties, municipalities, school districts, water districts, sewer authorities, and others. Confused as we are by our complex government, we sometimes lose sight of *the common denominator of all government — people.* If units are the trees of government, people are the whole forest. We shall first consider how politics arises from the human situation and define the major terms used throughout this book that relate to the study of politics.

## politics and people

Politics is what it is because people act as they do. Although this notion is neither startling nor new, it deserves continuing reexamination and persistent emphasis.

## the human situation

*The origins of politics lie in the human situation.* Man is limited by his physical needs and social wants, yet freed by his capacities, skills, and resources. To survive he must satisfy *physical needs,* including adequate

Political activity arises from physical
needs and social wants.

food, water, clothing, and shelter. Fortunately, the human animal has the
skills necessary to survive. His hands, his reason, and his speech have
enabled him to invent the tools and technology essential to survival and
development. By communication, people relate to each other and add
*social wants* to their physical needs.

Beyond the physical needs and social wants, human beings experience
a graduated diversification of preferences. *This diversity is a significant
source of political activity.* At the simplest level, all men require food,
but they desire different foods to enjoy living. In their yearnings for self-
respect, self-esteem, and equality, individuals differ in their social desires
as well. Inevitably, it seems, they disagree over how best to realize such
desires; moreover, they have different capacities and resources (talents,
intelligence, emotional makeup, and skills) to satisfy their needs and
wants.

In sum, men differ both in their physical and social traits and in their
personal preferences. To create a safe and stable environment in which
they can get more or less what they want, people make demands upon

one another. But resources are relatively scarce — never enough, really, to satisfy everybody. Therefore tension appears between classes or groups that compete politically. This human situation, in all its diversity, is the source of social conflict and the seedbed of politics.

## universality of human conflict

*Social conflict is universal and a normal part of the political process.* Social conflict arises when three conditions are fulfilled. First, the disputants (whether group or individual) must realize that their desires differ from those of others. Second, they must try actively to get what they want. Third, they must feel that the desires are incompatible. Because resources are limited, not all interests in conflict can be satisfied. Either one disputant's gains are achieved at the expense of the other or the disputants agree to alter their desires in such a way that neither gains all he seeks nor loses all he has.

Conflicting forces attempt to gain as much from each other as possible. Yet disputants characteristically have enough in common to permit compromise. A desire pushed to the no-compromise ultimate may destroy the very community in which a group seeks legitimate acceptance of its goals, as in the Civil War. More frequently, instead of rigidly adhering to extreme demands, each side becomes resigned to accepting half a loaf in preference to winning nothing at all; this is how most labor disputes are settled. As long as compromises can be engineered to satisfy *some of the wishes of all contenders,* negotiated "settlements" (often felt to be humiliating to national pride in wars) and "ties" (odious in competitive sports) are possible and acceptable in social disputes.

Social conflict, then, is a natural part of the human situation, but *the degree of conflict depends upon the characteristics of the society* — their diversity, commitments, and habits of settling disputes. The likelihood of social conflict decreases in a homogeneous society, particularly one in which resources appear to be fairly distributed. One source of the sporadic violence in metropolitan America in the 1960s was the disparity in economic well-being between the affluent urban and suburban middle class and the underemployed, debt-ridden tenants of the ghettos. Conflict is more likely if the disputants are well organized and if members of one side or another are committed to rigid ideological postures, like the intensely dedicated supporters of Barry Goldwater's presidential candidacy in 1964. Finally, societies tend to have more enduring internal cleavages when the rules of accommodating differences either are not generally understood or are not applied (as in disturbances on college campuses when police forces sometimes refrain from attempting to restore order).

Conflict is a universal aspect of the political process. Even though it may threaten social stability it often promotes social integration and change.

Conflicts also vary in method of reconciliation, visibility, and type of goal. First, they may be face-to-face confrontations between individuals or groups, or they may be resolved by third persons. In complex societies these intermediaries are institutionalized, which means that formal organizations such as legislatures, courts, political parties, and bureaucracies deal with social conflict by bargaining, application of rules, discussion, and voting. Second, the visibility of social disagreement varies. Open and publicized conflict is taken for granted in a democracy where public examination of a group's demands and public criticism of government policies are encouraged. A more authoritarian regime has less tolerance

6

of public conflict; it tries to maintain a façade of harmonious commitment to the ruler, ideology, or national goal. Third, topics that provoke disagreement may be specific and material (higher taxes) or less concrete, more symbolic, and ideological ("roll back communism").

*Social conflict tends to be contagious and to involve increasingly large proportions of the community,* which may in turn lead to compromising a dispute. Labor-management disputes over wages and working conditions in the first half of this century and the civil rights struggle illustrate that demands made by one group are usually met by counterdemands, resistance, and opposition. Escalated demands often lead disputants to seek support from the whole community. Often the price for such support is modification of the original demands that will win begrudged acceptance on the other side of the fence — and make the demands seem more "reasonable" to new supporters who are not ideological by nature and habit. The environmental crusade headed by Ralph Nader drew increasing public awareness and support because of "Nader's Raiders," dedicated people who traveled the nation speaking to public audiences and investigating environmental problems. As public support grew for environmental legislation, corporations and other groups accused of being responsible for pollution launched counterattacks of their own. They sought to convince the public that they were not only "doing something" to overcome pollution but also were being accused unjustly by save-the-environment zealots. Expanding public interest and support for governmental action led to legislation creating an administrative agency to set restrictions and penalties for environmental pollution. At the same time, the counteraction of business groups softened the extent and severity of new regulations and penalties.

It must be recognized also that *conflicts may be more quickly settled by not expanding public involvement.* The ability of university administrators and student activists to accommodate their differences has been limited in some instances by broad public involvement. As the general public, alumni, and parents took a more direct interest in campus affairs, university officials and student groups were less able to compromise their differences. New demands from the public often ran counter to the positions of *both* university and student interests. These demands injected new elements into the argument, e.g., a "get tough" posture that demanded disciplinary measures and police action. The deaths of students in clashes with police on several campuses made the cost of escalated conflict terribly high.

*Conflict is closely related to social change.* Conflict may promote social stability: a product of social change, it sometimes induces further change. And, it may threaten both social stability and social change. Let us examine *each* of these points.

Conflict divides people into opposing camps. Here, demonstrators exhibit "flower power" at the 1967 march on the Pentagon.

CONFLICT AND SOCIAL INTEGRATION. Conflict divides people into opposing camps. Paradoxically, cleavage can and often does promote social integration. If a society tolerates internal conflict, people can openly join groups that promote their personal values. They look to the group for definitions of goals that should be pursued, tactics that are legitimate, and issues that are worth contesting. In the struggle for civil rights, the National Association for the Advancement of Colored People has traditionally sued in the federal courts to redress black grievances. In the 1960s, the Southern Christian Leadership Conference of Dr. Martin Luther King, Jr., utilized nonviolent protests — demonstrations, marches, sit-ins — to achieve the same goals. By joining either or both organizations, members committed themselves to seeking equality of opportunity *within the existing community.* Conflict with current community practices thus served as an indirect means of displaying loyalty to the community itself.

SOCIAL CONFLICT AND SOCIAL CHANGE. The presence of dispute reminds us that changes are taking place in society and that emerging groups are pushing to achieve goals not necessarily accepted as part of the status quo. The "student power" movement and the conflicts associated with it suggest that articulate student groups increasingly desire to influence the governing of universities. As in other historical instances, groups seeking new goals and those protecting older ways make claims upon one another. In such ways are conflict and change interlocked, with competing groups constantly challenging the status quo.

SOCIAL STABILITY AND SOCIAL CHANGE. An overly cooperative society may be stagnant; however, a highly competitive society may be crippled unless it discovers some method for adjusting social disputes before they reach flashpoint intensity. Conflicts can and do intensify; positions harden; goals become dogmatically stated and tenaciously held. Social relations grow embittered, and adversaries seek one another's downfall, both physically and socially. The costs exceed any possible rewards if conflict is pushed to uncontrollable extremes. The result can be the attempt of one side to repress or annihilate the other; it may end in the total alienation of one side from existing arrangements for regulating conflict. *Politics is one means societies use to regulate disputes and prevent internal explosions.* Before turning to that point, let us explore briefly what advantages come to people who successfully regulate their social controversies.

## universality of human community

No less universal than human conflict is the tendency of people to join together and share their experiences. This is the fact of human community. Communities result from a collective disposition of human beings that cuts across regional, racial, religious, class, or other cleavages.

The sources of community are twofold. To begin with, people associate with one another to satisfy basic physical needs and fulfill their social wants. But, "a community consists of people who have learned to communicate beyond the mere interchange of goods and services."[1] People form communities because they share beliefs and values. Although a community usually originates in the simple wish of people to be together, in time shared *beliefs* (notions of what does and does not exist, what can and cannot be expected) and *values* (notions of what is right or wrong, good or bad, desirable or undesirable) develop. In Chapters Two and Three, we shall examine the beliefs and values that underlie the American community, e.g., the commitment to the ideal of "representative government." Representative government is one of the "self-evident" values that define the ways in which people think about politics in America. Although considerable debate takes place about which political practices are consistent with representative government, the notion itself is an overriding value in the American community.

The desire to live collectively implies no agreement to forego disputes; instead, a sense of community does imply a willingness to tolerate conflict, argue in the open, and adjust differences before their scope and intensity endanger common survival. A desire to share common territory implies that driving one's antagonists from the territory is rarely a feasible remedy for social controversies (although movie and television interpretation of the American West portray this as the usual solution of the struggle between farmers and cattlemen). Civil rights disputes cannot be adjusted by removing either segregationists or integrationists from the United States, even though some Americans have proposed just that. When disputants occupy the same territory other solutions usually must be discovered.

DIMENSIONS OF THE AMERICAN COMMUNITY. Three dimensions of the American community are particularly noteworthy: the personal, social, and politico-constitutional.

First, the *personal* dimension consists of individual beliefs and values about the community. We focus upon personal beliefs and values, but we are equally interested in the beliefs and values shared by large numbers of Americans. Shared beliefs and values constitute *ideologies* or *doctrines,* such as liberal democracy, socialism, or fascism. Such doctrines are not restricted to sets of ideas that are internally consistent and accepted by all members with equal dedication. Sometimes nothing is shared more than a fundamental agreement on the worth of the community; beyond that, members can disagree sharply over values and beliefs.

Second, the *social* dimension consists of the characteristics and relationships that draw persons together in groups — groups that reach back-

[1] Karl Deutsch, *Nationalism and Social Communication* (Cambridge, Mass.: Massachusetts Institute of Technology Press, 1953), p. 65.

ward and forward beyond the lifetimes of the current membership, including persons now dead and others unborn. Here we have in mind both the socially significant attributes of Americans (age, sex, ethnic, racial, and religious affiliations) and the relations between people in a social unit (group memberships, status, privileges, occupations). Not the individuals themselves but *aggregates of individuals,* joined by shared characteristics and activities, make up the social dimension.

The third dimension of the community that interests us here is the mechanism it possesses for settling disputes; we call this the *politico-constitutional* dimension. The political aspect has to do with the people involved in settling disputes; the constitutional aspect refers to the rules (written and unwritten) which govern this process.

PLURALIST COMMUNITY. The American community is pluralist in character. In pluralist communities *several interests conflict within the community,* of which the government apparatus is only one. Our community has an intermediate layer of stable, organized group life between the family and the government. From his earliest years when he leaves the family to attend primary school, the individual associates with a host of groups — religious, military, occupational, and voluntary professional, civic, fraternal, and social groups. *These associations are the backbone of a socially diverse America.* Because they have both complimentary and incompatible interests, overlapping memberships and the existence of tension among the many groups make it difficult for one group to control the community's policymaking.

Membership in diverse groups accomplishes several things. First, as members of several organizations, individuals are not totally dependent upon one social group or political agency to advance their interests. Citizens have different ways of getting action. Second, because multiple affiliations contribute to, as well as reflect, multiple interests, there is little tendency to invest any issue of public policy with extreme emotional attachment. In a pluralist community, the inclination is to "spread interests so that few defeats need to be final disasters."[2] Single-interest politics, single-issue campaigns, and single-principle parties are supplanted by bargaining and compromise between diverse interests. Third, multiple affiliation means that groups must compete for individual loyalty; they may find it difficult to dominate the behavior of their own membership. Union members who vote against a candidate endorsed by their local and doctors who support an expanded government health insurance program opposed by the American Medical Association illustrate the tendencies

[2] Rockefeller Brothers Special Studies Project, *The Power of the Democratic Idea* (Garden City, N.Y.: Doubleday, 1960), p. 35.

of people to ignore group demands and to express their own preferences.

In Chapter Four, we shall see how government institutions in America are divided by the principles of federalism and separation of powers. These divisions separate conflict regulation among multiple and often conflicting governmental units that often correspond to the plurality of social groups. Governing agencies are clusters of community officials participating in the struggle of other social groups for influence.

COMMUNITY INTEREST IN A PLURALIST SOCIETY. The notions of "community interest," "public interest," "national interest," and "common good" symbolize ideals of common purpose and striving. But it is often difficult to know where the interest of the community as a whole lies, or even whether there is any such thing as *the* community interest. Because of the many conflicting groups within it, *a pluralist society can only approximate a public interest or common good.* It relies upon its social and political diversity to ensure that many points of view will be represented in the regulations of conflict and the making of public policy decisions. To a degree, the American public interest — even when it cannot be spelled out precisely — is served by the processes of government itself. Selecting community leaders by popular vote decentralizes political power and influence and allows many competing groups to reach accommodation. But *the* public interest and *the* common good are symbolic concepts used in public debate more often than they are clearly defined in the minds of individuals living in a pluralist political community.

ANTIPLURALIST TRENDS. Although we consider the United States still to be basically a pluralist society, we must be aware of social tendencies that are modifying our traditionally pluralist character. The major tendencies are: an increasing division of our society into affluent and impoverished classes; a movement toward a mass response to public issues; and a movement toward elitist rule.

AFFLUENT AND NONAFFLUENT CLASSES. A pluralist society stakes its existence upon active citizen participation in diverse groups making political demands. We would expect the pluralist character of a nation to decline in proportion as its members refrain from such active participation. In America, as in other areas of the liberal democratic world, group participation is most widespread among the more affluent middle and upper classes. Those who have to spend all their waking hours maintaining the bare necessities for existence and satisfaction — a subsistence-level job, adequate diet, medical care, housing — tend to remain outside the political process. Not sharing in the benefits of the system, they can become a cancerous sore on the body of the pluralist community. For this class,

Outside the White House, demonstrators sing "We Shall Overcome." The
American sense of community is characterized
by willingness to tolerate conflicts and by faith in being able to regulate them.

the conditions of pluralist living are absent or unpleasant. Their interests
are less diverse than those of the affluent and better educated; their
group participation is confined to single-interest organizations; their
influence on policymaking is practically zero and they know it. Therefore
their faith in democracy is challenged, and they are so apathetic about
elections that many of them do not bother to register to vote.

It is no longer possible to ignore the gulf between the affluent and the
impoverished classes in America. In the 1970s, millions of persons are
still classified as "poor" (earning less than $3,000 a year); ten to fifteen
million Americans annually suffer or die prematurely from anemia, mental retardation, or secondary infections produced by malnutrition. The
coroner's certificate never reads "starved to death," but often that is

about what has happened. Employment, literacy, school attendance, and health care rates among the impoverished are far below those of the community as a whole. The difference is especially noticeable among minority groups — black, Chicano, Puerto Rican, and other ethnic minorities — as well as among the elderly living on inadequate pensions. The existence of poverty and want is a major factor modifying the pluralist character of America.

MASS RESPONSE TO PUBLIC ISSUES. The response of Americans to public issues reveals another modification of American pluralism. In a pluralist society, group affiliations and loyalties serve as mooring points for personal choices, although they do not necessarily dictate individual choices. Public opinion is created by an exchange of points of view by different groups or individuals attempting to influence persons who have not made up their minds on a particular issue. In a long debate over an issue like the Vietnam War, this process can become an emotional crucible. But the discussion process has at least a minimal amount of rational thinking; positions and counterpositions are debated, and people do share experiences. Out of such sharing, compromise and concessions usually come.

On the other hand, if social changes in America produce an aggregate of individuals who are not held together by any body of custom or tradition or organization, the conditions for a detached and alienated mass are present. Able to communicate even with each other only in very limited ways, such individuals are forced to act separately. Choices are made on the basis of purely individual interests and activity. The result is a *mass* society whose basic community choices stem from converging individual preferences rather than from group counsel (as when Americans simultaneously blame "the Communists" for causing our difficulties in foreign or domestic policy).

The one American family in four that moves to a different location each year contributes to the forming of a mass; and this nomadic trend has implications going far beyond the advantages accruing to moving van companies. Local identifications are dissipated, and regional attachments decline in significance. The proportion of "marginal people" — those who feel themselves part of no local community, but who are constantly moving in and out of many — rises. Unlike their grandparents, a formidable number of Americans mature nowadays without local ties, lifelong friendships, permanent church affiliations, or attachments to a coterie of intimate groups — relatives, schools, neighborhoods, or local congregations. Old traditions no longer have the same political or social weight when life is "detribalized," secularized, and nationalized.

Eᴌɪᴛɪsᴛ ʀᴜʟᴇ. In an elitist community, direct, popular participation in and influence upon policymaking is necessarily limited. Policy decisions are normally made by small groups that have fairly exclusive interests and are dominated by specialized leaders. An elitist politics maintains itself by taking policy decisions deemed suitable and by building mass support through sophisticated use of the communications media. Whereas pluralist politics implies popular rule by the interaction of a wide variety of conflicting interests, elitist politics connotes rule by the few for the good of the many. Theoretically, the elite in control is fairly stable in composition and self-perpetuating. Therefore powerful interests have guaranteed influence over policy regardless of changes in elected officials, party fortunes, or constitutional procedures.

A sizable amount of literature supports the proposition that specific types of individuals exercise disproportionate influence on local and national politics. One version of the elitist thesis argues that a business-scientific-technological elite, in alliance with political officials, charts America's course to its own exclusive satisfaction. A slightly different version of this view is that a power elite dominates decisionmaking whether or not other societal interests are in the majority. Further, it is argued that, because many key members of this power elite hold nonelective positions and are unknown to the public, it is virtually impossible to hold such an elite democratically responsible.[3]

A contrary argument concedes the presence of powerful interests such as those mentioned but holds that internal conflicts within and between them make a power elite impossible. This argument stresses that the concept of a unified, impenetrable, and monolithic elite is in error because it fails to recognize that different types of elites primarily influence only their own policy areas. Timber and lumber interests throw their weight around in conservation questions, as does the Council on Foreign Relations in foreign policy; but these interests have negligible influence in other areas. In short, this view holds that *the* American elite is nonexistent; rather, there is *an elitist element,* composed of the more engaged, affluent, and concerned group leaders, who are themselves divided and who do not necessarily think about the same things at the same time. We shall discuss "political influentials" in Chapter Seven. In the view of the authors, there is no permanent interlocking directorate of American political leaders. Instead, shifting groups of political activists, who come mainly from the middle and upper echelons of society, form *a pluralist elite.*

[3] This point of view is provided in C. Wright Mills, *The Power Elite* (New York: Oxford University Press, 1957); a slightly modified and more recent version appears in G. William Domhoff, *Who Rules America?* (Englewood Cliffs, N.J.: Prentice-Hall, 1967).

## politics: regulating social conflict

Politics varies from time to time and place to place; and no single definition mirrors its many facets. Yet it is possible, by using precisely the terms employed in ordinary political discussions, to construct a working definition of politics that will contribute to our understanding of American government. For that purpose *we define politics as the most inclusive process by which social conflict is regulated in a community.* In the remainder of this chapter, we shall examine the principal terms in this working definition.

When we speak of politics as a process, we mean that it is a *pattern of human activities* related to adjusting social disputes; that is, each activity in a series is related to those that precede and follow it. To see this pattern, we must investigate how the various activities relate to one another. There is a close connection between what happened yesterday, what happens today, and what will happen tomorrow. No act is an isolated event; each is related to other actions that, taken together, form a unified whole. The patterned quality of political behavior implies that these activities are reciprocal; that is, the acts of one person are fashioned by and contribute to the political responses others make to him. One of the highlights of any national political convention is the acceptance speech of the party nominee. It is generally agreed that one of the most effective acceptance speeches was delivered by Richard M. Nixon in 1968 when the Republican Party nominated him for President. As Nixon warmed to his task, he conveyed a sense of drama to his partisans in Miami Beach; in turn, the more enthusiastic their applause and cheers, the more vigorous, emotional, and stirring Nixon's presentation became. The setting, Nixon's appearance, demeanor, and prose combined with the crowd's scent of victory in November to produce an almost magical communion between speaker and audience. Few political relationships distill so much theatrical drama into one speech, although President John F. Kennedy's eloquent inaugural address in January 1961, powerfully affected millions of Americans who had not even voted for him. All political relationships have in them the element of reciprocity — between the leader and the follower, between the governor and the governed, between two individuals who merely exchange opinions on what has just been happening.

Political *activities* range in variety from the physical act of marking a ballot to the mental effort required to think about politics and discuss it intelligently. Normally these activities are manifested by the pursuit of individual and group interests. Because no person can satisfy all his desires simultaneously, people have to put their personal preferences into a selective order and put them into an order of priority. *The disposition of persons to achieve selected aims* is a specific interest activity.

*Conflict regulation is the way in which interest disputes are adjusted within a community.* By this means, community identity is preserved and developed. Now we shall go more deeply into the two stages of regulation: *conflict representation* and *conflict resolution*.

## conflict representation

When interests are defined, confront one another, and are expressed to public officials, we call this conflict representation. The critical element of representation is the existence of avenues through which people can make known their feelings, their shared and conflicting interests, to their elected agents and governors. "Write your congressman," to be sure; but he is not the only "representative" you have in the American system. Representation thus means the activities of any person who publicizes interest disputes for community resolution — whether he is congressman, journalist, voter, lobbyist, demonstrator, picket, administrator, teacher, or student.

Conflict representation occurs in every government, but its function as a link between governors and governed is of special importance in a representative democracy. A democratic system should not only implement the desires of the governed but provide the means by which the governed can hold their governors accountable. In a democratic society, the effectiveness of democratic control depends in large measure on communications between citizens and officials. If normal channels for expressing opinions to officials are closed, or if officials dismiss a significant number of complaints sent through open channels and refuse to do anything, alternative ways of voicing grievances may be found. Thus, people who had come to the end of their patience about American involvement in the Vietnam War resorted to massive marches and demonstrations, symbolic burials of the Constitution, and draft card burnings.

Relatively unrestricted conflict representation facilitates a free exchange of political ideas and thorough debate of the issues. Political ideas, as we shall see in Chapter Two, are sometimes statements of values and beliefs widely held in the community. But political ideas are also weapons in interest conflict. They rationalize interests, mobilize support, and justify or attack the political order. Ideologies, doctrines, and myths are frequently employed to sanction political action — e.g., the monumental sacrifices made by the Soviet Union in the name of communism, the gargantuan efforts made by the United States in two world wars as a protector of democracy. Dramatic political confrontations create oppor-

Federal and state authorities
clashed bitterly over the
admission of James Meredith to
the previously all-white
University of Mississippi in 1962.
Under heavy guard,
Meredith was forcibly admitted
into Ole Miss.

tunities to manipulate ideas as symbolic appeals: "higher standard of living," the "Communist menace," "mongrelization of the races," and "black power" have served as rallying cries to advance particular interests.

In Part Three of this book, we shall describe in detail the ways in which Americans inform their governors of what is happening by participating in politics. We shall examine how Americans take part in politics, then look specifically at how social conflict is represented when they express *political opinions,* exercise *political leadership,* make *voting choices* in elections, take part in *political parties,* and state their demands through *organized groups.*

## conflict resolution

In America, social conflict is resolved when governing institutions make public policies and make the decisions stick. *Public policies* are decisions, or courses of action, agreed upon by a variety of social interests to deal with a conflict. Usually these decisions are formalized in written statutes, or laws, but this does not always come about. No written statute calls for quadrennial Republican and Democratic conventions to nominate candidates for President, yet such conventions are standard procedure. Moreover, laws on the books do not always square with the policies

18

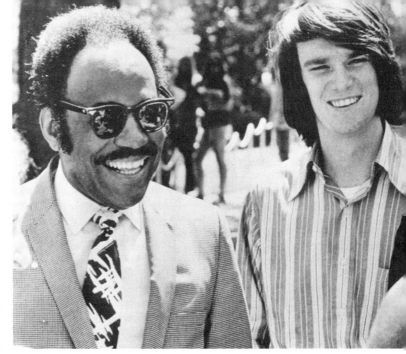

In 1972, a decade after Meredith's contested admission to the University of Mississippi touched off bloody rioting, he campaigned to unseat veteran Democrat, Senator James Eastland.

actually followed. The Eighteenth Amendment to the Constitution, effective in January 1920, made it illegal to manufacture and sell intoxicating liquor in this country. Yet law enforcement officers frequently ignored violations, and prohibition was scarcely the "law of the land." Because written statutes alone do not describe practiced policies, it is wise to keep in mind that *conflict resolution is a continuous process* that does not stop with a congressional vote or a presidential signature.

The policies intended to resolve conflict, then, are seldom definitive settlements of controversies. Rather, conflict resolution in America is better thought of as *a method of moderating social tensions to avoid community dissolution;* it is much less a way of curing social ills. The "war on poverty" pursued in the administration of President Lyndon B. Johnson produced a series of halfway measures to alleviate the plight of our most impoverished urban and rural citizens. The idea was to improve their lot sufficiently through job retraining, slum clearance, "head start" programs for preschool children, and low-cost housing, so they would "have a stake in" and not resort to violent outbursts against the community. With the heavy demands for federal spending in other areas — a war in Vietnam, farm subsidy programs, educational facilities, efforts to manage transportation, water and air pollution — this piecemeal war on poverty was a compromise between allowing conditions to worsen and committing much larger expenditures to meet the needs in all areas of poverty. In Chapter Eleven, we shall see that in poverty policies, and in many other areas of conflict, politics aims at a *modus vivendi* that keeps social disputes within tolerable limits.

CONFLICT RESOLUTION AND NEW CONFLICT. Not only is the resolution process imperfect, it frequently generates *new conflicts* if the outcome of policy controversies is disputed. During the Vietnam War, the American troop buildup made increasing demands upon the selective service system to supply new draftees. Prior to 1968, deferment procedures had been fairly liberal for young men seeking a college education, particularly for those who desired graduate and professional training. This proved a satisfactory, although not an ideal, arrangement for students who had money to attend college and for colleges and universities that depended upon a large pool of qualified students to expand their graduate programs. The burden of the draft thus fell upon the less affluent elements of the community who could not afford college.

Dissatisfaction with the selective service system led to the appointment of a presidential commission to study the problem, conflicting recommendations for change from sundry interests, and, ultimately, congressional-executive action. The new policy, designed in part to eliminate inequities in the old system, removed many young men, particularly those engaged in graduate and professional training, from the deferred category. It resolved practically nothing. This new policy drew fire from alarmed college educators and administrators, from Congressmen responding to constituents, and even from the armed services, which insisted that college graduates were unsuited for military discipline.

WHEN IS CONFLICT RESOLUTION "LEGITIMATE"? If conflict resolution is to produce effective community policy, citizens must be willing to accept community decisions as legitimate and binding. *Legitimate policies are those people feel they should obey.* Two sources of this feeling exist.

*First,* people may obey because they fear that, if they refuse, *force* will be used against them. Overt force actually may never be employed, but the threat of severe punishment or deprivation (jailing, death) is frequently sufficient. However, if the desire to disobey in pursuit of individual or group interests outweighs the statutory penalties, force has limited effectiveness. Civil disobedience and racial protests (violent and nonviolent) are evidence that neither imprisonment nor brutality always promotes compliance with the letter of the law. Frequently, however, compliance is achieved where force is neither employed nor threatened. This suggests a *second* source of political legitimacy, which is *consent*. Derived from an understanding between citizens and officials, consent is given when people agree to government according to specified rules and conditions. These may be written or unwritten, or manifested in traditions, habits, political doctrines, institutions, and ceremonies. To gain consent, government often substitutes the carrot for the stick, holding out the possibility of benefit instead of the threat of force. Such benefits may be tangible or symbolic. A decision to build a multi-million-dollar factory in an urban ghetto, with open employment policies, would have immediate tangible, economic, social, and political repercussions for local residents. Symbolic benefits seemingly lack direct relevance to people's lives, but they are crucial in determining the support people will give to community policy. For example, court decisions and statutes have declared racial restrictions on sale and occupancy of housing illegal, and political and group leaders have given much verbal support to the principle of "open housing." In some instances, the statutes and court rulings have been enforced; nevertheless the concept of "open housing" remains substantially a symbolic principle in the rule book of democratic equality. It is still an important one. If few blacks have been able to move into white suburbs because of the absence of real opportunity to purchase such property, the appearance of equal opportunity in housing may provide sufficient satisfaction for racial and ethnic minorities to remain reconciled to community policy.

As with conflict representation, conflict resolution in America consists of overlapping patterns. We shall examine these patterns in Part Four.

## american political patterns: a summation

In analyzing government, it is useful to think of politics as a human activity concerned with the regulation of social conflict. This usage is appropriate to our view of the human situation, of people who (1) are physical beings living in societies; (2) have different needs, wants, capacities, and resources; (3) pursue conflicting interests because of their very diversity; (4) associate in order to achieve interests that come from a shared human experience in the community; (5) endeavor to pursue their conflicting interests, but wish to do so without destroying the community; and (6) utilize politics as a method of regulating social conflict.

In America, conflict regulation consists of patterns of behavior by which social conflict is represented and resolved. Representation makes the conflict known through varieties of political participation — holding opinions, exercising leadership, voting, being partisan, and presenting organizing demands. Resolution is a policymaking process of reaching partial accommodations that keep the conflict within manageable limits. Officials make legitimate public policy through formulation, leadership, adoption, application, and adjudication. Politics is practiced within a community marked by social diversity, variations in doctrinal and politico-constitutional consensus, and policy disagreements. In short, politics is what it is because people are what they are. Bearing these points in mind, we now turn to a closer look at the American political community.

*bibliographical note*

The impetus for political change that was highly publicized in American politics at the close of the decade of the 1960s and opening of the 1970s is discussed in several works. Among these is Theodore J. Lowi, *The Politics of Disorder* (New York: Basic Books, 1971) that describes the strains placed upon American political institutions by the social movements of the decade. In his work *Ready to Riot* (New York: Holt, Rinehart and Winston, 1968), Nathan Wright, Jr., presents a case study of the underlying dissatisfactions contributing to urban violence. A comprehensive account of the nature of rebellion is Ted Robert Gurr, *Why Men Rebel* (Princeton, N.J.: Princeton University Press, 1970).

Several works available in paperback editions focus on the conflict-regulating functions of politics. In *The Semisovereign People* (New York: Holt, Rinehart and Winston, 1960), E. E. Schattschneider presents a very readable account of the role of American political parties and groups in representing social conflicts to decisionmakers. Equally readable is his *Two Hundred Million Americans in Search of a Government* (New York: Holt, Rinehart and Winston, 1969). A more general treatment of the relationship between politics and conflict is J. D. B. Miller, *The Nature of Politics* (London: Gerald Duckworth, 1962), which stresses the impact of human diversity on the development of political interests. Sophisticated discussions of the nature of human conflict in both national and international policymaking are found in Kenneth Boulding's *Conflict and Defense: A General Theory* (New York: Harper & Row, Torchbook Edition, 1963) and Thomas C. Schelling's *The Strategy of Conflict* (New York: Oxford University Press, 1963).

For accounts concerning the sources, consequences, and functions of conflict in human affairs, the following merit attention: Lewis Coser, *The Functions of Social Conflict* (London: Free Press, Paperback Edition, 1964); Georg Simmel, *Conflict and The Web of Group-Affiliations* (London: Free Press, Paperback Edition, 1964); and Edmund Stillman and William Pfaff, *The Politics of Hysteria* (New York: Harper & Row, 1964). Concerning the sources of human conflict, one should consult James C. Davies, *Human Nature in Politics* (New York: John Wiley, 1963). Finally, in this review of major works dealing with conflict theory one should not ignore the classic presentation by Thomas Hobbes, *The Leviathan,* available in several editions. Students interested in comparing human conflict with that of other species will find the following both readable and provocative: Desmond Morris, *The Naked Ape* (New York: McGraw-Hill, 1967); Konrad Lorenz, *On Aggression* (New York: Harcourt, Brace, 1966); and, Robert Ardrey, *The Territorial Imperative* (New York: Atheneum, 1966).

Treatises on the nature of human community are also abundant. After Aristotle's *Politics,* the following are noteworthy: Robert A. Nisbet's *Community and*

*Power* (formerly entitled *The Quest for Community*) (New York: Oxford University Press, 1962); the difficult but significant work by Ferdinand Tonnies, *Community and Society: Gemeinschaft and Gesellschaft* (New York: Harper & Row, Paperback Edition, 1963); Sebastian de Grazia's analysis of the sources of community in widely shared beliefs, *The Political Community: A Study of Anomie* (Chicago: University of Chicago Press, Phoenix Edition, 1963); and the classic of John Dewey, *The Public and Its Problems* (Denver: Alan Swallow, 1927). A useful textbook introduction to the sources and dimensions of the American community is Jessie Bernard's *American Community Behavior,* rev. ed. (New York: Holt, Rinehart and Winston, 1962). R. M. MacIver has devoted several works to interpreting the community bases of American social interaction including *The Web of Government* (New York: Free Press, Paperback Edition, 1965) and *The Modern State* (London: Oxford University Press, Paperback Edition, 1964). An abstract, but comprehensive, discussion of the relationship between political activity and human community is presented by Carl J. Friedrich in his *Man and His Government* (New York: McGraw-Hill, 1963).

A standard treatment of the essential functions of political concepts is T. D. Weldon's *The Vocabulary of Politics* (Baltimore: Penguin Books, 1953). Also useful is Thomas Landon Thorson, *The Logic of Democracy* (New York: Holt, Rinehart and Winston, 1962). If the student desires to sample the myriad definitions suggested for political activity, he may start with the following: Harold Lasswell, *Politics: Who Gets What, When, How* (New York: Meridian Books, 1958), relating politics and influence; Alfred de Grazia's definition of the politically relevant and his ensuing discussion of political ideas, institutions, and behavior in *Political Behavior,* rev. ed. (New York: The Free Press, 1962); Francis J. Sorauf, *Political Science: An Informal Overview* (Columbus, Ohio: Charles E. Merrill Books, 1963); Robert A. Dahl, *Modern Political Analysis* (Englewood Cliffs, N.J.: Prentice-Hall, 1963); Joseph Tussman, *Obligation and the Body Politic* (New York: Oxford University Press, 1960); Heinz Eulau. *The Behavioral Persuasion in Politics* (New York: Random House, 1963); and D. A. Strickland et al., *A Primer of Political Analysis* (Chicago: Markham, 1968).

For the attempts to suggest theories intended to explain political activity the reader should consult the following currently available paperback publications, each of varying quality and degree of difficulty: Lewis Froman's succinct description of the American polity, *People and Politics* (Englewood Cliffs, N.J.: Prentice-Hall, 1962); Karl W. Deutsch's related complex volume, *The Nerves of Government* (London: Free Press, Paperback Edition, 1966); and, Pendleton Herring's timeless and useful account of American political parties in a pluralist framework, *The Politics of Democracy* (New York: W. W. Norton, Paperback Edition, 1965). Currently available in standard editions are the volumes of David Easton's trilogy on the nature of political systems: *The Political System* (New York: Alfred A. Knopf, 1953), *A Framework for Political Analysis* (Englewood Cliffs, N.J.: Prentice-Hall, 1965), and *A Systems Analysis of Political Life* (New York: John Wiley, 1965). William C. Mitchell's *The American Polity* (New York: Free Press, 1962) demonstrates the use of systems analysis in interpreting American political patterns.

One of the influential interpretations of American politics as pluralist is David

A. Truman's *The Governmental Process* (New York: Alfred A. Knopf, 1951). Useful paperback critiques of pluralist politics include Henry S. Kariel, *The Decline of American Pluralism* (Stanford, Calif.: Stanford University Press, 1961); Abraham Kaplan, *American Ethics and Public Policy* (New York: Oxford University Press, 1963); and Robert A. Dahl, *A Preface to Democratic Theory* (Chicago: University of Chicago Press, Phoenix Books, 1963).

Various aspects of the controversy over whether America is pluralist or elitist are covered in the following: Robert A. Dahl's *Who Governs?* (New Haven, Conn.: Yale University Press, 1961) illustrates a pluralist power pattern in one community; C. Wright Mills in *The Power Elite* (New York: Oxford University Press, 1956) advances one of the more controversial views of an elitist-dominated government in America; G. William Domhoff's *Who Rules America?* (Englewood Cliffs, N.J.: Prentice-Hall, 1967) musters evidence in support of the Mills thesis; Arnold M. Rose in *The Power Structure: Political Process in American Life* (New York: Oxford University Press, 1967) views the American power structure as complex, diversified, pluralist, and accountable to popular control; finally, Peter Bachrach in *The Theory of Democratic Elitism* (Boston: Little, Brown, 1967) considers the impact that elite consensus has upon democratic views.

# how much consensus?

A community that has existed long enough to presume its own stability tends to develop distinctive political ideas. These ideas add up to a shared notion about how to conduct political business. Ideas need not be held rigidly or consistently; often they are so held. But they do contribute to a *community consensus, or a sharing of values and beliefs about human goals and conduct.*

## community consensus

Inevitably, *the content of community consensus will vary widely, especially in its political aspects.*

First, the values and beliefs on which agreement prevails cover a wide range. They can encompass ideas about the legitimacy of policymakers; constitutional arrangements; fundamental judgments about the desirability of free speech, majority rule, political equality, or popular election of policymakers; and such policy appraisals as the appropriateness of free medical care.

Second, each item in the consensus may be agreed to by different people. Agreement may be universal on the ideal of free speech, but fewer may agree to abide by the wishes of a majority, and only a handful may approve of the constitutional protection against self-incrimination which may be invoked by an accused criminal in the United States and Great Britain.

Third, intensity of agreement or disagreement varies. In the 1960s most young American males without strong feelings one way or another about military conscription acquiesced to the draft out of patriotism, expediency, or both; others protested by burning draft cards and going to jail; still others fled to Canada or Sweden.

Fourth, the items on which there is agreement may be consistent with one another or they may not. People agree that political equality is a "good thing," yet some insist that it is desirable to deny the vote to juveniles, Negroes, or others.

Fifth, the consequences of political consensus vary considerably. Consensus may actively support concepts like the Social Security programs; it may passively permit a specific action, such as allocating federal funds for school construction; or it may prohibit any decision at all; as it did when popular sentiment limited American involvement in World War II before Pearl Harbor.[1]

In its broadest sense, community consensus means *personal agreement* on a variety of matters; and in reaching such agreement, individuals are influenced by social and constitutional factors as well as by their beliefs. The types of community consensus may also be given several narrower definitions:

1. *Official consensus:* agreement with public officials. President Nixon's announcement in 1971 that he would visit Red China received general endorsement from the public and strengthened Nixon's efforts to open communications with the Chinese.

2. *Constitutional consensus:* agreement with rules and procedures. The general commitment to rules of procedure ("due process") in the handling of criminal cases is an obvious example.

3. *Doctrinal consensus:* agreement on democratic values.

4. *Policy consensus:* agreement on policy choices. Agreement is general that government ought to be active in alleviating social and economic problems such as unemployment, poverty, and old age.

## is there an american political consensus and an american ideology?

References to something called "Americanism" imply that our citizens either do — or should — share some ideas. "Americanism" is manifested by references to our forefathers, great moments in our history, *The Star-Spangled Banner*, pageants, and other reminders of our communal attachment. The relative absence of conflicting value symbols within the community leads us to suspect a general agreement on certain fundamentals. Current political commentators point out an "underlying consensus"

[1] V.O.Key, Jr., *Public Opinion and American Democracy* (New York: Alfred A. Knopf, 1961), p. 29.

People generally agree upon the value of democratic symbols and national holidays. Fourth of July flags remind us of our communal history.

within the American polity that enables it to survive continuing and serious disputes over policy alternatives.[2] The obvious fact that the federal community had, until the mid-sixties (with one major exception, the Civil War), managed to accommodate policy differences without serious disruption strongly supported the notion that a basic agreement over values and political processes buttressed peaceful regulation of social conflict.

The events of the current era, however, tell a somewhat different story, one that questions the proposition that America possesses a general polit-

[2] Robert A. Dahl, *A Preface to Democratic Theory* (Chicago: University of Chicago Press, 1956), pp. 132–133; Bernard Berelson et al., *Voting* (Chicago: University of Chicago Press, 1954), p. 313; and Sebastian De Grazia, *The Political Community* (Chicago: University of Chicago Press, 1948), p. ix.

ical consensus. Eruptions of violence and civil disorder remind us that, underlying the veneer of seeming agreement on fundamentals, America has long experienced turbulent unrest. Our violent past includes lynchings in the South, the relatively lawless "winning of the West," the frequently brutal removal of the American Indian from land he rightly owned, the forceful treatment of striking workers as recently as the 1930s, and, lest it be forgotten, the revolution out of which America was born.

Violence and disorder are not the exclusive properties of any segment of society or even of "the discontented." They can come from either "the left" or "the right," and they can be used to stamp out discontent as well as to express it. In recent years, a highly vocal if comparatively small number of discontented Americans have criticized the American polity as being unresponsive to social injustice (and therefore immoral), unrepresentative of popular wishes, and defective in its institutional structure which, it is claimed, is incapable of meeting or unwilling to meet the needs of the majority in America. The activists who seized university administration buildings, ransacked the files of draft boards, and marched on Washington had something in common with their ideological opposites who expressed disapproval of public policy by burning school buses and using cattle prods to disperse civil rights demonstrators. In each case, a minority group felt compelled to go outside "the system" of established procedures to redress grievances, and both rejected "the rule of law." One side did so out of conviction that the rules of the regime are rigged to destroy individualism and self-expression, and to achieve more "participatory democracy."[3] The other side behaved as it did out of hostility and fear.

Because the people who criticize the existing order but do not get violent about it are in the majority by far, violence and disorder are not the sole measurements of consensus denial. But such criticism, though it varies in scope and intensity, does indicate that assumptions about a "universal" consensus on doctrine or policy, or on constitutional rules and procedures, may lack foundation.

The juxtaposition of serenity, severe criticism, and violence in our history suggests that we might want to approach "Americanism" on different levels, returning to the distinctions between *official, constitutional, doctrinal,* and *policy* consensus introduced previously.

That at least *some* form of agreement exists in America is obvious to any reader of political news. Americans observe presidential campaigns

---

[3] See, for example, the first official statement of the Students for Democratic Society (SDS), adopted in the Port Huron, Michigan convention, June 11–15, 1962; see also Robert A. Goldwin, ed., *How Democratic Is America: Responses to the New Left Challenge* (Chicago: Rand McNally, 1971).

in which debate is heated, invective sparkles, and each side accuses the other of "selling America short." Candidates often grasp for uncomplimentary charges to devastate the opposition. At such times the likelihood that agreement will ever be reached on who should govern seems remote. Then on election eve, all sides remind Americans of their right and obligation to vote. Votes are cast, ballots are counted, and — seemingly in miraculous fashion — the winner is proclaimed and *accepted* by Americans as "our President."

Thus one form of *official consensus* over who shall govern is reached in election campaigns that are contested bitterly but within bounds of generally held ideas about what is fair and unfair, honest and dishonest. Here official consensus is tied to a prior agreement on how governors should be chosen, *reflecting an even deeper constitutional consensus.* There seems to be some, although less clear-cut *consensus on policy issues as well.* It would be surprising indeed for presidential candidates to debate seriously the proposition that an official church should be established in the United States. Yet, even that consensus on church-state separation is limited; when the Supreme Court decided in 1962 that the First Amendment forbade officially sanctioned prayers in public schools, controversy over church-state relations broke out, and there was even talk of a clarifying constitutional amendment.

We may assume from these different expressions of official, constitutional, and policy consensus that *there is a fundamental agreement on*

President Nixon is sworn in by Chief Justice Earl Warren with former President Johnson and unsuccessful challenger Hubert Humphrey looking on. The bitterness of national campaigns fades as the changing of the guard reveals our official and doctrinal consensus.

*some goals (separation of church and state, for instance), but the agree-*
*ment breaks down — sometimes violently — as soon as it becomes a ques-*
*tion of how to achieve these goals.*

Many debates in American history illustrate this point. Although it
seems less vivid to the students of this generation than to their fathers
and mothers, the New Deal debate during Franklin D. Roosevelt's presidency may be the most illuminating example of the twentieth century.
In 1934, former President Herbert Hoover declared that the continuance
of the New Deal would mark "a vast casualty to liberty," while President
Roosevelt himself conceived of the New Deal as an "extension of liberty."

Hoover and Roosevelt differed about means, not ends. Far more than
was apparent to their partisans at the time, both men were essentially
conservative. Both were clearly committed to the preservation of the
American free-enterprise economic system, but at a time of economic
crisis they differed over how to preserve the system. Hoover sincerely
believed that New Deal social and economic policies, particularly deficit
spending, threatened the democratic values of economic and individual
freedom; Roosevelt was also concerned with the individual, and he considered his policies a necessary means of preserving the same values. The
disagreement involved the means of achieving long-range goals, not the
goals themselves.

The same disagreement is found today in the argument about public
welfare. Hardly anyone thinks that the very poor and the very old deserve no more than a starvation death and a burial in the nearest potter's
field; beyond that, argument is copious. Should a minimum income be
guaranteed to each family, or to each individual? If so, what should the
minimum be? The goal, as expressed by the political slogans of yes-
teryear, is understood by all: the full dinner pail, two chickens in every
pot — that is, the abolition of poverty. But how to achieve the goal? Who
is to pay the cost?

Another contemporary example of policy consensus is found in the
argument about environmental quality. The issue is not the need for or
the desirability of clean air, water, and land. But there are serious
differences about the type of public policy required to achieve the policy
goal. Should antipollution laws be vigorously enforced and carry high
penalties for violation? Should the cost of restoring our waterways, land,
and air be borne by those most responsible for pollution or should government financially underwrite this effort?

As these questions suggest, usually some consensus agreement can be
seen in America about constitutional procedures and long-range values.
Agreement on short-term policies is less frequent. Some areas of conflict
are always visible, and we address ourselves here to the extent of our
consensus. *To ensure community stability, must all or nearly all citizens*

*hold identical values, or is it sufficient for only specific groups to accept them?* No systematic research provides complete answers to this question. The past decade, however, has seen increasing significant inquiry into the American political consensus. Despite frequent references to a fundamental consensus or "ideology" of Americanism, these provisional findings raise doubts about the extent to which Americans do hold common political values.

## ambivalent majority and active minority

The values Americans attach to politics condition their response to public officials, ideals and practices, and policies. What people think about politics and politicians is a critical factor in the climate of American opinion; it contributes to molding whatever fundamental ideals we hold. Community members react to decisions partly according to the esteem in which they hold the decisionmakers, and these reactions shape their opinions of the whole political community. But is there a consensus among Americans about politics itself? To the extent that there is, how is it related to their response to "democratic fundamentals" in the pluralist context?

### the image of politics

It has been said that when Americans "talk politics" they do so with invective and criticism, not reverence and awe. Perhaps the national pastime is not baseball but "damning politicians up hill and down dale ... as rogues and vagabonds, frauds and scoundrels."[4] A noted historian has written that Americans approach government as a "friendly enemy, a neighbor who will probably do well enough if you keep your eye on him."[5] Suspicion of those in power is not confined, however, to the holders of public office. Opinion surveys consistently show large majorities who feel that labor unions, political bosses, and corporations have "too much power."[6] Are these characterizations of American sentiment as quasi-hostile toward government accurate?

WHAT DO THE NOVELISTS SAY? Two themes emphasized by successful political novelists tell us something about American political attitudes.

---

[4] H. L. Mencken, *A Mencken Chrestomathy* (New York: Alfred A. Knopf, 1956), p. 148.
[5] Carl L. Becker, *Freedom and Responsibility in the American Way of Life* (New York: Vintage Books, 1960), p. 7.
[6] Key, *Public Opinion and American Democracy.*

**Although people generally agree on peace as a national goal, that agreement breaks down over specific policy alternatives.**

The first stresses the style individuals manifested in getting and keeping public office: "influence peddling" and the promise of jobs. Organized politics is seen as the domain of the "machine"; "persuasion" is looked upon as coercion (which it sometimes is); and the rewards of office are "spoils." This word has been in the American vernacular since the time of Andrew Jackson, but politicians rarely use it; when they speak of the subject at all, even in private, they use the word "patronage." It means the same thing: jobs. When politicians themselves are not sinful or born thieves, they are pictured as well-intentioned Pollyannas who, in order to accomplish beneficial ends, permit themselves to be used by calculating colleagues who really are sinful. Both strains of this theme run through the late Edwin O'Connor's *The Last Hurrah,* in which the political boss Frank Skeffington (obviously based on Boston's James Michael Curley) does indeed use coercion, the spoils system, and even chicanery

32

to their outer limits but is finally defeated by a Pollyanna type who is backed by men of less principle than Skeffington.

A second theme is what politicians must do to retain and conduct office. Allen Drury's President in *Advise and Consent* is forced to condone character assassination in order to secure Senate confirmation of a Cabinet appointee. Novelists are prone to write of politicians who sacrifice the public interest for personal gain, but political novels usually combine a romantic admiration of the politician's capacity to govern, even if he does so maliciously, with an implied condemnation of his actions.[7]

WHAT DO THE OPINION POLLS SAY? Although some political journalists, historians, and novelists continue to assume that Americans are negatively disposed toward politics, opinion surveys indicate that this picture is out of date. In 1944, the National Opinion Research Center reported that 69 percent of the Americans interviewed in a nationwide survey were opposed to politics "as a life's work" for their sons. Negative responses were critical of the "dishonest" and "dirty" aspects of politics; a few even felt that, at best, it was a "useless occupation." More recent surveys, however, reveal a slight decline in the percentage of negative responses. George Gallup reported in 1965 that more than one of every three Americans approved of a political career for their children; the proportion critical of politics because of its apparent corruption and lack of prestige, opportunity, and security — although still a majority — fell to 54 percent.[8]

Despite its tarnished image, politics as a profession has been gaining in public acceptance. Americans are growing more sensitive to the contributions politicians make toward individual happiness and the preservation of society. One crude indicator is the finding that 85 percent of the Americans in one representative sample cited their government and its political tradition as one aspect of the United States of which they were "most proud." This figure contrasts sharply with responses in four other nations. Only 3 percent of the Italians cited government or political traditions as aspects of their nation of which they were "most proud" — as compared to 7 percent for Germans, 30 percent for Mexicans, and 45 percent for Britons.[9]

Americans are also learning to regard politics as a professional under-

[7] Irving Howe, *Politics and the Novel* (New York: Horizons Press, 1967); Joseph Blotner, *The Modern American Political Novel: 1900–1960* (Austin Tex.: University of Texas Press, 1966); Allen Drury, *Advise and Consent* (Garden City, N.Y.: Doubleday, 1959): Edwin O'Connor, *The Last Hurrah* (Boston: Little, Brown, 1956).
nor, *The Last Hurrah* (Boston: Little, Brown, 1956).
[8] News Release, American Institute of Public Opinion (March 3, 1965).
[9] Gabriel A. Almond and Sidney Verba, *The Civic Culture* (Princeton, N.J.: Princeton University Press, 1963), p. 102.

taking requiring systematic performance of tasks rather than as a mere craft applying customs, conventions, and the pragmatic approach of trial and error. Whereas the NORC survey in 1944 revealed critical attitudes toward politics as highest among the better educated, many educated and distinguished citizens now go into politics as a challenging career. Sixty years ago, men with talent addressed themselves primarily to business and industry; today their sons and grandsons, free from financial worries, are more likely to devote their creative energies to public service. In the 1960s, two grandsons of the elder John D. Rockefeller simultaneously held governorships, one of them being the first Republican elected governor in Arkansas since Reconstruction. Depression, domestic disorder, and war, along with the expanded United States role in world affairs, have changed the popular view of government. More people than formerly regard it as a "channel for necessary change, not its obstacle."[10] Politics still has its wheelers and dealers, but the image has a new aspect: politics is an essential, honorable, and even prestigious activity in a civilized polity.

From still another point of view, mistrust of government and politics may indicate high but unfulfilled expectations. That is, we may expect — somewhat unrealistically — politicians to have standards of ethics and conduct superior to those of people in business or other private activities. Negative attitudes toward political parties "may grow from a . . . feeling of a faith betrayed, in that many sense that the party has not come near enough to fulfilling its unique contribution to the workings of democracy."[11] If we do set higher ethical standards for public men than for private individuals, this suggests that — rather than holding politics and government in contempt or suspicion — Americans actually have high hopes for the utility of politics to produce a better society. If they do, then negative reactions are explained by the failure of politicians to meet an expected standard.

SUMMARY. Although it appears that the trend is toward greater public acceptance of politics as a positive and useful endeavor, the negative perspectives of the past are still evident. The verdicts of popular literature and popular opinion surveys are ambiguous; we cannot conclude that politics is regarded as either a positive good or a necessary evil by Americans. Our attitudes toward politics combine respect and dismay. While politics becomes a prestigious profession for some, candidates for public office are still able to play upon popular disrespect for the activity.

[10] John Conway, "Politics as a Profession in the United States," *Daedalus* 92, no. 4 (Fall 1963): 845.
[11] Alan P. Sindler, *Political Parties in the United States* (New York: St. Martin's Press, 1966), p. 5.

An example was the adroit use of the slogan "Peace above Politics" in Hubert H. Humphrey's bid for the 1968 Democratic presidential nomination, a slogan designed to indicate he would unify the nation in time of civil disorder, work for peace in Vietnam, and not be deterred by "divisive" political considerations. In Nixon's 1968 presidential campaign, Republican campaign strategists made use of a photograph of a young schoolgirl at a Nixon rally holding a sign "Bring Us Together." This slogan was utilized to achieve much the same effect as Humphrey's, which was more extensively employed.

### sources of ambivalence

The ambivalence of the popular image of politics can be explained in several ways. The prestige of any activity or any individual is relative. The criteria used by Americans to evaluate occupations are vague. Frequently, the prestige of a job is determined by its label. A "politician" is scorned, but a "statesman" doing the same job is revered. When attitudes reflect ambivalence, there is good reason. The same government that provides a citizen's protection calls for sacrifice; payment of income tax is both a privilege and a burden.

OUR UNPHILOSOPHICAL APPROACH TO POLITICS. But the sources of ambivalence in the American response to government run deeper — touching our historical traditions and our unphilosophic reactions to most questions. Daniel Boorstin said that Americans live in "one of the most spectacularly lopsided cultures in all history."[12] They have experienced amazing success and vitality in the operation of their political system and have a firm belief in the superiority of democracy as the "best form of government." Yet they are distinctly uninterested in reflecting, speculating, and theorizing about politics. A reported exchange between President Franklin Roosevelt and a young journalist illustrates precisely how uninterested in philosophical questions most Americans (as well as most Presidents) are:

> "Mr. President, are you a Communist?"
> "No."
> "Are you a capitalist?"
> "No."
> "Are you a Socialist?"

[12] Daniel J. Boorstin, *The Genius of American Politics* (Chicago: University of Chicago Press, Phoenix Books, 1960).

"No," he said, with a look of surprise, as if he were wondering what he was being cross-examined about.

The young man said, "Well, what is your philosophy then?"

"Philosophy?" asked the President, puzzled. "Philosophy? I am a Christian and a Democrat — that's all."[13]

The reaction of Roosevelt was typical not only of the man but of Americans generally. Alexis de Tocqueville in his classic work, *Democracy in America,* observed in 1835 that Americans were not interested in philosophy but that they, nevertheless, were "in possession of one, common to the whole people."[14] He meant that Americans had a "consensus"; but today this "philosophy" is highly ambiguous and difficult to define.

Boorstin argues that three factors help to account for this unphilosophical bent:

1. *Our values were "preformed"* in the sense that the Founding Fathers and "certain facts of geography or history peculiar to us, supplied a set of principles to apply to all future matters." The leading example is the Constitution, a gift of the past, which is useful in dealing with current problems. Americans credit the Founding Fathers with amazing vision for, even following great domestic turmoil, constitutional consensus remains high. Despite controversy over the modern "meaning" of the Constitution, it is viewed as just about the final word in debate over political institutions and policies. Even when they recognize the necessity and desirability of change, Americans justify constitutional modifications on the ground that they are in accordance with the principles of 1789. Boorstin holds that because of preformed values, Americans are not interested in philosophical debates about whether the original principles themselves should be revised to suit contemporary problems.

2. *The "American way of life" is taken for granted.* American political values are deeply ingrained in our political institutions, which are still taken for granted by a majority of Americans. The "American way of life" is something special because it is built from a combination of soil, social arrangements, and cultural climate found nowhere else in the world. This concept of the "American way" complements the "preformation" theory in the sense that "Americanism" is something handed on to each generation born into the community or migrating into it. On the one hand, Boorstin argues, Americans look upon the Constitution as a permanent and nearly perfect governing framework; on the other, they see the values that the Constitution enshrines as leavened in the soil of America itself.

---

[13] Francis Perkins, *The Roosevelt I Knew* (New York: The Viking Press, 1946), p. 330.
[14] Alexis de Tocqueville, *Democracy in America* (New York: Oxford University Press, Galaxy Edition, 1947), p. 251.

3. *The continuity of American history is "unique."* Europe has been racked by revolutions, divisive ideological debates, and other cataclysmic changes. Americans are aware of the turbulence in their own short history, but they see a two-hundred-year line of progress linking past and present. Living in a community in which the "general truths" of politics are embedded in the land, in institutions and in sacred documents, and transmitted from generation to generation without disfigurement, Americans simply do not need a philosophy; they live it.

UNRESOLVED CONTRADICTIONS IN POPULAR OUTLOOK. The unphilosophical bent of Americans is revealed in their toleration of contradictory political ideas and political institutions. Robert G. McCloskey characterizes American ideology as "ambivalent." Americans hold "contradictory ideas simultaneously without bothering to resolve the potential conflict between them." Even those who could be classified as "ideologues" (persons who make choices on the basis of a specific doctrine) are uncertain about the nature of democratic values.[15] The statements of American folk heroes from Jefferson onward reveal this ambivalence toward the canons of democracy. Thomas Jefferson can be quoted with little difficulty in support of inconsistent propositions (compare his "the will of the majority in all cases to prevail" with "the minority possess their equal rights which equal law must protect"). Few Americans, fewer perhaps than in any other Western country, vote ideologically; and consistency in political ideas on the part of the great political leaders of American history is more atypical than normal.

If our regard for American political institutions is ambivalent, we should bear in mind that the Constitution itself is an ambivalent document. An instrument written to unify the nation and strengthen the central government, it also has been used to justify the "states' rights" argument — even though that expression is not found in the Constitution. We expect the legislative branch to determine policy by majority vote; yet many Americans support procedures such as Senate filibusters and the selection of standing committees in a manner that confers extra powers on legislators who have been in office long enough to achieve high "seniority." Some look to the presidency as a reflector of public opinion; others see the function of that office as molding and creating opinion.

Although few of our political leaders would oppose the "rule of law," the nation during the past two decades has witnessed southern governors openly defying the "law of the land" as interpreted by federal courts. McCloskey concludes that "it may be idle to seek for 'the' American

---

[15] Robert G. McCloskey, "The American Ideology," in Marian D. Irish, ed., *Continuing Crises in American Politics* (Englewood Cliffs, N.J.: Prentice-Hall, 1963), pp. 10–25.

The President represents the
American consensus. He speaks
for the nation and represents
the entire political community:
e pluribus unum.

tradition, for a 'consensus' in any usual sense of the word. Perhaps our
only really basic quality of mind is the pragmatic spirit that can tolerate
such a state of affairs and build an enduring polity upon it."[16]

THE EVIDENCE. Does our knowledge of American attitudes toward
fundamental political values support the assertions made above? Is the
American as a political thinker ambivalent toward politics, unreflective
in political thinking, and contradictory in his political judgments?

Data on the nature and extent of American political consensus are too

[16] *Ibid.,* p. 24.

scattered and incomplete to warrant more than an educated guess. Evidence does indicate that although American government normally operates *as though* there were a basic consensus on "democratic fundamentals," *little agreement exists beyond that on very general statements of democratic principles. Moreover, any consensus that does exist is more prevalent among the politically active than in the general population.*

A 1960 study permits the hypothesis that the more abstract the principle of democracy with which people are asked to agree, the greater the agreement; as principles are stated more specifically, consensus breaks down.[17] Support for statements about the principle of democracy itself ("Democracy is the best form of government"), majority rule ("Public officials should be chosen by majority vote"), and minority rights ("The minority should be free to criticize") ranged from 95 to 98 percent of the samples of registered voters in two localities — Ann Arbor, Michigan, and Tallahassee, Florida. But agreement failed to reach 90 percent on propositions that specifically applied these general principles. Fifty-four percent would not agree to allow a Communist to occupy the office of mayor even if "legally elected" — thus disowning one application of majority rule. Fifty-six percent disagreed that "if an admitted Communist wanted to make a speech in this city favoring communism, he should be allowed to speak" — an indication of a weak commitment to minority rights. A majority gave "undemocratic" responses to about half the specific propositions. Significantly, it was found in this study that agreement with specific applications of democratic values ran higher among better-educated and upper-income groups.

the elitist consensus

*Americans generally are not committed so strongly to democratic practices as they are to abstract democratic principles, but the politically active are more committed in both respects than most people.* This generalization is suggested by an extensive study in 1958 that examined the range of agreement on democratic values among two groups, one called "political influentials" and the other the "general electorate."[18]

THE 1958 STUDY. The influentials were 3,020 delegates and alternates to the 1956 Republican and Democratic national conventions who re-

[17] James W. Prothro and Charles M. Grigg, "Fundamental Principles of Democracy: Bases of Agreement and Disagreement," *The Journal of Politics* 22 (Spring 1960): 276–294.

[18] Herbert McClosky,"Consensus and Ideology in American Politics," *The American Political Science Review* 58, no. 2 (June 1964): 361–362.

sponded to questions aimed at determining the level of agreement on democratic ideals. A representative sample of 1,484 adults in the general population was asked to indicate agreement or disagreement with the same propositions. Consensus was defined as present where 75 percent or more of the respondents agreed with a "pro-democratic" proposition such as "People who hate our way of life should still have a chance to talk and be heard," or where 75 percent disagreed with an "antidemocratic" statement such as "The majority has the right to abolish minorities if it wants to."

Using the above criterion, the study revealed that political influentials expressed consensus on eight of twelve *"rules of the game"* put forward as democratic and fair play in political life. Only 25.6 percent agreed with "I don't mind a politician's methods if he manages to get the right things done." Solid majorities were found on respect for legal processes (almost 80 percent disagreed with "It is all right to get around the law if you don't actually break it") and the rights of minorities. Only 27.2 percent agreed that "We might as well make up our minds that in order to make the world better a lot of innocent people are going to have to suffer"). In contrast, the general electorate did not meet the consensus criterion on a single "rules of the game" item.

The differences between the two groups in their support of general *democratic principles,* as distinguished from *democratic practices,* was revealed by their answers and questions about free speech. On eight items dealing with principles of free speech ("I believe in free speech for all no matter what their views might be" was one), the influentials expressed consensus on all and the electorate on seven. But, when it came to statements indicating practical applications of these principles (such as "A book that contains wrong political views cannot be a good book and does not deserve to be published"), the influentials showed a more consistent commitment to democratic practices than did the general electorate. Neither group reached the 75 percent mark on all specific instances of free speech and procedural rights, but the influentials did reach consensus on five of the nine items, the general electorate on only one ("No matter what crime a person is accused of, he should never be convicted unless he has been given the right to face and question his accusers"). Finally, on fifteen statements reflecting belief in political, social, and economic equality, neither group expressed consensus; the split among both is typified by the agreement of 40 percent of the influentials and 60 percent of the general electorate that "There will always be poverty, so people might as well get used to the idea."

The findings reviewed here stress the equally overwhelming support political activists and the general population give to abstract statements about democracy and freedom; but the educational, social, and economic elitist elements of the population support the operating practices of democracy to a greater degree. It is possible to summarize by saying that "consensus and democratic ideology are poorly developed among the electorate and only imperfectly realized among the political influentials."[19]

Do our political attitudes reflect deep ideological views? Apparently they do not. Voters seldom respond to questions on policy issues along a "liberal-conservative" dichotomy. A study undertaken in the 1964 presidential campaign (Johnson vs. Goldwater) revealed that 26 percent of a national sample classified themselves as "liberal," 34 percent as "middle-of-the-road," and 30 percent as "conservative." Only 10 percent said they did not know. If such self-designations are accurate, we would expect a consistent pattern of liberals and conservatives lining up against one another on policy issues. They did not do so. By classifying respondents as liberal or conservative according to their reactions to carefully worded statements (such as "The federal government is interfering too much in state and local matters" and "We should rely more on individual initiative and ability and not so much on governmental welfare programs"), it was possible to compare self-designated ideologues with their positions on general propositions. Among those calling themselves "liberal," 28 percent actually took conservative positions. Of those calling themselves "middle-of-the-road," 46 percent emerged as liberals, 23 percent as conservatives, and the remainder of those polled straddled ideological lines.[20]

For most Americans, doctrinal views are so mixed, inconsistent, and confused that it is difficult to explain American political attitudes in ideological terms. Studies by the Survey Research Center of the University of Michigan show that Americans respond (or do not respond) to issues on their merits and not on the basis of a rigorously defined system of values. Less than 3 percent of Americans possess an "ideology" if we define that term as a fairly abstract and inclusive system of ideas against which political policies are evaluated.[21] The ambivalence so evident in American attitudes toward democratic values is also reflected by our lack of doctrinal orientation.

"POLITICAL SUBCULTURE" AND CONSENSUS. The evidence cited in this section suggests that few Americans have any kind of political philosophy, let alone a consistent outlook on democratic principles and prac-

[19] *Ibid.*

[20] Lloyd A. Free and Hadley Cantril, *The Political Beliefs of Americans* (New Brunswick, N.J.: Rutgers University Press, 1967), pp. 41–50.

[21] Philip E. Converse, "The Nature of Belief Systems in Mass Publics," in David D. Apter, ed., *Ideology and Discontent* (New York: Free Press, 1964), pp. 206–261.

tices. Those who do form what V. O. Key, Jr., has called the "political subculture" — a comparatively small group of Americans, generally of higher socioeconomic standing, who are politically involved, politically interested, and who go beyond mere lip service in their commitment to democratic values.[22]

Although no universal agreement is found within the activist subcommunity, consensus on democratic fundamentals lies primarily within this small core of the population.

## is political consensus necessary or expendable?

We have been speaking of several separate but related matters: (1) the ambivalent image Americans have of politics and politicians; (2) the generally unphilosophical approach most Americans take to politics; (3) the relative lack of agreement about the application, as contrasted with the acceptance, of democratic principles; and (4) the finding that the consensus about democratic practice that *does* exist lies within a political elite (an informed, activist minority), and even *its* members are ambivalent on some points. This conclusion, that there is little real consensus in America, is not easily reconciled with the classical theory of democracy or the long-held American assumption that the stability of a political community depends upon universal acceptance of fundamental values.

### consensus and political stability

Perhaps it is a mistake to assume that fundamental consensus is possible in a pluralist society that emphasizes individual autonomy. Potentially this emphasis may produce a "me" rather than a "you" viewpoint among community members, eroding the tolerance of diversity that is crucial to democratic practice. Hence we find the apparent inconsistency between the American "conscience" and practice that Gunnar Myrdal characterized as "an American dilemma" in his famous critique of our race relations. In pointing out that "the status accorded the Negro in America represents nothing more than a century-long lag of public morals," Myrdal argued that the contradiction between the ideals of equality and the treatment of blacks by whites in America created embarrassment and uneasiness among many whites. It was a dilemma that could not continue,[23] and recent civil rights disorders and remedial legislation support

[22] Key, *Public Opinion and American Democracy*, p. 51.
[23] Gunnar Myrdal, *An American Dilemma* (New York: Harper & Brothers, 1944), p. 24.

Almost all Americans accept the general concepts of human rights, including those ideals deemed necessary to maintain human dignity.

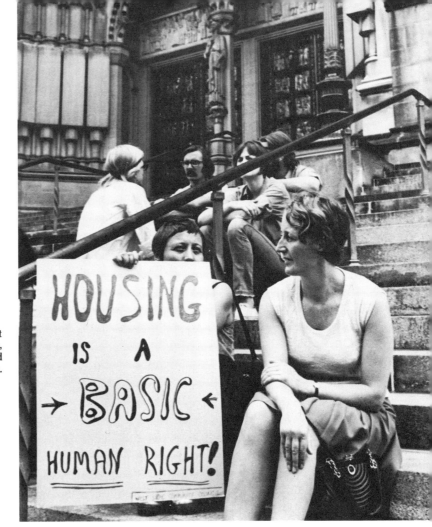

Despite adherence to general democratic ideals, conflict frequently erupts over the means to achieve them. Here, New York citizens protest a proposed housing project for low-income groups in Forest Hills.

Myrdal's conclusions. When we encounter a similar dilemma in other matters of community consensus, we see a parallel inconsistency. Having inherited a set of democratic principles from the past, we are willing to acquiesce to them but reluctant to apply them in the present.

One explanation for this inconsistency is offered by writers on "mass democracy." They say the democratic rhetoric to which we still give lip service is a relic of an earlier and essentially rural republic. What we now have is mass democracy, "a new phenomenon — a creation of the last half century — which it is inappropriate or misleading to consider in terms of the philosophy of Locke or of the liberal democracy of the nineteenth century."[24] The persuasiveness of such an argument is diminished by the fact that mutual recognition of "one another's rights" before the turn of the century was probably no greater than it is today; nor was consensus on fundamentals.

THE REAL QUESTION. It does not advance our inquiry to ask whether Americans ever shared an intense commitment to fundamentals. Evidence shows that they do not now and that they may never have done so. The real question is: *how much consensus is necessary to sustain the democratic polity and what is its extent, location, and content?* Perhaps stability of the political community is possible even without general consensus. There must be explanations for this stability, it would seem, other than mere assumptions about universal consensus either within the population as a whole or within elitist groups.

IS DEMOCRACY A HABIT? It may be that democracy is sustained more out of habit than out of conscious and articulate acceptance of principles. Habitual behavior, political or otherwise, is learned and may not be rooted consciously in acceptance and understanding of abstract ideology. Americans acquiesce in democratic values, and the failure of some people to support them in specific instances connotes no hostility to the values themselves. Quite the contrary. As "givens," the fundamentals are not subject to controversy. Americans feel no compulsion to explain or defend them; they merely observe them unthinkingly. When they do articulate them it is not for discussion, but in glorified patriotic forms like the traditional Fourth of July oration. *In short, despite the ambivalence of individuals, the collective community operates as if a general consensus does exist.*

HAS OUR CONSENSUS BROKEN DOWN? We might suggest that the widely publicized violence and disorder of America in the 1960s should not be

[24] Edward H. Carr, *The New Society* (Boston: Beacon Press, 1957), pp. 74–75.

interpreted as either a "breakdown of consensus" or an indication of "a sick society." Consensus, at least on democratic fundamentals, has never been sufficiently widespread for us to argue now that it is being torn asunder; if violence is an indication of malaise, then America has always been a sick society — a statement few would care to make. We suggest that it is less the American consensus that is changing, than the habits supporting it. Previously silent interests — the Negroes, the migrants, the dispossessed, the elderly, the young, the poor — have merely stopped being silent. These interests espouse many of the same ideals comprising the "American Dream" to which we have paid homage in the past. They are now articulating demands and protesting against their isolation from the consensus in unexpected, unconventional, and challenging fashion.

The protests and undisguised doubts about the American system are certainly not confined to the "have nots" and the "disadvantaged." Supporting criticism comes from many whose educational achievements and social and economic status put them in the upper bracket of American society. In colleges and universities, the affluent as well as the nonaffluent young have charged that the goals and priorities of our political system are both unrealistic and immoral. They think expenditures for national defense are vastly out of proportion to the sums spent on health care, poverty programs, the economic and social problems of our cities, and our worsening physical environment. Disaffection in the 1960s and early 1970s extended beyond explicit policy choices; it also seriously questioned whether the pluralist governing arrangement in America does, in fact, prevent rapid and adequate response to pressing needs. The critics charge that the groups that now participate in the public-policy bargaining process comprise an "establishment" that represents only the status quo; change, consequently, is difficult if not impossible.

Undoubtedly most Americans do not share this perspective. Nevertheless, probably never in our history have contradictions between the lives of ordinary Americans and the democratic concept of equality been so marked. The discontent over policy priorities also may reveal a potentially dangerous erosion of a sense of political stability. If large numbers of Americans were to display a lack of trust in the capacity of the political system to resolve social and economic problems, or if procedures were to be subordinated to the achievement of specific political goals, a breakdown of consensus might follow.

Evidence does not indicate that to be a probability. In their pioneering study of the political attitudes and beliefs of citizens in the United States and four other nations (Britain, Italy, Germany, and Mexico), Professors Almond and Verba found that both the Americans and the British tend to subordinate politics to more general social values that result in a tempering of political controversy. The Americans and the British display a high degree of social trust and cooperativeness and, although they are highly involved in partisan affairs, their involvement is not so intense as to produce irreconcilable attitudes on political differences. A "sense of community, over and above political differences, keeps the affective attachments to political groups from challenging the stability of the system."[25]

### our political consensus: some conclusions

It is misleading to assert that American political consensus alone must or does carry the burden of preserving the community. American political stability seems to rest on a number of factors:

1. *Democratic habits.* Americans behave *as if* they believe in democratic values.
2. *General acquiescence* in democratic principles. Americans accept them and do not oppose policy decisions reflecting these principles.
3. *Political activists.* These people believe in democratic tenets and act according to them.

By identifying that group of the population (political activists) most committed in practice to democratic fundamentals, we have provided one answer to the question of how much consensus exists within the system. In addition, there appears to be a strong commitment to existing institutional forms for the settlement of disputes. Despite criticism of particular policy choices (or failure to pursue specific policy goals) there is relatively little support for major alteration of existing institutions among either the political activists or the general electorate. We would argue that there is very considerable agreement on the appropriateness of existing arrangements for representation and resolution of conflict. Americans still accept such devices as federalism, separation of powers, the role of the courts, etc. In this respect the answer to the question of "How much consensus?" would be "A great deal."

In addition, there appears to be consensus on *the style of decisionmaking within the political system.* As one observer has stated:

> Group politics is not so much a politics without ideology as the politics of a specific ideology whose key premises are accepted by those who participate actively in the political process. These key premises of moderation in pressing demands, respect for the claims of all groups for representation of their inter-

---

[25] Almond and Verba, *The Civic Culture,* p. 357. For an exposition of the material referred to in this paragraph, see Chapters 9 and 13.

ests, a high degree of tolerance for delay, ambiguity, and waste as the necessary price to pay for the protection of individual freedom — in short, the premises of liberalism.[26]

Finally, although surveys that measure attitudes and values held by Americans have added greatly to our understanding of consensus, we still have difficulty defining its content and manifestation in American politics. The vagueness of our attempted definitions may derive at least in part from the close association of American cultural and political development with the ideology of democracy.

*bibliographical note*

There is extensive literature on the American character and political values. The following are available in paperback editions, Michael McGiffert, ed., *The Character of Americans* (Homewood, Ill.: The Dorsey Press, 1964), provides essays by historians and social scientists which explore the major features of American values and culture. Darryl Baskin, *American Pluralist Democracy: A Critique* (New York: Van Nostrand Reinhold, 1971), examines American pluralism and offers some interesting insights into the relationship between democratic theory and procedures and American political consensus; Donald J. Devine, *The Political Culture in the United States* (Boston: Little, Brown, 1972), presents extensive public opinion data in arguing the existence of a broad American consensus; Joseph Tussman's *Obligation and the Body Politic* (New York: Oxford University Press, 1960) is a relatively short and highly readable treatment of the role and responsibilities of the democratic citizen; Joseph L. Blotner, *The Political Novel* (New York: Random House, 1955), examines the novel as an instrument of expression and a shaping factor of American political values; Daniel J. Boorstin, *The Genius of American Politics* (Chicago: University of Chicago Press, 1960), argues that American politics is nonideological; David Riesman's important book, *The Lonely Crowd* (Garden City, N.Y.: Doubleday, abridged, 1955), presents a sociologist's view of an American people changed from "inner directed" to "other directed" personalities; another sociologist, Seymour M. Lipset, argues in his *The First New Nation* (New York: Basic Books, 1963) that the American character and values have not substantially changed over the past two hundred years. W. J. Cash, *The Mind of the South* (New York: Alfred A. Knopf, 1941) is a brilliant exposition of the political culture and values of a major region of the nation.

The 1960s and early 1970s have seen a wide-ranging and large amount of literature dealing with the themes of the "new left," radicalism, technology, and violence in the American system. A short book of essays which contains commentary by both critics and defenders of the present system is Robert A. Goldwin,

[26] Darryl Baskin, *American Pluralist Democracy* (New York: Van Nostrand Reinhold, 1971), p. 131.

ed., *How Democratic Is America?* (Chicago: Rand McNally, 1971); a work which offers essays by some of the most severe critics of the political system is Marvin E. Gettleman and David Mermelstein, eds., *The Great Society Reader* (New York: Random House, 1967); William P. Gerberding and Duane E. Smith, eds., *The Radical Left: The Abuse of Discontent* (Boston: Houghton Mifflin, 1970) is a collection of statements of writers, journalists, political leaders, and academicians who are highly critical of the position taken by the "radical left"; widely read and provocative in tone and perspective is sociologist Alvin Toffler's *Future Shock* (New York: Random House, 1970), which examines the broad perspective of change and technology on values, life-styles, and human relationships; not recent but still highly relevant is the novel by behavioral psychologist B. F. Skinner, *Walden Two* (New York: Macmillan, 1948), which is the fictional outline of a modern "utopia" in which human conduct and values are conditioned by a totally managed society. Arthur M. Schlesinger, Jr., *The Crises of Confidence* (Boston: Houghton Mifflin, 1969), discusses the impact of violence, Vietnam, and the cold war on the American people who have traditionally placed great confidence in American leadership and resources; Richard E. Rubenstein's *Rebels in Eden: Mass Political Violence in the United States* (Boston: Little, Brown, 1970) views violence in America from both the historical and contemporary perspective and argues that much of the contemporary violence finds its source in the failures of the political system itself. The changing character of democracy in the twentieth century is the concern of E. H. Carr, *The New Society* (Boston: Beacon Press, 1957); a different view, generated by the same concern, is the widely read and debated book by C. Wright Mills, *The Power Elite* (New York: Oxford University Press, 1956).

Those interested in exploring the empirical and behavioral research on political attitudes and consensual norms will find the following sources useful and suggestive of further reading. Gabriel Almond and Sidney Verba, *The Civic Culture* (Boston: Little, Brown, 1965) is available in paperback; Samuel Stouffer, *Communism, Conformity and Civil Liberties* (New York: John Wiley, Science Editions, 1966); and Lloyd A. Free and Hadley Cantril, *The Political Beliefs of Americans* (New Brunswick, N.J.: Rutgers University Press, 1967). Steven R. Brown, "Consistency and the Persistence of Ideology: Some Experimental Results," *Public Opinion Quarterly* 34 (Spring 1970): 62–71, raises some serious and provocative questions about methods used to measure the presence of an "ideology" among Americans. The gap between belief and practice in America is brilliantly illustrated in Gunnar Myrdal's *An American Dilemma* (New York: Harper and Brothers, 1944); V. O. Key, Jr.'s *Public Opinion and American Democracy* (New York: Alfred A. Knopf, 1961) contains perceptive discussion of the gap between theory and practice in American democratic values.

# II

# democratic ideals and constitutional government

The politics of any community evolve among the social characteristics of community members, their ideas about politics, and their political institutions. The pluralism in American society is reflected in ambivalent popular consensus on democratic values and institutions. Looking closely at our democratic ideals and constitutional government, we have seen how much Americans agree upon them and now will examine what those ideals and institutions are made of.

An important difference in ideals and practices distinguishes liberal democracy from other governments and makes liberal democratic government possible. We will trace the historical and philosophic sources of these liberal democratic ideals and practices; these sources have formed those principles by which our democratic way of life operates, and we shall encounter them often as we study civil liberties.

Liberal democratic ideals are partly embodied in the political institutions that the Constitution of the United States established. The Constitution is both an instrument of government and a symbol of American consensus. The way in which the document itself was formulated shows how social conflict is regulated and, as we shall see, the principles we have come to associate with constitutional government in this country — federalism, balanced government, republican government, and protection of civil liberties by the Bill of Rights — influence our ways of representing and resolving social disputes in politics.

# chapter 3

# liberal democracy

We in America think of ourselves as always having been practitioners of democracy, although for the first seventy-five years of our national existence we tolerated slavery, just as the original "demos" of ancient Greece did. We think of a "rule by ballot" but forget that the United States held its first nine national elections in a constitutional manner without a recorded popular vote for presidential candidates.

Nevertheless, most Americans believe — or think they believe — in "democratic values" institutionalized by the Declaration of Independence and the Constitution. These values, passed on from generation to generation as symbols of the "American way," shape the relationship that Americans consider to be proper between government and citizen.

The values may vary from one time to another in meaning and importance, but their continuing influence on the conduct of citizens always remains high. They strongly affect our notions about what is right and wrong political procedure and even help to determine the acceptable level of individual goals and claims on society. In other words, most Americans *act out* a kind of political theory, even though it may be vaguely defined and may not have been subject to conscious review by the individual on whose capacity for rational thinking the theory sets such importance. This is the theory of *liberal democracy* that goes back to our eighteenth-century history.

We broadly define democracy as *a system in which the governed are able to influence significantly public policy decisions made by those who hold formal positions of authority (the governors).*[1] It emphasizes repre-

---

[1] Joseph A. Schumpeter, *Capitalism, Socialism and Democracy* (New York: Harper, 1942), pp. 269–273; Seymour Martin Lipset, *Political Man* (Garden City, N.Y.: Doubleday, 1960), pp. 45–48.

*sentation* of those who are outside the formal structure of authority. Such representation is possible only if there are mechanisms (rules and procedures) that make access to decisionmakers possible. In turn, access depends upon a set of practices and attitudes that encourage political participation of individuals and organizations in conflict not only with each other but with government agencies. These practices and attitudes invoke legal and moral restraints even on a majority which is carried away by an idea or a personality of the moment.

## dimensions of democracy

We will use two basic yardsticks to measure the meaning of American democratic values. One is the *prescriptive dimension,* which includes the ideals and principles supporting the political theory. The second is the *procedural dimension,* the ways and means of putting the theory into practice and maintaining its viability.

We do not fully discuss here the great *ends or goals of government* — the "general welfare," "domestic tranquility," and the "blessings of liberty," all expressly included in the Preamble to the Constitution of the United States. They are linked to the prescriptive and procedural tenets, but primarily as the *objects* toward which democratic ideals and procedures are directed and which democracy as a system is perceived as capable of achieving.

So we shall concentrate on the prescriptive and procedural dimensions, which have in common the theory that the governors (the policymakers) are accountable to the governed (those affected by policy decisions). This theory stems from the proposition that the only acceptable way to enforce responsibility is to assure the governed the right to choose their governors. That is what "representation" is. It is the *process* that is supposed to give diverse individuals and groups a voice in public policy. Lack of representation can lead to frustration and violence, as the American Revolution itself attests.

The *prescriptive* tenets of responsibility and representation are made meaningful by commonly accepted *procedural* rules and arrangements. Thus open, competitive, and free elections in which votes are counted honestly, widespread suffrage, and the right to criticize policy freely and propose alternatives without government reprisals are essential elements in the theory of liberal democracy.

Two important qualifications must be spelled out here. First, although rule by the governed and representation of interests are essential to the democratic system, the procedural arrangements under which they are implemented may vary greatly. In parliamentary systems like those of

**Citizens discuss whether they will permit multiple dwellings in their town. Liberal democracy encourages active participation in governmental policymaking.**

Great Britain and the Federal Republic of Germany, the chief executive — a premier or prime minister — is chosen by a legislature elected by the voters. In the United States, a presidential system, the chief executive is chosen by the electoral college, which meets in January every four years to ratify the popular vote pluralities (*not* necessarily majorities) won by presidential candidates in their states in the preceding November. Since 1958, France has reflected both systems. It still has a premier, but because the president has the power to appoint or dismiss him the French system is now more presidential than parliamentary. Other procedural differences appear from one nation to another, and even among states in this country: voting qualification based on literacy tests or time of residence, nomination for office by convention or direct primary, whether a plurality or majority is required to elect a Governor, and others.

Second, not all procedural rules and practices adhere equally to liberal

democracy's prescriptive tenets. Voting laws or practices that discriminate against groups of voters are, by definition, inconsistent with the
right of the governed to choose their governors. Truly universal suffrage
is hardly ever granted and *practiced* anywhere; only recently did women
win the right to vote in Switzerland; and in the United States a turnout
of 70 percent of the eligible voters is considered good, even in a presidential year. We do know that restriction of suffrage to a specific minority — landowners, for instance, or members of the Caucasian race — is so
inconsistent with the prescriptive principle as to negate democracy. The
precise line between democratic and undemocratic rules and procedures
is extremely difficult to fix and may vary among political systems. That
is, a specific restriction on suffrage in one system may be considered
undemocratic because it conflicts with the inherited standards, or the
social habits of its people; the same practice may not be inconsistent with
democratic values in another system where different standards, habits,
and conditions prevail. It is not easy to separate the prescriptive and
procedural aspects of democratic theory and practice. One "prescribes"
what liberal democracy ought to be; the other is a collection of rules,
laws, and customs which define democratic procedures in a political system.

## democracy and individual dignity

Democratic ideals in the United States, rest upon the belief that every
individual deserves maximum opportunity to develop his intelligence,
his personality, his freedom of choice, *and his dignity*. He can develop
fully only when he is allowed to participate in the regulation of his own
conduct. John Dewey summed it up well: "The keynote of democracy as
a way of life may be expressed, it seems to me, as the necessity for the
participation of every mature human being in formation of the values
that regulate the living of men together."[2] Joint participation in social
choices is supposed to create a genuine sense of community, a sharing
of human experience worth preserving. So conceived, democratic politics has a distinctive purpose: "the education of an entire people to the
point where their intellectual, emotional, and moral capacities have
reached their full potential and they are joined, freely and actively, in
the genuine community."[3] Politics, whether practiced at its best or its
worst, is a distinctly human endeavor. Its quality therefore may be

[2] John Dewey, "Democracy and Educational Administration," *School and Society* 45
(April 3, 1937): 457.
[3] Lane Davis, "The Cost of Realism: Contemporary Restatements of Democracy," *Western Political Quarterly* 18, no. 1 (March 1964): 40.

judged by its contribution to human perfection. Political institutions and procedures (legislatures, periodic elections, etc.) can be designated democratic only to the extent that they make meaningful the democratic value of individual dignity.

Individual dignity has not been fully realized in any democratic polity. Yet the *idea* remains a goal to be sought by democratic societies. It also serves as a yardstick to measure the general quality of democratic life in the political system.

In our society, experience shows deviations from and outright denial of the ideals. Participation in the choice of officeholders and access to policymakers has been denied to various groups. Women have voted in presidential elections without restriction only since 1920, and the struggle of the Negro, the Chicano, the American Indian, and other minorities for political and social equality is a story known to all. Equality of opportunity and participation has not been fully achieved. Nevertheless, the ideal remains strong and viable, brightening the prospect for further achievement of democratic goals.

Having submitted a broad definition of democracy emphasizing the concept of representation, we now offer more specific criteria. A political community is democratic to the extent that (1) popular control of policymakers is broadly based; (2) open discussion and criticism of policy is tolerated; (3) political liberties are protected; and (4) political equality is recognized.[4] As we examine the historical roots of the democratic doctrine in America and the specific meaning of these four essentials, we must be aware that the ideals of democratic practices do not necessarily coincide with the realities. The ideals (prescriptive dimension) are measures with which we can assess the quality and effectiveness of rules and procedures in the democratic system (procedural dimension).

## liberal democracy in colonial america

The colonists brought to America many European concepts about the nature of man and government. The political ideas of John Locke, the seventeenth-century English philosopher, were perhaps the most profoundly influential. But other contemporary thinkers made themselves count. The less libertarian revolutionary leaders used some of the arguments Thomas Hobbes set out in his Leviathan (1651) to support their case for a strong centralized authority. Both James Harrington's thesis that political stability depended on the actual distribution of property

[4] See Henry B. Mayo, *An Introduction to Democratic Theory* (New York: Oxford University Press, 1960).

Recognition of each individual's worth is basic to American democracy, although democratic ideals and realities often diverge.

and Montesquieu's concept of balanced authority affected the thinking of many colonial politicians. More important than political theory, in the minds of the men who took up arms in 1775, was the idea that they were British subjects who had been shortchanged by a faraway government in London. They thought they had a natural claim to the rights of British subjects everywhere, including the right of petition and peaceful redress from Parliament. In the words of James Otis, a major American revolutionary figure, "every British Subject, born on the continent of America, or in any other of the British dominions, is entitled to all the natural, essential, inherent and inseparable rights of our fellow subjects in Great Britain."[5]

These notions soon changed. Less than fifteen months separated the battles of Lexington and Concord and the Declaration of Independence; in a little more than a year what had begun as a nasty little English civil

[5] Quoted in Alpheus Thomas Mason, *Free Government in the Making*, 3rd ed. (New York: Oxford University Press, 1965), p. 96.

war turned into something else entirely. Moreover, both before and after independence the old concepts were being modified by the unique experience of the colonists in the new American society, which contained no feudalism, no ingrown hereditary privilege, and no radical and underprivileged proletariat. Americans felt themselves to have been "born free," as de Tocqueville put it, and adopted a "natural liberalism" reflecting the absence of struggle against entrenched classes.[6]

De Tocqueville's remarkable *Democracy in America* appeared in French and English in the middle 1830s — significant timing, because this means he traveled in America during the presidency of Andrew Jackson when "democracy" finally was becoming an acceptable word. Nonetheless, from the early colonial period Americans had been developing a democratic liberalism on the John Locke model. Middle class in its profile, this liberalism emphasized the virtues of hard work and such rights as that of the individual to acquire and hold private property. Few American Presidents have thought of challenging that value outlook. It has characterized our nation throughout its history so intensely that Louis Hartz speaks of America as having the "moral unanimity of a liberal society" and as exhibiting the intolerance of a "dogmatic liberalism" toward any concepts not fitting into a Lockean background.[7] Thus, attacks by socialists on the concept of private property, whether or not made within the democratic framework of free expression and debate, have historically been considered "un-American" or "undemocratic."

Carl Becker shrewdly observes that "the strength of the Declaration [of Independence] was precisely that it said what everyone was thinking."[8] Locke used the expression "life, health, liberty or possessions"; Jefferson, writing the Declaration of Independence, apparently thought "the pursuit of happiness" more important than possessions. But the fact that Jefferson was wrongly accused in his own time of lifting the language of the Declaration from Locke certifies the influence of Locke on two centuries of American political thinking.

## locke's political theory and democratic values

John Locke (1632–1704) founded his political thought upon the concept of an initial *state of nature* preceding civil society in which all men were "free, equal, and independent" and governed only by *natural law,* which

[6] Louis Hartz, *The Liberal Tradition in America* (New York: Harcourt, Brace, Harvest Books, 1955).

[7] *Ibid.,* chap. 1.

[8] Carl L. Becker, *The Declaration of Independence* (New York: Harcourt, Brace, 1922), pp. 24, 26.

emanated from God.[9] Man gains knowledge of natural law by using his power to reason. This natural law is the basis of the fundamental and inalienable rights of life, liberty, and property. These natural rights reside with every man. Because they do not originate with man, it follows that no man or group of men may usurp them, nor can they be voluntarily given up.

THE NEED FOR A CIVIL SOCIETY. Unlike Hobbes, who thought man had been born a brute and had to be governed without what we now call "permissiveness," Locke thought of the original state of nature as happy and rational. If man's life in this state, as it developed, became quite inconvenient or insecure, it was because man tended to violate the fundamental moral law. In the state of nature, no one was obligated to obey man-made rules of authority, and the laws of nature could be enforced only through action taken by each individual who had suffered injury. This is a recognizable description of the "law of nature" by which individuals once lived on the American frontier, and Locke thought that both man and nature needed some help. In nature's raw state, the "want of a common judge" to protect individual rights created insecurity and brought man to recognize the need of a civil society authorized to make laws and enforce obedience. Because the individual was largely free in the state of nature (he was morally obligated only to respect others' natural rights), any provision under which his liberty was qualified or given up required his consent.

THE SOCIAL CONTRACT. Locke's means of bringing man from the state of nature into an orderly civil society was the "social contract." Each individual agrees with every other individual to a contract under which he forfeits some of his natural freedom in return for the benefits derived from man-made rules defining relationships among individuals. In short, the rights of the natural state from which men had come were replaced by those of the community. Locke held, however, that the rights of life, liberty, and property were universal and inalienable; the civil society created by the contract was prohibited from violating these rights. Its authority was limited to activities serving the common good.

 THE GOVERNMENT. But who was to decide which rules were to be made? Recognizing that unanimous consent would be impossible, Locke suggested rule by the majority as the only practical decisionmaking device.

Government exists, then, *only as a trustee of the people who have agreed to the contract.* It has no authority independent of that granted

---

[9] Locke's political thought is best represented in his *Two Treatises of Government* (1690).

by the people. If this arrangement is abused by political officials then, according to Locke, the right of revolution becomes the ultimate weapon. Whenever governors violate the natural rights of the governed, they for- feit the authority vested in them under the social contract. Disobedience and rebellion are justified, and the individual is freed of any obligation to obey civil law. But his rebellion, if successful, merely returns man to the state of nature. There he remains until he agrees to the creation of another government by contract.

## the declaration of independence

The Declaration of Independence incorporated two basic Lockean themes: rational individualism and republican government. Both have since been built into American institutions and beliefs.

### rational individualism

The first proposition underlying the Declaration is that man is a rational individual having inalienable rights, that he is politically equal to other men, and capable of rational choice between alternative courses of ac- tion. *He can therefore govern himself.* This concept of individualism, which emphasizes the right of each man to make his own choices and to have that right respected and protected, is the taproot of liberal de- mocracy. As the Declaration of Independence says, government exists "to secure these rights," and "whenever any Form of Government becomes destructive of these ends, it is the Right of the People to alter or to abolish it." This is an assertion of human dignity, founded on natural and hence inalienable rights that each individual has the right to defend, by revolu- tion if necessary.

The concept of individual rights and dignity has at least two important implications. One is that man is to be judged as an individual and not according to his economic or social position or his race or creed. In lib- eral democracy, "equality before the law" is a clear expression of indi- vidual worth. The second implication is equality of opportunity, meaning the conditions under which a person can compete for economic, social, or political benefits. It does not mean that all men are, or ought to be, equal in intelligence, ability, wealth, or status. It does mean that individ- ual choices ought to be free and that arbitrary limitations on opportunity are unacceptable.

The concept of rational individualism thus provides the moral basis — the prescriptive dimension — of liberal democracy. It indicates what ought to guide the actions of men in their political relationships. Two objections come immediately to mind, but neither negates either the value or the validity of the theme and its implications. It is true that the existence of natural rights and human dignity and individualism cannot be proved empirically. It is also true that real-life democratic governments dilute these moral postulates in practice. Nevertheless, no American government can ignore them entirely. Natural rights are presumed to exist — if only because Locke and Jefferson said so. Their triumph was to be credible when they asserted the existence of unchangeable and valid norms that were superior to man-made rules and provided the basis for judging government itself. Generations of Americans from the New England colonists on down have rallied to the Lockean standard in identifying public evils, promoting political and economic reforms, and generally insisting that any system that flouts these natural rights has forfeited its contractual right to exist.

## republican government

The second basic theme in the Declaration is that of republican or representative government. Assuming the political equality of men and the notion that community authority exists only to achieve the aims of the governed, it follows that the people must have an effective way of making their voices heard. Law-making is complicated, particularly when courts stand guard over the language of the laws, and it is impossible to conceive of a system under which all men participate directly in this process. The obvious alternative to direct democracy is representative democracy; the people choose public officials to act on their behalf and render themselves accountable by submitting to periodic reelection or rejection. Because the representatives, like the citizens, will not see eye to eye on most matters, the only practical way to operate is by majority rule. Liberal democratic theory clearly implies, however, that the minority may not be coerced by a majority that desires to violate *basic human rights and freedoms which are understood to be beyond the reach of the popular will.*

The relationship between majority rule and minority rights is an uneasy one, and it is a dilemma for democratic theory and practice. Ultimately, majority rule rests on the ethical and moral assertion that purely private interests should not override considerations of the "public good," "community interest," or the "national interest." When there is no *rational* basis for the will of the majority, then majority rule becomes a vulnerable if not indefensible proposition. The will of a majority, expressed in an arbitrary and irrational voice is morally unacceptable if the people — acting directly or through chosen representatives — violate the moral imperative of rational choice (which includes recognition of minority rights). Its decisions, under the higher law of liberal democracy, are illegitimate.

## democratic ideals and the american experience

In the summer of 1963, Dr. Martin Luther King addressed 200,000 persons who had marched on Washington, D.C., to protest against racial discrimination. King drew upon the Declaration of Independence to dramatize his philosophy of nonviolent change and his faith in democratic ideals. He spoke in the language of the American ideological consensus when he said, "I have a dream that one day this nation will rise up, live out the true meaning of its creed: 'We hold these truths to be self-evident, that all men are created equal.' "

For his listeners, King's eloquent reference to the ideological foundations of the American creed was a symbolic reminder of this country's democratic heritage. Beyond eloquence, the tie binding the social and economic life of the eighteenth and twentieth centuries was by no means self-evident. But the broad patterns of change which in two hundred years dramatically altered the face of America do relate to shifts in values or disputes over values that characterize the present era.

## the eighteenth century

The United States in its first years of independence was a nation of country dwellers. In 1790, more than 90 percent of a population of less than four million lived on farms. The wealth of the nation was its agriculture. Manufacturing was in the nascent stages, and New England had most of the little there was. By 1830, the American population had grown to thirteen million, of whom more than 95 percent were native born. Many national and ethnic groups were represented in the total population, including a lot of Germans and Scotch-Irish in Pennsylvania. But white American society in the early 1800s remained basically English and Protestant in its values and style of life. There were no large cities, even on the Eastern seaboard where the nation's people and power were concentrated. To the west lay the vast wilderness of the Louisiana Territory, purchased from France in 1803. It was hostile and largely unmapped, but it offered boundless economic opportunities to individuals dissatisfied with their surroundings. They could, if they chose, "get up and go."

"I have a dream that one day this nation will rise up, live out the true meaning of its creed: 'We hold these truths to be self-evident, that all men are created equal.' "

the nineteenth century

As late as 1860, agriculture still represented 50 percent of the nation's wealth, and by far the majority of Americans still lived on farms. But in the 1850s 300,000 emigrants had been arriving yearly, and thousands settled not only in New York and Boston but in the new cities farther west — Pittsburgh, St. Louis, Chicago. By 1900, about 15 percent of a population of seventy-six million were foreign born, and agriculture's share of the national wealth had fallen to 20 percent. The English and Protestant character of the white population had been permanently altered by millions of immigrants, including a high percentage of Roman Catholics. After 1880, they came mostly from southern and eastern Europe rather than from the English-speaking British Isles, and they brought with them new ethnic identities and new life styles.

By 1900, the industrial revolution, fueled by the Civil War and the invention of the Bessemer steel manufacturing process, was transforming America from a basically agricultural and rural nation into an industrial and urban society. The technological and demographic change deeply affected American life. A new "gospel of wealth," fashioned out of the Protestant ethic of hard work and individual achievement and the value of individualism in the democratic creed, preached that success and affluence went to those who were most fit to survive in the economic marketplace. Government was not supposed to interfere in the market-place; according to laissez-faire economic doctrine, artificial restraints ran counter to "natural" laws. By the twentieth century, the businessman not only symbolized the American success story but also dominated government; the United States Senate itself was a sort of millionaires' club. The giant corporations that dominated the new industrial economy were owned and controlled by a handful of people. About one-eighth of the population owned seven-eighths of the wealth, and more than half of the property belonged to 1 percent of the population. Until the presidency of Theodore Roosevelt, efforts to restore an economic balance were blocked by the United States Supreme Court, which protected laissez-faire economics by striking down laws that sought to regulate working conditions and employer-employee relationships. In 1886, the Court declared that a corporation was a "person" within the meaning of the Constitution and thus entitled to the same protections (and presumably controls) as individual citizens.[10]

## the twentieth century

As more and more wealth was concentrated in fewer and fewer hands, the distance between the top and bottom rungs of the economic ladder widened. The farmer, whose father and grandfather had prided themselves in being independent yeomen, often found himself a tenant tiller of soil because there was not enough land to go around. At best, he was a debtor businessman; the costs of new agricultural equipment and production forced him into dependency upon banking interests. Small bus-

---

[10] *Santa Clara County v. Southern Pacific Railroad Co.,* 118 U.S. 394 (1886). The most striking example of the application by the Supreme Court of the dominant business philosophy came in *Lochner v. New York,* 198 U.S. 45 (1905).

inessmen and professionals (doctors, lawyers, professors), once at the top of the class structure, were now outranked by the industrial ruling class. To compound their already great wealth, these industrial barons needed cheap labor, and they got it. The courts took a dim view of labor unions; effective minimum-wage legislation was far in the future; and the immigration laws that existed merely discriminated against Orientals. Immigration reached high tide in the ten years preceding the outbreak of World War I; an average of nearly one million people a year entered this country between the end of 1904 and the end of 1914. Thousands of unskilled Europeans quickly became part of an underpaid and exploited immigrant-laboring class. The world of individualistic entrepreneurs like the proud craftsman and the skilled worker began to come unstuck; the new working class was made up of men (and women) employed by huge industries and dependent upon them for a subsistence livelihood. Something else had disappeared from the scene: the frontier itself. Opportunities to "go West," were fewer and hardly any existed for the urban-bound immigrant who barely spoke English. The rise of huge industrial cities saw the beginning of tenement living and social deterioration marked by poverty, substandard working and living conditions, and disease. Despite the protests of farmers and relatively weak trade unions, the business ethic dominated national policy until the 1930s.

Analyzing the protests of the late nineteenth and early twentieth centuries against social, political, and economic conditions, historian Richard Hofstadter found that they were based on the old democratic ideal of equality of opportunity. "Because it was always possible to assume a remarkable measure of social equality and a fair minimum of subsistence, the goal of revolt tended to be neither social democracy nor social equality, but greater opportunity."[11] Assumptions that the system was balanced by competing economic and social interests capable of checking each other were clearly false. Only economic collapse and the worst depression in our history finally changed them.

The New Deal of Franklin D. Roosevelt in the 1930s represented an attempt to restore a balance between business and other interests within the system. Roosevelt's reference to a society that was "ill clothed, ill fed, and ill housed" was a clear rejection of laissez-faire philosophy. Through legislation, the New Deal sought not only to alleviate the social and economic ills of the depression but to create, through government regulation, a new and fairer balance of economic power. New legislation guaranteed

[11] Richard Hofstadter, *The Age of Reform* (New York: Alfred A. Knopf, 1955), p. 10. This is an excellent treatment of the reform movements of the late nineteenth and early twentieth centuries.

the right of labor unions to bargain with employers over wages and working conditions: to no one's surprise, people like steel and automobile manufacturers refused to give in easily, and violent strikes followed. Other laws were passed to regulate securities transactions, establish minimum wage rates, put ceilings on the number of hours worked, and provide social security and unemployment benefits. Such measures do not sound very revolutionary now, but they were hotly debated at the time. All reflected a belief that democratic ideals — equality, individualism, and government for the welfare of all — could be made meaningful only if government acted and intervened positively. The democratic concept of limited government did not, the New Dealers argued, mean government could not act to redress social and economic ills and an imbalance of political interests.

It took a new European war, which broke out in 1939, to end the unemployment problem, but by then the New Deal had brought about a new relationship between the corporate and industrial interests and other major economic groups like the farmers and organized labor. It had also established the responsibility of government to use its powers on behalf of the individual's security and welfare. Yet the groups that benefited most from the New Deal were largely in the middle levels of the system — farmers, small businessmen, white collar workers. These were more or less the same people who had participated in the American "political marketplace" since the eighteenth century. The New Deal achieved what it did because its legislation was *within the American system,* and since 1787 that system has mostly, or entirely, excluded conflict on issues that lay outside the traditional areas of policy. The Constitution, with its checks and balances and its loose dispersion of authority at the national and state levels of government, not only restrained majority power but also encouraged governments to act slowly or not at all. This constitutional framework, along with geographical expansions, rapid economic development, a social system that until the late nineteenth century provided the individual with opportunity to move up in the class structure, brought about almost universal acceptance of the political system. Even the New Deal brought no fundamental change in the structure or basic functions of government organization and procedure. It accepted both the prescriptive and the procedural tenets of liberal democracy that have been present throughout American history.

Then, in the 1950s and 1960s, it became apparent that dissatisfactions lay beneath the apparent acceptance of traditional processes and institutions. These grave dissatisfactions surfaced when active and sometimes violent protests were organized by blacks, the poor, Spanish-Americans, American Indians, migrant workers, and other elements (e.g., young

Standing before the statue of Massasoit the Great Sachem of the Wampanoags, "protector of the Pilgrims," an Indian reminds his audience of the Pilgrims' debt to the Indians.

Americans) who challenged the system and argued that it was ignoring (or incapable of solving) the serious problems of the second half of twentieth-century America.

This argument stemmed from the democratic notion of equality. A nation which "prescribed" equality for all imposed vast inequalities upon those who did not share in the economic abundance of the system. Nor, in fact, did they share equality of political rights. In 1968, the National Advisory Commission on Civil Disorders concluded that black Americans were reacting to circumstances that denied them "dignity, respect, and acceptance," and this had resulted in "alienation and hostility toward the institutions of law and government and the white society which controls them."[12]

The accelerating technological revolution of the twentieth century, particularly since the end of World War II, is difficult to grasp because of its magnitude and pace. For example, half the energy consumed by man during the past two thousand years for heating, cooking, transport, making war, etc., has been consumed in the last one hundred years.[13] Alvin Toffler has described the "disease of change" or "future shock,"

[12] *Report of the National Advisory Commission on Civil Disorders* (Washington, D.C.: Government Printing Office, 1968), p. 92.
[13] Cited in Alvin Toffler, *Future Shock* (New York: Bantam Books, 1970), p. 23.

a term he coined to describe "the shattering stress and disorientation that we induce in individuals by subjecting them to too much change in too short a time."[14] One change is less abstract and is statistically measurable. The American urban population in 1900 was only 40 percent of the total; by 1950 this had been turned around, and 60 percent of Americans lived in cities. *Only twenty years later more Americans lived in suburbs than in either the central cities or in rural areas.* One more example: As late as 1940, three-fourths of American blacks lived in the south, and most of them were rural. By 1970, seven out of ten blacks lived in metropolitan areas, and only 48 percent were residents of the South.

These factors have changed the American community in the 1970s in varying degrees and have influenced the subject matter of political conflict. We argue now about national "priorities" in a manner unheard of thirty years ago, but it is a natural thing to add new issues and interests to the political agenda. The current debate over priorities has much to do with our discussion of the ideological dimensions of democracy. Slum-lordism and the decay of our cities; the deteriorating quality of social and physical environment; white and black racism; the moral content of American foreign policy; population quality and quantity — all are now part of the national dialogue. They are there not only in the "procedural" context of setting action priorities but also because they closely relate to the prescriptive axioms of the democratic creed. As one scholar has observed,

> Black power, student power, peace power, these are watchwords of the multifarious radical factions who insist that political freedom, social freedom, economic freedom, and psychological freedom *now* are the indispensable conditions for the establishment of justice, the promotion of the general welfare, and the securing of the blessings of liberty; and that to whatever extent may be necessary such other constitutional goals as the assurance of domestic tranquility and provision for the common defense must be foregone, or even repudiated, in order to maximize the scope and the extent of the radical redistribution of our assets as a nation, in relation to the three criteria of Justice, Welfare, and Liberty.[15]

No broad agreement yet exists among individuals and interests about the new problems confronting the American system. A 1968 Harris poll showed that 67 percent of whites agreed that blacks "are asking for more than [they are] ready for." Yet *in the same poll*, 58 percent agreed that "America has discriminated against Negroes for too long." Harris also found that although whites associate blacks with crime, they *also* (by 63

---

[14] *Ibid.*, p. 2.
[15] Glendon Schubert, *The Constitutional Polity* (Boston: Boston University Press, 1970), p. 135.

percent) agreed that "Until there is justice for minorities, there will not be law and order."[16]

Can democratic ideals of equality, participation, and freedom be maintained through the procedures and institutions of the contemporary American system? This question must be analyzed within the framework of the operating principles that are essential to the meaning of liberal democracy.

## principles of democratic life

Four such principles are essential in a liberal democratic system: *popular control, political leadership, political equality,* and *political liberty.* Politics, we have said, is a human activity that seeks to regulate social conflict. The characteristic procedures of democracy represent a distinctive style of conflict regulation, marked by efforts to provide the widest possible personal choice through *open but nonviolent conflict.*

## popular control

The right of the voter to choose representatives and to hold them periodically accountable is essential in a liberal democracy. The heart of democracy is *the peaceful management of social conflict by channeling conflict into institutionalized competition for public office.* If the right to choose is to be exercised effectively, there must be universal suffrage, regular periodic elections, candidate competition, meaningful policy alternatives, and participation by all major interests. The American political system has added to its stability by broadening the suffrage, by eliminating property and sex as barriers and, in recent years, most racial barriers. Today more Americans than ever express their satisfaction or dissatisfaction with the way "things" are going. Taking part in elections is a symbol of individual consent to the policies which are adopted and — perhaps more important — to the democratic way in which they are *being* adopted.[17]

Popular control might not mean much, however, if it were exercised only through the vote. Since democratic theory assumes that human beings are fallible, it follows that public officials must be kept under constant public scrutiny and criticism. Therefore there are no sacred

[16] Richard M. Scammon and Ben J. Wattenberg, *The Real Majority* (New York: Coward, McCann & Geoghegan, 1971), pp. 97–99.
[17] Murray Edelman, *The Symbolic Uses of Politics* (Urbana, Ill.: University of Illinois Press, 1964), pp. 2–3.

In a liberal democracy, it is essential that citizens exercise their right and duty to vote. Voting channels conflict into institutionalized competition for public office.

cows in politics: nothing is immune to criticism, divergent views and opinions must be tolerated, and there must be ways and institutions through which they can be expressed.

In an opinion that struck down a state law compelling public school students to pledge allegiance to the flag, Supreme Court Justice Robert H. Jackson called the right of political unorthodoxy "a fixed star in our constitutional constellation."[18] In practice, proponents of unpopular views often run the risk of public vilification or repressive action taken by public officials on behalf of a majority that is less tolerant than it likes to think. Socialist Party candidates in the United States have always faced an unsympathetic and frequently hostile public because their proposals oppose such deeply held values as private property and limited government interference in economic matters. The Socialists polled their highest vote for President (919,000) in 1920 when their candidate, Eugene Debs, a pacifist during World War I, was in jail. In the 1960s, action by local police against the Black Panther Party was criticized as an attempt to eliminate the party altogether.[19]

These examples do not invalidate the point that our society has a variety of institutions through which the electorate can make known its pref-

[18] *West Virginia Board of Education* v. *Barnette,* 319 U.S. 624 (1943).
[19] For a statement of the position of the Black Panthers see the statement in Henry J. Silverman, ed., *American Radical Thought* (Lexington, Mass.: D. C. Heath, 1970). See also John Fisher, "Black Panthers and Their White Hero-Worshippers," *Harper's,* (August, 1970): pp. 18–26.

erences and modify or substantially alter policy. Periodic elections stimulate discussion between partisan groups seeking "a contract" to govern. Political parties display both similarities and dissimilarities of outlook as they mobilize popular support, woo potential followers, and encourage their sympathizers to go out and ring doorbells. By delineating the issues, parties make the voting act meaningful and consistent with the democratic concept of popular control.

Two other major institutional vehicles for popular control are the schools and the news media. One of the strongest reasons for supporting academic freedom is that it permits the free exchange of different ideas; an educated citizen with a knowledge of unpopular views is better qualified to make a rational choice. The press justifies its existence in a democracy by the service it performs reporting conflict and transmitting information. "Where the press is free," wrote Jefferson, "and every man able to read, all is safe."[20] In democratic theory, the legitimate function of newspapers, magazines, and radio and television commentators is the communication of information to assist in the popular discovery of truth. This was the crux of the argument of those who defended the publication, in June 1971, of the secret Pentagon Papers that exposed embarrassing and disturbing aspects of American policy in Southeast Asia during the 1960s. The oddities of this case brought about one of the severest tests the First Amendment had ever had, but a majority of the Supreme Court supported the right of the press to publish the papers in the interest of free inquiry and examination. Like the schools, the printed press and its airwave adjuncts have a contractual responsibility to make the "marketplace of ideas" meaningful.

## political leadership

Leadership is also a requisite of liberal democracy, but not just because the people cannot run the government themselves and therefore must choose leaders to run it for them. Leaders help make popular control effective by formulating policy alternatives and mobilizing electoral groups into winning coalitions. Popular participation is realized when political leaders define issues for community criticism and discussion, and conflict between political leaders helps preserve free choice in a democracy. The individuals who participate in political affairs by thinking up better ways to do things, recruiting candidates, and holding offices themselves are performing the vital function of "offering a choice."

[20] Letter to Colonel Charles Yancey, 1816, quoted in Saul K. Padover, *Thomas Jefferson on Democracy* (New York: The New American Library, Mentor Books, 1946), p. 89.

Party functions of leadership are discussed in later chapters. Although the American commitment to substantive democratic ideas is generally weak in practice, a political subculture of activists and leaders have a higher commitment to these ideas than the population at large. That this group also comprises the bulk of officeholders, opinion leaders, and policymakers does not mean that American democracy is a system in which an elite dictates terms to all the rest. These leaders are recruited from a variety of social classes, exhibit a diversity of social interests, and are not the only people able to influence those in policymaking positions.

### political equality and liberty

If popular control and leadership are to work as intended in democratic theory, two related but separate principles must be recognized. The first is that each voter should be *politically equal*. Essentially this means that

Both a new confidence and feelings of outrage appear in the charges minority groups have made in their jockeying for equal treatment.

every adult should have the franchise, each voter should cast only one vote per office, and each vote cast should be counted equally. The principle of "one man, one vote" leads to the corollary that a majority of votes should count for more than a minority in the final decision.

The second principle is that each voter should enjoy the *political liberty* that fosters the kind of individual participation essential to democracy. Specifically, each person should be free to exercise political choice, criticize policies (and perhaps the politico-constitutional system), organize groups, parties, and associations to win converts from within the opposition, and follow alternative political leadership. This is why constitutional guarantees of freedom of speech, press, and assembly are not just "prescriptive"; *they are procedurally essential.* Each guarantee is designed to make sure that (1) neither a majority nor a minority decision will block the opportunity of any community member to participate at some point in conflict regulation; (2) the voting community will be able to transmit preferences and opinions to leaders and get, in return, proposals and action; (3) political leaders will not have a legal opportunity to destroy the opposition; and (4) individual choice and assessment of existing policies, officials, and institutions will not suffer from artificial limitations placed upon free inquiry.

The tolerance of minorities is assumed in all four requirements. Majorities rarely need protection of their freedom to speak or write. Justice Douglas, defending the same rights of the minority, offered the eloquent argument that "freedom to differ is not limited to things that do not matter much. That would be a mere shadow of freedom. The test of its substance is the right to differ as to things that touch the heart of the existing order."[21] Today's minority can never hope to become tomorrow's majority unless it has the opportunity to argue its case in the marketplace of ideas. Government "by the people" demands, therefore, a commitment to the procedures through which minorities can act in a meaningful fashion. Liberal democracy cannot exist without minority participation.

### american ideology revisited

Commentators have frequently cited the "pragmatic mood" of Americans. We seem to be more interested in practical solutions, experiment, and "common sense" than in theories or doctrine.[22] Since their political ideas are "givens" rather than conclusions from ideological debates,

---

[21] *Beilan v. Board of Education,* 356 U.S. 399 (1958).
[22] V. O. Key, Jr., *Public Opinion and American Democracy* (New York: Alfred A. Knopf, 1961), p. 49.

Americans do not need to be highly conscious of a democratic ideology. Thus the average American knows what he is "against" better than he knows what he is "for." Abroad, he will see that the conduct of a Stalin negates democratic principles, as he and most other Americans understand these principles. In domestic affairs, he will see that an established state church or a law banning criticism of legislation clearly would violate democratic values and procedures.

In addition, the average American's concept of liberal democracy relies heavily on symbols. The American flag stirs an emotional attachment to the democratic values "America stands for." Even though these values may not be defined with precision, national holidays provide opportunities to emphasize them. We celebrate the birthdays of leaders like Washington and Lincoln because they are folk heroes who embody the highest virtues of the American past. But the Constitution itself is the outstanding symbol of the American liberal democratic faith. Those who favor or oppose a specific action on public policy invoke the great wisdom of the Founding Fathers and the instrument that reflects the meaning of democracy, freedom, and individual liberty. The language of the Constitution can be cited to support almost any argument — and usually is.

Most Americans, then, are at least loyal to liberal democratic values in their symbolic form. Despite deprivation and disagreement, symbolic loyalty alone is sufficient to promote contentment for many within the community. Indeed, democratic symbols become ends in themselves. Symbolic gratification may be a reward sufficient to keep the dissatisfied within the community; and for those who disapprove of the actual application of democratic ideals, attachment to the symbols demonstrates both to themselves and to others that, despite our disputes, we are all "Americans" and "democrats."

More often than not, the decisions of the politically active leadership, where commitment to liberal democratic ideals is more conscious, are accepted by the more inert mass.[23] There is therefore a very definite liberal democratic tone to American politics. Furthermore, in the United States social conflict generally is not a clash of ideologies but of interests. The political framework is taken for granted.

If ideological cleavage is not the basis of present dissatisfaction, then the sources of differences must be sought elsewhere. The theory, ideals, and symbols exist side by side with the realities of social and political inequality and with what critics see as an unresponsive system. Sociologist Scott Greer, remarking on the apparent stability of the American system, finds that even though the average man does not participate fully in democratic processes, freedom of choice is preserved for him by "the

[23] *Ibid.,* p. 50.

balance of 'countervailing forces' in the system."[24] The basis of American pluralism lies, then, in the struggle between diverse groups.

The protest movements of the 1960s and 1970s have leaned heavily upon the charge that men in charge of the system — the "power structure" — will not or cannot place the issues of the disadvantaged and the new dissenters on the agenda of national politics. The question, then, is not simply the *distribution* of influence. Control of policy and access to policymakers are not evenly distributed in the American system and never have been. More important, it is a question of assessing "influence over the range and types of alternatives considered. . . . In other words, what determines the agenda for political controversy within a community."[25] Because the distribution of influence over policy is distorted, the critics now ask how this balance may be changed and with what consequences.[26]

Such questions are related to ideology, but they do not indicate true ideological cleavage. As in the past, social conflict in America remains not a clash of ideologies but of interests competing within durable institutions and procedures. Unquestionably, the quality of democracy is related to the range of responses by government to minority dissatisfactions. We do suggest, however, that an ambivalent majority, an activist minority, and the promise of symbolic gratification all promote stability in the American political community. And despite some harsh and abrasive evidence to the contrary, this community possesses a liberal democratic tone as well.

*bibliographical note*

The literature on democratic theory is abundant. Leslie Lipson's *The Democratic Civilization* (New York: Oxford University Press, 1964) presents a helpful historical perspective on the development of democratic theory. For those interested in exploring further the theory of John Locke, see Thomas P. Peardon's introduction to John Locke's *The Second Treatise of Government* (New York: Liberal Arts Press, 1952).

To explore the range of views on the meaning and essential elements of democracy the following works, all available in paperback editions, will prove

[24] Scott Greer, "Individual Participation in Mass Society," in Roland Young, ed., *Approaches to the Study of Politics* (Evanston, Ill.: Northwestern University Press, 1958), pp. 340–341.

[25] Roger W. Cobb and Charles D. Elder, "The Politics of Agenda-Building: An Alternative Perspective for Modern Democratic Theory," *The Journal of Politics* 33 (Nov. 1971): 897, 905.

[26] *Ibid.,* p. 905.

useful. Henry B. Mayo, *An Introduction to Democratic Theory* (New York: Oxford University Press, 1960) identifies the major features of democratic theory and compares it with other points of view. A. D. Lindsay, *The Modern Democratic State* (New York: Oxford University Press, 1962), discusses the "operative ideals" of the modern democratic state. Thomas L. Thorson, *The Logic of Democracy* (New York: Holt, Rinehart and Winston, 1962), argues that democracy's essential element is the maintenance of an open marketplace for ideas and social change. Willmoore Kendall's *John Locke and the Doctrine of Majority Rule* (Urbana, Ill.: University of Illinois Press, 1941) is a provocative argument that Lockean theory is majoritarian and not individualistic in its emphasis.

Literature on American democracy and its development covers a wide spectrum. All the following are in paperback editions. Among the most important works is Alexis de Tocqueville's classic study, *Democracy in America,* available in several editions. Another classic study by a nineteenth-century foreign observor, James Bryce, *The American Commonwealth* (New York: G. P. Putnam's Sons, 1960) is less analytical than De Tocqueville's work. Neil Reimer, *The Democratic Experiment: American Political Theory,* vol. I (Princeton, N.J.: Van Nostrand, 1967) treats the major factors shaping American democratic theory from the seventeenth century through the first quarter of the nineteenth century. For a brilliant analysis and defense of democratic values from the perspective of one of the great philosophers of the twentieth century, see John Dewey, *The Public and Its Problems* (Denver, Colo.: Alan Swallow, 1954). Gunnar Myrdal's *The American Dilemma: The Negro Problem and Modern Democracy* (New York: Harper & Row, 1944) is an influential treatment of the American creed from the perspective of its ideals and its application. One of the finest explorations of the meaning and value of freedom is Felix E. Oppenheim's *Dimensions of Freedom: An Analysis* (New York: St. Martin's Press, 1961).

We can suggest only a small sample of the large body of material related to contemporary American patterns. It varies widely in its emotional content and analytical quality. Michael Harrington's *The Other America* (Baltimore: Penguin Books, 1964) presents a powerful analysis of the scope and effects of poverty in American society. Empirical data in the analysis of American values is presented in William Kornhauser's excellent work, *The Politics of Mass Society* (Glencoe, Ill.: Free Press, 1959) and in Lloyd Free and Hadley Cantril, *The Political Beliefs of Americans* (New York: Simon and Schuster, 1968). More argumentative in tone and content is Henry S. Kariel's *The Decline of Pluralism* (Stanford, Calif.: Stanford University Press, 1961), which maintains that corporate power has impeded democracy and pluralism is no longer a viable theory in American politics. Theodore Lowi, *The End of Liberalism* (New York: W. W. Norton, 1969), argues that because of the great power of private organizations popular control of government no longer exists as is supposed by the pluralistic argument. The argument for the pluralism of power in the American system is presented by Arnold Rose, *The Power Structure* (New York: Oxford University Press, 1967).

The literature about protest has significantly increased in volume over the past several years. Staughton Lynd, *Intellectual Origins of the American Revolution* (New York: Pantheon, 1968), finds that the radical thought of the present has intellectual roots as far back as Colonial America. Richard Hofstadter, *The Age of Reform* (New York: Alfred A. Knopf, 1955), analyzes the reform movements of the late nineteenth and early twentieth centuries.

Illustrative of the position of the radical left are: Eldridge Cleaver, *Soul on Ice* (New York: McGraw Hill, 1968), the argument of a major black leader; Thomas Harden, *Rebellion in Newark: Official Violence and Ghetto Response* (New York: Vintage Books, 1967); and Staughton Lynd and Thomas Hayden, *The Other Side* (New York: New American Library, 1966). An excellent dialogue between a conservative and a radical on the current revolutionary thought in America is Peter L. Berger and Richard John Neuhaus, *Movement and Revolution* (Garden City, N.Y.: Anchor Books, 1970). Responses to the radical challenge are many. See, for example, the essays in Robert A. Goldwin, ed., *How Democratic Is America?* (Chicago, Ill.: Rand McNally, 1971), and William P. Gerberding and Duane E. Smith, eds., *The Radical Left: The Abuse of Discontent* (Boston: Houghton Mifflin, 1970).

# the constitution:
# roots, principles, growth

The Constitution of the United States is probably the most revered document of its kind in the world. It symbolizes both the political unification of our community and its ultimate legitimizing force. If something is "constitutional," it is legitimate and usually acceptable to the groups in conflict. Great political issues generally have constitutional relevance. The principles of the Constitution are understood to be subject to changing interpretation but are regarded nonetheless as fundamental and durable. For two hundred years, the Constitution has served successfully first as the basic law for a small agricultural nation of a little more than three million people, then for an expanding continental state, and now for an industrial giant of more than two hundred million people who have new and difficult problems.

## american constitutionalism:
## instrument and symbol of government

When we speak of American constitutionalism, we mean at least two things — the constitutional system and the Constitution itself. The basic understandings and accepted procedures under which a community lives and regulates social conflict form its *constitutional system*. This system includes rules, customs, traditions, ideas, myths, and attitudes as well as any written constitutional documents. In America, the Constitution is a written document that describes the *constituted authority* in the polity. It defines the formal structure of government and the distribution of power among public officials and specifies the sources and limits of legal authority. This is the literal, or documentary, Constitution.

## the constitution as instrument

Men lend substance to the phrase "a government of laws" by actively accepting the restraints upon their behavior that laws imply. In this sense, the American Constitution is a great deal more than a hallowed parchment written at Philadelphia in 1787. It is *an instrument* for regulating social conflict as well as *a symbol* of consensus. As *an instrument*, the Constitution is not limited simply to its original text, which is surprisingly short, and its twenty-six amendments, which are also surprisingly short considering our experience with amending constitutions at the state level. Time and experience have altered American political institutions. Moreover, the actions of a dozen or more Presidents from George Washington to Richard Nixon and the rise of extraconstitutional agencies such as political parties and regulatory commissions have all shaped the "law of the land." So has the power of the Supreme Court.

## the constitution as symbol

Like many other symbols of American democratic values, the Constitution helps the citizen to identify with the political system. In accepting the Constitution, the citizen accepts the pattern of government it contains. Furthermore, the symbolic meaning of the Constitution as the expression of democratic values and the wisdom of the Founding Fathers makes it easier to accept as legitimate disputed public policy decisions subsequently held by the courts to be constitutional. Court decisions — such as those declaring racial school segregation unconstitutional — may be resisted, but usually with the argument that the Constitution has been misread by the judges, not that the Constitution itself is invalid.

The American Constitution, as both a symbol of consensus and an instrument of government obtains its life and meaning from the varied activities of people. American constitutionalism is not a series of fixed propositions but the product of continuing conflict and accommodation as a result of these activities. Let us look, then, at the molding of our Constitution.

The violence of the 1968 Chicago Democratic convention may have stemmed from a denial of the protestors' assembly rights by city authorities. Such conflict frequently stimulates us to reinterpret constitutional precepts.

## making the constitution

When the Constitution was written, fear of centralized control and a desire to limit its exercise were deeply rooted in the traditions and experience of the American people. John Locke and other theorists had emphasized the separation of powers in limiting the dangers of governmental authority.[1] The first volume of John Adams's *The Defence of the Constitutions of the United States* (1787–1788) was a strong reply to

---

[1] David C. Smith, *The Convention and the Constitution* (New York: St. Martin's Press, 1965), p. 54.

foreign observers who criticized the noncentralized power structure of the Articles of Confederation. Believing that the rights of property, the liberties of the people, and the welfare of all could be maintained only under a system of "balanced powers," the conservative leader wrote:

> The majority has eternally, and without one exception, usurped over the rights of the minority. . . . Self-interest, private avidity, ambition, and avarice will exist in every state of society, and under every form of government. . . . The only remedy is to take away the power, by controlling the selfish avidity of the governor, by senate and house; and of the house, by the governor and senate.[2]

Many of the new state constitutions closely reflected the principles of the Declaration of Independence. Seven states adopted bills of rights; and the Massachusetts constitution, which dates back to 1780, had in it a "free and equal" clause under which a black man successfully sued for his liberty in 1781. In varying degrees, all the new state constitutions incorporated popular rule, limited government, separation of powers, and checks and balances. By the late eighteenth century, these concepts all were firmly held in the American mind.

A desire for a common political community was also reflected in certain political arrangements from 1774 which kept the colonies united in a common endeavor. The first of these, the Continental Congress, which came into existence in 1774, adopted the Declaration of Independence, financed and prosecuted the war with England, carried on foreign relations, and submitted the Articles of Confederation to the thirteen states for ratification. Although this "first American experiment in reconciling unity with localism"[3] did not produce a "perpetual Union," as the Framers had hoped, and failed to solve problems that proved to be insurmountable, the Articles of Confederation did provide the framework of American government from 1781 to 1789.

## articles of confederation

The story of this "union of states," under which "each state retains its sovereignty, freedom, and independence," is one of difficulty and frustration. Representation in the single-house congress was based on equality of states — that is, one vote per state. Legislative, executive, and judicial functions were united in this single body. Control over taxation, commerce, and individuals was retained by each of the thirteen autonomous

---

[2] Quoted in Andrew M. Scott, *Political Thought in America* (New York: Holt, Rinehart and Winston, 1959), p. 109.

[3] Samuel Eliot Morison and Henry Steele Commager, *The Growth of the American Republic* (New York: Oxford University Press, 1950), pp. 1, 257.

states. Foreign affairs, postal matters, settlement of disputes between states, the power to borrow money, control of armed forces, and regulation of coinage, weights, and measures were vested in the central government. Lacking power to tax even imports or to regulate commerce and enforce its mandates, the Congress was hopelessly handicapped — even though a good many citizens did fairly well economically. The states refused to amend the Articles in order to give the central government adequate enforcement authority; unanimous consent was required, and this proved fatal.[4] In 1786, a conference of states, which met at Annapolis to consider state problems involving commercial transactions, called for a convention to consider a general revision of the Articles.

## the constitutional convention: consensus and conflict

The delegates to the Constitutional Convention faced a formidable task. Not only did they have to devise a scheme of government acceptable to themselves and to the states but they had to do so among strongly conflicting interests.

> The colonies were differently founded and governed, had different products and habits of life, and, with poor means of travel and transport, were distant from each other. They had little experience of self-government. Their knowledge of jurisprudence was theoretical. They were insistent on "the rights of Englishmen," but did not grasp their responsibilities to themselves. Freed of irksome parental oversight, they rejoiced in liberty without much thought of how to preserve it. They fought a war of Independence, but did not trouble to organize a nation as a result of it.[5]

The Founding Fathers thus had to accommodate widely diverse interests and confine conflict within manageable bounds. Their success is the story of the drafting and adoption of the Constitution itself.

## the delegates: profile of a leadership corps

The fifty-five delegates who convened in Philadelphia in May 1787, formed an elite of American politics. Seven had been governors of their states, forty-one had served in Congress, and eight had contributed to

---

[4] Disagreeing with much historical evaluation of the Confederacy, Professor Merrill Jensen has depicted the period as one of general optimism, economic progress, and stability. See Merrill Jensen, *The New Nation* (New York: Alfred A. Knopf, 1950).

[5] Broadus and Louise Mitchell, *A Biography of the Constitution of the United States* (New York: Oxford University Press, 1964), p. 7.

writing their state constitutions. They formed a nucleus of the influential men of their time — merchants, bankers, gentlemen farmers, lawyers, and investors. They were also men of differing talents and accomplishments.[6] George Washington and Benjamin Franklin lent great personal influence and prestige to the proceedings, and other delegates had outstanding ability and knowledge of political affairs. Among these were James Madison, who became "floor leader" of the convention, and his fellow Virginian, Edmund Randolph; John Dickenson of Delaware, who has been called the "Penman of the American Revolution"; and Alexander Hamilton of New York, the brilliant and controversial young advocate of strong government. Rufus King of Massachusetts and Roger Sherman of Connecticut were men of fair but not outstanding abilities. Elbridge Gerry of Massachusetts and New York's Robert Yates and John Lansing were men of stature, but Yates and Lansing feared the convention was about to destroy the liberty of the people and left early; Gerry stayed but in the end refused to sign the Constitution.

Some commentators have made much of the absence of the "common man" — the small farmer, the worker, the resident of the back-country rural areas — supposedly resulting in a document that reflected the interests of an aristocratic, propertied minority.[7] Certainly those who met at Philadelphia were the inner group who generally dominated postrevolutionary America. They deliberated in secret, a fact that did not sit well with many people when the argument for ratification had to be made. But these men also had helped shape the revolutionary consensus on individual liberty and the right of men to govern themselves, and the original language of the Constitution testifies that they felt committed to representative government.

John P. Roche has described the Founding Fathers as "first and foremost superb democratic politicians."[8] Although the delegates came from different states, different classes and economic interests, they shared a larger goal: the desire to establish for the American community a common government that would not be limited by the parochial and partial jurisdictions of each state. They also agreed on the need for an indirectly representative government and on the necessity to avoid putting total power in the hands of "popular majorities." Richard Hofstadter has de-

[6] For a brief sketch of each member of the Convention, see Max Farrand, *The Framing of the Constitution* (New Haven: Yale University Press, 1940), pp. 14–41.

[7] The classic argument for this position is by Charles A. Beard, *An Economic Interpretation of the Constitution of the United States* (New York: Macmillan, 1954); see also V. L. Parrington, *Main Currents in American Thought* (New York: Harcourt, Brace, 1930), pp. 279–291.

[8] John P. Roche, "The Founding Fathers: A Reform Caucus in Action," *The American Political Science Review* 55, no. 4 (Dec. 1961): 799.

scribed the Framers as "realists" whose political attitudes were shaped by a generally pessimistic view of the nature of man, a view of "reality" that they believed should be translated into the legal framework of government. Unless controlled by law, man would be unable to provide either stable government or protection of property. The delegates nevertheless viewed an unencumbered majority as destructive of stability and liberty. In Hofstadter's opinion, the Framers' concept of liberty "was linked not to democracy but to property," and the liberties they were attempting to protect were "chiefly negative." He argued that "they wanted freedom from fiscal uncertainty and irregularities in the currency, from trade wars among the states, from economic discrimination by more powerful foreign governments, from attacks on the creditor class or on property, from popular insurrection."[9] United in their desire for a stronger continental government and united in their opposition to "mob rule," the delegates sought to devise techniques of conflict regulation that would not lead to either extreme and that would still be acceptable to Americans. The conflicts that did arise in the convention were about the appropriate design of a political community that would fulfill the goals of authority and would be national in scope, republican in pattern, and most acceptable to those who would have to agree to it.

### the convention: a working caucus of politicians

The decision of American leaders to strengthen the bonds of national union carried over into framing the Constitution, but agreement upon procedural details was not easily achieved. Hence, the convention's approach combined the urgency, expediency, and cooperation characteristic of practical-minded men. The plan of union that came forth was produced by political craftsmanship rather than philosophical doctrine. The thorniest questions were on the distribution of power, such as whether the federal or state government would have the final say or whether the people or the states would have power in Congress.

The working plan of the Constitutional Convention was the Virginia Plan drafted by Edmund Randolph.[10] This plan, sympathetic to the interests of the larger states, significantly increased the national government's powers and sought to ensure the supremacy of those powers over state

---

[9] Richard Hofstadter, *The American Political Tradition* (New York: Vintage Books, 1958), p. 11.
[10] See *Documents Illustrative of the Formation of the Union of the American States* (Washington, D.C.: Government Printing Office, 1927), pp. 953–956.

authority. An opposing New Jersey Plan also favored a stronger central government but, reflecting small state fears, sought to preserve the equality of states.

The Virginia Plan contained a provision to give the national government power "to negate all laws passed by the several States, contravening in the opinion of the National Legislature the articles of the union." It also proposed granting the national government authority to use force against any state government "failing to fulfill its duty" to the Union — which was just what Lincoln did against the states of the Confederacy, Virginia included, seventy-four years later. The proposed authority to coerce state governments, although it was also part of the New Jersey Plan, was rejected early in the convention. A resolution, taken from the New Jersey Plan, deleted the legislative veto power and, as finally approved in Article VI of the Constitution, provided that the "Constitution, and the Laws of the United States" are the "supreme law of the land." Although speculation about "things that never happened" is always an uncertain matter, if the power of Congress to veto state laws that it believes unconstitutional had been granted, "no stable basis for state powers would have existed."[11] The final version of the supremacy clause modified the centralized power of the national government. However, the national government did acquire the authority to operate directly against *individuals.* Thus the power granted to Congress in Article I "to call forth the Militia to execute the Laws of the Union, suppress Insurrections and repel invasions." Thus the responsibility assigned to the President to "take Care that the Laws be faithfully executed." This language is directed to individual citizens, including, for example, governors and police chiefs who may try to disobey or nullify a school desegregation order. The principle of coercion against individuals who violate the laws of the United States is thoroughly consistent with the aim of the Framers to establish a national political community within a federal system.

## the federal scheme

The desire for stronger national authority and the unwillingness of the states to submit to totally centralized power dictated the organization of the new government on the federal principle. It was generally felt that the liberties of the people and popular government could be secured only if the powers of government were so divided that one unit could serve as a check upon another. There was also a belief, expressed best by James Madison, that power must be so distributed that despotic majorities

[11] Duane Lockard, *American Federalism* (New York: McGraw-Hill, 1969), p. 6.

would be unable to destroy or weaken the people's liberties. No serious question was raised about the need to divide power; the question was how. To get a constitution at all, the integrity of state governments had to be preserved against "centralized nationalism." This was the only way the delegates from small states could "have reasonable assurance of their continuance as efficient and effective members of an integral union."[12] Governmental powers were to be distributed by granting specified powers to the national government, leaving the remaining authority to the state governments.

The convention arrived at no consensus about the exact meaning of a federal division of powers. Studying what the Framers meant by "federalism," Martin Diamond concluded that they, "like all other men at this time . . . regarded federalism, not as a kind of government, but as a voluntary association of states who sought certain advantages from that association." The agreement of the delegates on so loose a concept did not stop them, of course, from dividing over the practical details. Diamond asserts that a compromise between conflicting positions would have been impossible had James Madison not persuasively insisted that a large-scale republic acting directly on the people in each state would not subvert the integrity of the individual states and would better protect the liberties of the people.[13]

## the connecticut compromise

The Virginia Plan proposed a national legislature of two houses, the lower to be based on population and elected directly by the people and the upper house chosen by the lower house from persons nominated by state legislatures. A national executive was to be chosen by the national legislatures — reflecting the fear of direct democracy. The New Jersey Plan, carefully guarding state equality, included a single-house legislature in which states were represented as units.

Faced with the possibility of an impasse, the delegates eventually accepted a "palatable alternative to the folks at home."[14] This was the Connecticut Compromise which blended both the Virginia and New Jersey proposals. It provided for a two-house congress, but only in the lower house was representation apportioned by population. In the upper house two senators were allotted each state, regardless of population.

---

[12] Andrew C. McLaughlin, *A Constitutional History of the United States* (New York: Appleton-Century-Crofts, 1935), p. 180.

[13] Martin Diamond, "What the Framers Meant by Federalism," in Robert A. Goodwin, ed., *A Nation of States* (Chicago: Rand McNally, 1933), pp. 24–41.

[14] Roche, "The Founding Fathers," p. 806.

The object in part was to achieve a balance between control of legislators by the people and control by the "aristocracy." In Madison's words, the Senate — elected by state legislatures until 1913 — would serve as a check against the "fickleness and passion" of the people and would, consequently, protect minorities by its veto over the "excesses of the first branch." Not all delegates were convinced that such an arrangement provided the necessary safeguards against reckless majorities; they fought hard to write a property qualification for suffrage into the Constitution. Others argued that a man ought not to be denied suffrage because he owned no land, and a compromise finally left voting qualifications to the individual states.

Agreement upon the definition of a federal republic in America came with the Connecticut Compromise, but the issue was not settled. Both the law-of-the-land clause and the later Tenth Amendment provided a basis for continuing dispute over the relationship between central and state jurisdictions. The question of "states' rights" appeared before the nineteenth century dawned, erupted in civil war in 1861, and remains today a basis for national debate. What is the "spirit of the Constitution" on the demarcation between legitimate and illegitimate exercise of state or national authority? There is no certainty about the Framers' intent. The convention's compromise over federalism was ambiguous, like that on balanced government. There is certainty that this was the only way in which the competing interests could have been accommodated at the time.

## indirect appointment and election

Compromises resulting from a fear of popular democracy are reflected also in provisions for the selection of federal judges and in the method of electing the President. Judges appointed by an indirectly elected President and approved by an indirectly elected Senate were granted life tenure; the idea was to insulate the judiciary from popular pressure. As for the presidential election, the electoral college seemed an ingenious way to placate conflicting interests that wanted the President selected by Congress, by the states, or by the direct vote of the populace — a rather extreme notion in those days. According to the original terms of the Constitution, the electoral college, whose members were to be chosen in each state as its legislature provided, was to choose the President. If one candidate received a majority of electoral college votes, he was elected. It was expected, however, that after George Washington, a certain choice as first President, no person would receive an electoral college majority and that most elections would actually take place in the House of Representatives as provided in Article II. This is another aspect of state equality in the federal pattern, because each state has one vote if the House selects the President. A four-year term for the President was provided in order to reduce further the effects of popular pressure.

The role of the House of Representatives in the indirect election system did not materialize as planned because of the unforeseen rise of political parties after Washington's retirement. In the close election of 1800, all seventy-three "Republican" electors cast their ballots for Thomas Jefferson *and* Aaron Burr and the result was a narrow victory for Jefferson after more than twenty ballots in the House. The Twelfth Amendment, ratified before the 1804 election, plugged the constitutional loophole by mandating electors to vote separately for President and Vice-President. The disappearance of the Federalists as a national party also threw the 1824 election into the House, which elected John Quincy Adams although Andrew Jackson had received a larger popular vote. After that the two-party system, for which the Twelfth Amendment had laid the foundation, and the party convention device became the "filtering process" which the Constitution's Framers had intended to leave in the hands of the electoral college and the House.

## trade, taxes, and slavery

The disputes over representation and power distribution were not the only ones resolved by compromise in Philadelphia. Northern commercial interests that loathed the control of commerce by individual states insisted on granting Congress full authority to regulate trade and navigation. Southern agrarians feared that this would lead to export duties on their agricultural products. This was settled by forbidding Congress to levy export taxes and giving the House of Representatives exclusive power to introduce all money bills.

The slave trade posed both a moral and an economic problem. Several delegates, including southerners, openly criticized slavery as immoral. Some delegates also appeared to believe that slavery was disappearing and could not continue for a long period at any rate. However, it was recognized that several southern states considered slavery essential to their agricultural economy and would not accept the Constitution if the practice was abolished or if continued importation of slaves was prohibited. The South also sought to count slaves for purposes of determining representation in the House of Representatives, whereas northern delegates objected to their being counted as persons when their owners legally regarded slaves as chattel property.

The South was trying to have it both ways, and the so-called Three-

fifths Compromise resolved the issue for the time being. It provided that
three-fifths of the slaves would be counted for purposes of representation
and *also* for the purpose of assessing direct taxes. The delegates agreed
to prohibit the national government from interfering with the slave trade
prior to 1808, by which time the slave population would be large enough
to reproduce itself.

The South came out ahead in this bargain but unwittingly set the new
nation on the long road to civil war. To understand the meaning of the
Constitution in the twentieth century we might keep in mind Roche's
assertion about its origins in the eighteenth century: "The Constitution,
then, was not an apotheosis of 'constitutionalism,' a triumph of architec-
tonic genius; it was a patchwork sewn together under the pressure of
both time and events by a group of extremely talented democratic politicians."[15] The Constitution has endured by receiving what it required —
constant reinterpretation by successive generations of political leaders
and interests that are in social conflict.

## the constitutional document:
## doctrinal principles and justification

The language of the struggle for ratification included terms that were not
actively argued until the Convention had adjourned. Expressions such
as "balanced government," "separation of powers," "checks and balances," and "federalism" were employed to describe and justify what
had been done in Philadelphia. These ideas still lie behind such "ideology" as Americans have — or think they have.

## balanced government

The most articulate effort to justify the Constitution as the very embodiment of the concept of balance is *The Federalist*. A series of eighty-five
letters written by James Madison, Alexander Hamilton, and John Jay, the
Federalist Papers appealed to broad doctrinal principles and "the common sense of the situation" to build support for ratifying the Constitution.

In Papers No. 10 and No. 51, the authors argued that the balance provided in the constitutional structure was the most practical guarantee for
the maintenance of liberty and a republican government.[16] In No. 51, the
authors made clear their conviction that the dangers to liberty and stabil-

[15] *Ibid.*, p. 815.
[16] James Madison, Alexander Hamilton, and John Jay, *The Federalist* (New York: Modern
Library, 1937).

ity arose from the very nature of man himself: "But what is government itself, but the greatest of all reflections on human nature? If men were angels, no government would be necessary." Said Madison: "In framing a government which is to be administered by men over men, the great difficulty lies in this: you must first enable the government to control the governed; and in the next place oblige it to control itself." The problem, then, was to balance the Lockean concept of representative government with the recognized tendencies of men to abuse power.

In No. 10, Madison argued that the great danger came from what he called "factions," or groups of people united for some purpose or cause "adverse to the rights of other citizens, or to the permanent and aggregate interests of the community." Because factions "were sewn into the nature of men," they could not be eliminated except by destroying liberty. Hence the means for controlling factions had to deal with confining their effects. The Constitution contains two such means: republican, or representative, government and the division of authority through federalism and the separation of powers.

## republican government

The institutional arrangement most suitable for controlling factions in a large and diverse country, the *Federalist* writers argued, was *republican government* – in other words, representative democracy. "Pure democracy," or direct rule by an assembly of citizens who "administer the government in person," provides no protection against unreasonable majorities. Representative democracy filters and refines popular views through representatives "whose wisdom may best discern the true interest of their country." Recognizing that the elected representatives may themselves "betray the interests of the people," Madison extended his argument by claiming that a large republic lessens the danger. A large republic not only has a greater number of "fit characters" to serve as representatives, but the larger the area to be governed, the more difficult it is for a majority to form. As Madison wrote in No. 10, "If such a common motive exists, it will be more difficult for all who feel it to discover their own strength, and to act in unison with each other."

## division of powers

Essays No. 10 and No. 51 both viewed the division of authority between the states and the national government as an added safeguard against the destruction of liberty by a majority. The argument is explicit in No. 51: "In the compound republic of America, the power surrendered by the

people is first divided between two distinct governments, and then the
portion allotted to each subdivided among distinct and separate departments. Hence, a double security arises to the rights of the people. The
different governments will control each other, at the same time that each
will be controlled by itself." Thus federalism and separated powers were
to complement one another.

## the federal principle

These constitutional provisions proved insufficient to contain conflict
only when different interests chose to interpret the meaning of the federal union so differently as to produce the Civil War.[17] The Confederates
argued that the federal Constitution was merely a voluntary compact
between separate states that rested on an unchanging balance between
national and state prerogatives and "states' rights"; individual states
could leave the Union should they feel their rights had been violated.

Lincoln's defense of the Union held that the Constitution of 1787 had
created a community of people within a federal framework that could
not be dissolved by the action of any state or group of states. His supporters cited the language of the Constitution under which states agreed to
a strong central authority operating directly on individual citizens. A
third view insisted that an organic political community, unifying its
members through the gradual assimilation of diverse traditions, habits,
and beliefs, had come into existence long before the Convention of 1787
or even the Articles of Confederation. Orestes Brownson, a leading journalist during the 1830s, asserted, "The Union is in each of the states, and
each of the states is the Union."[18]

Whatever the specific intentions of the Framers may have been, the
federal system has had a profound effect on the system of conflict representation and resolution.

## separation of powers

The separation of powers was another mechanism in the Constitution for
preserving balance and a republican government. In theory, allotting the
functions of government to separate institutions would prevent power

---

[17] One of the major contributions to the literature of political theory by an American was
a result of and itself provoked this crisis: John C. Calhoun's *Disquisition on Government*
(1853).

[18] Henry F. Brownson, *The Works of Orestes Brownson*, vol. 28 (Detroit: Thorndike
Nourse, 1832–1837), p. 114.

from falling into the hands of a single interest. Moreover, a system of checks and balances could be used to reinforce separation. Authority was assigned to three institutions — the executive, the legislature, and the judiciary — and restraints were put on the exercise of power by each.

In effect, in certain areas each branch of government was given authority to monitor the activities of the other two: the presidential veto is a restraint on legislative powers; congressional power of the purse limits presidential action; and the courts' power to review the constitutionality of laws or executive actions limits both President and Congress. The provision for a bicameral legislature, in which each house can veto the actions of the other, reflects the same principle. Further, federalism is itself a mechanism to achieve checks and balances by dividing authority between the national government and the states.

The argument that a distribution of the functions of government can prevent the concentration of power in a single minority or majority sounds plausible enough, but even *The Federalist* is not totally convincing on this point. Separation of powers and checks and balances can be quite unworkable. Given independence from the other two branches, the third can block policymaking and administration and a minority thus may effectively obstruct community action without ever capturing the whole apparatus. The refusal of a President to spend money appropriated by Congress could effectively block the implementation of a widely supported public policy choice. A decision of the Supreme Court upholding legislation requiring a specific action by government officials would be ineffective if the executive branch deliberately did nothing. If a majority faction captured all policymaking positions, the simple device of separation would not serve as a safeguard against majority tyranny. But the device of periodic elections makes it difficult for one faction to control the whole government long enough to smash up constitutional crockery.

## the doctrines accepted: ratification

Ratification of the Constitution did not come easily. Concious of how the unanimity requirement had made the Articles of Confederation unamendable, the Framers provided in the final article that the new document would go into effect upon approval by just nine, or two-thirds, of the thirteen states. To provide for wider popular participation — partly because the delegates believed state legislatures were less likely to approve the document — a requirement was included that each state ratify in conventions chosen by the voters.

Opponents attacked the proposed Constitution as a sacrifice of state autonomy, as a failure to secure the rights of Americans, as an "anti-

republican" arrangement, and as going considerably further than necessary to strengthen the Articles of Confederation. Some convention delegates returned home to fight against ratification. But the arguments for
limited government, balance, representative democracy, and federalism
proved persuasive, and, by June 1788, nine states had ratified. This
number did not include New York and Virginia, large and influential
states whose approval was essential, but both states ratified within a
month after a hard fight. The Constitution was now the law of the land
in a practical as well as a legal sense; and the constitutional principles
of balance, separation of powers, and federalism have become American
symbols. But they have produced conflict as well as consensus, and they
have injected tension into American political patterns.

## constitutional change by formal amendment

A brief glance at the formal Amendments to the Constitution reveals that
Article V, the amending clause, has been used infrequently and that some
of the twenty-six Amendments do not significantly affect conflict regulation in the American political community. The first ten Amendments — the
Bill of Rights — have been described as "perhaps the best known, most
cherished feature or portion of the Constitution [because they] are
thought of as absolute and moral, and not — like the remainder of the
Constitution — expressions of governmental policy."[19] Very little discussion took place in the Constitutional Convention about a Bill of Rights;
attention was focused on the need for a strong national government. In
meeting the subsequently heavy criticism of the proposed Constitution
for its lack of these protections, supporters of the Constitution argued
that such rights were protected by bills of rights in state constitutions.
But this did not seem enough; Massachusetts Federalists had to dangle
a Bill of Rights as bait to get their state's ratification, and the idea took
hold. Widespread public demand resulted in a Bill of Rights being added
to the Constitution by formal amendment shortly after the new government came into being.

## the amendments

Of the remaining sixteen Amendments, less than half have significantly
affected basic government structure. The Eleventh and Twelfth were
added as quick remedies for disruptive situations not foreseen by the

[19] Broadus and Louise Mitchell, *A Biography of the Constitution*, p. 187.

Framers. The Eleventh removed the jurisdiction of federal courts in suits brought against states by private individuals. The Twelfth was aimed at eliminating the possibility of a tie in electoral votes for President, which created the Jefferson-Burr deadlock in 1800. The Eighteenth ("prohibition") was repealed by the Twenty-First after years of frustrated attempts to enforce "dry laws." The Twentieth abolished "lame duck" sessions of Congress — sessions so designated because Congressmen defeated in the November elections continued to serve in the short session of Congress running from December to the following March. The Twenty-Third Amendment granted residents of the District of Columbia a voice in

White voting officials often openly intimidated southern blacks before the Amendment abolishing poll taxes and subsequent voting legislation made voting procedures conform to constitutional intent.

presidential elections. Finally, the Twenty-Fourth abolished payment of a state poll tax as a voting qualification in federal elections when only five states still required payment.

Three of the remaining eight Amendments (Thirteenth, Fourteenth, and Fifteenth) are labeled the Civil War Amendments because they abolished slavery and sought to guarantee the newly won rights of the Negro. Amendments Sixteen (permitting a direct tax on incomes), Seventeen (providing for the direct election of senators), and Nineteen (extending the franchise to women), ratified between 1913 and 1920, reflected the Progressive Movement's emphasis on extending democratic participation to all citizens. The Twenty-Second Amendment limited a President to two terms. The Twenty-Fifth, ratified in 1967, owes something to the assassination of President John F. Kennedy in 1963. It provided for succession to a vacancy in the vice-presidency and also established procedures under which the Vice-President becomes acting President in case of presidential disability. Most recently (1971), the Twenty-Sixth guaranteed the vote in all state and federal elections to those eighteen years or older, thus adding eleven million Americans to the voting rolls.

## why so few?

It is striking that only twenty-six constitutional Amendments have been approved, although since 1789 more than five thousand have been introduced in Congress. Relatively high procedural hurdles, which make minority opposition particularly effective, account in part for this small figure. Merely to *propose* an Amendment for ratification by the states, the sponsors of a draft must win approval by a congressional committee *and* a two-thirds vote in each house of Congress. An alternative method — through a national constitutional convention — has never been used. The additional requirement that at least three-fourths of the states must *ratify* a proposed Amendment further strengthens a minority in blocking change. All the states except Nebraska have two-house legislatures; because both houses must approve Amendments, a minority need only convince one chamber not to ratify. Amendment is not an easy process, but it was never intended to be too easy; nevertheless, despite the difficulties, the states have accepted all but six of thirty-one proposed Amendments. Only one, the Twenty-First, has been ratified by the alternative method of state conventions.

As Figure 4-1 shows, there has been a tendency to add Amendments in clusters. The political temper of the American electorate may partially explain this. The Amendments added to the Constitution between 1913 and 1933 reflected dissatisfaction with the government that had been ar-

| | | |
|---|---|---|
| 1971 | Twenty-Sixth | |
| 1967 | Twenty-Fifth | |
| 1965 | Twenty-Fourth | |
| 1964 | Twenty-Third | |
| 1951 | Twenty-Second | |
| 1933 | Twentieth, Twenty-First | |
| 1920 | Nineteenth | Progressive Era Amendments |
| 1919 | Eighteenth | |
| 1913 | Sixteenth, Seventeenth | |
| 1870 | Fifteenth | Civil War Amendments |
| 1868 | Fourteenth | |
| 1865 | Thirteenth | |
| 1804 | Twelfth | |
| 1795 | Eleventh | |
| 1791 | First through Tenth | Bill of Rights |

**FIGURE 4-1**
**Constitutional Amendments**

ticulated by liberals at the height of the Progressive Movement. Since that time, Congress has been more willing to enact legislation expanding federal activities based on broad construction of legislative powers; the presidency has grown in functions and status; and the Supreme Court has refrained from narrow interpretations of the constitutional powers of either Congress or the President while handing down a number of far-reaching decisions in civil rights and civil liberties that generally reflected a liberal outlook.

## constitutional change by informal modification

With the exception of the Twenty-Second Amendment limiting presidential tenure, no addition to the Constitution has significantly altered the original delineation of power. To be sure, procedures for majority rule have been marginally changed by Amendments extending the suffrage and providing for the direct election of Senators. Other developments — judicial review, expanded presidential power, growth of the administrative branch, independent regulatory agencies, and political parties — have had greater effect on our political balance.

judicial review

Article VI declares that the Constitution, laws of Congress, and treaties of the United States must be enforced by all courts, state or federal, as the "supreme law of the land." But nothing clarifies which branch should decide what constitutes conflict between documentary authority and official action. The great Chief Justice John Marshall, in the case of *Marbury v. Madison* (1803) asserted the Supreme Court's right to review legislative acts to determine their consistency with the Constitution. The Court held that because the Constitution was paramount any action contrary to its provisions must be null and void, and Marshall argued that the peculiar historical and constitutional role of the courts gives them the power and duty to say so.

Marshall's argument has stood up ever since, and judicial review as employed by the Supreme Court has significantly influenced the notion of balanced political authority. In ninety-four cases between 1803 and 1971, the Court declared unconstitutional 102 provisions of federal laws. Considering that Congress during this time passed more than seventy thousand laws, this is a very small number; but some decisions involved major pieces of legislation. Seventy-four were made between 1865 and 1937, when the Court's influence on policymaking was steadily expanding.

The peak of activity was reached in the middle 1930s when the court under Chief Justice Hughes invalidated thirteen New Deal measures in four years (1933–1937). During the same period, three presidential actions were also declared unconstitutional. The frequent use of the judicial veto led to President Roosevelt's attempt in 1937 to "pack" the court — to get legislation under which new justices could be added in order to produce a majority in favor of New Deal measures. But Congress refused to approve the proposal. Since 1937, the Court has declared provisions of federal laws unconstitutional in only nine cases.

To what extent has judicial review served as an effective check on the two other policymaking branches of the American government? Although the Court has used its authority sparingly, the fact that it *can* invalidate laws is a limiting factor in itself. Congress or the President may hesitate in the face of a strong expectation that the Court may rule an action unconstitutional. A potentially adverse decision does not, however, always prevent action. Behavior frequently depends upon the permanence of adverse Court decisions; that is, can the Court make its decision stick? Robert A. Dahl's study led him to conclude that "there is ... no case on record where a persistent law-making majority has not, sooner or later, achieved its purposes." Dahl found that one-third of the Supreme Court decisions holding congressional legislation unconstitutional ultimately were overridden by amendment or subsequent Court decisions. Many of the remaining cases involved minor legislation, temporary measures, or trivial sections of statutes.[20]

[20] Robert A. Dahl, *A Preface to Democratic Theory* (Chicago: University of Chicago Press, 1956), p. 110.

We may conclude that even without frequent declarations of uncon-
stitutionality, the possibility plays a checking role which is important if
not precisely measurable. But in the long run, the Court has not been
able to prevent determined legislative and popular majorities from ultimately achieving their goal — and has not often tried.

## the president's role

The rise of political parties transformed the electoral college into an
agency that simply reflects the popular choice in each of the states. Thus
the President is the only popularly chosen official whose constituency is
the whole American political community. What he does depends upon
who he is, but in the twentieth century the general trend has been toward
increased political leadership — the "active presidency." The President is
the leader of his party, the prodder of Congress, and a spokesman for
the "national interest" as opposed to the narrow interests of congressional constituencies. The presidential role has consistently grown in
scope and importance until it has cut across the technical limitations that
underlie separation of powers and checks and balances.

## administrative agencies

The administrative branch of the government has changed greatly both
in size and functions since the Constitution was written. The creation of
the Cabinet during Washington's first administration is an early example
of change without amendment. The proliferation of executive agencies,
especially in this century — about three quarters of the federal jobs have
been created since the 1930s — has brought about a whole new level of
policymaking not envisioned by the Framers. A relatively new term, "bureaucratization," is used to indicate the presence of "faceless" or "deper-
sonalized" government organizations in almost every aspect of American
life.

Of special importance are agencies such as the Interstate Commerce
Commission, the Federal Trade Commission, the Securities Exchange
Commission, and the Federal Communications Commission, created by
Congress and empowered to reach decisions that are partly legislative
and partly judicial. The President appoints the members of the agencies,
but they are not responsible to him. Nor are the agencies distinctively
legislative or judicial bodies. A mechanical definition of separation of
powers is not adequate as a means of fixing their place within the constitutional structure.

## political parties

The Constitution says nothing about parties. The Framers were fully aware that men join together to achieve common goals; they did that themselves in Philadelphia. But they had no idea that parties and party organizations would gain power, accumulate more power, and become a significant — perhaps indispensable — element in the balance of power itself. Among the functions of political parties, although certainly not realized perfectly, is the attempt to intermediate between citizens and government and translate popular desires into public policy. This is the function of representation and it must be considered as affected by party organization. Since the rise of the Whigs in the 1830s (followed by the antislavery Republicans in the 1850s), dissatisfied citizens have always had an alternative through which they could work to represent their demands to the party in control of the government.

Parties are organized to compete for public office and thus control positions of power. Occasionally the effect has been to alleviate — but by no means eliminate — conflict among the three branches of government. The organization of American parties follows the decentralized pattern of federalism, which means that policy choices — especially in the legislative branch — tend to reflect diverse sectional and localized economic, political, and social interests. In this respect, parties have been powerful in preserving the noncentralized distribution of power desired by the Framers. Partisan competition for the presidency does tend to make citizens aware of national issues and political events. But even if one party controls both the executive and the legislature, as it usually has until very recent years, the decentralized organization may produce strong disagreements within the party itself.

## the legal dimension

In 1869, considering whether the states of the southern Confederacy had ceased to be members of the Union during secession, the Supreme Court declared that they had not. The Constitution incorporated "an indestructible union composed of indestructible states." This decision, like the Civil War itself, affirmed the durability of the federal arrangement, but "proper" boundaries of national and state authority have been disputed continuously. The Tenth Amendment, which reserves to the states or the people "powers not delegated to the United States by the Constitution, nor prohibited by it to the States," is unchanged since its adoption in 1791. Instead federalism as originally constituted has undergone continuing reinterpretation.

Other major factors that have enlarged national policymaking include the increase in the electorate by the removal of restrictions on suffrage; the growing sense of national community; the development of common cultural patterns; the decrease of parochialism resulting from the high mobility of the American population; and the emergence of the President as a representative of national constituency. All of these factors are, at one time or another, reflected in the major Supreme Court interpretations of the federal mandate which we can best see by examining constitutional doctrines developed by the Supreme Court itself.

The case of *McCulloch* v. *Maryland,* decided in 1819, was the first major interpretation of the extent of national power under the Constitution. The issue was the creation by Congress of a national bank during Washington's administration and a second one in 1816. Both banks were bitterly opposed. It was argued that such action went beyond the delegated powers of Congress, and a number of states laid heavy taxes on the branches of the bank within their borders. The refusal of James McCulloch, cashier of the Baltimore branch of the bank, to pay such a tax precipitated a constitutional debate over national government jurisdiction under the federal arrangement. When the issue reached the Supreme Court, Chief Justice Marshall faced two major constitutional questions: Did a state have the authority to levy a tax on a national agency and thus, by implication, threaten its very existence, and could Congress create a bank when the Constitution did not specify its authority to do so?

The first question was answered by Marshall's assertion that "the power to tax involved the power to destroy." States could not levy a tax on a legitimate agency of the national government. But was the bank a legitimate agency?

In answer to this question, Marshall cited the principle of "implied powers." The "government of the Union," wrote the Chief Justice, "though limited in its powers, is supreme within its sphere of action." Under the supremacy clause, state laws in conflict with authorized policies of Congress must give way.

Was Congress, then, within its "sphere of action" in chartering a national bank? Yes, argued Marshall, even though nothing in the Constitution specifically authorized a national bank. Following the enumeration of the powers of Congress in Article I, section 8 of the Constitution, is the clause authorizing Congress "to make all Laws which shall be *necessary and proper* for carrying into Execution the Foregoing Powers."

The constitutionality of the bank, therefore, hinged on how narrow or broad an interpretation was to be given to the words "necessary and proper." The Framers, argued Marshall, had deliberately written a Constitution that broadly outlined congressional jurisdiction. A constitution that listed in detail all powers flowing from generally granted powers

# RANDOM SELECTION SEQUEN[CE]

## 1970

| No. | Date | No. | Date | No. | Date | No. | Date | No. | Date | No. | Date | No. | Date |
|-----|------|-----|------|-----|------|-----|------|-----|------|-----|------|-----|------|
| 092 | JAN 26 | 115 | JUL 3 | 138 | OCT 13 | 161 | SEP 2 | 184 | SEP 8 | 207 | SEP 16 | 230 | |
| 093 | JUL 1 | 116 | AUG 23 | 139 | MAR 6 | 162 | DEC 23 | 185 | NOV 20 | 208 | APR 30 | 231 | |
| 094 | OCT 28 | 117 | OCT 22 | 140 | JAN 18 | 163 | DEC 13 | 186 | JAN 21 | 209 | JUNE 30 | 232 | |
| 095 | DEC 24 | 118 | JAN 23 | 141 | AUG 18 | 164 | JAN 30 | 187 | JUL 20 | 210 | FEB 4 | 233 | |
| 096 | DEC 16 | 119 | SEP 23 | 142 | AUG 12 | 165 | DEC 4 | 188 | JUL 5 | 211 | JAN 31 | 234 | |
| 097 | NOV 8 | 120 | JUL 16 | 143 | NOV 17 | 166 | MAR 16 | 189 | FEB 17 | 212 | FEB 16 | 235 | |
| 098 | JUL 17 | 121 | JAN 16 | 144 | FEB 2 | 167 | AUG 28 | 190 | JUL 18 | 213 | MAR 8 | 236 | |
| 099 | NOV 29 | 122 | MAR 7 | 145 | AUG 4 | 168 | AUG 7 | 191 | APR 29 | 214 | FEB 5 | 237 | |
| 100 | DEC 31 | 123 | DEC 28 | 146 | NOV 18 | 169 | MAR 15 | 192 | OCT 20 | 215 | JAN 4 | 238 | |
| 101 | JAN 5 | 124 | APR 13 | 147 | APR 7 | 170 | MAR 26 | 193 | JUL 31 | 216 | FEB 10 | 239 | |
| 102 | AUG 15 | 125 | OCT 2 | 148 | APR 16 | 171 | OCT 15 | 194 | JAN 9 | 217 | MAR 30 | 240 | |
| 103 | MAY 30 | 126 | NOV 13 | 149 | SEP 25 | 172 | JUL 23 | 195 | SEP 24 | 218 | APR 10 | 241 | |

"The Congress shall have power . . . to provide for calling forth the Militia." The draft lottery was instituted in 1970 to make conscription more equitable and less subject to class privilege.

could "scarcely be embraced by the human mind." The criterion for interpretation established by the Chief Justice was: "Let the end be legitimate, let it be within the scope of the Constitution, and all means which are plainly adapted to that end, which are not prohibited, but consist with the letter and spirit of the Constitution, are constitutional. . . ." In this case, the enumerated powers to coin and borrow money and to regulate its value implied — made *necessary and proper* — the legitimacy of a national bank.

Marshall believed that if the Constitution was to endure, it must be adapted to fit the needs of each generation. Except for the years from about 1890 to the mid-1930s, the Supreme Court has used the implied-powers criterion to support the extension of communitywide authority into many new areas. Moreover, it has overturned a number of *state* statutes that were found to be inconsistent with the Constitution in order to preserve communitywide authority under the federal principle.

Three specific grants of power to Congress formed the base for these activities: the power to regulate interstate and foreign commerce, the power to declare war, and the power to tax and spend for the general welfare.

The federal laws stemming from the principle of communitywide authority today touch almost every phase of American life.

"Commerce ... among the several states" has been interpreted as including not only the movement of goods but matters that "affect" commerce. Thus, it is a crime under federal law to transport stolen automobiles across state lines, to kidnap, to sell adulterated goods, or to discriminate in employment or the use of public accommodations. Laws establishing minimum wages, prohibiting child labor, regulating labor-management relations, and controlling the production and marketing of agricultural commodities are justified as "necessary and proper" to carry out congressional responsibility for regulating commerce. In time of war, if national resources must be totally mobilized, congressional jurisdiction can be almost absolute. Military conscription, rationing of goods, control over production and consumption, and price control are "necessary and proper" in a concerted war effort. Finally, "to tax and spend for the general welfare" has been interpreted as including laws providing for social security, unemployment compensation, subsidization of agriculture, grants to states for highway construction, and support of education. The power to tax may be used in regulating or eliminating activities deemed harmful or undesirable. High taxes on the sale of sawed-off shotguns and narcotics are aimed not at producing revenue but at driving these activities out of existence.

Opponents of federal legislation based on the implied power principle have consistently charged that these statutes violated "states' rights." Underlying this constitutional dispute are conflicts of interest as well as principle that represent perhaps more mundane and practical considerations. Business interests may consider that extending governmental regulation of labor-management relations places an undesirable limitation on practices they consider useful or necessary for economic success. A labor union official, might on the other hand, see federal activity as enhancing his bargaining power with employers. One side may employ the rhetoric of "states' rights," the other that of "national needs"; yet in both cases the constitutional argument is often a surface justification for achieving more immediate goals.

## economic, social, and technological change

As technological, cultural, and economic change has altered the American style of life, it has also affected the federal pattern designed by the Framers of the Constitution. How has it affected the functional relationships between national, state, and local governments?

The 1970 census revealed that almost three-quarters of the American people now live in two hundred standard metropolitan areas.[21] Of these, more than 50 percent have populations exceeding one million and more than half live in suburbs. The northeastern seaboard has already developed into a "megalopolis" that crosses ten states and the District of Columbia and includes hundreds of overlapping counties, cities, and other units of local government.[22]

The same urban areas that produce the greatest wealth also present the nation's most pressing social, educational, economic, and environmental problems. Crime, drug addiction, poverty, unemployment, racial conflict, and environmental pollution are familiar to even the casual observer. While the large central cities in these metropolitan areas have grappled with expanding problems in mass transportation, housing, crime, sanitation, recreation, education, water supplies, and air quality, the more affluent citizens have moved to the suburbs. Left behind are the poor who most need better living conditions. The inner city is frequently unable to support the public housing, recreational, educational, and environmental programs needed by its residents. And as the suburbs become more crowded and suburban governments seek the financial resources to sustain the services necessary to their population, townspeople are complaining of an ever-growing tax burden.

How can government adequately respond to such needs? This is an extremely complex question. The American governmental structure was originally designed to protect its citizens by dividing power among state and federal governments, thus permitting a maximum of "local autonomy" that reflected the diverse interests of the "grass roots" level. Today these virtues are often a barrier to attacking problems that are local in origin but national in scope. The problems have no regard for the myriad complexities of state or local governmental boundaries, and their financial and human costs may overstrain the federal organization. Not only the organizational features of the federal principle but also the political

[21] The term "standard metropolitan area" is used by the Bureau of the Census to designate any county or counties containing a city or cities of fifty thousand people or more. In some cases such areas overlap state boundaries.

[22] Jean Gottman, *Megalopolis* (Cambridge, Mass.: Massachusetts Institute of Technology Press, 1961).

values that fostered it and continue to influence national public policy choices are deeply involved.

The federalist principle has been used to meet changing economic, political, and social conditions. Since the early eighteenth century, national and state governments have shared activities, power, and responsibilities. Morton Grodzins described the American system as a "marble cake" of mixed powers rather than a "three-layer cake" of national, state, and local governments. "In fact," he has written, "no important activity of government in the United States is the exclusive province of one of the levels, not even what may be regarded as the most national of national functions, such as foreign relations; not even the most local of local functions, such as police protection and park maintenance."[23] Since the early 1800s activities such as education, transportation, law enforcement, agriculture, and communications were shared by nation and states. This sharing or collaboration, also called *"co-operative federalism,"* has been consistent despite an opposing theory, *"dual federalism,"* developed in the eighteenth century. Proponents of dual federalism proposed that government functions be divided into state and federal levels, each with powers exclusive and independent of the other.[24] Dominant from about the 1860s, the concept lost its legal basis during the depression years of the 1930s, when greatly expanded federal participation brought general acceptance of federal state cooperation in meeting social and economic dislocations.

The major form of intergovernmental cooperation is the system of grants-in-aid. These are federal funds transferred to the states for specified purposes such as highway building and social welfare. States usually are required to match the federal funds by a prescribed formula. Such grants, however, usually are administered by the states and local governments, thus achieving joint government participation toward meeting social and economic needs.

Such federal activity now extends to most areas of government, causing sharp disagreement about its effects. Fears of "centralized government" and "destruction of the integrity of states" have generated many proposals to find new ways of meeting national problems while increasing state participation. President Lyndon Johnson called for "creative federalism," encouraging more direct cooperation between the nation and the states in attacking the social and economic problems of the 1960s. In 1969, President Nixon proposed a "new federalism" aimed at returning

[23] Morton Grodzins, *The American System,* Daniel J. Elazar, ed., (Chicago: Rand McNally, 1966), pp. 7–8.
[24] This theory was distinctly incorporated by the Supreme Court in *Hammer* v. *Dagenhart,* 247 U.S. 251 (1918).

A new highway is built through joint federal-state funding. Grant-in-aid programs encourage a "partnership" between the two levels of government to meet both local and national needs.

governmental functions to the states through a "revenue sharing" plan. The federal government would return to the states a percentage of personal income taxes based on the population of the state and the state's effort at raising revenue. Nixon's program is meant to relieve the so-called fiscal mismatch resulting from exclusive federal use of major tax sources (especially the income tax), which makes it difficult for states to find enough sources of revenue. Critics of the program have voiced fears that states would not distribute the funds in sufficient amounts to their cities, where aid is most needed, and have urged that the federal government give money directly to the cities.

The nation's problems belong to more than the federal government. Federal expenditures have increased steadily and dramatically since the 1930s, but so too have those of state and local governments.

Whether the Framers of the Constitution intended governmental functions to mesh as much as they do is conjectural. The accelerating change in American life makes uncertain the future direction of federalism. The crucial question today is not whether the states or the nation may or should undertake programs to meet present and future problems but which level can most effectively do so. Americans are traditionally attached to "grass roots" control and "local autonomy"; these, and the complex problems that overlap governmental boundaries, are integral to the American pattern of conflict. Federalism is rooted in the representation and regulation of conflict and, short of major alterations in the system, will continue to deeply affect policymaking.

## constitutional change and
## nationalization of the bill of rights

From the time of Chief Justice Marshall, the Supreme Court has been a primary force in constitutional change. The Court's decisions extending the guarantees of the Bill of Rights — more exactly, the first eight Amendments — against actions by state governments are among its striking products. This achievement is known as the "nationalization" of the Bill of Rights.

The Bill of Rights directly limits the authority of only the national government. State constitutions similarly prohibit state activity in a separate bill of rights or by other provisions. Presumably, therefore, the citizen is protected against both units of government. In fact, the states have differed greatly in the extent and interpretation of state-guaranteed substantive and procedural rights.

Before the Fourteenth Amendment was adopted, the Supreme Court took the position that the Bill of Rights protected the citizen only against actions of the national government.[25] Following the Civil War, the question arose as to whether the privileges-and-immunities clause or the due-process clause of the Fourteenth Amendment applied the guarantees of the Bill of Rights to state governments. Legal controversy early became centered on the due-process clause, which provides that "no state shall deprive any person of life, liberty, or property without due process of law." Until 1890, the Supreme Court held to its prewar view that the Bill of Rights limited national action only, but in 1890 it interpreted the Fourteenth Amendment's due-process clause as protecting property rights against state action. In other cases, the Court held to the position that the Fourteenth Amendment did not protect other guarantees of the Bill of Rights against the actions of state governments.

The first major break in this stand came in 1925 when the Court agreed

[25] *Barron v. Baltimore*, 7 Pet. 243 (1833).

Despite the 1962 Supreme Court ruling that declared school prayers unconstitutional, many school districts were slow to comply.

that the First Amendment guarantees of speech and press were among the "liberties" protected by the due-process clause of the Fourteenth Amendment.[26] Further "nationalization" of the Bill of Rights followed. In 1937, the right to peaceful assembly was guaranteed; and in 1940 the Court extended protection against state action abridging the free exercise of religion.[27] In 1947, the First Amendment prohibition against governmental establishment of religion was applied to the states when the Court ruled that a "wall of separation" must exist between church and state.[28]

Other provisions of the Bill of Rights remained outside the scope of the Fourteenth Amendment. Faced with the very important question of which, if any, of these guarantees were to be applied to the states, the Court gave an answer in *Palko v. Connecticut* (1937). Palko had been convicted of second-degree murder and given a life sentence. On appeal by the state, he was tried a second time, convicted of first-degree murder, and sentenced to death. He appealed this conviction on the ground that the due-process clause of the Fourteenth Amendment, which protected individuals against action of state governments, guaranteed the Fifth Amendment prohibition against double jeopardy (no person shall "be subject for the same offense to be twice put in jeopardy of life or limb"). Although Palko's appeal was denied, the Court, speaking through Justice Cardozo, laid down a general formula — known as the "fair trial rule" or "selective incorporation" — for determining which of the guarantees in the first eight Amendments applied to the states through the due-process clause. State actions that violated "fundamental principles of liberty and

[26] *Gitlow v. New York*, 268 U.S. 652 (1925).
[27] *De Jonge v. Oregon*, 299 U.S. 353 (1937); *Cantwell v. Connecticut*, 310 U.S. 196 (1940).
[28] *Everson v. Board of Education*, 330 U.S. 1 (1947).

justice" were prohibited by the Fourteenth Amendment. This "natural law" doctrine of selection was contrary to the belief of Justice Black and others that all the specific guarantees of the Bill of Rights were incorporated in the Fourteenth Amendment.

The "total incorporation" theory of Justice Black has never won majority support on the Supreme Court, but practically it has won out through the "absorption" of specific rights by the Court. Even *Palko* v. *Connecticut* was overruled by the decision in *Benton* v. *Maryland* in 1969. As shown in Figure 4-2, only a few provisions of the Bill of Rights are not now incorporated in the Fourteenth Amendment. The Second Amendment's guarantee of the "right to keep and bear arms," and the Third Amendment's prohibition against quartering of troops are of no real practical significance for state governments. Provision for indictment by a grand jury (Fifth) and the guarantee of holding trial in the district where the crime was committed (Sixth) are also not crucial. Only the Eighth Amendment's provision against excessive bail might be viewed as a right that should be brought to bear against state action.

As the Court has moved toward further general application of the provisions of the Bill of Rights against the states, it has also laid down more specific prescriptions in guiding state law-enforcement officers. In *Gideon* v. *Wainwright* (1963), the Court overturned the conviction of Clarence E. Gideon, sentenced by a Florida court for breaking and entering. Gideon had been convicted four times previously and had served prison sentences for felonies. A five-page, handwritten petition, drafted in prison and accompanied by a pauper's affidavit, represented his appeal to the Supreme Court. Gideon asked the Court to overturn his conviction on the ground that his request for state-appointed counsel should not have been denied by the Florida courts. Specifically, he urged that the Sixth Amendment provision of the right to counsel is a "fundamental right" and therefore applies to the states. Gideon won his appeal. A unanimous court ruled that in all criminal cases an accused must be allowed counsel — either his own or one appointed by the court if he is unable to afford his own.[29]

One year later, after state and federal courts had received thousands of petitions similar to Gideon's, the Supreme Court took another step in specifying what state courts must do to assure a fair trial. In *Escobedo* v. *Illinois* (1964) a five-to-four majority ruled that a confession obtained by police was not admissible during trial if the defendant had been denied his right to consult his attorney and had not been informed of his right to remain silent.

---

[29] For an excellent and fascinating account of the Gideon case and the issues it raised, see Anthony Lewis, *Gideon's Trumpet* (New York: Vintage Books, 1964).

| Provision | Applied to states? | Important decisions |
|---|---|---|
| **First Amendment** | | |
| Speech, press | Yes | *Gitlow v. New York* (1925) |
| Assembly and petition | Yes | *De Jonge v. Oregon* (1937) |
| Free exercise of religion | Yes | *Cantwell v. Connecticut* (1940) |
| No establishment of religion | Yes | *Everson v. Board of Education* (1947) |
| **Second Amendment** | | |
| Right to keep and bear arms | No | |
| **Third Amendment** | | |
| Quartering of troops in private homes without consent of owner | No | |
| **Fourth Amendment** | | |
| No unreasonable searches and seizures | Yes | *Wolf v. Colorado* (1949) <br> *Mapp v. Ohio* (1964) |
| **Fifth Amendment** | | |
| Indictment by grand jury for serious offenses | No | |
| No double jeopardy | Yes | *Benton v. Maryland* (1969) |
| No self-incrimination | Yes | *Malloy v. Hogan* (1964) |
| No denial of life, liberty, or property without due process of law | Yes[a] | |
| **Sixth Amendment** | | |
| Right to counsel in criminal prosecutions | Yes | *Powell v. Alabama* (1932) |
| Right of accused to confront witnesses against him | Yes | *Gideon v. Wainwright* (1963) <br> *Douglas v. Alabama* (1965) |
| Right to speedy and public trial | Yes | *Pointer v. Texas* (1965) |
| Trial in district where crime was committed | No | |
| Trial by impartial jury | Yes | *Duncan v. Louisiana* (1968) |
| **Seventh Amendment** | | |
| Trial by jury in civil suits | No | |
| **Eighth Amendment** | | |
| No excessive bail | No | *Robinson v. California* (1962) |
| No cruel and unusual punishments | Yes | *Louisiana ex rel. Francis v. Resweber* (1947) [b] |

[a] Same specific restriction in Fourteenth Amendment.

[b] Supreme Court assumed application against states.

**FIGURE 4–2**
**Nationalization of the Bill of Rights**

In June 1966, the Court went well beyond the *Escobedo* decision. In *Miranda* v. *Arizona* and three other cases decided at the same time, another five-to-four majority ruled that (1) a suspect taken into custody must be informed of his right to remain silent; (2) a suspect has the right to have a lawyer present during interrogation; (3) a court-appointed lawyer must be provided if the suspect requests one but is unable to pay for counsel; (4) a suspect may waive the right to counsel, but the prosecution must prove that the suspect knew his rights; and (5) if a suspect initially waives the right to counsel or starts to talk but later requests counsel or chooses to remain silent his wishes must be complied with. Perhaps mindful of the thousands of petitions from inmates of prisons throughout the country who had not been accorded these protections, the Court ruled one week later that the *Miranda* and *Escobedo* decisions would not apply retroactively.[30]

Decisions of the Warren Court on right to counsel stirred intense public and congressional controversy and criticism. Critics saw in the decisions an escape for the "guilty" and an "imbalance" between the law enforcers and the "criminal." In his campaign for the presidency in 1968, Richard Nixon charged that the Supreme Court had given the "green light to the criminal element" and pledged that he would take steps to rectify the imbalance. His appointment of Warren E. Burger to replace retiring Chief Justice Earl Warren was seen by many as a step toward slowing down or stopping the Warren Court's decisions of the 1960s in defendant rights. Three subsequent appointments by Nixon brought to the Court justices likely to be sympathetic to the Nixon position.

Strong differences on defendants' rights between Congress and the Warren Court were revealed by two actions — one by the Supreme Court and the other by Congress — in May and June 1968. In one day, the Court overturned five convictions in criminal cases, giving more rights to defendants or convicted persons. In June 1968, Congress, apparently responding to strong public pressures, overturned three rulings relating to the admissibility in *federal* courts of some kinds of evidence in criminal trials.[31] The action involved only matters related to federal rules of criminal procedure. Congress cannot overrule the Court's constitutional interpretation by simply passing a statute. It does, however, have the power to alter the federal court procedures based on prior decisions not involving a declaration of constitutional requirements. In this instance, then, Congress modified only the Supreme Court's rulings affecting crimi-

[30] *Johnson* v. *New Jersey,* 384 U.S. 719 (1966).

[31] The three cases relating to police interrogation and police line-up identification are *Mallory* v. *United States,* 354 U.S. 449 (1957); *Miranda* v. *Arizona,* 384 U.S. 436 (1966); and *United States* v. *Wade,* 388 U.S. 218 (1957).

nal *procedures* in the lower federal courts. The Court's power to interpret the Constitution was not at issue. In 1970, Congress again responded to public demands for a restoration of "law and order" by passing the Crime Control Act for the District of Columbia. Although this legislation provided for more judicial personnel and government-paid defense lawyers for indigents, it also reflected public clamor for "removing the handcuffs" from police. New rules permitted wiretap and electronic sensing devices to be used in investigating some types of crimes, obtaining search warrants for night searches, and allowing detention of an accused if the judge concludes that such detention is necessary to ensure community safety.

By 1971, the Warren Court's strong protective position seemed weaker, perhaps because of changes in court personnel, especially in the position of the Chief Justice, and also the increasingly complex issues raised in criminal justice. The change appeared in decisions involving guilty pleas, search and seizure, and the rights of juvenile defendants.[32] In *Harris* v. *New York* (1971), the Court, by a five-to-four majority, held that statements made by a defendant during police interrogation, inadmissible under the *Miranda* decision, might still be used to impeach his credibility if the statements at his trial were inconsistent with those made during police interrogation. Thus, although the Court did not directly reexamine *Miranda,* the *Harris* decision placed a major limitation on it.

Change by judicial action may draw reactions from other sectors of the political system. These counterpressures stimulate continuing constitutional change, either through formal amendments or alteration by informal means. Ths Supreme Court may further alter its position on the application of the Bill of Rights to the states and the imposition of new standards in federal matters.

## constitutional politics and liberal democracy

The evolving Constitution proves that the working principles of democracy are being realized more fully though still imperfectly. Part by intent and part by circumstance, constituted authority in American government restrains popular control and consultation, political leadership, equality, and liberty. Instead we have constitutional procedures of separate authority, balance, and federalism that qualify our liberal democracy. For example, majority rule, the corollary to political equality, is checked by the electoral college and can also be checked by court discretion and by state and other actions. Also, political liberty, the right to participate, has

[32] Otis H. Stephens, Jr., "The Burger Court: New Dimensions in Criminal Justice," *The Georgetown Law Journal* 60, no. 2 (Nov. 1971): 249–278.

The Warren Court (above) made strides in protecting defendants' rights
that have been slowed by the succeeding Burger Court.

been limited because the states in the federal union may determine voting qualifications.

But what of liberal democracy's substantive values? How well are they reflected in constitutional democracy? Constitutional restraints can be used to *liberate* the individual; constitutional democracy is a stepping-stone on the way to democratic ideals. The procedures underlying constitutional democracy can increase respect for human dignity, potential for human development, and freedom of intelligence. Thus court opinions and legislative acts protecting the rights of minorities and the accused are positive steps toward these goals. When procedures are used instead to restrict the development of individual potential — by local, state, national, or *any* level of the political community — then constitutional government is a guise for bondage, not liberation. The decentralized organization of federalism, for example, provides for representation of diverse interests, but it also enables state and local governments to resist the achievement of racial equality. To which ends our liberal-democratic procedures and organization will be put depends less on the institutions themselves than on the active dedication of Americans to their ideals.

We have seen that political differences within the American community are contained by a basic consensus marked by acquiescence to liberal-democratic ideals and procedures. Controversy seldom attacks the basic features and values of the constitutional system. If one side argues that a proposal will violate a constitutional ideal, the reply usually does not condemn that ideal. The proponents of the proposal instead deny that any violation is involved, affirm the validity of the ideal, and insist that their proposed action meets that ideal better.

The controversy over busing of public school children reached a peak of intensity in 1971 after several federal district court decisions had ordered busing to achieve racial balance. Proponents of the value of the "neighborhood school" clashed with those who argued that genuine educational development and opportunity could be achieved only by mixing children from predominantly black and underprivileged school districts with white children from more affluent neighborhoods. In March 1972, President Nixon proposed that Congress impose a "moratorium" on further court-ordered busing. Nixon saw court-enforced busing as not required by the Constitution; if it was, he argued, a constitutional Amendment banning it should be "considered." It was also "a bad means to a good end," the end being improved education for the poor. Equality could better be achieved by large expenditures of federal funds to improve substandard schools. Opponents of the President's plan, including educators, several of the Democratic party candidates in the presidential primaries, and the NAACP and other minority group spokesmen, responded that not only was busing a necessary means to achieve equal education for all but also that the President's proposals would be a step backward in the drive for political and social equality achieved by Supreme Court decisions and legislation since the early 1950s. No one questioned the value of the ideal: better education for an underprivileged minority.

Our attachment to liberal democratic beliefs and practices shapes and limits disputes, but does not eliminate them. We seem to have little difficulty in supplying the political agenda with continuing controversies over the best means to approach the ends we agree on. Diverse and conflicting interests in our society, as Madison argued in *Federalist* No. 10, underlies the permanency of individual and collective disagreements. Our political community is at least a partially open society that, by

The busing of public school children to achieve racial integration
is both politically and constitutionally controversial.

definition, encourages differences as well as agreement. Neither the number nor the status of groups remains static. Powerful interests lose their power (prohibition forces); relatively weak groups become stronger (labor unions, NAACP); new groups enter the political scene (John Birch Society, National Farmers' Organization, Students for a Democratic Society); and some groups disappear entirely (Whig Party). These changes are reflected in, and are affected by, constituted authority, and thus vitally influence the determination of policy and the resolution of conflict. So long as potentially destructive conflict is thus democratically adjusted, our continuously interacting system of fundamental values and operating rules can remain viable.

*bibliographical note*

Analysis and commentary on the background, formation, and development of American constitutionalism is extensive in scope and variety. Those interested in exploring the social, political, and economic forces that shaped values and ideas prior to 1787 should find Daniel J. Boorstin's *The Americans: The Colonial Experience* (New York: Random House, 1958) a useful source. Carl Becker's classic, *The Declaration of Independence* (New York: Harcourt, Brace, 1922), remains the most important source for understanding this important contribution to constitutional ideas. Clinton Rossiter, *Seedtime of the Republic* (New York: Harcourt, Brace, 1953) is among the best treatments of political history from the colonial period to 1776.

Charles A. Beard's influential *An Economic Interpretation of the Constitution of the United States with New Introduction* (New York: Macmillan, 1954), first published in 1913, questions the motives of the Framers and should be compared with Robert E. Brown's *Charles Beard and the Constitution* (Princeton, N.J.: Princeton University Press, 1956). An original source on the debates in the Constitutional Convention is Max Farrand's outstanding work, *The Records of the Federal Convention of 1787*, 4 vols. (New Haven, Conn.: Yale University Press, 1937). Farrand's *The Framing of the Constitution of the United States* (New Haven, Conn.: Yale University Press, 1915) is an easily read chronicle of the political struggles within the Convention. A more recent paperback by Broadus and Louise Mitchell, *A Biography of the Constitution of the United States* (New York: Oxford University Press, 1964), is an outstanding "life story of the Constitution."

*The Federalist,* available in paperback editions, is essential reading for a full understanding of the theory and political considerations that underlay the Constitution. A recent work, also in paperback, which treats this major work from an analytical perspective is Gottfried Dietze, *The Federalist* (Baltimore, Md.: Johns Hopkins Press, 1960). Charles S. Hyneman and George W. Carey, *A Second Federalist: Congress Creates a Government* (New York: Appleton-Century-Crofts, 1967) presents and analyzes the first forty years of congressional debates on "issues that were of critical importance in fixing the character of the American political system."

The profound influence of the federal pattern in American politics is illustrated by many excellent books. The following, all available in paperback, provide a range of views on the subject. William Riker, *Federalism: Origin, Operation, Significance* (Boston: Little, Brown, 1964) views American federalism from the persepective of comparative theory. Daniel Elazar, ed., *The Politics of American Federalism* (Lexington, Mass.: D. C. Heath, 1969) offers excellent readings with historical and analytical range. Debate over the meaning and purpose of federalism can be reviewed in Robert A. Goldwin, ed., *A Nation of States* (Chicago: Rand McNally, 1963). Among the best short treatments of the evaluation of federalism and divergent theories as to its functional influence is Duane Lockard, *American Federalism* (New York: McGraw-Hill, 1969).

The function of the judiciary in American constitutionalism is broad. We suggest only a few works among many excellent ones. Carl Brent Swisher, *The Growth of Constitutional Power in the United States* (Chicago: University of Chicago Press, 1963) is among the most insightful and readable accounts of developing court power as well as its limits. Walter F. Murphy's *Wiretapping on Trial* (New York: Random House, 1965) traces constitutional change through judicial action in an engaging case study of a major conflict. An excellent trio of short essays, written by scholars in layman's language, is Archibald Cox, Mark

DeWolfe Howe, and J. R. Wiggins, *Civil Rights, the Constitution, and the Courts* (Cambridge, Mass.: Harvard University Press, 1967). John P. Frank's study, *Marble Palace: The Supreme Court in American Life* (New York: Alfred A. Knopf, 1958), provides insight into the relationship of the Supreme Court to changing American social and economic patterns.

Assessments of the sixteen years of the Warren Court are the subject of Fred P. Graham's *The Self-Inflicted Wound* (New York: Macmillan, 1970), in which he treats the Warren Court years and the expanding procedural rights doctrines, and Alexander Bickel, *The Supreme Court and the Idea of Progress* (New York: Harper & Row, 1970). For other works on the courts and judicial politics see the bibliographical note at the end of Chapter Fifteen.

# III

# patterns of conflict representation: who takes part and how?

When their opinions differ, politically active people use every means possible to publicize them. Such "conflict representation" alerts the community to social conflicts that require resolution. To examine conflict representation, then, we must look at the question of who does what in politics and how he does it. The main patterns of popular participation in politics are affected by the basic components of the American pluralist community we have discussed — social diversity, which generates conflicts; contrasting personal values and beliefs within the framework of liberal democracy; and a fragmented constitutional order.

119

# participating in politics

What does it mean to *participate* in politics? We think it means taking part in the basic decisions about the common goals of one's society and finding the best ways to move toward these goals.[1] We know that in a pluralist community like America this means engaging in disputes over ends and means. *By participating in politics people air their disagreements and conflict is represented.* How much participation is there in American politics? How do people participate? Who is permitted to take part and who actually does?

## how much popular participation?

In liberal democratic theory, the citizen is pictured as rational, interested in politics, informed, capable, and desirous of taking part in his government. In one sense, this portrayal is fairly accurate. When Americans are asked if they think they have an *obligation to participate* in politics, they say they do. In a study of political views in five nations (the United States, the United Kingdom, Germany, Italy, and Mexico), samples of the population were asked the question:

> We know that the ordinary person has many problems that take his time. In view of this, what part do you think the ordinary person ought to play in the local affairs of his town or district?

Table 5-1 shows the percentages of citizens in each country who believe the ordinary man is obligated to take part in local affairs. Two varieties

[1] James C. Davies, *Human Nature in Politics* (New York: John Wiley, 1963), p. 23.

of participation are emphasized: *active* participation in local government, political parties, and voluntary organizations; and *passive* participation by keeping informed, voting, and taking an interest in politics. In the United States 59 percent of those interviewed thought the ordinary man was obliged to participate actively; 64 percent felt obliged to participate passively — at least to some degree. These totals are higher than those for any of the other four nations.

*But feeling an obligation to participate is not always matched by actual participation in American politics.* Table 5-2 lists the estimated proportions of Americans who take part in several types of political activity. This profile indicates (1) that *relatively few Americans actively*

|  | | **TABLE 5–1** |
|---|---|---|
|  | | **Obligation to Participate** |

| Form of participation | *Percentage who choose in* | | | | |
|---|---|---|---|---|---|
|  | United States | United Kingdom | Germany | Italy | Mexico |
| Active participation in local community | | | | | |
|    Take part in activities of local government | 21% | 22% | 13% | 5% | 11% |
|    Take part in activities of political parties | 6 | 4 | 4 | 1 | 5 |
|    Take part in nongovern-mental activity and in organizations inter-ested in local affairs | 32 | 17 | 9 | 5 | 10 |
| Passive community activities | | | | | |
|    Try to understand and keep informed | 21 | 11 | 24 | 6 | 29 |
|    Vote | 40 | 18 | 15 | 2 | 1 |
|    Take interest in what is going on | 3 | 13 | 6 | 15 | 4 |
| Participation in some form of politically related activity | 83 | 72 | 61 | 32 | 59 |
|        Number of cases | 970 | 963 | 955 | 995 | 1007 |

Source: Adapted from Gabriel A. Almond and Sidney Verba. *The Civic Culture* (Princeton: Princeton University Press, 1963), p. 171. Used with permission of Princeton University Press.

**TABLE 5-2**
**Profile of American Political Participation**

| *Means of political participation* | *Estimated percentage of Americans as participants* |
|---|---|
| Passive participation | |
| Expressing political opinions: | |
| Normally express opinions when asked | 70–90% |
| Normally express informed opinions when asked | 30–50 |
| Possess basic "textbook" information of politics | 15–40 |
| Making voting choices: | |
| Register to vote in presidential election years | 70–80 |
| Identify themselves as Republicans or Democrats | 65–75 |
| Registered and voted in recent presidential elections, 1960–68 | 60–70 |
| Registered and voted in recent congressional elections, 1960–70 | 45–60 |
| Register and vote occasionally in elections | 30–40 |
| Register and vote consistently in all elections — federal, state, and local | 25–30 |
| Do not register or vote in elections | 5–15 |
| Active participation | |
| Leading political opinions: | |
| Attempt to influence political views of others through informal discussions | 25–35 |
| Attempt to influence political views of others by taking part in political campaigns | 3–5 |
| Attempt to influence political views of others by regular participation in party precinct organizations | .25–1 |
| Participating in political parties: | |
| Attend political meetings, rallies, dinners | 5–10 |
| Financially support campaigns of parties or candidates | 4–10 |
| Active membership in a political club or organization | 2–3 |
| Joining voluntary organizations: | |
| Membership in organizations of any kind | 60–65 |
| Membership in organizations that sometimes take stands on political issues | 30–35 |

Sources: U.S. Bureau of the Census, *Current Population Reports*, Series P-20, No. 192, *Voting and Registration in the Election of November 1968* (Washington, D.C.: U.S. Government Printing Office, 1969); Survey Research Center and Interuniversity Consortium for Political Research, University of Michigan: Robert E. Lane, *Political Life* (Glencoe, Ill.: Free Press, 1959), pp. 45–94.

*participate in politics regularly,* and (2) *that the more passive the means, the greater the proportions of Americans who do participate.* Whereas many of our citizens express political opinions, think of themselves as Democrats or Republicans, and endeavor to influence others by discussion, far fewer vote in all elections, work for political candidates, or join political organizations.

We conclude that a sense of obligation to participate is widespread among Americans and that passive participation in conflict representation is relatively high; their activity in presenting demands and grievances is much less frequent and intense.

## how do americans usually take part in conflict representation?

The relatively few Americans who participate actively make us wonder how they seek to make policymakers hear their arguments. We have chosen to discuss six of the *principal patterns for representing conflicts* in American life. In the chapters that follow, we shall examine each in detail, but first an overall description is essential.

### expressing political opinions

The most effortless way of voicing disagreements in politics is to express a conflicting opinion on issues and personalities. A compilation of American public opinion surveys reported more than two decades ago that less than 15 percent generally expressed "no opinion" on a large variety of issues. "Americans," the authors of the study concluded, "are an articulate people and they express opinions on virtually every conceivable issue."[2] Is this generalization still accurate? The evidence strongly suggests that it is. Even a casual reading of hundreds of opinion surveys published annually in American newspapers suggests that, far from being a "silent majority," the citizens who happen to get interviewed are very vocal indeed.[3] People have opinions on almost any political subject, and the opinions are frequently *in conflict.*

Although relatively few Americans have "no opinion," many opinionated citizens would be more nearly correct to say "don't know" more

[2] Herbert H. Hyman and Paul B. Sheatsley, "The Current Status of American Public Opinion," in Daniel Katz et al., eds., *Public Opinion and Propaganda* (New York: Henry Holt, 1954), pp. 36–37.

[3] Many private polling organizations provide annual compilations of their surveys. See *The Harris Survey Yearbook of Public Opinion 1970* (New York: Louis Harris, 1971).

often than they do. *Although the average American is likely to have an opinion about anything, his opinion is not necessarily informed or based on supporting evidence.* Polls frequently report that more than 10 percent of the individuals expressing opinions answer "don't know" when asked why they feel the way they do. One significant study revealed that on the average only two American voters in three could be classified as familiar with public issues: that is, they both possessed an opinion *and* knew what "government is doing about" the matter in question.[4]

When does a statement of opinion on a public matter indicate the kind of personal involvement that can fairly be said to represent conflicting participation? When people express opinions on questions they have never heard of and know nothing about, they only confuse policymakers who are trying to learn what social conflicts underlie public opinion.[5] In 1971, *The New York Times* and *The Washington Post* began publishing a startling series of articles adding substantially to our knowledge of how the United States had become so heavily involved in Vietnam. The articles were based on the celebrated "Pentagon Papers" — documents and memoranda classified as secret, and acquired by the newspapers without official knowledge or sanction. The federal government sought a court injunction to prevent further publication. The injunction was granted, then canceled by a divided Supreme Court. During June and July of 1971, the conflict over publication of the Pentagon Papers was the leading news story in newspapers, on radio, and on television.

At the height of the controversy the Gallup organization conducted a nationwide opinion poll on publication of the papers. Asked if they thought the press was "too quick to print classified information whether or not it might hurt the nation's security," 56 percent responded affirmatively, 28 percent said no, and 16 percent had "no opinion." From such data a policymaker might conclude that there was a consensus among Americans against publication of classified information. Now, look at the answers to two related questions. One: "Have you heard or read about the articles first published in *The New York Times* about how we got involved in the Vietnam war?" Forty-five percent said they had not! Two, addressed to those who *had* heard about the story: "In your opinion, did the newspapers do the right thing or the wrong thing in publishing these articles?" Here 58 percent said it was the right thing to do, 30 percent the wrong thing, and 12 percent had "no opinion."[6] Informed opinion thus differed sharply from opinion across the board.

The situation was unusual, and the constitutional issue perhaps

[4] Angus Campbell et al., *The American Voter* (New York: John Wiley, 1960), pp. 171–176.
[5] Leo Bogart, "No Opinion, Don't Know and Maybe No Answer," *Public Opinion Quarterly* 31 (Fall 1967): 331–345.
[6] News Release, American Institute of Public Opinion (July 6, 1971).

Most citizens have definite
political opinions and are eager
to express them.

unique, but the difference between informed and uninformed opinion
was not unusual at all. Policymakers are always hard-pressed to distinguish opinions that reflect *active participation* from those that are simply
*passive responses* to political events; and surveys indicating the general
knowledge of Americans about politics provide striking evidence about
the low levels of information broadly shared. In 1970, only 53 percent
of a nationwide sample knew the names of their Congressmen, only 21
percent knew how their Congressmen had voted on major bills during
the year, and more than a third admitted they did not even know whether
their Congressman was a Democrat or a Republican. Knowledge about
state politics is even more meager. Many a state legislator would be cha-
grined to know that in 1967 only 28 percent of the respondents in a poll
knew who would represent their districts in the state senate in the following year, and only 24 percent could name their representatives in the
lower house of the state legislature.[7]

How meaningful is conflict representation through the expression of
opinions before such ignorance? From the policymakers' standpoint, it
obviously depends upon *who is expressing the opinion. All opinions
matter, but the opinions of active participants rather than passive ones
count most in conflict representation.*

## leading political opinions

We have seen that a person need not be engaged in politics to express
an opinion. To express an informed opinion, however, his involvement

[7] Norval D. Glenn, "The Distribution of Political Knowledge in the United States," in Dan
Nimmo and Charles M. Bonjean, eds., *Political Attitudes and Public Opinion* (New York:
David McKay, 1972).

126

must be greater. If he is to influence the opinions of others, he must have genuine enthusiasm for public affairs. Political leaders influence opinions: *they represent conflict not only by getting people to take part in politics but by getting them to take sides on issues.*

People do many things to influence the political opinions of others, but the most visible activities are the things people do *in election campaigns.* Table 5-3 presents the percentages of persons who have reported actively participating in recent political campaigns in nationwide surveys. The percentages are appallingly low; only one of three Americans, even in the superheated Nixon-Kennedy and Nixon-Humphrey campaigns of 1960 and 1968, tried to persuade a fellow voter even verbally. Passive conversation about politics, not really intended to change anyone's mind but simply to offer opinions and air gripes and frustrations about "them politicians," is more frequent and probably engages 70 percent of the population at one time or another. But the ratio of passive to active participation in political campaigns is always high.

Aside from electoral campaigns, citizens may *directly* make known their differing views to public officials in the hope of influencing policy-

| | | | | **TABLE 5-3** Varieties of Activities for Influencing Opinions in Political Campaigns | | |
|---|---|---|---|---|

| *Activities* | *1952* | *1956* | *1960* | *1964* | *1968* |
|---|---|---|---|---|---|
| Do you belong to any political club or organization? | 2% | 3% | 3% | 4% | 3% |
| Did you give any money to buy tickets or anything to help the campaign for one of the parties or candidates? | 4 | 10 | 12 | 11 | 9 |
| Did you go to any political meetings, rallies, dinners, or things like that? | 7 | 10 | 8 | 9 | 9 |
| Did you do other work for one of the parties or candidates? | 3 | 3 | 6 | 5 | 6 |
| Did you wear a campaign button or put a campaign sticker on your car? | a | 16 | 21 | 16 | 15 |
| Did you talk to any people and try to show them why they should vote for one of the parties or candidates? | 27 | 28 | 33 | 31 | 33 |

Source: Survey Research Center and Interuniversity Consortium for Political Research, University of Michigan.
a Question not asked in 1952 survey.

making. They do so by letters, telegrams, telephone calls, and personal contact. Again, however, few Americans exercise this political muscle. A 1950 study revealed that only about one American in five petitions a policymaker directly, and we have no reason to think the proportion is much higher today.[8] In 1964, only 15 percent of a nationwide sample could recall having written a letter to a public official. Of the letters officials receive, probably two-thirds are written by about 3 percent of the population. Only 3 percent of the 1964 sample could recall having written letters to newspapers and magazines; of "letters to the editor," two-thirds come from one-half of 1 percent of the population.[9]

Most Americans simply do not have the inclination, the time, or the knowledge to act as political leaders. In 1964, 63 percent of those interviewed in a national survey reported they had engaged in *none* of the activities described in Table 5-3; nor had they written letters to public officials, newspapers, or magazines. These people were either *apathetic*, with no interest in politics, casually interested or *spectators*: "they watch, they cheer, they vote, but they do not battle."[10] By the most generous estimate, *active leaders* are in the minority in American politics; and we shall want to know what they do and how people respond to them in conflict representation.

## making voting choices

The individual's most valuable political possession in a republic is the voting franchise. By voting, he makes his choice between candidates who are competing for the authority to make public policy; in some areas — constitutional amendments at the state level, referenda on taxes, bond proposals, and the like — the citizen's vote allows him to take part in making policy. By their votes, Americans declare their preferences for and against officials and policies, and *the distribution of their votes is a representation of their conflicts on these matters.*

We classify voting, however, as a relatively passive means of conflict representation in American politics. To be sure, voters must reach two decisions: whether to vote or not and, if they vote, whom or what to support or oppose. We might assume that in making these decisions voters are informed and actively engaged in politics, but the evidence demonstrates quite the reverse.

---

[8] Julian L. Woodward and Elmo Roper, "Political Activity of American Citizens," *The American Political Science Review* 64 (Dec. 1950): 872–885.

[9] Philip E. Converse et al., "Electoral Myth and Reality: The 1964 Election," *The American Political Science Review*, 59 (June 1965): 333.

[10] Lester W. Milbrath, *Political Participation* (Chicago: Rand McNally, 1965), p. 21.

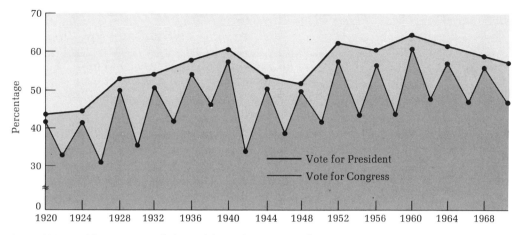

Source: U.S. Bureau of the Census, *Statistical Abstract of the United States: 1971* (Washington, D.C.: U.S. Government Printing Office, 1971).

FIGURE 5–1
Participation of the Electorate
in Presidential and Congressional Elections, 1920–1970

By and large, Americans are reluctant or simply careless about using their franchise. Only 25 to 30 percent of the adult population vote regularly in federal, state, and local elections. Another 30 to 40 percent cast votes so infrequently that they can be labeled fairly as nonvoters. The remainder never vote in any election.[11]

As Figure 5-1 illustrates, the overall picture of a relatively light vote is modified little by the fact that there has been a general increase in the turnout rate in federal elections during the past fifty years. In presidential elections, turnout levels rose prior to World War II, dipped moderately in the 1940s, increased again in the 1950s, and declined slightly in the 1960s. Turnout levels in congressional elections are consistently lower in off years when they do not coincide with presidential elections, and even lower in "special" congressional elections called to fill a vacancy created by death. Figure 5-1 does not take into account the restrictions on who is eligible to vote (that is, residence and registration requirements). It is safe to say, however, that from 10 to 15 percent of the eligible electorate are uninterested in voting or unwilling to go to the trouble even in presidential elections.[12]

---

[11] Robert E. Lane, *Political Life* (Glencoe, Ill.: Free Press, 1959), pp. 45–62.
[12] William G. Andrews, "American Voting Participation," *The Western Political Quarterly* 19 (Dec. 1966): 652.

## participating in political parties

American political parties compete for the authority to govern, and citizens take part in that conflict by affiliating themselves with political parties. They may do so passively or actively. At the passive level people simply have emotional loyalty or attachment to a party — they have a *party identification*. That identification varies according to which party people identify with and how strongly they feel about their attachment. Table 5-4 displays the distribution of Democrat and Republican party identification in the United States in recent years as measured by answers to standardized survey questions. Party identification significantly influences a citizen's voting behavior, and *attachment to party is a means of passive political participation engaged in by approximately three-fourths of Americans.*

Active party participation means taking a stand in the partisan battle

|  | | | | | | | | | | |
|---|---|---|---|---|---|---|---|---|---|---|
| | | | | | | | | **TABLE 5–4** | | |
| | | | | | **Distribution of Party Identification in the United States, 1952–1970** | | | | | |
| *Question:* | "Generally speaking, do you usually think of yourself as a Republican, a Democrat, an Independent, or what?" (If Republican or Democrat): "Would you call yourself a strong (R) (D) or a not very strong (R) (D)?" (If Independent): "Do you think of yourself as closer to the Republican or Democratic Party?" | | | | | | | | | |
| | *Oct. 1952* | *Oct. 1954* | *Oct. 1956* | *Oct. 1958* | *Oct. 1960* | *Nov. 1962* | *Oct. 1964* | *Nov. 1966* | *Nov. 1968* | *Nov. 1970* |
| Democrat | | | | | | | | | | |
| Strong | 22% | 22% | 21% | 23% | 21% | 23% | 26% | 18% | 20% | 20% |
| Weak | 25 | 25 | 23 | 24 | 25 | 23 | 25 | 27 | 25 | 23 |
| Independent | | | | | | | | | | |
| Democrat | 10 | 9 | 7 | 7 | 8 | 8 | 9 | 9 | 10 | 10 |
| Independent | 5 | 7 | 9 | 8 | 8 | 8 | 8 | 12 | 11 | 13 |
| Republican | 7 | 6 | 8 | 4 | 7 | 6 | 6 | 7 | 9 | 8 |
| Republican | | | | | | | | | | |
| Weak | 14 | 14 | 14 | 16 | 13 | 16 | 13 | 15 | 14 | 15 |
| Strong | 13 | 13 | 15 | 13 | 14 | 12 | 11 | 10 | 10 | 10 |
| Apolitical, don't know | 4 | 4 | 3 | 5 | 4 | 4 | 2 | 2 | 1 | 1 |
| Total | 100% | 100% | 100% | 100% | 100% | 100% | 100% | 100% | 100% | 100% |
| Number of cases | 1614 | 1139 | 1772 | 1269 | 3021 | 1289 | 1571 | 1291 | 1553 | 1802 |

Source: Center for Political Studies, University of Michigan.

and working within a party organization. Active partisans include precinct leaders, party chairmen, secretaries, fund raisers, professional organizers, campaign managers, convention delegates, and others who occupy a niche in the party hierarchy. *Relatively few Americans are active in party politics;* estimates run as low as less than 1 percent of the adult population.[13]

Although few citizens engage in party activity, the ones who do have an effect far out of proportion to their numbers. This effect varies with the *type of election* being held and with the general *strength of the party* in an area. When elections are contested by well-known personalities or involve clearly defined issues, precinct activists usually have less to do — but when such an election is close, they can still influence or even decide the outcome by getting out their own voters. They supply the margin of victory more often when candidates or issues are less well known, as in party primaries of contests for minor political offices. Every precinct captain knows which voters to start calling at noon on election Tuesday; he hopes the others will forget what day it is. He also knows their general health — that is, which of his voters need transportation or even need to be assisted physically into the polling place.

Activity on behalf of a minority party has more *noticeable* effects. The majority party needs only to hold and activate its own supporters to win. The minority party must convert voters to its cause, and when it does so it leaves the impression of striking accomplishment — even in defeat. The competition between political parties and the disagreements that occur within them as to who shall control nominations, policies, and programs combine to make parties significant arenas of conflict representation.

## joining voluntary organizations

One way in which Americans get policymakers to pay attention to their contrasting demands and grievances is by organizing to bring pressure on officials. Policymakers are sensitive to the conflicting pressures of organized interests. Strangely, however, *citizens do not generally think of joining voluntary organizations as the principal means by which they can influence governmental actions.* Table 5-5 shows percentages of citizens in five nations who would organize to influence government or who would prefer to act alone. Organized action is not overwhelmingly pre-

---

[13] Hugh A. Bone, *Grass Roots Party Leadership* (Seattle, Wash.: University of Washington Press, 1952).

TABLE 5–5
**How Citizens Think They Can Influence Government by Nation**

| What citizens would do | United States | United Kingdom | Germany | Italy | Mexico |
|---|---|---|---|---|---|
| Try to enlist aid of others | | | | | |
| Organize an informal group; arouse friends and neighbors to write letters of protest or sign petitions | 29% | 18% | 7% | 6% | 18% |
| Work through a political party | 1 | 2 | 6 | 2 | – |
| Work through a formal group (union, church, professional) | 4 | 3 | 7 | 2 | 3 |
| Total per cent who would enlist others' aid[a] | 32 | 22 | 19 | 10 | 20 |
| Act alone | | | | | |
| Directly contact political leaders (elected officials) or the press; write a letter to or visit a local leader | 57 | 44 | 12 | 7 | 8 |
| Directly contact administrative (nonelected) officials | – | 1 | 4 | 4 | 6 |
| Consult a lawyer; appeal through courts | – | – | 1 | 1 | 4 |
| Vote against offending officials at next election | 7 | 3 | 4 | 1 | – |
| Take violent action | – | – | 2 | 1 | 4 |
| Just protest | – | – | – | 3 | – |
| Other | – | 2 | – | 2 | 3 |
| Total per cent who would act alone[b] | 42 | 40 | 18 | 18 | 18 |
| Nothing | 21 | 32 | 56 | 50 | 50 |
| Don't know | 4 | 6 | 7 | 22 | 12 |
| Total percent[c] | 123 | 111 | 106 | 101 | 108 |
| Total number | 970 | 963 | 955 | 995 | 1007 |

Source: Gabriel A. Almond and Sidney Verba, *The Civic Culture* (Princeton, N.J.: Princeton University Press, 1963), p. 203. Reprinted with permission.

[a] Total percentages are less than the total of the individual cells, since some respondents gave more than one answer.

[b] This row includes only the respondents who said they could do something but did not mention working with others. The total is less than sum of the individual cells in which respondents may have mentioned both group and individual activity.

[c] Percentage more than 100 percent due to multiple responses.

ferred in any nation, and in both the United States and Great Britain individual efforts are clearly favored. We have seen that a small portion of Americans actually present their views to public officials directly; however, probably as many as two-thirds of Americans do belong to at least one voluntary organization of some kind, and about half of those belong to groups that take stands on political questions.[14]

How can we explain this seeming inconsistency: a generally expressed preference for individual means of influencing officials but a marked tendency to work through organized means? Probably there is no inconsistency. Approximately the same proportions of American citizens who would join with others to influence government (Table 5-5) are actually members of organizations that take part in political affairs. We have no way of knowing that the same people who prefer organized influence are members of political organizations, but we suspect so. Therefore it is reasonable to say that about a third of Americans prefer to take part in politics — and do — by joining political organizations.

Some voluntary organizations, such as the Southern Christian Leadership Conference or the Students for a Democratic Society, openly engage in political discussion, take positions on public issues, and protest against policies they find offensive. Others, such as the League of Women Voters, direct their efforts at stimulating greater citizen interest in public affairs. Moreover, any voluntary activity, such as working in a United Fund drive, creates greater interest in civic affairs. One survey revealed that 84 percent of the persons who were members of one or more voluntary groups said they took a great deal of interest in presidential politics, in contrast with 73 percent who were members of no organizations.[15]

Generally, then, *persons belonging to voluntary associations are more active in politics than nonmembers* and are likely to express themselves by voicing their opinions, voting, trying to influence others, and campaigning. Of the four in ten Americans who prefer to act alone (Table 5-5) in presenting conflicting interests to government, very few do so. These may be people who genuinely do not care about politics. It is more likely that most of them are citizens who are generally satisfied with government and with trust enough in political leaders to believe that *if necessary they could act alone to influence official decisions.* The apathetic portion of the community is reflected more properly in the 21 percent of Americans (Table 5-5) who could think of nothing they could do

---

[14] See Angus Campbell et al., *The Voter Decides* (Evanston, Ill.: Row, Peterson, 1954) and Gabriel A. Almond and Sidney Verba, *The Civic Culture* (Princeton, N.J.: Princeton University Press, 1963), pp. 302–307.

[15] Charles R. Wright and Herbert H. Hyman, "Voluntary Association Memberships of American Adults," *American Sociological Review* 23 (June 1958): 284–294.

to influence their national government. These people may be ignorant of how to take part in politics or, as we shall see momentarily, they may be not merely *dissatisfied* with government but so *disaffected* that they do not believe there is any conventional way to get politicians to listen to their grievances.[16] They write few letters to their leaders, make fewer telephone calls, and send no telegrams at all; but they frequently turn to protest as a way of representing their conflicting desires.

## protesting about grievances

The methods of political participation we have examined — opinion-holding, political influence, voting, participation in political parties, and membership in voluntary organizations — traditionally have been used by Americans to articulate their interests. When these channels have been open to all, they provided reasonably effective means for conflict representation even though used by most Americans only now and then. However, these conventional methods of participation have sometimes worked to the disadvantage of new interests whose demands conflicted with established ways of doing things. The impoverished have not the education to formulate informed opinions; migrant farm laborers have been disappointed by the failure of established labor unions to improve their lot; the black community until quite recently was excluded from effective party activity in the South; younger Americans have become disenchanted with the conservative and often unimaginative workings of party organizations. Such groups have sought new and dramatic methods to voice grievances. In the past decade, these have included sit-ins, lie-ins, the seizure of administration buildings on college campuses, marches on state capitals and to Washington, D.C., freedom rides, the burnings of men's draft cards, and a women's liberation march on the nearest men's bar. And we can scarcely overlook recent rioting in cities.

Such mass dissent — assisted by televised news coverage — had its effect on American politics. In the 1960s, such problems as civil rights, disaffection with the war in Vietnam, and urban poverty appeared significant partly because of the publicity given mass demonstrations. In this way, mass protests helped revise the agenda for national discussion and official action. Many officials have worried for a long time about man's deteriorating environment, but it became "good politics" to worry about it (and set long overdue legislative standards for environmental control) only after mass demonstrations such as "earth day," clean-up campaigns,

---

[16] Giuseppe Di Palma, *Apathy and Participation* (New York: Free Press, 1970).

During the 1960s, previously silent groups such as migrant farm workers
entered the political arena.

and the wearing of gas masks to protest against breathing foul air. And
who would deny that both favorable congressional and court actions on
civil rights during the 1960s were hastened by mass demonstrations and
reprisals?

It is too early to assess the merit of this mass protest, particularly in
its violent aspects, as a technique for expressing interests. But remember
the Boston Tea Party in 1773, and the Whisky Rebellion put down by
President Washington in Pennsylvania in 1794: *we have always used
protests to voice our grievances.*[17] They wax or wane as conditions dictate, like the strike and violence of an earlier era. Whether it represents
a periodic aberration or an emergent institution, mass protest is a recognizable means of conflict representation in contemporary America.

[17] Richard E. Rubenstein, *Rebels in Eden* (Boston: Little, Brown, 1970).

### why so little popular participation?

In the statistical sense, many Americans do participate in politics at least passively. The total vote in a presidential election exceeds the population of the United Kingdom or France; is not that mass, even massive, participation? It is, and it is important. But equally important is this question: Why do so many Americans not take part in conflict representation, even in a passive way? We think that there are three reasons: (1) they do not have the *opportunity;* (2) they do not have the *resources;* and (3) they do not have the *desire.*[18]

### who can participate?

We have said that one of the major characteristics of a community is its *politico-constitutional* aspect. By the political aspect we mean the activities of people seeking settlement of disputes; by the constitutional aspect we mean the rules that govern the process. Taking part in conflict representation implies the political aspect; *the opportunity to take part is governed by constitutional rules.*

*The opportunity to express and lead opinion (freedom of expression) is guaranteed by the First Amendment of the Constitution:* "Congress shall make no law . . . abridging freedom of speech, or of the press." But neither *freedom of speech* nor *freedom of the press* is total; the Amendment merely enjoins Congress from abridging them through restrictive legislation. The rest is left to the Supreme Court. It is the Court that must answer such questions as "Should government be permitted to prohibit spoken or written words that call for the overthrow of government, even though the words themselves constitute no immediate steps to implement that goal?"

THE CLEAR-AND-PRESENT-DANGER TEST. Justice Oliver Wendell Holmes, speaking for a unanimous court in *Schenck* v. *United States* (1919), laid down the "clear and present danger" test as a judicial formula for dealing with First Amendment cases involving freedom of speech and press. He wrote: "The question in every case is whether the words are used in such circumstances and are of such a nature as to create a clear and present danger that they will bring about the substantive evils that Congress has a right to prevent. It is a question of proximity and degree." In *Abrams*

---

[18] See James David Barber, *Citizen Politics,* 2nd ed. (Chicago: Markham Publishing, 1972), p. 27.

v. *United States,* also decided in 1919, Holmes gave a more precise definition in a dissenting opinion: a "present danger" is one that "imminently threatens interference with the lawful and pressing purposes of the law." Thus, danger would have to be imminent before government could prevent people from pressing their interests through freely expressed opinions; and the formula recognizes limits to the freedom to express and lead opinions. Although the First Amendment refers specifically to Congress, the Court held in *Gitlow* v. *New York* (1925) that the "liberty" protected by the Fourteenth Amendment against encroachment of the states includes the freedoms of the First Amendment.

Under the "clear and present danger" formula, any American could freely express and lead opinions as long as his acts did not form an imminent threat to society, but until the mid-1930s advocates of the formula did not again command a majority on the Supreme Court. When the Court in 1931 struck down a Minnesota statute *(Near* v. *Minnesota)* used to bar from further publication a newspaper that printed "malicious, scandalous, and defamatory" attacks, it did not rely on the clear-and-present-danger test. Instead the Court ruled that *freedom of the press prohibits prior censorship of publications.*

In 1938, Justice Harlan F. Stone breathed new life into the clear-and-present-danger test. Speaking in *United States* v. *Carolene Products Co.,* he argued that First Amendment freedoms should be accorded a special place, of "preferred position," in the Constitution. The *preferred position* test holds that because freedoms of speech, press, assembly, and religion are crucial to democratic government, government restrictions cannot be presumed constitutional: the Court must decide if a clear and present danger exists. This view found its way back into majority opinions of the Court during the early 1940s, but after the end of World War II new problems arose. Justice Felix Frankfurter repeatedly attacked both the test and the preferred-position doctrine and called for the Court to assume a more restrained position in dealing with First Amendment cases. Two difficult areas of law confronted the justices about free expression: the "hostile audience" and the "cold war" problem of dealing with groups that, according to Congress and the states, threatened national security.

The *hostile audience* issue was dramatically raised in *Feiner* v. *New York* (1951). During a street-corner speech, Feiner used derogatory language about the President of the United States, other public officials, and the American Legion. He was arrested when members of the crowd became unruly and threatened him. Feiner's conviction for disorderly conduct was sustained on the grounds that "a clear danger of disorder" existed. He could deliver the speech only if there was no danger of inciting a riot. It was the first time the Supreme Court had used the clear-and-present-danger test to *uphold* an action by government, and the Court was severely criticized. Some felt strongly that those who threatened the speaker should have been punished not the speaker, because he had not *advocated* violence.

In *cold war* cases arising out of government efforts to regulate subversive activity, the Court moved toward a new position on the First Amendment. In *Dennis* v. *United States* (1951) the Court upheld the conviction, under the Smith Act, of eleven leaders of the Communist Party who were charged with teaching and advocating the overthrow of the government. The defendants also were charged with conspiring to organize the United States Communist Party for the purpose of overthrowing the government by force and violence. None of the government's charges included overt activity with the immediate intention of revolution, but at the time the United States was actively engaged in the Korean War; Americans were being killed by bullets of Soviet manufacture in the hands of Chinese soldiers, and the popular mood was ugly. In rejecting the contention that immediate and clear danger must be established to justify any abridgment of the rights of free expression, Chief Justice Vinson laid down a new test: "Whether the gravity of the 'evil,' discounted by its improbability, justifies such invasion of free speech as necessary to avoid the danger."

The language did not sit well with the activist element on the Court. The grave-and-probable-danger test was qualified in *Yates* v. *United States* (1957) when the Warren Court distinguished between the instruction of abstract doctrine and actual incitement to dangerous action. Nevertheless the *clear-and-present-danger test has not been restored to its former eminence,* although in recent years the Court has moved back toward it slightly. In the 1971 "Pentagon Papers" case, decided in favor of *The New York Times,* Justices White and Stewart in a concurring opinion for a six-to-three majority (there was no signed opinion for the whole Court) used language reminiscent of the test. They wrote that they "do not say that in no circumstances would the First Amendment permit an injunction against publishing information about government plans or operations.... But ... the United States has not satisfied the very heavy burden which it must meet to warrant an injunction against publication in these cases."

RESTRAINING FREE SPEECH AND PRESS: LIBEL AND OBSCENITY. How free is a person to express and lead opinions if his actions constitute libel against others or are obscene? These issues have taken up a good deal of the Supreme Court's time during the past decade. The most significant libel ruling came in 1964. *Sullivan* v. *The New York Times* involved libel suits filed against the *Times* because of a paid advertisement criticizing the treatment of blacks in Alabama. The police commissioner of Montgomery, Alabama, pointed out that the advertisement contained factual errors and argued that the criticisms of the police were defamatory. He and another commissioner filed separate libel suits against the *Times* and were awarded one million dollars by an Alabama court. But the Supreme Court ruled that "erroneous statements honestly made" were not punishable as libel. Proof of "actual malice" was required to recover damages; that is, proof that the facts that were printed were known to be false or that there was "reckless disregard" of whether the material was false or not. The *Sullivan* rule has been extended to cover "public figures" so that "actual malice" would have to be proved against a politician before he could be found guilty of libeling an opponent — or a newspaper could be found guilty of libeling either.

Restrictions on free expression also can result if spoken, printed, filmed, or other material can be easily banned as obscene. In *Roth* v. *United States* (1957), the Supreme Court declared obscenity as "utterly without redeeming social importance" and thus not in the area of expression protected by the First Amendment. In *Roth,* the Court defined obscene material as that which "to the average person, applying contemporary community standards, the dominant theme of the material taken as a whole appeals to prurient interest." In *Manual Enterprises* v. *Day* (1962), the Court added that the material must be "patently offensive" and "self-demonstrating" in its indecency. Then in *Jacobellis* v. *Ohio* (1964), the Court exempted from its definition material "dealing with sex in a manner that advocates ideas . . ." in a literary, artistic, scientific, or other form with social importance. Publishers of erotic magazines and books occasionally go to jail, but a legal definition of obscenity and pornography is hard to come by.

FREEDOM OF RELIGIOUS EXPRESSION. The First Amendment also prohibits Congress from restricting the free exercise of religious expression. The Supreme Court's position is that there can be *no prior censorship on religious expression just as there can be none on free speech or press.* Even during World War II, in *West Virginia Board of Education* v. *Barnette* (1943), the Court used the clear-and-present-danger formula to strike down compulsory flag salutes, which Jehovah's Witnesses felt violated their free expression. The freedoms of the First Amendment, said Justice Jackson, "are susceptible of restriction only to prevent grave and immediate danger," a situation that he felt failure to salute the flag did not create. The Court also has taken a stand *against the establishment of mandatory religious practices* that might violate freedom of religious expression. In *Engel* v. *Vitale* (1962), it ruled against the "religious activity" in public schools of reading prayers, even though students who did not wish to participate could remain mute or leave the room. Following decisions held that reading of the Bible or the Lord's Prayer as part of an opening exercise in public schools was unconstitutional. Since *Mc-Collum* v. *Board of Education* (1948), the Court has held it unconstitutional for public schools to provide students with "released time" whereby they would be instructed in religious doctrines during school hours in school buildings.

THE OPPORTUNITY TO JOIN VOLUNTARY ORGANIZATIONS. Expressing and leading opinions and joining political organizations are overlapping opportunities, so we must turn there for a further understanding of who can take part in conflict representation. In the *Dennis* and *Yates* cases, the Supreme Court dealt in part with problems raised by the freedom of association. By virtue of the *Yates* principle people cannot be punished for mere membership in an organization such as the Communist Party. In *Aptheker* v. *United States* (1964) and *United States* v. *Robel* (1967), the Court extended this view, holding that Communists could not be forbidden to apply for passports or to work in defense plants.

The right of voluntary association, however, touches upon more than the Communist Party. Civil rights organizations, such as the National Association for the Advancement of Colored People, are also protected. In 1958, Alabama demanded that the NAACP register as an out-of-state corporation and supply the names and addresses of its members in the state. The organization refused to disclose its membership. The Supreme Court agreed with the NAACP, arguing that to compel an organization to reveal its membership lists could interfere unconstitutionally with the right of individuals to join in legitimate association with those of common beliefs *(NAACP* v. *Alabama)*. Similarly in *Gibson* v. *Florida Legislative Investigation Committee* (1963), the Court upheld the decision of an NAACP official not to reveal the organization's membership list to a committee investigating possible Communist activity in the NAACP.

Of course members of some militant organizations, such as the Weathermen faction of the Students for a Democratic Society or the Black Panthers, have been imprisoned or subject to surveillance, harassment, and litigation. But this does not truly restrict *a relatively broad freedom to associate.* Judicial action against members of militant groups usually has relied on grounds of violations of criminal statutes and has not been directed at the right to join voluntary organizations.

THE OPPORTUNITY TO PROTEST ABOUT GRIEVANCES. Public protest, as we have seen, is an American habit older than the Constitution itself. The "right of the people peaceably to assemble, and to petition the government for a redress of grievances" is guaranteed in the First Amendment.

In 1965, Martin Luther King led the well-known march from Selma to Montgomery and dramatized demands for equal voting rights. Legislation was enacted shortly thereafter.

In recent decades, which saw the labor movement achieve very great power, followed by civil rights demonstrations and antiwar protests, the opportunity to protest has become particularly important to individuals and to groups desiring to take part in politics.

How far can a protest go if it threatens public order? In cases dealing with the labor movement, the Supreme Court responded to this question by applying the clear-and-present danger yardstick. In *Thornhill* v. *Alabama* (1940), the Court ruled unconstitutional a state law that forbade peaceful picketing on the ground that the law violated freedom of speech: peaceful picketing, said the Court, posed no "clear danger of substantive evils." Because big labor unions now hold a stronger hand than they held in the 1930s, massive strike violence has vanished from the American industrial scene. Nonetheless "peaceful picketing" usually stops being peaceful when someone attempts to "scab" by crossing the picket line.

In any event picketing, marching, sitting-in, lying down in front of automobiles, and other such protests involve more than free speech. They combine speech with action and according to the Court some restrictions are legitimate. A government can require advance notification of demonstrations and can require permits for them. If they are too restrictive, permit ordinances may be declared unconstitutional as in *Walker* v. *Birmingham* (1967). Earlier, in 1965, when Martin Luther King, Jr., led his now famous march from Selma to Montgomery, Alabama to dramatize his demand for black voting rights, Alabama officials denied him a march permit but were overruled by a federal judge. At the 1968 Democratic national convention in Chicago, protestors were denied a parade permit. Mostly they supported the candidacy of Senator Eugene McCarthy for President, and they tried to parade anyway. Their ensuing confrontation with police illustrated how difficult it is to know how far a protest can go if it threatens public order.

So did the legal tangle that followed the violence. Seven participants in the demonstrations were charged with violation of the federal Anti-Riot Act, which makes it a crime to cross a state line to incite or participate in a riot. The trial of the "Chicago Seven" shed doubt on the constitutionality of such an act — a question still unresolved. Following the trial, members of the Chicago Seven were frequently denied permission to speak on college campuses. Federal judges, however, issued orders restraining college officials from denying such speaking rights on grounds that the mere possibility of trouble does not constitute a sufficient threat to justify the denial.

The distinction between protests which are *symbolic expressions* and those which are *speech and action* also was made when demonstrations against the Vietnam War became heated during the 1960s. In *Tinker* v. *Des Moines Community School District* (1969), the Supreme Court held that wearing a black armband to protest against the war was a symbolic expression protected by the First Amendment. If, however, symbolic expression is combined with actions that challenge the constitutional authority of the government, it is not so protected. In *United States* v. *O'Brien* (1968), the Court upheld a federal law making it a crime to "knowingly destroy" or "mutilate" a draft card. Congress has the constitutional power to raise and support armies; hence the symbolic expression of burning a draft card went too far.

The Supreme Court also has restricted the right of peaceful protest that disrupts the normal use of property. In *Adderley* v. *Florida* (1966), the Court upheld the conviction of a group of Florida students arrested for trespassing with malicious and mischievous intent when they assembled in front of a county jail to protest against the incarceration of several classmates. Justice Black, one of the firmest defenders of civil liberties in the Court's history, held that "The state, no less than a private owner

The Supreme Court has held that burning a draft card is not an extension of free speech and is not protected under the First Amendment.

of property, has the power to preserve the property under its control for the use to which it is lawfully dedicated." Among the opportunities for participating in conflict representation we have examined thus far, then, *those for protest are most closely restricted.*

THE OPPORTUNITY TO VOTE. The provisions of our written constitution, associated statutes, and unwritten political practices and traditions determine which persons in the community are eligible to participate in conflict representation by voting. In America, voting is restricted to *citizens,* as distinct from *noncitizens* of another nationality or no nationality at all. Noncitizens are not "nonpersons," but they must register annually with the government of the United States, they may be restricted in wartime, they can be deported for sufficient cause, and they may suffer other limitations on personal rights. No state has permitted noncitizens to vote since 1928.

How does a person become an American citizen? Article XIV of the Constitution and related federal statutes specify birth, naturalization, or congressional action as the ways. First, persons born in the United States, under its territorial jurisdiction, or of American parents residing abroad are automatically accorded citizenship. Second, by naturalization persons born to foreign parents outside the United States receive the rights of citizenship after following specified procedures. Third, Congress can award citizenship by collective grant (as it did to American Indians in 1924).

*Only citizens are eligible to vote, but not all are permitted to do so.*
Article I of the Constitution provides that the states shall establish their
own voting requirements. Individual states have periodically disfranchised groups — those without property, blacks in the South, Indians in
the Southwest, women, the young, residents of the District of Columbia,
and others. The extension of the franchise to each of these groups was
marked by controversy and conflict representation.

Property requirements were the first major restrictions states placed
upon voting. People were required to *own property* in order to vote.
Gradually the *poll tax* (the payment of a nominal fee that would prove
one's economic standing) supplanted property ownership as a voting requirement. Ironically, the poll tax was originally substituted for property
requirements as a liberalizing measure. Ultimately, it discriminated intol-
erably against southern blacks and other impoverished Americans. Beginning in the 1940s, civil rights groups representing the disfranchised
minorities were pitted against southern senators in a fight to ban the poll
tax. Frequently, the poll tax was defended as a revenue source necessary
to some states; in fact its purpose — to limit the voting franchise — was
about what its opponents said it was. In 1964, the Twenty-Fourth Amendment to the Constitution belatedly abolished the poll tax requirements
in elections for federal officials; federal court decisions also declared
state poll taxes (notably in Texas, Alabama, and Virginia) unconstitutional. Despite such reforms, property tax restrictions on local voting — in
some school board and bond elections — are reminders that the franchise
may still be limited to citizens who have an economic stake in the community.[19]

The opportunity to vote has been extended to disfranchised minorities
only after prolonged conflicts. The *American black* was guaranteed the
right to vote in the Fifteenth Amendment to the Constitution after the
Civil War. But for a whole century he has had to overcome discriminatory tactics. He fought the battle against *literacy tests* (see Figure 5-2)
by publicizing his grievances in federal court cases, in civil rights demonstrations, and in Congress. Prior to 1965, twenty states required potential
voters to prove their literacy before permitting them to cast a ballot.
Some states required only a signature from the voter; others requested
that applicants complete variously long and difficult registration forms;
still others required citizens to read and explain a passage from a state
constitution, statute, or other document before election judges (who were
prone to make far harsher demands on blacks than whites). Voting rights

[19] Chilton Williamson, *American Suffrage: From Property to Democracy, 1760–1860*
(Princeton, N.J.: Princeton University Press, 1960); Kenneth H. Vines and Henry Robert Glick,
"The Impact of Universal Suffrage: A Comparison of Popular and Property Voting," *The
American Political Science Review* 61 (Dec. 1967): 1078–1087.

### 1957 Civil Rights Act

1. Affirmed citizen's right to seek court injunctions to protect voting rights.
2. Authorized federal government to seek court injunctions to remove violations of voting rights.
3. Created federal Civil Rights Commission to investigate violations of voting rights.
4. Created Civil Rights Division in Department of Justice.

### 1960 Civil Rights Act

1. Authorized Attorney General to request court findings of patterns or practice of denial of Negro voting rights when violations warranted this.
2. Authorized courts to issue orders that Negroes were qualified to vote if voter discrimination was proved.
3. Authorized courts to appoint referees to aid Negroes in registration and voting.

### 1961 Twenty-Third Amendment

Extended the right to vote in presidential elections to citizens of the District of Columbia.

### 1964 Twenty-Fourth Amendment

Outlawed poll tax as voting requirement in federal elections.

### 1964 Civil Rights Act

1. Prohibited literacy tests in federal elections; prohibited unequal application of registration requirements; prohibited denial of right to vote because of voting-record errors or omissions where records were immaterial to qualification.
2. Required presumption of literacy where persons were educated through six grades in schools with instruction primarily in English.
3. Established special three-judge federal courts to hear voting rights suits.

### 1965 Voting Rights Act

1. Suspended literacy tests in states where fewer than 50 percent of voting age residents were registered or voted in 1964.
2. Appointed federal voting examiners to administer registration in states and counties using literacy tests in 1964 with voter participation below standards established by the act (registration or turnout of less than 50 percent of the population).
3. Authorized Attorney General to seek federal court findings of voter discrimination.
4. Authorized Attorney General to proceed against discriminatory state poll taxes.

### 1968 Civil Rights Act

Prohibited the injury or intimidation of any person because he was voting or campaigning for office in a public election, serving on a federal jury, working for a federal agency, or urging others to engage in these activities. (This last provision was aimed at protecting civil rights workers).

### 1970 Voting Rights Act

Extended the right to vote in national elections to eighteen-year-olds meeting normal home state requirements of citizenship, residency, and registration. (Act declared constitutional by the Supreme Court.)

### 1971 Twenty-Sixth Amendment

Provided that the right to vote of citizens eighteen years old or older shall not be abridged by the United States or by any state on account of age.

FIGURE 5-2
The Post–World War II Evolution of Voting Rights

legislation since 1957 has gradually corrected the most discriminatory aspects of literacy tests. The broadest legislation was the Voting Rights Act of 1965. As of now, fifteen states still use literacy tests as a voting qualification but — if challenged — must prove they are not discriminatory devices. Discrimination still exists, but the situation has improved vastly in the past ten years.

In addition, most controversy has surrounded other extensions of the opportunity to vote. *Women* achieved voting rights in 1919, when the Nineteenth Amendment to the Constitution was adopted, but only after fifty years of joining voluntary associations, petitioning Congress, engaging in marches and demonstrations, and organizing the suffragette movement. The *American Indian* was enfranchised in 1924 only after a long struggle in which his interests were represented by the Association of American Indian Affairs. Residents of the *District of Columbia* lobbied in Congress for decades before achieving, in 1961, the right to vote in presidential elections, and their mayor is still appointed by the President. It would be hard to deny that the extension of the franchise to citizens *18 years old and older* in 1970 and 1971 was not in part a response to the militant demands of American youth in the 1960s.

*Who then can vote?* Figure 5-3 identifies the general requirements for voting and their major variations among the states. How restrictive are these requirements? A precise answer to that question is not possible, but we can estimate the numbers of adults in the United States who are generally *ineligible* to vote.[20]

Between two and three million are noncitizens and thus have no opportunity to vote. Before 1972, an estimated five to eight million Americans were deprived of voting opportunities because they had not lived long enough in the locality in which they sought to vote. In March 1972, however, the Supreme Court ruled it unconstitutional to deny the vote on such grounds, saying that residency itself is a legitimate test but length of residency is not. A survey conducted in 1969 indicated that at least twenty-nine million Americans who were otherwise eligible had not registered. Failure to register is generally higher among the more mobile in our population, particularly those between eighteen and twenty-five years of age. Enfranchisement of younger citizens in 1970 and 1971 added a

---

[20] Estimates are based upon a variety of sources: William G. Andrews, "American Voting Participation," *The Western Political Quarterly* 19 (Dec. 1966), 639–652; *Congressional Quarterly Weekly Report* 29 (Nov. 6, 1971): 2296–2300; William B. Dickinson, Jr., ed., *Congress and the Nation*, vol. 2, 1965–1968 (Washington, D.C.: Congressional Quarterly, 1969), pp. 436–438; Elmo Roper, "How to Lose Your Vote," *Saturday Review* (March 18, 1961): 14–15; News Release, American Institute of Public Opinion (December 10, 1968); News Release, American Institute of Public Opinion (December 7, 1969).

| General requirement | Major variations |
|---|---|
| United States citizenship | |
| Minimum age: eighteen years | |
| Residency | |
| Registration[a] | Permanent registration in thirty-eight states. |
| | Periodic registration in one state. |
| | Combined permanent-periodic in ten states and no registration in one state. |
| Miscellaneous restrictions | All states deny the vote to inmates of penal institutions and the mentally ill. |
| | Citizens living on federal reservations may vote in California, Utah, and West Virginia. |
| | Loss of effective franchise for U.S. citizens residing overseas with no legal state of residence. |
| | Literacy tests in fifteen states. |

[a] Permanent registration requires that the voter establish his credentials only once, when he meets citizenship, age, and residency requirements; thereafter his registration is renewed by voting. Periodic registration has voters reestablish qualifications at selected periods (usually annually) throughout their lives.

**FIGURE 5-3**
**Who Has the Legal Opportunity to Vote?**

potential twelve million voters, of whom approximately four million did not register.

Finally, perhaps a million citizens are prevented from voting by the miscellaneous restrictions listed in Figure 5-3. Still more who go to the polls — perhaps as many as four million — have their ballots thrown out by election judges because they are marked improperly.

The estimates are rough, but it is safe to say that one in four Americans eighteen years old or older does not satisfy other requirements to vote. Thus, *universal adult suffrage is markedly restricted.*

The most restrictive requirements by far are residency and registration. The *residency requirement* is compounded by the difficulties a citizen has in voting when he is out of town on election day. The Voting Rights Act of 1970, as amended, does prohibit states from denying the right to vote absentee in federal elections; and all states permit absentee voting by members of the armed forces. In sixteen states, however, a citizen who is not in military service and who for personal or business reasons is absent on election day loses his right to vote in state elections. Traveling businessmen, students away at school or college, vacationers, the handicapped and incapacitated, and others often are unable to vote. When the eighteen-year-olds were enfranchised in 1970 and 1971, local residency requirements created another problem: Is a college student a resident of the community in which he attends college or of the community from which he comes? Most states insisted that students should vote in the communities from which they come, but by 1972 three-fourths of the states permitted them to vote where they attended college. In some college communities, students were even elected to public office.

To *register* to vote one must pay the price of inconvenience, which means finding out when and where he should register and actually taking the time to do it. Citizens sometimes are required to register as much as one year in advance of an election. If they do not register, they cannot vote no matter how much they have become interested in the candidates, issues, or campaign. The failure of young Americans to vote, along with the blacks, the Mexican-Americans, the lower socioeconomic classes, and people who just move around a lot, may reflect inactivity during registration periods rather than a lack of interest in elections.[21]

## who has the resources to participate?

Just as the politico-constitutional dimension of our community determines who has the opportunity to take part in conflict representation, *the social dimension* determines who has the resources to participate. By *resources* we mean the social position and characteristics that enable a person to acquire the knowledge, skills, and money that make participation in politics relatively easy and attractive.

*An individual's position in society is indicated by his social class, and social class is indicated by the levels of education, occupation, and income.* These resources control how much leisure time he has for politics, his awareness of what can be gained by taking part in conflict repre-

---

[21] Stanley Kelley et al., "Registration and Voting: Putting First Things First," *The American Political Science Review* 61 (June 1967): 359–379; Clifton McCleskey and Dan Nimmo, "Differences Between Potential, Registered, and Actual Voters," *The Social Science Quarterly* 49 (June 1968); 101–114; "Voter Qualification and Participation in National, State, and Municipal Elections," in Charles M. Bonjean, Terry Clark, and Robert Lineberry, eds., *Community Politics* (New York: Free Press, 1971), pp. 106–114.

**TABLE 5-6**
**Relation of Education Levels to Voter**
**Participation in Presidential Elections, 1948–1968**

| | *Percentage voting in election year* | | | | | |
|---|---|---|---|---|---|---|
| *Education level* | *1948* | *1952* | *1956* | *1960* | *1964* | *1968* |
| Grade school | 55% | 62% | 60% | 67% | 62% | 60% |
| High school | 67 | 80 | 74 | 81 | 73 | 78 |
| College | 79 | 90 | 90 | 90 | 81 | 84 |

Source: Survey Research Center and Interuniversity Consortium for Political Research, University of Michigan.

**TABLE 5-7**
**Relation of Education to Active and Passive Participation**

| | *Level of education* | | |
|---|---|---|---|
| *Means of participation* | *Grade school* | *High school* | *College* |
| Active | 21% | 28% | 46% |
| Voted and participated in one of the following — attempted to influence through discussion, supported campaign financially, attended political meetings or rallies, belonged to political club, wore a campaign button or used campaign sticker, or did other work for party or candidate. | | | |
| Passive | 32 | 46 | 44 |
| Only voted | | | |
| Failed to vote but participated in some other fashion as above. | 4 | 20 | 5 |
| No participation of any sort | 43 | 6 | 5 |
| Total | 100% | 100% | 100% |
| Number of cases | 542 | 880 | 330 |

Source: Survey Research Center and Interuniversity Consortium for Political Research, University of Michigan.

sentation, his group memberships, and his financial resources. As a rule, *lower social class is associated with reduced political participation.*

EDUCATION. Political awareness, civic obligation, and a feeling that one can influence government decisions are fostered by education. *Citizens with more years of formal schooling are likely to have more information about politics.* A 1970 Gallup Poll revealed that two-thirds of the respondents with college educations could name their Congressman, compared to about half of those with grade school educations.[22] The relationship of educational levels to voting turnout in two decades of presidential elections is depicted in Table 5-6. Again, *higher education levels imply more participation;* but three out of four voters are not college educated.

Is more education associated with more active participation in conflict representation? The data in Table 5-7, based upon surveys conducted in 1956, show a pattern that still holds — *persons with college educations are more likely to be active in politics than those with high school and grade school educations.*

OCCUPATION. If we divide occupations into higher status (the professions, managerial positions, business, and skilled occupations) and lower status (the unskilled, manual workers, farmers) in the United States and other nations, *persons in higher-status occupations generally are more politically active than those in lower-status occupations.*[23] This tendency manifests itself in the voting turnout (see Figure 5-4). Among the many reasons for this, one often is overlooked: participation in decisions about one's job provides experiences and leads to participation in politics generally. People in higher-status occupations are more likely to be consulted about decisions that affect their jobs; feeling free to protest job decisions, they receive training in participation that is related to political participation.[24] In many respects trade unions, by forcing employers to negotiate on employee working hours, wages, and retirement benefits, have supplied training in political participation for their members. Moreover, labor unions actively promote political participation among both skilled and unskilled workers. In the 1950s and 1960s, studies showed that the voting rate among union workers was approximately 75 percent, compared to 59 percent for unorganized laborers.[25]

The tendency of workers in higher-status occupations to participate

[22] *Gallup Poll Index* (October 1970), p. 10.

[23] Di Palma, *Apathy and Participation,* p. 144.

[24] Gabriel A. Almond and Sidney Verba, *The Civic Culture* (Princeton, N.J.: Princeton University Press, 1963), p. 345.

[25] Harry M. Scoble, "Organized Labor in Electoral Politics," *The Western Political Quarterly* 16 (Sept. 1963): 666–685.

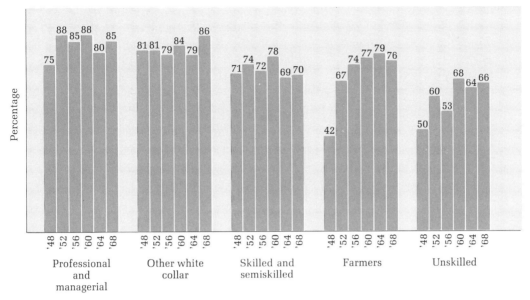

Source: Data from the Survey Research Center and Interuniversity Consortium for Political Research, University of Michigan.

FIGURE 5-4
**Relation of Occupational Status and Voting Participation
in Presidential Elections, 1948–1968**

more *is not limited to voting*. In *actively influencing opinions of others*, people in professional and managerial occupations and skilled workers do so more than do other white collar workers, the semiskilled and un-skilled, and farmers[26] (see Figure 5-4). *Leaders of political parties usually are lawyers or have professional or managerial careers.* Often Republican activists come from higher socioeconomic backgrounds than do Democrats, but the two parties do not differ appreciably in how their working politicians represent the social classes. Lower-echelon activists differ in their social and occupational makeup from region to region, from city to suburb, and from suburb to countryside.

We should not assume that individuals of higher occupational status comprise the bulk of American political participants. Far more voting Americans are in manual, service, clerical, and sales occupations than in corporate management and the professions. Although they participate less, *unskilled and semiskilled workers make up the largest part of the American electorate* year in and year out.

[26] Bernard Berelson et al., *Voting* (Chicago: University of Chicago Press, 1954), p. 377.

INCOME. Usually determined by a person's occupation or his family inheritance, income provides the financial resources that encourage political participation. More people with higher incomes express informed opinions, vote, support political candidates, contribute money to campaigns, and join political organizations. In the past, an annual income of about $7,500 has separated those likely to take part in political parties and clubs from those who have not.[27] More than two-thirds of those normally voting in presidential elections are in the middle-income bracket earning $5,000 to $15,000 a year.

Recently, however, signs have been clear that *income alone is not enough to indicate whether people will take part in politics.* Young blacks of low incomes are some of the most politically militant and active Americans. And younger people generally, many without regular incomes, have worked hard in the civil rights and peace movements, in drives to register the eighteen-year-old voter, and in the political campaigns of candidates like the late Robert Kennedy, Eugene McCarthy, George McGovern, John Lindsay, and George Wallace.

*The active political participation of more lower-status workers, blacks, and the young — regardless of social class — raises the question of how sociodemographic characteristics such as age, sex, race, religion, and residence relate to frequency of political activity.* If only because they are young or old, male or female, white or nonwhite, all people have different "resources"; and some find it easier than others to take part.

AGE. A person must be at least eighteen to vote; elderly people, on the other hand, are sometimes the most politically powerless because so many are unable to get out and help candidates, join political groups, articulate their grievances, and even vote. Table 5-8 illustrates the differences among three principal age groups in selected kinds of passive and active participation. Three facts are important. First, in passive participation such as keeping up with politics and voting, Americans over thirty take part proportionately more than do younger citizens; younger adults characteristically pay less attention to political issues and personalities. Second, in active participation younger Americans probably match those over thirty but do not surpass them. Third, the voting electorate tends to be middle-aged, neither young nor old.

SEX. Differences in passive and active political participation that depend on sex are also noticeable. If women voted in national elections with the same frequency and consistency as men, and if they voted "en bloc," their vote would decide almost any issue. After all, there are more

[27] Milbrath, *Political Participation,* pp. 120–121.

TABLE 5-8
**Varieties of Active and Passive Participation, by Age, 1968–1970**

| Means of participation | 21–29 years old | 30–49 years old | 50 and over |
|---|---|---|---|
| **Active** | | | |
| Worked for a political party or candidate | 17% | 17% | 21% |
| Willing to contribute $5 to campaign fund of preferred party | 42 | 49 | 39 |
| **Passive/Active** | | | |
| Know name of their Congressman | 44 | 55 | 54 |
| Know whether Congressman a Democrat or Republican | 54 | 63 | 64 |
| Know how Congressman voted on bills during 1970 | 16 | 23 | 21 |
| **Passive** | | | |
| Voted in 1968 | 54 | 82 | 73 |

Sources: News release, American Institute of Public Opinion (Gallup Poll), April 7, 1968; *Gallup Opinion Index,* October 1970; U.S. Bureau of the Census, *Current Population Reports,* Series P-20, No. 192, *Voting and Registration in the Election of November 1968* (Washington, D.C.: Government Printing Office, 1969).

adult females than males in America. But they do not vote en bloc, even in the age of women's liberation, and a smaller percentage of women than men vote at all. Seventy-eight men voted in the 1968 presidential election for every 74 women, and 57 men voted in the 1970 congressional races for every 51 women. Men generally are more knowledgeable than women about politics and are more likely to influence the opinions of others, attend political meetings and rallies, work for candidates, and join political organizations. Despite general differences, however, *men and women of approximately the same educational levels take part in politics in almost equal proportions;* indeed college-educated women are more politically active in some areas than college-educated men. The resources that facilitate political participation form a combination, and *no specific resource tells the whole story of why some people participate and others do not.*

RACIAL BACKGROUND. All by itself, race does not explain differences in political participation rates either. In American elections, black citizens register and vote in smaller proportions than whites; whites tend to know more often who their congressmen and United States Senators are and what political parties they represent. But *these differences are attributable to the low social standing* (education, occupation, and income) *of blacks rather than to "blackness" or "whiteness."* One recent study of black participation in the South revealed that if educational differences are taken into account, the rates of participation by whites and blacks — beyond simply talking about politics and voting — are nearly the same. A striking illustration of how we may be misled by looking at a single social characteristic is the fact that among college-educated southern males sampled in the study, a higher percentage of blacks than whites took part in politics.[28] Until the civil rights movement gained momentum in the South, low levels of black participation were also mandated by the intransigence of white-controlled commercial interests; the higher the percentage of black population in a locale, the more likely it was that steps would be taken to keep blacks from registering to vote. Civil rights legislation, although not a perfect solution, did provide blacks with the opportunity to use their resources effectively; between 1964 and 1968, the percentage of blacks registered to vote in the states of the old Confederacy more than doubled. Obviously, however, because blacks are less than 12 percent of the American population, they could not change the basically white orientation of the American national electorate even if they all voted. Massachusetts did elect a black senator, Edward Brooke, in 1968, but not with a "black vote"; only 2 percent of the state's electorate is black.

RELIGIOUS AFFILIATION. Another characteristic of political participation that is closely related to social class is being part of a religious group. The data on how the major denominations turned out in recent presidential elections is shown in Figure 5-5. Generally, *Protestants are the least active* (with Episcopalians and Presbyterians slightly more active than Baptists), *Catholics are more active, and Jews are the most active.* Bear in mind, however, that a lower rate of participation among Protestants does not alter the fact that they are the largest group of religious affiliates in this country. Two-thirds of the American electorate is Protestant. To some extent these differences in participation are attributable to the use of politics by Roman Catholics and Jews to combat religious or ethnic discrimination. The regularity of church attendance is also roughly related to participation; steady churchgoers are more likely to vote.

---

[28] Donald R. Matthews and James W. Prothro, *Negroes and the New Southern Politics,* (New York: Harcourt, Brace, 1966), pp. 68, 101–174.

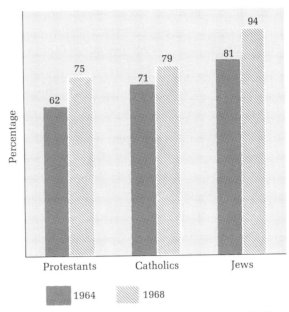

**FIGURE 5-5**
**Voting Participation by Leading**
**Religious Denominations**     Source: Interuniversity Consortium for Political Research, University of Michigan.

REGION OF RESIDENCE. Whether a person lives in a rural or urban area, the size of his community, and the region of the nation where he resides are all relevant to his political habits. In general, *political participation tends to be higher in the more commercial and industrialized urban areas of America's northeast, west, and upper midwest.* On the whole, people who live in the country are not so politically involved as city dwellers. They tend to be less well informed and less active in political groups. They vote less regularly than do urban residents. This is especially true in the South, where the voter turnout for all social groups is lower than in other regions (Figure 5-6). The highest level of political knowledge is found among residents of America's middle-sized communities (2,500 to 50,000), where about half the people can name their state senators and representatives, know how their Congressmen vote, and know something of political issues. Levels are lower among both rural residents (communities under 2,500) and persons living in cities of more than 50,000, where only about one in four is as well informed as his opposite number in a small city.[29]

[29] Glenn, "The Distribution of Political Knowledge in the United States."

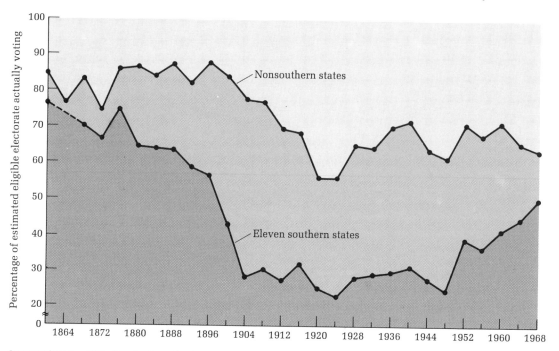

Source: Updated from Walter Dean Burnham, "The Changing Shape of the American Political Universe," *The American Political Science Review* 59 (March 1965): 11.

**FIGURE 5-6**
**Voting Turnout in Southern and Nonsouthern States, 1860–1968**

## who wants to participate?

Just as political and constitutional facts of life create the opportunities to participate in politics and social factors determine individual resources, the *personal element shapes the desire to be engaged in politics.* When, then, is a citizen motivated to do so?

*A citizen is motivated when he feels he can benefit by taking part.* People derive a variety of benefits from participating in politics. There is a bill to be paid too. The cost — in time, money, physical energy, or all three — is sometimes very high. *If the benefits outweigh the costs, people participate.*

ECONOMIC REWARDS. A person may use his vote to support a candidate who promises to cut his taxes. He may contribute money to a candidate's campaign in exchange for the promise that if the politician is elected he will reward the contributor with a sizable government contract for his business. But there are direct economic costs even to passive political participation. A person may shy away from taking a stand on a public issue because his boss, his clients, or his customers will not want to do business with a man who gets involved in controversy.

SOCIAL BENEFITS AND SACRIFICES. By taking part in politics, people can associate themselves with people they like, admire, and respect. A study in Detroit, Michigan revealed that among the party precinct leaders interviewed, more than two-thirds did their jobs because of the satisfaction they obtained in making social contacts and the social "fun" in politics.[30] But the desire to make or keep friends can inhibit political participation. Rather than threaten their friendships in a political argument, people avoid political discussion altogether. Married couples, for example, have been known to stay away from the polls on election day rather than cast ballots in opposition to one another.

INTELLECTUAL INTERESTS. People want to "understand what's going on," and being on the "inside" of a campaign provides enormous satisfaction. Thousands of young people worked around the clock to get Senator Barry Goldwater (1964) and Senator George McGovern (1972) nominated for the presidency. Many did so to put their political ideas into practice; others did so to learn at the most important working level — the bottom level — what politics is all about.[31] The politically curious try to develop informed, sophisticated opinions about politics; others find political discussion and campaigning a kind of rat race that is more confusing than enlightening. So they pursue less demanding avocations.

EMOTIONAL SATISFACTIONS. Politics bolsters the egos of winners and provides an exhilarating sense of self-importance about being an "in" person who has a private pipeline to city hall. Politically active people get a special thrill out of taking part in momentous decisions, even if they are merely on the periphery. But if a person is unwilling to endure criticism, frustration, failure, and defeat, he does not belong on the political playing field at all. He belongs in the stands, which is no disgrace; not everyone is physically equipped to play professional football.

*A citizen is also motivated when he feels politics "touches" him.* Unless people think politics touches their lives, they are not going to become

[30] Samuel J. Eldersveld, *Political Parties* (Chicago: Rand McNally, 1964), p. 278.
[31] See John H. Kessel, *The Goldwater Coalition* (Indianapolis, Ind.: Bobbs-Merrill, 1968), and Ben Stavis, *We Were the Campaign* (Boston: Beacon Press, 1969).

In 1912, New York women paraded for equal voting rights. The Amendment granting women suffrage was passed in 1920.

involved enough to achieve these economic, social, intellectual, and emotional rewards. *Every aspect of daily living is in some fashion touched by politics* — our economic chances, our right to walk the streets in safety, whether we are sent to fight in wars, what we can learn, think, and say. Do people sense this? The evidence indicates that they do. When Americans were asked, "thinking now about the national government in Washington, about how much effect do you think its activities, the laws passed, and so on have on your day-to-day life?" 90 percent responded that it had "great" or "some" effect.[32]

But this awareness is not matched by an equal awareness of how much

[32] Almond and Verba, *The Civic Culture*, p. 80.

Some state legislatures have liberalized their abortion laws
in response to women's protests.

effect they can have on governmental decisions. Voting in elections is an
example. Americans generally feel that *voting is a civic duty*. At the same
time, large portions of the American electorate do not believe election
campaigns are worthwhile or that their vote influences government decisions. Table 5-9 reports the percentages of persons surveyed in Wisconsin
who agreed and disagreed with selected propositions. More respondents
felt obliged to vote than found election campaigns meaningful or their
vote influential.

The typical relationship between civic duty, interest in the campaign
and the election's outcome, and voting is about what we might expect:
greater obligation, interest, and concern mean higher rates of voting. But
why do not all citizens regard elections as "meaningful"?

TABLE 5-9
**Popular Views of Voting in Elections, 1966**

| Questions | Percentage agree[a] | Percentage disagree[a] |
|---|---|---|
| Voting as a civic duty | | |
| "So many other people vote in the national elections that it doesn't matter too much to me whether I vote or not." | 7% | 89% |
| "It isn't so important to vote when you know your party doesn't have a chance to win." | 5 | 91 |
| "I generally get a feeling of satisfaction from going to the polls to cast my ballot." | 86 | 6 |
| "Many primary elections aren't important enough to vote in." | 19 | 72 |
| "A person should only vote in an election if he cares about how it is going to turn out." | 29 | 65 |
| Meaningfulness of elections | | |
| "Most of the effort, time and money spent in political campaigns could be better used some other way." | 59 | 24 |
| "Our political system would work a lot better if our leaders were chosen on the basis of merit in competitive examinations rather than by elections." | 30 | 47 |
| "Most election campaigns are silly or ridiculous." | 23 | 57 |
| "It is impossible for most voters to make informed decisions when they go to the polls." | 34 | 46 |
| The influence of voting | | |
| "The way people vote is the main thing that decides how things are run in this country." | 57 | 22 |
| "Voting is the only way that people like me can have a say about how government runs things." | 58 | 30 |

Source: Compiled from data reported in Jack Dennis, "Support for the Institution of Elections," *The American Political Science Review*, 64 (September 1970): 819–835.

[a] Percentages do not total 100 percent because of persons selecting neutral, don't know, or not ascertained positions.

THE LEVEL OF THE ELECTION. The less frequent federal elections, especially for President, get higher turnouts than local elections. Not since the 1920s has the presidential election failed to draw to the polls at least half those of voting age. But as many as 20 percent of those who vote in presidential contests do not do so in off-year congressional races. This is partly because presidential contests usually generate conflicts between commanding personalities; this can happen in congressional elections, but more often it does not. The national news media also pays less attention to congressional campaigns. Generally, elections for executive offices (president, governor, mayor) draw more voters than do those for legislative and judicial positions.

THE TYPE OF ELECTION. Nonpartisan elections (in which the party affiliations of candidates do not appear on the ballot) draw fewer voters than partisan contests which excite people simply because they *are* partisan. Special elections (such as referenda on constitutional amendments) attract fewer voters than regularly scheduled elections because the issues often confuse the mass of voters. General elections draw more voters than do primary elections.

ELECTION PROCEDURES. Burdensome registration or voting rules, long and complicated ballots (especially if they must be marked by hand), frustrating delays at the polls, or the scheduling of elections on workdays (they are held on Sundays in France) all inhibit participation. When too many different elections take place in one year, voters have neither the time nor the inclination to maintain a high level of interest.

THE DEGREE OF CONFLICT. Failure to take part in an election often reflects a belief that there is no meaningful choice to be made. If voters feel that the outcome of an election is a foregone conclusion (as it frequently is in cities or states dominated by one political party, faction, or interest), they can hardly be told that their vote "will count for something." The likelihood is greater that voters will go to the polls (especially when they have strong preferences) if they think the contest is close and the outcome doubtful.[33] But even in close contests their interest will lag if they think it makes no difference who wins. Apathy at the polls often does not reflect popular disinterest so much as a failure of the candidates to talk about the issues that voters believe are relevant, to offer alternative programs, and, once elected, to respond to complaints from their constituents.

[33] Campbell et al., *The American Voter,* p. 99.

INFLUENCING DECISIONS. Citizens participate in conflict representation when they believe that their voices will be heard and their demands will be taken seriously. People who feel this way have a sense of competence or *political efficacy*. Activists who lead opinions, join political parties, and take part in campaigns have a strong sense of political efficacy. In more passive participation, such as voting, those with a low sense of political competence are far less likely to vote than those with a high sense of competence (see Table 5-10).

Critical factors that contribute to a sense of political efficacy are the legal opportunity to participate and the social resources to do so. A person's relationships with others in social groups also bears upon his feeling of personal and political competence. *The family atmosphere is particularly important.* Children of politically active parents are more likely to become "political animals" themselves when they grow older than are those who come from politically indifferent families. The treatment of the child and the parental attention he receives contribute to his future political interest, his sense of political effectiveness, and his feeling of civic obligation. If public affairs are ignored in the home, or if their discussion engenders parental bickering, the child is likely to avoid politics, as a threat to family harmony.[34]

A low sense of political efficacy contributes to political disaffection — not just "dissatisfaction." A dissatisfied person does not like what politicians do, but he has enough faith in democratic processes to want to do something about it. A disaffected person has no such faith; he believes *all* participation is ultimately meaningless. He may turn to political cynicism,[35] expressing a strong distrust for the motives of politicians. If he votes at all, he does so not to change things but to make known what he is *against,* which may be practically everything in sight. He also may become politically *alienated,*[36] feeling that he should stay out of all politics. If he is sufficiently estranged and sufficiently angry, he may channel his frustrations into rational or irrational outbursts of protest.

How widespread is political disaffection in contemporary America? Any estimate is crude, but we have some clues. Table 5-9 gives one hint about how many people find elections meaningless. Cynicism is indicated by the fact that in a 1971 Harris poll, two-thirds of Americans believed that "only a few men are dedicated public servants" and 54

[34] Richard M. Merelman, "The Development of Political Ideology: A Framework for the Analysis of Political Socialization," *The American Political Science Review* 63 (Sept. 1969): 750–767.

[35] Robert E. Agger et al., "Political Cynicism: Measurement and Meaning," *The Journal of Politics* 23 (Aug. 1961): 477–506.

[36] Murray B. Levin, *The Alienated Voter* (New York: Holt, Rinehart and Winston, 1960).

**TABLE 5-10**
**Relation of Sense of Political Competence to Voting, 1970**

| | Low | | | | | High |
|---|---|---|---|---|---|---|
| | *0* | *1* | *2* | *3* | *4* | *5* |
| Voted | 31% | 43% | 45% | 51% | 64% | 65% |
| Did not vote | 69 | 57 | 55 | 49 | 36 | 35 |
| Total | 100% | 100% | 100% | 100% | 100% | 100% |
| Number of cases | 118 | 212 | 269 | 319 | 357 | 428 |

Source: Center for Political Studies, Institute for Social Research, University of Michigan.
[a] Respondents were classified according to the strength of their sense of political competence on the basis of a cumulative scale formed from responses to selected questions.

percent believed "most politicians take graft." A third of Americans thought politics is more corrupt today than it was ten years ago.[37] Two-thirds of Americans in a similar Gallup survey felt the American political system does not respond quickly enough to the needs of the people: 14 percent thought violence justified to bring about necessary changes.[38] Such figures provide evidence of a growing community of the politically disaffected.

Who are the disaffected? Research has made it clear that political cynicism and alienation are more likely to be found among the uneducated, the unemployed and impoverished, the frustrated, and the socially isolated. If there is to be a desire to get into the act of political participation, the apathetic must be convinced that they can use politics as a tool to fix what is wrong with their social environment. Active citizens feel a personal effectiveness in politics not shared by their indifferent brethren: "they know themselves and feel confident of their knowledge and skills; their ego is strong enough to withstand blows; they are not burdened by a load of anxiety and internal conflict; they can control their impulses; they are astute, sociable, self-expressive and responsible."[39] In short, they take to heart Socrates' dictum that "the unexamined life is not worth living." The activists examine political life and choose to pursue it; the apathetic withdraw.

[37] News Release, *The Harris Survey* (December 4, 1971).
[38] News Release, American Institute of Public Opinion (January 21, 1971).
[39] Milbrath, *Political Participation*, p. 89; Di Palma, *Apathy and Participation*, pp. 178–197.

When normal channels
of conflict representation
are closed, violence
often results.

### participating in conflict representation in the 1970s

Liberal democratic theory prescribes a high level of active participation, but Americans do not measure up well to the ideal. *Who then are our political participants?*

First, there are the *active participants,* who not only hold political opinions and vote but also keep informed, influence others, join political organizations, and petition their officials. A social profile of this group indicates that it consists primarily of middle-aged white men with better educations, more prestigious occupations, and reasonably good incomes. They reside in middle-sized and larger communities and have various religious affiliations. These are people who feel politics touches their lives, who gain personal satisfaction from politics, and who feel politically competent.

164

The riots at Attica State Prison
have initiated extensive
inquiry into prison reform.

Second, there are the *passive participants,* meaning primarily those who simply hold opinions and vote. The profile of this group in the 1970s is slightly more male than female; these people are predominantly Protestant, white, middle-aged, and generally have high school educations. They are in unskilled and semiskilled occupations, have moderate incomes, and reside in middle-sized cities and larger suburbs in the northeast, west, and midwest.

*Will these profiles of political participants change substantially in the 1970s?* This depends upon possible changes in the opportunities, resources, and desires underlying participation. Generally, the opportunity to participate is expanded or restricted on the basis of *continuing efforts to strike a balance between the rights of the individual and the need to maintain social order.* As they try to balance individual and social interest, policymakers are not insulated from conflicts or popular demands.

The proper balance involves neither what the Framers of the Constitution "really" intended nor the application of abstract theories of individual liberty. The basic issue of who will have the opportunity to participate is "the political one of what a certain governmental institution ought to do about a certain set of demands."[40] As time and circumstance change what people disagree about most, the content and meaning of constitutional guarantees of the opportunity to take part in conflict representation will also change. A strong popular consensus on democratic fundamentals (about which we raised questions in Chapters Two and Three) provides a framework within which the individual's opportunity to participate can be guaranteed; if there is no such consensus, that opportunity may turn out to be meaningless.

The opportunities to participate probably will not change much in the remainder of this decade. If more people go to college, move into higher-status occupations, increase their affluence, and reach middle-age, we might expect participation rates to increase. But the elementary social composition of active and passive participants will probably change very little. The enfranchisement of eighteen-year-old voters swelled the potential electorate by 10 percent in 1972; yet, because of lower voting rates among younger and older voters, the electorate that went to the polls in November was still predominantly middle-aged.

It is impossible to say if the personal desire to take part in politics will grow in the remainder of this decade. Straws in the wind suggest that things like the ecology movement and women's liberation are creating a greater sense of political involvement, but nobody knows how durable they will be. It seems unlikely that we will witness a dramatic increase in the popular sense of political competence during the next few years.

*How do present patterns of political participation affect conflict representation?* As long as participation is dominated by those who currently have the resources and the desire to capitalize upon their opportunities, disputes taken to policymakers will continue to be those that interest primarily the most consistent political activists. Therefore serious social tensions may go unnoticed until they touch the interests of citizens who are permitted to participate and are able and willing to do it. By that time, there may be a crisis beyond immediate resolution. One horrible example is the belated awakening of public officials to conditions in America's metropolitan ghettos. Those who live in the ghettos see little point in conventional political participation and resort instead to more dramatic methods — mass protests, demonstrations, riots, boycotts, and picketing. Disputes over civil rights, the relief of poverty, Vietnam policy, and earlier struggles over slavery and labor-management relations show

---

[40] Martin Shapiro, *Freedom of Speech: The Supreme Court and Judicial Review* (Englewood Cliffs, N.J.: Prentice-Hall, 1966), p. 61.

that our channels for conflict representation are not always sufficient.

A test of any polity's stability is the capacity to mediate urgent controversies or at least cope with them. America's democratic character is measured partly by its willingness to disclose and tolerate differences by political participation.

*Because of political design and social chance, plus the element of personal choice, America still has a host of unrepresented citizens.* But by removing discriminatory constitutional restrictions, supporting adequate living standards, and fostering creative political awareness it can maintain its pluralist character. It also can generate a working consensus not simply imposed by an active minority but arrived at by popular initiative. That is what conflict in the America of the 1970s is about.

*bibliographical note*

Two standard works describe in detail how Americans involve themselves in politics and their reasons for doing so. The first, Lester W. Milbrath's paperback edition of *Political Participation* (Chicago: Rand McNally, 1965), is a compilation of the communications — personal, social, political — and constitutional factors associated with citizen participation. Milbrath seeks to integrate and update the research summarized in Robert E. Lane's *Political Life* (Glencoe, Ill.: Free Press, 1959), still the best source of hypotheses on the actions and motives of political man. To compare American political participation with that of other polities, *The Civic Culture* (Boston: Little, Brown, 1965), by Gabriel A. Almond and Sidney Verba, is an indispensable report of research conducted in five nations at varying stages of democratic development. Also excellent is James David Barber, *Citizen Politics,* 2nd ed. (Chicago: Markham, 1972). See also Giuseppe Di Palma, *Apathy and Participation* (New York: Free Press, 1970).

Readable summaries of the opportunities for political participation discussed in Chapter Five include: H. Frank Way, Jr., *Liberty in the Balance,* 3rd ed. (New York: McGraw-Hill, 1971); C. Herman Pritchett, *The American Constitutional System,* 3rd ed. (New York: McGraw-Hill, 1971); and Alan P. Grimes, *Equality in America* (New York: Oxford University Press, 1964). Summaries of the social resources underlying participation, particularly voting, include: William H. Flanigan, *Political Behavior of the American Electorate,* 2nd ed. (Boston: Allyn and Bacon, 1972); Hugh A. Bone and Austin Ranney, *Politics and Voters,* 3rd ed. (New York: McGraw-Hill, 1971); and William C. Mitchell's book directed at younger voters, *Why Vote?* (Chicago: Markham, 1971). Angus Campbell et al., *The American Voter* (New York: John Wiley, 1964) is an introduction to the personal motives for participation. Two provocative accounts of the type of political participation we can expect in the 1970s are Richard M. Scammon and Ben J. Wattenberg, *The Real Majority,* rev. ed. (New York: Coward, McCann, & Geoghegan, 1971) and Samuel Lubell, *The Hidden Crisis in American Politics* (New York: W. W. Norton, 1971). For works treating specific forms of political participation, consult the bibliographical notes at the close of the remaining chapters of Part Three.

# chapter 6

# expressing
# political opinions

Of the ways in which they might take part in conflict representation, Americans are more likely to state political opinions than engage in any other political activity. To understand this, we must answer these questions: What are political opinions and what good does it do us to have them? What are their principal characteristics? On what political issues are Americans most likely to express conflicting views? Where do we get our opinions about politics?

## representing consensus and conflict
## by political opinions

When people talk politics, they state their views. Sometimes they agree; sometimes they disagree. If we add up the number of people expressing differing points of view on a matter, we have a representation of the social disagreements on that issue. If we find widespread agreement, we have a consensus; if there are two or more points of disagreement, we have a conflict. If an opinion *is a conclusion or judgment expressed about a specific issue* (including an idea, a person, group, situation, or proposal), then *a political opinion is simply a conclusion or judgment expressed about a political issue.*

Before considering the qualities of our political opinions, let us look a little more closely at this definition.

## how do political opinions differ from attitudes and interests?

We have defined politics (Chapter One) as a method for regulating conflicting interests. The relationship among attitudes, interests, and opinions in conflict representation is close and important.

*Attitudes* are relatively enduring personal preferences that people have about general matters. Feelings of pride in America, anxieties over war, worry about one's health, a belief in universal education — all these are personal *attitudes* of potential political significance.

*Interests* are general actions we take to pursue goals dictated by our personal preferences or attitudes. A belief in universal education causes a person to be aware of federally financed college scholarships: this indicates he has an *interest* in that proposal.

*Opinions* derive from the interplay of attitudes and interests, but focus upon specific topical and immediate matters.[1] Opinions are expressions of underlying attitudes and continuing interests that have been sharpened in response to concrete stimuli (see Figure 6-1). Senator Jones is up for reelection; he has always supported federal college scholarships; if a person decides Senator Jones should be reelected, he has an *opinion* on the matter.

This distinction between attitudes, interests, and opinions has three vital implications.

First, *personal attitudes and interests are the building blocks of political opinions.* Opinions are public statements stimulated by specific political objects. We form opinions when our attitudes and interests are "turned on" by contemporary political events, personalities, and issues. To understand where we get our opinions, we must understand how we acquire our attitudes and interests (which we will examine later in this chapter) and how politicians influence us (Chapter Seven).

Second, however, *our attitudes and interests influence what we see in politics.* If we are Republicans we are more likely to listen to Republican politicians and agree with what they say than we are to listen to or sympathize with Democrats.

Third, *we learn about a person's attitudes or interests by inferring them from his opinions.* If conflicts between people's interests flow from differing attitudes, we recognize them (and politicians recognize them) by listening to conflicting opinions.

Public opinions, like the personal attitudes and interests from which

[1] George Carslake Thompson, *Public Opinion and Lord Beaconsfield* (New York: Macmillan, 1886).

Immediate political context          Learned attitudes and interests          Political opinions

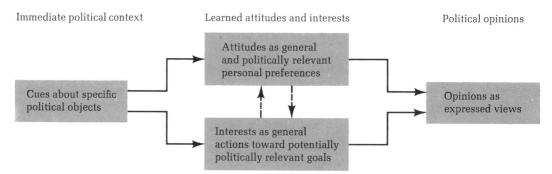

[a]Arrows indicate general direction of influence leading to opinion expression; one's attitudes and cues influence his perception of political objects as well.

FIGURE 6-1
**The Relationship of Political Attitudes, Interests, Opinions, and Influence**[a]

they originate, consist of three overlapping components.[2] First, *is a thinking component:* this is what people *know* and *believe* (rightly or wrongly) about a political object. When the United States in the 1960s committed armed forces to fight a war in Vietnam, many Americans believed this was necessary to prevent Communist domination of Southeast Asia; but others denied that necessity. The result was a conflict of political *thinking.*

Second, *is a feeling component.* People feel that something is either good or bad, desirable or undesirable. On the question of whether it was necessary in the 1960s to oppose communism in Southeast Asia, some Americans felt American and Vietnamese lives were worth more than any costly victory over Communist forces; others said they valued more the future generations who would be forced to live under communism if the current sacrifice were not made. Here was a conflict of political *feelings.*

Third, *is an acting component,* the things we do to realize our beliefs and values. Supporters of the American war effort in the 1960s voted for self-styled "hawks," called for increased military expenditures, and in other ways gave concrete expression to their views. Opponents of the Vietnam War refused to pay taxes, burned their draft cards, and otherwise demonstrated against the "immoral" war. This added a conflict of *actions* to those of beliefs and values.

*Generally the thoughts, feelings, and actions that form political opinions are consistent.* A man might value good roads and highways, believe government must raise taxes to provide these services, and vote to in-

[2] M. Brewster Smith, "The Personal Setting of Public Opinions: A Study of Attitudes Toward Russia," *Public Opinion Quarterly* 11 (Winter 1947): 507–523.

crease his taxes. But *consistency is not always the rule.* Consider the range of political opinions on race relations in America. A study in fifteen American cities[3] in 1968 showed that a majority of white respondents *thought* that blacks were discriminated against in housing and job opportunities, and a third thought they were victims of maltreatment by police. Smaller proportions of whites *felt sympathy* with black protests, whereas two-thirds of those felt that blacks were "trying to push too fast." Then, in questions designed to measure what *actions* whites would accept in racial contact, a third of the whites said they would prefer their small children to have only whites as friends and they would mind a "little" or a "lot" if a black family moved in next door. This study is not cited as evidence that white opinions about blacks are racist (indeed, the burden of the study was to demonstrate that they are not), but simply to illustrate that *beliefs* about a practice such as discrimination need not coincide with *feelings* about the practice or *acts* to change it.

## of what use are political opinions?

We know that most Americans, when asked, express opinions on political matters. They do so because having political opinions assists them in conflict representation.[4]

*Our opinions help us to understand politics.* Politics is confusing to most of us; so many things in politics seem contradictory. We are told that Communist China is our enemy. Then our President takes a goodwill trip there. Again, a President describes himself as a "fiscal conservative," then announces a budget to spend far more money than can be collected in revenues. Or, our Congressman says, "Washington should keep its hands out of local affairs," but urges the federal government to build a military installation in our district.

In all this confusion, we try to make sense of what is going on. Our opinions help us in the task — as political beliefs, they offer guidance for understanding. By helping us to understand politics, our opinions also help us to realize our interests. A union member has a favorable opinion of the Democratic party if he associates that party with lowering his taxes, keeping him employed, and otherwise supporting his economic demands. Opinions are thus instruments we use in taking sides in conflicts that involve our interests.

*Our opinions help us to relate to other people.* When we state our

---

[3] Angus Campbell, *White Attitudes Toward Black People* (Ann Arbor, Mich.: Institute for Social Research, 1971).

[4] See M. Brewster Smith et al., *Opinions and Personality* (New York: John Wiley, 1956) and Daniel Katz, "The Functional Approach to the Study of Attitudes," *The Public Opinion Quarterly* 24 (Summer 1960): 163–176.

Political opinions often reflect a preference for the absolute.

political views we know that some people will agree and others will not. We can use our opinions to join with those we like, respect, and want to be with, and conversely we can use them to fight or flee persons we do not like or want to avoid. Because opinions help us to adjust socially,[5] we may tailor our expressions to conform to what persons say with whom we want to get along. In this case, expressed opinions are one way of saying "I am like you," of putting into operation the old political adage that one must "go along to get along."

[5] Steven R. Brown and John D. Ellithorp, "Emotional Experiences in Political Groups: The Case of the McCarthy Phenomenon," *The American Political Science Review* 64 (June 1970): 349–366.

*Our opinions expose our personalities.* One of the classic formulations about politics is that people project their private motives upon public objects and rationalize them to conform with the public interest.[6] When a person states a political viewpoint, he expresses his inner personality — his psychic needs, emotions, tensions, frustrations, anxieties. Our stated thoughts and feelings defend our egos against hostile criticism and rationalize our pursuit of narrow interests, particularly those we do not think have general social sanction. Moreover, our stated opinions reveal the image we have of ourselves that we want others to accept. A man who thinks of himself as "liberal" or "conservative" wants others to accept that self-definition, so he takes every opportunity to express liberal or conservative opinions. His views on political issues reflect his definition of himself rather than any considered judgment of the merits of the proposals he supports.

Almost any political opinion performs these functions in some combination. An opinion guides our understanding, helps us to adjust to others, and assists us in expressing our motives. These three functions of opinions arouse parallel conflicts represented by political opinions. For instance, there are conflicting understandings of which tangible goals to pursue and how to achieve them (such as debates over permitting the sale of alcoholic beverages and taxing them to finance government services). Second are conflicts between social groups for political status (should "booze hounds" have as much to say about the sale of alcohol as "respectable, church-going citizens"). Third are conflicting private motives (as between politicians who rationalize selfish ambitions by campaigning to "wipe out sales of demon rum" or "let the people decide whether they want to pay taxes to drink"). When analyzing a debate on any political issue, it is helpful to remember that *all three levels of dispute usually surround the superficial disagreement. Conflicts of principle often mask a clash of understandings, social purposes, and personal motives.*

## what are political opinions?

Political opinions are useful not only to the people who express them. Politicians find out what is on the minds of people by paying attention to shared and conflicting opinions. Policymakers listen to and respond to political thoughts, feelings, and actions. But the relationship between political opinions and public policy is complicated; the people do not

---

[6] Harold D. Lasswell, *Psychopathology and Politics* (New York: Viking Press, Compass Books Edition, 1960), pp. 75–76.

always *want* exactly what government *does*. Some political opinions are easier for political leaders to heed than others. What characteristics of political opinions affect their influence in conflict representation?

*Direction* is an indication of whether an opinion is favorable, unfavorable, or qualified. People's opinions usually are influenced by their personalities, social backgrounds, or partisan affiliation rather than by the merits of the proposal. Regardless of the underlying reason — the issue itself or the predispositions — Americans usually line up clearly for or against proposals rather than give qualified reactions.

*Intensity* indicates how firmly people hold opinions. Some issues such as controversies over personalities excite public passion, and politicians respond quickly. When Lieutenant William L. Calley, Jr., was convicted in 1971 in a court-martial for the premeditated murder of Vietnamese civilians in the village of My Lai, the public was outraged that a "loyal American" was being used as a "scapegoat" — 80 percent of a nationwide sample disapproved of the verdict.[7] The protest was so intense that President Nixon ordered Calley removed from a military prison and returned to a comfortable apartment under house arrest. Nixon also agreed to review the case personally once all military appeals were exhausted. Eighty-three percent of Americans sampled approved of Nixon's action. On the other hand, policy questions that are less emotionally charged and more routine, such as the annual request of the President to Congress to raise the legal limit on the national debt, stir intense feelings among far fewer Americans.

*Stability* is a quality that opinions acquire when their direction and intensity is fairly constant over a period of time. In the 1950s and 1960s, typical nationwide surveys indicated that a majority of Americans favored foreign aid, about a third were opposed, and the remainder had "no opinion." But stability in the direction and intensity of political opinions depends upon two things: consistency of underlying personal attitudes and continuity in the conditions stimulating those attitudes. Thus, when America became involved in South Vietnam in the 1960s, opinions about foreign aid changed. They were no longer clearly pro or con, but qualified. Though percentages of support and opposition to foreign aid in opinion surveys were about the same as before, three-fourths of those sampled went on to say they wanted either to "reduce" or "cut off completely" aid to any country that did not support the United States "in a major foreign decision, such as Vietnam."[8]

When opinions are stable, politicians tend to identify their stands with

[7] News Release, American Institute of Public Opinion (April 6, 1971).
[8] Hazel Gaudet Erskine, "The Polls: Some Gauges of Conservatism," *The Public Opinion Quarterly* 28 (Spring 1964):168.

those opinions prevailing. Failure to estimate majority opinion correctly can be costly. Senator Barry Goldwater found this out in campaigning for the presidency in 1964. His reported stands reflected miscalculation on various issues: on Social Security (he urged substitution of a voluntary scheme for the compulsory one in operation); on the United Nations (he proposed a reduction of United States involvement in that organization); on the Tennessee Valley Authority (it was reported that he favored sale to private interests).[9]

When opinions on an issue are fluid and unstable, a leader can arouse support by proposing an attractive solution. In the 1952 presidential campaign, when dissatisfaction with the Korean War was growing, the Republican candidate, General Eisenhower, promised that if elected he would "go to Korea," a dramatic gesture that held out hope of a quick and positive end to the conflict to discouraged Americans.

## the big issues

Americans react most to five issues. These are things that interest them, things that worry them, and things about which they state opinions in conflict representation. Asked what worries them about their lives, they cite health, living standards, children, housing, and general happiness. When they are asked what worries them about America, they say war and peace.[10]

*Americans are nearly always worried about economic issues.* Economic issues include inflation, recession, and depression: whether or not a person can find work; how much money there is to spend; and how much money must be given to the government in taxes. Americans have worried about these matters often — in the economic depressions of the 1890s and again in the 1930s, in recessions such as the 1950s, in the inflationary trends of the 1960s and 1970s. They ponder President Nixon's freezing wages and prices for ninety days in 1971, the economic issues in the presidential campaign of 1972, and today's concern with tax reform.

*Americans worry increasingly about social issues.* As Figure 6-2 indicates, social and economic issues account for the majority of American worries. Social issues are (1) *the crime wave* with its fears of rising threats to life and property; (2) *the racial question* with whites resenting

[9] One elderly midwestern lady complained to a pollster in reference to the TVA issue that she would vote against Goldwater for he had threatened to sell her "TV."

[10] Hadley Cantril, *The Pattern of Human Concerns* (New Brunswick, N.J.: Rutgers University Press, 1965), pp. 34–44; Lloyd A. Free and Hadley Cantril, *The Political Beliefs of Americans* (New Brunswick, N.J.: Rutgers University Press, 1967), pp. 94–112.

Americans are nearly always worried about economic issues such as inflation, recession, and depression. Today, rising prices, minimum wages, and tax reform are on the minds of many people.

the too-fast pace of integration and blacks resenting that it is not fast enough; (3) *morality* and resulting worries about the decline in public morals indicated by widespread sales of pornography, permissive sexual codes, the controversy over sex education in schools, the decline in church attendance, etc.; (4) the *drug culture* — the use and abuse of alcohol, marijuana, LSD, and other drugs, and the accompanying controversy over legalizing sales and treatment of habitual drug users; (5) the *protest outbreak* leading to dismay over peaceful and violent protests in the 1960s about civil rights, the war in Vietnam, women's liberation, and the administration of colleges; and (6) the *life style debate* — how long should hair and skirts be, what is foul language, and what is proper respect for authority?[11]

*Americans worry about foreign issues primarily when American armed forces are directly involved in a war.* The Vietnam War aroused more worry than any other issue in international affairs. All other foreign issues, including the conflict in the Middle East, improve-

[11] On the "social issue," see Richard M. Scammon and Ben J. Wattenberg, *The Real Majority* (New York: Coward-McCann, Inc., 1970), pp. 35–44. See also David E. RePass, "Issue Salience and Party Choice," *The American Political Science Review* 65 (June 1971): 389–400.

ment of relations with the Soviet Union and the People's Republic of China, foreign aid, and American connections with the United Nations, seem less important. Americans rate "keeping out of war" as very important, but normally international issues do not touch them as closely as economic and social matters.

*Welfare issues are less important to most Americans.* These include expenditures for public education, old-age assistance programs, medical care programs, the fight against poverty, and others. Although large portions of the public do not express their feelings about these issues, interests do tend to organize around them and conflicts over them constitute some of the principal disputes brought to the attention of public officials.

*Ecological problems are highly publicized, but relatively few Americans consider them to be prominent issues.* Pollution of the air and water, destruction of forests, extinction of valuable wildlife, depletion of natural resources, and related matters such as the exploding population are important to organized interests but are secondary to the mass population.

The five issues in Figure 6-2 showed up as stable areas of worry in several opinion surveys (in fact, these areas are reflected in surveys dat-

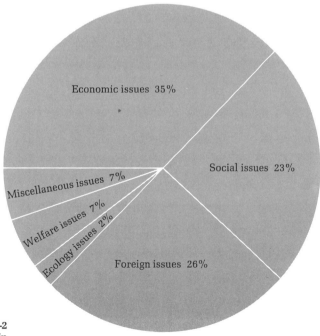

**FIGURE 6–2**
**Salient Issues in**
**American Political Opinion, 1971**     Source: News release, American Institute of Public Opinion (September 21, 1971).

ing as far back as the 1950s). Americans also worry most about the issues most publicized in the news. After President Nixon announced his highly publicized freeze on wages and prices, economic interest intensified. Finally, even if only a small proportion of those surveyed cite a specific worry, conflicts in that area are not necessarily unknown to policymakers. *The disputes that reach politicians depend not only upon people's interests but on how opinion is organized on these issues.* Frequently, an opinion expressed by a small number of Americans who form a cohesive group has influence quite out of proportion to the group's size. Minorities provoked civil rights legislation by their sit-ins, marches, and demonstrations in the 1950s and 1960s. To understand more fully how conflicts are represented by political opinions, we need to know more about how opinions are organized.

### how do we recognize consensus and conflict in popular political opinions?

*Opinions are distributed through the community in three distinctive ways: opinion consensus, opinion clusters, and opinion groupings.*

*Opinion consensus* requires three conditions: (1) citizens are willing to express an opinion on a specific issue in relatively large numbers; (2) at least two-thirds of those expressing an opinion agree on a course of action; and (3) relatively few persons — fewer than 20 percent — support alternative plans. Table 6-1, which reports the responses of Americans sampled in 1967 on two programs in President Lyndon Johnson's "War on Poverty," illustrates patterns of opinion consensus.

*Opinion consensus* forms two basic patterns, one *positive* and one *negative*. It is *positive* when citizens express enough *support* of a program to permit officials to act in a specific way.[12] When President Nixon announced in 1971 that he would make an unprecedented visit to the People's Republic of China, nationwide polls indicated that three out of every four Americans sampled *supported* his plan.[13] *Negative* consensus indicates widespread *opposition* to an action. Polls indicating that 90 percent of Americans *opposed* busing as a method of promoting school integration show a negative consensus.[14] The poll results on busing were used by several presidential aspirants in 1972, notably by Governor George Wallace of Alabama, to demonstrate that the conflict on that

[12] V. O. Key, Jr., *Public Opinion and American Democracy* (New York: Alfred A. Knopf, 1961), pp. 28–38.

[13] News release, Opinion Research Corporation (July 27, 1971); News release, *The Harris Survey* (September 9, 1971).

[14] News release, American Institute of Public Opinion (November 1, 1971).

**TABLE 6-1**
**Examples of Opinion Consensus, 1967**

| Issue | Present level or increased | Reduced | Ended altogether | Don't know |
|---|---|---|---|---|
| "As part of the anti-poverty program, the Federal Government is providing funds for retraining poorly educated people so they can get jobs. Do you think spending by the Federal Government should be kept at the present level, or reduced, or ended altogether?" | 75% | 13% | 8% | 4% |
| "Under the urban renewal program the Federal Government is making grants to help rebuild run down sections of our cities. Do you think government spending for this purpose should be kept at least at the present level, or reduced, or ended altogether?" | 67 | 10 | 11 | 12 |

Source: Compiled from data in Lloyd A. Free and Hadley Cantril. *The Political Beliefs of Americans* (New Brunswick, N.J.: Rutgers University Press, 1967), pp. 12–14.

issue was not among the mass of Americans but between the people and their officials.

*Opinion clusters* about issues occur when controversy rather than agreement arises over alternatives. The apparent consensus cited in Table 6-1 on methods for alleviating poverty breaks down when Americans are queried about the causes of poverty. When the same people whose opinions are displayed in Table 6-1 were asked, "In your opinion, which is generally more often to blame if a person is poor — lack of effort on his part or circumstances beyond his control?" 25 percent responded "circumstances," 34 percent said "lack of effort," 38 percent cited "both," and only 3 percent had no opinion. Opinion clustering typically consists of expressions on two sides of an issue, but there may be as many clusters as there are possible reactions. Multiple clustering appeared in the public's response to American policy in Vietnam. It was not until 1970 that a majority of Americans moved toward the opinion that United States troops should be completely removed from Vietnam. Earlier they had been divided among complete withdrawal, leaving a residual military force in Vietnam, and sending more troops to "win the war" (Table 6-2).

Two-sided clusterings are likely to form in conflict representation as debate progresses, positions harden, the alternatives are reduced, or proposed actions become more symbolic and less concrete and appeal to more people. Multiclustered distributions are more likely to appear among very well informed persons who are able to discern subtle differences in alternatives, rather than among the general community, where questions elicit simple pro or con responses.

Both the consensus and the clustering of political opinions form statistical patterns indicating the direction of opinions — how many people hold each of several opinions on an issue. But we know also that opinions vary in intensity, and here also we can see similar distribution patterns. Figure 6-3 illustrates positive consensus, negative consensus, two-sided conflicts, and many-sided conflicts on various issues. In each instance, the *intensity* with which people defend their opinions combines with the *direction* of those opinions to provide distinctive patterns that show the distribution of opinions in conflict representation.

Opinion consensus or clusters reflect patterns of individual opinions; they do not reflect the group affiliations or social characteristics of the persons. Opinion groupings, by contrast, are patterns based upon stands taken by organized groups or by identifiable segments of the population. Some theorists have argued that all political opinions are the products

**TABLE 6-2**
**Multiclustered Distribution**
**of Political Opinions on Vietnam, 1964–1970**

| Alternatives | Percentage in favor | | | | |
|---|---|---|---|---|---|
| | 1964 | 1966 | 1967 | 1968 | 1970 |
| Pull out of Vietnam entirely | 13% | 11% | 15% | 22% | 52% |
| Keep armed forces there, but try to end the fighting | 34 | 45 | 38 | 41 | 34 |
| Take a stronger stand | 43 | 44 | 47 | 37 | 14 |
| Total | 100% | 100% | 100% | 100% | 100% |
| Number of cases | 928 | 1046 | 1148 | 1362 | 1509 |

Sources: Compiled from data from surveys of the Survey Research Center, University of Michigan (available through the Interuniversity Consortium for Political Research) and of the American Institute of Public Opinion.

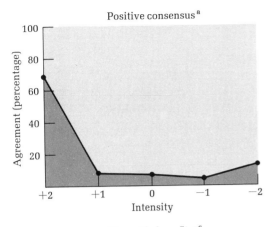

Positive consensus[a]

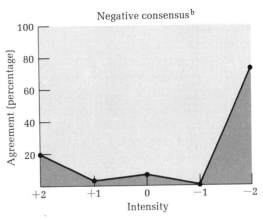

Negative consensus[b]

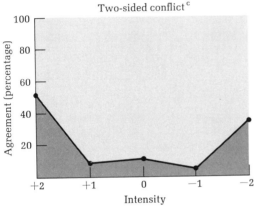

Two-sided conflict[c]

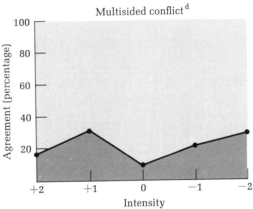

Multisided conflict[d]

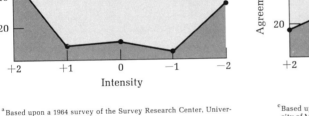

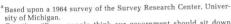

[a] Based upon a 1964 survey of the Survey Research Center, University of Michigan.
Question: "Some people think our government should sit down and talk to the leaders of the Communist countries and try to settle our differences, while others think we should refuse to have anything to do with them. What do you think?" Levels of intensity are (+2) favors talking and mind made up, (+1) favors talking but has reservations, (0) it depends, (−1) against talking but has reservations, (−2) against talking and mind made up.

[b] Based upon a 1966 survey of the Survey Research Center, University of Michigan.
Question: "Some say that a newsstand should be allowed to sell any kind of magazine to adults even if it's what people call indecent. How about you?" Levels of intensity are (+2) should be allowed, (+1) should be allowed, qualified, (0) it depends, (−1) should not be allowed, qualified, (−2) should not be allowed.

[c] Based upon a 1964 survey of the Survey Research Center, University of Michigan.
Question: "Some say the government in Washington ought to help people get doctors and hospital care at low cost; others say the government should not get into this. What is your position?" Levels of intensity are (+2) favors medicare and mind made up, (+1) favors medicare, but with doubts, (0) it depends, (−1) against medicare, but with doubts, (−2) against medicare and mind made up.

[d] Based upon a 1970 survey of Louis Harris and Associates.
Question: "If something happened to President Nixon and Vice-President Agnew became President, how would you feel about Spiro Agnew as President?" Levels of intensity are (+2) very high confidence, (+1) somewhat high confidence, (0) not sure, (−1) somewhat low confidence, and (−2) very low confidence.

**FIGURE 6-3**
**Examples of Opinion Consensus and Conflict, by Direction and Intensity of Political Opinion**

of group stands rather than the sum of individual preferences. Certainly group positions are visible on many political issues, but these group stands have clear characteristics.

First, a group's position is the product of internal bargaining between differing opinions to achieve unity before contending with rival groups and their opinions.

Second, such organized opinions usually fail to reveal the different views of factions or coalitions of factions still present within the group.

Third, although many individual opinions may be correlated with group stands, many others cannot be.

Opinion groupings are also identifiable by factors other than group membership. These include identification by geographical regions (South, East, North, West); residential areas (urban, suburban, and rural); social class (upper, middle, and working classes); religion (Baptists, Catholics, etc.); and ethnic origin (Mexican-Americans, Negroes, Puerto Ricans). Opinion groupings are potentially as numerous as the politically relevant groupings within the population. Actually, however, *the opinions people hold never match perfectly the stands taken by groups of which they are members.* Urban consumers do not without exception feel that farm subsidies should be abandoned, nor do all farmers think such payments are desirable. Conflicts within groups and consensus across groups makes it risky to generalize about the opinion predominant within a social category in conflict representation.

### how political opinions are distributed

We can better understand how the characteristics and distribution of political opinions are related if we extract the pattern of opinions typical of conflict representation. Let us assume that Americans face this issue: Do you or do you not agree with a bill passed by Congress requiring that all industrial plants install antipollution devices before the end of the year?

First, some Americans will express no opinions, the *nonparticipants.* Two groups do have opinions: those (frequently a majority) who "approve" or "disapprove" but are otherwise indifferent. This *indifferent majority* is likely to have opinions that are uninformed, of low intensity, and unstable.

A second group of opinion-holders will take the issue more seriously. This *informed minority* can be designated either *intense* or *moderate.* A particularly *intense minority* expressing a definite affirmative or negative response: namely, "I approve of the legislation because America has been

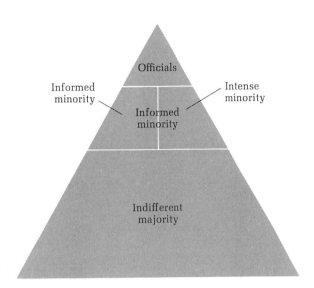

**FIGURE 6-4**
**The Distribution of Political Opinions**

entirely too complacent about its pollution problems; I am writing to my congressman to say so"; or, "I disapprove; I think the cost of installing antipollution devices in such a short time will be prohibitive." The preferences of these intense "approvers" and "disapprovers" are likely to be passionate, stable (perhaps even dogmatic), and better informed than those of the indifferent. Those with less passionate views qualify their replies: "I favor the regulation of polluting industries, but I think the bill should go further"; or "I oppose the fouling of the air that produced this bill, but I don't think that Congress should have placed so much blame on our industries." This *moderate minority,* by striving for realistic compromises between conflicting interests, frequently is significant as the controversy develops.

   This typical pattern of opinions in conflict representation is depicted in Figure 6-4. The triangle represents all those expressing a political opinion, excluding the "don't know" and "no opinion" group. At the apex are the officials who must resolve the conflict by some policy. Below them is the informed minority, both intense and moderate elements. The largest area in most disputes is occupied by the indifferent majority who have opinions, express them when asked, but are generally ignorant of the details. The people in the informed minority form an active public that both influences and is influenced by public officials who strive to build support for policies.

This triangle clearly shows that *give-and-take in conflict repre-sentation is generally more common between policymakers and the in-formed minority than between policymakers and the indifferent major-ity.*[15]

## acquiring political opinions

Personal attitudes and political stimuli interact to form political opin-ions. We need to know then how Americans learn their political atti-tudes, which we call *political socialization.*

Political socialization produces thoughts, feelings, and habits about the political community, the government, and political leaders; therefore, it *produces both consensus and conflict.* Citizens learn community loyal-ties that normally transcend conflicting group identifications. But they also learn loyalties to the groups to which they belong and they identify with fellow members in disputes with other groups. If we know what political attitudes people learn and *how* they learn them, we will know more about the sources of the agreements and disagreements that enter into conflict representation.[16]

Like any type of learning, political socialization continues throughout life, beginning in childhood and ending in death. Important learning af-fecting later political behavior frequently occurs quite early in life, *but* the early learning is modified in later years. If a person does not learn politically relevant attitudes early in life — say in the family or school — he may yet learn them in his church, job, or elsewhere. His socializing experiences need not be overtly political, but they may have political consequences in the future. Socializing influences are cumulative; the attitudes he learns reinforce one another.[17]

## political attitudes

The principal types of attitudes acquired through political socialization have to do with the political community, the political process, political leaders, civic obligation, and group identifications.

THE POLITICAL COMMUNITY. Identification with the political community is one of the first things a child learns in politics. Symbols such as the

---

[15] Donald J. Devine, *The Attentive Public* (Chicago: Rand McNally, 1970).
[16] Lewis A. Froman, Jr., "Learning Political Attitudes," *The Western Political Quarterly* 15 (June 1962): 305.
[17] Orville G. Brim, Jr., "Socialization through the Life Cycle," *Items* 18 (March 1964): 1–5.

A child learns early to identify with the political community. Symbols such as the flag reinforce emotional attachment.

flag, the national anthem, the Statue of Liberty reinforce the emotional attachment. The child of five is scarcely aware of any flag other than the Stars and Stripes. As one child put it: "God made the flag so they'd know who was the good people."[18] For vast numbers of American children, at least those in a middle-class environment, this early, intensely forged link between child and community endures and only partially erodes when

[18] Eugene A. Weinstein, "Development of the Concept of Flag and the Sense of National Identity," *Child Development* 28 (1958): 171.

it meets the frustrations and responsibilities of adult citizenship. In the view of some authorities, *this bond is possibly the most basic and essential aspect of socialization into involvement with the political life of the nation.*"[19]

THE POLITICAL PROCESS. American adults' ambivalent views about politics (see Chapter Two) are less characteristic of children. A survey study in the mid-1960s of predominantly white public school children in grades three through eight in selected metropolitan areas concluded that the American child's early trust in government exhibits a high acceptance of government as a necessary part of the natural environment. *If the child does develop discontent and a desire for change, his or her feelings are built upon an early base of high regard for government.*[20]

POLITICAL LEADERS. Although most children learn early in life to have deep affection for the community and for government, both "community" and "government" are abstract notions that are simply beyond their intellectual grasp. For youngsters, these abstractions are symbolized as personal figures to which children relate easily. *The typical American child's image of government is confined mainly to the President; and the child's idea of "law" is represented by the local policeman.* American children in grades two through eight usually express respect, faith, and warmth for the President and believe him to be a harder worker, more honest, more friendly, and more knowledgeable than most men; indeed, the majority of second graders frequently say he is the "best" man "in the world."[21] The uniformed local policeman (portrayed in children's books, in films, and on television) is one of the first political figures the child actually sees. Both black and white children learn to regard the policeman as dependable and trustworthy; this respect declines little among whites over the years, but erodes much more among black children.[22]

The sources of the child's early love for political leaders are not easy to trace. Respect for a political leader may come from two possible types of childhood experience: either the child who has had benevolent treatment from his parents transfers his love for that authority to, say, the President; or, the child who has been impressed with the coercive nature

[19] Robert D. Hess and Judith V. Torney, *The Development of Political Attitudes in Children* (Chicago: Aldine, 1967), p. 213. (Emphasis added.)

[20] David Easton and Jack Dennis, "The Child's Image of Government," in Roberta Sigel, ed., *Political Socialization: Its Role in the Political Process* (The Annals of the American Academy of Political and Social Science) 261 (Sept. 1965): 40–57.

[21] David Easton and Jack Dennis, *Children in the Political System* (New York: McGraw-Hill, 1969), pp. 165–245.

[22] Edward S. Greenberg, "Orientations of Black and White Children to Political Authority Figures," *Social Science Quarterly* 51 (Dec. 1970): 561–571.

of authority — as with parental punishment — respects political leaders because of his fear of disobeying. In either case, the average child learns to trust political leaders, to believe that they will protect and help him, and to respect them as powerful, competent, infallible, and benign. *Thus, an early trust in political leaders is typical of American children.*

But a child's warm response to a political leader such as the President is not just a reaction to a symbol of authority. As early as the fourth grade, children begin to associate a president with his political stands and to evaluate him by these as well as his personal qualities. A study undertaken immediately following the assassination of President John F. Kennedy indicated how children in primary and secondary grades in Detroit had felt about him as President. Although a majority recalled President Kennedy for his personal or symbolic qualities ("he looked after our country" or "he made me feel secure"), a third remembered him for political reasons. An eleven-year-old white girl remarked, "President Kennedy worked on programs for civil rights, less segregation, and physical fitness"; and an eleven-year-old Negro girl responded, "He tried to let Negro people live an intelligent life." The study concluded, "Detroit school children were by no means ignorant of their political environment; they seemed to have known the centrally important issues of their time and what transpired during the President's term of office. To be sure, their image lacked depth and detail as well as sophistication, but the same can well be said of most adults."[23]

CIVIC OBLIGATION. American public education emphasizes citizenship training to instill civic awareness and duty. Whether it is primarily the school that gets that message across is uncertain, but the evidence shows that a sense of the civic duty to participate in conflict representation is learned early in life. *By the eighth grade, children believe that it is every citizen's obligation to take part in politics by being interested in current events and by voting.*[24] As formal education increases, the sense of civic obligation increases also. Among college-educated persons, civic awareness is very high. But as we saw in Chapter Five, ideals and behavior in civics, as elsewhere, differ in the expected direction: more citizens feel they *should* participate than *do*.

GROUP IDENTIFICATIONS. Positive feelings toward the community, government, authority figures, and civic obligation are a principal source of political consensus. If time does not erode them, these attitudes help to

[23] Roberta S. Sigel, "Image of a President: Some Insights into the Political Views of School Children," *The American Political Science Review* 62 (March 1968): 226.
[24] Hess and Torney, *The Development of Political Attitudes in Children*, p. 67. Also see Charles F. Andrian, *Children and Civic Awareness* (Columbus, Ohio: Charles E. Merrill, 1971).

moderate conflicts. But what types of attitudes are sources of conflicts of opinion? The major ones are a person's identifications with conflicting groups such as partisan, religious, status, and racial groups.

*Party identification is acquired quite early.* By seven years of age, at least a majority of American children think of themselves as Republicans or Democrats; and by the time they are adults, 70 percent of Americans identify with a political party.[25]

*Religious identifications also appear early.* Partisan and religious preferences frequently complement one another throughout life, but when the two conflict, the less intense loyalty — often that of party — yields to the other.

*Children seldom acquire political ideologies that threaten partisanship.* Partisan attitudes are much more useful than ideological ones in enabling us to adapt to and handle new issues and unanticipated political situations.

*The child learns a sense of social status* that may bring him into conflict with others. Social class perspectives affect participation, as we saw in Chapter Five, and the direction of partisan loyalty as well.

Finally, studies of how racial identification is learned reveal that Americans do not acquire in equal measure durable positive attitudes toward political authority and their ability to cope with it. As early as the age of four, some *children recognize racial differences* along with a sense of their related social and political consequences. One young black child observed succinctly, "The people that are white, they can go up. The people that are brown, they have to go down."[26]

## how political attitudes are learned

How do people acquire their political thoughts, feelings, and habits? Political learning consists of the psychological process involved in learning and the stimuli or agents that influence what we learn. Most political learning results from a combination of a person's *genetic capacities* for learning, his gradual *physical-mental-emotional growth,* and his *exposure to politics.*[27] As his capacities and maturity permit, he reproduces

[25] Jack Dennis and Donald J. McCrone, "Preadult Development of Political Party Identification in Western Democracies," *Comparative Political Studies* 3 (July 1970): 243–263.

[26] Mary Ellen Goodman, *Race Awareness in Young Children* (Cambridge, Mass.: Addison-Wesley, 1952), p. 28.

[27] Richard M. Merelman, "The Development of Political Ideology: A Framework for the Analysis of Political Socialization," *The American Political Science Review* 63 (Sept. 1969): 750–767; Richard M. Merelman, "The Development of Policy Thinking in Adolescence," *The American Political Science Review* 65 (Dec. 1971): 1033–1047.

in himself the beliefs, feelings, and actions exhibited by real-life models (parents, friends, and others) or symbolic models (fictional persons, television figures, or persons with whom he has no direct contact). The psychological process of learning is thus a *modeling:* a person observes, compares, copies, imitates, and matches the behavior of others who are significant to him.[28]

Modeling begins in early childhood, continues throughout life, and is directed by many socializing agencies. *The general pattern is clear:* the family sets political socialization in motion; as the child grows older, parental influence decreases, and the family is gradually replaced by schooling, social groups, occupational influences, religion, and the mass media. Some new experiences reinforce the political convictions acquired in childhood; but as contacts with the social environment widen, exposure to conflicting views may modify attitudes learned much earlier.

THE FAMILY. One of the most influential socializing agencies, the family forms attitudes in the child's early years. Parents filter influences from the community at large and transmit political views to their offspring. Yet *though children's political attitudes generally conform to those of their parents, a correspondence in the political outlooks of the parent and child is in no way assured.* A major survey study in 1965 of high school seniors and their parents concluded: "There is considerable slack in the value-acquisition process. If the eighteen-year-old is no simple carbon copy of his parents — as the results clearly indicate — then it seems most likely that other socializing agencies have ample opportunity to exert their impact. This happens, we believe, both during and after childhood. . . . It is perhaps the intrusion of other and different stimuli lying outside the nexus of the family and school which has led to the seemingly different *Weltanschauung* of the post–World War II generation compared with its immediate predecessor."[29]

Why is the eighteen-year-old "no simple carbon copy of his parents"? Three characteristics of the family itself are particularly important.

First, *the way parents treat their children makes a critical difference.* During the late 1960s when militant students caused major disruptions on college campuses, a significant study explored the differences in the ways in which groups of young people had been treated by their families in childhood.[30] The groups were: *inactives,* who reported no participation

[28] Albert Bandura and Richard H. Walters, *Social Learning and Personality Development* (New York: Holt, Rinehart and Winston, 1963).
[29] M. Kent Jennings and Richard G. Niemi, "The Transmission of Political Values from Parent to Child," *The American Political Science Review* 62 (March 1968): 183–184.
[30] Jeanne H. Block, Norman Haan, and M. Brewster Smith, "Socialization Correlates of Student Activism," *Journal of Social Issues* 25 (1969): 143–177.

in political or social organizations or activities; *conventionalists,* members of sororities and fraternities involved in relatively little political activity who follow the traditional "Joe College" stereotype; *constructivists,* working in social service projects but infrequently involved in organized protests; *activists,* who protested their dissatisfaction with the status quo but who also joined in social service projects to correct the ills they perceived; and *dissenters,* young people involved primarily in organized protests. The differences in the personalities of their parents were clear:

*Inactives:* parents were anxious about their children's health and welfare but insisted upon obedience, conformity, and docility to parental demands.

Children absorb political attitudes before acquiring the information to support them.

*Conventionalists:* parents adhered to traditional social values (responsibility, conformity, achievement, and obedience), demanded socially appropriate behavior and achievement, and made those demands clear by invoking physical or psychological punishment.

*Constructivists:* parents emphasized discipline, achievement, and dependability, restricted self-expression, and used nonphysical punishment. They were more warmly regarded by the children than parents of conventionalists.

*Activists:* parents encouraged children to be independent and responsible — as did parents of constructivists and conventionalists — but encouraged self-expression short of physical aggression and emphasized discipline less. Parent-child relations were considered less than good by activists.

*Dissenters:* parents were inconsistent in child-rearing practices, permissive in certain areas and highly restrictive in others; they emphasized independence and early maturity less but pressed at the same time for achievement and encouraged competition. Parent-child relations were evaluated most negatively by dissenters. Two major conclusions were reached: (1) dissenters, those whose parents inconsistently combined permissive and restrictive practices, were in far greater rebellion against parental attitudes than others; and (2) it is a mistake to lump together all student protestors as products of permissive upbringing, for activists also protest, but not simply as adolescent rebellion against all authority.

Second, *the relative influence of the mother or father within the family influences political orientations.* Most children grow up in homes where the two parents are alike in political orientations. In these families, the mother usually transmits that consensus to the child. Where parents differ, the father appears more influential, but children do not gravitate in disproportionate numbers to his preferences. The evidence is that children from mother-dominated families, especially males, are less likely to be politically interested and engage in politics than those from father-dominated families.[31] Not being politically interested in the home, these children have more opportunity to be influenced by other agencies (schools, friends) whose outlooks may conflict with parental convictions.

Third, *the extent to which parents are interested in politics at all makes a difference.* When politics is not important in the family it is not a very good target for the child's protest or rebellion. If politics is important, however, the child may adopt political convictions contrary to those of his parents as a symbolic protest against their authority.[32]

---

[31] M. Kent Jennings and Richard G. Niemi, "The Division of Political Labor Between Mothers and Fathers," *The American Political Science Review* 65 (March 1971): 69–82.

[32] Kenneth P. Langton, *Political Socialization* (New York: Oxford University Press, 1969).

TABLE 6-3
**Resemblance in Party Identification between Parents and Children, 1964**

| Party identification of offspring | Parental party identification | |
|---|---|---|
| | Mother Democrat, Father Republican | Mother Republican, Father Democrat |
| Democrat | 69% | 44% |
| Republican | 31 | 50 |
| Independent | 0 | 6 |
| Total | 100% | 100% |
| Number of cases | 32 | 52 |

Source: Survey Research Center and Interuniversity Consortium for Political Research, University of Michigan.

Whether rebellious or conformist, *children acquire their initial sense of political awareness in the family.* The more politically active Americans have parents who voted regularly, discussed politics, were politically informed, and attempted to exert political influence. Such families implicitly teach their children that political participation, along with earning a living, playing, and other experiences, is important and rewarding.

*The family is crucial in orienting children toward political parties.* Most pairs of parents share partisan loyalties and most children adopt the partisan affiliation of their parents. Deviation from the party attachment of their parents is higher among children when the parents are "weak" rather than "strong" party identifiers. Where the party loyalties of the parents differ, as the figures in Table 6-3 illustrate, the mother's partisanship is somewhat more influential. However, adults with only a grade school education and working class adults are more likely to have the party affiliation of their father than their mother.

Once the child grows to adulthood and has a job and family of his own, his social interests may diverge from those of his parents because he has improved or lowered his social class. We say such a person is socially mobile. *Social mobility is related to learning political attitudes different from those acquired in the parental family.* Those who improve their social position are often less interested in politics, less liberal on questions of foreign policy and civil liberties, more liberal on economic questions, and more often Democrats than those above them in the social ladder. The downwardly mobile — those whose social position is lower than that of their parents — are more interested in politics, more conservative on economic questions, more liberal on foreign policy and civil liberties, and more often Republican than persons below them on the social ladder.

*The socially mobile, then, change their attitudes in the direction appropriate to their new status so that their views are intermediate between those typical of their family upbringing and their new station in life.*[33]

SCHOOLING. Just how much formal education affects political attitudes is difficult to gauge. Still, it is possible to consider the effects of each level of education — primary, secondary, and college.

The *primary grades* give each child an early opportunity to compare his views with those of his peers. School environments that include those from diverse social classes expose the student to a range of opinions different from his family's convictions. The results of this exposure are not random, however; lower-class children tend to learn the values of children from higher-class backgrounds. The consequence is a resocializing upward of lower-class and working-class students in the direction of more conventional American middle-class norms, political attitudes included.[34]

This result is cited by many who advocate racially balanced schools as an effective way of reshaping the motivation of children from minority groups so as to improve their learning and school performance. The sources and themes of disagreement with that position are many. One camp urges that the home and neighborhood environments are the major determinants, and that the school cannot be expected to offset their influence. A counterargument is that it is wrong to assume that middle-class norms are superior or desirable; such beliefs can lead only to alienation of nonconforming sectors of the community, which feel rejected and despised. Readers should have no difficulty in fleshing out a list of disputants and themes for this, one of the most intensely controversial domestic political issues of our day — the meaning and extent of racial desegregation in the schools and whether and how to achieve it.

The *secondary school* years provide opportunities for political socialization. Maturing involves growing ability to integrate diverse attitudes

[33] James Alden Barber, Jr., *Social Mobility and Voting Behavior* (Chicago: Rand McNally, 1970).

[34] Bernice L. Neugarten, "Social Class and Friendship Among School Children," *The American Sociological Review* 51 (Jan. 1946): 305–313. Kenneth P. Langton, "Peer Group and School in the Political Socialization Process," *The American Political Science Review* 61 (Sept. 1967): 751–758.

with consistent outlooks. Textbook knowledge and information about current events intrude upon one's political views. A systematic effort at citizenship training occurs. Finally, newly acquired secondary school friends are more likely than primary school friends to have outlooks different from those taught by the family.

The politically relevant attitudes generally formed in high school strengthen the appreciation for democratic values, a sense of partisan loyalty, and civic awareness. The attempt to indoctrinate students with democratic values is undertaken in American high schools in "citizenship" courses, but *the effect of the civics curriculum varies with the social background of the student*. It is most effective for children from lower- and working-class families, who are more susceptible to political influence because of the limited political interest, information, and involvement in their family environment. Middle- and upper-class students enter high school aware of how active political participation can contribute to their lives, so that formal courses may well be less important in shaping their political socialization.[35]

The socializing effect of *college* on political attitudes, which is probably quite large for many, results from the young adult's exposure to increasingly diverse acquaintances, increased political information, and the opportunity – presented, by definition, to students reading this book – to compare the world "as it is" with the picture presented in the classroom. A college education increases the student's tolerance for diversity of opinion and social nonconformity, heightens his sense of civic awareness and competence, improves his aptitude in expressing informed political opinions, increases the probability of voting, and lessens partisan loyalties. High school graduates who go to college already differ from their schoolmates who terminate their formal education with high school graduation. Hence, *differences in political attitudes of adults with high school and college educations may be attributed both to lingering social class differences in the types of people who go to college and to the college experience itself.*[36]

What are the political attitudes of college students? For one thing, *they are not as avidly* partisan as people in other generations. Figure 6-5 illustrates the increase in students in recent years who call themselves "independent" rather than identifying with either major party. Contrary to widely publicized views, surveys indicate that *most college students are not radical*. The great majority of students reject far left or right political

[35] Kenneth P. Langton and M. Kent Jennings, "Political Socialization in the High School Civic Curriculum in the United States," *The American Political Science Review* 62 (Sept. 1968): 852–867.

[36] Langton, *Political Socialization*, pp. 115–116.

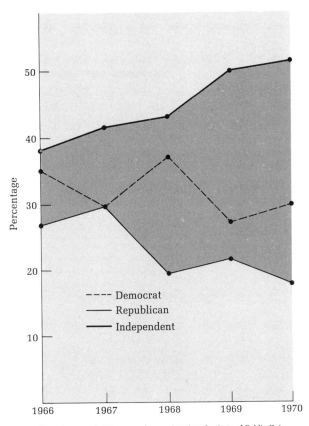

**FIGURE 6-5**
**Party Identification**
**of College Students, 1966–1970**

Source: From data reported in news releases, American Institute of Public Opinion (December 14, 1969, and February 14, 1971).

positions. Those who regard themselves as simply "left" outnumber those on the "right" by two to one, but most of the student population is in the middle of the road.[37] Only about one student in eleven classifies himself as far left or far right. Extremism for its own sake appeals to these students. Many students who think of themselves as on the far left or far right have favorable views of *all* such organizations as the Ku Klux Klan, the John Birch Society, the Students for a Democratic Society, the Black Panthers, and the Weathermen.[38] Finally, college students regard a variety of techniques, both direct and indirect, as effective ways of influencing government, but *most reject violence as ineffective* (see Table 6-4).

[37] News release, American Institute of Public Opinion (February 14, 1971).
[38] News release, American Institute of Public Opinion (February 7, 1971).

TABLE 6-4
Attitudes of College Students
toward Selected Political Tactics, 1970

Question: "To bring about real improvement in the problems facing the country, how effective do you feel each of the following is?"

| Tactic | Very effective | Somewhat effective | Not effective | Not sure |
|---|---|---|---|---|
| Writing letters or sending wires to public officials | 17% | 62% | 21% | |
| Visiting public officials in person | 29 | 60 | 10 | 1% |
| Demonstrating or protesting peacefully to influence the policies of elected officials | 22 | 63 | 14 | 1 |
| Demonstrating or protesting peacefully to bring about basic changes in the system | 18 | 56 | 24 | 2 |
| Resorting to violent tactics, if necessary, to bring about basic changes in the system | 11 | 21 | 63 | 5 |

Source: Compiled from data reported in Louis Harris and Associates, Inc., *The Harris Survey Yearbook of Public Opinion 1970* (New York: Louis Harris and Associates, 1971), p. 342.

SOCIAL GROUPS. When a person joins a group, he exposes himself to more norms and values than are normally represented in his immediate family. A child's *peer groups* (his circle of friends and people he considers to "like" him) are critical influences that affect his attitudes. A middle-class child often reinforces his middle-class norms and values first acquired in his family. Children raised in ghetto or poverty areas do not learn such middle-class attitudes; studies indicate that they grow up with negative attitudes toward political institutions and leaders.[39]

SECONDARY GROUPS. Voluntary associations and civic clubs also help to reinforce an individual's views because he usually joins groups with whose aims and attitudes he agrees. Frequently, however, he joins these groups because he wants to improve himself economically or socially. When groups enforce conformity to their norms and values, individuals are often reluctant to challenge the dominant views for fear of social ostracism. Generally, the individual adjusts his attitudes to others if he

[39] Herbert Hirsch, *Poverty and Politicization* (New York: Free Press, 1971).

feels strongly about being accepted as an equal and has a strong need to be liked, is frequently in personal contact with others, finds important issues discussed in the group, has no alternative way of gathering political information and defining political positions, and is swayed by the arguments of leading members of the group. If he belongs to groups that hold conflicting opinions on issues, he may respond to the cross-pressures by making a choice between groups, attempting to strike a compromise that will permit him to stay in all the conflicting groups, ignoring the issue in dispute, ignoring the conflict, or by withdrawing from all groups if he finds the controversy intolerable.

**Construction workers demonstrate their support for the Vietnam War. Employees who have opportunities to join in making decisions affecting their organization are frequent political participants as well.**

OCCUPATION. Your job influences your political attitudes in several ways. Work associates are a group that you want to join; the day-to-day functions of your job therefore exercise a powerful political influence by setting the agenda for political discussion. Jobs that require a great deal of interaction with the public (sales, advertising, and service occupations) are much more likely to bring the jobholder into contact with politics than are isolated occupations like farming. Some jobholders (civil servants and schoolteachers) are prohibited by law in some states from engaging in partisan politics.

As we saw in Chapter Five, those whose jobs bring opportunities to take part in decisions affecting an organization, a company, a union, or fellow workers — even though the participation may not be directly political — demonstrate favorably the usefulness of participation in civic affairs. Although such occupational influences come later in life than do the opportunities to take part in family or school affairs, they come precisely when the worker sees the connection between politics and his economic improvement.

RELIGION. Although more than 90 percent of the adult population identify themselves as either Protestant, Catholic, or Jewish, the number to actually go to church is much lower. Nonetheless, organized religion still is important in the political socialization of Americans. The dignity of the individual and the value of moral behavior are only two examples of politically relevant teaching by organized religion. On the other hand, religion may also reinforce a dogmatic attitude on some questions; a study of the relationship between Christian beliefs and anti-Semitism, based upon a random sample of the adult population, indicated a dogmatism that, if not tempered by religious liberalism, produced intolerant attitudes toward religious minorities such as the Jews.[40]

The conservative influence of many churches derives from absolutist doctrines that are not always congenial to democratic politics and lead to a preference for the status quo. Any social or political perspective, conservative or whatever, which characterizes a religious body, can affect the attitudes that members learn and influence their assessment of political issues. Evaluation of policies toward crime, the death penalty, alcoholism, gambling, divorce, birth control, abortion, communism, education, and numerous other matters is colored by religious convictions as well as other attitudes.

THE MASS MEDIA. Because they are a primary source of information about the world, the mass media affect a person's outlook. No longer is

[40] Charles Y. Glock and Rodney Stark, *Christian Beliefs and Anti-Semitism* (New York: Harper & Row, 1967).

Father Daniel Berrigan addresses
supporters following his release from
Danbury State Prison. To varying degrees,
religious attitudes influence
our assessment of political issues.

a citizen forced to accept a secondhand description of a battle by a war correspondent; his television set brings the war into his home, in vivid color. Awareness of the items on the current political agenda — a political campaign, a presidential trip to foreign lands, riots, threat of nuclear attack, hope of peace — comes from watching television, listening to "spot news" on the radio, scanning the headlines, or reading a favorite magazine.

How much socialization does this bombardment from the communications media achieve? *The mass media are symbolic models from which children acquire political beliefs and feelings.* In rural and urban poverty areas, the media are more important models for children to follow politically than parents, peers, or teachers. And, even in middle-class families, the mass media serve as "parents" in transmitting attitudes toward political figures, war, political candidates, and the use of violence in obtaining goals.[41]

By and large, *the mass media affect political socialization in shaping political expectations, but they do not stimulate many people to take an active part in politics.* Preparing for a major news event such as a national political convention, a presidential election, or a landing on the

[41] Bradley S. Greenberg and Brenda Dervin, *Use of the Mass Media by the Urban Poor* (New York: Praeger, 1971); Gary C. Byrne, "Mass Media and Political Socialization of Children and Pre-Adults," *Journalism Quarterly* 46 (Spring 1969), 140–141; June E. Foster, "Father Images: Television and Ideal," *Journal of Marriage and the Family* 26 (Aug. 1964): 353–355; Neil Hollander, "Adolescents and the War: The Sources of Socialization," *Journalism Quarterly* 48 (Autumn 1971): 472–479; Steven H. Chaffee et al., "Mass Media and Political Socialization," *Journalism Quarterly* 47 (Winter 1970): 647–659.

moon, the news media give us a background against which we expect events to occur. In viewing, hearing, or reading what happens, we interpret events from the perspective provided by the media. Rarely do we break out of the context within which the media places us, so that we can reach independent interpretations.

Television is the latest and probably the most powerful instrument for shaping political socialization and Americans. If television influences our notions of the "way things are" (or, far more accurately, the way news commentators think the mass public wants to think things are), then our view of the world will be only as clear as the presentation of politics on television. But politics is scarcely as important as professional and collegiate sports, women's fashions, advice to the lovelorn, or simple fantasy in television coverage. Time and space limitations of the electronic and printed media reduce coverage of politics to superficiality and accent sensational events and controversial personalities rather than subtle details in political issues. Despite claims of objectivity, the content of the news media — notably of network nightly news programs — reveals parti-

**President Nixon responds to a question at a televised news conference. As a primary source of information about the world, television shapes a person's political awareness.**

san bias.[42] Yet even though the depiction of politics is frequently incomplete and romanticized, the mass media, notably television, provide standards, norms, and values in socialization.

summary

Although significant and politically relevant attitudes (images of the community and its leaders, party loyalty, religious preference, political awareness) are acquired early in life, *the child is not the sole father of the political man.* Changes in attitude occur, and no person is destined to continue through life viewing government in ways dictated in his youth. *Attitudes do not dictate political opinions;* they are but one element in the formation of opinions that include diverse and frequently contradictory appeals from leaders as well as the personal predispositions of followers. Attitudes are tendencies to action but action is not inevitable.

## representing political opinions

By expressing political opinions, the most widespread form of political participation in our society, citizens let public officials know what is on their minds. However, *expressed opinions do not always represent interest conflicts accurately.* Several reasons lie behind this distortion.

*Most political opinions expressed by individuals do not represent social conflicts nor are they intended to influence policymaking;* instead, *they represent private, personal interests flowing from the desire to relate to other people and to relieve inner tensions.* Expressed opinions often have little to do with the subtleties of the issues. Opinions are uninformed; people *choose* to be ignorant about most political matters and to be informed about only a few. The indifferent majority generally pays marginal or peripheral attention to politics. Is it because Americans are basically apathetic, passive, insensitive people who do not want to govern themselves? We think not. Too often those who castigate citizens for their political apathy forget that expressing *informed opinions about politics is hard work.* It is hard because it takes time and effort to gather and understand relevant facts about issues, especially when significant details are not readily available in the news. It takes time and energy away from our private life to think about public issues, perhaps sacrificing financial gains, leisure activities, and more rewarding ven-

[42] Edith Efron, *The News Twisters* (Los Angeles, Calif.: Nash, 1971).

tures. And, it is threatening. It takes courage to open our minds to information that clashes with our attitudes and is at odds with our current, secure understanding of things; it takes courage to pronounce informed views if these antagonize our friends; it takes courage to assimilate significant facts that muddy clear-cut alternatives with confusing ambiguity.

A person normally learns politically relevant attitudes before he acquires the political information and knowledge that support them. His attitudes color his perception of government and his political judgment. Learned *political attitudes can be a source of distortion in conflict representation.* We know that the politically relevant attitudes American children learn are strongly influenced by family, schools, and peer groups. For the most part these childhood attitudes are *positive acceptance* of the community, government, authority figures, and middle-class values as they are. The child acquires a sense that he should influence policymaking, but primarily in passive ways — by voting, by affiliating with political parties, and by being interested in politics. He learns that politics involves *individual* effort (loyalty, obligation, responsibility), but he learns little about *organized* influence, how he can join with others to take part in groups. Small wonder that he retires to the relative peace of political indifference, responding to political events with his preferences for the status quo and individual action and perhaps condemning those who dissent from the way things are and organize to change it.

Political socialization helps distort conflict representation in another way. *Children are exposed not only to an overemphasis upon individual ways of expressing opinions; they may fail to learn that it is worthwhile even to do so.* Family background, education, and occupation encourage some citizens to take part in politics, but discourage many others. Children whose parents insisted upon conformity, docility, obedience, and punishment; the young who do not go beyond high school; the ghetto black; the impoverished in both urban and rural America; the worker with no control over his destiny — these are the types of people who grow into adulthood with little interest and faith in politics and, equally important, with little respect for their own political efficacy. When opinions are counted by policymakers, these people's ideas probably will not even have been expressed.

*Political leaders influence opinions that people express through conflict representation by handpicking the issues stimulating personal attitudes and interests.* Seeking support for themselves and their causes, political leaders are selective in choosing issues and do not always choose those of deepest interest to citizens. People may feel uneasy about rising rates of divorce, suicide, or highway fatalities, but political leaders must emphasize these issues first, before the public can respond.

Once expressed, opinions are funneled into many channels (including elections, newspaper editorials, party platforms, group stands, politicians' speeches, and opinion surveys by the dozen ranging from haphazard guesses to systematic samplings), where *it is easy to misinterpret the direction and intensity of political views.* Distinguishing between the opinions of indifferent majorities and informed minorities, measuring them, and deciding which (if any) deserve greater weight is difficult. Even when political opinions are expressed, there is no assurance that all will be considered or that they will be effective in influencing policy.

Representing conflict by political opinions is highly selective work that covers many conflicts but overlooks or ignores many others, actual and potential. Expressing political opinions makes up much of conflict representation, but it does not involve everybody. Everyone is not called upon for opinions, given opportunity or resources to express opinions, or even wants to express opinions, particularly informed ones. *The political opinions that are voiced are only imperfectly drawn samples of all the underlying attitudes and interests on issues confronting the community.*

Imperfect though it seems in composing an accurate picture of diverse social interests in this nation, however, the means by which political opinions are expressed to policymakers is a rich source of political consensus. American loyalties breed disagreements: they learn to be loyal to some groups and critical of others; they learn partisan loyalties that both unite and divide them; they grow acutely aware of racial and ethnic differences; and they acquire religious sentiments that are sometimes tolerant, sometimes bigoted. Can these loyalties be so intense and divisive that they endanger community consensus? It is possible, but traditionally our political institutions have tried to moderate these disputes. Americans, of many races, religions, generations, and political outlooks often are suspicious and intolerant of dissenters; rival interests are generally unwilling to compromise. But here the sense of loyalty to "America," to its political institutions (the Constitution, President, Congress, and courts), major political parties, and "rules of the game" — acquired by political socialization in childhood — is vital. *Loyalty promotes a politics of compromise and conciliation that permits a peaceful conflict of interests.* But, if the institutional mechanisms fail to respond to groups trying to advance their interests (particularly new groups such as the young or impoverished), or if they think the mechanisms are useless in the struggle, then *the thin consensus provided by constitutional loyalties may vanish and violent conflict may follow.* For the political consensus to persevere, support for constitutional mechanisms must come from both opinion holders and opinion leaders. Just how do opinion leaders fit into conflict representation?

Several brief paperback books introduce the role personal opinions play in politics. One of the best is Robert Lane and David O. Sears, *Public Opinion* (Englewood Cliffs, N.J.: Prentice-Hall, 1964). James N. Rosenau presents a view of how opinions are linked to policies in his *Public Opinion and Foreign Policy* (New York: Random House, 1961). Still very useful is Walter Lippmann's classic work, *Public Opinion,* first published in 1922 and now available in several editions. Two introductory texts in clothbound editions that are useful are V. O. Key, Jr., *Public Opinion and American Democracy* (New York: Alfred A. Knopf, 1961) and Bernard Hennessy, *Public Opinion,* 2nd ed. (Belmont, Calif.: Duxbury Press, 1970). The most informative pieces on political opinion are in article form and are reprinted in current anthologies. See Edward C. Dreyer and Walter A. Rosenbaum, eds., *Political Opinion and Behavior* (Belmont, Calif.: Duxbury Press, 1970); Dan Nimmo and Charles M. Bonjean, eds., *Political Attitudes and Public Opinion* (New York: David McKay, 1972); and Norman R. Luttbeg, *Public Opinion and Public Policy* (Homewood, Ill.: Dorsey Press, 1968).

The contrast between the opinions of attentive minorities and apathetic majorities is developed in Donald J. Devine, *The Attentive Public* (Chicago: Rand McNally, 1970). See also Gabriel A. Almond, *The American People and Foreign Policy* (New York: Praeger, 1960). Summaries of opinion surveys of American views on a variety of issues are regularly published in *Public Opinion Quarterly.*

How opinions serve people who hold them is reviewed in M. Brewster Smith et al., *Opinions and Personality* (New York: John Wiley, Science Editions, 1956). One should also read Kenneth E. Boulding's excellent little book, *The Image* (Ann Arbor, Mich.: University of Michigan Press, Paperback Edition, 1961). For a review of how personality influences attitudes and opinions see Fred I. Greenstein, *Personality and Politics* (Chicago: Markham, 1969). Also noteworthy are Robert E. Lane, *Political Thinking and Consciousness* (Chicago: Markham, 1969) and Milton Rokeach, *The Open and Closed Mind* (New York: Basic Books, 1960).

Political scientists' growing interest in how people acquire politically relevant attitudes and opinions is reflected in these summaries: Herbert Hyman, *Political Socialization,* rev. ed. (New York: Free Press, 1969); Richard Dawson and Kenneth Prewitt, *Political Socialization* (Boston: Little, Brown, 1969); and Kenneth P. Langton, *Political Socialization* (New York: Oxford University Press, 1969). Results of research projects include Fred I. Greenstein, *Children and Politics* (New Haven, Conn.: Yale University Press, 1965); David Easton and Jack Dennis, *Children in the Political System* (New York: McGraw-Hill, 1969); Robert D. Hess and Judith V. Torney, *The Development of Political Attitudes in Children* (Garden City, N.Y.: Doubleday, Anchor Edition, 1967); Herbert Hirsch, *Poverty and Politicization* (New York: Free Press, 1971) and Charles F. Andrian, *Children and Civic Awareness* (Columbus, Ohio: Charles E. Merrill, 1971). Among the anthologies of relevant articles are Roberta Sigel, ed., *Learning About Politics* (New York: Random House, 1970) and Norman Adler and Charles Harrington, eds., *The Learning of Political Behavior* (New York: Scott, Foresman, 1970).

# exercising
# political leadership

The distinction between leaders and followers is fundamental to government. In the regulation of social conflict, not everyone can be a regulator. As molders of opinion, political leaders take part in conflict representation; as makers of policy, they contribute to conflict resolution. We will explore the relationships between opinion leaders and opinion holders, specifically examining leadership in conflict representation, public officials as leaders, and how political leaders influence opinions.

## leadership in conflict representation

Political leaders publicize social disputes — and often generate them as well — by getting people to take sides in disagreements over what goals to seek and how to achieve them. How do they represent conflicts in American politics? The attributes of political leadership, the types of political leaders, and how well they represent the social composition of those they lead are facts that will help answer that question.

## what is political leadership?

*Leadership means mobilizing and coordinating the activities of others in pursuing collective goals.* Political leadership has three major attributes: reciprocity, a specific setting, and influence.[1]

[1] See Murray Edelman, *The Symbolic Uses of Politics* (Urbana, Ill.: University of Illinois Press, 1964), chap. 4.

RECIPROCITY. The interested minority governs a nation; the indifferent majority responds to leadership out of habit, conviction, fear, or the hope of personal gain. Yet *reciprocity is crucial to political leadership*. Leaders once were thought to induce others to follow them by their superior traits: appearance, intelligence, knowledge, morals, or skills. Social scientists now emphasize a reciprocal relationship in which the leader's options are defined by the demands and needs of his followers. Followers bestow obedience and thereby legitimacy upon their leaders and, in exchange, the leaders act on their responsibility to govern, to humanize governance, and to maintain social order. Mutual obligations link leaders and followers.

By making citizens feel that someone cares and projecting distinctive personalities in public statements, *political leaders inject humanity into an apparently impersonal government*. Franklin Roosevelt's fireside chats, Harry Truman's "give 'em hell" oratory, Lyndon Johnson's homilies about boyhood on the Pedernales River in Texas, and Richard Nixon's talk of football days in college, add the human touch to politics. Faith in presidential leadership, vital in national crises, is made by impressions of the leader's personal qualities as well as appraisal of his proposals.

By their individual styles, leaders get close to — form a human relationship with — followers. Style is simply those distinctive ways of behaving that their followers associate with them: the *demagogue* plays upon his followers' fears, frustrations, and illusions (Senator Joseph McCarthy rose to national prominence in the 1950s by investigating alleged Communist influence at "high levels of government"); the *democratic* leader appeals to the people's positive aspirations and to their desire for self-respect and well-being by consulting with them on public matters; a *charismatic* leader elicits passionate dedication from his followers by forging a deep emotional bond; the *traditional* leader tries to make his policies look legitimate by showing that they conform to his followers' customs. A leader frequently combines or alternates styles. Richard Nixon, seeking support for his Vietnam policies, appealed to American fears of a Communist takeover of all Southeast Asia, but he also beckoned to the American tradition of nonaggression and to Americans' democratic aspirations by emphasizing South Vietnam's right to self-determination.

SETTING. Circumstances mold the relationship between a leader and his followers. Presidential influence is easiest to gain in times of crisis — in war, during economic depressions, or when public confidence is shaken. *Effective political leadership requires its own brand of skills.* Some of those who have taken on important public posts with limited political experience have found it hard to adjust to government service

Spokesman for the United Farm Workers,
Cesar Chavez. A leader's options are
largely defined by the needs of his followers.

where constitutional restraints limit their activities and where their behavior faces public disclosure and criticism. The characteristics they
bring to their political jobs matter less than their ability to adapt appro-
priately to the task, its setting, and the mood of their followers.

INFLUENCE. A political leader exerts influence by his power to shape
opinion. Opinions are formed when citizens respond to stimuli — appeals, issues, or whatever (see Chapter Six). The leader's task is
to apply those stimuli to his followers in a way that will induce them
to respond favorably to him and his goals. When President Nixon announced his freeze on wages, prices, and rents as one means of curbing
inflation by a televised appeal for a positive consensus, according to
opinion surveys he received it — 73 percent of Americans were shown
to approve of his policy.[2]

[2] News release, *The Harris Survey* (September 6, 1971).

In releasing the Pentagon Papers, Daniel Ellsberg appealed to a national sense of guilt. The ensuing controversy encouraged people to take sides on both goals and means regarding the Vietnam War.

But leaders must also adjust to prevailing opinions when it is in their interest. President Nixon, in keeping with widespread opposition to busing of students to promote racial integration (polls indicated three-fourths of Americans opposed), promised a policy that would end busing.[3] Leadership implies a mutual adjustment between leaders and followers, but *in influencing opinions, the leader normally modifies the views of his followers to conform to his own interests.*

People will take part in actions that bring conflicts to the attention of policymakers when they have the opportunity, the resources, and the desire to do so. These conditions are most likely to be fulfilled for those in positions of formal authority, or in responsible positions in private organizations, or for those who enjoy the trust of their peers. Each position contributes to a different kind of political leadership.

Those who exercise leadership because they occupy positions of formal authority are called *public officials.* The prominence of their posts ensures publicity for their official actions and works, giving them a strategic advantage for influencing opinions. Individuals who exercise leadership because they have important jobs in large, private organi-

[3] News release, American Institute of Public Opinion (November 1, 1971).

208

zations we refer to as *group leaders,* such as figures in political parties; presidents of farm organizations, large corporations, and labor unions; lobbyists; and television commentators or newspaper columnists. *Personal leaders* have influence because fellow citizens trust them and respect their political knowledge. Without official position in either the government or private organizations, they are likely to be influential only in their immediate environment.[4]

*How do the three types of political leaders differ from nonleaders?* Naturally, leaders are more active politically; they are more committed to democratic ideals, somewhat more ideological in outlook, and more partisan. They communicate in a give-and-take way with one another as leaders, but "pass the word" down to their followers more often than they listen to followers' ideas. Political leaders' opinions are more intense and stable than those of their followers: their opinions are better informed and involve political events and issues rather than simply personalities. Finally, leaders find material issues more meaningful than symbolic ones.[5]

## social characteristics of political leaders

Social background is only one clue, and not an infallible one — to the interests leaders represent. One antipluralist trend in America is the development of elitist rule (see Chapter 1): a business-scientific-technological elite, in alliance with public officials, makes policy in its own special interests. Elitist theories of politics postulate that similar background welds the elite into a dominant group. If so, meaningful conflict representation is not possible. Public disputes between elites — such as electoral campaigns — become nothing more than a façade; and "political power, properly so called, is merely the organized power of one class for oppressing another."[6] Is this true of American political leadership?

PUBLIC OFFICIALS. Most public officials in America are members of the middle and upper classes. Most have more formal education than the average American; they are professionally trained, and many have a legal background. Normally they come from families with better than average socioeconomic status. Public officials are typically male, native-born,

---

[4] See Elihu Katz and Paul F. Lazarsfeld, *Personal Influence* (Glencoe, Ill.: Free Press, 1955).

[5] *Lewis A. Froman, Jr., People and Politics* (Englewood Cliffs, N.J.: Prentice-Hall, 1962), pp. 38–48.

[6] Karl Marx and Friedrich Engels, *The Communist Manifesto,* Samuel H. Beer, ed. (New York: Appleton-Century-Crofts, 1955).

white, Protestant, and fifty to sixty years old.[7] The social backgrounds
of our public officials have not been typical of Americans as a whole.

GROUP LEADERS. Group leaders are more representative of the American community than are public officials. The local leaders of our two
major parties have varied backgrounds highly representative of the social
and economic characteristics of their locality. In the early 1960s, Detroit's
Democratic leadership was disproportionately composed of the Irish,
business and professional groups, and unorganized labor; while Republican leadership overrepresented business and managerial groups, predominantly white labor unions, and blacks.[8]

Many minorities inadequately represented among public officials develop spokesmen within their own associations. Black leaders represent
a variety of racial points of view in such organizations as the National
Association for the Advancement of Colored People, the Southern Christian Leadership Conference, the Urban League, the Black Panthers, and
the Black Muslims. Social characteristics of American black leaders do
not differ markedly from those of leaders in the larger community. However, *black* women and *young* males are more often leaders in black
politics than white women and young males in the larger community.[9]

Underprivileged, indifferent, or passive Americans are not represented
fully or equally by group leadership. More militant spokesmen have
charged older black organizations with being too modest in their demands and not representing oppressed blacks seeking "Black Power."

PERSONAL LEADERS. Personal leaders who influence the opinions of
peers — friends, colleagues, and neighbors — are perhaps most generally
representative, although still not fully so. They have many occupations.
Social class differentiates even personal leaders, however. Those who
have more formal education and those most likely to be in professional
or managerial positions are also more likely to be personal leaders. Because formal education builds knowledge, well-educated citizens are
often consulted for information and advice in political affairs. People
generally are more likely to be influenced by those whose social status
is the same as or higher than their own than by those with lower status.

By definition, *personal leaders influence opinions only within their*

[7] Wendell Bell et al., *Public Leadership* (San Francisco: Chandler, 1961); Donald R.
Matthews, *The Social Background of Political Decision-Makers* (Garden City, N.Y.: Doubleday, 1954); Charles O. Jones, *Every Second Year* (Washington, D.C.: Brookings Institution,
1967).

[8] Samuel J. Eldersveld, *Political Parties* (Chicago: Rand McNally, 1964), chap. 4.

[9] Norval D. Glenn and Charles M. Bonjean, eds., *Blacks in the United States*, Part 1 (San
Francisco: Chandler, 1969).

Speaking for the AFL–CIO, George Meany declared the independence of his organization from both political parties in the 1972 national election. Group leaders frequently modify the views of their constituents to conform to their own interests.

*immediate group.* Women influence other women more than they do men, Protestants influence Protestants, and so on. People rely on those of the same age for political counseling. Once in a while younger persons go to older persons for political advice, but rarely does the reverse happen: "Youth seems to have much more respect for elders' opinions than the elders do for youth's."[10] Student discord in the late 1960s and early 1970s was an exception; many issues voiced by militant students later were debated by their elders — morality of the war in Vietnam, extension of the franchise to eighteen-year-olds, reform of the selective service system, ecology issues, and others.

[10] Bernard Berelson et al., *Voting* (Chicago: University of Chicago Press, 1954), p. 104.

A GOVERNING ELITE? The middle and upper classes occupy most leadership positions in American politics. Social advantage makes it easier to pursue a political career and devote oneself to public service as an avocation. High social status, high income, a college education, and politically related occupations make it easier to obtain "coin of the political realm" — money, social contacts, experience in dealing with people, spare time for politics, public esteem, and a reputation for success in all endeavors.

Because of such tendencies, some observers have argued that America is governed by an economic elite. Their argument is that a group of entrenched, modern aristocrats — labeled variously as a "ruling elite," a "power elite," an "establishment," a "corporate elite," or an "invisible government" control the President, Congress, the bureaucracy, and the judiciary.[11] *That more affluent economic interests directly affect policymaking is unquestionable. It cannot be proven, however, that an elite rules the community in its own interest.* The difference is great between constructing a statistical profile of the people who exert political leadership and proving that political power rests with one class united by a common interest and coordinated by a functioning directorate that dictates policies to both elective and appointive officials.[12]

Although American political leaders are similar in social characteristics, their common interests are not strong enough to create a governing class. Leaders of corporations do have a common interest in obtaining preferential tax policies or policies regulating labor unions, but the *specifics* of such policies generate disagreement among business leaders. The interests represented by corporate managers, bank presidents, bond lawyers, and others are not always the same, despite general agreement that capitalism is the preferred way of ordering the economy. These disputes end up being resolved by the disputants, union leaders, popularly elected Congressmen, and officials in regulatory agencies. Faced with conflict among themselves and with others over specific policies, economic leaders are not in a position to impose their views on policymakers.

The disproportion of upper-class persons in the leadership suggests government by the affluent even if affluent groups do differ over policy matters. Whether one believes there is an affluent elite — pluralist and divided though it may be — depends in part upon one's perspective. The

[11] For example, see G. William Domhoff, *Who Rules America?* (Englewood Cliffs, N.J.: Prentice-Hall, 1967); C. Wright Mills, *The Power Elite* (New York: Oxford University Press, 1957); and Richard Rovere, *The American Establishment* (New York: Harcourt, Brace, 1961).

[12] See Arnold M. Rose, *The Power Structure: Political Process in American Life* (New York: Oxford University Press, 1967); Grant McConnell, *Private Power and American Democracy* (New York: Alfred A. Knopf, 1966).

black or Mexican-American, the poverty-stricken of all ethnic backgrounds, alienated youth, consumers weary of paying exorbitant prices for poor quality products, the low-income worker who has reached the breaking point on taxes, and many others feel that government is not responsive to their needs. Government certainly seems to them to be run by the affluent. But things are not as bad as they could be.

The relatively large size of the middle class (compared to the upper and lower classes) reduces, though it does not prevent, sharp cleavages between the wealthy and the impoverished. The American community has been able to adjust the most serious economic disputes between classes. The adjustment so urgently needed today was not brought on by a reactionary governing elite refusing to adjust to change but by (1) *sharp conflicts within all classes over solutions,* (2) *general satisfaction with the status quo,* and (3) *apathy among middle-class Americans about things political.*

American political institutions frequently make it difficult to stimulate unified action and to coordinate conflicting views. The authority to generate solutions to pressing social problems is scattered among levels of government and political agencies. The *federal arrangement* divides authority among local, state, and federal jurisdictions, and these governments often battle over the revenue to support programs that alleviate social injustice (states and cities compete for federal funds to operate antipoverty programs). Moreover, *separation of powers* scatters authority among congressional committees and bureaucratic agencies that compete for support among special clienteles, affluent or not.

To acquire mass support, even elites must broaden their appeals and adjust to the diversity of American political opinion. *The votes of the affluent will not alone elect candidates, although the affluent are the most likely to vote.*

The quest for social justice in the 1960s and 1970s has gotten somewhere. Tangible gains have been made in advancing racial equality by the civil rights movement; urban majorities have more influence because of legislative redistricting; voting rights have been broadened by legislation and constitutional amendment; the consumer has greater protection because of pricing and packaging regulations, automobile safety legislation, or banning of harmful nonprescription drugs; and various programs have helped in the struggle against poverty. *Much is left to be done —* in prison and welfare reform, public education, and countless other areas. Today's controversy is *how* it can be done, not *whether* it should be done.

One side says the defects in our society can be corrected only at a slow, orderly pace, avoiding unrealistic hopes for massive spending of funds that simply are not available. Another feels that we must reorder our priorities, turning the money we have away from space exploration and military commitments and into social reform. Between these views are others that provide the issues for political leaders to deal with in the 1970s — for instance, whether the federal government should share its tax revenues with states, so they can assume responsibility for correcting social evils. Progress in alleviating social ills suggests that government can respond to interests other than those of the affluent. But, so much remains to be done that we must question the pace of reform and whether future progress will dispel the notion that America is governed by an affluent elite.

We cannot yet judge whether America is run by a governing elite. We suggest that *political leadership is a deck stacked in favor of some social groups, but their control is hardly absolute.*

## public officials as political leaders

Many group and personal leaders take part in conflict representation, but public officials are the most visible of our political leaders. We know their social characteristics. How is our idea of these officials shaped and how does their recruitment shape their leadership?

### what do we think of our public officials?

A political leader's *influence* is fed by the esteem he inspires in his followers. His *reputation* is affected by his engagement in a political enterprise, the position he holds, the decisions he makes, and his ability to satisfy his followers' demands. Public officials as well as other political leaders are equally subject to what we think of them; that is, upon a *personal dimension of the community* as well as upon the social dimension in their backgrounds.

The American attitude toward politicians and politics is ambivalent. Although politics seems to be gaining in prestige, we generally think less of public service than careers in business, the military, the church, or even sports. American political folklore has led to a distrust of political power and support for "the less government, the better." Americans, then, do not completely trust governing officials.

Confidence in them varies with the governmental position occupied. *The office of the presidency is respected in its own right;* anyone assuming the office is heir to a long tradition of public devotion. *Respect for the office, however, does not imply approval of the incumbent through-out his term.* As Figure 7-1 illustrates, of the presidents in the last forty years, at one time two-thirds of the public approved of their conduct in presidential office. That proportion during their tenure declined to a low of 23 percent for Truman and 35 percent for Johnson. Through 1972, approval for President Nixon's presidential conduct ranged from 48 percent to 68 percent. Nixon's highest popularity came in 1969 immediately after his speech announcing gradual withdrawals of American forces from Vietnam, again in the same year following America's successful landing of men on the moon, and in 1972 following his return from a visit to the People's Republic of China. His low point in popular esteem came in midsummer of 1971, when inflation and unemployment were high.

The variations in Nixon's popularity illustrate the expected fluctuations in public approval of presidential conduct. First, approval of a newly elected President usually is high but declines gradually as the interests that comprised his winning coalition grow critical of his failure to meet their demands. Second, as his tenure continues, his popular support is colored by partisanship — Democrats approve of the conduct of a Democratic President, but disapprove of a Republican, and vice versa.

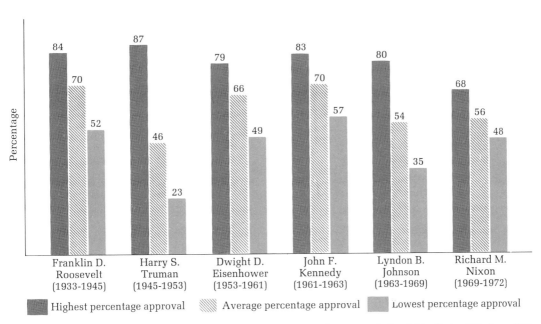

Source: News releases, American Institute of Public Opinion (July 10, 1971, Dec. 27, 1971); John M. Fenton, *In Your Opinion* (Boston: Little, Brown, 1960).

FIGURE 7-1
**Presidential Popularity, 1933–1972**

Third, short-term boosts in presidential popularity follow international crises — as when President Kennedy dealt with the removal of Soviet missiles from Cuba in 1962 — or national achievement, such as the moon landing. Fourth, presidential popularity is lowered by continuing economic problems (recession, unemployment, inflation) and continuing involvement in seemingly unending wars, as in Korea in the Truman era.[13]

*Americans also generally express approval of appointive federal executives* (secretaries and heads of Cabinet-level departments, heads of independent agencies and commissions, presidential staff aides, and various kinds of advisers).[14] *The popular evaluation of Congress is less positive.* Annual surveys of political opinion in the 1960s were undertaken to determine how Americans rate "the job Congress has done" each year. A general drop in esteem for Congress showed up, particularly since 1965. By the close of the decade, only 34 percent of those sampled expressed favorable views of Congress in contrast to 71 percent in 1965.[15] *The general evaluation of the Supreme Court is more favorable than that of Congress,* although here also judgment of the institution is colored by the respondent's partisanship and his current feeling about the decisions of the justices.

Leadership images thus derive from the policies public officials pursue as well as from the offices they hold. Southern Democrats prior to 1954 agreed with the rest of the country in their support for the Supreme Court, but the decisions prohibiting school desegregation prompted a quick decline in the confidence expressed by southerners. Further, the official's choice of a leadership role and his avoidance of a confusion of roles have significant impact upon his popular esteem. Does a President see himself as a passive broker of political forces or an aggressive initiator of policies? If he acts nonpartisan, does he assign many of the necessary partisan activities to his subordinates (as Eisenhower and Nixon did) or does he confuse the two, with mixed effects (as Truman did)?

## recruiting public officials

Performance in conflict representation depends on social background and popular esteem but also on how officials are selected for leadership from the community, introduced to political office, and trained to govern.

---

[13] John E. Mueller, "Presidential Popularity from Truman to Johnson," *The American Political Science Review* 64 (March 1970): 18–34.

[14] Franklin P. Kilpatrick et al., *The Image of the Federal Service* (Washington, D.C.: Brookings Institution, 1964).

[15] Louis Harris and Associates, *The Harris Survey Yearbook of Public Opinion 1970* (New York; Louis Harris and Associates, 1971), p. 21; News release, *The Harris Survey* (January 22, 1968).

We call this *political recruitment.* It reflects the community's political and constitutional influence upon political leadership.

By specifying the political offices, both elective and appointive, which are available, the Constitution and its supporting legislation influence political leadership: they structure the opportunities and incentives open to politically ambitious men. The most prestigious political offices are at the federal level or in the largest states; those least desirable for the ambitious politician are at the local level (mayoralties of large cities are the exception).

Career advancement is clearly patterned; it flows from state office to Congress or the presidency.[16] Two-thirds of recent officeholders in the presidency and the top levels of the national bureaucracy held some state office before attaining a national position. The general movement is from state legislature to state governor, to the Senate, or from the House of Representatives to the Senate.

Political recruitment then is semihierarchical. Local officials who aspire to higher elective political office must be particularly attentive to the demands made upon them by the electorate and must influence the opinions of their constituents. Those aiming for national appointive office must build reputations as able local or state administrators or as judicial officers; usually they must also ally themselves with a rising political star. As one moves up the electoral ladder, constituencies become larger and the rewards of office, especially in status, increase. The higher the office the ambitious politician seeks, the more critical it is that he be able to lead political opinions, a subject to which we now turn.

## leading political opinions

A successful politician is able to influence the opinions of those who follow him. Americans, however, are really not very interested in politics. A politician's chances of getting his followers' attention is enhanced if he is skilled at presenting important issues as symbolic appeals, skillful at political campaigning, and can maintain good communications with those who follow him.

### symbolic persuasion in politics

Of all the nations, the United States selects the greatest number of its public officials by election. Even political leaders in appointive federal positions – Cabinet members, agency heads, ambassadors, judges – are

---

[16] For empirical evidence relating political careers to political structure, see Joseph A. Schlesinger, *Ambition and Politics* (Chicago: Rand McNally, 1966).

In 1968, Eugene McCarthy campaigned largely on the peace issue. His candidacy
mobilized others, notably youth, in support of that cause.

chosen by elected leaders and are thus affected by the electoral process.
The constitutional requirement that officials must win elections to obtain
and retain office generally means that *politicians emphasize persuasion
and minimize coercion in exercising leadership in conflict representation as they seek to influence the opinions of those who follow
them.*

Coercion and persuasion are different, albeit overlapping, forms of
influence. *Coercion* describes the reprisals used to get people to do what
they would prefer not to do; *persuasion* means promising benefits and
using minimal threats of deprivation to achieve consent. In reality, of
course, coercive and persuasive tactics are mingled in American politics;
some voters have been intimidated or kept from the polls; others are
promised rewards such as lower taxes if they vote as specified. Although

218

they occasionally revert to coercive tactics, political leaders generally prefer to gain influence by persuasion because they prefer active consent to reluctant compliance.

*To persuade followers, a leader manipulates appropriate symbols in varying political contexts, which we call symbolic persuasion.* The successful political leader can identify himself with popular causes (anticommunism, a balanced budget, peace, and prosperity); his goal is to convert approval of the cause into support for himself. Similarly, the effort to devise succinct slogans which give expression to favored symbols is commonplace in presidential politics, although the memorable successes are few. "Get America moving again" was John Kennedy's slogan in 1960; "the war on poverty" and "the Great Society" were slogans of Lyndon Johnson in 1964; and "bring us together" was Richard Nixon's contribution in 1968. President Eisenhower got his popularity from his reputation as a war hero, but he also symbolized an American preference for nonpartisanship. Popular ambivalence about politics apparently makes Americans receptive to candidates who seem to rise above politics.

Political leaders employ symbolic persuasion to project qualities they think their followers will find attractive: *the sum total of the qualities that followers see in a leader constitute his image.*

The leader's image has two origins. First are the impressions followers have of his ability to perform: his performance as a *public official* (his training, experience, philosophy, policies) and as a *politician* (connections among party members, relationships with influential people). Second is the impression he gives of his *political style,* which is made up of his personal qualities (appearance, personality, honesty, integrity) and rhetorical skill as a public speaker, as a television performer, and as a man who is able to inspire mass confidence.

Leaders strive to manipulate the images followers have of them by carefully controlling the *expressions* they give off as leaders.[17] Some techniques of image management are easy to recognize in the public performances of political leaders.[18]

DRAMATIC ENCOUNTER. It is difficult for political leaders to avoid controversy; indeed, their part in influencing and representing conflicting opinions makes them leaders. Confronting controversy, however, they must dramatize their command of every situation. President Nixon's freeze on wages, prices, and rents, meant to stabilize the economy, was opposed by organized labor. Rather than avoid the conflict, Nixon con-

---

[17] Erving Goffman, *The Presentation of Self in Everyday Life* (Garden City, N.Y.: Doubleday, Anchor Books, 1959).

[18] For an account of other techniques, see Orrin E. Klapp, *Symbolic Leaders* (Chicago: Aldine, 1964).

fronted members of the American Federation of Labor–Congress of Industrial Organizations (AFL–CIO) in addressing their national convention and reaffirming his policies. His reception by union members was
sometimes cold, sometimes tumultuous, but he impressed his nonlabor
supporters with his intention to enforce his economic policies regardless
of the strident demands of special interests. His critics said he had culti-
vated such an encounter precisely to leave that impression.

CONTROLLED AMBIGUITY. In earlier days, it was possible for a politician
to take differing, even contradictory, stands on public issues before competing interests in widely scattered parts of the country. Mass communication, however, has made it difficult for a leader to tailor his stands
to suit all special interests. Yet take a stand he must. To avoid alienating
followers, the stand is frequently ambiguous, committing the leader to
no specific policies but indicating that he is "concerned," is "studying the
issue," and shortly will have a "plan." Returning from his trip to the
People's Republic of China in 1972, President Nixon encountered two
criticisms. One side maintained that the trip was an effort on Nixon's part
to call attention to himself and curry public favor and that it accomplished no substantial alteration in opposing policies of the United States
and China. The other side accused him of turning his back on the policy
of opposing communism everywhere in the world and of selling out our
traditional allies, the nationalist Chinese on Taiwan. Nixon's report on
his China trip, both to congressional leaders and to the public, was ap-
propriately ambiguous. He stated that the trip was only a first *necessary*
step to "bridge the gap" in relations with China and that American military forces would not be removed from Taiwan until, in keeping with
the "Nixon Doctrine" of decreasing military commitments, a demon-
strable "relaxation of tensions came about." In short, *something* had been
changed by the trip, but *what* was left unclear.

CONFORMING TO EXPECTATIONS. People expect things of their leaders
and their expectations often seem contradictory. Leaders must be strong-
willed but flexible, decisive but not rash, coolly efficient yet human. The
appropriate posture is a precarious balance of qualities. Senator Edmund
Muskie of Maine discovered this in seeking the Democratic presidential
nomination in 1972. Campaigning in New Hampshire, Muskie openly
challenged a newspaper publisher who had described Muskie as alleg-
edly making fun of Americans of French-Canadian extraction and who
had criticized the Senator's wife. This dramatic encounter happened on
the front steps of the publisher's offices. Muskie began his charges in firm,
calm language, but then lapsed into anger and was unable to continue.
Opinion soundings found that many New Englanders were pleased to see
this display of the "human" side of Muskie and approved of his posture;

but Americans in western states, who had seen Muskie's performance on televised newscasts, were astonished at such a display of "weakness" in a man who wanted to be President.

## the political campaign:
## exercise in symbolic leadership

We can get a better picture of how political leaders try to influence opinions, particularly by symbolic persuasion, by studying a major conflict in American politics: the competition for public office. Here the political candidates and their campaign managers are the principal leaders representing conflicts between interests, usually political parties, for the authority to govern.

In American politics, *election campaigns are contrived, not spontaneous*; every phase is designed to be reported to the public. As little as possible is left to chance, although things do not always go as planned. Selected qualities of the candidate — his image — are publicized in an appealing fashion. His activities are staged for maximum exposure in the mass media (baby kissing, whistle-stops and airport fly-ins, handshaking, televised interviews, factory tours, walks through shopping centers, consuming locally famous foods, and speeches). All are filmed for television. The whole campaign is designed to identify the candidate with the community's most revered symbols — the Constitution, the democratic way, justice, peace, prosperity, prudence. Simple catch phrases are coined to symbolize the candidate's intention to provide a "return to normalcy," a "new frontier," or a "new prosperity."

Campaigns are not just a sham intended to dupe the people. Candidates have only so much time, money, manpower, and energy to devote to persuading people to vote for them; they must budget their resources to achieve optimum publicity for themselves, their policies, and their philosophy. Planning the campaign, political leaders must consider three phases: organizing, testing, and critical.[19]

## the organizing phase

No nominee can hope to wage a successful campaign without an effective political organization working on his behalf. Besides trusted advisers of long standing, the campaign organization of a political aspirant includes

[19] Charles O. Jones, "The 1964 Presidential Election — Further Adventures in Wonderland," in Donald G. Herzberg, ed., *American Government Annual, 1965–1966* (New York: Holt, Rinehart and Winston, 1965), pp. 1–30.

specialists in public relations, surveyors of political opinions, and party leaders. Each brings different skills to campaign management, and each plans to reach the voter in different ways.

The *public relations expert* attempts to merchandise the candidate to a mass audience. He makes these assumptions about mass behavior: (1) a mass audience exists and is composed of individuals sharing attitudes and social characteristics; (2) this audience selects products, candidates, or policies on the basis of qualities emphasized in mass advertising; (3) an appeal will be effective if it conforms to what voters are predisposed to accept (if they believe a President should be dynamic, the candidate should appear in settings that dramatically emphasize his dynamism); (4) the candidate's image must be sufficiently colorful to attract the citizen's attention and get him to vote; and (5) dramatic and sensational presentations, repetition, and finally saturation of the mass audience with campaign appeals will penetrate the audience's indifference and break down resistance. The public relations expert brings to the campaign the most modern communication skills for influencing opinions.

The candidate's *political opinion analyst* must determine: (1) what qualities the ideal President, Congressman, Senator, governor, mayor, or other public official should have; (2) how closely voters think the candidate matches the ideal; (3) what worries, problems, and issues are uppermost in voters' minds; (4) whether the candidate is leading or trailing his opponent in public favor, and why; and (5) the likelihood that the candidate's supporters and opponents will actually vote.

The political opinion analyst also has pollsters conduct opinion surveys — face-to-face interviews, telephone interviews, and mail questionnaires — of representative samplings of the eligible voters in the election district. In analyzing responses, the pollster does not look at voters only as a mass. He also examines how categories of voters — farmers, suburbanites, union members, men, women, Democrats, Republicans — respond to the candidate. His analysis suggests the image and issues the candidate should emphasize before the electorate.

The experienced *party organizer* mobilizes a vigorous grass-roots organization that will complement the candidate's impersonal, media-oriented efforts. His target is the individual voter, and his technique is personal contact. He sends out a large number of people who will ring doorbells and explain to prospective voters what the issues are and how the candidate stands on them. His aim is to arouse interest in campaign issues, both foreign and domestic, to stimulate political discussion among friends, and to get as many people as possible to vote.

Recent campaigns for the presidency have shown dramatically how significant these specialists are in popular elections. All major presidential aspirants in recent years — Richard Nixon, Hubert Humphrey, Ed-

Chicago's Mayor Daley has proved to be an effective coordinator of people in pursuit of partisan goals. He presides over a vigorous grassroots organization.

mund Muskie, Lyndon Johnson, Barry Goldwater, John Kennedy, George McGovern, George Wallace, and others — have employed professional public relations firms. All have also used professional pollsters. A major theme of the 1972 McGovern campaign (that Americans were distrustful of their government and would support a candidate offering fundamental reforms in governmental institutions) was formulated on the basis of recommendations of McGovern's pollsters. Campaign specialists also work in most major statewide contests, congressional elections, mayoralty elections, and even campaigns for minor elective posts.

the testing phase

The effectiveness of the candidate's strategies and those of his organization is assessed during the testing phase of the campaign, and necessary tactical adjustments are made then. The nominee strives to hold his partisan adherents by leading their cause while projecting a nonpartisan image and taking moderate stands on issues to win wavering voters among the undecided and the opposition.

Acceptance speeches by presidential nominees herald the beginning of the testing phase. They are designed both to heal preconvention wounds and to publicize the new party leader. Republican nominees traditionally emphasize party stands against centralized authority, the desirability of individual initiative and freedom, and their support of free enterprise. Democratic nominees stress their willingness to promote social welfare, to seek continued prosperity, and to exert leadership in foreign affairs. Having identified themselves with traditional party themes, nominees inject their own ideas on the issues that they hope will be foremost in the campaign. In 1968, Richard Nixon, playing upon a widespread fear about the breakdown of "law and order" in the 1960s, promised if elected to appoint a strong attorney general and fight crime; Hubert Humphrey in 1968, faced with a badly split party, pleaded in his acceptance speech for party unity.

*Providing an opportunity for defining major campaign themes, the testing phase also permits the candidate to prove that he measures up to the voters' idealized image of political leaders.* Senator John Kennedy, entering the campaign against Vice-President Richard Nixon in 1960, seemed to many Americans to be too young, inexperienced, and impudent to make the weighty decisions called for in the presidency; Nixon, on the other hand, had experience in the vice-presidency, had been involved in the decisions required after President Eisenhower's heart attack in 1955, had "debated" with Soviet Premier Nikita Khrushchev in Moscow in 1959, and had visited numerous foreign countries. Clearly Nixon's image matched that which Americans expected a President to present. Then the candidates engaged in four televised debates. Kennedy entered the debates rested, tanned, and with the benefit of careful planning; Nixon was tired, fatigued by the strain of campaigning and a bout with staphylococcus, and he had not done his homework. The ensuing exchange projected an image of an informed, witty, confident Kennedy challenging an indecisive, subdued, and haggard Nixon. Although partisan Democrats and Republicans were generally unmoved by the performances, staying with their party's nominee, independent voters were impressed with Kennedy (by nearly two to one) to feel that he had "won" the debate. Much of Nixon's later campaigning was devoted to recapturing his lost image.

*A vital part of testing is finding issues that inspire popular support.* Candidates campaign on issues primarily because their stands on the issues and the emphasis they give them are the principal factors determining a voter's choice that they can manipulate during a campaign. If the issues the candidate planned to use prior to his campaign fail to elicit enthusiastic response, he must keep searching. Republican candidate Barry Goldwater tested several issues in 1964, but with little success: foreign policy (Vietnam, Cuba, the threat of communism); domestic affairs (big government, civil rights, violence in the streets); and personalities (Johnson's wealth and Humphrey's connections with liberal organizations such as Americans for Democratic Action). None touched off enough support to counter Democratic claims of "moderation" and "peace" in foreign affairs and "prosperity" at home. Goldwater selected issues to overcome the Democratic lead (samplings of opinion indicated a two-to-one majority for President Johnson). The Democrats were able to wage their campaign with the knowledge that victory was theirs if no one rocked the boat.

Richard Nixon's campaign in 1968 exemplified the careful organizing and testing typical of modern campaign management. The planning involved two assumptions: the bloc of votes indispensable to victory consisted of American suburbanites discontented with crime and violence, mass protest, increasing taxes, and the style of Lyndon Johnson's "Great Society" (projections indicated that four million more votes would be cast in the suburbs than in the cities in 1968); and Nixon would have to win independents and dissident Democrats in all regions because Republicans alone could not supply needed pluralities.

Among the techniques aimed at winning the suburban vote were nominating Spiro Agnew for Vice-President (he had a record of strong suburban support as Governor of Maryland); filmed question-and-answer sessions with Nixon before all-white high school students in typical suburbs; highly organized "spontaneous" demonstrations in both affluent and working-class suburbs; and saturation television commercials, each one minute in length, attacking the Johnson administration, not in specifics but by pleading that America needed "new leadership." Nixon exposed his strategy to refrain from direct partisan appeals immediately after his nomination: "I will do nothing that will divide the country geographically, racially, or on a party basis." In keeping with this theme — and so long as the opinion polls indicated that he was easily leading both Hubert Humphrey and George Wallace — Nixon avoided direct confrontations with his opponents or direct attacks on either. Throughout the testing phase, Nixon kept himself aloof from criticism, refusing to make the types of retorts so characteristic of him in earlier, unsuccessful campaigns. He was able to maintain the "new Nixon" stance until the closing weeks of the contest — the critical phase.

## the critical phase

All campaigns reach a crucial point at which the only voters still undecided are nonpartisan, frequently uninformed citizens who pay little attention to politics, but whose votes can make the difference between victory and defeat. A candidate frequently tries to capture the imagination of these indifferent voters with a particularly dramatic gesture that displays his ability to take advantage of unexpected events. During the Kennedy-Nixon campaign of 1960, Martin Luther King, Jr., the prominent Negro civil rights leader, was sentenced in Atlanta to four months at hard labor in the state penitentiary for sitting-in at a segregated restaurant. At his campaign advisers' suggestion, Senator Kennedy telephoned the distraught wife of the imprisoned civil rights leader, expressing his concern and suggesting that he would intervene if necessary. When the press spread this dramatic news, it was immediately effective. Martin Luther King, Jr.'s father, who had come out for Nixon earlier, switched his support to Kennedy and urged all blacks to do the same. Civil rights leaders across the nation, impressed by Kennedy's gesture (and by King's release after Robert Kennedy's plea to the judge who had pronounced sentence), followed suit. "One cannot identify in the narrowness of American voting of 1960 any one particular episode or decision as being more important than any other in the final tallies," Theodore H. White wrote later; yet

> when one reflects that Illinois was carried by only 9,000 votes and that 250,000 Negroes are estimated to have voted for Kennedy; that Michigan was carried by 67,000 votes and that an estimated 250,000 Negroes voted for Kennedy; that South Carolina was carried by 10,000 votes and that an estimated 40,000 Negroes there voted for Kennedy, the candidate's instinctive decision must be ranked among the most crucial of the last few weeks.[20]

But it is not always easy to take advantage of events quickly enough to profit by them. In 1968, President Johnson announced a halt to the bombing of North Vietnam a few days before the presidential election. It appeared that Hubert Humphrey might benefit from the move by winning the votes of antiwar dissenters. Although there was a late surge in Humphrey's support, the halt in the bombing appears to have been too late to bring him victory over Nixon.

[20] Theodore H. White, *The Making of the President, 1960* (New York: Atheneum, 1961), p. 323.

## the costs of campaigning

Running for public office has always been expensive. As Will Rogers once remarked, "It takes lots of money to even get beat with." Assembling a competent campaign organization – including public relations specialists, political opinion analysts, and party organizers – and managing the organizing, testing, and critical phases of an election campaign are expensive enterprises. Figure 7-2 illustrates the striking rise in the cost of political campaigns in presidential election years in the last two decades. The cost per vote cast in presidential campaigns increased from 19 cents in 1952 to 60 cents in 1968; even adjusting for economic inflation, campaign costs rose 45 percent from 1952 to 1972.

The cost of campaigning has climbed so high that Congress has had to act. How important should money be in politics? Advocates of limitation of funds feel that campaign costs are so high that those who run for public office must either be affluent or willing to accept support from wealthy special interests. Others think that, despite increased costs, the money goes for a good and necessary cause: to inform the public about candidates, issues, and policies. If campaign costs are to be regulated, say advocates of the latter opinion, it should be made easier for the average American to contribute money.

In the Federal Election Campaign Act of 1971, Congress limited the amounts that candidates for Congress and the presidency could spend for television and other communications media. Congress also provided for disclosure of campaign expenditures and contributions. Among its provisions governing campaign spending, the act (1) limited the amount that could be spent for advertising to 10 cents per voter with a limit of 60 percent of this amount to be spent for broadcasting; (2) required broadcasters in the 45 days prior to a primary election and in the 60 days prior to a general election to sell candidates advertising time at the lowest rate for the time and space used; and (3) strengthened requirements for reporting expenditures. Provisions of the act, however, refer to candidates, not to persons and committees acting on their behalf.

Congress also dealt with campaign fund-raising in 1971, limiting the amount a candidate or his family could contribute to his own campaign to $50,000 for President or Vice-President, $35,000 for a Senator, and $25,000 for a Representative. Congress refused, however, to pass a proposal that would have made it relatively easy for Americans to take part in financing presidential campaigns by authorizing that a portion of their income tax be put into a general campaign fund. Instead, Americans are permitted a tax credit of half of each person's contribution to a political campaign, with a maximum credit of $12.50 for each individual.

*Most Americans, then, do not contribute financially to campaigns* and

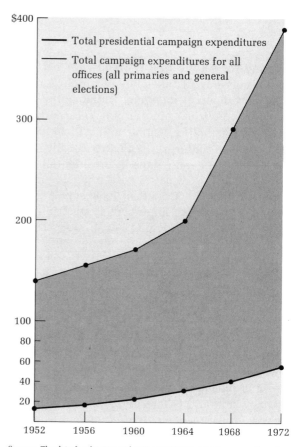

$400

300

200

100
80
60
40
20

1952    1956    1960    1964    1968    1972

Total presidential campaign expenditures

Total campaign expenditures for all offices (all primaries and general elections)

**FIGURE 7-2**
**Estimated Costs of Political Campaigns**
**in Presidential Election Years, 1952–1972**
**(Millions of Dollars)**

Sources: The data for the 1952 and 1956 presidential campaigns come from the Report of the President's Commission on Campaign Costs, *Financing Presidential Campaigns* (Washington, D.C.: U.S. Government Printing Office, 1962); data on total campaign expenditures for 1952 and 1956 come from Alexander Heard, *The Costs of Democracy* (Chapel Hill: University of North Carolina Press, 1960); all other estimates come from reports of the Citizen's Research Foundation.

are not likely to do so in the future. Campaign funds come from wealthy business, labor, and professional organizations. Among such groups, the Committee on Political Education (COPE) of the AFL–CIO has been especially helpful to Democrats and the American Medical Political Action Committee (AMPAC) has done much for the Republican cause. Also, nominees who can pay their own way are more likely to be chosen — supporting their campaigns both within and by circumventing legal limitations. The strongest representation of conflicting opinions in political campaigns is likely to be that of interest groups with the financial resources to support sympathetic political leaders.

## mass communications and opinion leadership

The campaign to win public office has a side benefit for the community as a whole: by taking stands on issues, candidates represent social conflicts. To make their messages heard they and other political leaders need not just skill in persuasion but also access to publicity. Political leaders rely mainly on mass communications to publicize their views, so that most Americans hear those views at second hand, as reported in the mass media.

### what are mass communications?

By mass communications we mean the activities of organizations that use the printed word (newspapers, magazines, mailed brochures) and those that use electronic media (radio, television, movies, telephones) to communicate with a relatively large, heterogeneous, and anonymous audience timing the message to reach most people simultaneously.[21] In America *news organizations — The New York Times, The Washington Post,* the Associated Press and Universal Press International wire services, and the news departments of major broadcasting networks — are the largest participants in such political communication.

*The mass media expose controversy and provide a forum in which conflicting interests may criticize the actions of officials.* Ideally, the media perform this function on behalf of all citizens; freedom of the press is a citizen's right guaranteed by constitutional and statutory law as well as by unwritten agreements. The basic protection of a free press, guaranteed by the First Amendment (see Chapter Five), limits official interference in the activities of the communications media. Those activities are restricted. Television cameras are barred from courtrooms in the interest of impartial litigation; individuals may seek redress for libelous utterances by the press; and movies are sometimes censored by local authorities. The communications media supply unfettered channels for political information, persuasion, and entertainment. Deliberate distor-

[21] Melvin L. De Fleur, *Theories of Mass Communication,* 2nd ed. (New York: David McKay, 1970).

The fireside chats of Franklin
Roosevelt stimulated public
confidence during the
Depression. His use of radio
enhanced his leadership.

tion of news is frowned upon by most newsmen and politicians, but news
organizations are free to interpret and comment as they see fit.

*The ideal of socially responsible communications media is tempered
by economic and political realities.* The sheer cost of media operations,
particularly television, prevents all but the most affluent from using it,
except for free coverage in news stories, interview programs, or televised
debates. Cost also prevents the press from presenting all significant social
conflicts for open discussion. Newspapers wanting to increase their cir-
culation may publicize conflicts that are of interest and importance to
readers, slighting stories of less immediate appeal such as hunger, pros-
titution, or the plight of the American Indian. *The interests of the news
audience condition the types of conflicts presented by political communicators; minority interests are passed over in efforts to attract
readers or a high audience rating.*[22]

Access to communications channels is a factor in a political leader's
capacity to influence opinion; the leader's occupation, in turn, governs
the access he has to the media. A person in a prestigious position can

[22] See Robert Cirino, *Don't Blame the People* (Los Angeles: Diversity Press, 1971).

easily exercise political persuasion because of his entree to the media — labor leaders usually have easier access than businessmen, whereas teachers and scholars have little access.

The President has automatic access to the media in that any action of his is news. In news conferences, he publicizes his stands on controversial issues; by timely releases to the press, he can dominate the headlines and ensure a few minutes of exposure on each evening's televised news (a favorite technique of President Johnson); and he can have time on radio and television almost for the asking to speak "directly to the people" (frequently done by President Nixon).

How effective are such presidential appeals? It is impossible to say with real accuracy, but as Table 7-1 suggests, being able to report directly to the people on television directly affects public approval given a President. Subordinates, rivals within the presidential party, or members of the opposition without such easy access to the news media find it more difficult to circulate their criticism of presidential policies. This access to publicity through the news media is one of the factors that makes any incumbent President a formidable opponent to challengers.

In their efforts to secure information, reporters and their parent news organizations come to be special interest groups in their own right. Like pressure groups, they make claims upon officials for information, demand unencumbered access to policymakers, and expect freedom from official control. Their claims generate conflicts between the media and public officials. So long as democracies cherish public disclosure of conflict, tension between the press and public officials is inevitable. Whether out of conviction, principle, or economic considerations, the communications industry is continuously at odds with policymakers, as newsmen publicize matters that officials prefer to keep secret. This *basic conflict between government and the press* has been highlighted repeatedly in recent years — Vice-President Agnew in 1969 charged that public officials were subjected to "instant analysis and querulous criticism ... by a small band of network commentators and self-appointed analysts"; the Nixon administration sought to prevent publication of a secret report of American involvement in Vietnam (the Pentagon Papers) in 1971; in the same year, a committee of the House of Representatives attempted (unsuccessfully) to cite the Columbia Broadcasting Company for contempt after the network refused to cooperate in an investigation into the background of "The Selling of the Pentagon," a documentary film about the expensive public relations programs of the Department of Defense.

Just as public officials are critical of the news media, reporters often charge government with "managing the news." Bureaucratic agencies have offices of public information designed primarily to control the flow of news and avoid unauthorized news leaks. So long as these offices give

**TABLE 7-1**
**Presidential Television Appearances**
**and Changes in Presidential Popularity, 1963–1970**

| Date of TV appearance | Event | Poll results |
|---|---|---|
| July 26, 1963 | President Kennedy announces nuclear test ban treaty | Before: 73% favored treaty<br>After: 81% favored treaty |
| August 1, 1965 | President Johnson explains Gulf of Tonkin incident | Before: 42% positive on LBJ Vietnam policy<br>After: 72% positive on LBJ Vietnam policy |
| January 31, 1966 | President Johnson announces resumption of bombing on North Vietnam | Before: 61% favored resuming bombings<br>After: 73% favored resuming bombings |
| May 14, 1969 | President Nixon announces phased troop withdrawals from Vietnam | Before: 49% favored phased withdrawals<br>After: 67% favored phased withdrawals |
| November 3, 1969 | President Nixon asks for support of Vietnam policy | Before: 46% positive on Nixon's handling of war<br>After: 51% positive on Nixon's handling of war |
| April 30, 1970 | President Nixon announces Cambodian strike by U.S. troops | Before: 7% favored sending U.S. troops into Cambodia<br>After: 50% favored sending U.S. troops into Cambodia |
| May 27, 1970 | President Nixon announces withdrawal of U.S. troops from Cambodia | Before: 47% said Cambodian move not wrong<br>After: 56% said Cambodian move not wrong |

Source: News release, *The Harris Survey* (September 3, 1970).

reporters a convenient place for securing prepared releases covering agency events, newsmen accept them. But when such offices attempt to manipulate newsmen by concealing what is taking place or by releasing news that tells only one side of a controversy, reporters object. In 1971, India and Pakistan engaged in a brief war resulting in the establishment of a new nation, Bangladesh. Columnist Jack Anderson insisted that the

Vice-President Agnew repeatedly has charged
that the press has excessive
influence in molding public opinion.

Nixon administration had twisted its accounts of the war to place blame
on India and thus to curry favor with the People's Republic of China (a
nation that had long had border disputes with India and that Nixon was
shortly to visit). One measure of the extent to which a free press is com-
promised is how much "official information" the press carries without
securing all the evidence relevant to the political issue, even if it is
damaging to public officials. As both channels of news and active participants, political communicators create conflict when they expose and represent it.

233

### television and politics

In 1950, only about one American household in ten had a television set; two decades later, more than nine in ten owned them, many of them color sets. Americans today turn to television as their prime source of information and entertainment. Young Americans are particularly prone to do so: a nationwide survey in 1970 indicated that more than 40 percent of those fifteen to twenty-one years of age reported watching television from two to ten hours each week and as many spent more than ten hours at it per week.[23] Not only is it a major news source, both generally and in political campaigns, for most Americans (as Table 7-2 illustrates), it is their most believable news source. Because it is everywhere — and it is believed — television must influence political awareness.

Television has reshaped the style of political campaigns. In adapting television (and to a lesser degree, radio) to their political campaigns, candidates rely on specialists in the television industry. (When Nixon campaigned for President in 1968, he hired Roger Ailes, known for his preparation of material for television's popular *Laugh-In,* as a consultant.) Television specialists generally bring to the political campaign the attitude that the *basic task of television is not to inform but to entertain.* Television viewers are not interested in devoting their leisure hours to serious programs demanding concentration and reflection. Consequently, the specialist's basic task is to present an image of the candidate that an audience accustomed to entertaining and dramatic television personalities will accept. Television viewers acquire from the mass media attitudes toward what is entertaining and what is dull, the dramatic and the bland, the romantic and the deadening. Candidate images as projected on television, therefore, must conform to these highly subjective evaluations, which viewers make on the basis of their *media predispositions.*[24] A politician such as the former movie actor Ronald Reagan, who can "act" the role of the candidate, makes an ideal television campaigner.

*How do mass communications affect political opinions?* Television specialists are probably correct in assuming that entertaining rather than informative communications are most influential in politics. The person most likely to be swayed by mass communications is the "floating voter," the person who pays little attention to politics, who does not scan the news for political information, who is influenced at the last minute in a campaign by a dramatic event or personality, and who from election

[23] Louis Harris and Associates, *The Harris Survey Yearbook,* p. 422.
[24] Gene Wyckoff, *The Image Candidates* (New York: Macmillan, 1968).

**TABLE 7-2**
**Sources of Political Information in Selected Years, 1952–1971**

| Sources | 1959 | 1961 | 1963 | 1964 | 1967 | 1968 | 1971 |
|---|---|---|---|---|---|---|---|
| Most used news sources | | | | | | | |
| Television | 51% | 52% | 55% | 58% | 64% | 59% | 60% |
| Newspapers | 57 | 57 | 53 | 56 | 55 | 49 | 48 |
| Radio | 34 | 34 | 29 | 26 | 28 | 25 | 23 |
| Magazines | 8 | 9 | 6 | 8 | 7 | 7 | 5 |
| People | 4 | 5 | 4 | 5 | 4 | 5 | 4 |
| Don't know, no answer | 1 | 3 | 3 | 3 | 2 | 3 | 1 |
| Most believed news sources | | | | | | | |
| Television | 29 | 39 | 36 | 41 | 41 | 44 | 49 |
| Newspapers | 32 | 24 | 24 | 23 | 24 | 21 | 20 |
| Radio | 12 | 12 | 12 | 8 | 7 | 8 | 10 |
| Magazines | 10 | 10 | 10 | 10 | 8 | 11 | 9 |
| Don't know, no answer | 17 | 17 | 18 | 18 | 20 | 16 | 12 |

| Sources | 1952 | 1956 | 1960 | 1964 | 1968 |
|---|---|---|---|---|---|
| Most information about political campaigns | | | | | |
| Newspapers | 22.9% | 24.3% | 22.3% | 24.5% | 23.1% |
| Radio | 28.1 | 10.6 | 5.3 | 3.7 | 4.0 |
| Television | 31.9 | 49.4 | 60.9 | 57.8 | 64.3 |
| Magazines | 5.2 | 4.6 | 4.3 | 6.9 | 6.0 |
| Newspapers and radio | 2.2 | .6 | .1 | .2 | .2 |
| Newspapers and TV | 1.0 | 1.2 | 1.7 | 1.8 | 1.5 |
| Radio and TV | 1.2 | .2 | .2 | .4 | .2 |
| Magazines and one other | .9 | .2 | .5 | 1.1 | .4 |
| Any other combination | .2 | .5 | .2 | .4 | .3 |
| Did not follow campaign | 6.4 | 8.4 | 4.5 | 3.2 | |

Sources: Data on news sources from Report of the Roper Organization, Inc., "An Extended View of Public Attitudes Toward Television and Other Mass Media, 1959–1971." (Percentages do not total 100 percent because of multiple responses.) Data on political campaigns from Survey Research Center, University of Michigan, through facilities of the Interuniversity Consortium for Political Research.

**TABLE 7-3**
**Time of Decision and Voting Choice**
**in Presidential Elections, 1948–1968**

| Time of decision | 1948 | 1952 | 1956 | 1960 | 1964 | 1968 |
|---|---|---|---|---|---|---|
| Before party conventions | 37% | 35% | 57% | 30% | 40% | 35% |
| During party conventions | 22 | 30 | 18 | 30 | 25 | 24 |
| During campaigns | 26 | 31 | 21 | 36 | 33 | 41 |
| Don't know, no answer | 15 | 4 | 4 | 4 | 2 | 0 |
| Total | 100 | 100 | 100 | 100 | 100 | 100 |
| Number of cases | 421 | 1251 | 1285 | 1445 | 1126 | 957 |

Source: Survey Research Center, University of Michigan; data supplied through facilities of the Interuniversity Consortium for Political Research.

to election shifts his allegiance between parties.[25] If America is undergoing a trend away from party loyalty, then we might speculate that *television campaigns will increase their influence on voting in the future.*

*The effectiveness of mass communications is limited by the characteristics of the mass audience to whom their appeals are directed.* In typical political campaigns, as illustrated by Table 7-3, most voters make their choice before the campaign starts. If mass communications have affected voters, they probably have done so between elections by providing general impressions of politics on which voters judge the adequacy of the incumbent administration. It is more likely that the choice of the voters has been determined by their basic party loyalties. *Political candidates are wise to direct their mass appeals to the uncommitted voters who can swing the vote in a close election.*

*Mass communications do not operate in isolation but complement, supplement, or counter personal communication* — among friends, in the family, on the job, or elsewhere. Mass communications probably gain their effect principally from an intricate network of personal leaders, not from direct messages to citizens. Even such a shocking event as the assassination of President John Kennedy was learned of by only half of the

[25] Philip E. Converse, "Information Flow and the Stability of Partisan Attitudes," *The Public Opinion Quarterly* 26 (Winter 1962): 578–599.

adult population through the mass media; the remainder learned from telephone calls and personal communications.[26]

In determining how strongly mass communications influence political persuasion, we must distinguish between the different effects the mass media can have in forming opinions. They can *activate* an otherwise passive voter. Mass communications frequently *reinforce* political views. Our attitudes help to determine the types of communication to which we expose ourselves and which we perceive and remember; our friends and family also influence our reading, listening, and viewing habits. We expose ourselves to what we want and expect to read, hear, or see. Small wonder then that the messages that filter through are not likely to impose views contrary to our preferences; as loyal Democrats or Republicans we seek and find in mass communications reasons for voting as we intended to all along. Finally, mass communications can *convert* a voter from one position to another, but do so infrequently. Only those without clear-cut preferences, with unstable opinions, or faced with contradictory choices are markedly influenced solely by mass communication.

## representing and influencing political opinions

Political behavior is not determined solely by the attitudes and interests people bring to politics from their political socialization. Cues from political leaders interact with these predispositions. Political leaders help to initiate disputes by stimulating mass attitudes and mobilizing diverse interests; as a result, *leaders represent conflicting opinions.* Moreover, relying upon the resources at their disposal — derived from their social characteristics, the esteem they have in the eyes of their constituents, and the constitutional opportunities to achieve higher office — and using many techniques, particularly symbolic persuasion, *leaders influence political opinions.* In representing and influencing political opinions, public officials, group leaders, and personal leaders perform a necessary task in the community.

But political *leaders are not free to create and change opinions at will.* Calls for revolution, though well publicized, are rare for good reason: it is unlikely that political leaders could get many Americans to accept a major social revolution. In recent years the status quo has been fundamentally challenged in political debate; and steps have been taken to

[26] Paul B. Sheatsley and Jacob J. Feldman, "The Assassination of President Kennedy: A Preliminary Report on Public Reactions and Behavior," *The Public Opinion Quarterly* 28 (Summer 1964): 192–193.

alleviate some of the worst forms of social injustice. Yet other tasks remain, for even now the number of Americans pleading the cause of the poor, deprived, sick, elderly, and even simply the average consumer is relatively small.

*The influence of political leaders* in conflict representation is restricted by: (1) the repository of semifixed attitudes of followers that leaders must take into account; (2) the indifference of Americans to politics generally; (3) the many social groups represented in the leadership despite a relative overrepresentation from the middle and upper classes, which provides for conflicts among leaders themselves; (4) the limited access many leaders have to mass communications as a tool for persuasion, certainly compared with that of the President; (5) the need for leaders — certainly in this television age — to adjust to the expectations and conceptions, or images, which their followers have of an ideal leader; and (6) the conflict of officials and newsmen in a democracy.

There are two further restrictions upon leaders' influence. First, *leaders willingly restrict themselves.* American politicians, with rare exceptions, uphold the rules that make possible democratic representation and resolution of conflict. By practicing fair play — accepting defeat at the polls and looking toward the next contest — political leaders preserve free elections and enable Americans to choose between competing rulers. Politicians may still "humbug the people," but they stop short of the most extreme demagoguery (stirring animosities in religious groups, arousing class against class) that might draw support from the disaffected. Second, perhaps the greatest restriction, is the *widely distributed functions of political leadership,* limiting the influence politicians can exercise: official leadership is dispersed among governing branches, agencies, departments, and bureaus; group leadership is exercised by persons in competing organizations and factions; and personal leadership occurs in a very large number of social circles, most of them isolated from one another. The concentration of leadership in a small band of influential persons is difficult in such a pluralist setting. This dispersion is inherent in the way we elect our leaders, conduct our partisan affairs, and pressure officials to do our bidding. Each is a distinctive pattern of conflict representation linked to political opinion and leadership.

*bibliographical note*

Social scientists have studied political leadership for some time. At first they simply prepared biographies of notable leaders, but in recent decades they have examined the characteristics, skills, and styles of political leaders. Many of their findings are summarized by Wendell Bell, Richard J. Hill, and Charles R. Wright,

*Public Leadership* (San Francisco, Calif.: Chandler, 1961). One of the most entertaining accounts of the images of leaders is Orrin E. Klapp, *Symbolic Leaders* (Chicago: Aldine, Paperback Edition, 1968). Perhaps the leading work by a political scientist on the subject is Murray Edelman, *The Symbolic Uses of Politics* (Urbana, Ill.: University of Illinois Press, 1964). James D. Barber in his *Political Leadership in American Government* (Boston: Little, Brown, 1964) includes selections illustrating presidential, congressional, and judicial leadership.

A useful study of the social characteristics of American public officials is Donald R. Matthews, *The Social Background of Political Decision-Makers* (New York: Random House, 1954); also consult David T. Stanley et al., *Men Who Govern* (Washington, D.C.: Brookings Institution, 1967). The general problem of political elites is explored in Suzanne Keller, *Beyond the Ruling Class* (New York: Random House, 1963). The question of whether there is a governing elite in America is considered in G. William Domhoff, *Who Rules America?* (Englewood Cliffs, N.J.: Prentice-Hall, 1967). The topic of personal leadership is developed in Elihu Katz and Paul F. Lazarsfeld, *Personal Influence* (New York: Free Press of Glencoe, Paperback Edition, 1964). The leading work on the relationship of political structure to leadership is Joseph A. Schlesinger, *Ambition and Politics* (Chicago: Rand McNally, 1966).

The theory, nature, and techniques of influencing political opinions are explored in works dealing with propaganda, public relations, opinion formation, and campaigning. Among those dealing specifically with political matters are Terence H. Qualter, *Propaganda and Psychological Warfare* (New York: Random House, 1962); Stanley Kelley, Jr., *Professional Public Relations and Political Power* (Baltimore: Johns Hopkins, Paperback Edition, 1966); Nelson W. Polsby and Aaron B. Wildavsky, *Presidential Elections,* 3rd ed. (New York: Scribner, 1971); Dan Nimmo, *The Political Persuaders* (Englewood Cliffs, N.J.: Prentice-Hall, 1970); John Kingdon, *Candidates for Office* (New York: Random House, 1968); Robert J. Huckshorn and Robert C. Spencer, *The Politics of Defeat* (Amherst, Mass.: University of Massachusetts Press, 1971); and Ray Hiebert et al., eds., *The Political Image Merchants* (Washington, D.C.: Acropolis Books, 1971).

The role of the mass media in politics, especially television, is discussed specifically in Kurt Lang and Gladys Engel Lang, *Politics and Television* (Chicago: Quadrangle Books, 1968); Bernard Rubin, *Political Television* (Belmont, Calif.: Wadsworth, 1967); Gene Wyckoff, *The Image Candidates* (New York: Macmillan, 1968); Harold Mendelsohn and Irving Crespi, *Polls, Television, and the New Politics* (Scranton, Pa.: Chandler, 1970); Joe McGinnis, *The Selling of the President, 1968* (New York: Trident Press, 1969); and Richard W. Lee, ed., *Politics and the Press* (Washington, D.C.: Acropolis Books, 1970). Studies of the effects of mass communications on activating, changing, and reinforcing political attitudes are summarized in Joseph T. Klapper, *The Effects of Mass Communication* (New York: Free Press, 1960).

# chapter 8

# voting choice

Americans express their conflicting social interests by casting votes for political leaders competing for public office; that is one way. Selecting people to govern for limited terms of office is the primary purpose for holding elections but not the only one. They also go to the polls on local matters — to accept or reject city charters, approve or refuse constitutional amendments, grant authority to tax, vote revenue bonds, or create governing districts. Elections are numerous and their purposes varied, but we will limit ourselves here to federal elections for the President, Senators, and members of the House of Representatives.

## elections and conflict representation

Free elections help represent social conflict in America in two ways: they permit citizens to take part indirectly in policymaking by allowing them to decide between candidates; and they provide governors with an indication — if only an imperfect one — of public concerns, satisfactions, and irritations. In mobilizing support, political leaders try to attract attention to their stands on specific issues; and by voting for a candidate, citizens let public officials know their positions on these issues. These positions are often difficult to determine because politicians modify them to attract as many voters with diverse interests as possible. Voters are more interested in the personalities or party labels of the candidates than in their stands. Furthermore, when there is more than one significant political issue in the election — and typically there is — just what does the candidate's victory or defeat mean as a verdict across the whole range

of issues? It is clear that the choices of the electorate can be but ambiguous expressions of policy preferences.

*Election mandates are often difficult, if not impossible, to ascertain.*
To see why, let us examine the principal constitutional, sociodemographic, and personal influences on voting behavior.

## the constitution and american elections

The Constitution influences American elections in representing conflict
in three ways. Elections are regulated by (1) mechanisms provided in
the written Constitution, notably the federal system and the electoral
college; (2) formal statutes; and (3) the customs and habits that make up
our *unwritten constitution,* particularly those affecting our political parties.

### how does the written constitution affect elections?

By leaving it to the states to determine voting requirements, the Constitution implies that the states have the authority to regulate some aspects
of elections. The restrictions on state authority are the constitutional
amendments that prohibit the states from denying to citizens the right
to vote because of race, color, previous condition of servitude, sex, age,
or nonpayment of a poll tax. Beyond these prohibitions, however, the
federal Constitution directly influences elections because it created a federal system and the Electoral College.

THE FEDERAL SYSTEM. As an operating feature of American government,
the federal system divides political authority among several levels of
government. Citizens elect public officials for each level; we choose a
President, Senators, and Representatives for national office; governors,
legislators, and sometimes judges for state office; mayors and aldermen
or councilors for city office. Partisan support develops for candidates
at each level.

*The federal system's divisiveness is modified by regional alignments,*
*forming one of the most enduring patterns of American voting behavior.*
Regional loyalties to a party have prevailed throughout American history. Democratic dominance in the South and Republican ascendancy in
the Northeast were taken for granted for decades. Alignments in recent
presidential and congressional elections, however, portend modifications
in these regional patterns. Areas outside the South that were once strongly

Republican now send many Democratic Congressmen to Washington; since 1950, the excess of Republican over Democratic Congressmen elected from outside the South and border states fell from eighty-five to an almost even split between the parties. Republicans are replacing Democrats in the South, though not so many.

*State patterns of partisan alignment underlie these regional patterns.* Because the federal system requires the citizens of each state to elect their own governing officials, it is possible for a political party to establish itself as the major force in one or several states even though it has less strength nationally. One-party domination of states — Maine and Kansas by the Republicans, and South Carolina, Mississippi, and Alabama by the Democrats — is an old, accepted political fact. The change in regional political alignments is occurring, however, because of shifts in traditional state alignments. One-party domination has given way in states like Maine, which has elected three Democrats governor since 1955; Kansas, which has elected a Democratic governor for three successive terms in the last decade; South Carolina, Mississippi, and Alabama, all of which voted for Republican Barry Goldwater in the 1964 presidential election; Virginia, which elected a Republican governor in 1969, and even Vermont, which in 1964 gave its electoral votes to the Democratic candidate for President for the first time in American history.

These shifts in partisan strength have several causes. *Critical issues* such as desegregation made southerners take a sharp look at the Democratic party; and though unable to stem the tide of integration, southerners expressed symbolic protests by their support for Republican candidates and for George Wallace. Concurrently, blacks in both North and South — traditionally loyal Republicans — learned to appreciate the Democratic party since 1936 because of its stand on civil rights. *Population shifts* between and within states have also changed traditional patterns. *Presidential nominees* themselves have brought new supporters into their party and alienated former loyalists. (Some southern Democrats preferred Protestant Richard Nixon to Catholic John Kennedy in 1960, and Republicans in the Northeast in 1964 found Lyndon Johnson preferable to Barry Goldwater.) *The regional and state strongholds of our two major parties are being revised.*

THE ELECTORAL COLLEGE. The voting support for our two major parties varies between regions and states. The electoral college established by our Constitution magnifies these variations in presidential elections. The Founding Fathers arranged that the President of the United States would be chosen by a majority of the votes of electors chosen within the states, each state having as many electors as it has delegates in the House of Representatives and the Senate. Currently in each state each party runs a slate of electors, pledged to support its presidential candidate in the electoral college, who are chosen by popular vote at the time of the presidential election. The candidate receiving a plurality of popular votes thus receives all the electoral votes of the state.

*Regional and state alignments have deeply affected selection of the President by the electoral college.* Urban America, outside the South and Southwest, was a center of Democratic support after the New Deal, which gave the Democrats an advantage in competition for the electoral votes of the populous urban states: New York, California, Pennsylvania, Illinois, Ohio, and Michigan. A combination of electoral majorities in a few of these states and the traditional support for the Democratic nominee in the South gave Democrats a clear advantage in presidential elections from 1932 to 1952. Republicans were at a disadvantage because their support was strong in states with few electoral votes — in agrarian midwestern states and the smaller northeastern states.

With our two major parties changing geographic alignment — and formerly one-party states becoming competitive in presidential elections, at least — *neither Democrats nor Republicans are now sure of their traditional support in the electoral college.* Candidates for President have designed their strategies to appeal to new groups. Barry Goldwater hoped in 1964 to combine victory in the South with winning margins in the traditional Republican states of the Rocky Mountains, the Midwest, and northern New England for an electoral majority. He managed to carry only five states of the deep South and his own Arizona. In 1968, George Wallace of Alabama campaigned to win the electoral votes of the South for his American Independent party, hoping to keep both the Democratic and Republican nominees from winning a majority of the electoral votes; the House of Representatives, where Wallace supporters might have bargaining power, would have selected the President. Despite substantial support within the South and scattered strength elsewhere, Wallace carried only five states of the deep South. His forty-five electoral votes were not enough to prevent Richard Nixon from winning the required majority.

## how do written statutes affect elections?

Elections are covered by extensive statutory regulation, including devices such as control of absentee voting, residence and registration requirements, provision for tabulating votes, placement and position of candidates' names on the ballot, write-in voting, and the length of the ballot. *State statutes are seldom impartial in their effects upon electoral competition:* each favors or hurts interests jockeying for electoral advantage; each may be manipulated to help or harm a candidate, faction, or party by the ballot form used, the scheduling of elections, and the nature of constituencies affecting voters' options and conduct.

*Two major forms of ballot are used in American elections* (see Figure 8–1). The *party-column* ballot lists the candidates for each party in a separate column. This ballot form facilitates "straight-ticket" voting, for the voter may select one party's entire slate merely by pulling the lever for all candidates in a column. The *office-column* ballot groups candidates by the office sought. Party affiliation is indicated next to each office seeker's name rather than at the head of a column, requiring the voter do a little more thinking.

Party-column ballots promote party competition by providing voters with a choice between sets of party candidates; the office-column ballot makes party preference less significant. About 15 percent of those who would be straight-ticket voters on a party-column ballot split their vote between the parties on office-column ballots.[1] Providing space to *write in* the names of candidates the citizens wish to support instead of those listed on the ballot also can influence voting patterns. In 1964, Henry Cabot Lodge became a serious contender for the presidency by winning the New Hampshire presidential primary with write-in votes.

*The scheduling of elections affects voting.* Local and statewide contests are often held in conjunction with federal elections. The more elective offices they vote upon, however, the less citizens know of the positions, qualifications, and loyalties of each candidate. Consequently, voting choices are often determined by easily recognized symbols, such as party affiliation, which simplify the voter's selection. When federal, state, and local elections are scheduled simultaneously, the forces producing victory for a slate of candidates at one level frequently carry over into races for other offices. Where ballot forms facilitate straight-ticket voting and federal elections coincide with state and local contests, several party candidates may ride to victory on the "coattails" of a winner at the head of the ticket. In 1952 and 1956, some victorious Republican Senators and governors probably benefited by Dwight Eisenhower's popularity, although Democratic dominance of the House of Representatives was not much reduced. The important coattails may be those of a senatorial candidate rather than the presidential aspirant. In 1968, Hubert Humphrey might have carried even fewer states against Richard Nixon had not more attractive Democratic candidates (such as Senator Abraham Ribicoff in Connecticut) provided helpful coattails.

*The extent and nature of coattail voting are hard to determine because they deal with the voter's motivations,* which are hard enough for

[1] Angus Campbell et al., eds., *The American Voter* (New York: John Wiley, 1960), pp. 266–289.

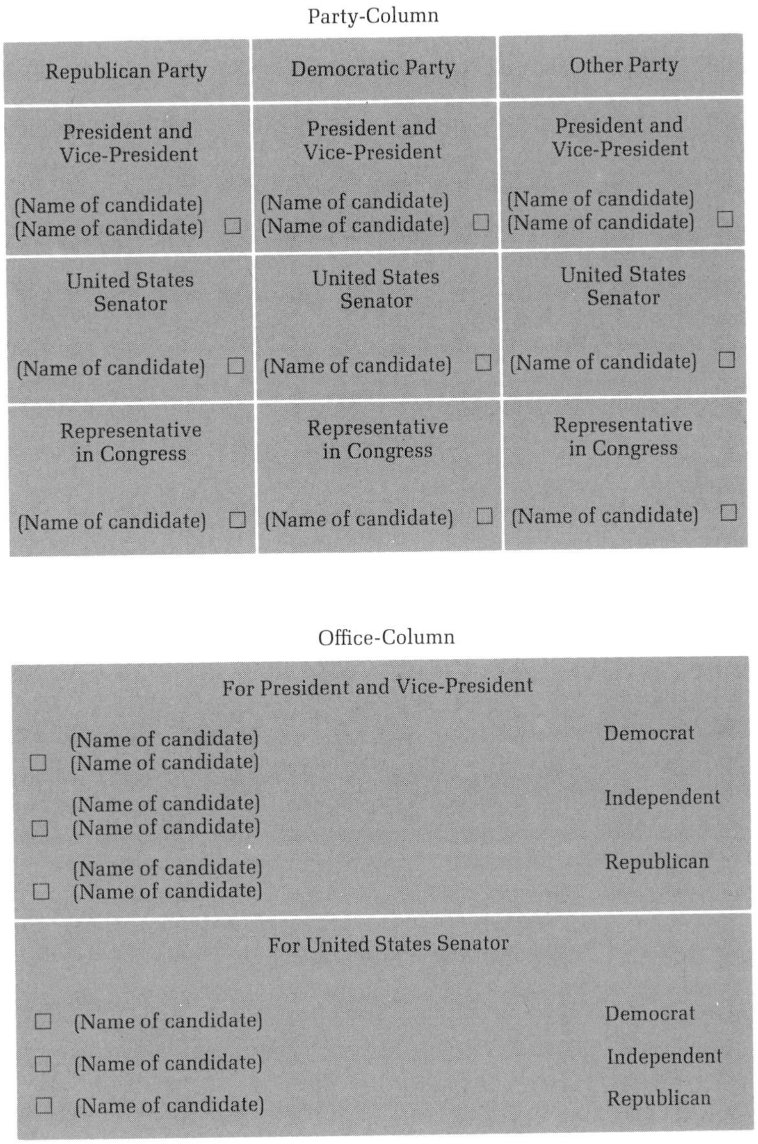

Party-Column

| Republican Party | Democratic Party | Other Party |
|---|---|---|
| President and Vice-President<br><br>(Name of candidate)<br>(Name of candidate) ☐ | President and Vice-President<br><br>(Name of candidate)<br>(Name of candidate) ☐ | President and Vice-President<br><br>(Name of candidate)<br>(Name of candidate) ☐ |
| United States Senator<br><br>(Name of candidate) ☐ | United States Senator<br><br>(Name of candidate) ☐ | United States Senator<br><br>(Name of candidate) ☐ |
| Representative in Congress<br><br>(Name of candidate) ☐ | Representative in Congress<br><br>(Name of candidate) ☐ | Representative in Congress<br><br>(Name of candidate) ☐ |

Office-Column

**For President and Vice-President**

☐ (Name of candidate)
  (Name of candidate)    Democrat

☐ (Name of candidate)
  (Name of candidate)    Independent

☐ (Name of candidate)
  (Name of candidate)    Republican

**For United States Senator**

☐ (Name of candidate)    Democrat

☐ (Name of candidate)    Independent

☐ (Name of candidate)    Republican

FIGURE 8-1
A Comparison of Party-Column and Office-Column Ballots

the person himself to disentangle and just about impossible for the out-
sider to assess. Clearly straight-ticket voting for reasons other than coattails — especially party identification — is very common.[2] In close contests, though, relatively few voters may make the difference, so party
leaders welcome an attractive candidate at the head of the ticket, because
some of his popularity may rub off in voter support for the party's lesser
nominees.

Politicians have had such faith in the drawing power of a popular
candidate that they have tried to schedule elections either to facilitate
or thwart the coattail effect. In the late 1930s, when Franklin Roosevelt
was at the height of his popularity, legislatures in Republican-controlled
states scheduled elections for state offices at times different from the
presidential elections, hoping to get around Roosevelt's popularity. But
in the 1950s, when Eisenhower's popularity would have assisted Republican nominees in these same states, they were deprived of his pulling
power by changes in scheduling.

*Statutes regulating the boundaries, size, and composition of electoral
constituencies also affect patterns of preference.* Political choice is tied
to such factors as party identification and place of residence. Constituencies can be designed to make one party dominant over others. When
this occurs, social interests normally compete within the primary election of the dominant party rather than align with lesser parties that have
no chance of winning the general election. Often the vote of blacks,
Mexican-Americans, and other ethnic groups is split into several constituencies, instead of remaining concentrated in an electoral unit that could
form a majority in the struggle for political control.

## how do unwritten partisan traditions affect elections?

Constitutions reflect political habits as well as being collections of statutes and written principles. One of the habits of the American electorate
is enduring loyalty to one of the two major parties in federal elections.
*The distribution of votes between the Republican and Democratic par-
ties has been remarkably stable.* Republican majorities in presidential
elections were typical from 1864 to 1932. Since then Democratic majorities have been the rule. Exceptions to both patterns were Democratic

---

[2] Angus Campbell and Warren E. Miller, "The Motivational Basis of Straight and Split
Ticket Voting," *The American Political Science Review* 51 (June 1957); 293–312; Warren E.
Miller, "Presidential Coattails: A Study in Political Myth and Methodology," *The Public
Opinion Quarterly* 19 (Spring 1955): 26–39.

victories in 1876, 1884, 1892, 1912, and 1916, and Republican victories in 1952, 1956, and 1968.

Control of Congress has alternated fairly consistently between the parties, although some congressional seats have been held by the dominant party without real challenge. One-party dominance in "safe" districts has helped a party continue to function despite a national landslide won by the opposition, preserving two-party competition. In 1964, Republicans found solace in having elected Congressmen in the Midwest and West when Lyndon Johnson achieved an overwhelming victory over Barry Goldwater.

Party voting in presidential elections since 1789 clearly reveals a cyclical trend in shifting party fortunes.[3] One party enters a period of *ascendancy,* while a minority of the voters favors the opposition or an occasional minor party. So long as party identifiers stick to their loyalties the dominant party continues in the ascendancy and the result is *maintaining* elections.[4] In the 1924 and 1928 elections, the Republicans maintained their ascendancy.

A second stage of the cycle begins when new voters come into the electorate and identify with the opposition; when a few partisans are converted; or when normally indifferent citizens — attracted by a personable candidate or stimulated by a dramatic issue — vote against the ascendant party. With the two parties more evenly balanced, close competition begins a new period of two-party *equilibrium.* Presidential and congressional elections from 1872 to 1896 reflected such an equilibrium. In equilibrium stages, elections usually are either deviating or reinstating rather than maintaining. In a *deviating* election, issues, candidates, and other influences produce enough temporary defections among majority party identifiers for the minority to win — as in 1968 — or an unusually high turnout by normally indifferent or independent voters who vote for the minority party. The presidential elections of 1952 and 1956 illustrate such elections; Eisenhower attracted many Democrats and independent voters as well as loyal Republicans to his cause and became the first Republican President since 1933. A *reinstating* election returns to power the party defeated in a deviating election; party loyalists who had defected return to the fold at the same time as the indifferent voters lose intense interest in the electoral outcome. The victory of John F. Kennedy in 1960 reinstated the Democratic majority that had prevailed from 1933 until 1952.

Periods of equilibrium also break down and often are followed by

---

[3] Charles Sellers, "The Equilibrium Cycle in Two-Party Politics," *The Public Opinion Quarterly* 29 (Spring 1965): 16–37.
[4] Campbell et al., *The American Voter,* 531–538.

party realignment, reflecting a new long-term shift in party allegiance. During this phase a *critical* election reveals the realignment and installs the opposition as the newly ascendant party.[5] Sometimes critical elections follow serious disturbances in American social life, disturbances resulting in permanent personal defections from one party to another. An example was the presidential election of 1932 held in the midst of the Great Depression. Following the critical election, the cycle begins anew with another period of party ascendancy.

Party ascendancy, equilibrium, and realignment periods, and the type of election common to each are based on the traditional American loyalty to one of the major parties. Several indicators suggest, however, that *partisan voting may be on the way out.* First, partisan identification still is a most common form of political participation, but the proportion of self-designated independents is rising and that of partisans is declining slightly (Table 8-1). Second, split-ticket voting is increasing, suggesting that fewer voters enter the voting booth with strong partisan convictions; indeed, many voters split their choices for President, governor, and Congress between parties and then do not bother to mark the remainder of the ballot.[6] Third, deviating elections are more frequent, an indication that weak partisans and peripherally involved voters are moving back and forth across party lines. Fourth, party identification is generally associated with high rates of voting in elections; that is, partisans vote more often than do independents. But turnouts in American presidential elections have dropped, which may mean that partisan attachments are weakening. Moreover, partisans are more likely to vote both in presidential election years and in congressional elections in years with no presidential contest. The voting rate in off-year congressional elections is relatively low, however, which may prove that many voters who take part in presidential elections are without partisan leanings and do not vote two years later.[7]

*If these indicators are valid, what can we predict about patterns of voting choice in the 1970s?* The possibilities are many.

Despite the long-term trend, *American elections will continue to reflect extensive partisan choice.* Even with defections among weakly identified Democrats to George Wallace and Richard Nixon in 1968 (a

    [5] V. O. Key, Jr., "A Theory of Critical Elections," *The Journal of Politics* 17 (Feb. 1955): 3-18.

    [6] Walter DeVries and V. Lance Tarrance, *The Ticket-Splitters: A New Force in American Politics* (Grand Rapids, Mich.: William B. Eerdmans, 1972).

    [7] Walter Dean Burnham, *Critical Elections and the Mainsprings of American Politics* (New York: W. W. Norton, 1970).

TABLE 8-1

Shifts in Self-Designations
of Partisanship and Independence of American Voters, 1960–1970

| Self-designation | Year | | | | | | | | | | | | Decade shift | |
|---|---|---|---|---|---|---|---|---|---|---|---|---|---|---|
| | 1960 | | 1962 | | 1964 | | 1966 | | 1968 | | 1970 | | | |
| | SRC | AIPO | SRC | AIPO | SRC | AIPO | SRC | AIPO | SRC | AIPO | SRC | AIPO | SRC | AIPO |
| Republican | 27% | 30% | 28% | 29% | 24% | 25% | 25% | 27% | 24% | 27% | 25% | 29% | −2% | −1% |
| Democrat | 46 | 47 | 46 | 48 | 51 | 53 | 45 | 48 | 45 | 46 | 43 | 45 | −3 | −2 |
| Independent | 23 | 23 | 22 | 23 | 23 | 22 | 28 | 25 | 30 | 27 | 31 | 26 | +8 | +3 |

Sources: SRC: Survey Research Center, University of Michigan, and Interuniversity Consortium for Political Research; AIPO: American Institute of Public Opinion (Gallup Poll). Data need not total 100 percent because of "don't know" responses.

deviating election in an era of declining equilibrium) and again to Nixon in 1972, strong and moderately intense partisans remained loyal. It was the new voters who exercised independence and divided their support between Humphrey, Nixon, and Wallace in 1968 and between McGovern and Nixon in 1972.

We can anticipate some *realignment in partisan patterns.* Barry Goldwater, despite his loss in 1964, was able to overcome the standing party commitments of Democrats in the West and deep South, just as Lyndon Johnson did among Republicans in the Northeast. The national alignment in 1964 closely resembled that in the elections from 1896 to 1932 with a sectional polarization of sorts. The West and the South against the Northeast. In the earlier era, Democratic strength lay in the South and West and Republican strength in the Northeast. In 1964, precisely the *reverse* was true; Democrats captured the Northeast handily, and Goldwater's votes were concentrated in clusters of counties in the South and West. Traditional partisan patterns were reversed, so we may speculate that partisanship alone no longer guarantees a stable ordering of voters' preferences independently of sectional and class loyalties.

The personalities of the candidates themselves (as projected by the mass media) will become more important in elections. *The number of deviating elections reflecting short-term shifts in party loyalties will increase.*[8]

[8] Donald E. Stokes, "Party Loyalty and the Likelihood of Deviating Elections," *The Journal of Politics* 24 (Nov. 1962): 689–702.

Education, age, sex, ethnicity,
as well as class and
status, influence party preferences.

## social bases of voting choice

The American electorate's fluctuating performance in representing its conflicts — in voting — is affected by its social groups and its demographic characteristics: they do not impel anyone to vote Democratic or Republican any more than they impel him to vote at all, but they do affect his choice. Our political guides often are like us in some way and they may be our intimates.

## demographics of voting

Americans' responses to elections depend on their sex, age, education, ethnic background, religion, residence, and social class. The proportions of demographic groups associated with partisan choice in some presidential elections appear in Table 8-2.

Neither of the two major political parties
has a firm base
of support in any demographic group.

SEX. As voters in presidential elections, women are less loyal to their parties than men. They are more likely to vote Republican than are men (see Table 8–2), but the difference is so slight that it could reflect other social characteristics (age, residence, social class) rather than intrinsic political differences.

AGE. No age group shows a consistent partisan preference, but age does influence political choice. Maturity brings with it opportunities for greater political involvement and participation, leading older citizens to vote more readily in federal elections than younger citizens. Party loyalties intensify with age. The longer one supports a party, the more inclined he is to continue to do so — with exceptions, of course. Maturity also brings more social and economic reasons for shifting party allegiance: a person in his thirties with a record of lukewarm support for Democratic candidates may acquire a preference for the Republican party because of his upward social mobility.

Many young people enter the voting population in an election with partisan leanings imparted by family, church, and school. But more and more, they are politically independent and switch party preferences from one election to another. Issues and candidates' personalities frequently provide their cues for voting.

EDUCATION. Many consistently Republican voters have more formal education than Democratic voters; and because education is part of class status, many Republicans are from the upper class. Although many Republicans are college graduates, not all college graduates are Republicans; there is a party split by occupation within this group. Persons with postgraduate training as lawyers, medical doctors, and engineers seem to

TABLE 8-2
Partisan Voting Choices of Demographic Groups, 1952–1968

| | | | | | | Presidential election | | | | | |
|---|---|---|---|---|---|---|---|---|---|---|---|
| | 1952 | | 1956 | | 1960 | | 1964 | | 1968 | | |
| Demographic group | D | R | D | R | D | R | D | R | D | R | Wallace |
| National | 44.6% | 55.4% | 42.2% | 57.8% | 50.1% | 49.9% | 61.3% | 38.7% | 43.0% | 43.4% | 13.6% |
| Men | 47 | 53 | 45 | 55 | 52 | 48 | 60 | 40 | 41 | 43 | 16 |
| Women | 42 | 58 | 39 | 61 | 49 | 51 | 62 | 38 | 45 | 43 | 12 |
| White | 43 | 57 | 41 | 59 | 49 | 51 | 59 | 41 | 38 | 47 | 15 |
| Nonwhite | 79 | 21 | 61 | 39 | 68 | 32 | 94 | 6 | 85 | 12 | 3 |
| College | 34 | 66 | 31 | 69 | 39 | 61 | 52 | 48 | 37 | 54 | 9 |
| High school | 45 | 55 | 42 | 58 | 52 | 48 | 62 | 38 | 42 | 43 | 15 |
| Grade school | 52 | 48 | 50 | 50 | 55 | 45 | 66 | 34 | 52 | 33 | 15 |
| Professional and business | 36 | 64 | 32 | 68 | 42 | 58 | 54 | 46 | 34 | 56 | 10 |
| White collar | 40 | 60 | 37 | 63 | 48 | 52 | 57 | 43 | 41 | 47 | 12 |
| Manual | 55 | 45 | 50 | 50 | 60 | 40 | 71 | 29 | 50 | 35 | 15 |
| Farmers | 33 | 67 | 46 | 54 | 48 | 52 | 53 | 47 | 29 | 51 | 20 |
| Under 30 | 51 | 49 | 43 | 57 | 54 | 46 | 64 | 36 | 47 | 38 | 15 |
| 30–49 years | 47 | 53 | 45 | 55 | 54 | 46 | 63 | 37 | 44 | 41 | 15 |
| 50 years and older | 39 | 61 | 39 | 61 | 46 | 54 | 59 | 41 | 41 | 47 | 12 |
| Protestant | 37 | 63 | 37 | 63 | 38 | 62 | 55 | 45 | 35 | 49 | 16 |
| Catholic | 56 | 44 | 51 | 49 | 78 | 22 | 76 | 24 | 59 | 33 | 8 |

Source: American Institute of Public Opinion (Gallup Poll).

prefer the Republican label; voters with graduate degrees in the sciences, humanities, and social sciences, particularly academicians, are more frequently Democrats.

ETHNICITY. America is often described as a "melting pot" into which people of all races, national origins, and religious backgrounds "have been poured"; in a generation or two, the notion goes, ethnic traits recede, and the sons and daughters of immigrants are "Americans." Voting studies prove the melting pot theory more myth than fact; ethnic groups retain their individuality through many generations. Democrats draw electoral support from voters of Irish, Polish, Italian, and Slavic descent; Republicans still appeal to Americans of English, Scottish, Welsh, German, and Scandinavian ancestry. Since 1936 or earlier and most markedly in 1964, black voters have shifted from Abraham Lincoln's party to that of the Democrats (see Table 8-2).[9]

RELIGION. Although there are both Catholic Republicans and Protestant Democrats, Protestants are more often affiliated with the Republican party; Jews vote Democratic; and Catholics support Democratic candidates less than Jews, but still are a major source of Democratic voting strength.

In some campaigns, religion is really significant. John F. Kennedy's candidacy aroused pro- and anti-Catholic sentiments. The Michigan Survey Research Center estimated that in the 1960 campaign "Kennedy won a vote bonus from Catholics amounting to about 4 percent of the national two-party vote." Yet losses from Protestant Democrats and Independents were about 6.5 percent. Overall the religious issue caused a loss of 2.2 percent of "normal" Democratic support — the percentage of votes a Democratic candidate could have received had everyone acted solely on the basis of partisan affiliation.[10] This loss was more than offset, however, by the peculiarities of voting in the electoral college. The Catholic shift to Kennedy helped him win the electoral votes of populous states; defections by Protestant Democrats occurred in states with fewer electoral votes. Overall, Kennedy's religion provided a windfall of ten electoral votes.[11]

RESIDENCE. Generally, the *urban* areas of the North have been strongholds of the Democratic party, particularly in the East and portions of

[9] For a detailed breakdown of ethnic traditions in voting in America, see Kevin Phillips, *The Emerging Republican Majority* (New Rochelle, N.Y.: Arlington House, 1969).

[10] Philip E. Converse et al., "Stability and Change in 1960: A Reinstating Election," *The American Political Science Review* 55 (June 1961): 269–289.

[11] Ithiel de Sola Pool, Robert Abelson, and Samuel Popkin, *Candidates, Issues and Strategies* (Cambridge, Mass.: Massachusetts Institute of Technology Press, 1964).

the Midwest. Republican strength has grown appreciably in urbanized communities in the South, especially in the last decade. Both parties have support in the small towns of America; southern hamlets are traditionally Democratic (aside from pockets of Republican strength in east Tennessee and Kentucky), and Republicans receive votes in the small towns of the East and Midwest.

*Suburban* America is neither predominantly Republican nor Democratic. Despite folklore to the contrary, few people who move to the suburbs enjoy (or suffer) political conversion; they retain their party loyalties. Many suburbs have distinctive class colorations, with associated party leanings and urbanites who resettle in the suburbs frequently select a suburb congenial to their class and political outlook. Hence there are strongly Democratic suburbs and strongly Republican suburbs, and some are mixed.

*Rural* America, unlike our cities, is primarily Republican. In 1964, more farmers voted for Barry Goldwater than any other major occupational group. The small towns in rural areas are the Republican heartland. Democrats, however, are not without support in agrarian areas, particularly in the rural South. But that support does not always go to the nominee of the Democratic party in presidential elections. In 1968, the independent candidacy of George Wallace got much of its support from the traditionally Democratic strongholds of the rural South.[12]

OCCUPATION. Neither political party can count on exclusive support by any occupational group and yet tendencies are clear. Businessmen, both large and small, generally favor the Republicans, although that depends on the type of business, locale, and so forth. Republicans attract the votes of white collar, managerial, professional, and executive workers; other workers, whether unskilled, organized, or unorganized, lean toward the Democrats (see Table 8–2).

SOCIAL CLASS AND STATUS. Both *objective measures* of social class — the social standings of citizens as indicated by their occupations, incomes, and education — or *subjective* measures of social status — people's classifications of themselves as members of a social class — reveal a fairly stable pattern of class and status voting: *consistent Republican support is more probable from the upper and upper-middle classes than from the middle and lower classes, which tend to vote Democratic.*[13] With subjective measures, the relationship is more ambiguous, but the direction is

[12] See Irving Crespi, "Structural Sources of the George Wallace Constituency," *Social Science Quarterly* 52 (June 1971): 115–132; Anthony M. Orum, "Religion and the Rise of the Radical White: The Case of Southern Wallace Support in 1968," *Social Science Quarterly* 51 (Dec. 1970): 674–688.
[13] Robert R. Alford, *Party and Society* (Chicago: Rand McNally, 1963).

the same. Americans seem quite willing to classify themselves as belonging to, say, the "propertied," "middle," or "working" class, but the penchant for self-classification does not go so far as to produce intense class awareness that would intensify the link to party preference. It is unlikely that an American consistently votes Republican or Democrat because he identifies with the upper, middle, or working class. We simply do not know whether an automobile worker sees himself as a "working man" and votes Democratic because he believes that party protects the workers' interests, or whether he sees himself as a Democrat first and judges his class position from that standpoint. *A complex mingling of party, class, and status conditions voting.*

Political parties do make distinct appeals to class consciousness; and those appeals have influenced electoral outcomes, as in the depression period of the 1930s. The apparent consensus of voters in all socioeconomic categories for a candidate or party (Eisenhower in 1952 or Johnson in 1964) has led many observers to conclude that class issues are no longer relevant in American politics. Yet class differences once again sharply faced the parties in 1972 as presidential aspirants had to deal with the class issues implicit in the Nixon administration's regulation of wages, prices, and rents and in reports of poverty and malnutrition in both urban and rural America.

THE ROLE OF DEMOGRAPHICS. Table 8–3 recapitulates the voting tendencies of major demographic groups. Do not be misled by these general profiles of support for each major party and conclude that any social category belongs exclusively or permanently to Republicans or Democrats. Neither party stakes its destiny on these tendencies. Each group has shifted its support from one party to another between elections (Table 8–2). *Neither of the two major parties has a secure base of support in any demographic group.* Neither can appeal to deep-seated animosities between categoric interests — rich and poor, educated and uneducated, Protestant and Catholic. Instead, both must help to mold a consensus among people with different social backgrounds by blunting the conflicts between diverse interests.

Finally, we must remember that no American is simply middle class, or Protestant, or thirty years of age, or a southerner. *Any voter combines varied, often conflicting, social characteristics.* One that may predispose him to vote Democratic (his religion) may conflict with another that turns him to the Republicans (his career). Most influences are inconsistent, so we cannot identify which of many social characteristics are crucial in deciding voting choice.[14]

---

[14] D. Stanley Eitzen, "Social Class, Status Inconsistency, and Political Attitudes," *Social Science Quarterly* 51 (Dec. 1970): 602–609.

**TABLE 8-3**
**Partisan Tendencies of Demographic Groups**

| *Democratic* | *Republican* |
|---|---|
| Middle and lower income | Middle and upper income |
| Organized and unskilled workers | Managerial and professional persons |
| First and second generation Americans: Irish, Polish, Italian, Slavic minorities | |
| Nonwhites and whites | Germanic and Scottish stock Whites |
| Farm operators | Prosperous farmers |
| Roman Catholics and Jews | Protestants |
| Both low formal education and with graduate training | College educated and professionally trained |
| Residents of cities, lower- and middle-class suburbs, rural southerners | Residents of middle- and upper-class suburbs, small towns, rural midwesterners |
| Young to middle-aged | Middle-aged to elderly |

## social groups and voting

Demographic breakdowns such as rural or urban residents, ethnic categories, and the like are categoric social groups that differ from *primary* face-to-face social groups such as the family or friends. Generally they complement one another in their influence on voting. People with similar social characteristics and backgrounds are more likely to mingle socially, defining and sharpening amorphous demographic interests by intimate group membership.

*Families* and *groups of friends* are politically homogeneous social units. American husbands and wives agree remarkably well in voting opinions; less than 10 percent of couples disagree on candidate preferences in presidential elections and are very similar in party loyalties, political knowledge, interest in politics, and active participation in elections.[15]

*Co-workers* probably have less influence over a person's vote than do members of his family or close friends because the bonds are weaker.

---

[15] Robert E. Lane, *Political Life* (Glencoe, Ill.: Free Press, 1959), pp. 208–209; M. Kent Jennings and Richard G. Niemi, "The Division of Political Labor Between Mothers and Fathers," *The American Political Science Review* 65 (March 1971): 69–82.

Furthermore, if relations between a person and his family or friends become tense and uncomfortable in the heat of an argument, he may simply leave. But his selection of co-workers is not voluntary and he must remain on the job throughout the work day. He may form only casual friendships, if any, on the job. Personal leadership in political discussions, based on the respect for leaders in intimate social groups, is more likely in the family and among friends than among fellow workers.

## personal factors and voting choice

The personal factors underlying voting decisions include both an individual's views of politics in general — his *political perspectives* as shaped by the attitudes learned throughout life — and what he thinks is important in an election, his *political perceptions* of opposing candidates, issues, and parties. Conflicting perspectives and perceptions are normally reflected in their voting choices. Partisanship is a principal factor governing the voter's perspective on elections and upon the candidates, parties, and issues that are the objects of his perceptions.

### party identification

*Of all the things that condition voting behavior, none has proved so vital as enduring partisan loyalties.*[16] Attachment to a major political party is one of the most widespread and consistent ways in which Americans take part in conflict representation (see again Table 5–4). Although party loyalties declined slightly in the 1960s (Table 8–1), about three Americans out of four are still willing to classify themselves as Democrats or Republicans; many who call themselves "independents" say they feel closer to one of the major parties than to the other.

Whatever the source of party loyalties — conscious reflection, habit, emotional satisfaction, early family socialization and subsequent reinforcement by friends and other primary groups — they are personally meaningful symbols that simplify the choice between candidates. A person's *psychological attachment to a political party* colors his long-term political perspective and guides his perceptions of candidates, issues, and campaign events.

If Americans were to cast votes in presidential elections solely in ac-

[16] Philip E. Converse, "Of Time and Partisan Stability," *Comparative Political Studies* 2 (July 1969): 139–171.

Responses to the candidates are the major source of defection from party loyalty in presidential elections. In 1950, voters preferred the popular and reassuring image of Dwight D. Eisenhower to the more removed, intellectual Adlai Stevenson.

cordance with partisan sentiments, the normal distribution of the two-party vote between Democrats and Republicans would be 56 to 44 percent.[17] This estimate does not contradict the fact that of those identifying with a political party Democrats outnumber Republicans slightly less than 5 to 3; it simply takes into account the greater tendency of Republicans to vote and the higher rate of nonvoting among self-declared Democrats. But in no presidential election between 1952 and 1972 has the division of the two-party vote actually produced the 56 to 44 split (see Table 8-2 again). Partisan attachment then seems to be imperfectly correlated with actual voting behavior, a supposition confirmed by the data reported in Table 8-4. In presidential elections, some party loyalists (usually from a fifth to a third of party identifiers) defect to the opposition because of specific characteristics of the election.

Commitment to a political party may be weak, moderate, or strong. This actual vote is predicted inexactly by party identification: "weak" and "moderate" Democrats and Republicans are especially likely to defect when faced with the ballot, because of a highly attractive candidate or a striking issue. In 1952 and 1956, many "weak" and "moderate" Democrats voted for Eisenhower, whose image as a victorious general transcended party loyalties.[18] Many Protestant Democrats voted for Richard Nixon in 1960, but only 5 percent of Republicans voted for Kennedy; in 1964, two of every ten Republicans defected to the Johnson-Humphrey ticket; and, in 1968, many Democrats *and* Republicans voted for George Wallace's independent candidacy. (As Table 8-4 illustrates, a higher proportion of Democrats did so.)[19] Party attachment that is weakening from strong to moderate to weak may slowly be converting to identification with the other party; such voters are very likely to vote at variance with their declared party loyalty and then, after they reassign their identification to the new party of their choice, they once again vote in line with their party commitments. More rigid and intense party conversions can happen: the shift of blacks and other have-not groups from Republican to Democratic in the 1930s under Franklin Roosevelt; the new Republicanism of southern interests disenchanted with the complexion and policies of the national Democratic leadership.

Even if voter partisanship were automatically translated into matching

[17] Warren E. Miller, "Who Voted for Whom in 1970," report of the Center for Political Studies, Institute for Social Research, University of Michigan (May 18, 1971).

[18] Philip E. Converse and Georges Dupeux, "De Gaulle and Eisenhower: The Public Image of the Victorious General," in Angus Campbell et al., eds., *Elections and the Political Order* (New York: John Wiley, 1966), pp. 292–345.

[19] Philip E. Converse et al., "Continuity and Change in American Politics: Parties and Issues in the 1968 Election," *The American Political Science Review* 63 (Dec. 1969), 1083–1105.

| | TABLE 8-4 |
| --- | --- |
| | **Partisan Voting Choices of Party Identifiers, 1952–1968** |

| | Partisan voting choices in presidential elections | | | | | | | | | | |
| | 1952 | | 1956 | | 1960 | | 1964 | | 1968 | | |
| Party identification | D | R | D | R | D | R | D | R | D | R | Wal- lace |
| Republicans | 8% | 92% | 4% | 96% | 5% | 95% | 20% | 80% | 9% | 86% | 5% |
| Democrats | 77 | 23 | 85 | 15 | 84 | 16 | 87 | 13 | 74 | 12 | 14 |
| Independents | 35 | 65 | 30 | 70 | 43 | 57 | 56 | 44 | 31 | 44 | 25 |

Source: American Institute of Public Opinion (Gallup Poll).

votes, the many independents in the electorate would vary the national distribution of votes between the major parties. As clearly illustrated in Table 8-5, independents — those who choose not to identify with a party — are increasing, especially among young voters. The distribution of party identifications prior to the elections of 1972 appears in Table 8-5. Note the proportion of independents among those eligible to vote in their first presidential election (eighteen to twenty-four years of age). Those independents, however limited their political interest and information, are unpredictable in their voting because they respond more to the short-term forces of an election than to partisan appeals.

Because they do respond to specific appeals of candidates regardless of party, independents are very likely to be split-ticket voters. Fewer than 15 percent of them vote straight party tickets, whereas more than 80 percent of party identifiers do so. Independents who split their tickets share demographic characteristics: they are younger, more educated, and more

| | TABLE 8-5 |
| --- | --- |
| | **Party Identification of Americans, by Age** |

| | Age | |
| --- | --- | --- |
| Party identification | 18–21 years | Over 21 years |
| Republican | 18% | 27% |
| Democratic | 38 | 45 |
| Independent | 42 | 28 |

Source: Survey conducted for *Newsweek* by American Institute of Public Opinion, *Newsweek* 78 (Oct. 1971): 41.

often white-collared and suburban than the average voter. Moreover, they get more of their political information from the mass media than from partisans and, for this reason, they are more responsive to the images of candidates and issues as portrayed in the media than to party definitions. As the percentage of independents rises, therefore, we expect to see symbolic persuasion (see Chapter Seven) increasingly affect election outcomes.[20]

*Party identification, despite the increase in independents, still is the strongest influence upon voters' long-term perspectives on elections.* The chief alternative — identification with an ideological point of view (Liberal or Conservative) — is much less important. Relatively few get their political outlooks from an ideological commitment, and most are political activists. Within each party, voters with ideological convictions form intense minorities bent upon converting all partisans to their views, to the end that in elections the Democratic-Republican alternative will be a liberal-conservative one as well. In 1964, definite ideological disputes marked the preconvention maneuvering of the Republicans. The victorious conservative faction, united behind Barry Goldwater, carried its doctrinaire message into the campaign only to find that it fell on deaf ears, or, worse yet, was heard and led to negative judgments on Goldwater. The "conservative vote" in 1964 could hardly have exceeded a fourth of the Goldwater total of twenty-seven million.[21]

## reaching a voting decision

In a political campaign, then, the voter looks at the election from a perspective primarily dictated by party identification. Whether he votes his party loyalty or defects depends upon how he responds to the short-term inducements offered by the candidates, competing parties, and issues.

CANDIDATE IMAGES. The campaigner's style and voters' expectations combine to form an image. The popular and reassuring image of Dwight Eisenhower; the peppery image of Harry Truman; the "intellectual grace" and youth of John F. Kennedy; the "calculating politician" image of Lyndon Johnson; and the "loser" reputation of Richard Nixon before he won in 1968 — all show how voters develop a picture of a presidential, senatorial, or congressional candidate that usually sticks and significantly af-

---

[20] DeVries and Tarrance, *The Ticket-Splitters.*
[21] John Osgood Field and Ronald E. Anderson, "Ideology in the Public's Conception of the 1964 Election," *The Public Opinion Quarterly* 33 (Fall 1969): 380–398.

fects the election. Voters express more interest in the candidates than in abstract programs or notions of the public interest; moreover, so long as parties do not present voters with clear-cut policy alternatives, voters are forced to emphasize competing personalities. *Responses to the candidates probably are the major explanation of why voters defect from party loyalty in presidential elections.*[22] Candidate imagery is less important in congressional than in presidential campaigns; in the former, most voters do not know the contenders, and for those who do, the incumbent candidate's image is generally more persuasive.

The interplay between voters' partisan loyalties and their images of competing candidates is complex. *Party loyalties color perceptions of candidates* (voters regard the candidate of their party far more positively), but *voters affiliate with parties because of the candidates nominated* as well as other factors. If they believe that their party no longer offers candidates who appeal to them, their loyalty to the party may weaken. And when younger voters see one party consistently offering more attractive candidates, their long-term party allegiance tips toward the party with the more appealing candidates. The lasting appeal of the major parties is tied to the images of party nominees — images, which are significantly influenced by television campaigning.[23]

PARTY IMAGES. Party images are made of the things people like and do not like about the major political parties. They are not the same as party identifications, for a person may identify with a party yet not like some of what the party is doing.[24]

The structure of a party image includes references to party candidates ("I like Ike" or "I don't trust tricky Dick Nixon"), evaluations of the performance of the party candidates ("they spend less money," "times are better under them"), references to the groups the parties favor ("they are good for the common people," or "they are good for big business"), and general expressions ("I just don't like them"). From 1952 to 1972, the ratio of favorable to unfavorable comments about Republicans was about one to one, but for Democrats that ratio has been about two to one.[25] Among newly enfranchised younger voters (18- to 21-year-olds), the image of

[22] Richard W. Boyd, "Presidential Elections: An Explanation of Voting Defection," *The American Political Science Review* 63 (June 1969): 498–514.

[23] Herbert F. Weisberg and Jerrold G. Rusk, "Dimensions of Candidate Evaluation," *The American Political Science Review* 64 (Dec. 1970), 1167–1185; Donald E. Stokes, "Some Dynamic Elements of Contests for the Presidency," *The American Political Science Review* 61 (March 1966): 19–28.

[24] Donald R. Matthews and James W. Prothro, *Negroes and the New Southern Politics* (New York: Harcourt, Brace, 1966), chap. 13.

[25] Ratios based upon presidential elections studies, Survey Research Center, University of Michigan; data supplied by the Interuniversity Consortium for Political Research.

The campaigner's style and voters' expectations combine to form an image. The "intellectual grace" and youth of John F. Kennedy was but one example.

neither party is as positive as it is among the general electorate. A nation-wide survey of younger voters revealed that only 15 percent of their comments about the Republican party were favorable (only 22 percent of their comments favored Democrats).[26]

Party images also include public assessments of how well Republicans or Democrats can handle the problems facing America. When Americans are asked to name the most critical problems facing the country and then designate the party "they think can do a better job of handling" them, neither party comes off very well. In 1971, Americans pointed to the state of the economy, Vietnam, drug abuse, and race relations as the leading problems. Asked which party could best handle these matters, 32 percent

[26] News release, American Institute of Public Opinion (August 15, 1971).

favored the Democrats, 22 percent the Republicans, and 36 percent thought it made no difference (the remainder had no opinion).[27] That the largest percentage fell in the "no difference" category may mean that the mass public cannot distinguish differences in policy and that Americans are simply disenchanted with current partisan approaches to problems.[28]

*The general image of the two political parties shows that public feeling is lukewarm and mixed,* but the Democrats are slightly better regarded by voters of all ages than are Republicans.

POLITICAL ISSUES. Generally, most voters in national elections care little about and are unfamiliar with many of the campaign issues; in congressional elections, they are even more aloof. *Yet in some campaigns, issues are significant short-term forces.* In 1964, differences between Johnson and Goldwater on major issues were publicized — civil rights, nuclear responsibility, social welfare legislation, the role of "big government," and foreign policy. Those issues affected the vote in four ways. (1) Most Democrats, except those strongly opposed to civil rights legislation, voted for Johnson. Defections of Democrats occurred primarily in the South where the racial issue cut across traditional party loyalties, but in the North Goldwater's position on civil rights probably cost him votes among some Republicans. (2) Republicans defecting from Goldwater disagreed not only with his stand on civil rights but also on nuclear responsibility and social welfare questions. (3) Independents generally voted according to candidates' stands on issues; most of them were influenced in the pro-Democratic direction on domestic issues. (4) The minority of voters who detected differences between the foreign policy stands of the two candidates favored Johnson by two to one. This was in marked contrast to the elections of the 1950s when, for example, the Republican foreign policy position as represented by Eisenhower was supported by five to one.[29]

On political issues, the public is not always a uniform whole. It is pluralist and divided into groups that have their own interests and conflicts with other groups that are based on its issue stands. Although the *mass* public often finds it hard to discern differences between parties and candidates on issues — 1964 being a significant exception — *specialized publics do spot party differences on issues that are important to them* (blacks see differences on civil rights issues, businessmen on regulation of the economy, the elderly on health care issues). In explaining the vot-

[27] News release, American Institute of Public Opinion (December 19, 1971).

[28] Jack Dennis, "Support for the Party System by the Mass Public," *The American Political Science Review* 60 (Sept. 1966), 600–615.

[29] Ithiel de Sola, Robert Abelson, and Samuel Popkin, *Candidates, Issues and Strategies,* pp. 164–182; Philip E. Converse et al., "Electoral Myth and Reality: The 1964 General Election," *The American Political Science Review* 59, no. 2 (June 1965): 321–337.

ing choices of members of these specialized publics, *pertinent issues have almost as much weight as party identification.*[30]

A voter does perceive the issue stands of his party and candidate within the framework of his party identification. How acceptable he finds his party's candidate depends on how strongly he feels about what his party traditionally stands for and how the candidate's position conforms to that position. In 1968, in both the North and the South many Democrats defected either to Richard Nixon or George Wallace because they preferred those candidates' firm stands on "law and order" to what they considered to be a weaker position of the Democratic party.[31] Such defections indicate that *issues can influence voting independent of party identification.* If voters become displeased with their party's issue stands, they may shift their loyalties to the opposition permanently. (Some indications show that many former southern Democrats have done so over the civil rights issue.)

Political issues influence voting choices in another way. *Voters reach general appraisals of the goodness or badness of the times;* if times are good, they may approve of the party in power but if they are bad they hold it responsible. In 1952, voters were uneasy over the war in Korea and inflation; although many had once supported the New Deal and Fair Deal Democratic administrations, they registered their growing disenchantment by voting Republican. In 1968, we saw similar defections of Democrats because of uneasiness over the Vietnam war, civil disorder, and race relations. Shifts in long-term party fortunes often follow the tendency of "weak" and "moderate" partisans, as well as independents, to switch their support from the "ins" to the "outs" because of general impressions about policy performance.[32]

Politicians know that voters make such general appraisals. Incumbents attempt to "time" the voter's memory by pushing through clearly unpopular policies (tax increases) early in their terms in office. They then pursue popular causes in election years (promising tax reductions if re-elected), hoping the voter has forgotten what took place earlier.

---

[30] David E. RePass, "Issue Salience and Party Choice," *The American Political Science Review* 65 (June 1971): 389–400; Ruth S. Jones and E. Terrence Jones, "Issue Saliency, Opinion-Holding, and Party Preference," *The Western Political Quarterly* 24 (Sept. 1971): 501–509.

[31] The American Institute for Political Communication, *Anatomy of a Crucial Election* (Washington, D.C.: The American Institute for Political Communication, 1970); David M. Kovenock et al., "Status, Party, Ideology, Issues, and Candidate Choice: A Preliminary, Theory-Relevant Analysis of the 1968 American Presidential Election," paper delivered at the Eighth Congress of the International Political Science Association, Munich, Germany, Aug. 31–Sept. 5, 1970.

[32] V. O. Key, Jr., *The Responsible Electorate* (Cambridge, Mass.: Belknap Press, Harvard University Press, 1966).

**THE PRESIDENCY**
NATIONAL POPULAR VOTE **92**%
(AS COUNTED)

NIXON REP.
**28,991,339    43%**

HUMPHREY DEM.
**28,800,091    43%**

WALLACE A.I.P.
**9,036,420    14%**

Popular votes provide a rough index of conflicting opinions on issues of policy, but determining which issues helped voters make up their minds is a difficult, often impossible, task.

HOW THE VOTER DECIDES. We have argued that *relatively stable party identification influences the way in which voters look at candidates, parties, and issues* in political campaigns. Voters' evaluation of these three short-term forces is consistent with their party loyalties, particularly when they are "strong" partisans. If all voting choices depended upon strong partisanship and the tendency to act consistently with it, the winners and losers would be determined simply by how many voters of each party went to the polls to express their fixed loyalties. Campaigns would then be designed not to switch voters' decisions but to retain the support and increase the turnout of those who had already made up their minds.

But *voting choices are not foreordained merely by the party loyalties* voters bring to campaigns. The campaign itself sometimes changes hitherto standing decisions, getting people to defect from their party identifications, especially if the voter must choose between conflicting but very important loyalties.

During a campaign, voters may learn that their party's candidate has a quality or a position they find disagreeable, as did some Protestant Democrats in 1960. They were torn between Kennedy, the Democratic but Catholic candidate, and Nixon, the Republican but Protestant contender. How do voters decide when faced with such conflicts?

*People confronted by contradictory influences try to put in order their personal attitudes and their perceptions of reality — their emotions and their intellect — composing a consistent outlook.* Social psychologists call

266

this effort a "strain toward consistency," a "drive toward congruity," or a "reduction of dissonance."[33] In a political campaign, people try to hold consistent views of candidates, parties, and issues. Citizens who enter the campaign with consistent views are not likely to be swayed by conflicting appeals because they filter out information that contradicts their consistent outlooks. But *people who have dissonant views* and are therefore cross-pressured are more susceptible to change. The voter changes his opinions, if any, depending on the intensity and direction of his precampaign views, their consistency, and the harmony or discrepancy he notices between his political preferences and those of his friends, the party's candidates, the political parties, and political groups.

The cross-pressured voter achieves personal consistency by *changing a previous attitude,* as did some southern segregationists who foreswore their long-term Democratic loyalties rather than vote for a presidential nominee pledged to end segregation. But for a voter deeply committed to supporting the candidate of his party, a *shift in perceptions* may prove easier than a change of perspective. Some staunch anti-Communist Republicans adjusted to President Nixon's trip to China in 1972 by convincing themselves that it was only a token gesture and would never lead to recognition of the Communist regime in China, despite utterances by Nixon to the contrary.

Finally, the voter may find it impossible to resolve the conflict between his attitudes and the contradictory views of the leaders he respects. He may *choose then simply not to vote,* thus neither distorting his perceptions of what is going on nor changing his personal views, but relieving himself of the need to settle his conflict.

## constitutional, social, and personal factors and voting choice: the election of 1972

The reelection of President Richard Nixon in 1972 over his Democratic opponent, George McGovern, by a 3 to 2 ratio vividly illustrates the forces that combine to produce deviating elections. Recall that a deviating election occurs when short-term factors (especially candidates, issues, and party images) produce temporary defections among majority party iden-

---

[33] See Leon Festinger, *A Theory of Cognitive Dissonance* (Stanford, Calif.: Stanford University Press, 1957), Carolyn W. Sherif, Muzafer Sherif, and Roger E. Nebergall, *Attitude and Attitude Change* (Philadelphia: W. B. Saunders, 1965), and Denis G. Sullivan, "Psychological Balance and Reactions to the Presidential Nominations in 1960," in M. Kent Jennings and L. Harmon Zeigler, eds., *The Electoral Process* (Englewood Cliffs, N.J.: Prentice-Hall, 1965), pp. 238–264.

tifiers. These defections produce victory for the minority party. In 1972 Democratic identifiers outnumbered Republicans by about a 5 to 3 ratio. That George McGovern did not win suggests that key factors encouraged massive defections from standing Democratic loyalties and influenced independents to support Richard Nixon. What were these factors?

*The candidates' images made a difference.* According to polls, voters favored neither candidate markedly, but Nixon fared better than his challenger. Nixon capitalized on being the incumbent, striking a pose of the nonpartisan statesman, and minimizing active campaigning. He relied on Cabinet members, governors, and others to speak on his behalf and attack the opposition. Slogans avoiding reference to Nixon as a Republican, e.g., "Reelect the President" and "Four More Years," symbolized Nixon's campaign style. Opinion polls indicated that citizens viewed Nixon as "experienced" and "responsible" despite proclaiming him "devious" and "an opportunist." By comparison McGovern appeared "too radical," "not experienced," "indecisive," and "always complaining." McGovern's greatest problem (if we believe the polls) was people's unwillingness to trust his judgment. Particularly after the disclosure that the Democratic candidate for Vice-President, Senator Thomas Eagleton, had previously sought psychiatric assistance — a disclosure leading to Eagleton's resignation from the ticket — people perceived McGovern as having made "too many mistakes" leading to "doubts about his judgment." They voiced doubts about the credibility of a presidential candidate who had promised to stand behind Eagleton "1,000 percent." All in all, about half of those sampled in polls said Nixon fit their image of an ideal President; only one-fourth said that of McGovern.

Many voters simply perceived George McGovern to be on the *wrong side of important issues.* Regarding Vietnam, opinion polls consistently indicated support for Nixon's handling of the war; McGovern's attacks on the Nixon foreign policy made little headway. On economic issues, McGovern promised to end price and wage controls, but opinion polls indicated that the electorate favored some even stricter controls. And on social issues, including stricter law enforcement, regulation of drug traffic, and forced busing to achieve integration of public schools, the majorities surveyed approved of Nixon's positions. On such social issues Nixon gained the support of many backers of George Wallace after the latter's withdrawal from presidential politics for 1972. Finally, McGovern's attacks on corruption in the Nixon administration failed to stir widespread popular response.

*Direct appeals by Nixon strategists to Democrats also increased Democratic defections.* John Connally, a Democrat and former governor of Texas as well as a former member of Nixon's Cabinet, directed "Democrats for Nixon." Attacks on McGovern (especially on television) came not from Nixon but from Connally's organization. Moreover, the Republicans appealed extensively to various Catholic groups, Jewish voters, and members of organized labor — all formerly Democratic stalwarts.

The McGovern candidacy also suffered from a *failure to rally broad support from independents,* even among first-time voters, 18–24 years old, on whom McGovern's strategists relied so heavily for victory. Although McGovern did well on college campuses, young noncollegians leaned toward Nixon. Turnout rates well below those of recent presidential elections, especially among independents as well as weakly identified Democrats, further assisted the Nixon cause.

Despite the overwhelming defeat suffered by Democrats in the electoral college (winning only 17 of the 538 votes), the party continued its twenty-year majority in Congress. Surveys indicated that the Democratic party retained its image as the party better able to handle problems considered most salient by people. Probably Nixon's victory did not reflect a long-term shift of partisan sentiment leading to a Republican majority of party identifiers. Rather, short-term forces — the appeal of an experienced incumbent running for reelection, the problems associated with perceptions of McGovern and his stand on issues — contributed to Democrats' and independents' votes for Nixon and to the deviating outcome of the election.

## voting choice and conflict representation in america

On the surface, it seems that voting has relatively little to do with making the policies that resolve social disputes in America. After all, except for local elections (voting on constitutional Amendments, bond issues, tax increases, and the like), popular votes do not decide policies at all. Yet voting choices do help to regulate interest conflicts.

To the extent that we can tell which issues helped voters make up their minds — admittedly very difficult and often impossible — *popular votes roughly represent conflicting opinions on policy questions.*

Second, *the distribution of votes is a resolution of the conflict over who shall govern:* winning candidates acquire the authority to make decisions for the entire community by competing for the people's vote.

Third, *voting provides for participation in a vital, though symbolic, democratic ritual:* the popular election that symbolizes the liberal democratic consensus on the virtue of self-government and permits people to express and reinforce their deep emotional loyalties to political leaders, parties, and the American way of doing things.

These three ways in which voting aids conflict regulation parallel some of the levels on which the citizen takes part in elections. And at each level of participation, distinct demands are made upon the citizen. On *the issue level,* the voter must have enough interest in the election to discern salient issues: enough information to detect differences on those issues between competing candidates and parties (if there are differences), enough interest to form an opinion on those issues, and reason enough to decide which candidate represents that opinion.

On *the candidate level,* the voter must decide which candidates have the ability to govern. This decision is difficult because we do not always know which qualities are best suited to governing and, if we did, it would still be difficult to get a clear picture of which candidates have them, despite the vast resources devoted to campaigning.

Finally, at *the partisan level,* long commitment to a political party provides both an emotional and intellectual standard to assist us in voting.

American voters take part on all three of these levels of voting. All voting behavior occurs within *boundaries* established by constitutional and statutory regulations and party traditions. The individual voter is influenced by his *social and demographic* background and personal *perspectives,* which are greatly affected by party identifications. These are lasting, relatively stable factors that influence voting. In each election, these factors and voting decisions themselves are affected by the citizen's impressions of the *candidates, parties,* and *issues.*

It would be easy to conclude that for most Americans voting is only a symbolic exercise, that their perspectives are so laden by partisan prejudices, their images of candidates, parties, and issues are so colored, and their interest in elections is so low that they simply are not able to vote rationally on the candidate and issue levels. We believe that that conclusion is too harsh. It ignores the fact that *party identification, although it is a screen through which people view elections, gives many Americans a rational understanding of politics.* Partisanship is not simply blind; it can serve as an instrument for coping with political facts.

Recently enfranchised eighteen-year-olds register to vote on the Berkeley campus. Pollsters find this group largely independent of party identification and more prone to vote on personalities or issues than party labels.

Candidate images, party images, and political issues have had effects independent of party identification, even causing defections from old partisan loyalties. Americans do differentiate between their partisan ideas and their perceptions of short-term forces. They can and do determine which are more important in specific elections, and they represent their considered opinions by voting.

Even if party identification dictated voting choices (and we know it does not), more and more Americans vote without firm partisan loyalties. These independents are different from those uncovered by the voting research of the 1940s and 1950s. The latter were generally uninformed about politics, apathetic, had little confidence in their ability to influence government, and were easily swayed by emotional appeals. The independent voters of the 1970s are of two kinds: the "old independents" characteristic of earlier decades and the "new independents," who identify with neither party not because they are politically passive but because they believe that neither political party adequately represents their interests in electoral conflicts to warrant permanent loyalty.[34] The "new independent" is particularly prone to act on the issue and candidate levels rather than on the partisan level.

The general factors affecting voting do not demonstrate that Americans are incapable of rational choices, because old loyalties and independence *both* contribute to rational understanding. Also one cannot insist that extensive and continuous electoral involvement by most of the citizenry in politics is essential for American democracy to survive. Certainly, if people are to present their disputes for public resolutions, high levels of voting are one way of representing those conflicts.

Voting choice, however, is very much like the other major patterns of conflict representation we have looked at — expressing opinions and exercising leadership. The absence of extensive and continuous involvement by the mass citizenry does not prove that American elections are undemocratic. Rather, voting choice — like expressing opinions and exercising leadership — as a method of representing conflicts, shows America's pluralist character. People participate on many voting levels just as they do on opinion and leadership levels (by expressing opinions as members of intense or moderate minorities or as members of indifferent majorities; by exercising official, group, or personal leadership; by voting on issue, candidate, or partisan levels).

The test of whether the opinion, leadership, and election processes are democratic is not simply to count the number of people who take part in them. *The crucial test of democratic representation* is whether those who do take part (1) permit others to do so if they want to; (2) encourage

[34] Burnham, *Critical Elections*, p. 127.

others to do so by assuring that constitutional opportunities, social resources, and personal benefits are available; and (3) respond peacefully when others join them in political participation, even when cherished interests are challenged. When these conditions prevail in the electoral arena, we suspect that more and more Americans will take part in elections on all levels and voting choices will more truly represent the interest conflicts inherent in our pluralist society.

*bibliographical note*

Several concise summaries of voting studies are useful to the undergraduate. Among these are William H. Flanigan, *Political Behavior of the American Electorate,* 2nd ed. (Boston: Allyn and Bacon, 1972) and Hugh A. Bone and Austin Ranney, *Politics and Voters,* 3rd ed. (New York: McGraw-Hill, 1971). Of the major voting studies themselves, one should consult Angus Campbell et al., eds., *The American Voter* (New York: John Wiley, 1964), *Elections and the Political Order* (New York: John Wiley, 1966), *The Voter Decides* (New York: Harper and Row, 1954), Bernard Berelson et al., *Voting* (Chicago: University of Chicago Press, Pheonix Edition, 1966); and Paul F. Lazarsfeld et al., *The People's Choice,* 2nd ed. (New York: Columbia University Press, 1948).

The constitutional, statutory, and conventional influences upon elections are discussed in A. J. Milnor, *Elections and Political Stability* (Boston: Little, Brown, 1969), Douglas Rae, *The Political Consequences of Electoral Laws* (New Haven, Conn.: Yale University Press, 1967), Gerald M. Pomper, *Elections in America* (New York: Dodd, Mead, 1968), and Wallace S. Sayre and Judith H. Parris, *Voting for President* (Washington, D.C.: Brookings Institution, 1970), which discusses problems associated with reform of the electoral college. In *Competition in American Politics* (New York: Holt, Rinehart and Winston, 1970), Andrew M. Scott discusses electoral behavior through the use of competition borrowed from economics.

The social bases of voting are treated in a variety of works. Among those having an influence upon students of voting behavior and politicians alike are Richard M. Scammon and Ben J. Wattenberg, *The Real Majority* (New York: Coward-McCann, 1971), Kevin Phillips, *The Emerging Republican Majority* (New Rochelle, N.Y.: Arlington House, 1969), Ithiel de Sola Pool, Robert Abelson, and Samuel Popkin, *Candidates, Issues and Strategies* (Cambridge, Mass.: Massachusetts Institute of Technology Press, 1965), Seymour Martin Lipset, *Political Man* (Garden City, N.Y.: Doubleday, 1959); and Samuel Lubbell, *The Hidden Crisis in American Politics* (New York: W. W. Norton, 1971).

The strength of partisanship over voting behavior is discussed in V. O. Key, Jr., *The Responsible Electorate* (New York: Random House, Paperback Edition, 1970), Walter DeVries and V. Lance Tarrance, *The Ticket-Splitter* (Ann Arbor, Mich.: William B. Eerdmans, 1972), and Walter Dean Burnham, *Critical Elections and the Mainsprings of American Politics* (New York: W. W. Norton, 1970). The impact of candidates, parties, and issues upon voters in 1968 is described in the American Institute for Political Communication publication, *Anatomy of a Crucial Election* (Washington, D.C.: American Institute for Political Communication, 1970). For studies discussing the relative impact of campaigning upon voting behavior, see the selections mentioned in the bibliographic note to Chapter Seven. Readers interested in exploring some of the problems voters have when their views of candidates, issues, and parties conflict will find a useful introduction in Phillip Zimbardo and Ebbe E. Ebbesen, *Influencing Attitudes and Changing Behavior* (Reading, Mass.: Addison-Wesley, 1969).

# chapter
# 9

# party politics

Americans begin to acquire partisan leanings early in life; this identification with a party definitely influences voting choice. Let us examine how *parties as organizations* contribute to conflict regulation: the types of political participation labeled partisan, how political parties are put together, and what the parties do in representing conflict.

## parties and partisans in conflict regulation

Political parties contribute to both conflict representation and its resolution. By competing for control of government in elections, party politicians publicize social disagreements. Between elections, party leaders select issues on which to take stands and attack the opposition. Party leaders in government offices formulate policies to adjust social disputes. Before we see how parties are led to make these contributions, we will examine the partisans and their parties.

## who are the partisans?

A follower of any political cause or faction is a partisan. In this broad sense, all political participants are partisans whether they are party members, group affiliates, or candidates for public office. Partisans are involved even in "nonpartisan" elections, the difference being only that in such elections no party label is used. However, we will give the word a narrower meaning: in discussing American partisanship, we shall call the *partisan* one *who is directly involved with an organized political party.*

Three levels of partisan activity are visible in America. The *party identifiers* (see Chapter Eight) are the voters who identify, either intensely or casually, with a party and who may even vote consistently for it. *Public officials* are party members elected or appointed to public office; usually they exercise political leadership (see Chapter Seven). As governing officials, the decisions partisans make are not motivated only, or even primarily, by partisan considerations; their personal convictions, the influence of pressure groups, their experience in government — many things contribute to the decisions they make on policy. *Party activists* devote their time, money, skills, and other resources to advancing the party's interests; they occupy positions in the formal party bureaucracy (such as national chairman, national committeeman and committeewoman, county chairman, precinct leader); they make and implement decisions in the party's name. These are the people who operate "the machine," or "the organization"; this chapter is about them.

## a definition of party

*A political party is a coalition of fairly stable, enduring, and frequently conflicting interests, organized to mobilize support in competitive elections in order to control policymaking.* This definition covers the two principal American political parties, Republican and Democratic, and those third parties that may affect two-party politics. Every major element in this definition distinguishes political parties from other political groups.

PARTIES AS COALITIONS. America has traditionally had but two major political parties, which generally have been organized as coalitions. If either party appeals only to narrow social interests, its chances for electoral victory are slim. To build electoral majorities, both parties must recruit, represent, and exploit a large and diverse following. By doing so America's dominant parties act as inclusive, or multi-interest organizations instead of exclusive, special-interest groups like factions. Frequently, each major party coalition has several factions. They can disrupt party unity and promote change in the balance of power between the parties. Intraparty cleavages over platforms, programs, and candidates (such as dissension among Democrats over the party's position on the Vietnam war in 1968) can be more bitter than the campaign between parties.

PARTY STABILITY. As stable organizations, our parties "exist for politics on a full-time, overt, and continuous basis."[1] Unlike pressure groups (see Chapter Ten) that sporadically devote their work to specific issues, parties are involved with *all* issues. By maintaining continuous political activity, the party does two things beyond the reach of most pressure groups: it molds a durable organization that directly contributes to the management of popular elections, and it builds enduring loyalty among its followers, who react with warm support to party appeals and party candidates.

PARTIES AND PUBLIC OFFICE. Parties also differ from other political groups in their ways of seeking to control policymaking. Parties nominate and rally support behind candidates seeking the presidency, congressional seats, and state-level elective posts; from those bases of power they determine appointments to other executive and judicial positions. Pressure groups, whose work is influencing office-holders, refrain for the most part from entering into direct electoral competition and rarely seek to place their own spokesmen in office. Pressure groups restrict their electoral activity primarily to financial and voting support for the party's candidates for public office.

## party politics: what is it?

The characteristics of the American community — social diversity, doctrinal inconsistency, and constitutional pluralism — have produced a socially and ideologically diverse two-party arrangement in which power is spread through all levels of the organization. Three major features — two-party politics, decentralization, and the diverse social base of each party — will help us to analyze American party organization.

## two-party politics

The competition for political office has traditionally been between two major parties, which have "adhered to the same basic values and sought the same basic goals in a virtually 'bipartisan' fashion even though they have differed over the best means of achieving those goals."[2]

[1] Allan P. Sindler, *Political Parties in the United States* (New York: St. Martin's Press, 1966), p. 6.
[2] Harvey Wheeler, " 'Duocracy' or the Imperfect Competition in Our Party System," in Joseph R. Fiszman, ed., *The American Political Arena* (Boston: Little, Brown, 1962), p. 304.

ORIGINS OF THE TWO-PARTY SYSTEM. After they ratified the Constitution, American politicians faced the tough problem of making their scheme work. The Constitution had deliberately divided the governing authority among separate institutions of government, the several states, and localities on the municipal and even village level. This constitutional arrangement had to be made to work in a pluralist society. Popular demand made necessary broadened suffrage and the representation of many and diversified interests. Nothing like this had been attempted in man's history: to build and integrate a community of continental size within a newly constructed, entirely untested framework that had to consider the complicated terms of the constitutional bargain, the realities of a newly formed society of free men, and their visionary democratic expectations.[3]

*In this pluralist setting, a two-party arrangement then developed to achieve the task.* Alexander Hamilton and his colleagues needed support in Congress to enact centralizing programs in the Washington and Adams administrations. The Federalist Party filled this need: it closed the gap between the President and Congress and altered their relationship with the judiciary, making it easier for Hamilton to build support for his programs in all branches of the government. To effectively oppose the Federalists, the Democratic-Republican party was formed by the followers of Jefferson and Madison, who recruited partisan assistance within the states.

The split between the Federalist and Republican parties in the republic's formative years laid the groundwork for the party competition that began in federal elections as early as 1796. Americans accepted a basic idea: *coalitions of interests could differ legitimately over policy aims and compete for the authority to advance those aims, under restraints imposed by the Constitution.*

That idea meant two things: *victorious partisans do not try to destroy the vanquished with far-reaching reprisals* (a notion never challenged despite the Federalist-enacted Alien and Sedition Acts and Jefferson's attempted purge of federal judicial officials); and *the losers in competitive elections become the "loyal opposition,"* criticizing the party in power and its policies, confirming their commitment to the two-party bargain by contesting the next regular election, but not attempting to overthrow the government by force (a notion of loyalty by no means accepted in many nations, then or now). Conflict over the acceptability of the Constitution was displaced by a consensus recognizing that policy and electoral differences under that Constitution were legitimate. The two-party system that has evolved, particularly since 1865, reflects a *bipartisan*

---

[3] Joseph Charles, *The Origins of the American Party System* (New York: Harper and Brothers, Torchbook Edition, 1961).

*sanctification* of the Constitution but has produced sharp *partisan disagreements* over who should govern, how, and for what policy goals.

Our two-party system has gone through four stages at the national level: (1) the *Federalist-Republican* era, from the 1790s to the 1820s, when the Federalists as a party gradually went into eclipse; (2) the *Democratic-Whig* era from 1828 to 1860; (3) the *Republican* era from 1860 to 1932; and (4) the *Democratic* era from 1932 to the present. Each of these eras has seen periods both of one-party domination and vigorous two-party competition.

Some speculate that we are entering a fifth stage of development in which the Republican party will realign itself to obtain support in the South, Midwest, and far West, while the Democratic party will rely heavily upon votes in the populous centers of the East and upper Midwest, forging an alliance between blacks and newly affluent middle class in all sections. It is premature to say which party will dominate the next stage of party development,[4] if such a realignment of the two parties is indeed occurring, but it is reasonable to say that it will be marked by primarily two-party competition with one-party and multiparty variations.

ONE-PARTY VARIATIONS. The two-party pattern in national politics has not been matched by equivalent competition in the states. Within the states, party competition varies by level of office. Generally *presidential elections produce closer two-party competition than contests for United States Senator or Governor, whereas many congressional and state legislative races are dominated by one party.* Taking into account these variations in party competition by office level, we find the pattern of Democratic and Republican one-party states and competitive two-party states depicted in Figure 9-1. Because party competition at all office levels is changing rapidly, such a classification has to be rough. The complex relationships among our three types of partisans — party identifiers, public officials, and party activists — show up in voting in one-party states. Most party identifiers in one-party states side with the majority party; in local, state, and congressional elections, they transform their party loyalties directly into votes for their party's candidates. Also, in one-party states, more and better organized party activists work for the dominant party. (Indeed, the minority party's activists may not even contest local, state, and congressional elections.)

---

[4] For a discussion of the possibilities of party realignment see Walter Dean Burnham, *Critical Elections and the Mainsprings of American Politics* (New York: W. W. Norton, 1970); for the thesis that the next state of party development will be dominated by Republicans, see Kevin Phillips, *The Emerging Republican Majority* (New Rochelle, N.Y.: Arlington House, 1969); for a challenge to the Phillips thesis see Everett Carll Ladd, Jr., *American Political Parties* (New York: W. W. Norton, 1970), Ch. 6.

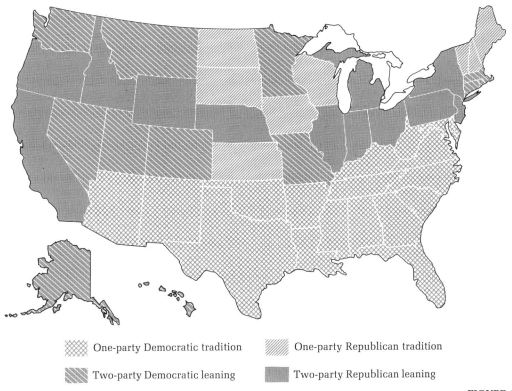

| | | | |
|---|---|---|---|
| One-party Democratic tradition | | One-party Republican tradition | |
| Two-party Democratic leaning | | Two-party Republican leaning | |

FIGURE 9-1
**Patterns of Interparty Competition in the Fifty States**

In elections for the presidency, governorships, or United States Senate seats, however, the relationships between types of partisans in one-party states differ. Most identifiers are still with the dominant party; but activists are working for both parties, and voters frequently defect to the opposition. Several such defections have happened in recent years. Democratic control of state legislatures has not been threatened in Florida, Tennessee, and Virginia, yet each state elected a Republican governor in the past decade and all three were carried by Nixon in 1968. In the same period, the legislatures of Kansas and South Dakota were heavily Republican, yet Kansans elected a Democratic governor for three successive terms and South Dakotans elected Democrat George McGovern to the Senate twice.

*As a rule, then, voters in one-party states have increasingly split their tickets and followed national trends in presidential and major statewide*

*elections while holding firmly to party loyalties in local and congres-*
*sional races.* By providing a locally based congressional opposition in
eras of Republican or Democratic control of the presidency, one-party
states have helped preserve two-party government at the federal level.
But as local areas begin to respond to the same forces affecting national
politics — population migrations, economic changes, urbanization, the
gradual slackening of loyalties that were produced in the South by the
Civil War and afterward, the reapportionment of state and congressional
legislative seats — even contests for lesser offices in the one-party states
will lose their insulation from national influences. Thus we will probably
see a great erosion of single-party dominance.

MULTIPARTY VARIATIONS. Also marring the tidiness of the two-party
scheme are *minor parties — those with sufficient durability to retain an*
*identity and organization separate from the two major parties.* Generally, minor parties reflect the claims of special interests that feel unrepresented in two-party politics. They rarely attract a large following away
from the two major parties; since 1900, in all presidential elections except
1912, 1924, and 1968, no minor party has won more than 10 percent of
the vote.

Minor parties are of two main types: doctrinal and splinter. *Doctrinal*
*parties push for an ideological cause,* which may be narrow, like that
of the Prohibition party, or broad, like the Socialist party's doctrine. The
doctrinal parties have very different techniques. The Socialist party follows democratic procedures and pushes for economic, social, and political reforms by means of propaganda, public discussion, education, and
by putting up candidates for office. Early in this century, the Socialist
party got broad support in elections when neither major party responded
to demands from many segments of the community. In 1912, it received
6 percent of the presidential vote by appealing to populists, progressives,
and reformers frustrated by the lack of innovative programs in the
Republican and Democratic parties. Other doctrinal parties (the Socialist
Labor party and the Communist party) run candidates from time to time,
but do not use elections as the principal means of advancing their aims.
They advocate agitation, infiltration, and violent overthrow, which has
not helped those parties obtain power. Generally, *doctrinal parties have*
*not prospered in the diverse American social and ideological setting.*

*Splinter parties originate as dissident factions of a major party.*
Splinter parties suggest — and rightly so — an unresolved internal party
conflict. Their basic character has gone through several variations. The
Populists, a party of dissident Democrats in the Midwest and South in
the late nineteenth century, advocated a specific program of economic
and political reform, including public ownership of railroad, telegraph

and telephone industries, free and unlimited coinage of silver, direct election of United States Senators, women's suffrage, and other measures. After 1896, when both the Democratic and Populist parties advocated free silver coinage and nominated William Jennings Bryan for President, Populists began to decline as a separate political force.

In contrast, the Bull Moose, or Progressive, party of 1912 had no real program but united around Theodore Roosevelt after he had failed to obtain the Republican nomination for President. The party polled a larger popular vote than the Republicans; but the Democrats won the presidency with Woodrow Wilson, and the Bull Moose party quickly vanished.

The most recent substantial splinter party effort was made by the American Independent party in 1968. It supported George Wallace of Alabama for President. Composed mainly of southern Democratic dissidents, the party articulated protests against racial integration, growing federal power, massive federal spending, crime and violence, and decisions of the Supreme Court.

We can say that *whether splinter parties are parties of program, personality, or protest, they try to persuade one or both major parties to adopt their views; both success and failure in that quest facilitate their passage into political obscurity.*

NONPARTISAN ELECTIONS. Many local elections are *nonpartisan* — that is, *candidates appear on the ballot without party designation.* Two forces join in these elections: the nonpartisan ballot is one way states have of shutting parties out of local elections. They make it illegal to designate the party on the ballot or for candidates to make partisan appeals, reflecting an antiparty sentiment for electoral reform. Also, nonpartisan local elections are most common in one-party states. Removing the party label from elections reduces the party organization's stake in the outcome of local races, so parties make little effort to play even a covert role.[5] The threat to the two-party tradition in state and federal elections is not disabling.

TWO-PARTY PERSISTENCE. Despite the one-party, multiparty, and nonpartisan variations, the basic two-party system persists for party identifiers, activists, and officeholders. The persistence appears in the differences on policy questions between Republicans and Democrats. *Identifiers' opinions on policy differ, but not as much as the opinions of party activists or officeholders of the two parties.* Republican identifiers

[5] Eugene Lee, *The Politics of Nonpartisanship* (Berkeley and Los Angeles: University of California Press, 1960).

are slightly less internationalist than Democrats (more Republicans favor reducing or terminating foreign aid), are somewhat more apt to favor a "hard line" in dealing with foreign nations, and are more opposed to the federal government's involvement in regulating the economy, financing schools, and providing social welfare programs.[6]

*Differences also occur in the opinions of party activists.* Among delegates to presidential nominating conventions, more Democrats than Republicans favor federal regulation of public utilities, public ownership of natural resources, federal aid to education, taxes on corporate income, and regulation of business.[7]

Finally, *roll-call votes in Congress reveal consistent differences between the two parties' public officials* on social welfare, federal regulation of the economy, and foreign affairs. Despite divisions between southern and northern Democrats, the party has recently been fairly unified in supporting programs for social welfare, more participation by the national government in the economy, and an internationalist posture in foreign affairs, all of which require greater federal spending. Republicans more often vote to reduce federal spending for domestic and foreign programs. To some extent, these differences represent party alignments responding to the incumbent President's proposals. In 1971, the average

[6] See Lloyd A. Free and Hadley Cantril, *The Political Beliefs of Americans* (New Brunswick, N.J.: Rutgers University Press, 1967), pp. 134–156.

[7] Herbert McClosky et al., "Issue Conflict and Consensus among Party Leaders and Followers," *The American Political Science Review* 54 (June 1960), 406–427.

Richard Nixon and George McGovern making appeals to construction workers. To build electoral majorities, parties often compete in charming and exploiting various constituencies.

Republican supported President Nixon on 64 percent of the votes in the Senate and on 72 percent in the House; Democrats supported the President on an average of 40 percent of the votes in the Senate and 47 percent in the House.[8]

Granted, then, that the two-party tradition persists among identifiers, activists, and governing officials and that differences between the parties are reflected in the opinions on policy of partisans. *Why has the two-party tradition persisted?* Perhaps because of the conditions provided by our constitutional system, our social structure, and our personal attitudes.

*Our constitutional system reinforces two-party politics.* States make it difficult by law for new parties to enter electoral competition, requiring either that they have received a specified percentage of electoral support in past elections or that they have the support of a percentage of the electorate, proven by signatures on a petition.

New parties also find it difficult to elect candidates under the *single-member, plurality electoral system,* which means that the candidate with the most votes in the district wins the election but trailing candidates win nothing. In contrast, *multimember constituencies with proportional representation guarantee seats to minority parties.* Whereas single-member, plurality systems discourage minor parties from entering elections, the

[8] "Congress and the President; Support Level Steady," *Congressional Quarterly Weekly Report* 30 (Jan. 8, 1972): 31.

multimember, proportional representation procedure rewards minority efforts. If a party wins 30 percent of the popular vote in a ten-member district, it may receive up to three of the seats in that district.

American congressional and presidential elections use the single-member, plurality system (remember that the presidential contest is for the electoral votes of each state, and the plurality winner takes all the electoral votes). Under this arrangement, the two major parties can always muster enough loyal partisans to limit the success of an intruder. Despite minor party influence in state politics — notably the Nonpartisan League in North Dakota, the Farmer-Labor party in Minnesota, or the Conservative and Liberal parties in New York — most new parties have been squeezed out of federal elections by the major parties.

*The absence of really deep and enduring social cleavages in American life has made it difficult for new parties that base their appeal on one overriding issue, to get a foothold.* The two major parties have won adherents from all social groups by promising some satisfaction to each upon winning office. The very need to reward supporters from such diverse interests discourages multiparty politics and also makes one-party politics less likely. If either party has too many diverse groups in its membership, it finds it hard to reward any of them because a policy favored by one group will be opposed by another. Because either party usually needs only a majority of the votes to win, each tones down its appeals to diversity: it might not be able to satisfy all its members. An oversized majority can be a bane as well as a boon. In 1964, President Lyndon Johnson, less than a year into his new term, began to find it impossible to satisfy all sections of his huge following. By attempting to hold down price increases to aid the consumer, he offended his business supporters; holding wage increases within suggested guidelines (to the joy of business leaders), he angered union members. "While most politicians do not consciously prefer minimal majorities to overwhelming ones, the pressures of a system of competing coalitions built on such a diversity of groups compel them to behave as though they did."[9]

*At the personal level, voters' party commitments support two-party politics.* In national politics, the Republican and Democratic parties are personally meaningful symbols for many Americans, and there is a positive consensus on the two-party arrangement. Although voters frequently split their tickets, they generally split between the two major parties. Minor parties competing for state offices but unaffiliated with the major national parties cannot draw upon such widely accepted symbols as

[9] Charles Sellers, "The Equilibrium Cycle in Two-Party Politics," *The Public Opinion Quarterly* 29 (Spring 1965): 30.

"Republican" or "Democrat" to win adherents. As a result, they often find it difficult to continue as an independent force in state-local politics. The tradition of two-party loyalties helps to preserve domination by two parties at all levels of government.

## decentralization

*A singular feature of the two major parties is the fragmentation of power within them.* Party members are controlled by many local leaders; no central power delegates authority to subordinate units. We will compare their formal structures with the forces that work against centralization.

CENTRALIZED HIERARCHY: A FICTION. Throughout American government — national, state, and local — party organizations are at work for both parties. On paper (see Figure 9-2), each party is a hierarchical organization of committees, chairman, and conventions binding local parties to national party headquarters. Some organization of party activists is supplied for each voting and electoral unit: precinct, constituency, coordinating, and national level organizations.

*Party organization begins with the precinct.* The principal functionary is the precinct committeeman, captain, or leader. He is elected either in the party primary or by the precinct party members assembled in convention; in some areas, he may be appointed by party leaders of countywide organizations. The precinct leader works for high voter registration and a respectable turnout of party identifiers on election day. Moreover, he preaches party doctrine, passes along information, and performs social and economic services.

*The constituency is next above the precinct;* it is the lowest level from which a public official is elected. In larger cities, this level is the ward; in rural areas, it is the township; in some sections of the country, it is a state legislative district; and in some states, it is the congressional district. The basic organization is the *county committee,* usually composed of the precinct leaders. The head of this committee is the county chairman, who is chosen either by the committee or in the party primary. He is charged with seeing that precinct leaders mobilize majorities in their precincts and that the party as a whole carries the constituency for local, legislative, congressional, senatorial, gubernatorial, and presidential candidates.

*The coordinating level is above the precinct and constituency;* it is usually composed of the state central or executive committee and includes representatives from constituency committees. The *state party*

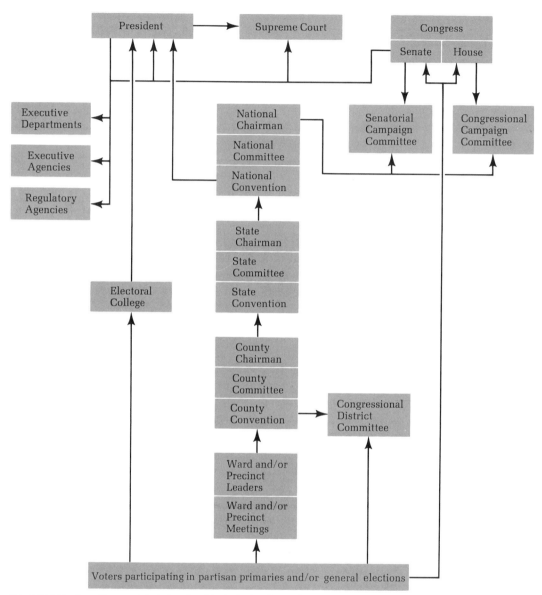

Note: Solid linking lines with arrows indicate formal participation in the selection of leaders through direct election, nominating, appointing, or approving persons for positions.

FIGURE 9-2
**Formal Relations between Public Officials, Activists, and Identifiers
of the Major Parties**

*chairman* ordinarily is either the leader of a dominant party faction within the state or the governor's hand-picked spokesman. Sometimes he is both. As at the precinct and constituency levels, conventions are regularly scheduled; at the coordinating level, they are attended by delegates from wards, counties, legislative districts, and so forth. *State conventions* perform tasks ranging from merely ratifying decisions made at other levels to nominating candidates for statewide office and preparing party platforms.

*National organizations are at the top of the party hierarchy,* and each party has a number of them. Both major parties have a *national committee.* In the Republican party, it is composed of a man and a woman from every state and the Canal Zone, District of Columbia, Guam, Puerto Rico, and the Virgin Islands; the state chairman of any state which was carried by the party's last presidential nominee or which elected a Republican senator or a majority of Republicans to its House of Representatives delegation is also a member. In its 1972 presidential nominating convention, the Democratic party agreed to this makeup for their national committee: (1) the chairman and the highest ranking officer of the opposite sex of each recognized state Democratic party; (2) additional national committee members apportioned to each state on the basis of that state's representation on the standing committees of the 1972 Democratic national convention; (3) the chairman and two others designated by the national conference of Democratic state governors; (4) Democratic leaders in the United States Senate and House of Representatives; and (5) additional members not to exceed twenty-five to provide balanced representation of all Democratic voters.

*The national chairman* is selected by the presidential nominee, although formal approval comes from the national committee. If the party suffers electoral defeat, a new chairman may be chosen by dominant party interests to reintegrate and unify the party. Regardless of how he is selected, the chairman's duties are extensive. With his staff, he administers and directs fund raising, maintains liaison between activists and officeholders, conducts public relations, criticizes the opposition, and manages the presidential candidate's campaign if asked.[10]

A third element is the quadrennial *national convention.* Made up of party activists from states, counties, and congressional districts, its tasks are to nominate a presidential and vice-presidential candidate, formulate a platform, resolve internal disputes, and conduct party business.

Finally, the party that loses the presidency usually sets up some device to permit its elected governing officials to formulate political stands. In

[10] Cornelius P. Cotter and Bernard C. Hennessy, *Politics Without Power* (New York: Atherton Press, 1964), pp. 67–80.

1969, the Democratic Policy Council — composed of governors, United States Senators, mayors, and leading state legislators of the party — was created to determine party stands on major issues. After defeat in the presidential election of 1964, a Republican Coordinating Committee performed a similar function for that party.

THE REALITY OF FRAGMENTATION. A tight hierarchical structure describes the local parties' earlier years — the classic urban "machine" was built of precinct workers supervised by county, ward, or district leaders who, in turn, worked for the party "boss" — but *it was never typical of the major national parties.* In fact, relations between levels of party organization are so reciprocal, discontinuous, loosely coordinated, and sporadic that they are at best only a modified hierarchy. Authority is diffuse within and between all levels, and lower-level activists are not generally responsible to upper-echelon members. State and local units are the influential elements of the national parties, and these lower-level organizations frequently ally with one another, with higher-level agencies, and with nonparty forces to oppose party leaders. Because committee positions at the constituency level often go unfilled or are occupied by politicians with no active interest in party work, the detailed work of party organizations frequently remains undone. *Actual party organization is decentralized and some of it is as good as disorganized.*

WHY ARE PARTY ORGANIZATIONS DECENTRALIZED? There are many reasons for lack of centralization; but among the most important are the multiplicity of constituencies, the character of the electoral system, and the statutory regulation of parties.

Political parties try to win as many elections as possible by focusing their efforts on the individual constituencies that elect public officials. *Elective offices are so numerous that the party inevitably shatters into many separate party units, each of which feels that it can most effectively compete for votes by maintaining its autonomy.* The numberless semipermanent constituency organizations are matched by a host of affiliated groups. Some of these are adjuncts to the party organization, reflect many of its conflicts, and compete with it for influence. Such groups include the Young Republicans, Young Democrats, New Democratic Coalition (a group of liberal Democrats formed after the 1968 election), and volunteer organizations (Independents for Eisenhower, Citizens for Nixon) that are created temporarily to handle specific problems in a campaign, raise funds, broaden the base of voting support, or even prepare policy statements.

*Constituency organizations for each electoral unit respond to the basic political fact of federalism:* it "creates separate, self-sustaining centers of power, privilege, and profit which may be sought and defended as desira-

Behavior at national nominating conventions clearly indicates that parties are an alliance of local organizations rather than hierarchies directed from the top.

ble in themselves, as means of leverage upon elements in the political structure above and below, and as bases from which individuals may move to places of greater influence and prestige in and out of government."[11] By following the federal pattern, however, partisans deprive the national party leadership of the means for enforcing party discipline. The local autonomy of state, county, and district party organizations assigns the fate of policy decisions to locally responsible governors, mayors, county commissioners, or congressmen, who are pretty much free of central control.

Pressure-group leaders understand this party fragmentation; and when they want to influence Congress, they go to the congressman's local constituency and party politicians within it, not to the national party organi-

[11] David B. Truman, "Federalism and the Party System," in Nelson W. Polsby et al., eds., *Politics and Social Life* (Boston: Houghton Mifflin, 1963), pp. 518–519.

zations. Parochial interests often have a voice in the party's affairs that is out of proportion to their size, particularly if the local organization depends upon pressure groups for financial aid and electoral support.

*The splitting of political authority shapes social conflict representation by channeling disputes and demands through local party organizations.* As a result, democratic responsibility is often so diffuse that parties cannot respond to broad social changes. Though civil rights was a problem in the 1930s and 1940s, southerners were able to keep civil rights statements out of Democratic platforms because they controlled local party organizations and threatened to bolt the national party. Ever since President Harry Truman was elected in 1948 despite a southern defection, this tactic has been less effective, but it is not yet dead.

*Decentralization is further reinforced by staggered elections and single-member districts.* The many offices created by the separation of powers and federalism are made even more independent of one another by provisions for nonconcurrent terms of office: the President serves four years; Senators serve six years and Representatives two years; governors and state legislators serve either two or four years depending upon the state; terms of mayors, city councilmen, county commissioners, and other officials vary similarly. Because of the nonconcurrent terms officials are elected at staggered intervals and voters respond to forces peculiar to each election. Local party organizations, bent upon winning their own contest, seldom have to unify their efforts to win a single national office. Only in presidential election years do they show much unity as they try to adjust to the presidential contest's effects on state and local races; even then the national party is more a working alliance of local party organizations than a hierarchy directed from the top.

American elections are won by the candidate with a plurality of votes in single-member districts. Such a district is one from which one candidate is elected with a simple plurality of votes. There is no carry-over of votes from one district to another. Parties concentrate their efforts where they know they have enough identifiers to win a simple plurality. They restrict their efforts to constituencies in which they are dominant or at least competitive, preferring not to waste resources where they at best can come in only second, winning nothing. Where it is sure to win lopsided victories because it has the most party identifiers, the party does not need strong organization. Here neither party is likely to have a strong organization, the minority party because it has no chance and the majority party because it does not need to be organized.

States are more active in regulating political parties than the federal government so they tailor their organizations to fit state regulations. *Statutory regulation decentralizes party organization.* The *intent* behind state regulation has been to promote broad participation in party affairs by the rank and file in place of tight control by party leaders. Almost three-fourths of the states require that the parties hold regular conventions — city and county — of precinct members. Many also require that parties nominate candidates through primary elections, removing nominations from the control of party politicians. But primary elections do not necessarily give control of nominations to party identifiers, because party lines are crossed easily in primaries. (In some states voters are given ballots for both parties, requiring no test of party membership. In one state primary contests of all parties are on one ballot.) The primaries are but one more force weakening central organizational control within our major parties.

CENTRALIZING TENDENCIES. Although our two major parties are highly decentralized, centralizing tendencies overcome more and more barriers such as separation of powers, federalism, and localism. It is in the continuing interest of partisans to stick together. Although they have no abstract belief in the merits of centralization itself, party politicians recognize that some party unity is essential for electoral victory. The dissension in the Republican party in 1964 and among Democrats in 1968 shows how disunity in presidential elections contributes to defeat.

Another tendency is clearly related: as one-party politics declines and two-party competition spreads, more effective organizations are required for victory. Constituency-level parties, no longer assured of victory in safe districts, see an advantage in affiliating more closely with national organizations that might provide financial help or send a popular party figure to campaign for local candidates.

Politics at state and local levels is shaped more and more by national issues. The local issues (unemployment, inflation, racial integration, drug control, law and order) are now national; making it increasingly difficult for local and state politicians to ignore or defect from positions that national party leaders take.

Finally, the parties themselves are slowly providing their national-level organizations with sanctions to enforce party discipline. After 1968, the Democratic party adopted guidelines making it more difficult for dissident elements to refuse support for the presidential ticket selected by the national convention.

*Forces within both major parties bind partisans in a common cause, although they do not command party discipline.*

### the perils of diverse social interests

By diversifying their membership, parties have made it harder to achieve organizational unity. The price they pay for a disparate following is the likelihood of factional disputes. The more inclusive the party is, the more likely it is that internal struggles will reflect interest disputes throughout America — *the major parties' social compositions and conflicts are microcosms of the larger society.*

Instead of trying to settle their internal disputes, which can lead to damaging factional warfare, party leaders try to bridge the differences by appealing for unity within the party. They pass the task of conflict resolution on to their elected public officials, so that the parties are primarily mechanisms for representing, not resolving conflict. Internal wrangles cannot always be quietly ignored, however; sometimes party leaders must work for internal peace, as did followers of Barry Goldwater and the more "moderate" Republicans in 1964. After an overwhelming electoral defeat, they agreed to replace the Goldwater-appointed chairman of the Republican National Committee with a compromise candidate.

If adjustments cannot be worked out, factions may rebel, as George Wallace's American Independent party defected from the Democrats in 1968. A political party in America endures only so long as it is able to counter schismatic tendencies inherent in too diverse a following.

THE REWARDS OF PARTY MEMBERSHIP. A party's clientele is diverse partly because people engage in active party work for many reasons. Each party differs in social composition from region to region, reflecting the ethnic or occupational groups that dominate each area, but party leaders of both parties usually are lawyers or have professional, managerial, or governmental jobs. Precinct leaders of both parties obtain about the same satisfactions from party activity: social contacts, patronage, privileged administrative treatment, financial rewards, career opportunities, and ideological convictions. *The rewards and incentives for party activity are found at the local level,* contributing to decentralization, because local activists and locally elected officials, including Congressmen, are inclined to respond to their constituency organization rather than to the national party when the two conflict.[12]

Although party activity offers some incentives, *parties have difficulty recruiting members.* Unlike a business firm or football team, parties have no special staff to scout applicants for party membership. Because citizens generally are not too interested in party work and the parties have relatively few inducements to offer activists (who are expected to repay the party with hard work), parties must rely on means other than systematic recruitment to attract new members.

Generally, new activists come to the party by either of two routes. *Self-starters* seek direct rewards and incentives in party participation. Self-starters may wish to advance their careers by engaging in politics,

---

[12] William H. Riker, *Federalism* (Boston: Little, Brown, 1964), p. 101.

As the 1972 convention closed, Democrats joined hands in the traditional victory pose.
Party unity is essential to win a national election.

like the many lawyers who become party activists. Governmental appointments are not the incentive they once were; the civil service, relying on competitive merit appointments, removes partisan influence from the selection of many administrative personnel.

*External recruits* join parties because they have been persuaded to do so by other activists, friends, relatives, or fellow workers. By far the greatest number of party activists are recruited through informal contacts with friends or colleagues; self-starters comprise only 10 to 30 percent of local party ranks.[13]

IDEOLOGICAL DIVERSITY. Because of the extremely diverse interests represented in our two major political parties, neither is able to make

[13] Frank J. Sorauf, *Party Politics in America,* 2nd ed. (Boston: Little, Brown, 1972), p. 97.

narrow ideological appeals for fear of alienating other bodies of support. The parties cannot therefore recruit and hold members with strong ideological commitments, but their diverse appeal permits them to retain widespread support among the electorate. The broad ideological differences between our two major parties rarely harden into direct ideological appeals to the electorate simply *because most voters do not care about ideological conflicts.*[14] Party leaders compensate for any ideological gap between themselves and their followers by obscuring their ideological stands in ambiguous campaign oratory (symbolic persuasion — see Chapter Seven).[15] *The disdain of American voters for political ideology further reinforces party decentralization.* The fact that party members have little or no ideological commitment, finally, means that ideological appeals have little coordinating value.

## what do parties do in conflict regulation?

By the work its activists do, the American political party helps greatly in regulating social conflict by mobilizing the support of diverse interests, particularly — but not exclusively — in elections for public office. Three of their activities are nominating candidates, conducting election campaigns, and influencing policymaking.

### nominating candidates

Nominating candidates to run for public office is a critical part of the parties' contribution to government; it is vital also to their own interests. Party activists can control the distribution of patronage better if the victorious candidate owes his nomination and election to the party rather than to wealthy backers, a major interest group, or another power base. If he is indebted to the party for his nomination, he will be more likely to carry through on party programs. Controlling nominations also enables party leaders to discipline factions.

*Three methods of nominating candidates have been used.* The earliest was the *party caucus,* a meeting of select party leaders (often dominated by legislative officeholders) to choose the candidates for the next elec-

[14] See Philip E. Converse, "The Nature of Belief Systems in Mass Publics," in David Apter, ed., *Ideology and Discontent* (New York: Free Press, 1964), pp. 206–256; compare John Osgood Field and Ronald E. Anderson, "Ideology in the Public's Conceptualization of the 1964 Election," *The Public Opinion Quarterly* 33 (Fall 1969): 380–398.

[15] See Gerald M. Pomper, *Elections in America* (New York: Dodd, Mead, 1968), chaps. 7 and 8.

tion. "King Caucus" expired in national politics after Andrew Jackson triumphed over John Quincy Adams in 1828. The caucus had selected Adams as the official party candidate, but the national convention nominated Jackson instead, a turning point in political history. The legend of the "smoke-filled room" persisted long afterward, however.

The *convention* spread partisan conflict by including state factional leaders as well as legislative officeholders in the nominating process. *Primary elections,* theoretically open to all party members, further enlarged the nomination process. Both Populists and Progressives justified it on the grounds that the reform would make party leaders responsive to all party members and the party's officeholders responsible to all voting citizens. Their responsiveness and responsibility were to be ensured by converting nominations from bargains arrived at by party "bosses" to victories in electoral competition.

Party primaries are of three types. In the *closed primary,* used by forty-three states, only those who have registered as party members or who declare their party identification at the polling place may participate. Six states permit the *open primary,* in which the voter is given a ballot for each party at the polls; he marks only the ballot of the party of his choice. In the state of Washington, the ballot lists every party's contestants under the office they seek; in this *blanket primary* a voter may choose a Democratic candidate for one office, a Republican for another.

Nominating procedures have been made more democratic by the primary, but some results were not anticipated. *Although the party's public officials and its activists no longer control nominations, neither does the full party membership.* Turnout in primaries is low, so the party nominee usually is chosen by a small proportion of the party's members. These are the hard-core loyalists who are not necessarily representative of the diverse interests of voters in general elections.[16] This may handicap the party in the general election if the winning candidates were chosen because of narrow appeals to the interests of party loyalists. Again, if a large number of candidates enter a primary, or even if the turnout is large, the winner usually receives only a plurality, not a majority, of the primary vote. Where runoff primaries (a second primary to choose between the two candidates receiving the most votes in the first primary) are not provided, it is not uncommon that candidates who receive less than one-third of the votes are nominated. Such nominees frequently owe their victories to a small band of faithful friends, relatives, neighbors, or to uninformed primary voters attracted by a popular family name. (In Massachusetts one John Kennedy was nominated for state trea-

[16] Austin Ranney and Leon D. Epstein, "The Two Electorates: Voters and Non-Voters in a Wisconsin Primary," *The Journal of Politics* 28 (Aug. 1966): 598–616.

surer; he was a political unknown and not related to President John F.
Kennedy, yet the name drew votes.) Finally, many primary candidates
are not opposed, so the voter has no choice; from a third to a half of the
primary candidates for state legislative seats are unopposed.[17]

The primary does not truly turn control of nominations over to party
identifiers, but it has achieved a second aim of its advocates — weakening
the party "machine." Public competition between leaders of factions for
nominations exposes the party's factional conflicts. Once publicized,
such conflicts are not easily resolved by private bargaining; and the dis-
gruntled losing factions may refuse to support the primary victor in the
general election. A major Republican breakthrough in the one-party
South came in the 1960s when Republican John Tower of Texas was
twice elected to the United States Senate because liberal Democrats in
the state voted for him rather than for the more conservative nominee
selected in their own party's primary.

Parties survive by winning elections. Parties threaten that survival if
they produce candidates with little chance to win the general election.
A reformed convention system could promote participation by *minorities*
(rarely achieved fully in primaries) and representation of all *major
factions* and interests, by selecting nominees in open, give-and-take
competition. Nominations by conventions of party activists might then
produce candidates more representative of the party membership and
therefore more likely to win the general election.

Party leaders have several tactics for restoring some bargaining to the
nominations. Half a dozen states permit some form of preprimary convention that allows the party to endorse a candidate in the primary election. Some local party organizations also use screening committees of
factional leaders, who meet in caucus, sort the desirable candidates from
among those who have filed (assuming that the party has tried to get
desirable candidates to file in the first place), and announce a party slate.
Efforts to control the nominating process by controlling the primary,
however, are only partially successful. Some interests may be disenchanted with the promises made in preprimary bargaining; they can
force a primary fight and publicize the divisions within the party.

The primary is the principal method for nominating candidates for
Congress. The President, however, is still nominated by delegates meeting in convention (see Chapter Twelve). In 1972, twenty-three states held
presidential primaries, but fewer than a third of those states required the
convention delegates to support the primary winner. A presidential

---

[17] Frank J. Sorauf, *Party and Representation* (New York: Atherton Press, 1963), p. 111;
V. O. Key, Jr., *American State Politics* (New York: Alfred A. Knopf, 1956), p. 178.

aspirant therefore cannot hope to win his party's nomination merely by winning presidential primaries. Careful wooing of delegates chosen by state and local conventions is indispensable. In fact, a prospective nominee may lose several primaries and yet end up with the nomination if he has the support of delegates in the nonprimary states, as George McGovern did in 1972.

## conducting election campaigns

Two questions must be answered now: How do party activists contact voters, and how do they help finance election campaigns?

PRECINCT ACTIVISTS. In all elections, the precinct worker is important: he stimulates party sympathizers to vote, reinforces partisan loyalties, and wins new adherents to the cause. Precinct canvassing, traditionally associated with the local party's campaign efforts, aims at turning out party identifiers by distributing literature, ringing doorbells, making

**Stimulus for and satisfaction from party activity are found at the grassroots level. To survive, a political party must continuously recruit new members from all age groups, particularly the young.**

phone calls, operating car pools, and even providing babysitting on election days. *Such grass-roots efforts do produce somewhat higher turnouts;* a party may increase its vote by about 5 percent by such activity.[18] Beyond winning votes in specific elections, *precinct activists have a long-term effect on partisan attitudes;* the loyalties of party identifiers are intensified by frequent contact with party organizers. In this sense, the party organization is as important an agent in reinforcing political attitudes as the family, friends, and co-workers. Finally, *precinct activists win new adherents by performing a variety of services.* Although they do so less than in earlier days, precinct leaders — especially in the poverty pockets of rural America and in the cities — obtain legal counsel for constituents in trouble with the police, find political jobs for the unemployed, and help clothe and nourish the needy, all in exchange for support. In more affluent suburbs, they offer other incentives — giving people social status, assisting their careers through social contacts, and promoting congenial friendships.

In electoral campaigns, the party activist shares responsibility with specialists: public relations men, public opinion analysts, mass media technicians, and computer experts. They are as valuable as the activist because they supply essential services to candidates, but that in turn raises new problems of organizational control for the party. A candidate who can successfully employ such specialists independently of the party in primary or general elections can challenge party discipline. In 1966, Ronald Reagan relied heavily upon nonparty campaign specialists to win first the Republican nomination for Governor of California, then the governorship. By becoming Governor, Reagan captured the party leadership from the outside. Like any major public official (President, Governor, Senator, Congressman, Mayor), Reagan exercised party leadership by virtue of his office, another example of the problems parties have in controlling public officials.

FINANCING CAMPAIGNS. We know that campaign costs are so high that federal and state regulations are imposed on fund raising and campaign spending. *Party activists at all levels devote a major portion of their energy to raising the money to finance campaigns.* Their techniques are many: fund-raising dinners; personal appeals to party members by visits,

---

[18] Gerald H. Kramer, "The Effects of Precinct-Level Canvassing on Voter Behavior," *The Public Opinion Quarterly* 34 (Winter 1970–1971): 560–572; John C. Blydenburgh, "A Controlled Experiment to Measure the Effects of Personal Contact Campaigning," *Midwest Journal of Political Science* 15 (May 1971): 365–381; William J. Crotty, "Party Effort and Its Impact on the Vote," *The American Political Science Review* 65 (June 1971): 439–450; Daniel Katz and Samuel J. Eldersveld, "The Impact of Local Party Activity upon the Electorate," *The Public Opinion Quarterly* 25 (Spring 1961): 1–24.

phone calls, and door-to-door canvassing; solicitation by mass mailing of letters; television, radio, newspaper, and periodical advertising; demands addressed to patronage appointees; special events such as cocktail parties and theater parties; and appeals to affluent nonparty groups.

*Who finances campaigns?* Only about 10 percent of Americans contribute money to campaigns in presidential election years (see Chapter Five). With campaigning so costly, parties and their candidates depend upon large donations from a relatively small percentage of wealthy citizens. In 1968, $1.5 million was contributed to political campaigns. It came from forty-six of the sixty-six Americans who had fortunes in excess of $150 million. In this campaign, when Nixon was so highly favored to win, these wealthy donors favored Republicans over Democrats in donations by about thirteen to one. Moreover, of the twenty-five top defense, space, and nuclear contractors doing business with the federal government in 1968, officers and directors of all but one made political contributions in 1968, totaling $1.2 million and favoring Republicans over Democrats six to one.[19]

Such figures make it easy to conclude that parties — particularly winning parties — find it fairly easy to get money from wealthy patrons. Actually, the reverse is true. Much as party leaders would like to have the money raised in a campaign go directly into the party treasury, major donors often bypass the party, contribute their money directly to the candidate, and hope thereby to gain favorable access once the candidate wins the public office. Party organizations suffer: so long as the candidate looks elsewhere than to the party for financing, he is not inclined to accept party discipline. Unless the party can find a way of guaranteeing financing that will free candidates from dependence upon large-sum donors (such as some form of federal subsidy, attracting more contributors of small sums, recruiting dues-paying members), it may continue at the mercy of nonparty rivals in trying to control its successful candidates, the elected public officials.

## influencing policymaking

*Party activists represent social conflict by organizing elections* — nominating candidates with different views promoting discussion of political issues, and exposing interest disputes within the party itself. *As public officials, party members also take part in all phases of conflict resolution:* through the presidency, they exercise *leadership* in making policies;

[19] Robert A. Diamond, ed., *Dollar Politics* (Washington, D.C.: Congressional Quarterly, 1971), pp. 28–35.

Presidents cannot dictate strategy, but must appeal to party unity. Here, President Johnson meets with top Democratic congressional leaders and advisers.

in Congress they offer policy proposals and bargain among themselves, *the process of adoption;* by occupying appointive positions in the federal bureaucracy, they apply policy; and, although partisanship is less apparent in the courts, they also influence the *adjudication* of policy disagreements in judicial bodies.

PARTIES AND THE PRESIDENCY. Political parties exercise policy leadership during and between elections. A focal point of that leadership is the presidency, occupied by the leader of one party and continuously sought by leaders of the opposition. When *publicizing selected social conflicts to hold or win the presidency, the major party leaders promote policies that go beyond the interests of any one group.* As leader of his party, President Nixon proposed legislation to reform federal social welfare programs, restructure the federal administrative bureaucracy, create a national health insurance plan, share federal revenues with the states, and restrict forced busing of children to promote racial integration in public schools. Leading Democratic contenders for the presidency, such as Senators Edmund Muskie, George McGovern, Hubert Humphrey, Representative Wilbur Mills, and Alabama Governor George Wallace, responded with their own proposals. In this way, the President and his critics defined the social problems that became major political issues of the early 1970s.

*The political party is a base of support for the President from which he can get more influence in policy leadership.* Despite its difficulties in disciplining members, the party provides the President, if he has a large party following, with a means of getting cooperation from executive officials and congressman. Following his overwhelming reelection in 1964, President Lyndon Johnson, partly because the Democrats had large majorities in both the House and Senate (with 295 Representatives and 68 Senators), was able to win congressional approval for an impressive number of his administration's proposals — voting rights legislation, medical care for the aged, federal aid to education, a departmental agency for urban affairs, foreign aid authorization, and several other measures hitherto stalled in Congress. In the midterm elections of 1966, however, the Democrats lost forty-seven members of their House majority and three Senate members. Without the oversized party majority of 1965 and 1966, Johnson was unable to match his earlier success in leading Congress to adopt his programs.

For the party that controls the White House, the decentralizing tendencies in American politics are offset by the unity spurred by the President's leadership and program. The "out-party" — the major party whose presidential candidate lost — lacks such a unifying force, has more factionalism, is less able to provide alternatives to the President's policies, and pronounces its programs in discordant voices, each claiming to be its authoritative spokesman. The Democratic party's experience in the 1972 elections shows how the out-party's leadership becomes dispersed. Differing — sometimes conflicting and sometimes compatible — policy statements on such problems as defense spending, busing schoolchildren, regulating wages and prices, consumer legislation, taxation, and American policy toward both Nationalist and mainland China came from party "spokesmen" including Senator Hubert Humphrey (the party's previous presidential nominee), Senator Edmund Muskie (the party's previous vice-presidential nominee), Senator George McGovern (who became the nominee), Mayor John Lindsay of New York City (earlier he had renounced his Republican status and had become a Democrat), Senator Edward Kennedy, Congressman Wilbur Mills of Arkansas (Chairman of the powerful House Committee on Ways and Means), Florida's Governor Reubin Askew, and Alabama's Governor George Wallace (who in 1968 had campaigned for President on a third-party ticket). It is difficult enough to generate party unity behind presidential leadership; without it, a united partisan policy is almost impossible.

PARTIES IN CONGRESS. *Most American legislative bodies, including Congress, are organized in keeping with partisan considerations* — members of the majority party control committee chairmanships and comprise the majority of each committee, choose the presiding officer of the legislative body, and control the order of business. Other influences on legislation inspired by party considerations depend on parochialism among Congressmen, pressures exerted by the President as a party leader, and constituency and pressure group demands and partisan interest.

*Party voting* in Congress on substantive issues (agreement by members of each major party in roll-call votes) varies. Table 9-1 displays the proportion of roll-call votes in both houses of Congress for a decade in which majorities of Democrats voted against majorities of Republicans; for individual legislators in 1971, we find that the average Democrat in Congress voted with his party 62 percent of the time, whereas Republi-

TABLE 9-1
Party Voting in Congress, 1961–1971

| Year | Percentage of roll calls in which majority of one party voted against majority of other party | | |
| | Both houses | Senate | House |
| --- | --- | --- | --- |
| 1961 | 58% | 62% | 50% |
| 1962 | 43 | 41 | 46 |
| 1963 | 48 | 47 | 49 |
| 1964 | 41 | 36 | 55 |
| 1965 | 46 | 42 | 52 |
| 1966 | 46 | 50 | 41 |
| 1967 | 35 | 35 | 36 |
| 1968 | 33 | 32 | 35 |
| 1969 | 34 | 36 | 31 |
| 1970 | 32 | 35 | 27 |
| 1971 | 40 | 42 | 38 |

Source: Compiled from *Congressional Quarterly Almanacs* of each year.

cans voted with their party in 66 percent of roll calls. Party affiliation is an imperfect indicator of legislative voting. In Congress from 1967 to 1971, *bipartisan voting* (votes on which a majority of Democrats and a majority of Republicans agreed) occurred in more than 60 percent of roll calls. *Although far from infallible, however, party labels are generally the best indicator of how the legislative body will divide on substantive issues.*

PARTIES AND ADMINISTRATIVE BUREAUCRACY. When the President uses his discretion to appoint partisans to administrative posts, his party can strongly affect the application of public policies. But presidential discretion in making appointments extends only to top administrative posts; below these, the rules of career civil service dictate procedures of selection. Career officials frequently develop loyalty to their agency and its established programs, resisting both partisan and presidential appeals for policy innovations. Congress supervises agency operations and expenditures and is at least a partner with the President in controlling the administrative branch (see Chapter Fourteen).

PARTIES AND THE COURTS. Partisan considerations weigh heavily in the selection process in states that elect judicial officials. In appointing persons to federal judgeships, particularly in federal district courts (see Chapter Fifteen), the President normally selects qualified individuals from his own party. Since the 1930s, a scant 5 percent of the federal circuit and district judgeships have been filled with appointments from the opposition party. However, *a President cannot automatically appoint qualified party members as he wishes to judicial positions.* The tradition of "senatorial courtesy" permits a Senator of the President's party to oppose an appointment to the federal bench in his state on grounds that the nominee is "personally objectionable" to him. The rest of the Senate, regardless of party lines, is prepared to reject the nomination, not merely to please a colleague but to protect each other's power in such situations in the future. The President is thus forced to use authority to appoint in ways that strengthen his Senate partisans, at the direct expense of his own power. Here is yet another example of the dispersion of party controls.

The influence of political parties on the judiciary is restricted by the widespread belief that judges should be "nonpolitcal"; that is, partisan considerations should not enter into their judicial decisions. President Franklin Roosevelt proposed in 1937 that he be allowed to appoint additional justices to the Supreme Court for each judge over the age of seventy who did not retire after ten years of service and that the maximum number of justices for the court be raised from nine to fifteen. This proposal was interpreted as an attempt to "pack" the Court with judges amenable to presidential programs previously declared unconstitutional by the justices. The proposal was criticized by many as violating the nonpartisan tradition of the judiciary, and it failed.

Early in his tenure, President Richard Nixon also ran afoul of the nonpolitical tradition associated with the courts. In nominating to the Supreme Court on separate occasions two southerners, Clement Haynesworth of South Carolina and G. Harrold Carswell of Florida, the President drew criticism from many Senate Democrats *and* Republicans for attempting to remake the Court to the South's liking in exchange for southern support for his programs and reelection. When the qualifications of both appointees were questioned, the Senate refused to confirm either. These incidents and the "court-packing" episode show that *party leaders influence the appointment of federal judges, but only so long as partisanship does not then enter into the judges' decisions or result in party discipline over members of the judiciary.*

## party politics and american democracy

Ideally the task of democracy is to organize conflict in such a way that public officials are subject to popular control and the entire political process is open for public debate. Political parties can serve that ideal by making their elected and appointed public officials responsive to social conflicts and responsible to the people.

*Do American parties create a responsive and responsible officialdom? We believe that in general they do.* In competing for political authority, each of our major parties appeals to and absorbs many conflicting interests. Neither party resolves these disputes, but each does unite its factions enough to contest elections. Once the election is over, the social conflicts inherent in the two parties surface once more and are brought to the attention of public officials; in the resolving of those conflicts by government, partisanship is important but not supreme. Operating in this fashion for the past century, the Democratic and Republican parties have demonstrated to Americans that party rivalry is an acceptable way to select our governing officials. Two-party politics is as much a part of the constitutional consensus as the written Constitution itself, although no provision is made for parties in the written document. And so long as partisans carry the liberal-democratic creed, the parties help bind Americans to substantive as well as procedural tenets of democracy.

*But American political parties have been only partly successful in making public officials responsive and responsible to social interests.* Our major parties exploit primarily interests that provide electoral majorities in localized constituencies; except in presidential elections, they seldom make nationwide appeals to encompass Americans in all walks of life. By appealing to a majority of the voters, party leaders sometimes overlook the interests of resentful ghetto blacks, impoverished migrant workers, and exploited Mexican-Americans because the parties themselves have not adequately *represented* those interests. And, when party members do respond to the interests of the unrepresented, the party's diverse composition makes it hard to unify behind corrective programs. Moreover, the dispersion of power within the party makes it impossible to force public officials to support legislative and executive programs.

Our political parties, then, do make indispensable contributions to the democratic regulation of social conflict in America, even though they alone have not produced an ideally responsive and responsible government. *Parties are the only large-scale, continuously active, open, and inclusive organizations in politics that represent a highly diverse clientele.* Other means of bringing pressure on public officials and making them responsive may augment political parties, but they do not supplant them.

*bibliographical note*

A number of detailed descriptions, analyses, and interpretations of American political parties are now available in paperback editions. Each defines party politics (albeit in a slightly different way), spells out the characteristics of American parties, and includes examples and anecdotes illustrating the function of partisan politics. Among the best are the following: Frank J. Sorauf, *Political Parties in the American System* (Boston: Little Brown, 1964); Allan P. Sindler, *Political Parties in the United States* (New York: St. Martin's Press, 1966): Fred I. Greenstein, *The American Party System and the American People* (Englewood Cliffs, N.J.: Prentice-Hall, 1963); Everett Carll Ladd, Jr., *American Political Parties* (New York: W. W. Norton, 1970); Clinton Rossiter, *Parties and Politics in America* (Ithaca, N.Y.: Cornell University Press, 1960); John H. Fenton, *People and Parties in Politics* (Glenview, Ill.: Scott, Foresman, 1966); and Kay Lawson, *Political Parties and Democracy in the United States* (New York: Charles Scribner's Sons, 1968).

Moreover, several of the earlier perceptive treatments of partisanship are now also conveniently available in paperback editions, including Pendleton Herring's *The Politics of Democracy* (New York: W. W. Norton, 1965), detailing the consequences of American pluralism for party organization; E. E. Schattschneider's account of the problems of party decentralization, *Party Government* (New York: Holt, Rinehart and Winston, 1942); V. O. Key, Jr.,'s study of party politics in the American South, *Southern Politics* (New York: Random House, Vintage Books, 1949); and Austin Ranney, *The Doctrine of Responsible Party Government* (Urbana, Ill.: University of Illinois Press, 1962).

Two succinct publications have directed attention to the origins of the American two-party system: William Nisbet Chambers, *Political Parties in a New Nation* (New York: Oxford University Press, 1963) and Joseph Charles, *The Origins of the American Party System* (New York: Harper and Brothers, Torchbook Edition, 1961). Present-day aspects of each of the two major parties are treated in Ralph M. Goldman, *The Democratic Party in American Politics* (New York: Macmillan, 1966), and Charles O. Jones, *The Republican Party in American Politics* (New York: Macmillan, 1965).

Among the standard works available for reference, one should certainly consult Samuel J. Eldersveld's combined text and report of research in Wayne County, Michigan, *Political Parties: A Behavioral Analysis* (Chicago: Rand McNally, 1964). Other excellent references are Avery Leiserson, *Parties and Politics: An Institutional and Behavioral Approach* (New York: Alfred A. Knopf, 1958); Maurice Duverger, *Political Parties* (New York: John Wiley, 1954); V. O. Key, Jr., *Politics, Parties, and Pressure Groups* (New York: Thomas Y. Crowell, 5th edition, 1964); Hugh A. Bone, *American Politics and the Party System*, 3rd ed. (New York: McGraw-Hill, 1965); and Frank J. Sorauf, *Party Politics in America*, 2nd ed. (Boston: Little, Brown, 1972).

Additionally, several compendiums of essays concerning American partisan patterns are noteworthy: William J. Crotty et al., *Political Parties and Political Behavior* (Boston: Allyn and Bacon, 1966); John R. Owens and P. J. Staudenraus, *The American Party System* (New York: Macmillan, 1965); Frank Munger and Douglas Price, *Political Parties and Pressure Groups* (New York: Thomas Y. Crowell, 1964), and Robert A. Goldwin, *Political Parties U.S.A.* (Chicago: Rand McNally, 1964); William J. Crotty, ed., *Approaches to the Study of Party Organization* (Boston: Allyn and Bacon, 1968); Garold W. Thumm and Edward G. Janosik, eds., *Parties and the Governmental System* (Englewood Cliffs, N.J.: Prentice-Hall, 1967); Charles G. Mayo and Beryl L. Crowe, eds., *American Political Parties* (New York: Harper & Row, 1967); and Seymour M. Lipset and Stein Rokkan, eds., *Party Systems and Voter Alignments* (New York: Free Press, 1967).

# chapter 10

# organizing interest demands

We have examined in detail four ways in which Americans participate in conflict representation: how they express political opinions, exercise political leadership, reach voting choices, and take part in party politics. They also act in politics by joining voluntary organizations and bringing their demands and grievances directly to government officials. *These organized efforts to influence government are called interest group politics.*

### organized interests in conflict representation

How do people organize their demands by joining interest groups and how do they exert organized pressure to influence government? To answer these questions, we must consider two others: What are interest groups, and who takes part in them?

### a definition of interest groups

We distinguished among attitudes, interests, and opinions, so that we can now say that in politics *an interest group is any organization of persons, bound by attitudes that they share, who make demands upon others and express group opinions to influence policies that affect themselves.* Let us consider each principal element in this definition further.

SHARED ATTITUDES. An interest group is not just any collection of people. They must share some characteristic that brings them to interact or to react in a common way to a problem, if we are to say they are an interest group.[1] Persons of the same age are a demographic group with a common attribute, but they are not an interest group. If their age leads them to share some attitudes, which inspire them to make a common response to a specific question (like eighteen-to-twenty-year-olds seeking the right to vote at the close of the 1960s), people in the same age category become an interest group.

When people interact because they share attitudes, they generally organize; but two things characterize organized interest. *People need not be members of a formal organization to pursue the interests represented by it.* A person can be interested in eradicating poverty without joining an organization attempting to achieve that goal. Our subject here is group interests represented by formal organizations.

*Organization is not the same as unity of purpose.* Although enough attitudes are shared to make the group possible, interest groups often consist of different and competing elements or subinterests, striving to define, as well as achieve, organizational goals. Because unity promotes strength, group leaders develop formal organizational hierarchies and procedures to reconcile diverse elements. Tidiness in the organization is easily disrupted, however. Subgroups vie for control and form temporary alliances to direct group policy. Within the National Association for the Advancement of Colored People, controversy is continuous over the organization's traditional approach, advocating a moderate pace of racial integration, or a more militant stand. Also, the interests of group members are not always in harmony with the stated goals of the group. The American Medical Association reflects the goals of many doctors, but certainly not all of them; many research specialists and general practitioners do not share its opposition to a broad increase in federal programs for medical care.

MAKING INTEREST DEMANDS. Demands usually begin as goals sought primarily on behalf of group members. Interest groups, however, are not inherently "selfish." *Frequently, the demands of special interests are of ultimate benefit to larger sectors of the population.* Among the legislative proposals pushed through Congress by the administration of Lyndon Johnson in 1965 were bills to beautify the cities, establish new national park areas, regulate highway billboards, eradicate unsightly highway junkyards, and prevent air and water pollution. Although specialized environmental groups advanced these proposals (symbolically led by Mrs. Lyndon Johnson), the measures were designed to benefit all Americans.

[1] See David B. Truman, *The Governmental Process* (New York: Alfred A. Knopf, 1952), pp. 33–39; compare E. E. Schattschneider, *The Semisovereign People* (New York: Holt, Rinehart and Winston, 1960), pp. 23–24.

Often the claims of special interests ultimately benefit the population at large. Participants in Earth Day, 1970, made a nationwide appeal for environmental caution.

The same might be said of other policies that at first were special demands of narrow interests — particularly policies of welfare legislation such as social security, minimum wage legislation, and medical care for the aged.

*Many interest groups are organized to advance general rather than narrow demands,* such as John Gardner's Common Cause, an organization designed to promote participation in politics, change American political institutions to make them more responsive to social needs and produce a major reordering of national priorities; Ralph Nader's Center for the Study of Responsive Law works for consumer protection; and Saul Alinsky's Industrial Areas Foundation helped organize low-income communities for political protest in the 1960s.

*To be durable and effective, interest groups must continuously adapt their demands to meet current political realities.* Because their aims often conflict, some demands generate counterdemands. When environmentalist groups got congressional legislation requiring antipollution devices for cars, the manufacturers countered by requesting that some taxes on automobile sales be dropped to help raise money for necessary research and development.

The goals pursued by private interests may not parallel the public interest as public officials define it. To win approval for their position, organized interests often recruit support from other groups or rationalize their narrow demands to make them acceptable to the community. The

309

price of recruiting outside support is accepting modification of their initial claims to avoid conflict with other groups they want as allies. An appeal to mass public opinion, claimed to be in the public interest, may require that the original position be changed. Many members of the American Medical Association have vociferously opposed any government-sponsored medical insurance program. When almost two-thirds of the Americans surveyed in 1960 said they approved of such programs, the AMA changed its position to oppose only federal programs, thus allowing for state participation or sponsorship. It endorsed a bill providing matching federal grants to reimburse the states for medical aid to needy aged persons. In 1965, over AMA opposition, a medical care program for the aged, financed under the federal social security program, became law. (After losing the Medicare battle, the AMA tried and generally succeeded in influencing and even controlling the program's operation. Thus interest groups may keep going on an issue they consider vital.)

INFLUENCING GOVERNMENTAL DECISIONS. Interest groups seek access to public officials in order to express to them group opinions and to obtain favorable policies. Because they apply pressure on governing officials to influence policy, organized interests are often referred to as *pressure groups,* a term we shall consider as synonymous with *interest groups.* Interest groups have several ways of getting access to policymakers: administrative agencies, congressional committees, and presidential advisers. Some are easier to reach than others, so interest groups plan carefully to gain whatever advantage they can get where they do gain access. A major interest may find it far easier to work through the most influential people in a congressman's home district (automobile manufacturers in Michigan or farming interests in the midwest), thus reaching him by way of his constituents rather than approaching him directly as a public official.

Organized interests care less about having their own spokesmen elected or appointed to government offices (though this sometimes occurs) than about getting elective or appointive officials to recognize their claims. They do not, of course, divorce themselves from electoral politics. One way of access is having sympathetic candidates selected. If party control is diffuse or party leaders are divided, interest groups significantly affect party decisions, and perhaps even win nomination for their own members. But if a group spokesman is a political candidate, he runs as a Republican or Democrat, not as a leader of the Audubon Society, the Hardwood Plywood Institute, or the Marble Industry of America. The appeal of organized interest is too narrow to compete directly with the major parties, so group leaders prefer to work through party organizations rather than confront them directly.

*Interest groups thus differ from political parties in their goals and methods.* An American political party's goal is to control governmental authority; its method, mobilizing support behind candidates for office. The interest group's goal is to influence policy in a specific area; its methods include identifying with dominant community values, seeking the support of allied groups, lobbying with officials, endorsing and financing party candidates — always stopping short of offering a group spokesman for office.

## who participates in interest groups?

Two of every three Americans belong to some formal organization, and at least half of these belong to groups that take stands on political issues. Who joins and why?

*Group membership varies with social class,* because members of more affluent classes have more time, money, and resources to devote to group activity. Taking *occupation* as an indicator of social class, we find that professional and business people almost always belong to interest groups; clerical and skilled workers are less likely to join; unskilled workers, unless required to be members of trade unions, are unlikely to join.

*Education* also affects group membership — more group members come from the more educated. Those with higher *incomes* are more likely to join interest groups; membership in avowedly political clubs — neighborhood groups performing both social and political functions — has little to do with one's income, however.

The politics of organized interests and interest groups do not represent all social interests, so class bias is real. Currently, though, *representation from hitherto unorganized sectors is clearly increasing.* Before 1965, grape workers in southern California earned a yearly pay that was scarcely above the poverty level; they had no assurance of employment, no unemployment insurance, and no trade union. Cesar Chavez organized the workers well enough so that they could call a strike, march to the state capital to protest about grievances, and cause a nationwide boycott of grapes. Labor organizations and civil rights groups helped the grape workers behind Chavez to get broad public support; and by the end of 1970, two-thirds of the grape growers agreed to contracts favorable to the workers. With more and less success, black Americans, Mexican-Americans, young people, women's liberation proponents, and other formerly unrepresented elements have also organized to present their interest demands.

People join interest organizations for many reasons. Certainly one is their desire for political expression. Generally people do not exercise political initiative individually, but respond to group leaders who demonstrate their common interests, that these can be represented in politics, and that organized expression will influence policymakers. Such leaders as Martin Luther King, Jr., Cesar Chavez, Ralph Nader, and the late Saul Alinsky have articulated for blacks, farm laborers, consumers, and the poor that something can be gained by collective action. People also join groups for social and personal reasons — a need for meaningful camaraderie, to improve their social status, to enhance their sense of personal worth, or to respond to those making demands upon them. *Whatever their reasons for joining, group members obtain allies in pursuing their interests that they would not have if they stuck to purely individual techniques* such as voting, writing officials, keeping informed, or simply holding political opinions.

## organized social and economic interests in politics

The social and economic interest groups that represent conflicting interests to policymakers are hard to count (in Washington alone registered lobbyists represent more than a thousand organizations).[2] We can only suggest the variety among the largest groups that organize important social and economic demands in America and describe some of their interests.

### social demands

Some enduring problems of the 1960s and 1970s show up best when we look at interest groups in two policy areas: education and veterans affairs. Another type are the significant and much-publicized policy demands made by major organizations in recent years: civil rights, environmental quality, and consumer protection.

EDUCATION GROUPS. A principal group interested in educational policy is the National Education Association, an organization of schoolteachers, which has sought support for federal aid to education. In particular, the NEA has advocated channeling aid directly to local school agencies rather than through the states. The National Congress of Parents and Teachers (PTA), the American Council on Education, and the educa-

[2] For an inventory and description of major economic interests, see Harmon Zeigler, *Interest Groups in American Society* (Englewood Cliffs, N.J.: Prentice-Hall, 1964).

tional bodies of all major religious denominations have also expressed interest in federal aid and shared many of the NEA's ideas on aid to local districts. Federal aid to higher education has been a policy goal of several organizations such as the National Association for Equal Opportunity in Higher Education, which has proposed direct grants to institutions enrolling large numbers of students from low-income families to ensure that funds go to those students most in need of them. Interest groups in higher education have taken stands on proposals to allow a tax credit for the expenses of a college education, federal aid to college libraries, work-study programs, funding for construction of college classrooms, bills designed to deal with student unrest, and many others.

VETERANS' ORGANIZATIONS. Groups representing veterans have sought such benefits as low-cost hospital and medical care, low-cost housing, free land, education benefits, pensions, assistance to families of prisoners of war, and privileged treatment in competing for public employment. Among the most influential are the American Legion, the Disabled American Veterans, and the Veterans of Foreign Wars. Like most organized interests, they do not confine themselves to seeking material benefits for members; they also take stands on issues of symbolic importance. The American Legion and the Veterans of Foreign Wars were among the chief opponents to admission of mainland China to the United Nations.

CIVIL RIGHTS ORGANIZATIONS. Perhaps the most unrelenting efforts to influence policymaking on behalf of hitherto unrepresented interests have come from civil rights groups working on behalf of blacks, Mexican-Americans, women, young people, the poor, and the elderly. Civil rights groups illustrate the tendency of all interest organizations to use varied techniques to publicize their cause and to influence public officials. The National Association for the Advancement of Colored People and the Mexican-American Legal Defense and Educational Fund have used nonmilitant approaches, seeking redress for grievances in the courts and Congress. The Black Muslims have advocated a separate community for their people, and the Black Panthers have urged alliance with all sympathetic minority parties to contest elections. Women's liberation groups such as the National Organization for Women, the National Women's Political Caucus, and the Women's Equity Action League have employed marches, demonstrations, and boycotts as well as court and congressional hearings to publicize their causes, such as equal rights for women and policies pertaining to abortion, employment opportunities, child care, and the draft. Young people have campaigned for political candidates, demonstrated, occupied public buildings, disrupted college campuses, and used other tactics to publicize their complaints about war, the anonymity of mass education, drug use, and the deteriorating environment. Civil rights groups working on policies toward the poor have allied with other organizations to promote the economic as well as social and political rights of members, as has the National Welfare Rights Organization formed a coalition with the National Association of Manufacturers and the AFL-CIO to urge a major overhaul of welfare legislation and achieve a minimum annual income for poor families. Finally, groups representing the interests of the elderly, such as the Senior Citizens Council, have employed mass televised rallies and television documentaries to call attention to the need for improved health programs for the aged.

Many of the civil rights organizations also illustrate the *tendency of interest groups to diversify their interests* to fully represent their members. Until the mid-1960s, the Southern Christian Leadership Conference was interested primarily in obtaining federal legislation to guarantee voting rights for southern blacks. Its leadership corps, particularly the late Martin Luther King, Jr., recognized, however, that federal policies in areas other than voting also affect blacks, such as the burden of the draft to provide troops for the Vietnam War, which fell heavily on black youths; moreover, funds to finance that war were drained away from projects designed to alleviate black poverty. By the close of the 1960s, the SCLC was no longer interested only in the black's political rights; it had become deeply involved in urging Congress to fight poverty — as in the Poor People's March on Washington in 1968 — and to cut expenditures for defense and space exploration as one means of doing so.

Although these civil rights groups have gotten the most publicity in the 1960s and 1970s, others have been both active and influential. The Americans for Democratic Action and the American Civil Liberties Union have pressed for expansion of human rights, changes in the selective service laws, fair and impartial judicial hearings, and other measures. The American Jewish Congress, the Anti-Defamation League (also Jewish), the National Council of Catholic Men, and the Protestant National Council of Churches have also been involved in civil rights causes.

ENVIRONMENTALIST GROUPS. Interest in and demands for measures to protect man's environment from the deteriorating effects of water, air, noise, and other forms of pollution and from the threat of overpopulation have grown in the 1970s. Among the main environmentalist interest groups are the Sierra Club, which engages in organization at the grassroots level to influence congressional constituents, brings suits against major polluters, and engages extensively in publishing. In the 1970s, the Sierra Club has fought the development of a supersonic aircraft transport, underground testing of nuclear devices, timber cutting in national

Hitherto unrepresented interests can achieve influence through organized expression. Ralph Nader is credited with having influenced both government and industry to adopt stricter standards of consumer protection.

forests, and the building of oil pipelines in the Alaskan wilderness. The Center for Law and Social Policy, the Friends of the Earth, the Conservation Foundation, and organizations for young people have staunchly battled for policies to clean up the environment. To protect the environment from overpopulation, several interest organizations, such as the Council for Planned Parenthood, the Association for the Study of Abortion Laws, and Zero Population Growth, have proposed legislation favoring birth control, liberalized abortion, and the distribution of information about contraceptives.

CONSUMER INTERESTS. Groups have been organized to speak for the average consumer who is the victim of unfair sales practices, inadequate packaging, faulty products, low-quality goods, and over-the-counter sale of vitamin and food supplements of questionable effectiveness. The most vocal advocate of consumer protection has been Ralph Nader, organizer of "Nader's Raiders" (the Center for the Study of Responsive Law), urging legislation to improve automobile safety, the quality of prescription and nonprescription drugs, household detergents, and numerous other products. Both Consumer's Union and Common Cause have taken up the cause of the previously unrepresented consumer.

## economic demands

The most influential organized interests in this country have been those devoted to economic matters — business, labor, agricultural, and professional interests. The two leading business organizations in America are the Chamber of Commerce of the United States and the National Association of Manufacturers. Both have particularly dealt in policies on foreign trade, corporation taxes, federal minimum wage legislation, Social Security and unemployment policies, and government contracting. The Chamber of Commerce is an association of local chambers of commerce and thus represents many local business interests. The NAM is especially responsive to the interests of large industries. Many other groups representing small businessmen, the retail trades, the building trades, banking, transportation, and motel and hotel interests are active in politics.

LABOR ORGANIZATIONS. Labor organizations have greatly expanded their involvement with policy since the 1930s when legislation on minimum wages and maximum hours were their big interests. Unions still are deeply interested in such bread-and-butter matters as labor-management relations, wage and hour legislation, Social Security, and income tax legislation, but other issues — federally sponsored health insurance programs, legislation dealing with problems raised by automation, foreign aid, federal aid to education, a guaranteed annual wage, policies dealing with housing and government contracts — also occupy their attention. Among the most influential labor organizations have been the AFL–CIO, the United Mine Workers, the International Teamsters Union, the United Automobile Workers, the International Ladies Garment Workers' Union, and the International Telecommunications Union. Government employees have also been represented in the labor movement by such organizations as the American Federation of Government Employees (an AFL–CIO affiliate), the National Alliance of Postal and Federal Employees, and the National Postal Union.

THE MILITARY-INDUSTRIAL COMPLEX. During and after World War II, federal spending for military purposes, defense preparations, space development, and weapons technology increased immensely. Many industries relied on federal contracts for economic survival and prosperity; workers in these industries depended entirely on continued federal defense spending. An alliance of interests grew up, seeking high levels of defense expenditure: business firms seeking government contracts, labor unions in defense industries, government agencies urging new spending programs, military officers seeking support for the armed services, and congressmen in whose home districts the defense industries were located. *Industrial, labor, bureaucratic, military, and congressional interests have combined to form the most powerful influence on defense policies for the last two decades.*

At the top of the military-industrial complex are the Pentagon (Department of Defense), the House and Senate Armed Services committees, and prime defense contractors. Their interests are closely allied: 69 percent of the members of the Senate Armed Services Committee represent districts in which Pentagon expenditures are the prime source of federal funds. Though the committees in both houses reduce the Pentagon's budget request each year, the requests are often padded in anticipation of the cuts. When the two armed services committees have made budgetary recommendations for the Department of Defense, the Senate has approved its committee's recommendations all but three times and the House Armed Services Committee has never been overridden. Thus both committees effectively advocate the Pentagon's interest. Finally, the Department of Defense now spends about three times as much money as any other federal agency.

The potency of this alliance, even facing one of the severest challenges to its influence, showed in its ability to win approval in 1969 and 1970 of an elaborate research and development program for an antiballistic missile system (ABM) to deter Chinese or Soviet missile threats. Environmentalist, scientific, antiwar, religious, and other groups opposed it; even opinion polls indicated a gradual increase in general public opposition during the controversy. Opponents of the program argued that the ABM would be unworkable and excessively expensive (perhaps amounting to a total cost of $400 billion), that it would be a threat to communities near ABM sites which would be targets of enemy missiles, and that it would make it impossible to achieve effective world disarmament. But the military-industrial interests were able to convince enough Congressmen of the need for such a deterrent and of the economic benefits to their constituencies, and they received substantial approval in the House of Representatives and a one-vote victory in the Senate.

THE FARM BLOC. Before farmers began to migrate from the land to urban areas, farm groups were among the most influential in American politics. They still exert great pressure, particularly over programs that set farm subsidies and crop allotments and deal with farm laborers. The American Farm Bureau Federation has generally opposed strict production controls and favored high price supports, the National Farmers Union has supported both programs, and the National Grange has varied its position. The National Farmers Organization, was organized mostly to force food processors to pay higher prices for agricultural products.

PROFESSIONAL GROUPS. The interests of major professional groups encompass both social and economic demands. Among those with much influence are the American Bar Association (judicial, legal, and welfare issues) and the American Medical Association, which has been particularly vocal about proposals for national health insurance. The National Association of Realtors and the National Association of Home Builders are professional and business groups that take stands on such issues as federal subsidies for home building, urban redevelopment, open-housing legislation designed to end racial discrimination in sales of homes, and even drug abuse (local organizations of realtors developed "Turn in a Pusher" programs to report to local authorities anyone suspected of illegally selling drugs).

Organizations of scientists have been increasingly active in politics in recent decades. An informal group of nuclear scientists was instrumental in persuading Congress to establish a civilian agency, the Atomic Energy Commission, to control the development of nuclear power after World War II instead of letting the military manage it. In 1969 and 1970, the American Federation of Scientists was one of the most active anti-ABM groups; it was unable to keep the ABM on the ground but it did reduce funds committed to the project.

## techniques of organized interests

Each social and economic interest takes a stand on any issue affecting its membership. Organized interests thus represent diverse and frequently conflicting points of view to executive, legislative, and judicial officials. Representing social conflict to policymakers, interest groups engage in two general activities: first, to win support and to counter claims made by opposing interests, *groups publicize their demands and thus influence political opinion;* second, to inform government of their members' interests, *groups present their demands directly to public officials and thereby influence public policy.*

## publicizing group interests

All organized interests use varied tools to influence political opinions. Among the principal ones are organizing opinions among their own members, socializing members, exercising leadership in calling public attention to issues, electioneering, and protesting grievances.

ORGANIZING GROUP OPINIONS. Interest groups are important in organizing political opinion for good reason. Before they can recruit outside aid in pursuit of their goals, they must first mobilize internal support for those goals and for the means and strategies to realize them. Because large social and economic organizations (such as education groups or large labor unions) have many interests, they must often work hard to reconcile divergent opinions. When the techniques they use to achieve those adjustments are democratic, members are more likely to support democratic ways of settling disputes within the larger community, including the occasional need to accept compromise on their own position.[3]

*Internal democracy in private interest organizations, however, is not the rule.* Many organized interests are governed by oligarchic controls; although most members participate relatively little in running the organization, an *active minority* makes decisions and speaks for the group.[4] It is always wise in studying group stands to recognize that the opinions of group leaders and the rank and file may differ substantially. Oligarchic and nondemocratic though it may be, rule by an active minority is necessary to the organization. The active minority usually is a stable, experienced leadership core that sees to the necessary day-to-day detailed operations, about which most members do not care. In the group's conflict with other interests, a small core of leaders can respond more quickly and effectively to outside pressures than can the mass membership; and concentrating the responsibility for making public statements in group leaders leaves the impression of organizational unity in making demands on public officials, in spite of internal rifts. (George Meany, head of the AFL-CIO, could say that he speaks for *all* his members despite internal dissension about his political ideas.)

SOCIALIZING THE MEMBERS. Attitudes and opinions mingle. People who share attitudes join interest groups that respond as one to problems, but simply being in the group reinforces one's own attitudes. Group life thus

---

[3] See John Dewey, *The Public and Its Problems* (New York: Henry Holt, 1927), chap. 1.

[4] Abraham Holtzman, *Interest Groups and Lobbying* (New York: Macmillan, 1966), chap. 2.

Senior citizens have mobilized to dramatize demands for better and cheaper health care.
The goal of most interest groups is to influence policy in one area.

helps socialize members. Generally, taking part in an organization makes members more aware of politics, reinforces their awareness of political self-competence, and stimulates them to be politically active. The closer a person's affiliation with a group is, obviously the more the organization will affect his thinking.[5]

EXERCISING LEADERSHIP. Interest groups and group leaders identify problems and alert a larger public to them, influencing opinions outside their own organizations. In 1965, Ralph Nader wrote *Unsafe at Any Speed*,[6] in which he called attention to the problem of automobile safety,

[5] V. O. Key, Jr., *Public Opinion and American Democracy* (New York: Alfred A. Knopf, 1961), p. 507.
[6] Ralph Nader, *Unsafe at Any Speed* (New York: Grossman, 1965).

which was not new or ignored by public officials. Yet the public was not worried about it until Nader's revelations prompted General Motors to investigate him, expecting to discredit both him and his book. The publicity generated by the Nader–General Motors controversy focused the public's attention on the real problem, safety in automobiles, providing an impetus in Congress for more stringent safety requirements.[7]

ELECTIONEERING. Interest organizations advance their aims during election campaigns by mobilizing their own members to support candidates, by endorsing candidates, or by making financial and other contributions. Organized labor, particularly the AFL–CIO, has been particularly effective in mobilizing votes on behalf of candidates it favors. During the 1968 presidential campaign, it became apparent that George Wallace, candidate of the American Independent Party, was winning support from members of organized labor and threatening to siphon votes away from the AFL–CIO's preferred candidate, Hubert Humphrey. To counter the Wallace appeal, the AFL–CIO's Committee on Political Education (COPE) distributed a brochure to union members recounting that "George Wallace's Alabama" had one of the worst records of any state in supporting policies favorable to organized labor. It is doubtful the COPE effort was the sole cause, but in the last weeks of the campaign, Wallace's support among union workers decreased substantially.

Many interest groups endorse candidates for public office, thus informing their members and nonmembers of their preferences. The National Committee for an Effective Congress, composed of leaders of both political parties, operates primarily by making endorsements. Although this interest has little formal organization, the dedication of its members to the cause has brought much success in congressional elections.[8]

The financial contributions of major organized interests to political campaigns are usually channeled through "political action committees," organizations designed to solicit members for funds. The big contributors in recent years have been the National Association of Manufacturer's Business-Industry Political Action Committee (BIPAC), the Bankers' Political Action Committee, the American Medical Political Action Committee, and the AFL–CIO's Committee on Political Education. In the 1970 congressional elections, political action committees alone collected and disbursed almost 40 percent of the contributions reportedly received by candidates for the House of Representatives.[9]

[7] Charles O. Jones, *An Introduction to the Study of Public Policy* (Belmont, Calif.: Wadsworth, 1970), chap. 3.

[8] Harry M. Scoble, *Ideology and Electoral Action* (San Francisco: Chandler, 1967).

[9] Robert A. Diamond, ed., *Dollar Politics* (Washington, D.C.: Congressional Quarterly, 1971), p. 60.

The money supplied to political candidates by interest organizations is only part of the story. Interest groups also contribute the "free time" of paid secretarial and administrative staffs, postage and stationery, private airplanes, and numberless other items. On election day, interest organizations provide message services, car pools, and babysitting for voters. These tactics are significant because they are normally channeled through the local precinct organizations of the two major parties, augmenting party efforts in return for consideration that interest groups hope will be sympathetic from the party's elected public officials.

PUBLIC PROTESTS. Protest activity has been most commonly associated with the civil rights movement, but public protests have a long history (the Boston Tea Party of 1773). Protest tactics are designed to publicize the grievances and demands of both economic and social interests. These include strikes, boycotts, peaceful demonstrations, picketing, sit-ins, lie-ins, mass moratoriums, and violence. Many of these tactics constitute civil disobedience.

The *strike* is a tactic employed most often by organized labor, though it has been used by other groups (in the nationwide Vietnam Moratorium of October 15, 1969, students on many college campuses refused to attend classes as a protest against the war). As a technique in labor-management disputes, the strike is regulated by federal law. Under specified circumstances, the President may seek a court injunction enjoining a labor union from striking if the work stoppage would imperil the national health or safety.

A *boycott* is a collective refusal to purchase commodities or services from a manufacturer, merchant, firm, or utility whose economic or social policies are considered unfair. Boycotts have been used primarily as a form of economic reprisal by labor unions and consumers to force changes in wages, prices, and the like. One of the most widely famous boycotts, however, was meant to publicize social demands; that is, the boycott of buses in 1955 organized by Martin Luther King, Jr., in Montgomery, Alabama, to give force to a demand for racial equality. Similarly, women's liberation groups have sometimes refused to purchase cosmetics, undergarments, laundry soaps and other products, not to force price changes but to demonstrate their dissatisfaction with what they regard as a demeaning image of women in the advertising of such products.

*Peaceful demonstrations* proved an effective attention-getting device in the 1960s and 1970s, especially for civil rights groups, environmental interests, and antiwar protestors. Generally, civil rights advocates have selected a policy they considered unjust, such as the practice then widely accepted in the South of refusing to serve blacks and whites together in restaurants, and they protested by disobeying the policy (black and white

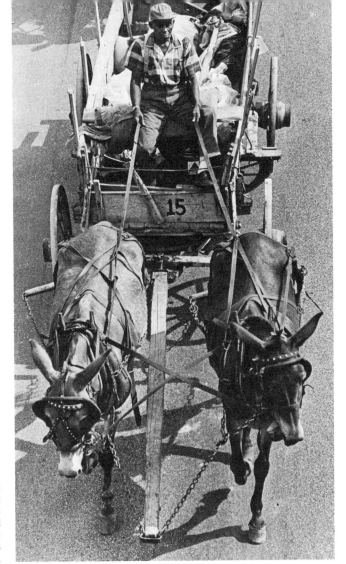

The "Poor People's" march in 1968 called national attention to persisting poverty. Ancient farm wagons pulled by floppy-eared mules symbolized that the American poor do not yet share the benefits of our society available to the affluent.

civil rights workers would occupy restaurant seats for hours). Mass marches and rallies, like the civil rights march on Washington in 1963 and the "Poor People's" march in 1968, dramatically demonstrated minority grievances.

Opponents of legislation designed to hasten racial integration also turn to peaceful demonstrations to publicize their positions. In 1972, mass caravans of cars and school buses moved along highways in some states of both North and South to protest against the busing of school children to achieve racial balance in public schools. Groups interested in cleaning

323

up the environment have used nonviolent demonstrations, such as wearing gas masks to publicize the dangers of air pollution, organizing the nationwide appeal that culminated in Earth Day in 1970, holding cleanup campaigns, and establishing collection points for recycling bottles, cans, and newspapers.

Many peaceful demonstrations are meant to test the legitimacy of laws by disobeying them, being arrested, and arguing a case in the courts as in some antiwar demonstrations. When Congress passed a law in 1965, forbidding young men to burn their draft cards, several youths protested against both the Vietnam War and the law by holding public burnings. David P. O'Brien, one young man who burned his draft card in 1966, was arrested, tried, and convicted. He appealed the decision on the grounds that the 1965 law was an unconstitutional abridgment of freedom of speech. Although the Supreme Court ruled against O'Brien, the publicity given the case effectively demonstrated the antiwar point he wished to make.

*Violence,* said a protest leader of the 1960s, is as American as cherry pie. To be sure, violence was used many times in American history to protest against grievance: the Whiskey rebellions of the 1790s, the use of terrorism in the post–Civil War South by such groups as the Ku Klux Klan, violent conflict in labor-management disputes in the 1890s, assassinations of public figures, periodic riots in urban areas throughout our history, and student disruptions on college campuses in the 1960s.[10] Violence, however, is not a preferred tactic for publicizing group interests. Dissident groups — despite the widely publicized use of Molotov cocktails, bombing, and airplane highjackings have only a limited capacity to mount an open revolt so long as governing authorities have the guns, planes, tanks, and manpower to repress it.[11] Moreover, violence, whether used by protestors against or enforcers of the law, raises the moral question of whether the end justifies the means, which applies to violence and to civil disobedience as well.

CIVIL DISOBEDIENCE. Many of the tactics, both peaceful and violent, which have been employed to publicize interest demands have been justified by dissident groups as legitimate forms of civil disobedience; that is, as *deliberate, public infractions of the law aimed at changing policies.* Agreement on just what *civil* disobedience is has been anything but universal. Protestors, politicians, lawyers, judicial officers, philosophers, and interested citizens disagree on several important points.

[10] See Richard E. Rubenstein, *Rebels in Eden: Mass Political Violence in the United States* (Boston: Little, Brown, 1970).

[11] On the impracticalities of violence as a technique in the face of counterviolence by government, see Martin Oppenheimer, *The Urban Guerrilla* (Chicago: Quadrangle Books, 1969).

*Civil disobedience involves illegal acts; is it thereby inherently violent?* Infractions of the law do not in themselves constitute violence so long as they do not involve physical injury to persons and are carried out with consideration for the rights of others.[12] Much political rhetoric, however, has equated violations with violence and thereby urged repression of all civil disobedience.

*Does the illegality of civil disobedience imply that people using it must willingly suffer the consequences of violating the law?* One side says yes, because this willingness demonstrates that the disobedient are sincere; they suggest that objectionable laws be reconsidered in the courts. Another side says that it is the citizen's *duty* to disobey in order to make an extraordinary appeal to the community's conscience. As an act of political obligation, they say, civil disobedience entitles the disobedient person to legal immunity or lenient punishment. Following this reasoning, some militant students who occupied campus buildings, denied access to college campuses for military or industrial recruiters, and performed similar acts were not willing to be arrested or stand trial. And, postulating that it takes political courage to disobey, Senator Edward Kennedy in 1972 urged amnesty for young men who fled the country in protest against compulsory military service in a war that they and he considered immoral.

*Is civil disobedience not justified until all other legal means of protest have been exhausted?* Some advocates of the tactic argue that it should be a last resort against injustice; others argue that infractions of the law are necessary precisely because the system against which they protest is unresponsive and immoral and provides no ethical, legitimate means other than disobedience to redress grievances.[13]

*Which laws are subject to protest?* Some civil rights lawyers argue that disobedience is civil only where laws of doubtful constitutionality are challenged; the breaking of "innocent" laws such as traffic regulations and of laws against murder is not condoned. Others feel that *all* laws of a corrupt government are subject to civil disobedience.

*Is civil disobedience justified if it is not intended to test a law or to change a policy?* Responsible dissent is assumed to have a reformist end, to alleviate ills within the established system. Yet the dissenter, more interested in revolution than reform, more in overthrowing the government than improving its policies, often practices agitation for its own sake.[14]

These questions about civil disobedience as a technique used by inter-

[12] Paul F. Power, "Civil Disobedience as Functional Opposition," *The Journal of Politics* 34 (Feb. 1972): 37–55.

[13] Herbert Marcuse, *An Essay on Liberation* (Boston: Beacon Press, 1969).

[14] Sidney Hook, "Neither Blind Obedience Nor Uncivil Disobedience," *The New York Times Magazine* (June 5, 1966).

The Berkeley Free Speech Movement was the parent of later sit-in strikes, some of which entirely disrupted academic life during the 1960s and raised serious questions about the justifiable limits of civil disobedience.

est groups will not quickly or easily be resolved. It is best that they should not be. They are the very heart of democratic government — how minority dissent works under popular majority rule — and they deserve continued public debate.

*Two functions of civil disobedience in representing interests* conflict with established ways of doing things. First, civil disobedience strikingly demonstrates to established regimes that grievances about the status quo have been overlooked or ignored by governmental leaders but they must be alleviated. When civil rights, women's liberation, and antiwar groups in the 1960s turned to civil disobedience, it was no longer possible for political leaders simply to return to business as usual without trying to

326

meet some of the interest demands. Second, civil disobedience stimulates interest organizations and elected officials to reexamine their popular followings and institutions to find out why they failed to represent dissident interests. It forces them to reform both themselves and political institutions to regain the confidence they have lost. The franchise was extended to young people not long after the campus demonstrations. Civil disobedience has resulted in some functional benefits that cannot be discounted in organizing interest demands.

## presenting group interests

Many techniques by which organized interests publicize their demands are also used to present those demands to policymakers. Occupying government office buildings (sit-ins) is a direct confrontation with officials as well as an effort to call public attention to grievances. Other techniques, such as lobbying, influencing the appointment of public officials, and working within government, are designed to influence public officials, not public opinion.

LOBBYING. *A lobbyist is a paid representative of an interest group whose principal function is to link organized interests with public officials.* He does his work by contacting public officials, by performing services for them, and by giving services to the organization.

Lobbyists work for enactment, alteration, or defeat of policies by personal contact with governing officials. They contact the officials by presenting testimony to administrative officials and legislative committees, stimulating group members and sympathizers to write letters to policymakers, making financial contributions to election campaigns, becoming personal friends with lawmakers, and so forth. Lobbyists usually try to contact officials already sympathetic to their views. Officials return the favor.[15] The stereotype of special interests dictating policy to lawmakers is unrealistic; instead, lobbyists and officials are brought together because they have the same interests and help each other toward the same goals.

By their services to governing officials, lobbyists try to keep open the channels of communication between groups and government, to establish mutual respect between themselves and policymakers, and to build personal reputations for honesty, knowledgeability, and efficiency, They supply specialized information to legislators and administrators, counter

[15] Raymond A. Bauer, et al., *American Business and Public Policy* (New York: Atherton, 1963), p. 353.

the pressures of opposing groups on the lawmakers (supporting a Congressman's denunciation of an opposition interest), and encourage officials to solicit their opinions. In a survey of Washington lobbyists, only 14 percent said that their views were solicited regularly by officials,[16] but another study of Congressmen's feelings about lobbyists (see Table 10-1) shows that they do make some use of the lobbyists' services even if they rarely solicit their views.

Many lobbyists, instead of contacting public officials or providing services for them, inform their organizations of policy developments and assist the organization in inquiries, discover loopholes in the laws, and negotiate with other interests. Some spend far more time trying, often without success, to warn about the implications of policies than to influence policies themselves.

The popular idea of the lobbyist has him as a shady character getting officials to do his bidding by bribery if all else fails. Actually, both lobbyists and Congressmen condemn bribery as a method of securing influence.[17] In 1968, both the Senate and the House of Representatives, as a guard against unethical tactics, passed resolutions calling for limited disclosure of honorariums received by legislators for performing any service (such as addressing a convention) for organized interests. In recent years, a few Congressmen (Representative John Dowdy of Texas was convicted in 1972 of accepting a $25,000 bribe to prevent a federal investigation of a Maryland home improvement company) have engaged in blatantly unethical conduct, keeping public suspicion alive despite evidence that such conduct is relatively rare and that the Congress has taken initial steps to deal with it.

INFLUENCING GOVERNMENT APPOINTMENTS. Organized interests obviously think about the views of those appointed to public office, so they support or oppose any nominee. The American Bar Association has made it a practice to comment on the legal background and qualifications of anyone selected for a judicial position. Other major interests do the same. A leading candidate for nomination to the Supreme Court in 1971 was Representative Richard H. Poff of Virginia, who had once said, "I'd rather be on the Supreme Court than be President." The Nixon administration saw many qualities in Poff: he was from a southern state, had a conservative voting record, and his long membership in the House Judiciary Committee had given him experience in constitutional law. The American Bar Association's federal judiciary committee met to discuss his qualifications, and the White House prepared a lengthy memorandum

[16] Lester W. Milbrath, *The Washington Lobbyists* (Chicago: Rand McNally, 1963), p. 340.
[17] *Ibid.*, pp. 274–281.

**TABLE 10-1**
**Congressmen's Perceptions of Lobbyists**

| View | Percentage |
|---|---|
| **Personal Aid** | |
| "Most lobbyists are helpful to me because they supply detailed facts on complicated legislative questions." | 62% |
| "Some lobbyists are helpful to me because they supply detailed facts on complicated legislative questions." | 7 |
| "Most lobbyists confuse the issue because they distort the facts." | 3 |
| "Lobbyists neither help nor hinder me in my work." | 17 |
| No response | 11 |
| **Aid to Congress** | |
| "Lobbyists help Congress to legislate with maximum intelligence." | 41 |
| "Congress would be better off without lobbyists." | 5 |
| No Response | 54 |
| **Pressure** | |
| "I have often felt unreasonable pressure from lobbyists." | 11 |
| "I sometimes have felt unreasonable pressure from lobbyists." | 21 |
| "I have never felt unreasonable pressure from lobbyists." | 33 |
| No response | 35 |
| N=122 | |

Source: Data taken from a *Congressional Quarterly* survey conducted in 1957 reported in *Congress and the Nation, 1945–1964* (Washington, D.C.: Congressional Quarterly Service, 1965), p. 1554.

describing his abilities. But when the possibility of the appointment was publicized, opposition was raised at once by key interest groups: civil rights organizations opposed Poff because he had voted against the Civil Rights Acts of 1957, 1960, 1964, and 1968; the AFL–CIO objected to his conservative voting record, and George Meany, president of the organization, said, "I understand Mr. Poff is a very nice gentleman, but on his record he's a racist"; the National Organization for Women (NOW) announced it would join other women's liberation groups to oppose Poff because of his "sexist" stand in the House Judiciary Committee, which helped to weaken a proposed constitutional amendment giving women rights equal to those of men; and the Americans for Democratic Action questioned Poff's judicial qualifications. Facing this publicized opposition, Poff asked that his name be withdrawn from consideration for nomination to the Supreme Court, and President Nixon acceded to his wishes.

WORKING WITHIN GOVERNMENT. Political interest groups are not just private groups trying to put pressure on public officials. Officials try to further their own interests by applying pressure to their colleagues and private organizations.

At least three varieties of organized interests work within the formal governmental structure. *Government agencies work in consort and in conflict with other agencies to serve a special clientele.* The Veterans Administration promotes the interests of veterans, frequently joining with veterans organizations in urging Congress to provide more money for programs to aid veterans. Private interest organizations are represented within government when *interest group leaders are appointed to government positions.* If a labor lawyer is appointed Secretary of Labor or a railroad executive is appointed to the Interstate Commerce Commission (the agency charged with regulating the railway industry), those interests acquire appointed administrative spokesmen. *Many government agencies and legislative bodies develop their own interests, which they pursue in competition with others.* Thus, under the chairmanship of Senator William Fulbright, the Senate Committee on Foreign Relations in the late 1960s acted as an interest group in demanding that the President and the Secretary of State consult the committee on relations with South Vietnam and the conduct of the Vietnam War.

## what determines a group's effectiveness?

Because of the many interest groups in our highly pluralist society, it is hard for any organization — competing with all the others for the citizen's and public official's attention, support, and loyalty — to mobilize the people's interests into an effective majority. The effectiveness of interest groups in representing demands is influenced by popular views, internal characteristics, and political and constitutional considerations.

## popular thoughts on interest groups

Political groups are able to organize popular support for their demands depending on popular conceptions of how effectively collective action influences policymakers, the causes that groups espouse, and their tactics in publicizing and presenting demands.

Led by William Fulbright, the Senate Committee on Foreign Relations has performed as an interest group in insisting on presidential consultation regarding conduct of the undeclared Vietnam War.

ASSESSING INTEREST GROUP EFFECTIVENESS. *Collective action is considered to be an effective way of influencing policy, but organized activity is not generally the preferred way of influencing government.* A representative sample of Americans were asked what action they would take if Congress were considering a law they believed unjust or harmful. Their choices in order of preference were: (1) contact elected leaders as individuals, (2) arouse friends and neighbors, (3) do nothing, (4) vote, (5) work through a formal group, and (6) work through a political party. People are generally reluctant to turn to formal organization to publicize and present their interests; as many as 43 percent of Americans do not belong to political organizations of any type.[18]

They believe it is effective, but they prefer not to take part. The reasons are not complex. They simply prefer to spend their leisure time doing something other than joining organizations. They distrust organized activity because the stereotype associates shady activities with special (often thought to be "selfish") interests. The preference for individual methods of influencing government is probably left over from attitudes learned in childhood. American children emphasize the individual side of civic duty (voting, keeping informed, contacting officials) and know little about the positive contributions organized efforts make. And, of course, American indifference to active politics in general makes it tough

[18] Gabriel A. Almond and Sidney Verba, *The Civic Culture* (Princeton, N.J.: Princeton University Press, 1963), p. 191.

**TABLE 10–2**
**Popular Respect for Black Civil Rights Organizations**

| Organization | A great deal | Some, but not a great deal | Hardly at all | Not sure |
|---|---|---|---|---|
| | | *Degree of respect* | | |
| National Association for the Advancement of Colored People | 75% | 18% | 3% | 4% |
| Congress of Racial Equality | 42 | 28 | 6 | 24 |
| Southern Christian Leadership Conference | 73 | 18 | 3 | 6 |
| Urban League | 53 | 24 | 5 | 18 |
| Black Panthers | 25 | 24 | 36 | 15 |

Source: Louis Harris and Associates, *The Harris Survey Yearbook of Public Opinion, 1970* (New York: Louis Harris and Associates, Inc., 1971), p. 255.

for groups to arouse interest in special causes. Political groups thus appeal primarily to an already participating and intensely involved minority.

ASSESSING INTEREST GROUP DEMANDS. To organize interest demands effectively political groups must have popular support. Some groups have found their goals acceptable. The most effective groups representing blacks in the civil rights movement have been those supported by both blacks and whites. The Black Panthers have had limited popular support (see Table 10–2). Blacks did not believe militant organizations like the Panthers represented their views as well as more moderate black interest groups like the NAACP, the Urban League, and others.[19]

ASSESSING INTEREST GROUP TACTICS. Many organized interests sacrifice popular support because their techniques for publicizing and presenting their demands do not have public approval. A nationwide survey in 1970 revealed that a third of the adults agreed in general with the goals of student protestors, but only about one in ten approved of their tactics.[20] Popular opinion supports a way of protesting against grievances if it ap-

[19] Louis Harris and Associates, Inc., *The Harris Survey Yearbook of Public Opinion, 1970* (New York: Louis Harris and Associates, 1971), p. 258.
[20] *Ibid.*, p. 274.

proves of the group using it. Asked if workers should have the right to strike, two-thirds said they felt workers should have that right. When asked about specific types of workers (postal workers, air traffic controllers, schoolteachers, newspaper employees, and hospital employees), however, they said that only postal workers and newspaper employees should have that right, and at that only a slim majority approved.[21]

### groups: characteristics and effectiveness

The size, motivations of members, goals, quality of leadership, politically relevant resources, and capacity to act in concert help to determine how well organized interests do in influencing government. *Sheer numbers always mean a great deal in a democracy:* the spokesman for sixteen million union workers gets more deference from public officials than the president of a neighborhood civic club. But bigness may be offset by the difficulty of achieving solidarity. The disputes that racked the Students for a Democratic Society (SDS) at the close of the 1960s threw that organization into a decline that has just about made it vanish. It was formed in 1962 to promote individual participation in decisionmaking and to encourage an independent spirit in men. It sharply criticized rampant materialism, the loss of individual identity in mass institutions, racism, and militarism in American life. As it expanded, goals and tactics were disputed. Moderate members favored reforming American institutions from within; more militant elements such as the "Weathermen" urged drastic challenges to the institutions themselves — challenges such as the "days of rage" in Chicago in 1969 which resulted in destruction of property and confrontation with police. Another faction, the National Officer Collective, dedicated itself to class warfare in the Communist tradition. By 1970, the extremist tactics of the most militant had so alienated the moderates that no compromise was possible. The moderates withdrew, the national headquarters closed, and the militants went underground.

*The commitment of members is often as important to effectiveness as group size.* Intensely committed members in small organizations can recruit broader support. The women's liberation movement began with a relatively small number of women in organizations scattered throughout the country. Their loyalty and dedication were so great that, even though they were ignored by many men and women, the members were able to publicize their demands, expand their membership, and by 1972 win approval of Congress to submit a constitutional amendment forbidding discrimination based on sex.

---

[21] *Ibid.,* pp. 74–75.

*Group effectiveness depends too on flexibility in defining goals.* Groups dedicated to moral causes (such as those devoted to purging America of materialism) are increasing in America. Many attempt to build internal solidarity by insisting on ideological purity among members, which calls for an absolutist position (such as eternal opposition to the "establishment" or "you can't trust anyone over thirty"), limiting their ability to bargain and compromise with other groups who may share common ends but whose members cannot accept moral absolutism. Overly doctrinaire groups lose their popular appeal. The American Medical Association, fighting proposals for compulsory national health insurance programs, made a moral issue out of protecting the confidential doctor-patient relationship. Its intransigence on this issue in the 1960s cut into its support and damaged the medical profession's reputation for avoiding partisan politics.

If doctrinaire interests do compromise their stands, they risk alienating their most dedicated members simply because of the purity they demand. Professional organizations of educators, such as the American Association of University Professors, are constantly faced with the problem of whether their position as impartial seekers of knowledge permits them to join organizations that take political stands. Portions of the membership of the AAUP have vowed to leave that organization if it should take stands on political issues.

*Group leaders influence the effectiveness of their organizations* by their ability to define group goals, mobilize support among both members and nonmembers, contest and negotiate with other groups, and present group demands to policymakers. In doing these things, many group leaders develop specialized interests that may not reflect those of other group members. For several years, some miners argued that the United Mine Workers union leaders had lost touch with the membership's interests and above all had failed to press for improvement in mining safety and treatment for black lung disease caused by inhaling coal dust. After a West Virginia mine explosion in 1968 trapped and killed seventy-eight miners, protesting miners took their grievances not just to the federal government but to their own union by forming the West Virginia Black Lung Association, demanding that the United Mine Workers seek better health and safety standards. The union's leadership responded favorably, and the miners ultimately were rewarded with the Federal Coal Mine and Safety Act in 1969, which acceded to their principal demands.

*An organized interest's politically relevant resources also contribute to its ability to influence policymakers.* Material resources are money, manpower, permanent office space near legislative and administrative halls, facilities for regular meetings both en masse and individually with key personnel, and perhaps even ownership of a popular newspaper.

The National Welfare Rights Organization has diversified its initial concern for economic rights to concerns for social and political rights as well. As with many organized interests, a broadened appeal helps ally it with other political groups.

Because many groups are not involved in politics full-time, however, most lack financing, skilled personnel, information, and time to do an effective job of pressuring policymakers. Although great sums of money are spent by interest groups to influence officials, the overall expenditure is divided among uncoordinated, sometimes even conflicting, organizations. Most organizations can afford to spend relatively little on political activities. Swiss watch manufacturers budget more than $2 million annually for advertising and public relations, but only about one-eighth of this amount is spent campaigning against United States tariff increases. Less tangible resources also have their value. Among these are personal "contact" and friendships with public officials and knowledge of how the decisionmaking machinery works.

Any group is better off in a policy struggle if it has public respectability. The American Medical Association has used the medical profession's positive image (some of it deliberately created, including the homely appeal of the doctor-patient relationship) as a weapon in combating legislative proposals on medical care until its stand became too intransigent and it was forced to accept the Medicare program.

*To strengthen their specific claims, groups often form alliances for common action.* To get cooperation, however, they must bargain and perhaps accept positions they did not originally intend to take. Varied groups reconciled their differences in the battle to obtain federal aid to education and won in the Elementary and Secondary Education Act of 1965.

The principal interest groups were the National Education Association (representing teachers and school administrators), the American Federation of Teachers (affiliated with the AFL–CIO), and the Americans for Democratic Action. To win support for an aid bill, they sought support from religious organizations such as the National Council of the Churches of Christ and the National Association of Evangelicals, and other groups that favored federal aid to public schools. But they also had to oppose such groups as the National Catholic Welfare Conference, the Council of Catholic Men, and others that strongly favored aid to parochial schools. Representatives of all these groups met with officials of the Johnson administration and approved an arrangement giving aid to school districts with many children from low-income families and permitting private schools to share in some of the federally aided services through special programs. Only after the administration got organized interests to approve the proposal did it submit the bill to Congress, where it won rapid approval. Thus, a major religious conflict over education policy was resolved by negotiating with contending interests before Congress began handling the bill.

## political and constitutional factors

Organized interests are affected by guarantees granted by the Constitution, the Constitution's structure, and public policies.

CONSTITUTIONAL GUARANTEES. It is a commonplace in American political rhetoric to belabor the "special interests" that are thought to be responsible for undesirable community conditions and policies. The crowds enjoying President Truman's attacks on "the interests" in the 1948 campaign urged "Give 'em hell, Harry." Yet interest group politics has its utility — whatever its defects — because it represents social conflict to public officials and provides ingredients essential for resolving these conflicts. Though some activities of interest groups shock us, a healthy democracy could not operate without them. The Founding Fathers fretted over the "mischieviousness of faction," but they provided specific constitutional guarantees giving interests the opportunity to organize, publicize, and present their demands (see Chapter Five). James Madison wrote in Federalist No. 10: "Liberty is to faction what air is to fire, an ailment without which it instantly expires." *The First Amendment guarantees of freedom of speech, association, and petition provide the liberty that makes interest group politics possible.*

CONSTITUTIONAL STRUCTURE. Like all large organizations, including political parties, interest groups are affected by the separation of powers, the system of checks and balances, and some federal features of our governing arrangement. *These determine the access of organized interests to policymakers.* The United States Chamber of Commerce, with its federal base and its physically dispersed local units, matches the federal structure of government, a feature which has greatly helped the organization by affording access to Congressmen who depend, in part, on the type of business support represented by the local chambers. Many other interests are similarly organized to work not only through lobbyists in Washington but through local Congressmen and field offices of federal agencies.

The effectiveness of interest groups also depends in part on whether their goal is to get legislation passed or to prevent its passage. *It is much easier to keep legislation from being passed than to get it passed, because policymaking authority is scattered among many semiautonomous agencies.* The chance that a proposal will be vetoed increases directly in proportion to the number of official agencies that must agree before a policy is adopted. Separation of powers, checks and balances, federalism, and other forces dispersing power thus work against interests seeking significant alterations of the status quo, even as they favor interests trying to prevent change.

Federalism frequently sharpens conflict between interests. The ones that have favorable access to officials in state governments seek support there; those who can obtain favor through federal action concentrate their energies at that level. In the conflicts over civil rights, segregationist and integrationist forces had different access points in the federal structure. Segregationists often found that state and local officials, local courts, and local school boards were sympathetic; so they could delay or dilute school desegregation, integration of public facilities, or the removal of literacy tests for voting. Integrationists successfully take their case to federal officials, particularly the President and Congress, which passed civil rights acts in the 1960s. Moreover, they have asked the Department of Justice to investigate cases of discrimination and have appealed judicial decisions of state courts to federal courts. The quarrel over "states' rights" versus "national authority" is more rhetoric than reality; the dispute simply reflects the disputants' different leverage points within the federal structure.

LINKS BETWEEN PRIVATE INTERESTS AND PUBLIC OFFICIALS. In this century, bureaucratic agencies charged with specialized functions in policymaking have proliferated, resulting in a pluralist bureaucracy that closely complements the social pluralism reflected by the diversity of organized interests (see Chapter Fourteen). Some operate with a minimum of supervision from either the President or Congress. Agencies at all levels of the administrative establishment have developed close relationships with constituent interests, the very groups the agencies were designed to regulate. Among these are the radio and television broadcasting networks and the Federal Communications Commission, major oil interests and the Federal Power Commission, financial interests and the Securities and Exchange Commission, and the military-industrial complex described earlier. *Such favored access of organized interests to policymakers is not only permitted but promoted by the dispersion of governing authority* which is inherent in the contemporary constitutional structure.

POLICIES AFFECTING ORGANIZED INTERESTS. The tactics that organized interests may use and their access to public officials are regulated by legislation and administrative rules. The Federal Regulation of Lobbying Act, part of the Legislative Reorganization Act of 1946, was designed to publicize the lobbying activities of interest organizations. It required any person who hired himself out for pay as a lobbyist on behalf of someone else to register with the clerk of the House of Representatives and the secretary of the Senate, to file quarterly reports of his receipts and expenditures, and to list the bills in which his organization was interested. It also required quarterly statements on receipts and spending from organizations conducting lobbying. Other statutes forbid bribery (making it a crime to offer a Congressman "anything of value" to influence him), prevent some types of organizations such as corporations and labor unions from making direct contributions to finance candidates' election campaigns, and require Congressmen to disclose their sources of outside income. Also, administrative rules define the legitimate channels of communication between group leaders and officials. Many administrative agencies specifically restrict congenial informal contacts between their officials and parties interested in agency decisions. The owner of a television station who seeks access to federal communications commissioners by offering them trips on his yacht may find himself without the license he hoped to retain, because the commission forbids such tactics.

Most of these legislative and administrative requirements and restrictions contain loopholes that free organized interests from close scrutiny. Interest organizations must report their lobbying expenditures, but they can determine what portion of those expenditures should be reported; corporations are prohibited from contributing to political campaigns, but officers of corporations are not. Policies directly regulating interest activities still provide ample opportunity for groups to exercise political influence.

Acts of Congress, administrative edicts, and judicial decisions determine the influence of pressure groups in a less obvious way too. Policies specify which officials are responsible for decisions that apply to particular interests. Laws authorizing special programs serve as a road map — informing groups about access routes and, more important, about residence of key officials — and thus make it easier to concentrate pressure rather than disperse it. In bidding for federal contracts, a potential contractor may be asked to submit a design of the missile guidance system he proposes to develop. More than a dozen agencies, departments, and administrative bureaus make recommendations on this subject, each with a specialized function and numerous personnel dealing with the details of the proposal. A potential contractor must be selective; he cannot get to each responsible official. Other firms are seeking such contracts, so he goes for support to the officials authorized to recommend his project. He has to know just who makes the decisions and learns it by studying authorizing legislation and by experience in negotiating the administrative labyrinth in Washington.

## organized interests and democratic representation

Judged by the tenets of procedural democracy — the procedures designed to implement popular control, political leadership, political equality, and political liberty — we must conclude that *interest group politics decidedly contributes to democratic government, but the representing of social conflict by way of organized interests has its defects.* Interest groups advance popular control and political leadership in several ways: they organize and express political opinions on public issues; they stimulate their members to active participation by urging them to vote, to take stands on issues, and to support group leaders; they provide a means for collective political action supplementing individual political efforts; and they inform policymakers about demands made by people who might otherwise be ignored. Interest groups that have organized have publicized, and presented to governing officials for reconciliation the demands of many hitherto unrepresented "have-nots" in our society: the blacks, migrant laborers, tenants, low-income consumers, ghetto dwellers, and others. These contributions help democratic government in its task, "not to express an imaginary popular will, but to *effect adjustments among the various special wills and purposes which at any given time are pressing for realization.*"[22]

But even as they advance social interests, some of the characteristics of interest group politics raise a reasonable doubt about whether they conform to the ideals of political equality and liberty. *Not everyone fares*

[22] John Dickenson, "Democratic Realities and Democratic Dogma," *The American Political Science Review* 29 (March 1930): 291–293.

*equally well in the give-and-take of interest group politics.* Though the have-nots are more effectively organized and policymakers are more responsive to their demands than in the recent past, most of the politically organized are the better educated people from the upper and middle classes. The most influential interests are the ones that can afford expensive techniques (contributions to election campaigns, mass advertising, lobbying) for publicizing and presenting their views. The advantage in interest group conflicts still lies with the more affluent.

A second problem in interest group politics conflicts with democratic theory: *in their internal organization, interest groups do not always promote the freedom of members to take part in organizing demands.* Many are oligarchic, run by an active, elitist minority, and do not always represent their rank-and-file members' interests. They are controlled by active minorities for strong reasons — the indifference of their members, the tactical advantages of having disciplined workers, and the flexibility offered by centralized decisionmaking. But group leaders can lose touch with the rank-and-file and act on their own behalf, either instead of or in spite of their members' interests, and then the organization is not giving democratic representation.

The politics of organized interests is the essence of government by a pluralist elite: group leaders represent diverse interests vying to influence policymaking. Its deficiencies reveal a large defect in the American pluralist way of representing social conflict — representation is very selective, even distorted. Only a few social disputes and problems get enough public attention to be resolved by policymakers.

Perhaps a method of representation that fixes only the most pressing problems is not all bad because it keeps manageable the policymakers' task of reconciling differences. But it also fails to reflect the plurality of American interests and is, instead, biased, favoring some and penalizing others. A painful question comes out: Does the selectivity in conflict representation so distort reality that policymakers ignore major social problems — environmental pollution, hunger, overpopulation, mass disaffection from government — until they have reached a critical, perhaps unresolvable, stage? That question demands that we examine the implications for presenting conflict inherent in our pluralist society and the effects of social and governmental pluralism on our way of resolving social disputes by formulating policy.

*bibliographical note*

There are several excellent descriptions of the role of interest groups in the representation of social demands. The standard source on the subject is David B. Truman, *The Governmental Process* (New York: Alfred A. Knopf, 1958). For a discussion of interest activity generally, see Arthur F. Bentley, *The Process of Government* (Chicago: University of Chicago Press, 1908). See also John Dewey, *The Public and Its Problems* (Denver: Alan Swallow, 1927); J. D. B. Miller, *The Nature of Politics* (London: Gerald Duckworth, 1962); Harmon Zeigler, *Interest Groups in American Society*, 2nd ed. (Englewood Cliffs, N.J.: Prentice-Hall, 1972); and Mancur Olson, *The Logic of Collective Action* (Cambridge, Mass.: Harvard University Press, 1965).

In recent years, there has been considerable controversy among political scientists regarding the desirability of pluralist politics and, more specifically, whether interest groups are functional or dysfunctional to a democracy. The nature of this controversy can be sampled in Robert A. Dahl, *A Preface to Democratic Theory* (Chicago: University of Chicago Press, Pheonix Edition, 1963); E. E. Schattschneider, *The Semisovereign People* (New York: Holt, Rinehart and Winston, 1960); Henry S. Kariel, *The Decline of American Pluralism* (Stanford, Calif.: Stanford University Press, 1961); Murray Edelman, *Politics as Symbolic Action* (Chicago: Markham, 1971); Theodore J. Lowi, *The Politics of Disorder* (New York: Basic Books, 1971); and, the same author's earlier work, *The End of Liberalism* (New York: W. W. Norton, 1969).

Among the studies that provide a useful assessment of how influential organized interests are in publicizing and presenting their demands, the following should be examined: Abraham Holtzman, *Interest Groups and Lobbying* (New York: Macmillan, 1966); Raymond A. Bauer et al., *American Business and Public Policy* (New York: Atherton, 1963); Lester W. Milbrath, *The Washington Lobbyists* (Chicago: Rand McNally, 1963); and R. Joseph Monsen, Jr., and Mark W. Cannon, *The Makers of Public Policy* (New York: McGraw-Hill, 1965). Among the works that focus on the areas of public policy of concern to organized interests in the 1970s, see Reo M. Christenson, *Challenge and Decision* (New York: Harper & Row, 1970).

The movement for civil rights among blacks, students, women, and others in the last decade resulted in several works attempting to capture and explain the nature of minority grievances and tactics. Among these the student will find the following particularly instructive: Nathan Wright, Jr., *Ready to Riot* (New York: Holt, Rinehart and Winston, 1968); Norval D. Glenn and Charles M. Bonjean, eds., *Blacks in the United States* (San Francisco: Chandler, 1969); Ted Robert Gurr, *Why Men Rebel* (Princeton, N.J.: Princeton University Press, 1970); Martin Oppenheimer, *The Urban Guerrilla* (Chicago: Quadrangle Books, 1969); Richard E. Rubenstein, *Rebels in Eden: Mass Political Violence in the United States* (Boston: Little, Brown, 1970); Richard P. Young, ed., *Roots of Rebellion: The Evolution of Black Politics and Protest Since World War II* (New York: Harper & Row, 1970); and Theodore Lowi's aforementioned *The Politics of Disorder*.

Scholarly and popularly written articles on the theory, functions, and tactics of organized interests appear in a variety of anthologies. Among the best is Robert H. Salisbury, ed., *Interest Group Politics in America* (New York: Harper & Row, 1970). See also H. R. Mahood, ed., *Pressure Groups in American Politics* (New York: Charles Scribner's Sons, 1967) and Berry H. Zisk, ed., *American Political Interest Groups* (Belmont, Calif.: Wadsworth, 1969).

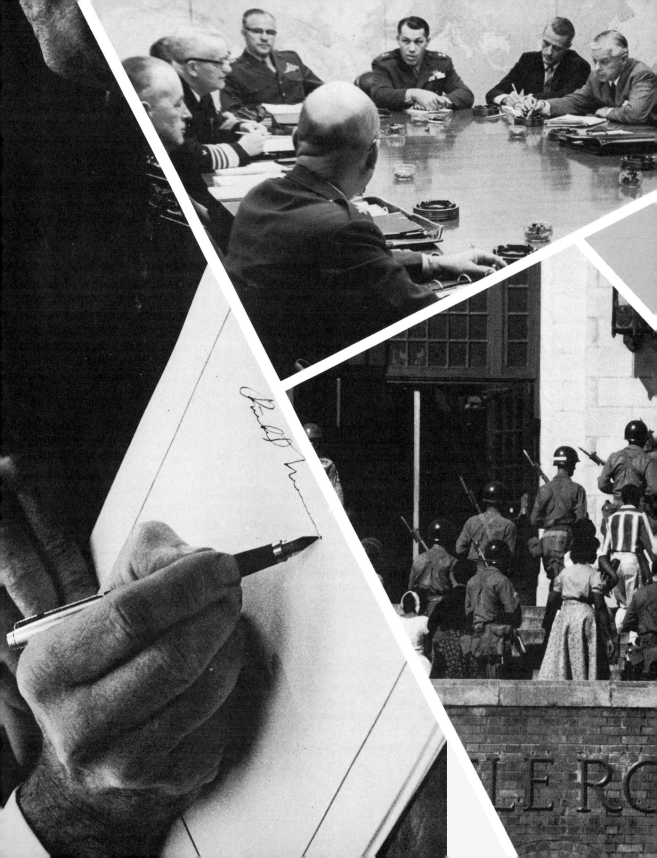

# IV

# patterns of conflict resolution: who makes public policies and how?

In Parts One and Two we defined politics and described the doctrinal and constitutional background against which American politics takes place. Politics, we said, is the most inclusive way in which social conflict is regulated, consisting of both conflict representation and conflict resolution. In Part Three we considered the principal ways in which Americans take part in representing social disputes to governing officials. It is now time to turn to the actions those officials take in making public policies that adjust differing interests, which we have designated as conflict resolution. In the chapters of Part Four we will examine how public policies are made in America: in Chapter Eleven we will introduce the overall method of conflict resolution, examine how policies are formulated, and study particularly

343

what makes conflict regulation pluralist; in Chapter Twelve we will see how presidential leadership contributes to policymaking; in Chapter Thirteen we will describe how Congress adopts public policies; how the administrative bureaucracy applies general policies to individual cases is our topic in Chapter Fourteen; and in Chapter Fifteen we discuss the function of the judiciary, especially the Supreme Court, in interpreting the appropriateness, legitimacy, and adequacy of public policies in resolving interest disputes. The personal, social, and political and constitutional features of our pluralist community that influence political participation as we remarked upon in Part Three are equally important in shaping the key patterns of policymaking in America; therefore, throughout the chapters in Part Four, we will consider that influence and how it limits policymaking to a few of the many social disputes and resolves even fewer.

# chapter 11

# formulating policies

Public policy properly arrived at may not directly end disputes or solve problems, but it does keep social tensions from destroying the community. Studying how policy is formulated, the method is important, the content less so. We will look into characteristics of public policies, how they come to be formulated, and the merits and defects of pluralist conflict resolution.

## public policies: key characteristics

What is public policy? What is policy formulation, and who does the formulating? What types of policies are formulated? When these questions are answered, we can turn to the problem of what features of our society and political institutions influence policy formulation.

## what is public policy?

*Public policies are legitimate decisions made by political institutions that resolve disputes affecting the general community.* Decisions that are called "public policies" are *public, legitimate,* and made by *political institutions.* What is implied in these notions?

People faced with problems find ways of coping with them. So long as their acts affect only one another — the parties immediately involved — the problem and acts are private. A quarrel between a husband and wife and their negotiating to resolve the dispute are clearly private matters. If the steps they take affect others and these others think the ramifications are important, then the problem and consequent actions are public. If the husband and wife decide to dissolve their partnership, their divorce becomes a public matter. *Problems and actions affecting people beyond the immediate parties to a dispute are public.*

*Public policies are legitimate when the people affected accept the decisions as binding.* That acceptance may be brought about by government, which can get obedience by threatening to use force or punishment, or by promising tangible or psychic rewards. Legitimacy requires that people accept public decisions as binding on their own behavior as well as that of others affected by them. Refusal to obey proclaims, among other things, a desire to test a law's legitimacy, as in civil disobedience.

Binding public policies are made by our political institutions, but policymaking is not limited to people acting in official capacities. *Public policies generally result from coalitions of diverse interests* that have something to gain by associating instead of acting alone. Such an alliance usually consists of official interests, private interests, or both, working to achieve legislative majorities, favorable administrative treatment, or judicial support for their proposed courses of action, proposals that develop out of policy formulation.

## what is policy formulation and who are the formulators?

To solve public problems, some planning and resources are necessary. *Policy formulation consists of developing relevant and acceptable courses of action to resolve social disputes.*

Policymakers do not know all the problems. They may know about a problem but may not think it pressing enough to require action. Not until the late 1950s did many governing officials recognize how automobile exhausts contribute to air pollution, and only in 1965 did Congress think the problem important enough to call for corrective action, the Motor Vehicle Air Pollution Control Act. *A relevant course of action is not always the passage* of a law or the issuance of an administrative edict or court decision. Policymakers frequently react to public problems, even though they are aware of them and their importance, by leaving them untreated or by taking actions designed to mollify disputing interests without resolving the conflict. During his first two and one-half years in office President Richard Nixon was well aware of the acute difficulties in the American economy, such as inflation and unemployment, but made no major policy decisions until August 1971, when he froze wages, prices, and rents. *Relevant action is that action deemed relevant by key policymakers,* and their decisions may or may not respond to the underlying sources of public problems.

Policymakers can devise courses of action that cope with public problems if they work out *acceptable* policies whose terms the formulators find agreeable. The next question is: Who takes part in policy formulation? In a democracy, policy is supposed to be formulated by officials freely chosen and authorized to act for the community. In practice, however, *policy formulation involves both public officials and the leaders of private groups,* sometimes acting separately but more often in concert and conflict with one another.

The most widely publicized public officials who formulate policy are the *President and his chief advisers* who, at least in this century, have become primary initiators of action on public problems.

Second are the *appointed and career public officials in the administrative bureaucracy.* In carrying out programs, they help to formulate policies by keeping abreast of problems within their responsibility (such as health, education, welfare, labor-management relations, and quality of the environment), develop proposals to cope with them, and submit these to presidential and congressional scrutiny.

*Legislators* also formulate policy. In congressional hearings and by informal contact with organized interests and administrative officials, legislators identify problems, solicit suggested proposals, and formulate courses of action.

The courts too take part. Often *judicial officers* are the first officials to deal directly with pressing problems, particularly in lower courts where cases originate. Federal district court judges have helped resolve disputes on racial integration, apportionment of legislative bodies, opportunities for citizens to vote, and the rights of people who objected to taking part in the Vietnam War.

*Leaders of private interest organizations also formulate policy,* sometimes acting on the government's behalf. In "Phase Two" of President Nixon's program to combat inflation and unemployment in 1971 and 1972, he appointed two boards, composed of representatives of labor, business, and consumer interests, to administer guidelines for authorizing wage and price increases affecting any major sector of the economy.

*Generally, however, group leaders present to government proposals that their organizations have formulated — as alternatives* to the courses of action requested by executive, administrative, legislative, or judicial formulators. As a result, competing proposals come from separate formulators, like major proposals for establishing a national health insurance program in the 1970s. Senator Edward Kennedy, with Representative Martha Griffiths, formulated and presented to Congress a proposal for a

The Kennedy cabinet meets during the Cuban missile crisis in October 1962. In time of international crisis, the President and his chief advisers must respond quickly.

comprehensive national health insurance system for all Americans, to be financed partly by increased taxes and funds from federal general revenues. The Nixon administration submitted the National Health Insurance Partnership Act, proposing that employers make approved health-care plans available to their employees, that government-sponsored health insurance be available to low-income families with children not covered by employment-related insurance, and that health maintenance organizations be established to improve health services. The American Medical Association offered the Health Care Insurance Act (Medicredit), providing income tax credits for the purchase of private health insurance and a federally subsidized health insurance or group insurance plan for low-income persons. Finally, the Health Insurance Association of America, an interest organization of insurance companies, proposed a National Healthcare Act providing for an insurance system in which employers and employees would contribute to insurance costs, with government subsidies for state-sponsored programs for the poor. Policymakers thus had four major proposals to choose from, or to compromise on, each of them supported by different private or official formulators jockeying for advantage in the national health insurance controversy. *This mixture of public officials and private interests in formulating policies is typical of policymaking in America.*

## types of policies

Three varieties of policies can be distinguished by their general effects: *distributive, regulatory,* and *redistributive* policies.[1]

*Distributive* policies take natural, social, and economic resources and award them to specific interests. In the nineteenth century, the federal government provided tracts of land to farmers, ranchers, railroaders, speculators, and others settling the frontier.

*Regulatory* policies are designed to ensure that specific activities — such as operating an air line, a bank, a public school, or even a person's automobile — are in the public interest, not for selfish advantage. It is characteristic of regulatory policies, however, that public officials and representatives of organized interests cooperate in their formulation, and the latter sacrifice little of their prerogative to decide how best to utilize their resources to their own advantage.

*Redistributive* policies reallocate resources, taking from the "haves" and benefiting the "have-nots": taxation policies designed to provide financing for welfare, antipoverty, educational, public health, and similar programs.

DISTRIBUTING ECONOMIC BENEFITS: FIGHT FOR THE SST. In 1959, aviation authorities in the federal government proposed that the United States subsidize the development of a supersonic transport (SST), a high-speed (1,800 miles per hour), long-range aircraft capable of carrying large freight or passenger cargos. In 1961, President John Kennedy, sensitive to demands of the aircraft industry for an American SST to compete with the Concorde then being built by joint British and French interests, sup-

---

[1] These are categories employed by Theodore J. Lowi, "American Business, Public Policy, Case-Studies, and Political Theory," *World Politics* 18 (July 1966): 677–715.

ported the proposal and requested congressional funds. Under the administration's plan, the federal government would contribute 75 percent of the costs of development, and private interests the remainder. It was argued that the economic benefits from development of the SST (in the form of government contracts to firms employing workers in more than fifty communities located in twenty states) would more than recompense the federal share of the estimated $1 billion cost. Congress agreed, and prior to 1965 distributed economic benefits by appropriating $91 million for the project.

In the second half of the 1960s, the project ran into trouble when environmental groups suggested that the earth's atmosphere might be altered by SST flights and noise pollution from its sonic booms. Their opposition found a sympathetic congressional ear, and in 1970 the Nixon administration was unable to secure full funding for the project. Administration forces vowed to save the SST, and the way was prepared for an intense conflict over a major distributive policy.

By 1971, the interests opposed to the SST were led by the Coalition Against the SST, an alliance of fifteen national and fourteen state and local political, conservation, and environmental organizations. The national groups included the Citizens League Against the Sonic Boom, Environmental Action, Federation of American Scientists, National Taxpayers Union, Sierra Club, Wilderness Society, Zero Population Growth, Friends of the Earth (which raised $20,000 to fight the SST), and Common Cause; state and local organizations included the Committee for Green Foothills (California), Ecology Action for Rhode Island, and the Texas Committee on Natural Resources. The anti-SST arguments were environmental and economic. The environmental effects were uncertain, but John Gardner, chairman of Common Cause, summed up the argument: "There remains much to be proven about possible atmospheric dangers," but "there is one environmental consequence that is virtually certain, and that is noise pollution." The coalition stressed that the SST in flight would create a continuous shock wave fifty miles wide.

Along with such officials as Senator William Proxmire of Wisconsin, the Coalition opposed the SST on economic grounds as well, arguing that the project would cost more than $1.3 billion, and no matter what the alleged economic benefits, the investment could bring no adequate return. Arthur Oken, chairman of the Council of Economic Advisers during the Johnson administration, testified, "The very fact that proponents of the SST have turned to the federal government for funds is evidence itself that the SST does not pass the market test."

Proponents of the SST included the Nixon administration, many Representatives and Senators from districts with aircraft industries, and the National Committee for the SST (with its adjunct, Industry and Labor for the SST). The Committee set up a fund of $350,000 to convince the public and Congress that the SST would create aerospace jobs and sales and that the predicted environmental problems had been either solved or "grossly exaggerated." On the committee were major labor leaders like George Meany, AFL–CIO president; I. W. Abel, president of the United Steelworkers; J. J. O'Donnell, president of the Air Lines Pilots Association; and business leaders such as the president of Fairchild Hiller Corporation, which had received $34 million in contracts connected with the project. The committee argued in newspaper ads, organized letter-writing campaigns, and business and labor publications that the death of the SST would eliminate 50,000 jobs, add unemployed to the welfare rolls, reduce the nation's tax resources, and adversely affect the balance of trade.

But the effort to save the SST failed. The Senate voted fifty-one to forty-six to discontinue federal funding (after a lengthy filibuster by anti-SST Senators), and the House too voted it down.

When first conceived, the SST project was a classic example of government's allocation of economic resources to enhance the interests of specific groups — aerospace companies, workers, and others. The project had the support of three Presidents — Kennedy, Johnson, and Nixon — as well as Congress and major organized interests. But it shows too how by organized publicity opposition interests can rescind what they believe to be costly and potentially dangerous distributive policies. As an example of policy formulation, the SST case carries an important lesson: *policy-making is ceaseless, and the policies formulated and adopted at one time can be undone by interests formulating and pressing contrary courses of action.*

REGULATING A SOCIAL PROBLEM: CONTROLLING FIREARMS. The federal regulation of interstate traffic in firearms began to arouse interest after a study in 1961 by the Senate Judiciary Subcommittee on Juvenile Delinquency, headed by Democratic Senator Thomas J. Dodd of Connecticut. It was found that neither federal nor state laws effectively restrained mail order sale of firearms to juveniles, felons, and narcotics addicts. The assassination of President Kennedy in 1963 stimulated intense interest in gun control legislation. Dodd had introduced a bill to restrict the mail order sales of handguns and to prohibit interstate sales to persons under eighteen. Because the assassination was carried out with a mail order, military surplus rifle, Dodd proposed an Amendment to his bill to cover rifles and shotguns as well as handguns. Advocates of stricter controls consisted of an unorganized group of Congressmen such as Dodd, Democratic Senator Joseph Tydings of Maryland, Senator Edward Kennedy of Massachusetts, and Senator Robert Kennedy of New York. In 1965, President Lyndon Johnson also proposed strict gun control legislation to prohibit the interstate mail order sale of all firearms to private individuals and the over-the-counter sale of handguns to persons not living in the dealer's state. He also called for limitations on the importation of firearms to the United States, and asked for a minimum age for purchasers of guns.

The opposition to strict regulation, led by the National Rifle Association representing 900,000 members, was well organized. The NRA's principal tactic was to encourage its members to write to Congressmen protesting against regulation as an infringement on the "right to bear arms." The NRA was assisted by its close ties with military officials. The Department of the Army supported its national rifle matches and even provided ammunition; moreover, since 1903 members had been able to purchase surplus firearms and ammunition from the army at a discount, because such privileges were supposed to improve marksmanship in the armed forces by civilian training.

Opponents of the NRA's lobbying activities, however, claimed that only 3 percent of the army's trainees were members of the NRA and that the average age of NRA members was thirty-nine, beyond the draft age. The NRA's position drew support in Congress from Senator Strom Thurmond, Republican of South Carolina, Senator Frank Church, Democrat of Idaho, and Senator Bourke Hickenlooper, Republican of Iowa. The Wildlife Management Institute and the Isaac Walton League also opposed strong federal regulation. Such organizations are supported financially by excise taxes on the manufacture of sporting arms and ammunition to aid state fish and game agencies. Gun manufacturers themselves, of course, also opposed regulation of firearms, particularly through such trade associations as the Sporting Arms and Ammunition Manufacturers' Institute (SAAMI), which consists of the nine largest gun and ammunition manufacturers.

Between 1963 and 1967, efforts to pass federal legislation placing strict controls on the sales of firearms were unsuccessful. During that time, however, events continually brought to public attention what gun control advocates called the consequences of unregulated sales. Among these they cited the summer riots in major cities in which some law enforcement officers claimed mail order guns had been confiscated. Investigations revealing that from one hundred to two hundred Americans die every week from gunshot wounds reinforced the case of the gun control advocates. In early 1968, a nationwide survey revealed that more than eight out of every ten Americans favored some type of federal regulation.

The impetus for strict regulation intensified in 1968. Dr. Martin Luther King, Jr., was assassinated in April. An amendment was added to the Omnibus Crime Control and Safe Streets Act of 1968 prohibiting the interstate shipment to individuals of pistols and revolvers and the over-the-counter purchase of handguns by individuals not residing in the dealer's state. The bill, however, specifically exempted rifles and shotguns from regulation. During the formulation of this measure, the combined efforts of the NRA and independent gun owners produced a massive amount of mail opposing strict regulation. Senator Charles Percy, Republican of Illinois, received 3,500 letters, most of them against gun controls; Senator James Eastland, Democrat of Mississippi, reported his mail ran five to one against controls.

Then, almost three months to the day following the King assassination, Senator Robert Kennedy was slain with a .22 caliber pistol that cost $30.95. After that assassination, advocates of strict gun control organized their own campaign in response to that of the "gun lobby." The Council for a Responsible Firearms Policy sought ten million signatures on a petition favoring registration of all firearms; former astronaut John Glenn announced that he was forming a nationwide group to stimulate a letter-writing campaign aimed at swaying Congress, and President Johnson proposed banning the mail order and out-of-state sale of rifles, shotguns, and ammunition, and requiring registration of all firearms and licensing of all gun owners.

We cannot know how much public officials and group leaders were influenced by the Kennedy assassination and the campaign for strict gun controls that followed, but some actions were clearly related: (1) On the day of Kennedy's death, Congress passed the Omnibus Crime Control Act with its gun control provisions. (2) After the assassination, Congressmen began to report a new trend in their mail and on June 10, Senator Percy's office received 1,300 letters favoring stronger regulations. Representative G. Elliot Hagan of Georgia reported that, whereas his mail had been "overwhelmingly against" gun controls before the assassination, it now ran "50-50." (3) A number of Congressmen shifted their positions on gun control. Senator George McGovern, Democrat of South Dakota, worked against strict legislation in May, but said in June he would support restrictive legislation; Senate Majority Leader Mike Mansfield of Montana had been cool toward regulation but declared in June that he would support proposals for strict regulation. (4) Other governing officials moved to restrict the shipment and use of firearms. The Postmaster General announced new regulations requiring all firearms sent through the mail to be clearly identified, and he instructed local postmasters to notify police before delivering guns. (5) The Department of the Army, acting on a recommendation by the National Board for the Promotion of Rifle Practice (a group composed of both military and civilian officials), announced that it would limit its support to rifle clubs whose members still had their service obligations ahead of them, would limit the sale of rifles to clubs specifically designed for rifle competition, would sell only to clubs affiliated with the army's program, and would hold to its earlier decision not to supply men or ammunition for the 1968 national rifle matches. (6) The heads of such firearms manufacturing firms as Remington, Savage, and Winchester-Western urged Congress to prohibit the sale of shotguns and rifles by mail to individuals. (7) Finally, on October 10, 1968, Congress extended the restrictions placed on handguns by the Omnibus Crime Control Act to long guns and ammunition. Specifically, it banned mail order sales and interstate shipments, set licensing standards for parts of the firearms and ammunition business, and established minimum ages for the purchase of firearms and ammunition.

This policy conflict illustrates many typical features in policy formulation, especially the way in which regulatory policies are formulated. Gun control legislation was like *many policy disputes that cut across party lines,* placing Republicans and Democrats on both sides of the controversy; party lines did not vanish, of course, for there was still party division over the recommendations of a Democratic President. Second, *the conflict pitted informal coalitions of major interest groups against each other. Alliances of political leaders may shift when opposed by counterpressure;* the Department of the Army, firearms manufacturers, and many Congressmen sympathetic to the NRA changed their ideas when popular interest in the gun control issue spread — popular interest not always typical of legislative disputes. Like many regulatory policies, the 1968 legislation contained *loopholes to protect the prerogatives of organized interests.* On the surface, it made small caliber handguns unavailable by banning their importation from abroad, but manufacturers and dealers were able to get around the law by importing gun parts and attaching them to frames made in the United States. Moreover, the act did not require that firearms be registered or the owners licensed. Finally, the legislation *temporized the dispute, but neither laid it to rest nor solved the problem.*

In 1971, Senator Birch Bayh proposed a ban on the transfer or sale by any federally licensed dealer of any firearm other than rifles or shotguns to anyone except law enforcement officers; the "Saturday night special" (a handgun costing about $10–$20), he said, accounted for most of the country's murders, and twenty-two people die in America each day from wounds inflicted with such weapons. The attempted assassination of Governor George Wallace of Alabama while campaigning in Maryland in the 1972 presidential primaries stimulated interest in firearms control. Again a coalition of interests, headed by the NRA, opposed legislation and once more the controversy over regulation of firearms was resumed. A bill passed by the Senate forbade the sale of "Saturday night specials," but the House failed to act on the measure.

Chairman of the Federal Price
Commission, C. Jackson Grayson,
checks meat prices
at a Los Angeles supermarket.
Administrative agencies often have
far-ranging regulatory and
judicial powers.

REDISTRIBUTING RESOURCES: THE WAR ON POVERTY. In 1964, President Lyndon Johnson declared a "national war on poverty," an innovative proposal designed to accomplish something unusual in American life — redistributing basic resources to solve a chronic social problem. Poverty had been a plague for many generations, but only modest policies to alleviate it had been tried, most of them for the aged, the handicapped, the orphaned, and similar groups. But, it became apparent that poverty was not limited to the aged or otherwise dependent population; there was widespread poverty among residents of urban ghettos, rural areas such as Appalachia, and numerous ethnic minorities including blacks in the North and South, Mexican-Americans in the Southwest, and the American Indians. Born into poverty, children of impoverished parents lacked the resources to leave their environment, get an education, and acquire the skills that could "break the poverty cycle"; instead the children of poverty grew up to beget more poverty-stricken children.

Because poverty was becoming more severe and awareness of it was growing, Presidents Kennedy and Johnson gave executive agencies responsibility for formulating a policy to deal with chronic poverty. Among these were the President's Council of Economic Advisers, the Bureau of the Budget, the White House Staff, the Peace Corps, the Small Business Administration, and the agency that later became the Department of Housing and Urban Development. Private citizens complemented their efforts through the Ford Foundation and the President's Committee on Juvenile Delinquency and Youth Crimes.

Officials and citizens in these agencies and groups formulated this policy: (1) a Job Corps with centers located in rural and urban areas would provide young men and women aged sixteen through twenty-one with education, vocational training, and work experience; (2) federal assistance for state and local programs would provide local work experience; (3) grants to institutions of higher education would enable students from low-income families to obtain part-time work to support their schooling — the work-study program; (4) federal grants to community action programs conducted by state or local public and private nonprofit agencies — with the maximum participation of local residents — would develop job opportunities and improve working, learning, and living conditions; (5) federal grants would support adult education programs; (6) financial assistance would be given needy children; (7) money would be provided for loans to low-income rural families, assistance to migrant workers, business incentives for small business in poverty areas, and various work experience programs. The Office of Economic Opportunity was created to recruit, select, and train volunteers in cooperation with state and local agencies to assist such groups as Indians, migratory workers, the mentally ill and retarded, and the poor of the District of Columbia and of United States territories.

The Economic Opportunity Act, most of it formulated by executive leaders, was sent to Congress although prior consultation with members of that body was minimal. The Senate acted quickly on the bill, but the Democrats narrowly defeated a "states' rights" amendment that would have required state governors to approve all federal-local community action projects. The Chairman of the House Committee on Education and Labor moved the bill quickly through committee despite Republican protests; it then passed the House quickly (with a southern conservative as its chief sponsor). President Johnson had declared the war on poverty in March of 1964; by August, the Congress had adopted the necessary legislation, a remarkably quick response to executive proposals.

The Economic Opportunity Act of 1964 suggests how redistributive policies may be successfully formulated and passed. Relevant and acceptable courses of action clearly were facilitated by consensus among the formulators (primarily executive officials) that the problem was real

and that sweeping, innovative action had to be taken to allocate resources and deal with it. The policy was formulated, of course, without
the interests most affected by it: the poor. Perhaps things would not have
gone so smoothly if the affected interests had been consulted; the rivalry
that developed between blacks and Puerto Ricans for control of such
local action programs as in New York City strongly suggests that some
intense conflicts would have come about.

But broad redistributive legislation was proposed and adopted, a new
agency was created, and large sums were appropriated. Carrying out the
program then became the job of officials and group leaders at all levels
of government, who had not been privy to the formulation. Conflicts soon
sundered these interests, especially in community action programs. Interest rivalries produced criticism of the program that quickly reached Congressmen from their constituents. Congressional enthusiasm began to
wane, and appropriations declined.

But the blow that crippled the antipoverty program was the channeling
of funds to support the Vietnam War. President Dwight Eisenhower had
said a decade before the war on poverty was dreamed of: "Every gun that
is made, every warship launched, every rocket fired signifies, in the final
sense, a theft from those who hunger and are not fed, from those who
are cold and are not clothed." So the struggle to break the poverty cycle —
an innovative effort to allocate resources and solve a chronic social problem — lost most of its redistributive strength.

## pluralism and policy formulation

In each of these three cases of policymaking many interests had a hand;
the fact that many diverse interests take part in formulating policies reflects our *pluralist social and political context.*

### the pluralist society

Those who advocate high tariff rates on imported raw materials, industrial goods, and agricultural products are in a difficult position. They may
try to broaden their appeal by urging that all major economic interests
in America can benefit from high tariff policies. But high tariffs do not
benefit all economic interests. A large building contractor wants low-
priced steel, whether purchased domestically or from European or Asian
producers. This contractor would oppose a high tariff on imported steel,
however pleasing that tariff would be to an American steel producer.

Conflicting group interests in a pluralist society thus compel any group to choose between narrowing its appeal by holding fast to an uncompromised position, and broadening its appeal by moderating its demands to attract allies. Relationships between a group and its environment are similar. A trade association for an industry made up of many "Mom and Pop" retail stores and a few large chain stores may find that it either has to straddle many industry issues on which its members are divided or elect to narrow its membership to one or the other.

In a pluralist society, groups also compete for the attention of officials. A politician has a choice of the groups to which he listens, or he may listen to more than one side. A Congressman considering a proposal to eliminate discrimination in the sale and rental of houses and apartments can draw his information from opponents and proponents of such legislation, including realtors, civil rights groups, mayors of large cities, and congressional colleagues. The many groups seeking his vote give him a chance to take a more independent stance toward each, legitimizing whatever position he does take, because some groups push for that view.

Because claims made by interests are channeled through group leaders, contacts between them and public officials are vital. In a pluralist society, influence is spread widely among leaders both inside and outside of the formal government. In formulating policy, citizens acting as members of organized interests control their leaders and are controlled by them; in turn, their leaders influence other group leaders and public officials are influenced by them. These reciprocal relationships among citizens and private and public leaders arrange that *popular control over policymaking will at best be exerted indirectly,*[2] as in our cases showing how distributive, regulatory, and redistributive policies are formulated.

### the pluralist government: federalism

Over the years, governments at the various levels of our federal system have grown stronger and the national government has gained power much faster than the states. Responding to demands that it regulate business, alleviate social and economic ills, improve education at all levels, and preserve and restore the environment, the federal government has expanded its influence.

This tendency toward centralized power still leaves protection for state autonomy in both the party system (see Chapter Nine) and the Constitution (see Chapter Four). The states have been beneficiaries, as well

[2] Robert A. Dahl and Charles E. Lindblom, *Politics, Economics and Welfare* (New York: Harper & Row, Torchback Edition, 1963).

as victims, of the federal government's growing dominance; programs of *cooperative federalism* enable the states to prosper too. The network of interstate highways on which we now drive grew from this cooperation. Congress authorized the federal government to pay 90 percent of the cost of the interstate system, yet the states retained authority over construction. Compliance by all states made it possible for the federal government to initiate construction of this highway network that benefits interstate commerce and national defense. In return, the states profited by the program's distributiveness from the money poured into local economies and from increased tourist travel. Moreover, the automotive industry, tire manufacturers, petroleum companies, trucking firms, motels and restaurants, and others gained indirectly.

Although the federal arrangement has changed since 1789 because the national government is more powerful and federal-state programs have been developed, federalism still influences policy formulation. *The federal arrangement and the separation of powers facilitate corporate conflicts — conflicts between governing officials at different levels* (national, state, local) *or in different political institutions* (executive, legislative, judicial), who seek to advance or safeguard their interests and authority at the expense of others. By *corporate conflict* we mean disputes between officials as distinguished from disputes among private interests. State officials see their authority threatened by federal expenditures for schools, highways, and other facilities within the state; often they demand control over federal money spent in their states (money which federal officials collected as taxes from their states' residents).

By providing separate national and state governing authorities, *federalism gives interests many chances to try to influence policymaking.* Failing to gain satisfaction at the local level, an interest can take its demands to Washington; or, if it is dissatisfied with federal policies, it can attempt to block them by appealing to state and local officials. Organized interests frequently advance their demands by promoting corporate conflicts over who has the authority to make a decision affecting them. The interests that opposed strict gun controls argued that only the states had the authority to set regulations. They took this position because of their strong influence with state officials and because the states have no authority to prohibit the interstate sale of firearms. Arguing that the prohibited federal regulation — "the right of the people to keep and bear arms, shall not be infringed" — the gun lobby really hoped to avoid any regulation at all. Advocates of gun control aimed at the national government, arguing that the right to bear arms was intended only to assure "a well regulated Militia," which surely involved the federal government. But federal officials were not completely successful in overcoming objections by state agencies to gun control legislation.

## the pluralist government: separation of powers

Although American government is much changed since 1789, the separation of powers, and its corollary principle, checks and balances, still strongly influence policy formulation. Figure 11-1 shows how constitutional authority is distributed among legislative, executive, and judicial branches. Each branch now has several divisions, such as the General Accounting Office under congressional authority, the various offices, departments, and agencies linked to the executive, and the several levels of the judicial system.

The mere presence of separate institutions that restrain and balance one another in the exercise of authority makes conflicts inevitable in relations between the institutions, their divisions, and the political subunits — such as bureaus and committees — attached to each. To settle these conflicts, political subunits forge coalitions that perform crucial functions in formulating policy.

CORPORATE CONFLICT. Built into our provision for three branches of government and the division of government functions among them, corporate conflict requires that the President win legislative approval for his appointments, proposed legislation, and financial requests. Yet, for each of the years between 1953 and 1971 (Eisenhower through Nixon), with few exceptions, Congress has accepted less than half of the President's proposed programs. Both the House and the Senate have institutional interests or prerogatives that its members try to protect against encroachment by the President, the courts, or the other legislative body. These may take the form of Senate resentment of undue presidential control of foreign policy and the war and treaty powers (as the Senate was dissatisfied over President Johnson's and President Nixon's conduct of the Vietnam War). Another type is the belief and practice that a Congressman can be disciplined only by his colleagues, and has immunity from many forms of legal action. Controversies between the courts and either the President or the Congress also dot our history. President Roosevelt's attempt to enlarge the Supreme Court in the 1930s and the late Senator Everett Dirksen's attempt in 1965 to override the Supreme Court's decision that both houses of state legislative bodies must be apportioned according to population clearly show corporate conflict between the major branches of government.

SUBUNIT AUTONOMY. Units within each major institution of government (particularly legislative committees and executive agencies and bureaus)

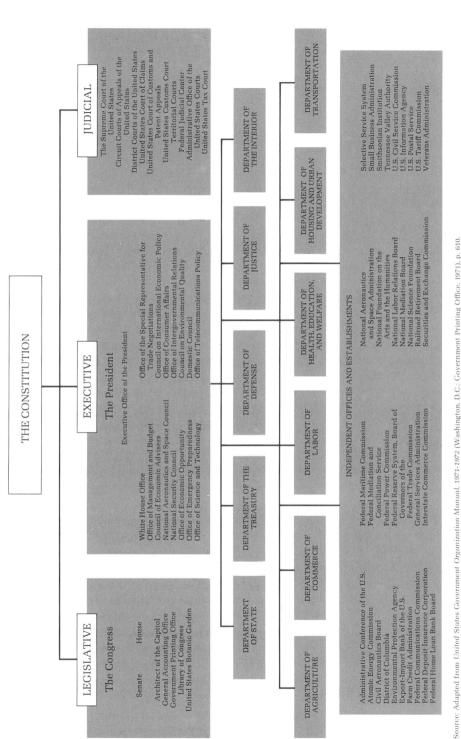

Source: Adapted from *United States Government Organization Manual, 1971-1972* (Washington, D.C.: Government Printing Office, 1971), p. 610.

**FIGURE 11-1**

**Governmental Organization of the United States**

have gathered much autonomy. Policy decisions often reflect clashes between interests represented by these subunits.

Interests diversify in Congress as committees and subcommittees in each chamber get authority of their own and win the deference of the rest of the chamber. Committees gain autonomy because legislators assume that committee members are expert in the committee's specialized areas, from which it follows that the committee's judgment on bills should be given great weight by the rest of the chamber: the Armed Services committees of the House and Senate seldom have had their recommendations for the defense budget overridden by their chambers. Tenure on committees automatically confers status and respect for the competence of members and increases as veteran legislators remain with their committees despite changes in party control. Longevity, specialization, and congressional acquiescence promote the development of semi-autonomous policymaking committees, or subcommittees.

*The chairmen of congressional committees are key leaders in initiating or blocking policy in the legislature.* They often compete with the President and his legislative leaders. In 1969, President Nixon proposed the Family Assistance Plan, which would guarantee annual federal benefits for poor families. Wilbur Mills, Chairman of the House Ways and Means Committee, was only lukewarm in supporting the measure; and it was not until he changed his views that his committee reported a bill similar to the Nixon administration's proposal (it guaranteed an annual income of $2,400 to a family of four). The measure passed the House in 1970. In the Senate, however, Finance Committee Chairman Russell Long, Democrat of Louisiana, opposed a "guaranteed annual income for not working" and argued that the Family Assistance Plan would "undermine the moral fiber of the country." Long's committee delayed action, promising to conduct hearings only after "tough work requirements" were added to the bill.

In theory, the administrative branch simply applies and enforces the laws adopted by negotiations among legislators and other officials. *In practice, administration involves so much discretion that it gives lawmaking authority in fact, and at times in form, to that branch as well.* A regulatory agency charged by Congress with providing "a fair rate of return" for the firms it regulates has plenty of leeway in determining what that criterion means and how to apply it. So, too, does the Office of Economic Opportunity in figuring out how the congressional instruction to provide for "maximum feasible participation of the poor" at local levels can be worked out. Even when a statute is more precise, "gray areas" of interpretation remain, meaning that the administrative unit's handling of them makes the law on the point.

Finally, no sizable administrative unit can hope to enforce with equal energy all of its abundant statutory obligations and rules that have the force or effect of law. In choosing which to enforce and to what extent, and which to slight, the bureaucracy in practice determines what is effective law and what is not, such as the incidence of categories of crime in a community, which depends partly on which categories of crime engage the attention of the police.

*Administrative discretion continuously reshapes policies,* especially when regulatory agencies are empowered to make, apply, and interpret rules. A quasi-judicial regulatory agency such as the Interstate Commerce Commission is a *subgovernment*[3] in that it combines executive, legislative, and judicial tasks. It sets railroad rates, sees that they are enforced, and decides when rules have been violated by railroad companies. The National Labor Relations Board not only applies labor legislation aimed at eliminating unfair labor practices but investigates complaints from labor and management, promotes collective bargaining, and may prescribe rules and regulations advancing the purposes of major labor statutes.

Each regular administrative department, such as the Department of Health, Education and Welfare, is made up of many subunits, which are administrative bureaus with considerable autonomy. Bureau leaders can often keep their superior department heads from direct control by developing their own links to Congress and interest group supporters. By developing political "clout" in their own right, combining it with their technical knowledge and protected civil service status, they insulate themselves from presidential or departmental control. *Bureaucratic leaders thus can be significant formulators of policy.*

COALITIONS OF POLICY FORMULATORS. Separation of powers, which contributes to corporate conflicts and subunit autonomy, also promotes the formation of coalitions by those who formulate policy. Such coalitions contain both public officials (from relevant executive bureaus and congressional committees) and leaders of powerful organized interests. These coalitions operate as subgovernments, each developing an exclusive and autonomous sphere of policy on matters important to the members of the coalition.

Among examples are the military-industrial complex of congressional leaders, military and bureaucratic officials in the Department of Defense, and major defense contractors; the National Rifle Association's alliance with state officials, members of Congress, and officials in the Department of the Army; the alliance of the House Committee on Government Information with public information officers in administrative agencies and

---

[3] J. Leiper Freeman, *The Political Process*, rev. ed. (New York: Random House, 1965).

Secretary of Defense McNamara meets with the Joint Chiefs of Staff and other department officials. Bureaucratic leaders are often significant formulators of public policy.

Washington journalists trying to find out what is going on; the alliance of the House Agriculture Committee, the Sugar Division of the Agriculture Department, and leaders of the sugar industry formed to determine the prices and quotas of imported sugar; or the coalition of the Bureau of Indian Affairs, the Association on American Indian Affairs, and the House and Senate Committees on Indian Affairs.

A specific case will show how coalitions of policy formulators form. In the early 1960s, some consumers complained that food products were packaged and priced so that purchasers could not compare prices, make a reasonable choice, and obtain full value for their dollar. Packaging in "regular," "family," or "jumbo" sizes, odd package shapes, not filling packages to capacity, and offering goods at "cents-off" the regular prices were typical packaging and pricing techniques that consumers found confusing and misleading. Senator Philip Hart, Democrat of Michigan, introduced a bill in 1961 which prohibited deceptive packaging as a restraint of trade. This bill came under the jurisdiction of the Senate Antitrust and Monopoly Subcommittee of the Senate Judiciary Committee. Food industry spokesmen had much influence with the Judiciary Committee, but advocates of consumer legislation, despite the support of President Kennedy and his twelve-member Consumer Advisory Council, were ineffective. Through 1964, therefore, the coalition of opponents of truth-in-packaging legislation prevailed, chiefly because the Senate Judiciary Committee failed to report a bill.

In 1965, Hart introduced a new bill to authorize the Food and Drug Administration and the Federal Trade Commission to issue regulations requiring clear statements of net quantity in packages. It also provided standards for weights, quantities, sizes, and shapes of packages; and it prohibited offering a product at less than the customary retail price. Hart designated the new bill as intended to prohibit deceptive packaging and labeling in interstate commerce, thus attempting to transfer jurisdiction of the bill from the unresponsive Judiciary Committee to the Senate Commerce Committee. By voice vote, the Senate sent the bill to the Commerce Committee over the objections of Minority Leader Everett Dirksen, Republican of Illinois. The Senate Commerce Committee held hearings; and in 1966 Congress passed a truth-in-packaging law, but only after a coalition of interests (lobbyists for the food industry, several southern Democrats, and the Republican members of the House Interstate and Foreign Commerce Committee, together with officials in the Department of Commerce) won deletion of the key provision that authorized officials to establish standard package sizes. Instead manufacturers were required, through the Secretary of Commerce, to develop their own standards. The House Committee reported that it had substituted the voluntary procedure to meet the "recurrent objections raised by industry that mandatory standards would result in greatly increased cost to the consumer and would stifle package innovations." The Commerce Department also agreed with the substitution in order to placate the food industry. In the words of Representative Leonor Sullivan, Democrat of Missouri and supporter of consumer legislation, the final legislation that proved acceptable to the food industry and its allies in the Congress and executive agencies was so far removed from what had been sought by consumers that "we can all voice a very mild cheer — for very little."

Partial autonomy describes the two legislative houses and their subcommittees and committees, agencies and bureaus within agencies, and interest groups and factions within them. Diversification of interests at every level of authority generates give-and-take that results in two levels of policy formulation: in specialized areas (regulation of the railroad industry, or setting quotas for the importation of sugar) and in general areas (the SST, regulation of firearms, or the war on poverty). Because of the pluralist influence, *select minorities rule in specialized areas and a collection of diverse minorities rules in more general policy matters; popular majorities in either case are rare in policy formulation.*

## how are policies formulated?

Policies are formulated in American government in distinctive *styles,* which comprise methods used to reach decisions on courses of action and to obtain compliance, and *traditions,* which are the habits, expectations, conventions, and guidelines customarily involved in making policy choices.

styles of policy formulation

Although we can distinguish three other styles — persuasion, command, and competition — the policy style most used in reaching decisions and achieving compliance is bargaining. By bargaining, conflicting leaders reach a common policy position — they *explore and accept mutually beneficial adjustments of their differences.* Policy formulators attempt by means of bargaining to adjust conflicts by modifying their own demands no less than those of their opponents. In America, mutual adjustment is inescapable because of constitutional features as well as social pluralism. The separation of powers requires that policy decisions receive the approval of executive, legislative, and, at times, judicial branches to be legitimized. *The anomaly of legal separation but actual interdependence underlies all political bargaining.*

It is a truism of bargaining that both sides must be willing to negotiate and must have something to negotiate about; they must be able to offer something others want and they must want something others have. Some problems are easily negotiable; others, very difficult. On the question of minimum wages, it is easier to find a compromise between those who urge a $2.50 minimum and those who want a $3.00 minimum than it is to negotiate the question of whether there should be any minimum wage at all.

Two broad types of bargaining can be distinguished. In *explicit* bargaining, the policy formulators minimize the chances of misunderstanding by clearly formalizing their agreement.[4] Treaties are explicit bargains in international affairs; wage contracts and government defense contracts, in domestic affairs. *Implicit* or *tacit* bargaining is more significant for most American policymaking. At times, ambiguity is desirable and the responsibilities of formulators to one another are purposely couched in such vague notions as "future support," "good will," or "favorable disposition." The most common implicit bargain is an exchange of support between legislators whereby one legislator agrees to "go along" with another in voting for a bill in exchange for the latter's cooperation at some unspecified future time. The convertibility of such political I.O.U.s into actual support when requested rests more on mutual respect for playing by the rules than on the clarity of terms in any formal agreement.

At the heart of political bargaining of either type is exploring for mutual advantages: bargains are made by pleasing everyone somewhat. If

---

[4] Thomas C. Shelling, *The Strategy of Conflict* (New York: Oxford University Press, 1963), pp. 21–52.

one accepts that bargaining is the principal style of policy formulation, then politics is the art of compromise. Compromise is one way in which agreements can be reached, because if disputants hold to their initial claims, none is likely to profit; impasse or total defeat are the more likely outcomes. If all sides decide to give in a little, none is completely satisfied but none is completely unhappy with the result.

*Bargaining can end in less commendable consequences.* Elected leaders may find after a while that the men they have appointed to regulate groups are finding bases of support within those groups; they become difficult to control, and make regulation of the groups very difficult. Popular control over the policymakers is diluted as well. Another effect is the length of time it takes to make policy. Bargaining often makes it impossible to fix responsibility for public policy on any individual, group, party, or legislative body. Also, policymaking often is costly in wasted effort and resources as well as in uncoordinated and inefficient policies.

Finally, the issues resolved by political bargaining are necessarily only a small part of the almost limitless number of social conflicts facing the arbiters of conflict representation. The political circuits would be grossly overloaded if all actual and potential conflicts had to be attended to. Similarly, political bargainers must conserve their resources and efforts for issues of most importance to them. The bargainer's need to pick and choose his issues thus complements the need of the political system to filter social conflicts. The items that do not get on the political agenda may be just as vital for the continued health of the community as the ones that do.

ALTERNATIVES AND SUPPLEMENTS TO BARGAINING. Bargaining is the principal style of policy formulation in America, but others sometimes replace and at other times underpin it. By *persuasion,* formulators influence one another by holding out promises of gratification and reward. Recent Presidents, for example have made a practice of holding occasional "White House breakfasts" with congressional leaders. Some are negotiating sessions designed to forge policies, but more often they permit the President to outline his already set program, point out its advantages for Congressmen and their constituents, and ask for their support in obtaining congressional approval, which he hopes will result from the merits of his persuasive arguments.

If a policy leader regularly threatens reprisal as well as promising rewards, his style is one of *command.* A policy leader commands as much support as he has sanctions to apply. Some of the formal sanctions that the President holds over administrative subordinates include his authority to review their budget requests, appoint administrative personnel,

Presidents prefer techniques of bargaining to command, but occasionally they are forced to decree. In 1971, Richard Nixon invoked the Taft-Hartley Act as the dock strike snarled West Coast ports.

clear their legislative proposals, and limit the information they may release to the press.

The authority to review and cut agency budget requests is of particular importance. Because agencies and bureaus cannot *formally* request more funds from Congress than are authorized in the President's budget, their autonomy is limited. Bureaucratic leaders are often able to circumvent such formal restrictions, however, by testifying before sympathetic legislators in congressional committees. President Nixon regularly requested less federal spending for public education than some education interests, both in Congress and in the executive, would otherwise request. Although instructed to support the President's requests publicly, a few administrators in the Office of Education expressed their desire for more funds before congressional committees. Congress responded by budgeting more federal aid to education than requested by the President, prompting him to use his ultimate sanction, the veto, on several education measures.

Within administrative agencies, conflicts arise between the administrator seeking to command support and his subordinates who have outside help in refusing to obey. In 1967, Secretary of Defense Robert S. McNamara announced that the United States would begin developing a limited antiballistic missile system costing $5 billion to defend against a possible nuclear attack by Communist China. The dissatisfaction of portions of the army and air force, who wanted a more elaborate program costing $40 billion, was shared by members of the House Armed Services Committee who criticized the "austerity" of the McNamara plan. The military and congressional proponents of a major antiballistic missile system thus remained free to lobby against the secretary's decision.

When political interests strive for the same prize and resources are limited or scarce, policy formulators must choose between courses of action. This makes for the style called *competition*. We see it in legislative bodies when political leaders compete for the legislative votes to approve or reject a proposal; we also see it in court cases; one side wins the decision and the other loses. The adversaries in policy disputes, however, are not usually so unalterably opposed, and courses of action are not so clear that zero-sum competition ensues (that is, competition in which one side clearly wins everything and the other loses everything without achieving some hoped-for benefits). More often, competition is combined with other styles of policy formulation.

Bargaining, persuasion, command, and competition, although "pure" styles of policy formulation, seldom appear alone in policymaking. They overlap and supplement one another, although bargaining is the characteristic style in American politics. The words used to describe the political style of Mayor Richard Lee, an energetic leader dedicated to urban renewal and other policies to invigorate New Haven, Connecticut, typify the American style of policy formulation:

> The mayor was not at the peak of a pyramid but rather at the center of intersecting circles. He rarely commanded. He negotiated, cajoled, exhorted, beguiled, charmed, pressed, appealed, reasoned, promised, insisted, demanded, even threatened, but he most needed support and acquiescence from other leaders who simply could not be commanded. Because the mayor could not command, he had to bargain.[5]

## traditions of policy formulation

Tradition in policy formulation is the habits, expectations, conventions, and guidelines customarily associated with making public policies. The three most important traditions are: *reciprocity*, referred to colloquially as the custom of "you scratch my back and I'll scratch yours," *incrementalism*, "muddling through," and the *public interest*.

[5] Robert A. Dahl, *Who Governs?* (New Haven: Yale University Press, 1961), p. 204.

RECIPROCITY. Perhaps no activity sets apart the politician as much as bargaining. His selection and subsequent success as a policymaker (by election or appointment) depends upon his skill at negotiating. His life and energy are then devoted to continuously reshaping coalitions of policy formulators. In arranging political bargains the politician cares only about finding solutions that work, not perfect ones. All policymakers are committed to mutual accommodation, even when they are spokesmen for divergent interests, so they are willing to adjust to each other's demands rather than push their differences beyond reconciliation.

Just recently, Americans have begun to appreciate that the give-and-take of the politician's job has its good side. We often used to think of reciprocal influence as the shady side of politics, though we should realize that, however implicit and subtle, *compromise and bargaining are part of our day-to-day relationships.* (When was the last time you refrained from arguing because to do so would jeopardize your relations with a friend or group?) Bargaining is just as vital in the welter of social interests making legitimate claims on government and policy.

INCREMENTALISM. Many critics argue that bargaining is not a rational way to formulate policies, for the bargains usually work to the advantage of the bargainers and seldom solve social problems. They advocate a more *rational* and *comprehensive* approach to policy formulation: (1) Clarify policy goals before considering alternative courses of action to reach those goals. (2) Search for *all* alternative means of achieving the agreed-on policy objectives. (3) Comprehensively test each alternative course of action against the criterion that the most rational (and hence, "best") policy will be the most appropriate and efficient means of reaching agreed-on ends. Finally, (4) select this most rational policy.[6]

A rational, comprehensive procedure of formulating policies may seem desirable, but its requirements contradict all we know about how human beings reach decisions, particularly in American politics. It is rarely easy, and usually impossible, to get people to clarify and agree on policy goals. Our pluralist society and government restrict political consensus to the most vaguely defined and abstract goals — "government by the people," "justice, " "freedom," "a better standard of living." We cannot comprehensively analyze alternative ways of achieving goals if those goals are not agreed on in advance. Comprehensive policy analysis also requires knowing what courses of action are available. Seldom, however, do we

---

[6] A detailed comparison of the rational-comprehensive and incrementalist approaches to decisionmaking is Charles E. Lindblom, "The Science of 'Muddling Through,' " *Public Administration Review* 19 (Spring 1959): 79–88; see also Charles E. Lindblom, *The Intelligence of Democracy* (New York: The Free Press, 1965).

Close advisers meet with President Johnson. Policy formulation is less
a matter of finding perfect than working solutions.

know all the options. Finally, the comprehensive approach requires us
to anticipate the consequences of each conceivable option in order to
select the policy most apt to advance our goals. But it is unrealistic to
believe that even the most knowledgeable person can correctly predict
what will happen if he adopts any possible course of action. (Let the
reader, for instance, think of how many times he has chosen the right
course of action and then found that the result he expected did not follow.) Unanticipated consequences have a way of frustrating even the best
laid plans.

Political scientists call the behavior of American politicians in formulating policy the *incrementalist* approach to change, or "muddling
through." In this approach, goals are not agreed on before considering
how best to achieve them; rather *the selection of ends and means over-
laps.* To design policies, it is not enough to know that most Americans
favor racial integration in principle — in the abstract. That vague "majority support" provides no real guidance to which means will be favored
in attempting to achieve that goal — the contrary occurs. The true meaning of the goal, and a better way of knowing how much support it has,

appears only in the reactions to each of the proposed means. When a goal, racial integration, is cast in the form of school integration, one set of pro and con forces develops; when the means is open housing, another set comes forth; equal voting rights produces still another configuration of forces, and so on.

The alignment of interests on the various proposed means will overlap, of course, but significant differences will come out as well. For the "rational" model it is assumed that policy goals are clear and independent of proposed means, and that dispassionate and technical analysis can determine the best (most efficient) means to agreed-on ends. As our example indicates, however, it is only in the conflict over *means* that *goals* become clarified. *Public policy, therefore, is not simply a matter of devising effective means to reach known and shared ends; it is a simultaneous search for means and ends on which disagreement is widespread.*

Following the incrementalist approach the parties to a dispute frequently agree on a *"good" policy without agreeing on what it is good for;* although unable to agree on ends, conflicting interests still agree on means. Take as an example Congressmen. Liberals want to extend old age benefits through social security as a means of having the federal government provide equal welfare opportunities to all elderly Americans (to achieve the principle of equality). Conservatives support the same policy, but for a different reason. They see it as a way of reducing labor demands on private corporations for support of union pension plans (to protect private enterprise). In the rational-comprehensive approach to formulating policy, it is assumed that a "good" policy is that which achieves agreed-on goals; the incrementalist approach has no criterion for a "good" policy apart from saying that it serves the separate, perhaps conflicting, goals of specialized interests.

In selecting an appropriate policy, *the incrementalist approach usually neglects to analyze in detail the consequences of adopting a policy.* Important policy outcomes are often neglected. When the policies leading to the development of the SST were formulated, the consequences for the environment of operating large numbers of supersonic aircraft were ignored. Only *relevant* consequences were analyzed: the stimulus the SST would give business and employment, and the prestige the United States might lose to other nations developing such an aircraft. In the incrementalist approach, alternative policies that might accomplish a specified goal in a better way than the proposed policy are seldom considered. Not that after a time alternative policies are not offered; clearly they are (the all-volunteer army has been offered as an alternative to selective service in sustaining a defense force; the Nixon administration offered a comprehensive alternative to current welfare programs for the needy). In initial policy conflicts, relatively few proposals are considered and they look very much alike; fresh approaches to old problems are relatively rare.

In the incrementalist approach *policies are changed by successive comparison.* Instead of examining policies to see if they have been successful, retaining the ones that accomplish stated goals and scrapping the ineffective ones to start anew, policies already chosen are periodically adapted to changing conditions to patch up obvious mistakes. In the budgetary process, for instance, last year's appropriation for an agency is typically considered to be the base for change, which the Bureau of the Budget or the Congress will seldom question. Only the size of the increase will be attacked.

The disadvantage is that programs and agencies seldom die or are severely cut back, that coordination of policy is made much more difficult, and that the President can control only a small fraction of the total budget with which he can implement his own priorities and policies. The advantages are that review efforts and conflicts are cut down and stability and continuity is assured in policies and agency programs and activities. No one has to go back to the beginning each year to justify why the program or agency or policy should continue to exist. If government activities were continuously open to basic reconsideration, the burden on officials, groups, and citizens would be intolerable. *The adjustment of social conflicts in traditional, incremental change means that policies are allowed to evolve and that great basic shifts in policy are the exception.*[7]

The incrementalist way of formulating policy appears to be chaotic. It reveals no deliberate effort to coordinate the disparate efforts of policy leaders. But such procedures do simplify the complex business of making policy. Instead of considering all alternative policies in a conflict, leaders limit themselves to those which differ little from current policies. The worth of each policy is measured by what diverse interests demand, insulating the policymaker from more demanding interests.

Policymaking is simplified in yet another way. The "best" policy is the one on which bargained agreement has been achieved. The complex task of estimating how specific policies will affect distant goals gives way to a more simplified accounting, determines which immediate interests are pleased and displeased, whose support is won and whose lost. *Policymaking thus develops into a search for workable solutions, which satisfy though they do not maximize the demands of interests, rather than the more difficult, and perhaps impossible, search for perfect solutions to public problems.*

[7] Allen Schick, "Systems Politics and Systems Budgeting," *Public Administration Review* 29 (March/April 1969); 137–151.

THE PUBLIC INTEREST. But if bargaining and incrementalist policy formulation is an attempt to satisfy diverse private interests, what happens to the general interest? The public interest has a history of being many things to many people. Most often it is thought of as substantive ideals — goals — against which all policy proposals should be judged, such as "equality of opportunity," "equal justice," or "fairness to all." As symbols or norms, such goals spell out the aspirations of a society. Special interests tie their claims to these symbols to rationalize their desires and to increase support for their position.

It would be misleading, however, to suggest that organized interests cynically manipulate public interest theories to suit their knowingly selfish aims. Is it so clear or obvious, after all, what "the public interest" requires in any major social conflict? In public welfare policies? In taxation? In education? In defense spending? In relations with other nations? Because "the public interest" is an ambiguous idea, special interests often are genuinely persuaded that their demands are indeed in the public interest — and the same applies to the special interests opposing them.

Another conception of the public interest emerges. Public interest as affected by the substance of policy is not some external and autonomous standard "out there," but the result of bargaining by group interests seeking to resolve their conflicts. *The public interest, like substantive policy itself, constantly evolves in the continuing adjustment caused by social conflicts; it is not a fixed, permanent entity.* Procedurally, however, the public interest may be said to require viable decisionmaking by the community to facilitate the conciliation of clashing interests. Bargaining and policy incrementalism shape and sustain this conciliation and so promote the public interest.

## conflict resolution by pluralism, bargaining, and incrementalism

Public policy must be made within our pluralist society and our constitutional arrangement; policy formulation is greatly influenced by a bargaining style and the incrementalist tradition. Critics of American democracy have suggested major defects in this method of resolving social disputes. What are their criticisms?

Our pluralist system consists of innumerable semiautonomous fiefdoms — coalitions of policymakers protecting their own interests and beyond control by any central authority. Rarely is a leader under our fragmented constitutional arrangement able to call attention to the many social problems, to formulate adequate responses, and to mobilize widespread public interest and effort. Instead, government is prone to formu-

A government so paralyzed by negotiations that it cannot respond to dire needs, such as controlling industrial pollution, is the real threat in a liberal democracy.

late policies that distribute resources to favored interests and permit special clienteles to regulate affairs on their own behalf than to try to devise redistributive policies directed at removing the causes of pressing social tensions.

Incremental change is very slow and often stifles or delays the search for solutions to deep problems. All too often the delay is long; and social evils are allowed to grow so intense that it becomes difficult, perhaps impossible, to formulate relevant responses. Bargaining and incremental change can be quite unreceptive to innovative policies; and formulation descends into a routine, unimaginative, conservative approach that sustains the status quo for its own sake. The real threat may be not a government quick to act in a tyrannical way but a government unable to act at all, immobilized by its tendency to reach negotiated settlements in response to the demands of privileged interests and not reacting to hitherto unrepresented groups challenging the very legitimacy of the establishment. The government does respond to such challenges; but often the response is symbolic, giving discontented interests the illusion that their voices are heard in formulating policies, but seldom responding to the substance of their demands.

Such are representative criticisms that have been leveled against the process of formulating policies described in this chapter. (We have, of

course, cited other criticisms of the pluralist process of conflict representation in Part Three.) A good deal of controversy rages over the validity of these representative criticisms. Some point to crises in race relations, disaffection among youths, intensification of poverty, and
deterioration in the environment as evidence that our way of making
policy has been tried and found wanting. Basic reforms are needed, they
say; some call for moderate reforms to compensate for weaknesses,
others say the whole system is faulty and demand that it be discarded.

Others argue that the pluralist-bargaining-incrementalist system can
resolve social conflicts and has done so. They point to civil rights legislation passed in the 1950s and 1960s as fruitful incremental change; they
cite antipoverty and Medicare legislation as indicative of innovative
though defective programs that affect the redistribution of resources.
They deny that social ills are ignored (pointing to major proposals calling
for welfare reform, national health insurance, environmental improvement, tax reform, and other basic policy changes that Congress is considering). They point to examples of policy formulation (the antipoverty
program) in which initiative for program development was centralized,
not dispersed among conflicting interests. Nor are they willing to accept
the charge that our way of formulating policy is beyond repair; they cite
new techniques of budgeting that reform the conventions of incremental
change by involving the President in the early stages of policy development, providing for him to scrutinize existing programs, and giving him
authority to do more than simply cut some agency requests and add a
few items of his own.

This controversy reflects a basic tension always found in American
government: it opposes coordination and fragmentation, centralization
and decentralization, majority rule and minority rights. Each of the major
policymaking institutions reflects this tension. In weighing the defects in
policymaking, their consequences, what can be done and is being done
about them, and their origin in the pluralist character of American society and government, it is well to keep in mind that for all its faults, its
defenders say, it does manage conflict by building a consensus stronger
than any we could imagine if every group received precisely what it
demanded of the community.

*bibliographical note*

In recent years political scientists have taken an increased interest in describing
not only the content of specific public policies, but in policymaking. As a result
several brief paperbacks are now available that describe how policies are formu-

lated. Despite the spate of new works, the best single introduction to the pluralist character of policymaking remains J. Leiper Freeman, *The Political Process*, rev. ed. (New York: Random House, 1965). A popularization of many of Freeman's theses is Douglass Cater's *Power in Washington* (New York: Random House, 1964). Among more recent works, each with a different focus, are Charles O. Jones, *An Introduction to the Study of Public Policy* (Belmont, Calif.; Wadsworth, 1970), which provides a general framework for analyzing policymaking; Roger W. Cobb and Charles D. Elder, *Participation in American Politics: The Dynamics of Agenda-Building* (Boston: Allyn and Bacon, 1972), which is concerned with how public problems are brought to the attention of policymakers; and Charles E. Lindblom, *The Policy-Making Process* (Englewood Cliffs, N.J.: Prentice-Hall, 1968) that focuses on the general context of policymaking. A basic textbook introduction is Joyce M. Mitchell and William C. Mitchell, *Political Analysis and Public Policy* (Chicago: Rand McNally, 1969).

Several works examine the consequences for policymaking of social pluralism and constitutional fragmentation. The standard treatment is Robert A. Dahl and Charles E. Lindblom, *Politics, Economics, and Welfare* (New York: Harper & Row, Torchback Edition, 1963). Still a valuable work on the subject is Pendleton Herring, *The Politics of Democracy* (New York: W. W. Norton, 1965), first published in 1940. That the seeds of constitutional fragmentation and, hence, the pluralist-incrementalist tradition in policymaking were sown early in the Republic's history is indicated in discussions of our constitutional arrangement, notably David G. Smith, *The Convention and the Constitution* (New York: St. Martin's Press, 1965) and Arthur N. Holcombe, *The Constitutional System* (Chicago: Scott, Foresman, 1964).

Recently there has been considerable criticism of the pluralist-incrementalist method of making public policies in America. A good example of this criticism is Theodore J. Lowi, *The End of Liberalism* (New York: W. W. Norton, 1969). See also Henry S. Kariel, *The Decline of American Pluralism* (Stanford, Calif.: Stanford University Press, 1961). A succinct statement of the positive side of the pluralist-incrementalist tradition is Abraham Kaplan, *American Ethics and Public Policy* (New York: Oxford University Press, 1963). The functions of bargaining, mutual adjustment, and incremental changes in policymaking are discussed in Charles E. Lindblom, *The Intelligence of Democracy* (New York: Free Press, 1965) and David Braybrooke and Charles E. Lindblom, *A Strategy of Decision* (New York: Free Press, 1963).

There are several brief accounts of how specific policies have been made in America. Among these are Clyde E. Jacobs and John F. Gallager, *The Selective Service Act: A Case Study of the Governmental Process* (New York: Dodd, Mead, 1967); Daniel M. Berman, *A Bill Becomes a Law*, 2nd ed. (New York: Macmillan, 1966); Demetrios Caraley, *The Politics of Military Unification* (New York: Columbia University Press, 1967); Donald F. Hadwiger and Ross B. Talbot, *Pressures and Politics* (Ames, Iowa: Iowa State University Press, 1965); Richard Art, *The TFX Decision* (Boston: Little, Brown, 1968); James E. Anderson, *The Economic Opportunity Act of 1964: Analysis and Effects* (Belmont, Calif.: Wadsworth, 1971); Stephen K. Bailey and Edith K. Mosher, *ESEA: The Office of Education*

*Administers a Law* (Syracuse, N.Y.: Syracuse University Press, 1969); Raymond Bauer et al., *American Business and Public Policy* (New York: Atherton, 1963); James W. Davis and Kenneth M. Dolbeare, *Little Groups of Neighbors: The Selective Service System* (Chicago: Markham, 1968); A. Lee Fritschler, *Smoking and Politics* (New York: Appleton-Century-Crofts, 1969); Daniel P. Moynihan, *Maximum Feasible Misunderstanding* (New York: Free Press, 1969); Aaron Wildavsky, *The Politics of the Budgetary Process* (Boston: Little, Brown, 1964); and Alan P. Sindler, ed., *American Political Institutions and Public Policy* (Boston: Little, Brown, 1969).

# chapter 12

# policy leadership

The framework for resolving conflicts, as set forth in the first three articles of the Constitution, is simple: the legislature passes laws, the executive enforces them, and the judiciary interprets them. But we now know that things are not that simple. Authority and influence are so dispersed throughout the constitutional structure that it is difficult to trace the origins of public policy and fix responsibility for its execution. In this mosaic of policy activity, it is the President who most often coordinates the disparate efforts of the many subgovernments. The degree to which he can do so, however, constantly fluctuates; his influence on policymaking hinges on his varying relationships with other major participants in politics. In this chapter, we examine the President's power and influence in representing and regulating conflict in the American community.

## the president and policy leadership

Policy leadership defines the community's goals, initiates policy proposals to achieve these, and obtains both official and popular compliance in their execution. The President takes the lead in establishing a continuing reconciliation of diverse interests within the community. It is fair to say, therefore, that the presidency has come to dominate the American political system.

## development of the presidency

The dominant presidency was not foreseen by the Founding Fathers and was achieved only after a long and sometimes bitter struggle between the governing institutions. The men who wrote the Constitution focused on the legislative branch, but they nevertheless wanted an executive with great independence and potential. So they rejected selection of the President by the legislature except in extraordinary circumstances (when no candidate receives a majority of electoral votes), and provided a fixed term of office, subject only to removal by impeachment. The President was given control over foreign relations, was made chief of the administrative branch, and was provided a veto over legislation. These formal powers assigned by Article II have not been changed by amendment.

We cannot understand the presidency by studying its legal status only. "The executive Power shall be vested in a President of the United States of America" are the opening words of Article II. This Article provides for, but does not define, the extent of such power, which has led Edward S. Corwin to remark that for those who seek certainty in a constitution the clause is a "nightmare" and for those who prefer broad language it "should be a vision realized."[1] All Presidents have been charged with the constitutional responsibility to "take Care that the Laws be faithfully executed," but the meaning of this obligation has undergone marked changes.

Daniel Webster, during the administration of Andrew Jackson, charged that "the President carries on the government; all the rest are subcontractors." The presidency grew steadily in significance until 1865, but during the several decades that followed the Civil War it was in eclipse. The trend was reversed in this century, so that Harry S. Truman could say in the 1940s that the presidency is "the greatest and most important office in the history of the world."

## the president and other policymakers

The modern President, by definition of his office, cannot be a neutral force in conflicts of interest. Problems that were once purely local matters — race relations, urban slums, education — are now among the national government's biggest problems. Politics reflects more and more clashing of national social and economic interests, and national programs and goals now are clearly felt even in congressional contests. The President has been at the center of this trend toward nationalized politics because his constituency alone (except for that of the Vice-President) is national.

Because their constituencies are local and policy leadership is dispersed within each chamber, the pressures Congressmen respond to

---

[1] Edward S. Corwin, *The President: Office and Powers* (New York: New York University Press, 1948), p. 2.

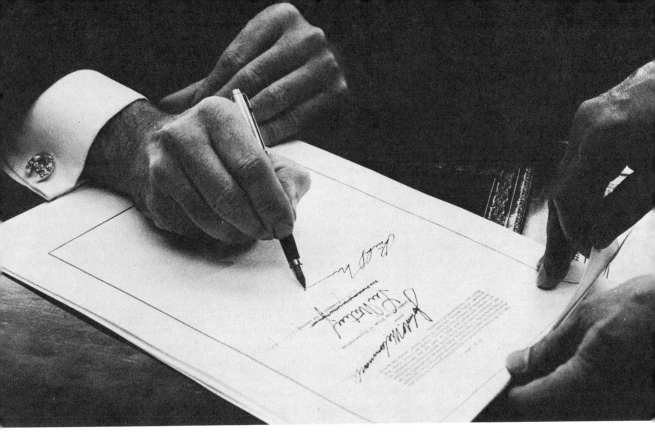

The presidency today is the fulcrum of leadership in the American system.

are different from those felt by the President. Legislative policy goals, too, are often different from those of the President. But the two branches do have incentives for cooperating: party ties and the need to respond to both pressing domestic problems and foreign crises. Cooperation, not command, characterizes relations between presidential and congressional leaders, involving them in the mutual negotiation and accommodation so characteristic of the entire political system. A President, then, must shelter the autonomous interest claims of congressional leaders within his overall policy.

Although judicial interpretations of presidential power have generally expanded the scope of the presidency, the judiciary also indirectly threatens presidential leadership. The Supreme Court's restrictive interpretation of national power in economic regulation before 1937 severely hampered President Roosevelt's attempts to meet the problems of the depression. Later, a change in the court's position opened the way for new policies and further extension of federal programs.

Courts can make policy as well as block it. In *Brown* v. *Board of Edu-*

*cation* (1954), the Supreme Court made policy in overturning racial segregation in public school systems. This was a major decision of the court, and in the next decade it presented important problems of policy leadership to Presidents Eisenhower, Kennedy, and Johnson. The decision had to be enforced in parts of the South where both state governments and community sentiment were hostile to integration; and federal troops had to be used to achieve integration in Little Rock, Arkansas, and at the University of Mississippi, showing how *executive* action may be used to enforce policy initiated by the judiciary. The precedents set by the Brown decision and others that followed led to the busing of public school children across school district boundaries in order to achieve racial integration. President Nixon resisted these decisions by asking Congress to impose a moratorium on busing orders issued by federal district courts.

Presidential leadership is challenged at other points within the governmental structure. Because a President cannot control all policy decisions in a large bureaucracy, he must leave specific decisions to subordinates who may not follow his general directives or wishes. Leadership is further complicated by regulatory agencies with policymaking authority that are not directly responsible to the President. Coordination is hampered by multiple layers of decisionmaking, even in executive agencies that are legally responsible to the chief executive. By yielding to or allying with external groups, administrative bureaus develop independent support for their goals, weakening the President's control over the executive hierarchy. The strong influence on Congress of the Army Corps of Engineers is one important example. Presidents have had little success in preventing congressional approval of flood control and other projects urged by the corps but contrary to presidential programs.

The President as a policy leader depends on a set of relationships — formal and informal — between competing interests and institutions in the political community. He molds policy, but he is also subjected to continuing conflict. The manner in which he leads is heavily influenced by the man himself, by the environment in which he finds himself, and by the demands that flow from that environment. The presidency, however, must also be understood as a continuing force in defining national goals and translating these into specific policy choices. A significant aspect of that role is the symbolic nature of the office itself.

### symbolism in presidential leadership

President Taft's description of the President as "the personal embodiment and representative of [the people's] dignity and majesty" pinpoints, albeit somewhat pompously, an inherent function of the President as a community leader. Filling a number of related symbolic roles, the President enjoys status unequaled by any other leader. Fred I. Greenstein classified the "pyschological functions of the presidency": First, the President "*simplifies perception* of government and politics" by serving as "the main cognitive 'handle' for providing busy citizens with some sense of what their government is doing." By utilizing the communications media, he can dramatize his control and knowledge of difficult situations and focus the nation's attention on the *President*'s programs and the *President*'s policy decisions. Second, he provides *"an outlet for emotional expression"* by his ceremonial activities and public interest in his and his family's private and public life. Third, he is a *"symbol of unity"* despite differences of opinion over his policies. Fourth, he provides citizens with a *"vicarious means of taking political action."* During international crises Americans identify closely with him as their leader, who acts decisively for them. Finally, he is a *"symbol of social stability"*; he represents the order and security of the "ship of state."[2]

As the focal point of leadership, the President is strengthened by the symbolic roles the public assigns him, but he has obligations: the public's expectations. When major decisions are to be made, no President can escape the necessity of making them; he is expected to act. Like President Nixon's wage-price freeze in 1971 to control inflation, or President Kennedy's handling of the Cuban missile crisis in 1961, his actions may unalterably affect his prestige and popularity for ill or for good, *but act he must.* Whatever his response to the problems he will be listened to closely and will be seen by most as the nation's leader, not just as the chief spokesman for his party or other interests.

By capitalizing on this unique attribute, a skillful President can modify our pluralistic and fragmented policymaking. Thus, President Kennedy, as the symbol and representative of the larger community, in 1962 forced the steel industry to revoke its increased prices. President Nixon in March 1972 signed a bill ending a West Coast dock strike. The strike was already over, but the legislation was important as "a symbolic gesture" that emphasized the need for legislation setting up permanent machinery to avert crippling strikes.

### constituted authority

The Constitutional Convention of 1787 debated over how it could create an executive strong enough to enforce national laws but not so strong as to become a threat to republican government. Under the leadership

[2] Fred I. Greenstein, "The Psychological Functions of the Presidency for Citizens," in Elmer E. Cornwell, ed., *The American Presidency: Vital Center* (Chicago: Scott, Foresman, 1966), pp. 30–36.

The President assumes many symbolic roles. Americans identify closely with him as their leader.

of James Wilson, James Madison, and Alexander Hamilton, the Framers decided on a single executive rather than a collegiate body and gave to the President prerogatives independent of the other branches.

We are not sure how much authority they intended to give the President. At least one of the Framers, Alexander Hamilton, foresaw a strong chief executive. In *Federalist* No. 70, he argued, "Energy in the executive is a leading character in the definition of good government. . . . A feeble executive implies a feeble execution of the government . . . and a government ill executed, whatever it may be in theory, must be, in practice, a bad government." He urged that Article II laid the foundation for strong leadership: "that the *executive power* of the nation is vested in the President; subject only to the *exceptions and qualifications* which are expressed in the instrument."

He saw the office as the fulcrum of leadership in the American system, drawing its legal foundations from the specific grants of power in the

Constitution and its vitality from the person who occupies the office and puts his powers to use. Hamilton urged upon President Washington vigorous executive action in foreign affairs and in organizing the administrative branch of the new government. The presidency today is Hamilton's hope fulfilled.

The great powers and resources the President derives from the Constitution and the statutes are not without limit, of course. He cannot force solutions unacceptable to other sources of power in the system. And sometimes it seems his responsibilities are too great for the resources granted him. He has other powers, though; these are based on interpretations of presidential authority by incumbents and by the courts, and the development of the office by custom and usage. Although the Constitution draws seemingly distinct boundaries between the symbolic, administrative, strategic, international, and legislative dimensions of the presidency, the President can join these forces when he chooses to act. The "seamless unity" uncovered by students of the presidency makes distinctions of this kind meaningless.[3]

## administrative leadership

The constitutional mandate that the President faithfully execute the laws is a responsibility that is often difficult to meet. His administrative subordinates, legally subject to presidential control, often operate outside it; many of his orders fail to elicit an obedient response; his lines of command are often tenuous. Louis Koenig distinguishes between an "imagined Presidency," which is vested in our minds with more power than the President really has, and the "real Presidency" which is "what the Presidency effectively is in the present, what it can do in a given situation."[4]

As leader of the administrative bureaucracy, the President must consolidate policy activity taking place in thousands of administrative units around the nation and involving three million civilian employees. Programs range from efforts to alleviate poverty to confining criminals in federal prisons. In 1800, nonmilitary federal employees numbered around three thousand; when the Capitol was moved in that year to the District of Columbia, the complete files of the executive branch were

[3] See Clinton Rossiter, *The American Presidency*, rev. ed. (New York: Harcourt, Brace Jovanovich, 1960), p. 41; Richard E. Neustadt, *Presidential Power* (New York: John Wiley, 1960); Donald B. Johnson and Jack L. Walker, eds., *The Dynamics of the American Presidency* (New York: John Wiley, 1964).

[4] Louis W. Koenig, *The Chief Executive*, rev. ed. (New York: Harcourt Brace Jovanovich, 1968), p. 3.

shipped in seven packing cases. In 1970, about five thousand people worked in President Nixon's Executive Office alone, only one of hundreds of agencies. Directing, controlling, and coordinating the executive branch of government as well as the responsibility for what goes wrong with it, constitutionally falls to the President.

## power to appoint and remove

How much control over the bureaucracy does the President's power of appointment and removal give him? The Constitution and statutes grant him broad appointment power, subject to Senate approval. High-ranking officials such as department heads, executive office personnel, and members of regulatory agencies are appointed by him. But more than 90 percent of federal employees are under the merit civil service which establishes entrance requirements, conditions of work, and grounds for dismissal.

The Constitution says nothing about his removing executive branch officers and employees, but the Supreme Court has ruled that his removal power extends to all "purely executive officials"; it does not include members of quasi-judicial or quasi-legislative agencies such as the Interstate Commerce Commission, delegated by Congress to carry out duties not a part of the executive function.[5]

Despite his legal authority to hire and fire, the President is under strong *political* restrictions in exercising it. One study of how sub-Cabinet officials are appointed observes that "practice and expediency dictate that presidential control over appointments has to be shared with others who also have a stake in the administrative branch of government."[6] Party leaders, Congressmen, interest group representatives, and agency and department heads cannot be ignored in choosing appointees for important posts. Appointments to high executive posts are also exchanged for political support of major groups or in payment for political debts incurred during a campaign.

Political considerations similarly limit the President's power to fire. J. Edgar Hoover's position as chief of the FBI was impregnable for many years because of his strong support from Congress and the public. The political cost of removing an official such as Mr. Hoover, even after he passed retirement age, seems greater than any President would be willing

---

[5] *Myers* v. *U.S.*, 272 U.S. 52 (1926); *Humphrey's Executor* v. *U.S.* 295 U.S. 602 (1935).

[6] Dean E. Mann, *The Assistant Secretaries* (Washington, D.C.: Brookings Institution, 1965), p. 76.

to pay. Removing important appointees may result in lost support for his programs. "The ends of bureaucratic control and of acquiring political support," as Grant McConnell wrote, "are often mutually exclusive."[7]

## other presidential controls over the bureaucracy

The limits on power of appointment and removal are balanced by formal power to control the budget and to alter the administrative organization. These are more important but by no means without political limitations.

The Budget and Accounting Act of 1921 created the Bureau of the Budget, now called the Office of Management and Budget. Initially within the Treasury Department, the bureau functioned largely as an agency through which departmental requests for funds were filtered and sent to Congress. In 1939, the bureau was moved to the Executive Office of the President and became a major arm of his control over the administrative branch. The budget represents his overall program for action. Being able to recommend appropriations is a powerful weapon of administrative control; his recommendation can mean life or death for proposals made by agencies, perhaps even for the agencies themselves. The budget is also a proposal for legislative action, so a President will carefully consider what he can and cannot achieve in Congress, which holds the power to accept or reject budget proposals. If Congress appropriates more or less than he requests for a program or agency, he can either accept that action or veto the entire bill; he cannot veto individual items. An administrative agency can bypass presidential strictures on spending by getting sympathetic congressional interests to support its request.

Presidents were authorized to reorganize executive agencies by altering their structure or redistributing functions by the Reorganization Act of 1939. President Roosevelt used this authority to create the Executive Office of the President, which initially housed five major offices to assist him in administrative and policy management.

Other offices have been added by other Presidents. Except for the Office of Management and Budget, the White House staff is probably the most important unit in the Executive Office. This "lengthened shadow" of the President includes assistants such as a press secretary, appointments secretary, and special assistant for national security. They write his speeches and correspondence; communicate his wishes to departments, Congress, party leaders, and interest groups; and they analyze domestic and foreign affairs problems confronting the President.

[7] Grant McConnell, *The Modern Presidency* (New York: St. Martin's Press, 1967), p. 58.

To alter structure is to change points of influence and power. James W. Davis writes:[8]

> To organize means to allocate power and responsibility and to reorganize means to change the existing pattern of allocation. Certainly, just who exercises power may have little to do with who has what powers on paper. But even though there have been weak or ineffective Presidents, no one would argue that the formal powers of the President are meaningless. Formal powers give the man who has them an advantage in seeking actual power. They provide stepping stones to actual power.

Clearly, organizational and political conflict are reflected in structure. An administrator may find that the prospect of losing his authority or influence because of organizational change is an incentive to comply with presidential wishes. On the other hand, congressional, bureaucratic, party, and private interests will consider proposals for change in organization or personnel heading major offices and agencies for their effect on *their* goals and policy preferences. Considering potential gains and losses for *his* goals, a President seeks to achieve command over the administrative structure.

## delegated powers and presidential leadership

The President's responsibilities as chief administrator have been considerably expanded by congressional action authorizing or requiring his action (or that of his designated administrative subordinates) in economic matters or during wartime emergencies. Although such delegation of power may infringe upon the constitutional principle of separated powers, it is part of the President's responsibility as chief administrator.[9]

In 1911, Congress authorized the Secretary of Agriculture to regulate the use of federal grazing lands. Other delegations of authority have involved wartime controls over prices and rent, agricultural marketing agreements between the Secretary of Agriculture and producers of farm commodities, presidential action under the Taft-Hartley Act of 1947 to prevent strikes from taking place for at least ninety days, and the imposition of wage and price controls in 1971 and 1972.

In exercising his discretionary authority and responsibilities in these

[8] James W. Davis, Jr., *The National Executive Branch* (New York: Free Press, 1970), p. 196.

[9] Generally, the Supreme Court has held that although Congress may not abdicate its constitutional function to make laws, the limits of delegation are broad and general in scope. See, for example, the discussion in *Yakus v. United States*, 321 U.S. 414 (1944); for an example in which the Court declared that congressional delegations exceeded constitutional bounds, see *Schecter Poultry Corporation v. United States*, 295 U.S. 594 (1935).

matters, the President depends on the bureaucracy as well as the cooperation of other governmental and private interests. President Nixon's wage and price boards, established to achieve control over economic inflation, were politically controversial agencies. Although their actions received broad public support, major interest groups challenged, questioned, or opposed strong controls.

Formally, the President could order these boards to apply specified wage-price policies. He appointed and could dismiss their members. But organized labor's fierce resistance to limitations on wage increases and the insistence by agricultural interests (including the Secretary of Agriculture) that farm prices not be controlled, gave the President less room to maneuver. The economic and political complexity of such measures drew conflicting advice from his advisers and high-level administrators. As chief administrator, the President had formal authority to act but he was limited by the demands and influence of conflicting interests. Legal and formal power is just one important element in the dynamics of interest conflicts.

## leadership in military and foreign affairs

### commander in chief

The Constitution names the President "Commander in Chief of the Army and Navy ... and of the Militia of the several states, when called into the actual Service of the United States." May he, then, employ armed forces whenever he wishes? Although Congress alone is constitutionally empowered to declare war, the President may precipitate conflict by using troops, leaving Congress no choice but to appropriate funds to bring the conflict to a successful conclusion. In 1907, when relations with Japan were strained, Theodore Roosevelt ordered the navy to sail around the world to show our peaceful intentions and the right of the American Navy to sail in Pacific waters. Roosevelt had funds enough for only half the trip, so Congress was forced to appropriate money to bring the fleet home.

American involvements abroad since the end of World War II have raised more serious questions over the extent of presidential powers as Commander in Chief. Since that war ended, no American military involvement has been based on a formal declaration of war. Presidents have acted either when authorized by congressional resolutions to use troops if necessary or on their own initiative. Using the argument that Russia and China had violated post–World War II agreements on Korea,

President Truman meets with British Prime Minister Attlee, Secretary of State Dean Acheson, and Secretary of Defense George Marshall during the Korean crisis in 1950. No President can escape making necessary decisions in crisis situations.

President Truman ordered troops to defend South Korea. President Johnson's steady escalation of the Vietnam War after 1964 followed several years of American involvement using "military advisers" and military aid to South Vietnam. Johnson relied heavily upon the Tonkin Gulf Resolution of 1964, in which Congress declared itself prepared "as the President determines, to take all necessary steps, including the use of armed force" to defend the peoples of Southeast Asia. A congressional resolution empowered President Kennedy to take military action in the Cuban missile crisis in 1962. But President Eisenhower sent troops to Lebanon in 1958 and President Johnson ordered troops to the Dominican Republic in 1965, both on their own authority, with the justification that such action was necessary to prevent Communist takeovers.

Public and congressional dissatisfaction with the Vietnam War brought Congress to try to control presidential actions involving the United States in armed conflicts. Senator William Fulbright and others charged that the President had turned the Tonkin Gulf Resolution into authorization for a major war, contrary to the intentions of Congress. In early 1971, Congress approved a resolution attached to another legislative bill that repealed the Tonkin Gulf Resolution. Other congressional actions have been aimed at restricting the President's discretionary powers in the use

390

of troops. The National Commitments Resolution, adopted by the Senate in 1969, declared that American troops could not be committed to hostilities abroad without approval by Congress. Congress also threatened, with very little success, to use its appropriations power to control use of American troops overseas. After President Nixon ordered American troops into Cambodia in April 1970, both houses approved a measure forbidding expenditures to support these operations after July 1, 1970. The troops were withdrawn by that date, so the real effectiveness of such legislative power remained untested.

Although the unpopular nature of the Vietnam War is the major policy issue, the basic constitutional issue goes deeper. How far can the President go with his power as commander in chief to involve the nation in war? The experience in Vietnam has sharpened congressional efforts to limit such power, but the United States is committed by treaties and other agreements to defend more than forty nations and maintains military bases in about thirty countries. It seems impractical to impose major congressional controls on presidential actions.[10] Nevertheless, the President must take into account public sentiment on the use of military power and also congressional attempts to legally limit such power.

## wartime emergency powers

As a strategic commander in time of war, the President has authority to do much more than issue military orders. Presidents Wilson and Franklin Roosevelt extended wartime controls over the American economy, the labor force and transportation, and approved government seizure of strike-bound or strike-threatened plants and industries. In February 1942, the army, acting in the name of the Commander in Chief, evacuated seventy thousand Japanese-Americans from three west-coast states and part of Arizona on the grounds that a danger of espionage and sabotage existed.[11]

During the Civil War, President Lincoln combined the powers of Commander in Chief with his constitutional duty to faithfully execute the laws and formulated the "war power," with which he justified unprecedented measures, including suspension of the writ of habeas corpus in designated areas and spending unauthorized funds from the federal treasury. Moreover, using powers granted under Article II and by congres-

---

[10] For a brief but excellent review of the history of President-Congress relations, see *Congressional Quarterly's Guide to the Congress* (Washington, D.C.: Congressional Quarterly Service, 1971), pp. 213–225.

[11] This action has subsequently been considered one of the most deplorable deprivations of civil liberties in American history.

sional statute, Presidents may use force to compel compliance with federal law and to prevent domestic disorder and violence. In 1894, Grover Cleveland broke the Pullman strike by ordering federal troops to protect the movement of the United States mails. Both Presidents Eisenhower and Kennedy used federal troops to quell disorders arising from resistance to court orders to integrate public schools.

Although the courts have recognized and upheld presidential "emergency powers" in wartime, the Supreme Court in *Youngstown Sheet and Tube Co.* v. *Sawyer* (1952) denied President Truman's assertion that "inherent" emergency powers of the presidency justified his seizure of the steel mills to avoid a crippling strike. How well does this decision fit the realities of cold-war politics? Because twentieth-century life is one long crisis and foreign and domestic problems are so closely related, permissible action by a President probably hinges more upon circumstances than it does upon legal distinctions under the Constitution. At the focal point for national action, the President must have broad prerogatives in time of emergency, but their scope remains unclear.

## international leadership

The increasing involvement of the United States in world affairs during this century and the grave risks inherent in foreign policy decisions in the nuclear age place the President in a crucial position as an international leader. He cannot avoid the task.

## formal limitations in foreign affairs

President Truman affirmed presidential dominance of foreign affairs when he said in 1948, "I make American foreign policy." In 1799, John Marshall, then a member of the House of Representatives, described the presidency as "the sole organ of the nation in its external relations, and its sole representative with foreign nations."[12] Marshall's statement accurately describes the President's role. The Supreme Court has repeatedly affirmed his primacy in foreign affairs. Justice Sutherland commented that the President has not only specific constitutional and statutory authority in these matters but also "the very delicate plenary and exclusive power of the President as the sole organ of the federal government in the field of international relations."[13]

The President has the top job in foreign affairs because he is Com-

[12] Quoted in Corwin, *The President: Office and Powers,* p. 216.
[13] *United States v. Curtiss-Wright Export Corporation,* 299 U.S. 304 (1936).

mander in Chief and has constitutional authority to make treaties, appoint diplomatic representatives, and recognize foreign governments. Checks on these formal powers are not very significant. The Senate must confirm his major appointments and the House retains the power of the purse. Congress may also pass laws that affect foreign policy.

These checks have not substantially interfered with presidential actions. Although Senate concurrence in treaties may be withheld or qualified, only eleven proposed treaties have been completely rejected. The most famous was the Treaty of Versailles, rejected in 1920 mostly because of fears about United States entry into the League of Nations. The Senate may also alter or amend the provisions of proposed treaties, thus requiring resubmission to other parties to the agreement. Such actions have been frequent since the end of World War II. For example, in 1946 the Senate added reservations to its approval of United States participation in the International Court of Justice.

The *executive agreement* has given Presidents a way of avoiding formal congressional concurrence in proposed treaties. An executive agreement — between the President and the head of a foreign state — does not require approval of either house of Congress. The President as chief executive can make executive agreements because of indirect constitutional powers or authority granted by Congress. In 1940, fifty United States destroyers were exchanged for long-term leases to naval bases on British territory by executive agreement based on presidential powers. International postal agreements and American participation in a number of international associations are also statute-based executive agreements. About two-thousand executive agreements were concluded between 1940 and 1972.

Since World War II, large appropriations for foreign aid and defense have increased the power of the purse. Presidents have defended requests for foreign aid, consisting primarily of economic and military assistance programs, as "essential" to American foreign policy. Congress has supported these requests but not without close scrutiny. The President must mobilize bipartisan support for these appropriations and must bargain with powerful Congressmen such as Representative Otto E. Passman, chairman of the House Subcommittee on Foreign Operations Appropriations. As a leading opponent of foreign aid, Passman has consistently succeeded in cutting presidential requests.

## foreign policymaking: the political context

The President's political importance in foreign affairs overshadows his formal, legal status as chief arbiter of foreign policy. The tone is set for his leadership by "national interest," which is more evident here than

in domestic policy. His control of information and communications with
other nations and his symbolic position as representative of the nation
enable him to define the "national interest" for both the nation and the
international community. Other nations recognize the President as the
sole spokesman for the nation, enabling him to define the "national interest"at home. Fewer challenges to the President's primacy are thrown up
by other subsystems in the community in foreign affairs than in domestic
affairs. He is *the* authoritative spokesman for the nation, and although
his actions must take into account criticisms of his policy, no one challenges his right to initiate that policy and set the agenda for debate in
Congress and in the public sector of the community.

To be sure, he is limited, but more by the realities of political relationships than by constitutional limitations. When he defines the "national
interest," he must do no more than the community will accept. Although
he controls information and so can significantly influence public attitudes, he does not always succeed. President Roosevelt tried in the late
1930s to get American opinion to support the British against Nazi Germany, but he failed to overcome strong isolationist sentiments throughout the nation. Only the Japanese attack on Pearl Harbor in 1941 so-
lidified public opinion behind American involvement against both Japan
and Germany. President Johnson's inability to achieve high consensus in
support of his Vietnam policies certainly played a role in his decision
not to become a candidate in 1968.

Each President inherits his predecessors' policies and finds that changing their direction is very difficult and slow. Commitments made to other
nations are not easily broken. Dwight Eisenhower's campaign promise in
1952 to shift American policy from "negative" containment of Communist advances to "positive" emphasis on the "liberation" of areas behind
the iron curtain failed to materialize. President Nixon's visit to Communist China in 1972, aimed at reducing tensions between the two nations,
was carefully reported by the White House to avoid suggesting that
American support of Nationalist China was being abandoned.

President Truman's remark "I make foreign policy" is, then, still an
accurate statement of the presidential role, if the political limits of his
choices are understood. The President will be effective in foreign affairs,
as in his other duties, only if he gets and keeps support from many interests. Congress has control of appropriations, power to investigate, and the
right to criticize, and so commands the President's respect when he
chooses alternatives. He must also weigh the opinions of other national
leaders — friendly, unfriendly, or neutral — in assessing American goals
and actions in international matters. He deals with international treaty
organizations — the North American Treaty Organization, the Southeast
Asia Treaty Organization, and the United Nations — and he heads a nation whose domestic programs are closely related to foreign affairs. Eco-

President Nixon confers with Chairman Mao Tse-tung and Premier Chou En-lai in
Peking, 1972. The President defines
the "national interest" for both the domestic and foreign communities.

nomic or social crises at home may shake the confidence of leaders of
other nations in his ability to lead the free world. Conversely, whatever
he does in exercising his international leadership may well affect his
ability to maintain his support at home.

The President's alternatives in dealing with other nations are conditioned by long-standing domestic ideology as well as public opinion. The
American experience has produced ideological public support for political and moral ideals based on liberal democratic concepts such as the
right to self-government and basic individual rights and freedoms. Americans have felt comfortable in claiming leadership of the free world and
in accepting a foreign policy aimed at combating communism. Although
American involvement in Southeast Asia was defended as an obligation
to meet our "moral commitments" to non-Communist peoples, *opposition*
to this involvement has been based on feelings that traditional American
democratic and moral values were being ignored.

Just how public opinion reacts to foreign policy decisions is difficult to
assess. Studies have shown that most Americans are uninterested in and
not knowledgeable about foreign policy issues. Less than 15 percent are
classified as "attentive," meaning well-informed, articulate, and interested. Gabriel Almond has found, however, that the public as a whole
has a foreign policy "mood"; that is, a combination of very general attitudes or predispositions.[14] The predominantly isolationist mood in the

[14] Gabriel Almond, *The American People and Foreign Policy* (New York: Harcourt Brace
Jovanovich, 1950).

1930s and the fear and hostility toward communism in the 1950s certainly limited the policy alternatives available to Presidents. The scope of public involvement in foreign affairs enlarges in crisis situations and tends to produce opinion consensus, a fact that also reduces the options available to the President.

To manage all these interests and to arrive at a long-range foreign policy depend more on a President's ability to persuade and to bargain than on his ability to command a course of action. Above all, his control over the nation's foreign affairs is political, not constitutional. Enhanced and also limited by constitutional provisions, the shape and substance of foreign policy are formed by the political environment.

# legislative leadership

The President gets his power in legislative affairs mostly from the development of his office, and less from constitutional grants. Article II enjoins him to provide Congress with information in a State of the Union Address and special messages, authorizes him to call special sessions of Congress "on extraordinary occasions," and permits him to set adjournment dates whenever the two houses cannot agree on one. He also has the power of the veto over legislation. Within ten days of receiving a bill, he may sign it into law, allow it to become law without his signature, or return it to Congress with a message stating his reasons for vetoing it. If Congress adjourns within the ten days, he may exercise the so-called pocket veto by simply failing to sign the bill. (Congress cannot override this type of veto by a two-thirds vote of both houses.) Presidents have vetoed 2,277 bills, up to mid-1971, almost half of them (1,137) in the past six administrations. Congress has been able to override only 3 percent of the vetoes and only 2.3 percent of those exercised by the last six Presidents.[15] We do not know how many times a presidential *threat* of veto has prevented congressional action on legislation, but this threat has often induced Congress to comply with presidential wishes.

The President is much more influential in legislative matters than his formal powers indicate. This power has been formed by the development of the office, especially during this century. Speaking and acting as representatives of a national constituency, Presidents have seized the initiative in proposing legislative policy and guiding it through Congress. Woodrow Wilson broke tradition by delivering a special message asking for currency-reform legislation. Franklin D. Roosevelt sent a message to Congress in 1942 saying in effect that if Congress did not pass price-and wage-control legislation by a date he specified, he himself would estab-

---

[15] *Congressional Quarterly's Guide to the Congress,* p. 583.

lish such controls by executive order. The tact, vigor, and style of a President are crucial factors in obtaining major legislation. For example, President Johnson's proposal for voting rights legislation in 1965 followed national shock and outrage over the treatment of civil rights marchers in Selma, Alabama. This time, the mood in Congress and the President's vigor together brought about major legislation giving further protection to the right to vote.

Techniques introduced by such strong Presidents as Wilson and Franklin Roosevelt are the common stock of their successors. When they are not used, people complain about lack of presidential leadership. Cries of "dictatorship" directed at a strong President are not uncommon, but the public usually sees in them political rhetoric rather than responsible criticism.

Legislative leadership is not synonymous with dominance of Congress. A President may utilize his prestige, powers of persuasion, and his formal powers to achieve his goals. He is, on the other hand, limited by the institutional, social, and constitutional pluralism of the system. Congress is jealous of its constitutional mandate to legislate, so Presidents must bargain within these limits; and their success depends on their tactics and the strength of their party in Congress. However, both Congress and the public still expect that he will initiate most of the legislative policy proposals.

## partisan leadership

Unlike his other responsibilities, the President's leadership of his party is not imposed by the Constitution. Political parties were the conscious creations of politicians like Hamilton, Madison, and Jefferson, and were designed specifically to support presidential commands and persuasions. Party loyalty has served well in supporting presidential leadership.

The President's connection with his party contributes to his outlook on public policy. Certainly the process of his selection as the party standard bearer and, later, the election campaign influence his behavior as President. The campaign is a testing ground for his leadership. His capacity for organization, decision, bargaining, command, and persuasion are revealed under pressure; from the campaign we also find out what he thinks of American political sentiments.

## politics of presidential nominations

Winning the presidency is the goal of both major parties. It follows that a candidate for nomination must be able to convince his party that his qualifications and appeal to voters are superior to those of all other candidates. Specifically, he must convince a majority of delegates to the national party convention. An incumbent president has little difficulty in doing so; in this century no incumbent who wanted it has been denied renomination. The nomination may be sought by several major contenders, whose strategy must include deciding on which state primaries to enter, how to win delegates selected by state party conventions, and when to bargain, negotiate, and accommodate the demands of opposing groups.

Professors Polsby and Wildavsky suggest that convention delegates generally share these desires: "to gain power, to nominate a man who can win the election, to unify the party, to obtain some claim on the nominee, to protect their central core of policy preferences, and to strengthen their state party organizations."[16] What type of men have met, or have come close to meeting these demands? Until the 1960s, the successful nominee would have been a governor from one of the more populous states of the North, a Protestant of Anglo-Saxon origin whose family and personal life were unimpeachable, who appealed to broad economic and political interests within his party.

The nominees of the 1960s and 1970s changed the pattern. None of five presidential candidates (Nixon was nominated three times) from 1960 through 1972 was a state governor. Lyndon Johnson succeeded to the presidency in 1963 after a distinguished Senate career and service as Vice-President. Richard Nixon was a Senator and Vice-President before winning the nomination in 1960.[17] Hubert Humphrey followed the same career as Nixon and was reelected to the Senate after his defeat in 1968. John F. Kennedy, Barry M. Goldwater, and George McGovern were serving in the Senate when they were nominated.

Other changes in nominees included John F. Kennedy, a Catholic, who won the Democratic party nomination in 1960 despite the convictions of some party leaders that a Catholic could not be elected President. The political careers of Humphrey and Goldwater strongly identified them with wings in their parties — Humphrey (1968) as a liberal closely associated with the goals of organized labor, and Goldwater (1964) as a conservative with strong ties to business interests. Humphrey (Minnesota), McGovern (South Dakota), and Goldwater (Arizona) came from states with comparatively few electoral votes. In fact *all* the major candidates for the Democratic nomination in 1968 and 1972 were from states without large numbers of electoral votes. One geographical restriction continues

[16] Nelson W. Polsby and Aaron B. Wildavsky, *Presidential Elections*, 3rd ed. (New York: Charles Scribner's Sons, 1971), pp. 121–122.

[17] Until the nomination of Richard Nixon in 1960, no *incumbent* Vice-President had been nominated as a presidential candidate since Martin Van Buren's nomination in 1843.

to operate. Southerners are not likely to be nominated. Lyndon Johnson of Texas was from the South, but by succeeding to the presidency his claim to the Democratic nomination in 1964 was supreme.

Two crucial decisions on strategy face candidates for their party's presidential nomination: How many presidential primaries should they enter and how can they get maximum support for the candidacy in states that do not use the primary to select delegates or in which primaries do not bind delegates who are selected?

### presidential primaries

States and territories choose their delegates to the national conventions either in primary elections or in conventions. In 1972, twenty-three states, the District of Columbia, and the Virgin Islands held primaries to select delegates. States differ in the extent to which their delegates are bound or pledged to vote for a presidential candidate. Some bind delegates who are selected to vote for the winning candidate in the presidential prefer- ence poll; others permit delegate slates on the primary ballot that are either pledged or unpledged to vote for a candidate. Most of the eighteen states that hold presidential primaries also simultaneously hold a *presidential preference poll* separate from the selection of convention delegates.

States also differ in their way of getting a candidate's name on the ballot. Consent by the candidate is required in six primaries. In other states, a name may be placed on the ballot by designated state officials on the basis that the candidate is nationally recognized or his candidacy is generally advocated. In some states, an unwilling candidate may with- draw his name; but in others, he must sign an affidavit that he is not a candidate for President.

The decision to enter a state's primary may be crucial for a candidate. If he lacks wide support among party leaders, he may choose the pri- maries to demonstrate his popular appeal. John F. Kennedy did so in 1960 to overcome fears among party leaders that his Catholicism would bar his election. His victory in heavily Protestant West Virginia helped estab- lish him as a strong vote-getter throughout the nation. Vice-President Richard Nixon chose to enter all the Republican primaries in 1960 but for a quite different reason. Generally conceded the clear Republican choice for nomination, he faced no serious opposition but thought of the primaries as an opportunity to show that he was not taking the presiden- tial nomination for granted.[18] He repeated this strategy in 1968, again run-

---

[18] Richard M. Nixon, *Six Crises* (Garden City, N.Y.: Doubleday, 1962), pp. 308–309.

ning unopposed after his major primary opponent, George Romney, withdrew from the race.

Although important to all candidates, primary victories may be of little practical value to a candidate. Estes Kefauver ran unopposed in the 1952 primaries because other potential Democratic candidates were reluctant to oppose popular Dwight Eisenhower, the likely Republican nominee. Kefauver's victories were considered of even less value because he lacked support among Democratic party leaders, who preferred Adlai Stevenson.

Eugene McCarthy entered the Democratic primaries in 1968 to convince party leaders that his opposition to the Vietnam War had wide grass-roots support. Despite an impressive record in the primaries, McCarthy lost the nomination to Hubert Humphrey who had several primary successes of his own and was supported by state party leaders. Though Barry Goldwater's primary campaigns in 1964 were dotted with failures he marched steadily toward the Republican nomination assisted by a narrow victory in the crucial California primary.

The Democratic primaries in 1972 were strategically unavoidable for the major contenders because no one was supposed to be strong enough to win without showing evidence of voter appeal. Senator Edmund Muskie, identified by the press as the clear front-runner before the primaries, announced that he would enter almost all of them. He not only had to stretch his campaigning rather thin but made a poor showing in the important early primaries, throwing voter appeal in doubt. George McGovern had no such support from the party organization as Muskie and Humphrey had, so a strong primary effort was essential. Victory in the important Wisconsin primary established McGovern as a serious contender; and even though his record in other primaries was not spectacular, he became identified as a candidate with broad voter appeal.

Future candidates other than incumbent Presidents probably will be unable to avoid entering at least some of the important primaries. But the practical consequences will be no less variable for each candidate. As with Muskie, the front-runner risks most because his opponents and some supporters as well will interpret poor showings as a sign of weak voter appeal. If he wins several major contests, however, he reinforces his claim for party leadership.

### are primaries more representative?

The divisive struggle between Hubert Humphrey and Eugene McCarthy for the Democratic nomination in 1968 raised much criticism of the convention system for not representing the preferences and sentiments of party rank-and-file in the choice of a nominee. In response, the 1968 Democratic Convention created a Commission on Party Structure and Delegate Selection, chaired until early 1971 by Senator George McGovern. In its report and recommendations in 1970, the commission agreed that the 1968 convention had "exposed profound flaws in the presidential nominating process" and that "meaningful participation of Democratic voters was often difficult or costly, sometimes completely illusory, and, in not a few instances, impossible." Finding that the convention system did not fairly represent blacks, women, and young people and did not accurately represent the preferences of party members on issues and candidates, the commission proposed binding "guidelines" for selection of candidates.[19] Essentially, the rules governing the 1972 convention ensured procedures for selecting delegates that prohibited discrimination against 18-to-30-year-olds, or on the basis of race, color, creed, or national origin.

Many who advocate that the nominating process be reformed assume that the presidential primary is the best device for achieving a more representative system of selecting presidential nominees. Austin Ranney, a member of the McGovern Commission, has raised doubts about this.[20] Using survey data on voter opinions on issues in the 1968 New Hampshire and Wisconsin primaries, intensity of party attachments, and the extent to which voters participate in primaries, Ranney concludes that: (1) people who vote in presidential primaries do not fully represent the opinions and policy preferences of those who do not vote; (2) voters in primaries are demographically unrepresentative of party members who do not vote (that is, participants are older, come from higher social status groups, and are more active in civic, religious, and political organizations); (3) these patterns of unrepresentation are much the same as those found among national convention delegates (at least through 1968) when delegates are compared to their parties' rank-and-file members. Although Ranney warns that these relationships need much closer examination, his findings suggest that it may be wrong to assume that primaries are more "representative" for nominating Presidents.

## winning delegate support: strategy and organization

Because delegates chosen in primaries are not bound to cast their convention votes for the winning primary candidates, the candidates must concentrate on these delegates as well as those selected by party conven-

[19] Commission on Party Structure and Delegate Selection, *Mandate for Reform* (Washington, D.C.: Democratic National Committee, 1970). Quoted material on pp. 9, 10.

[20] Austin Ranney, "Turnout and Representation in Presidential Primary Elections," *The American Political Science Review* 66 (March 1972): pp. 21–37.

tions. Without a smooth-functioning, effective campaign organization these convention votes will be lost. The interim between party conventions affords candidates time to develop and maintain party ties and to build a campaign organization throughout the nation. Normally, presidential candidates wait until about a year before the presidential election to announce their candidacy, but the formation and activity of the campaign organization begins long before. John Kennedy began to work for the Democratic nomination in 1956 after his unsuccessful bid for the vice-presidential nomination in the 1956 convention. Senator Barry Goldwater emerged as a contender for the 1964 nomination at the 1960 Republican convention when he withdrew his name as a possible nominee and admonished conservatives to "get to work" and recapture control of the party. Senator George McGovern's campaign organization was formed about eighteen months prior to his nomination and included key members of John F. Kennedy's 1960 campaign. This strong and effective organization was a decisive factor in McGovern's winning the Democratic nomination in 1972.

Careful attention to a well-financed and professionally run organization also paid off in nomination for Kennedy in 1960, Goldwater in 1964, and Humphrey and Nixon in 1968. The strategy in these efforts is clear. By building a strong communications and intelligence network and by establishing valuable personal contacts, a candidate builds a public personality and also hopes to establish himself as the front-runner for his party's nomination. Because of these preparations, primary defeats may be less injurious since party organization support may be enough to overcome primary setbacks. Since about half of the delegates to the 1972 conventions were chosen by state conventions, the stakes obviously are high. Some candidates must build national recognition and can do so only by cultivating the mass media, fulfilling numerous speaking engagements, making personal visits to party leaders, and other means aimed at making themselves nationally visible.

The policy goals that delegates and party leaders seek are not necessarily the same. A candidate has to build broad support for his candidacy by adjusting differences among delegates, but he must also avoid attacks on his opponents that endanger or destroy party unity. Within this framework, delegate votes become a resource in a bargaining environment. They may be used to win platform concessions, promises for future action (or not), or assurances of consideration in political appointments.

Money is a resource that cannot be overlooked. In the 1972 Illinois primary, Senator Eugene McCarthy spent $250,000 only to lose and Mayor John Lindsay spent $180,000 in an unsuccessful Florida "media blitz."[21] These sums are modest compared with the funds available to

---

[21] *Newsweek* (April 3, 1972), pp. 21–22.

leading contenders. In March 1972, four months before the Democratic convention, Senator Muskie released the names of 13,982 persons who contributed more than $2 million to his campaign. Senator McGovern spent more than $5 million in his successful campaign for the nomination and Governor George Wallace reported almost $1 million in contributions and funds raised by campaign activities. Clearly, a candidate for nomination must have financial resources to effectively wage increasingly expensive nomination campaigns.

## the convention phase

Nomination culminates in the national convention. Each step of the proceedings — the report of the Credentials Committee and seating delegates, selecting temporary and permanent convention officers, the report of the Platform Committee, the call for nominations, floor demonstrations, and ultimately the balloting — may be crucial in the conflict over who the party's standard bearer will be.

In the Republican convention of 1952, several southern state delegates who supported Senator Robert A. Taft were challenged. Both the Republican National Committee and the Convention Credentials Committee voted to seat these delegates despite opposition by Eisenhower supporters. Ultimately, the Eisenhower forces succeeded in getting the issue to the convention floor where they were (correctly) confident of winning reversal of prior decisions. Dramatic proof that convention rules and procedures are vital could be seen at the 1972 Democratic Convention. A critical issue was exposed when the Credentials Committee ruled that California's 271 delegates — won by Senator George McGovern in a winner-take-all presidential primary — would have to be apportioned among McGovern and Senator Hubert Humphrey, according to the proportion of the primary vote received by each candidate. McGovern lost 151 delegates. At the same time, the Committee denied seats to fifty-eight Illinois delegates controlled by Mayor Richard Daley of Chicago, a Humphrey supporter. The Credentials Committee ruled that, although the delegates had been selected in a primary, the delegate-candidates in the primary had been chosen in a manner that violated Democratic party rules.

Senator McGovern went to court but lost the legal battle when the United States Supreme Court, following a hastily called special session, ruled that the issue had to be decided by the convention and not by the judiciary. A bitter convention floor battle was resolved by seating the challenged McGovern delegates from California. The Credentials Committee decision on the fifty-eight Illinois delegates was also upheld. McGovern's victory in both struggles was crucial: Senators Humphrey and Muskie both withdrew from the race for the nomination, thus assuring McGovern's nomination.

Platform provisions can cause serious disagreement; the Democratic platform statement on the Vietnam War in the 1968 convention did so. These disputes may also indicate the relative strength of candidates. In 1964, the Goldwater forces in the Republican convention proved strong enough to resist all efforts by less conservative forces to alter the Goldwater-dominated platform.

If the party is to be a useful tool supplying the presidential candidate later with tactics of persuasion and command, he must be assured that his nomination has not damaged that task. A nominating campaign filled with rancor, a convention struggle over seating delegates, or arguments about platform provisions may spawn lukewarm partisans, as it did for the Republicans in 1964 (Goldwater), the Democrats in 1968 (Humphrey), and the Democrats again in 1972 (McGovern).

The balloting for nomination in the convention is also part of the strategy. Polsby and Wildavsky point out that the front-runner at the convention must win an early victory or his chances decline rapidly. If victory does not come on the first or second ballot opposing candidates may convince the leader's supporters that their candidate has peaked and their votes should be switched to another candidate.[22] Keeping a strong front-runner from winning on an early ballot is a slender hope. In the twelve conventions from 1928 to 1972, the Democrats have nominated their candidate on the first ballot ten times. In 1932 and 1952 (four and three ballots respectively), no incumbent President was a candidate for renomination. The Republican pattern is similar: only twice, in 1940 and 1948 (six and three ballots) did the nomination go beyond the first ballot. Even when early nomination is not assured by the time the convention meets, it seems that bargaining among party leaders produces an early victor. The bargain may include choosing a vice-presidential candidate, a traditional way of producing party harmony, and a method for strengthening the appeal of the party ticket. Vice-presidential candidates have been chosen from an opposing wing of the party (Lyndon Johnson in 1960) or they may be picked to appeal to a geographical area, "balancing the ticket." (Spiro Agnew was chosen by Nixon in 1968 because of his acceptability to southerners.) When a candidate feels sure of victory, however, he may refuse to accept a vice-presidential nominee from the opposing wing of the party, as Goldwater did in 1964.

The unprecedented withdrawal of Thomas Eagleton as the Democratic vice-presidential candidate in 1972 was forced by press disclosure that Eagleton had been hospitalized three times during the 1960s for nervous

---

[22] Polsby and Wildavsky, *Presidential Elections*, p. 147.

exhaustion and had undergone electric shock treatment. Senator McGovern's decision to recommend to the Democratic National Committee that Sargent Shriver replace Eagleton followed McGovern's conclusion that the disadvantages of Eagleton's medical history outweighed the advantages of having a Catholic border-state (Missouri) Senator as a running mate.

The convention thus is more than an instrument for formally choosing the party leadership. It can smooth over differences within the party and rally the party faithful for the election's struggle. Also, it may reflect the passing of party control from one party group to another. Many heralded the choice of McGovern in 1972 as wresting control from "old-style" Democratic liberals by reform-minded "new politics" Democrats.

If the party candidate is elected President, he assumes both party and national leadership. Party choice, as revealed in the struggle for nomination, is directed by considerations of costs and benefits in pursuing strategies for nomination: bargaining gets support by the delegate, assurances of party unity if the nomination is won, and representation for diverse party and electoral interests in shaping the image and policy positions of the next President.

## partisanship and presidential goals

A President can carry out his foreign or domestic programs only if he wins and keeps the support of the coalition that elected him to office. His party's nationwide success depends on the quality of his leadership and the support his programs get within Congress and the electorate. A highly popular President is a distinct asset to party candidates at other levels, and party fortunes rise and fall with his success. Thus, Congressmen of his party have a significant stake in strengthening the public's favorable image of the President; it is a good way of improving their own chances of electoral success.

A President has partisan controls of his own, some overt and others created by changing patterns in party politics that enhance his bargaining position. The overt type stems from the President's power to dispense patronage and political favors of all kinds. The second type results from the steadily increasing strategic power of the President as the national leader. The increasing nationalization of politics is reflected in the presidential technique of appealing to the public at large to mobilize opinion on behalf of his program and to pressure members of both parties in Congress. Thus, presidential leadership can counteract the localism of legislators and the recalcitrance of local party leaders and organizations.

The President has yet another resource for exercising party leadership:

President Johnson with Minority Leader Everett Dirksen. The President cannot be an extreme partisan without soldifying opposition. At times he must seek the opposition's support in order to pursue his programs.

the "presidential party," a group that helps him shape and execute his program. Its nucleus is made up of the President's staff and several Cabinet heads, most or all of whom have been highly active in his nomination and campaign efforts. Members of Franklin Roosevelt's so-called "brain trust" occupied key positions in his administration and helped to formulate New Deal policy. Lyndon B. Johnson surrounded himself with advisers and Cabinet members sympathetic to his "Great Society" program.

The Executive Office of the President now includes the White House Office, the Office of Management and Budget, the Office of Emergency Planning, the Central Intelligence Agency, the Council on Environmental Quality, the Office of Science and Technology, and six other units. All give him information and assistance in formulating policy. Staffed by presidential appointees chosen for their ability to contribute to presidential programs, the Executive Office makes policy far removed from the influence of interests that operate in the legislative branch. Often the interests which enjoy access to these agencies are the ones that most closely represent the center of the presidential party.

The political party that the President leads, however, is fragmented in organization and leadership, so he is limited in providing direction for the congressional party and commanding support from it. Legislative alignments typically reflect party lines and presidential partisanship, but they do so imperfectly, so that it is commonplace for some legislators of the President's party to refuse to vote for one of his major programs. Legislators have found their problems with their local constituency modified, but by no means displaced, by the nationalizing trend in politics.

To get his programs through, a President often has to depend on the votes of opposition party members in Congress. He cannot appear to be an extreme partisan or he risks solidifying the opposition and defeating his program. When he does pursue partisan ends, he is expected to refrain from putting too much pressure on his own party's Congressmen and to recognize that congressional constituency interests must sometimes be given preference over presidential demands.

The President, in short, must balance the interests of the major party groups that make demands upon him. He must satisfy interests both as party leader and as President of all the people. He cannot look like a blind partisan who seeks narrow goals nor can he be indifferent to partisan demands. He must adjust his use of the great resources available to him to the decentralized and diverse American party system, but he must also keep the support of the coalition of voter groups that put him into office.

## conceptions of the presidency

The President who is aware of the varied and conflicting demands made upon him considers those demands in the light of his own image of the office. Richard Neustadt, both adviser to Presidents and student of presidential politics, identifies five major presidential constituencies, each of which makes different claims upon the President's time, energy, and influence: the administrative bureaucracy, Congress, fellow partisans, the general citizenry, and foreign groups. Each depends on him for benefits but does not always support him in exchange. His bureaucratic clients and congressional allies have their own constituencies and interests to represent. The demands his partisan friends present are usually narrower than he can accept without compromise. Community leaders may go somewhere other than Washington for help. And, Neustadt concludes, "friends abroad are not compelled to run in our elections."[23]   Each Pres-

---

[23] Neustadt, *Presidential Power*, p. 8.

ident must define his own part in our diversified political community. Building support for a policy that reflects his own goals he gradually moves closer to some constituents, alienating others. He will respond to some community conflicts and pay little attention to others. Many of the pressures he encounters are of his own making to the extent that, in defining his role, he chooses the areas of conflict from which demands will come.

Knowing what he ought to do and can do depends on the President's concept of the office. Professor Corwin, describing the background of the presidency as "a history of aggrandizement," shows how the office developed under five major personalities: Jackson, Lincoln, Wilson, and the two Roosevelts. These men all used well a keen sense of history, circumstances, and timing to achieve their goals; and each had a clear idea of the presidential role. Theodore Roosevelt's theory of presidential powers is useful today in describing the "strong" President; he called it the "residuum of powers" theory:

> I insisted upon the theory that the executive power was limited only by specific restrictions and prohibitions appearing in the Constitution or imposed by Congress under its Constitutional powers. My view was that every executive officer, and above all, every executive officer in high position, was a steward of the people bound actively and affirmatively to do all he could for the people, and not content himself with the negative merit of keeping his talents undamaged in a napkin. . . . I did not care a rap for the mere form and show of power; I cared immensely for the use that could be made of the substance.[24]

President Hoover's contrasting approach was more in harmony with strict constitutional edict. Although he modified his views toward the end of his term, Hoover's style reflected a strong moral and legal commitment to formal limits on power, buttressed by an equally strong belief in "American individualism." He felt that the "executive" must not encroach on the "independence of the legislative army," and he confessed that he had "little taste for forcing Congressional action or engaging in battles of criticism."[25] Although he exercised the veto, he disapproved of using it to defeat congressional will or force legislative action into desired channels; rather, the veto was to be used to protect the fundamentals of the Constitution.

Hoover's perspective and that of Franklin Roosevelt contrast strikingly. Roosevelt believed that a President must be "alert and sensitive

---

[24] Theodore Roosevelt, *An Autobiography* (New York: Charles Scribner's Sons, 1946), p. 35.
[25] Herbert C. Hoover, *Memoirs, the Cabinet and the Presidency, 1920–1933* (New York: Macmillan, 1952), p. 217.

Federal troops compel integration in Little Rock, Arkansas, 1955. Executive action
may be used to enforce policy initiated by the judiciary.

to change." He forcefully used the prerogatives and the prestige of the
presidency to lead the nation to ends he thought desirable. Roosevelt's
biographers have agreed that he thoroughly enjoyed exercising leadership. According to Neustadt, "he saw the job of being President as being
F.D.R. He wanted mastery, projected that desire on the office and fulfilled it there with every sign of feeling he had come into his
own."[26])

Whether, like Dwight Eisenhower, a President has a "dislike for the
rough and tumble" of politics[27] or, like Harry Truman, he knows that he
must be "constantly on top of events, or . . . events will soon be on top of
him,"[28] a President must exercise the initiative in policy. The public has
come to expect the President to exercise more and more policy leadership, cutting into or perhaps even making impossible strong congressional initiative in policy formulation. The President acts and Congress
is forced to react, and this relationship shows little sign of change.

[26] Neustadt, *Presidential Power*, p. 162.
[27] Nelson W. Polsby, *Congress and the Presidency* (Englewood Cliffs, N.J.: Prentice-Hall,
1964), pp. 20–21.
[28] Harry S Truman, *Memoirs: Years of Trial and Hope*, vol. 2 (Garden City, N.Y.: Doubleday, 1956), p. 1.

No occupant of the White House can escape the demand for action as he faces almost continuous crises. He may not act just as he wants, but has to choose among realistic alternatives determined by his limited power and resources.

## the president and policy choice

Whether a President is thrust into policy conflict by force of circumstance or whether he deliberately initiates policy disputes, he "must always be setting priorities and measuring costs."[29] His choices are limited by the resources he can command as opposed to the interests in conflict. The decision he finally makes will be based on the data he has, immeasurable factors such as hunches, and sheer conviction that one alternative is "right" and others "wrong."

## flow of information and policy choice

As representative of all the people, a President must be sensitive to demands that reach the White House from all sectors of the electorate, but the breadth of the interests that seek access to him means a policy that pleases one group will be anathema to another. They may seek access to Congress and often to the courts, though, and sometimes get there what a reluctant or opposing President refuses to give. His power to initiate policy is no guarantee that he will have his way.

A President is not master of all around him. He depends on those closest to him for information and advice; and although he can seek it whenever he wishes, both time and his style of leadership limit how far he can go in the search for information. He communicates information as well as receiving it. How he communicates, to whom, and when are of great importance. His decisions, reflecting broad or particular interests, will produce confidence and support among other decisionmakers and the public.

The Pentagon Papers controversy of 1971 was thought of as a crisis of confidence, since the information these documents revealed raised questions about where several Presidents got their advice and how much information had been kept from Congress and the public or whether they had been deliberately deceived. Although a President must choose, he

---

[29] Theodore C. Sorenson, *Decision-Making in the White House* (New York: Columbia University Press, 1963), p. 28.

does so in part as a leader limited by the need for decision and in the isolation resulting from dependency on those around him with whom he chooses to consult and communicate. The Pentagon Papers controversy also revealed the potential hazards faced by a President who ignores the public's right to know.

## sources of information and policy choice

Pressure-group goals and demands are seldom presented directly to the President. He listens carefully to selected legislators, especially those in key positions, and to Cabinet heads and other major executive officials, who may act as a channel for various social interests. Party leaders and the press also provide contacts for the President and put pressure on him too.

Conflicts may arise within the President's own circle of advisers or within the bureaucracy, forcing him to decide between the interests represented. The State and Treasury Departments sometimes fundamentally disagree on the proper approach to world trade; the Defense Department and the State Department may see matters affecting foreign policy quite differently; and the Agriculture Department and the Bureau of the Budget may look on farm subsidy programs from entirely different perspectives. The President must bridge all such conflicts, which lie far beyond the boundaries of the administrative hierarchy and involve interest groups at many levels.

Some Presidents go out of their way to get close advisers to clash so they will hear all points of view before making a policy choice. Franklin Roosevelt delighted in stirring up the strong convictions of his very diverse subordinates. Dwight Eisenhower preferred that his advisers present him with one policy that he could accept or reject. Roosevelt's approach provided several perspectives on policy issues, but it also carried controversies beyond the point of presidential decision, potentially weakening the policy position both inside and outside the executive branch. Eisenhower's style limited his perspectives but also produced recommendations that reflected the need for compromise among diverse views.

Presidential decisionmaking is continuous, ranging from the routine to decisions carrying profound consequences. Some are "programmed" in that they cannot be avoided or delayed, such as nominations of Supreme Court justices, Cabinet officers, and other officials. The preparing and presenting of the budget and the State of the Union Address are fixed by the Constitution and statutes. Most decisions are not on this kind of

timetable. Some, such as the need to respond quickly to Soviet missile
bases in Cuba in 1962, demand immediate action. Others, such as the
question of American policy in Vietnam, are long debated within and
outside of the executive branch. Others are initiated by Presidents themselves. President Kennedy pressed the attack on poverty during the campaign of 1960 and proposed extensive legislation to deal with it after he
entered the White House. As the presidency has grown in prestige and
prerogatives, more conflicts have gravitated toward that office. The President finds that he cannot have free choice in selecting the conflicts that
he will attend to.

He can, however, exercise some control by timing his response. He
may wait until he feels that the moment is right for maximizing his preferences. President Nixon was under strong pressure to act on the busing
of public school children long before he did act in March 1972. His proposals came in a climate of opinion that was highly receptive to his proposal that forced busing of children be ended or strongly limited.

## planning the president's program

Under continuing pressure to make decisions, a President also works to
get his policy goals formulated — and his program implemented. A wide
assortment of agencies and a group of hand-picked advisers help him.

The presidential institution is a vast array of agencies, offices, bureaus,
special advisers, and committees. Many people in the administrative hierarchy look on policy matters through the interests of the agencies they
represent. To remain above such narrow interests and to serve the aims
of the bureaucracy he heads and is responsible for, the President needs
a staff of advisers who are close to and loyal to him and serve him alone.
From whom does a President seek assistance in coordinating administrative interests, and how does he use his staff?

### the cabinet

The Cabinet developed as an extraconstitutional body to "consult" with
the President. Some Presidents have treated it as an important policymaking body; others have used it as a means of gathering information
by means of reports, discussions, and debates on major issues. The common estimate of the Cabinet as the board of directors of the nation or
the President's major source of advice on policy formulation is mistaken.
Richard F. Fenno stresses that the Cabinet does not coordinate relations
between executive departments and that it is an effective forum for

"well-informed, well-organized discussion of policy alternatives." Its principal uses include advising the President and serving as a sounding board for a variety of alternatives that are suggested by competing interests.[30]

A President cannot regularly rely on the Cabinet because he has to choose many of his department heads to satisfy his external political needs instead of his need for close friends and advisers. President Kennedy named Douglas Dillon, a highly respected Republican businessman who had served in the Eisenhower administration, as Secretary of the Treasury. Robert C. Weaver, appointed by President Johnson to head the new Department of Housing and Urban Development, was the first Negro in a Cabinet post. President Nixon chose as his Secretary of the Treasury a conservative Democrat, John Connally. The administrative or legislative experience of the appointee or the need to mollify an opposing faction within the party also may determine a President's selection of Cabinet members.

The pluralistic pulls of American politics also work against the functioning of the Cabinet as a collective body with collective responsibility. As the head of a major executive department, each Cabinet member inevitably concentrates on the special needs and quasi-autonomous politics of his own department. The Secretary of such "service" departments as Commerce, Labor, or Agriculture is caught among conflicting interests. His departmental bureaucracy and the outside interests his department serves expect him to represent them, but the President expects him (according to the model of collective Cabinet responsibility) to rise above such parochialism. If he comes too close to the latter, he will alienate his own constituency and soon will be an ineffective department head. No occupant of the White House could bear such a cost. Little wonder, then, that Presidents are both unable and unwilling to rely on the Cabinet, and instead selectively use individual Cabinet members and a variety of non-Cabinet personnel for continuing advice and counsel.

All Presidents have had unofficial cabinets. President Jackson was the first to draw advice and counsel from a small group of close advisers who helped him win the presidency, who reportedly entered the White House through the kitchen door, earning the popular name "Kitchen Cabinet." Franklin Roosevelt gathered a small group headed by Harry Hopkins, former social worker and long a confidant. President Nixon has relied on a few close advisers such as Henry Kissinger, his special adviser in foreign affairs.

[30] Richard F. Fenno, Jr., *The President's Cabinet* (Cambridge, Mass.: Harvard University Press, 1959), p. 20.

### the white house staff

Besides the Cabinet, about five thousand people, many of them specialists of one kind or another, make up the President's staff. The chief executive's personal staff in the White House forms his eyes and ears. The press secretary, the appointments secretary, and the staff members assigned for liaison with members of Congress have clearly defined duties. The remainder serve in whatever capacity the President desires. Chosen for their loyalty to the President as well as their ability to perform essential services, the White House staff members assist him by gathering information, reading the sentiments of Congressmen, bureaucrats, and the public, and serving as instruments in formulating and carrying out his program. Since the White House Office was formed in 1939, journalists have paid more attention to the men around the President, his way of using them and how much responsibility he delegates to them.

President Nixon confers with
Henry Kissinger. Recent Presidents
have relied heavily on special
advisers. The boundary between
using staff as an aid and delegating
to it a policymaking role must be
guarded by the President.

A President sometimes relies heavily on an aide, as Woodrow Wilson did in his especially close relationship with Colonel Edward M. House, who represented the President in important domestic and foreign assignments. President Nixon's great trust in Henry Kissinger has pushed Secretary of State William Rogers into a secondary position in formulating and executing foreign policy. Such associations surround the President with a dilemma — he has to maintain the line between using his staff as an aid and delegating to it the authority to *make* policy choices. The boundary must be guarded by the President

## the office of management and budget

One of the major agencies in the Executive Office, the OMB is appointed by the President — Senate consent is not required. The director of OMB is directly responsible for (1) drawing up the budget by reviewing departmental requests for appropriations; (2) controlling the rate of expenditures after Congress has passed on appropriations; (3) clearing executive-agency requests for legislation to see that they conform to the President's program before they are submitted to Congress; (4) studying and recommending changes in the organization and management of executive agencies; and (5) reviewing and improving, with the Treasury Department and the General Accounting Office, financial-management practices.

Recent Presidents have used the OMB in such a way that it is now crucial in executive policymaking. Harry S Truman had it prepare a comprehensive and integrated legislative program. Under President Eisenhower, the OMB, assisted by key personnel in the White House staff, coordinated the proposals of all federal agencies in preparing a thoroughly defined and complete legislative program. Formulating a comprehensive presidential policy package will almost certainly become an institutional pattern.[31] For coordinating administrative interests and programs, the OMB's review of budget requests is invaluable. It provides a centralizing influence to counter the separation built into the semiautonomous policy coalitions that form around executive bureaus and congressional committees. Congressional leaders, mindful of this threat, periodically reveal OMB attempts to "strangle" the initiative and discretion of executive policy formulators. Congress complained in 1971 that the Nixon administration's refusal to spend $13 billion for domestic programs (the funds had been impounded by President Nixon) violated the

[31] Richard E. Neustadt, "Presidency and Legislation: Planning the President's Program," *The American Political Science Review* 59 (Dec. 1955): 980–1021.

separation-of-powers principle. Some Congressmen felt that this type of action, also used by the four previous Presidents, negated or modified laws of Congress. In 1972 the Senate rejected a House-approved bill that would have given President Nixon unrestricted power to cut federal programs in order to keep total spending in 1973 under $250 billion. The Senate majority felt that such power would directly challenge congressional power of the purse under the Constitution.

All executive agencies are not, however, easily subjected to control through the OMB. An agency will respond most readily to the institutional device best able to control its economic life. Is the OMB or is Congress, through its powers of appropriation, best able to exercise such control? The answer to the question depends upon the particular agency. For some, the appropriation requested by the OMB usually prevails or is reduced by appropriations subcommittees of Congress. Thus an agency in this position will view the OMB as not supporting its appropriations goals; and in fact, the OMB does not usually protect them against legislative cuts. Other agencies enjoy quite a different relationship. They have "political clout" with Congress and often are able to win from Congress what the OMB has denied. Because the OMB wants to keep its control over executive agencies it will attempt to win congressional endorsement of its recommendations for the various agencies or at least prevent Congress from increasing recommended spending. The political effect of this orientation is that politically strong agencies can "force" OMB to endorse their requests, but politically weaker agencies are heavily dependent on OMB because they lack access to congressional appropriations subcommittees. A President may find it almost impossible to control programs of agencies he deems less important to his goals, and programs marked with great importance may not win adequate financing from Congress.

## the president and the vice-president

The Vice-President is often said to be superfluous. Constitutionally, his job is presiding over the Senate, which is far less significant than the speakership of the House of Representatives. The Constitution also designates him as successor if the President dies, is removed, resigns, or is unable to discharge his duties.

The Vice-President was an early victim of the American party system. By the early 1800s, vice-presidential candidates were selected less for their presidential potential than for their usefulness in winning sectional or factional support for the presidential candidate. President Truman said he was unaware of the atomic bomb when he succeeded Roosevelt.[32]

The sudden death of President Roosevelt in 1944, the heart attack suffered by President Eisenhower in 1954, and the assassination of President Kennedy in 1963 have made the American public acutely aware that the Vice-President might have to assume the presidency. In 1967, the Twenty-Fifth Amendment was ratified, establishing procedures for determining presidential incapacity and for allowing the Vice-President to act as President during the interim. The President is also empowered to name a Vice-President, subject to approval by a majority vote in both houses of Congress, if that office becomes vacant.

The vice-presidential job has gained public esteem. The occupants have been unusually active in recent administrations. Eisenhower sent Vice-President Nixon on important foreign-policy missions, and had him advise in domestic matters as well. Lyndon Johnson was appointed chairman of President Kennedy's Committee on Equal Employment Opportunity, which increased his contacts with Negro interests and enhanced his political image with minority groups. Vice-President Agnew's overtly partisan role in attacking the press and critics of Nixon's policies let the President act as President and statesman. Because the Vice-President can do little by himself to develop his importance, he depends on the President to determine the meaningfulness, if any, of his role.

The "life of the Crown Prince is likely to be hard."[33] The adoption of the Twenty-Second Amendment, limiting a President to two terms in office, may buoy the political aspirations of the Vice-President, especially if he has been chosen for a second term. But the possibility that the President might choose another running mate after the first term reduces the Vice-President's ability to develop his own image outside the President's shadow. A Vice-President may not be able to maintain an image within the party and among the electorate independent of the President. Vice-President Humphrey, long identified with the liberal wing of his party, was severely criticized by liberals because of his support for President Johnson's Vietnam policies. President Johnson said of the Vice-President: "He's in a difficult place. He has no troops; he has no real power; he's at the mercy of the President."[34] The vice-presidency is still an instrument of the presidency, although recent occupants of the office have been impressive.

[32] Harry S Truman, *Memoirs: Year of Decisions,* vol. 1 (Garden City, N.Y.: Doubleday, 1955), pp. 10–11.

[33] Paul T. David, "The Vice Presidency: Its Institutional Evolution and Contemporary Status," *The Journal of Politics* 26 (Nov. 1967), p. 74.

[34] Transcript, CBS News Special, "LBJ: Lyndon Johnson Talks Politics," CBS Television Network (January 27, 1972), p. 9.

# presidential leadership

The President's power is great. Legal authority has proved flexible enough to permit a vast expansion of presidential action within the prescribed framework. The continually growing sense of national community, enduring political crises, nationalization of politics, popular feeling that the President is *the* leader of America, formal delegations of authority, and ever-broadening presidential notions about their responsibilities have expanded the office.

The President also "wears many chains from which he cannot escape." The same forces that shape his power restrict his ability to act. He is bound by constitutional and policy traditions and is also liberated by them. His constitutional jurisdiction in administrative, military, state, foreign, legislative, and partisan affairs overlap and sometimes collide. With all his limitations, he may find it better to muddle through, to bridge disagreements, exploit controversies, and even avoid rather than reconcile opposing forces. What *must* be left undone today is better put off until tomorrow. For the conflicts he chooses or is forced to grapple with, the President must accept restrictions and do what he can within them. As a leader in making policy, he must persuade because he can seldom command; he must bargain because he cannot coerce. President Truman said, "I sit here all day trying to persuade people to do the things they ought to have sense enough to do without my persuading them. . . . That's all the powers of the President amount to."

The presidency will continue to grow in importance as America grows in complexity and impersonality and the people focus their anxieties and aspirations on the President. It looks unlikely that the modern presidency heralds an end to our most sacred governing principles: separation of powers, checks and balances, and federalism, although that fear is often expressed. Moreover, even if the President does dominate policy leadership, policies must be adopted by Congress before they become the law of the land.

*bibliographical note*

The presidency covers virtually all aspects of American politics. This is abundantly illustrated by histories of the United States as well as day-to-day news stories and commentaries by journalists. For the student who wishes to explore the presidency in more systematic fashion, the following works should prove helpful.

General treatments of the presidency range from Edward S. Corwin's classic and thoroughly documented *The President: Office and Powers,* 4th ed. (New York: New York University Press, 1957) to Richard Neustadt's analytical *Presidential Power* (New York: John Wiley, Science Editions, 1960). Neustadt illustrates the bargaining context in which presidential power can be utilized. Grant McConnell, *The Modern Presidency* (New York: St. Martin's Press, 1967) discusses the presidency from the perspective of the myth and symbol of that great office.

*The Presidency* (Boston: Little, Brown, 1969), edited by Aaron Wildavsky, presents several stimulating interpretations of various aspects of the relationships between the President and the bureaucracy as well as other excellent essays on presidential style, decisionmaking, and leadership. The diffusion of leadership and the difficulties of achieving unity in the executive branch are well presented in Norton Long, "Reflections on Presidential Power," *Public Administration Review,* 29 (Sept.–Oct. 1969) and Chapter 14 of David B. Truman's *The Governmental Process* (New York: Alfred A. Knopf, 1951). Patrick Anderson, *The Presidents' Men* (Garden City, N.Y.: Doubleday, Anchor Books, 1969) presents a highly readable analysis of the backgrounds, roles, and responsibilities of White House assistants from F. D. Roosevelt to Lyndon B. Johnson.

Among the best analyses of the politics of presidential nomination, for both the serious student and the casual reader, is Nelson W. Polsby and Aaron B. Wildavsky, *Presidential Elections,* 3rd ed. (New York: Charles Scribner's Sons, 1971). James W. Davis, *Presidential Primaries: Road to the White House* (New York: Thomas Y. Crowell, 1967) concentrates solely upon presidential primaries and discusses the strengths and weaknesses of this system.

Presidential relationships with Congress and the Courts are well reviewed in Lawrence H. Chamberlain, *The President, Congress and Legislation* (New York: Columbia University Press, 1956) and Glendon Schubert, Jr., *The Presidency in the Courts* (Minneapolis, University of Minnesota Press, 1957). Crises and the range of presidential power is the focus of Cornelius F. Cotter, *Powers of the President During Crises* (Washington, D.C.: Public Affairs Press, 1960).

Autobiographies, biographies, and works on particular Presidents and their administrations provide a "feel" for that office that is difficult to acquire through other reading. The student will appreciate the range and variety of this type of literature by simply examining the card catalogues in any library.

# chapter 13

# how congress
# adopts policies

The chairman of the House Foreign Affairs Committee admonished an administration witness before his committee: "Don't expect us to start from scratch on what you people want. That's not the way we do things here — *you* draft the bills and *we* work them over."[1] The Congressman's remark is striking confirmation that in modern times it is the executive branch and not Congress that leads in initiating legislation. Congress' role, although more disposing than proposing, remains important: it has the power to pass, to modify, or to reject the President's proposals, and so contributes significantly to the management of social conflict.

But neither the President nor Congress makes decisions independently of other forces in the political system. Public policy is a continuing series of decisions, an interplay of interests operating inside and among the three branches. Throughout the system, both formal and informal power relationships reflect the pluralism of the American structures, sustaining bargaining and compromise among conflicting social interests, which is nowhere better illustrated than in the functioning of the legislature.

## policy adoption and patterns of representation

As the most representative branch within the constitutional structure, Congress is the major institutional symbol of the democratic creed. The Framers of the Constitution provided for an executive removed from the

---

[1] Quoted by Richard E. Neustadt, "Presidency and Legislation: Planning the President's Program," *American Political Science Review* 49 (Dec. 1955): 1015.

Although thousands of bills
are introduced
during each session of Congress,
less than 5 percent
ever become law.

direct control of the people and a judiciary that would be independent and insulated. The Constitution formally assigns the enactment of policy to the legislature in Article I. Citizens are integrated into the community by accepting the actions of their representatives — consenting to proposals that become the law of the land.

Congress gives legitimacy to public policy by passing bills and in other ways. Part of the executive's role in adjudicating disputes are based on authority granted by Congress. The President's power to initiate the national budget is based on the Budget and Accounting Act of 1921; the independent regulatory agencies in the administrative branch make rules under authority granted by Congress; and the right of courts to hear appeals is to a large extent based on the action of Congress creating appellate courts and regulating their jurisdiction.

Democratic theory holds that the will of the people (practically speaking, the will of the majority) is to be translated into law by popularly chosen representatives. Some questions show up immediately. How can representatives know what their constituents want? Which system of election best achieves the goal of representing the will of the people? Does the majority's will always have to be followed, or does a "national interest" transcend that will and must it be given preference? On what basis should a legislator decide to cast his vote? Finding answers, or partial answers, to these questions will give us some feeling for the things that affect legislators' behavior and also help us understand how Congress works.

## bias in congressional representation

No method for apportioning representatives is neutral; any arrangement will favor some interests and slight others. The federal bargain of 1787 provided for representation by state in the Senate and by population in the House of Representatives. Because the Constitution requires that each state be equally represented in the Senate, regardless of its population size, striking disparities show up, as in Table 13-1.

The twenty-six least populated states hold 52 percent of Senate seats and the nine most heavily populated — with more than 50 percent of the United States population — elect only 18 percent of the Senators.

Four states — Ohio, Michigan, New Jersey, and Florida — have almost as many people (98 percent) as reside in the twenty-six least populated states. Yet in the House of Representatives, these twenty-six least populated states hold four more seats than the four that, together, have almost as large a population — another disparity. House districts in the states vary in population, too, making another kind of inequity.

| | Twenty-six least populated states[a] | Nine most populated states[b] |
|---|---|---|
| **TABLE 13-1** **The Bias in Congressional and Electoral College Representation** | | |
| Percentage of total U.S. population | 16.8 | 52.2 |
| Number and percentage of total house seats | 76 (17.5) | 227 (52.2) |
| Number and percentage of total electoral college votes | 128 (23.8) | 245 (45.5) |

Source: Population data from 1970 United States Census Reports.
[a] Alaska, Wyoming, Vermont, Nevada, Delaware, North Dakota, South Dakota, Montana, Idaho, New Hampshire, Hawaii, Rhode Island, Maine, New Mexico, Utah, Nebraska, West Virginia, Arizona, Arkansas, Oregon, Colorado, Mississippi, Kansas, Oklahoma, South Carolina, Iowa.
[b] California, New York, Pennsylvania, Texas, Illinois, Ohio, Michigan, New Jersey, Florida.

The bias in Senate and House representation reappears in the apportionment of electoral college votes. Measured by population size, the twenty-six least populous states are again overrepresented, because each state has as many electoral votes as it has Senators and Representatives. Thus the nine largest states in the Union have only 45.5 percent of all electoral votes, even though more than half the population live there.

The Senate and House were designed to represent different interests. Overlapping six-year terms for Senators and indirect election by state legislatures were meant to be a conservative check on the popularly elected House. All members of the House would reflect the popular will more directly. The Seventeenth Amendment, ratified in 1913, finally provided for the direct election of Senators, but the Senate remained a conservative body. In recent years, especially since World War II, the House has become the more conservative force. Legislative proposals on federal aid to education, aid to economically depressed areas, housing, and unemployment are more likely to get favorable treatment in the Senate; civil rights does better in the House.[2]

The Senate probably has grown more liberal because more social interests are represented in state constituencies (like the diverse national population) than in the more homogeneous constituencies of House districts. About 70 percent of House seats are politically "safe" for one or the other major party, whereas only about 45 percent of Senate seats can currently be so characterized.

### legislative apportionment: the key to power?

Since 1930, the 435 seats in the House have been automatically redistributed among the states according to the latest population count. State legislatures draw congressional districts within the states and traditionally have discharged that obligation with exquisite sensitivity to partisanship. The resulting distortions typically have been either unequal district populations or strangely shaped districts designed to include some categories of population and to exclude others, or both. The first type is called *malapportionment*, the second, *gerrymandering*; but both are used to inflate the electoral strength of the majority party in the state legislature and minimize that of the minority party. As a result of malapportionment over the past three or four decades, suburban, and to a lesser extent urban, sectors of America have been underrepresented. Rural districts, generally smaller in population, often are drawn so as to make the district "safe" for the incumbent Congressmen.

[2] Lewis A. Froman, Jr., *Congressmen and Their Constituencies* (Chicago: Rand McNally, 1963), pp. 71–84.

In 1963, Andrew Hacker found that 41 percent of the congressional districts were inequitably drawn.[3] He derived a standard for equitable representation by finding the average number of people who ideally should be included in each state's congressional districts if the state were apportioned in direct proportion to population. He computed how much districts varied from this norm: a 15 percent variation from this average, either up or down, was considered equitable; larger variations were considered inequitable. In 1964, the United States Supreme Court ruled in *Wesberry* v. *Sanders* that wide discrepancies in the number of persons living in each congressional district violated the requirement (Article I, section 2) that Congressmen be chosen "by the People of the several States." By 1970, thirty-nine of the forty-five states with more than one Representative had redistricted as required by the *Wesberry* ruling.[4] A 1969 Supreme Court decision, *Kirkpatrick* v. *Preisler*, declared that any variation in district population, "no matter how small," must be justified. A Missouri variation of only 3.1 percent was held to violate the one-man, one-vote principle. States have been required to eliminate almost all disparities in district populations that existed before the *Wesberry* decision.

Although the *Wesberry* decision outlawed excessively malapportioned districts, state legislative majorities can still manipulate the electoral strength of the parties without creating wide discrepancies in district populations. *Gerrymandering*, already practiced in the eighteenth century, is the drawing of district lines by the majority party in the state legislature so as to create a maximum number of districts that would be expected to elect candidates of that party. For example, in 1961 the Democratically controlled North Carolina legislature drew congressional district lines in such a way as to force the sole Republican Congressman into an election with a strong Democratic opponent. Gerrymandering is not affected by the Supreme Court decisions on apportionment, and the Court has shown no inclination to deal with the practice.

## apportionment and legislative policy decisions

Clearly, these practices have contributed to the maintenance of one-party districts: about 85 percent of incumbent candidates in House and Senate elections are reelected. Barbara Hinckley found in studying congressional seniority that from 1947 to 1966, 44 of 48 states had Senators who

[3] Andrew Hacker, *Congressional Districting: The Issue of Equal Representation* (Washington, D.C.: Brookings Institution, 1963), p. 104.

[4] In at least three states — Florida, Indiana, and Tennessee — districts were drawn by a federal district court after the state legislature failed to meet court-ordered deadlines for equitable districting.

had served for ten years or more, and in the House 139 members had won nine or more consecutive elections.[5] About half of the 435 House seats have been held by the same party, and another fourth rarely change from one party to the other.

Most Democratic "safe"[6] districts are in predominantly rural areas of the South and in the urban North. Republican one-party districts are concentrated in the rural Northeast and Midwest. Because incumbent Congressmen from one-party districts are reelected with little or no opposition, they acquire seniority, the major factor in obtaining committee chairmanships and memberships on the most desired committees.

Redistricting and changing patterns in party competition are, however, reducing the dominance of southern Democrats. Whereas 79 percent of "safe" Democratic districts were in the South in 1946, in 1964 there were only 36 percent.[7] A gain in safe districts outside the South will produce more Republican southern representatives and will bring more nonsouthern Democrats to committee chairmanships. Northern urban Democrats may rise to leadership, so that legislative policy should reflect more urban interests. We may speculate further that because the relative power of key Congressmen from rural and small-town districts will be reduced, there will be greater harmony between committee leadership and party leadership, which usually are more responsive to urban-based groups.

*Such speculation is intriguing, but we counsel great caution in assuming its validity.* The *Congressional Quarterly* has concluded that "there is no statistical evidence to substantiate the assumption that equal district populations will materially 'liberalize' the U.S. House." The exploitation of issues by political parties and a higher caliber of congressional candidates were considered more important in changing the ideological orientation of Congressmen.[8] Nor does any significant relationship appear in state legislatures between malapportionment and support of such legislation as welfare programs, aid to large cities, tax policies, or aid to education.[9] Studies of state legislatures suggest caution in assuming that a change such as imposing numerical equality in House

[5] Barbara Hinchley, *The Seniority System in Congress* (Bloomington, Ind.: Indiana University Press, 1971), pp. 25–26.

[6] A "safe" district is usually defined as one in which the majority party wins by a margin of at least 65 percent of the vote.

[7] Raymond W. Wolfinger and Joan Heifetz, "Safe Seats, Seniority, and Power in Congress," *American Political Science Review* 59 (June 1965): 347.

[8] Representation and Apportionment (Washington, D.C.: *Congressional Quarterly*, 1966), p. 60.

[9] Richard I. Hofferbert, "The Relation Between Public Policy and Some Structural and Environmental Variables in the American States," *American Political Science Review* 60 (March 1966): 73–82. See also, Thomas R. Dye, "Malapportionment and Public Policy in the States," *Journal of Politics* 27 (Aug. 1965): 586–601.

President Nixon addresses a
joint session of Congress.
Congress responds to national policy
more than it initiates it.

districts will affect public policy. Reapportionment of congressional districts has most benefited the growing suburban population, not the inner cities of metropolitan America. The social, political, and economic problems and interests of these two demographic areas are significantly different; therefore, we cannot assume that reapportionment will elect House members more sympathetic to welfare and other legislation.

## political conflict and the congressman

A Congressman[10] brings to his office values and attitudes acquired from many sources: his own political socialization, his social and political environment, and his own expectations of how a Congressman ought to behave as well as those of the public and his colleagues. The pattern of expectations — of others and of the individual Congressman — define his *role*.

## social background

Congress is not a representative sample of the population at large. Although legally any person meeting the age, residency, and citizenship requirements under Article I of the Constitution is eligible to serve, eligi-

[10] We use "Congressmen" to refer to members of both House and Senate.

bility in practice is more narrowly defined. Congressmen are better educated than the average American, and about three-fourths have had prior experience in public office. A majority are professionals, businessmen, and farmers; lawyers constitute about 1 percent of the general labor force, yet they occupy about half of the legislative seats. The average age of Representatives and Senators is ten to twenty years greater than that of the average American. More than 10 percent of the population are blacks, yet only thirteen served in Congress in 1972. In 1966, Edward W. Brooke of Massachusetts became the first Negro Senator since the Reconstruction era almost one hundred years ago. About 35 percent of church members in America are Catholic, yet only 26 percent of congressmen serving in 1972 were of that faith. Women are in the majority in the electorate, yet only twelve women served in the House and only one in the Senate in 1972.[11]

These statistics suggest certain characteristics that are necessary for success in seeking legislative office. For example, in large northern urban areas with large concentrations of blacks or Catholics, successful candidates for House seats reflect the characteristics of these minority groups. Although senatorial constituencies are larger and include a larger number and variety of social groups, these factors may still apply. A Catholic is more likely to be elected in Massachusetts than in Mississippi, which is predominantly Protestant. As the franchise is extended to the South, it is likely that more black candidates will be recruited and elected there.

These broad trends show up in Table 13–2, but the data must be looked at cautiously. These shifts in population may bring important changes: (1) Congressional membership and, ultimately, legislative policy will better reflect the interests and needs of urban populations; (2) black voters will be in a better position to swing the balance of power in urban Congressional district elections; and (3) increased participation by black voters will replace southern Congressmen traditionally opposed to legislation in favor of black and urban interests.

*Social background and experience affect policy but it is difficult to determine how much.* One author says that "although it is true that in the general population class position correlates with opinion on a variety of public issues, many people deviate from the majority opinion on every class level."[12] More systematic studies are needed on the relationship of background to behavior. In social and economic backgrounds, Congressmen *are* an elite among the American population. But does background

[11] On the implications of the lack of representativeness in Congress, see the Report of the Twenty-sixth American Assembly, *The Congress and America's Future* (New York: American Assembly, 1964).
[12] Thomas R. Dye, Herbert Jacob and Kenneth N. Vines, eds., *Politics in the American States,* 2nd ed. (Boston: Little, Brown, 1971), p. 176.

**TABLE 13–2**
**Urban Population, House Seats, and Standing**
**Committee Chairmen, by Geographical Region, 1950–1970**

| Region[a] | Percentage of total population in urban areas | | | Number of House seats | | | Number of Standing Committee Chairmen, House | | | Number of Standing Committee Chairmen, Senate | | |
|---|---|---|---|---|---|---|---|---|---|---|---|---|
| | 1950 | 1960 | 1970 | 1950 | 1960 | 1970 | 1950 | 1960 | 1970 | 1950 | 1960 | 1970 |
| Northeast | 79.5% | 80.2% | 80.4% | 115 | 108 | 104 | 2 | 4 | 3 | 0 | 0 | 0 |
| North-central | 64.1 | 68.7 | 71.6 | 129 | 125 | 121 | 5 | 2 | 3 | 0 | 1 | 0 |
| South | 48.6 | 58.5 | 64.6 | 134 | 133 | 134 | 12 | 13 | 13 | 9 | 10 | 12 |
| West | 69.5 | 77.7 | 82.9 | 59 | 69 | 76 | 0 | 1 | 2 | 6 | 5 | 4 |
| Total | 65.4 | 71.3 | 74.9 | 437 | 435 | 435 | 19 | 20 | 21 | 15 | 16 | 16 |

[a] Northeast: Pennsylvania, New Jersey, New York, Connecticut, Rhode Island, Massachusetts, Vermont, New Hampshire, Maine. North central: North Dakota, South Dakota, Nebraska, Kansas, Minnesota, Iowa, Missouri, Wisconsin, Illinois, Indiana, Michigan, Ohio. South: West Virginia, Maryland, Delaware, Virginia, North Carolina, Kentucky, Tennessee, South Carolina, Georgia, Florida, Alabama, Mississippi, Louisiana, Texas, Oklahoma. West: Washington, Oregon, Idaho, Montana, Wyoming, Colorado, Utah, Nevada, California, Arizona, New Mexico, Alaska, Hawaii.

promote some interests and hurt others? Legislators are drawn from occupational groups particularly suited for legislative jobs, but that does not invalidate the principle of the representative system. That parties recruit more politically active members from some social and economic groups as candidates for office does not mean that they are insensitive to constituency demands. Our discussion of consensus on democratic values and practice in Chapter Two indicated that the better educated, higher income, and more politically active groups in the population are the "carriers of the democratic creed." They also occupy political offices, reflecting the democratic goal: representing the will of the governed.

## how do congressmen see their jobs?

A midwestern Republican Senator, charged during a campaign with consistently voting against President Eisenhower's legislative program, said he voted the way "his people" felt about the issues. Clearly, he viewed himself as an agent of his constituency instead of an ally of the President.

WHAT INTERESTS SHOULD A CONGRESSMAN REPRESENT? Edmund Burke, following his election from Bristol to the British House of Commons, told his constituents in 1774 that "Parliament is a *deliberative* assembly of *one* nation, with one interest, that of the whole — where not local purpose, not local prejudices, ought to guide, but the general good, resulting from the general reason of the whole. You choose a member, indeed; but when you have chosen him, he is not a member of Bristol, but he is a member of Parliament."[13] Where Burke emphasized conscience and independent judgment, others feel that constituents should be given what they want.

Which of these positions best describes how legislators see their jobs in relationship to their constituencies? In a study analyzing members of the state legislatures in California, New Jersey, Ohio, and Tennessee, each legislator was classified according to his own views as to how he should make decisions: trustee, delegate, or politico. The *trustee* sees himself as a free agent, "votes as he sees it" after appraising all sides of an issue, and bases his decisions on what he thinks is morally right or just. The *delegate* sees himself as a "servant of the people" and defers to the instructions of his constituents. The *politico* is more flexible in behavior, at times acting like a trustee and at others like a delegate, or a combination of the two.

The study found that 63 percent of the legislators were trustees, 14 percent considered themselves delegates, and 23 percent were politicos. The authors concluded that the trustee may be a "functional necessity" because modern government is so complex. If they cannot understand the problems of government, people are likely to entrust decisions to their better informed representatives.[14] Also, a legislator often finds it difficult to find out what his constituents think about issues, reinforcing the idea of trusteeship.

## norms of behavior

Legislators pursue policy decisions according to behavioral norms set by both the public and the legislative body. The public expects a Congressman to observe — at least openly — standards of conduct: avoiding relationships and associations that open to question his honesty or ability to weigh evidence impartially, defending orderly procedures so that the opposition gets its day in court, and observing generally accepted norms of personal behavior. The legislative body itself expects conformity to its informal standards of behavior. David. B. Truman writes that

[13] Edmund Burke, *Works*, vol. 2 (Boston: Little, Brown, 1886), pp. 95–96.
[14] Heinz Enlau, John C. Wahlke, William Buchanan, and LeRoy C. Ferguson, "The Role of the Representative: Some Empirical Observations on the Theory of Edmund Burke," *American Political Science Review* (Sept. 1959): 742–756.

Congress "has its standards and conventions, its largely unwritten system of obligations and privileges. . . . The neophyte must conform, at least in some measure, if he hopes to make effective use of his position."[15] These traditions of behavior, important in both chambers, are especially so in the Senate. There they govern participation in debate, specialization in a particular area of legislative interest, observing rules of courtesy, being loyal to the Senate, and serving an "apprenticeship" before assuming full status in the Senate.[16] Senator Robert F. Kennedy, already nationally known before his election to the Senate, waited six months before delivering a major address on the floor of the Senate. Even then, some of his colleagues thought he had spoken too soon.

What else affects a Congressman's opinions about his job as policymaker? His position toward his party's programs and executive proposals and his impression of himself as a member of a congressional committee are also relevant to the legislative process. Informal and unofficial groups may help them to define their jobs; they may develop special friendships with their colleagues or join specialized social or political groups. In 1959, the Democratic Study Group was formally organized by liberal members of the House who felt that the Democratic House leadership was too cautious and conservative. It has since raised money for the campaigns of liberal Democrats in marginal districts, served as a fact-finding group, and coordinated support by Congressmen for liberal measures.[17] Similar groups are the "Boll Weevils," an informal organization of conservative southern Democrats, and the Wednesday Club formed by House Republicans of the Eighty-ninth Congress.

## authority, procedures, and structure of congress

The executive branch, interest groups, and political parties initiate most major policy proposals. They work within a formal procedural structure fixed by the Constitution and by the rules of Congress itself. Structure and procedure cannot, of course, be easily isolated from the larger patterns of political conflict. We separate these features for purposes of greater clarity, but the real world of legislative policymaking is made of continuing, changing relationships among structure, procedures, institutions, and political actors, all of which affect the content and direction of legislative policy.

[15] David B. Truman, *The Governmental Process* (New York: Alfred A. Knopf, 1955), p. 344.

[16] Donald B. Matthews, *U.S. Senators and Their World* (Chapel Hill, N.C.: University of North Carolina Press, 1960).

[17] Kenneth Kofmehl, "The Institutionalization of a Voting Bloc," *Western Political Quarterly* 17 (June 1964): 256–272. Randall B. Ripley, *Party Leaders in the House of Representatives* (Washington, D.C.: Brookings Institution, 1967), pp. 176–179.

Congressional power of the purse is an important weapon in the legislature's ability to maintain a check on the executive branch.

## powers of congress

Article I, Section 8 of the Constitution gives Congress broad legislative authority to raise and support an army and navy, to tax and spend for the general welfare, to borrow money, regulate commerce, coin money, establish courts, declare war, establish post offices, and govern the capital district. This section also contains the "necessary and proper" clause, which laid the basis for the doctrine of implied powers that John Marshall voiced in *McCulloch* v. *Maryland*. We have seen in Chapter Four how this doctrine laid the foundation for the extension of national legislative authority into almost every corner of community affairs.

The power of Congress is nevertheless limited by the working principle of balanced government. The presidential veto and judicial review are major potential limitations. The separation-of-powers doctrine also prohibits legislative encroachment on the jurisdiction of the other two branches, limiting the legislative matters that Congress may delegate to administrative or judicial agencies. Eight *specific* limitations are imposed by Article I, Section 9 of the Constitution, two of which are of minor importance. Four limit the taxing and appropriations powers, and two — prohibiting bills of attainder and ex post facto laws and limiting suspension of the writ of habeas corpus — are protections of individual rights.[18] Individual rights and liberties are more completely protected against legislative violation by the Bill of Rights: Congress is prohibited by the First Amendment from abridging the rights of free speech, press, assembly, petition, and free exercise of religion.

Four other constitutional provisions govern legislative authority. Congress may propose constitutional Amendments by a two-thirds vote in both houses and may admit new states to the Union. Its power to investigate and hold hearings enables the legislature to educate and inform the public, as well as itself, on social and economic problems and other important public matters. It also has an elective function: if no candidate wins a majority of electoral votes, the House selects the President from among the leading three candidates and the Senate selects the Vice-President from among the top two candidates.

## judging qualifications and disciplining members

The Constitution specifies the minimum qualifications of members of Congress: minimum age (thirty in the Senate, twenty-five in the House); United States citizenship (at least seven years for the House and nine years for the Senate); residency in the state from which a Senator or Representative is elected; and holding no other "Office under the United States" during service as a member of Congress. Under the last provision, a Congressman would be required to resign his seat if he were appointed to a position in the executive or judicial branches.

Article I grants each house the power to "be judge of the elections, returns and qualifications of its Members," and to "punish its Members for disorderly behavior and with the concurrence of two-thirds, expel a Member."

---

[18] A *bill of attainder* is a legislative act inflicting punishment without judicial trial; an *ex post facto law* imposes punishment for an act which was not punishable at the time it was committed. *Habeas corpus* is a writ issued by a court directing an official to show cause why an individual is being held; it thus prevents arbitrary imprisonment.

May Congress impose additional qualifications for membership, and does the constitution limit the grounds for discipline or expulsion?[19]

QUALIFICATIONS OF MEMBERS. Until at least 1969, Congress apparently assumed that its power to judge the qualifications of its members extended to the right to *add* qualifications beyond those specified in the Constitution. Since 1789, fourteen Senators-elect and thirty-one Representatives-elect have been challenged as unqualified to serve. Of these, the Senate has voted to exclude three (the last in 1867) and the House has excluded ten, four since 1900. Grounds for denying a seat have included failure to meet the constitutional requirements on citizenship, age, or residence, but also such matters as misconduct before election, polygamy (Mormons in the nineteenth century), and charges of sedition.

The controversial case of Representative Adam Clayton Powell, Jr., of New York City raised a deep constitutional question: How broad is congressional power to judge membership qualifications? Powell was first elected to the House from his Harlem district in 1944, and regular reelection by large majorities ultimately brought him seniority and the chairmanship of the powerful House Education and Labor Committee. Powell used his influence to achieve legislation that benefited the economically disadvantaged and socially deprived. A stormy and flamboyant Congressman, he became involved in the 1950s in court cases on income-tax evasion and libel charges. He was also accused of misusing committee funds for costly pleasure trips (accompanied by a female employee) and of putting his wife on the committee payroll, although she was living in Puerto Rico.

Responding to demands from both in and outside Congress, the House in January 1967 removed Powell as Chairman of the Education and Labor Committee and began proceedings questioning his qualifications to be seated (he had been reelected in November 1966). The House Committee appointed to investigate Powell's qualifications recommended that he be seated, but that he also be censured for "gross misconduct," that he be fined $40,000, and that he be stripped of his committee seniority. The full House rejected this recommendation and instead voted to exclude him from House membership. Because he was a highly influential black Congressman, this action resulted in strong criticism by many of his supporters, both black and white, who saw the action as racially motivated. Powell went to court, challenging the constitutional validity of the House

[19] The following discussion is based on data and analysis presented in the Congressional Quarterly's *Guide to the Congress of the United States* (Washington, D.C.: Congressional Quarterly, 1971), pp. 300–317.

action on grounds that Congress lacked power to refuse him his seat because he met the age, citizenship, and residency requirements. In June 1969, the United States Supreme Court upheld his claim,[20] holding that matters relating to qualifications of Congressmen are not exclusively the province of Congress; i.e., courts may intervene if Congress imposes qualifications beyond those listed in the Constitution.

CENSURE AND EXPULSION. For serious offenses, each House of Congress can impose censure or expel a member. Since 1789, eighteen Representatives and seven Senators have been censured for charges such as bringing the Senate into disrepute, assulting another member, financial misconduct, or offensive and insulting utterances. No House member has been censured in this century, but five Senators have been punished. Most recently (in 1954), Senator Joseph McCarthy was censured for conduct arising in his investigations of an alleged "communist conspiracy." In 1967, Senator Thomas J. Dodd of Connecticut was censured by the Senate for misconduct in diverting campaign funds to his own use.

Either of the two houses may *expel* one of its members for serious misconduct, but only fifteen Senators and three Representatives have been expelled. All but one (the exception occurred in 1797) took place during the early 1860s when Congress formally charged southern Congressmen who supported secession from the Union.

Congress has been cautious in exercising its right to discipline, expel, or exclude members. The Powell case has raised doubts about whether grounds for excluding Congressmen-elect may go beyond age, residence, and citizenship; yet this case may not prevent a future confrontation between the Supreme Court and a Congress determined to have its way. Could a Communist be refused a seat? Or could either chamber legally impose moral or political requirements not provided in the Constitution? Both houses have refused to seat members-elect on such grounds. The ultimate question may be: Does a constituency have the right to elect and be represented by a person who meets the minimum constitutional qualifications?

## the two houses: similarities and differences

SIMILARITIES. With two exceptions, the legal authority of both branches of Congress is about the same. The exceptions are the special prerogatives of the Senate in foreign affairs and presidential appoint-

---

[20] *Powell* v. *McCormick,* 395 U.S. 486 (1969).

ments, and the constitutional requirement that all revenue bills must originate in the House. Because both houses must concur on legislation, either can block bills passed by the other. The overall procedures and organization of the two houses, with some significant exceptions, operate in much the same way. Both are highly decentralized by the committee system, which gives great power to committee and subcommittee chairmen. Reinforced by a weak party structure, this decentralization has produced a policymaking system that needs compromise among divers and local interests.

The Senate's smaller size enhances the public awareness and prestige of the individual Senator; rarely, and certainly not in recent years, have Senators aspired to membership in the House. On the other hand, Representatives often seek the greater prestige and long term of a Senate seat. Nonetheless influence in the legislative process does not necessarily depend on which house a member serves in. His legislative perspective and importance are governed far more by his position in the House of Representatives or the Senate.

DIFFERENCES. The bargain of 1787 that produced a two-chamber legislature built into the policy-adoption process a tension that has never been relieved despite partisanship, presidential coordination, and policy coalitions. Different constituencies give them different perspectives on legislation, and it is relatively rare that legislation is not a compromise between the two houses.

From the point of view of House and Senate members, the two houses differ in several important features. The great difference in size of the two houses significantly affects procedural rules and the effectiveness of leadership. The House needs more rigid procedures and a hierarchical leadership more than the Senate. The Senate also enhances the power and prestige of each Senator: because of more committee assignments and the greater importance of his one vote, he can exert greater influence over more issues than a member of the House.

Because the House is larger, its leadership has more power over its members. The House leadership schedules legislation with little or no consideration of House members other than committee or subcommittee chairmen, which makes the House a more impersonal body and isolates leaders from the rank and file.

Finally, the differences in constituencies between House and Senate members is important. A Senator represents a whole state and must listen to more interests and more diverse interests than the House member, whose constituency is smaller and who necessarily concentrates on more local interests.

## political parties and policy adoption

### party control

The role of parties in Congress can be appreciated by comparing the American and British systems. A member of Parliament is expected to support his party's positions on issues designated by party leaders as partisan matters. Party structure is highly disciplined, so the party's leadership is directly responsible for policy: for the majority party, the Prime Minister, and the Cabinet. The voting discretion of individual legislators is therefore reduced, and interest groups have much less effect on legislation in the British system.

Biennial American congressional elections produce a majority and a minority party, but about the only time all Republicans vote in opposition to all Democrats is at the beginning of each session. The first item of business for each chamber is to "organize": to select the Speaker of the House, the President Pro Tempore of the Senate, majority and minority floor leaders, and members of the standing committees. The candidates previously selected by the majority party are elected by the House, of course; and the majority party gains the chairmanship and a majority in all committees. Once the key posts are safely in the hands of the majority party, partisan behavior is fragmented.

The power of party leaders in Congress depends on their skill and persuasion more than on formal powers or direct commands. Lyndon Johnson, a very effective majority leader during his tenure in the Senate, commented: "The only real power available to the leader is the power of persuasion. There is no patronage; no power to discipline; no authority to fire Senators . . . a President can fire his members of Cabinet."[21] Although both parties in the Senate and the House provide for a formal party caucus, these meet infrequently and rarely attempt to bind their members. Party leadership is somewhat tighter in the House than in the Senate, because the Speaker of the House has favors and benefits to dispense. But overall, coercion is rare and bargaining, persuasion and exchanges of favors are the norm.

The majority party has trouble guiding a program through Congress because Congressmen in key legislative posts often are jealous of their prerogatives and responsible neither to the leadership in Congress nor to influential party spokesmen outside Congress. It is very hard to weld

[21] "Leadership: An Interview with Senator Lyndon Johnson," *U.S. News and World Report* (June 27, 1960), p. 90.

Speaker Sam Rayburn presides over the House of Representatives. The power of congressional party leaders depends more on their ability to persuade than on any formal authority.

a coalition of semi-independent Congressmen, even of the same party. Further, party leaders cannot and will not insist on a legislator's support when his constituency's preferences are contrary to the party's position. A legislator's defection from his party majority's vote to represent his constituency is understood and tolerated by all legislators; it is considered only a technical defection. Where party leadership is effective — that is, where the persuasiveness and personal appeals of leaders succeed in winning the support of party members — the influence of other factors is reduced. But if there is no unified party influence, legislators are more likely to operate autonomously, or interests can get unobstructed access to legislative policymaking by exchanging support between themselves and Congressmen.

Congressmen claim that importance of local interests justifies their resisting demands by legislative party leaders. Relatively little is known about how a Congressman finds out what his constituency thinks and whether his vote on legislative matters is determined more by his own preferences or those of the people he represents. One study found that

Congressmen usually voted as they believed their constituents wanted, but often they were wrong about what the constituents wanted. Further, the survey showed that voters know little about their Congressmen's voting record, contradicting legislators' belief that their voting record is crucial to their reelection.[22] Even if one assumes that it is better that a Congressman "vote his constituency, not the party," the representative function of his vote may lie more in what he *believes* his constituents want; his may be no more than a rough approximation of their wishes.

The elected legislator comes to Congress not as a eunuch subject to external forces but as a developed personality with his own personal attitudes and relationships. His social background, group associations, and convictions help define his constituency relationships, his relations with colleagues, and his attitudes toward the political community itself. His membership in the House or Senate adds one more group loyalty. Some pressure groups have special influence because many Congressmen are members of them. Since a third to a half of the members of Congress are members of the American Legion, the influence of that organization is considerably enhanced. Similarly, on the state level, it presumably helps the state's law school that a high proportion of legislators are its alumni.

### party affiliation and voting behavior

To what extent does party affiliation determine the voting behavior of Congressmen? Analyses show that constituency influences reduce partisan voting. Table 13–3 shows two traditional voting alignments that work against party unity. North-South Democratic splits are frequent. In the fifteen sessions covered in the table (1957 to 1970), these two wings of the party differed on roll-call votes from 21 percent of the time in 1962 to 40 percent in 1960. Also, a coalition of Republicans and southern Democrats, generally conservative in nature, consistently opposed northern Democrats in these sessions, and the number of Republican-Democratic coalition votes in both houses ranged from 28 percent in 1961 to 14 percent in 1957 and 1962. Although these were a minority of the roll calls, it is significant that when the coalition operated it *usually* got its way. The coalition victories ranged from 89 percent in 1957 to 33 percent in 1965.

Democrats controlled both House and Senate during the entire period, although a Republican President served for six of the fourteen years

---

[22] Warren E. Miller and Donald E. Stokes, "Constituency Influence in Congress," *The American Political Science Review* 57 (March 1963): 45–46.

**TABLE 13-3**
**Constituency Influences and Party Cohesion, 1957-1970**

| Year | Total roll calls | Republican-Democratic "conservative coalition"[a] | Coalition victories | North-South Democratic splits[b] |
|---|---|---|---|---|
| 1957 | 207 | 14% | 89% | 31% |
| 1958 | 293 | 18 | 79 | 29 |
| 1959 | 302 | 17 | 71 | 27 |
| 1960 | 300 | 22 | 58 | 40 |
| 1961 | 320 | 28 | 55 | 33 |
| 1962 | 348 | 14 | 62 | 21 |
| 1963 | 348 | 17 | 50 | 24 |
| 1964 | 308 | 15 | 51 | 24 |
| 1965 | 459 | 24 | 33 | 35 |
| 1966 | 428 | 25 | 45 | 29 |
| 1967 | 560 | 20 | 63 | 26 |
| 1968 | 514 | 24 | 73 | 34 |
| 1969 | 422 | 27 | 68 | 36 |
| 1970 | 684 | 22 | 66 | 34 |

Source: *Congressional Quarterly Almanac*, 26 (1970): 1145, 1156; *Congressional Quarterly Report*, 50 (December 30, 1966): 3078.

[a] Roll calls on which the majority of voting southern Democrats and the majority of voting Republicans opposed the stand taken by the majority of voting northern Democrats.

[b] Roll calls on which a majority of voting southern Democrats took a position opposite to that of a majority of voting northern Democrats.

(1957 to 1960 and 1969 to 1970). The conservative coalition was much more successful during these years; also, North-South Democratic splits occurred relatively often. This pattern may be attributed in part to the appeal to conservatives of both parties of the more conservative domestic programs of Republican Presidents. For example, the conservative coalition has been both more frequent and more successful during the Nixon years, which have also been characterized by relatively small Democratic majorities. On the other hand, the *lowest* percentage of coalition victories (thirty-three) occurred in 1965 even though the number of coalition and North-South Democratic splits were among the *highest* during the fifteen-year period. The overwhelming victory of President Johnson in 1964 was accompanied by very large Democratic majorities in both houses — a margin of one hundred and fifty seats in the House and thirty-six in the Senate. The strong resistance of conservatives to Johnson's Great Society program was no match for this oversized Democratic majority.

Just as loyalty to the constituency may cause a legislator to defect from the party line, it may also promote party cohesion — if the wishes of the constituency and those of the party coincide. Lewis A. Froman examined party support for President Kennedy's liberal domestic policy programs and found that Democratic Congressmen who supported Kennedy came from urban districts with few owner-occupied dwellings, many nonwhite voters, and high populations. Republicans who opposed the Kennedy programs represented districts with more owner-occupied housing, a lower population, and fewer urban and nonwhite voters. The interests of both legislative supporters and opponents matched their own voting direction, so Froman's findings lead us to think that constituency characteristics may reinforce party unity as well as fragment it on Congressional roll calls.[23] This inference in turn implies that if a party's legislators came from districts with the same pronounced characteristics, whether conservative or liberal, but not both, party unity would be enhanced because constituency and party pressures would coincide. Constituency characteristics, however, are not so uniform that they do not work against party unity as well as for it.

Although party affiliation does help greatly to explain congressional voting, the explanation is incomplete because (unlike the British system) other things affect it too: sectionalism, constituency differences, the intensity of group demands, legislative norms and customs, personal attitudes, reciprocal relations with administrative officials, and congressional leadership. All these limit partisan voting in Congress.

## party leadership

### speaker of the house

The majority party in each house controls the selection of legislative officers, and each party chooses its own leaders. The presiding officer in the House, the Speaker, is more pivotal in getting policies adopted than either of his counterparts in the Senate, the Vice-President or the President Pro Tempore. During the nineteenth century, the Speaker gained almost unlimited power over House proceedings and policymaking. In 1910, his powers were severely restricted by the House. He remains powerful, but his power today depends heavily on the skills of the man himself.[24] As leader of the majority party, he can strongly influence the

[23] Lewis A. Froman, Jr., *Congressmen and Their Constituencies* (Chicago: Rand McNally, 1963), pp. 71–84.

[24] See Ripley, *Party Leaders in the House of Representatives*, pp. 16–24.

choice of standing committee members, although the formal choice rests elsewhere. Republican Speaker Joseph Martin said about his power during his four years as Speaker that "no Republican went on an important committee without my approval."[25]

Perhaps the Speaker's most important function is to facilitate policy, which is necessary because diffuse leadership requires sharing functions. He can use his power and influence to move legislation through the House by mediating between interests and between the two parties. Also, when both the President and the House are controlled by the same party he is usually the main contact between them. This position encourages a sense of independence from the President and also builds the Speaker's prestige in the House. Sam Rayburn occupied the speakership for eighteen years duing four administrations, and he used the power of his position to great advantage in the formulation of legislative policy.

## majority and minority leaders

The major partisan spokesmen in both houses are the majority and minority floor leaders, who are chosen by their party caucuses. They have little formal authority, but they have persuasive influence in the legislature. The House majority floor leader is to work in conjunction with the Speaker, the minority floor leader, and the Rules Committee to set the schedule for debate. As chief strategist and tactician he is a "middleman in the sense of a broker"; he must negotiate as well as harmonize diverse interests within his own party while cooperating with the opposition to ensure legislative action on policy proposals.[26]

Majority and minority leaders also carry communications to their own party members and to the press and public. They are in the midst of legislative conflict and strategy and must deal with complex legislative machinery and procedures. They are sources of information to and from rank-and-file members, and they present to the press and public their party's position on policy issues.

## party whips

Each party selects a whip, or assistant floor leader, who keeps the members informed of the weekly legislative schedule and sees that members are on the floor for important votes. He cannot command members

---

[25] Joseph W. Martin, Jr., *My Fifty Years in Politics* (New York: McGraw-Hill, 1960), p. 181.
[26] David B. Truman, *The Congressional Party* (New York: John Wiley, 1959), pp. 106–116.

Senate Minority Leader
Hugh Scott and Majority Leader
Mike Mansfield preside
over a bipartisan gathering.
Cooperation despite opposition
characterizes the best
congressional behavior.

to follow the party position, but tries to persuade them to do so and communicates partisan strategy and position on specific measures.

The most significant unifying force in legislative party leadership is the President. Although his influence is greater when his party controls either or both houses, decentralized legislative leadership limits presidential influence under any circumstances. When the majority is of the President's party, the President speaks for his party, but his role is still more bargaining than command. The pull of presidential preferences is, of course, considerably lessened when legislative control rests in the hands of the opposition party. Leadership is scattered among several party leaders, committee chairmen, and influential legislators, making the initiation and formulation of a distinctly "legislative" program unlikely. The scattering of legislative leadership shows even more clearly within the legislative minority party when that party does not control the presidency. "Divided leadership hurts the minority party's functioning as an 'alternate government,' [and] is a defect in the party system that merits more attention than the absence of tight party lines on many roll-call votes."[27]

[27] Allan P. Sindler, *Political Parties in the United States* (New York: St. Martin's Press, 1966), p. 86.

## party policy committees

Each party in both houses has a party policy committee. These committees have never functioned as instruments for formulating overall legislative policy. Membership consists of elected party leaders who serve ex officio and party members chosen by the leadership (the Senate Republican Policy Committee is chosen by the party conference). The party of the President is mainly bound by executive initiative. Although the policy committees of the opposition party may provide a means for developing alternative legislative proposals, it does not usually happen that way and the committees' main functions are to provide communication with party members.

## congressional organization and procedure

## the committee system

The critical work of Congress is done primarily by four general types of committees: (1) *standing* committees are the workhorses of Congress and are permanently provided for by House or Senate rules; (2) *special* or *select* committees are appointed by the Speaker of the House or by the President of the Senate for a specific task, usually an investigation, and are dissolved when their task is completed; (3) a *conference* committee, consisting of members of both houses appointed by the presiding officers, irons out differences in Senate and House versions of a bill; and (4) a *joint* committee, with members of both houses appointed by the presiding officer in each, usually conducts investigations, research, or supervisory activities of Congress. Joint committees are permanent, and one of them, the Joint Committee on Atomic Energy is as powerful as some standing committees. It is the only joint committee that can report legislation, and it supervises and directs the activities of the Atomic Energy Commission.[28]

## standing committees

In *Congressional Government* (1885), Woodrow Wilson described American politics as "government by the Standing Committees of Congress," and said the fate of all legislation lay in the hands of these "little leg-

[28] The powers of this joint committee are so great that at least one student of Congress has questioned whether the committee is not "a massive and unconstitutional invasion of executive branch prerogatives." Stephen K. Bailey, *The New Congress* (New York: St. Martin's Press, 1966), p. 53.

islatures."[29] Standing committees do the work of Congress itself, and they have not changed much in this century. Every legislative matter is covered by one or more of the standing committees in each house, and the adoption of every bill lies in the hands of committee members. Standing committee power is great: only 10 to 15 percent of bills referred to committees are reported out for further consideration. Administration-sponsored legislation is usually considered and reported, but a committee or one of its subcommittees may amend or change a bill to suit its own purposes.

The number of standing committees has varied; the House now has twenty and the Senate sixteen. Some are very important — Appropriations, Ways and Means, Agriculture, Foreign Relations — and membership in them is coveted more than service in less significant committees such as House Administration, Government Operations, and District of Columbia.

To expedite business, each standing committee creates subcommittees that handle work within its jurisdiction. This division of labor is necessary, but it further splinters legislative leadership. Since the full committee customarily accepts subcommittee recommendations, subcommittees and particularly their chairmen are powerful.

Proposed legislation must go through the committee stage in both the House and Senate. After a bill is introduced, it is referred to a standing committee, which subjects it to review (including hearings on major bills). The committee may recommend the bill for adoption as submitted, or as changed — sometimes a little, sometimes extensively. Or it may kill the bill. If a House committee refuses to report a bill to the floor, a *discharge petition* signed by a majority of the House membership (218) can force the bill out of the committee. The discharge method is not often successful; used 835 times, it has succeeded only 24 times since the discharge rule was adopted in 1910, but party leaders may threaten to use it to speed up committee action.

Committees also investigate. They may request or subpoena witnesses as they look into the operations of executive agencies, the effects of a law, problems and conflicts requiring new legislation, etc. The House Committee on Un-American Activities (now titled the Internal Security Committee) has raised much judicial, legislative, and public controversy over the authority of Congress to investigate matters of political action and belief. Hearings by the Senate Committee on Foreign Relations, many of whose members were highly critical of administration policies, prompted wide public interest in review of Vietnam policies.

---

[29] Woodrow Wilson, *Congressional Government* (New York: Meridan Books, 1956 [originally published in 1885]).

### assignment of members to standing committees

The majority party in each house fills a majority of the seats on all standing committees, a practice intended to ensure partisan control. The parties' respective share of seats on each committee is generally set at the same ratio as the comparative numerical strength of the parties in the chamber as a whole. The majority party wants to ensure at least formal control of some of the major committees, so it claims a disproportionate number of seats, as in the House Rules Committee. Each party determines the assignments of its partisans, limited by the Legislative Reorganization Act of 1970, which says that each Senator may serve on no more than two major and one minor committee and that he may serve on only one of these: Armed Services, Appropriations, Finance, or Foreign Relations. Representatives rarely serve on more than two standing committees.

**Investigations such as this one conducted by Robert Kennedy,
counsel for the Senate Rackets Committee,
focus public attention on national problems and help generate support for legislative action.**

A freshman Representative must serve on a minor committee before winning a more important assignment. Each party assigns freshmen Senators to one major committee. A new Congressman will naturally seek a major committee assignment that is congenial to his own or his constituency's interests. Transfers between committees may be made when vacancies occur, or when members agree (with party approval) to switch committee assignments.

Assignments to the three major House committees — Appropriations, Rules, and Ways and Means — are usually based on factors such as representing a fairly "safe" district, geographical balance of committee representation, and the Representative's reputation as a "responsible" member of the House. Assignments to other House committees are based on such factors as the desire to place each party member on a committee that will help him win reelection (the most important consideration), the Congressman's interest group support, his professional background, and the geographical area he represents.[30] In the Senate, the major committees do not accurately reflect either geographical or ideological balance, but regional balance is considered. A vacancy is normally filled with a member from the same state, if the Senator wants membership on that committee.

Some standing committees — Agriculture, Labor, Interior and Insular Affairs, Judiciary — clearly reflect specific interests. Congressmen from farm states control the agriculture committees; western Senators dominate Interior and Insular Affairs; Congressmen from urban and industrial states compose the labor committee; and lawyers dominate the judiciary committees. Pressure groups are deeply interested in which committee is given jurisdiction over legislation. Although bills usually fall clearly within one committee's jurisdiction there are occasions when a choice exists as to which of two committees might be assigned major legislation. If the attitudes of the respective committee majorities differ markedly on the bill, then its fate can be determined by which committee gets the bill.

## the seniority rule

The seniority rule is crucial in the selection of standing-committee chairmen. A chairman has power over the committee's agenda, appointing its staff (the administrative specialists who serve the committee), choosing subcommittee chairmen and members, deciding whether hearings will be held on the bill, representing the committee on the floor, and designating who will handle a bill once it reaches the floor.

[30] Nicholas A. Masters, "Committee Assignments in the House of Representatives," *The American Political Science Review* 55 (June 1961): 345–357.

The seniority rule automatically awards the chairmanship to the member of the majority party with the longest uninterrupted service in the committee; the member of the minority party with the longest continuous committee service becomes chairman when his party gains a majority. A member may acquire high seniority not only by winning reelections but also by the death, transfer, or resignation of more senior members from a committee. Building seniority through reelections is considerably easier for Congressmen in states and districts dominated by one party. Those from areas where party competition is close rarely survive long in Congress, so that most committee chairmanships and ranking minority member positions are controlled by Congressmen from a few states and few regions; most of these are conservative. Between the Eightieth and Eighty-ninth congresses (1947 to 1966), southern Democrats controlled 53 percent of the chairmanships and ranking minority member positions in the Senate and 61 percent in the House. Midwestern Republicans held 51 percent of these positions in the House and 46 percent in the Senate.[31] Many safe districts that are represented by conservative Congressmen are in the Midwest and South.

## seniority and party leadership

The seniority rule weakens the legislative party's leadership. The legislator's claim to key committee positions is determined by his party label and his own ability to be reelected, not by his record of party loyalty in congressional voting. Because they amassed seniority "on their own," they have little incentive to be grateful to or feel dependent on the party leadership. Furthermore, having safe districts often means that they serve a pronounced constituency interest. The President is no more able to get a hostile committee chairman of his own party removed than the Congress is to force a President with whom it disagrees to resign.

## should the seniority system be retained?

The undesirable effects of the seniority rules have long been recognized by political analysts and commentators. They have held that it weakens the parties and their influence and enthrones unrepresentative and minority interests from safe districts, like Woodrow Wilson's "little legislatures." The rebuttal against the torrent of negative criticism is that continuous committee service of high-seniority legislators gives them

[31] Barbara Hinchley, *The Seniority System in Congress*, p. 27.

experience on their committee's specialities that makes it possible for Congress to exercise effectively the powers assigned to it by the Constitution. That argument seems questionable at best, if only because a rigid seniority formula is not the only way of making experts.

The real utility of the seniority rule and the reason that Congress quietly and stubbornly retains the rule despite nearly universal criticism is its secure fit with the legislative party's character. A centralized party's major source of power would be control over distributing key committee posts among its partisans; a decentralized party would not. Conversely, if committee posts were assigned by the party leadership, a party caucus, or according to criteria such as party loyalty in voting, these measures would describe a centralized party system. Because American legislative parties — like the national parties themselves — are too weak to perform in that manner, the other major reason for assigning committee positions would have to do with personal attributes and talents. Yet, could we find a better guarantee of an enfeebling free-for-all conflict within each legislative party than to equate committee assignments with judgments of the personal qualities of individual legislators? Or, if conflict were to be minimized, could we find any better guarantee of endless horsetrading of support for personal advancement, unrelated to any interest in "fairer," "better," or "more effective" than those produced by the present seniority rule?

The seniority rule then is an *impersonal* and *nonparty* formula for distributing power among legislators who operate within a fragmented party system and who are generally equal in legal and political standing as elected representatives. Reforms would have to change the kind of party system as well as the way of choosing chairmen. Changes in the way committee positions are allotted, in short, are not a matter of insulated tinkering but relate to central characteristics of the legislative and party process.

Whatever the basis for the selection of both members and chairmen of standing committees, it clearly affects the ability of groups to influence policy choices. Committees are autonomous centers of power and their chairmen are often in competition with party leaders for legislative leadership. Leadership in policy formulation and adoption is thus diffused further and the opportunity for veto of proposals is increased.

## public hearings

Standing committees and their subcommittees do their crucial work in closed sessions with much bargaining among interests. Yet all major committees spend many hours holding public hearings, supposedly to take evidence from all interested parties. What purpose do hearings serve if the real decisions turn on other considerations?

Hearings are mediums through which committees perform their expected function as fact-finding bodies. While information is being gathered, interest groups and individuals are formally given an opportunity to present their own version of the facts and their position on proposed policies. This procedure accords with the democratic principle of representation, but committee members are not always impartial judges. A chairman may give priority to witnesses sympathetic to his own ideas, or he may not give opposing groups a chance to be heard. Furthermore, a committee member may put his questions in such a way as to show a group in its most favorable light, or to make its image unfavorable.[32]

These proceedings may be meant to persuade other committee members or to generate public support (or the *appearance* of support) for the committee's position. Hearings may, however, perform an important democratic function: providing information and an official medium for raising dissent to current or proposed policies. Widely publicized hearings on American policy in Southeast Asia, conducted by the Senate Committee on Foreign Relations beginning in the late 1960s, gave opponents of the administration's policy opportunities to publicly oppose decisions on the Vietnam War. A sympathetic committee chairman, Senator J. William Fulbright, also used the hearings to suggest alternative policies.

## the house rules committee

The most crucial standing committee in either house of Congress is the House Rules Committee. Normally the Rules Committee determines not only the order in which bills are considered but whether they will be considered by the full House at all. Because the committee channels the flow of legislation to the floor by determining limits on debate and fixing the number and kind of amendments that may be offered, it can force changes and concessions in legislation before permitting it to reach the floor.

House membership is so large that the need is clear for a "traffic cop" to direct and manage the flow of legislation. Although this function is essential, who should do it and for what ends? To answer the question we have to consider the advantages and disadvantages for competing partisan and legislative interests.

The Rules Committee has been a strong obstruction to liberal legisla-

[32] David B. Truman, *The Governmental Process*, pp. 372–379.

tion for many years. From the late 1930s to the early 1960s, it was dominated by a coalition of Republicans and southern Democrats who successfully blocked domestic legislation that was supported by the White House and often a majority of the House membership. House liberals, supported by President Kennedy and Speaker Rayburn, in 1961 succeeded in adding three members to the Committee, giving liberal forces a one-vote majority. In 1965, after Johnson's landslide victory and capitalizing on the oversize liberal Democratic majorities in the House, the House approved two changes in rules which substantially weakened the authority of the Rules Committee. The twenty-one-day rule (abandoned in 1967) permitted a committee chairman or committee member to introduce a bill that had been before the Rules Committee for twenty-one days without being considered by the full House. The other rule weakened the committee's power to block or delay sending a bill to a conference committee by permitting the House to send it to conference by a majority vote. A 1970 rule change removed the power of standing committee chairmen to block reporting of legislation that had been approved by a majority of the committee and also prevents a chairman from refusing to call a meeting of the committee, gives greater potential power to the majority of members, and reduces still further the autonomy of the chairman.

The *discharge petition* may also be used to force a bill out of the Rules Committee, although it is rarely successful. The formal procedure of *Calendar Wednesday*, which permits a standing committee to call up bills blocked by the Rules Committee, is a cumbersome and ineffective way of overcoming Rules Committee opposition to legislation.

The Rules Committee still is a powerful force in the House. By misusing its function as a clearinghouse to block and delay, it can give special access to some groups in the House, frustrate the majority's goals, and force negotiation and compromise. Most of the advantage goes to conservative forces, and they have succeeded in fighting off most attempts by liberal forces to remove that advantage.

## floor consideration and final passage of bills

House floor debate on bills reported from standing committees is rigidly controlled by time limits and other procedural rules set by the Rules Committee. The whole House may name itself as a special committee — the Committee of the Whole — to discuss a proposal without members being subjected to all the formal rules of parliamentary procedure. Important decisions and compromises can be reached that could not be so easily negotiated under more rigid conditions.

Senators nap outside the
chamber during a civil rights
filibuster in 1960.

The smaller Senate does not have the restrictive schedules and controls
of the House. Control of floor debate rests mostly with the majority
leader, but he lacks the power to limit debate. Once a Senator has the
floor, he may talk as long as he pleases and he may yield the floor to
whom he chooses. A group of Senators may prevent a bill from coming
to a vote by exploiting this "free and unlimited speech" to kill time, a
tactic known as the *filibuster*. As a weapon of the minority, the filibuster
has had many dramatic successes, and the threat of using that tactic has
won many concessions from the majority. Although it is more frequently
used to prevent the passage of civil rights legislation, the filibuster has
also been employed by liberals. It was used in 1970 to prevent Senate
votes on the supersonic transport, and in 1972 to block passage of an
antibusing bill.

Debate can be limited by invoking *cloture,* otherwise known as Rule
Twenty-two. Cloture limits each Senator to one hour of speech on a bill,
but it must be passed by a two-thirds vote. It is presented to the Senate
on the second calendar day after a petition has been filed, signed by at
least sixteen members in favor of cloture. Of sixty-nine efforts to invoke
the rule, however, only twelve have been successful.

## voting methods in congress

Four methods of voting on measures are used in the House and three in
the Senate. In the House, the *voice vote* is the most common — members
simply respond to the call for "aye" or "nay" and no individual votes
are recorded. Voice votes may be challenged by demanding a *teller vote*
by one-fifth of a quorum (twenty in the Committee of the Whole and
forty-four in the House). Members pass between tellers who count those
on each side of the issue. Since 1970, individual votes on a teller vote
taken in Committee of the Whole may be recorded, but no recording is
made of these votes on final passage of the legislation. A *roll-call vote* is
taken if one-fifth of those present demand it. Roll-call votes are recorded
and published in the *Congressional Record,* the official proceedings of
Congress.

The Senate does not use the teller vote and only one method of voting
may be used on a proposition. Roll-call votes are easier to obtain (usually
on request by one Senator) and employed more often than in the House,
probably because it is easier to handle roll-calls in the smaller Senate.
The votes of individual Senators are recorded only when roll-calls are
taken.

## conference committees

When House and Senate pass a legislative proposal but disagree on some
features, an ad hoc joint committee called a conference committee is
created. Members are appointed by the presiding officers of each house
and are usually drawn from the two standing committees that handled
the bill on the floor. Each house may instruct its conference members.
Because conference committees freely ignore the procedural rules prohibiting them from making major changes in the legislation and because
their report must be voted on without change by both houses, they represent "committee power in its most concentrated form."[33]

## the work of congress

Decentralization is found everywhere in the legislative process. A bicameral legislature reflects the built-in parochialism of federalism. Representation grants distinct advantages to some interests because of single-

---

[33] Bertrom A. Gross, *The Legislative Struggle* (New York: McGraw-Hill, 1953), p. 317.

member districts, malapportionment, and gerrymandering. Party leadership reinforces localized and segmented control of policy adoption. Legislative procedures provide multiple points of decision so that exclusive interests, official and nonofficial, can block, delay, frustrate, and sometimes force through legislative policy. The consequences are the same as in other parts of the system: limited presidential coordination, partisan ineffectiveness, negotiated decisions, difficulty in fixing responsibility for policy, and policy by incrementation.

But legislative decentralization gives the average Congressman much freedom to choose alternative policies. On the surface, fragmentation seems to provide perfect conditions for pressure groups to dictate policy. We might expect legislators to be mere pawns of exclusive interests. Yet each legislator filters out the pressures he does not want to bear, admits those which support him in his work, and colors others. In short, the legislator "unconsciously chooses which pressures to recognize."[34] Pressure groups succeed by exploiting the common ground they share with some legislators, not by overt pressure. A Congressman whose constituency is mostly agricultural does not have to be "pressured" by farm groups: his goals are already compatible with theirs. He considers "sound" or "in the public interest" demands that parallel or support his own views; and inversely, pressure organizations nurture mutually beneficial relations with legislators on whom they can rely.

The relatively great autonomy of Congressmen does not mean that Congress dominates or controls policymaking. Policy is initiated elsewhere, for one thing. Congress legislates less than it ratifies, formulates less than it adopts, and leads less than it responds. Legitimate community policies require that congressional majorities be mobilized behind them, but the policies usually are initiated elsewhere.

## congress and the executive branch

The executive's growth as a regulator of social conflict is both a fact and a problem. Congress surrendered to the executive conflicts that it could not resolve, delegating much of its policy leadership and altering its function of representing conflict. We hear little about a congressional policy program, but much about the President's program. Conflict between the branches has long worried students of government.[35] Some suggest re-

---

[34] Raymond A. Bauer, Ithiel de Sola Pool, and Lewis Anthony Dexter, *American Business and Public Policy* (New York: Atherton Press, 1963), p. 416.

[35] See for example, James A. Robinson, *Decision-Making in Congress* (Washington: American Enterprise Institute, 1965).

forming Congress by eliminating obstruction by committees and tightening partisan leadership; they believe that Congress should reduce its autonomy and fragmentation and move closer to presidential leadership. Many critics suggest that Congress has become too much of a negative institution and an obstacle to presidential power.

If a co-equal legislative branch depends on the ability of Congress to seize the function of formulating policy, then Congress is probably not co-equal with the executive and judicial branches. Fragmented leadership, decentralized power, and localized interests are the legislature's burden; they do not add up to a body that can easily exercise policy initiative. This suggests that Congress should stop emphasizing its legislative function and concentrate on two others equally vital: *overseeing* and *representation*.

The power to investigate, to approve of presidential nominations, to impeach, to review and recommend changes in organization of the executive branch, to advise and consent, and the vital power of the purse are all varieties of *oversight* by which the Congress holds the executive branch responsible for its actions and exercises the prerogative to alter, amend, and propose changes in programs and organization.[36] It does not interfere with legitimate executive functions and prerogatives.

The *representative* function closely parallels oversight. The President has become more and more the focal point in representing the broad and changing patterns of a national constituency, and a change in administrations changes representation and access. "A thousand new officials descend on Washington, coming fresh from the people, representing the diverse forces behind the President, and bringing with them new demands, new ideas, and new power."[37] Congress's representative role cannot be the same. It can, however, represent the citizen and the unorganized interests of society. In fact, localized congressional constituencies and decentralized congressional power are important assets to such representation. The average citizen appears to be increasingly unable to understand or appreciate big government and is cynical about his chance of "being heard." Congress may be the major link between government and citizen. The Congressman is a mediator between the individual and the bureaucracy (sometimes described as the "errand boy" function); together with the larger congressional oversight, he is vital to democratic pluralism. He may also be the best way of balancing the power and influence of the presidency.

[36] An excellent brief discussion of the dimensions of legislative oversight is Cornelius P. Cutter's "Legislative Oversight," in Alfred de Grazia, ed., *Congress: The First Branch of Government* (New York: Doubleday, 1967), pp. 24–79.

[37] Samuel P. Huntington, "Congressional Responses to the Twentieth Century," in David B. Truman, ed., *The Congress and America's Future*, p. 17.

There is abundant literature on Congress and the legislative process. Standard treatments of Congress are well represented by George B. Galloway's *The Legislative Process in Congress* (New York: Thomas Y. Crowell, 1953) and the more recent work of Malcolm E. Jewell and Samuel C. Patterson, *The Legislative Process in the United States* (New York: Random House, 1966). Shorter treatments are found in Dale Vinyard, *Congress* (New York: Charles Scribner's Sons, 1968) and Nelson W. Polsby, *Congress and the Presidency* (Englewood Cliffs, N.J.: Prentice-Hall, 1964). More analytically oriented, with provocative essays on a variety of topics, is David B. Truman, ed., *Congress and America's Future* (Englewood Cliffs, N.J.: Prentice-Hall, American Assembly Series, 1964).

Studies in social backgrounds of Congressmen, representational patterns, and Congressional roles comprise a growing part of the literature. Donald R. Matthews, *The Social Background of Political Decision-Makers* (New York: Random House, 1954) is a seminal work in the use and limitations of social background analysis. Heinz Enlau and John D. Sprague, *Lawyers in Politics* (Indianapolis: Bobbs-Merrill, 1964) is one of the best studies of the relationship of the legal profession to the legislative process. Nelson W. Polsby, ed., *Congressional Behavior* (New York: Random House, 1971) includes several excellent essays on the congressional career and the contemporary role of the Congressman. The perspective of the Congressman is presented in Charles L. Clapp, *The Congressman: His Work as He Sees It* (New York: Doubleday, 1963), a work based on roundtable discussions with and between representatives. James D. Barber's *The Lawmakers* (New Haven: Yale University Press, 1965) provides an analytical framework for viewing the relationship of social background and legislative behavior. Stephen K. Bailey, *Congress in the Seventies* (New York: St. Martin's Press, 1970) offers useful insights in the role of Congress in the present decade. Lewis A. Dexter's *The Sociology and Politics of Congress* (Chicago: Rand McNally, 1969) argues that an active citizenry can influence congressional behavior.

Case studies offer a useful medium to understand the dynamics of the legislative process. Among the better ones are Daniel M. Berman, *A Bill Becomes a Law: Congress Enacts Civil Rights Legislation,* 2nd ed. (New York: Macmillan, 1966), and Eugene Eidenberg and Ray D. Morey, *An Act of Congress: The Legislative Process and the Making of Educational Policy* (New York: W. W. Norton, 1969).

The vital role of congressional committees and procedures in the legislative process are analyzed in a number of the works cited above and also in in-depth studies. Specific committees are the subject of David N. Farnsworth, *The Senate Committee on Foreign Relations* (Urbana, Ill.: University of Illinois Press, 1961); James A. Robinson, *The House Rules Committee* (Indianapolis: Bobbs-Merrill, 1963); and John F. Manley, *The Politics of Finance: The House Committee on Ways and Means* (Boston: Little, Brown, 1970). A short but excellent treatment of rules and procedures and their relationship to policymaking is Lewis A. Froman, Jr., *The Congressional Process* (Boston: Little, Brown, 1967).

The nature and role of congressional leadership and the party function is considered in Stephen K. Bailey's *The New Congress* (New York: St. Martin's Press, 1966). Bailey argues that Congress is more influenced by presidential and party than by constituency demands. Roger H. Davidson, David M. Kovenock, and Michael K. O'Leary, *Congress in Crisis: Politics and Congressional Reform* (Belmont, Calif.: Wadsworth, 1968) provide a dimension on the relationship of congressional reform and the representation of constituent interests. Charles O. Jones, *The Minority Party in Congress* (Boston: Little, Brown, 1970) and Randall B. Ripley, *The Majority Party Leadership in Congress* (Boston: Little, Brown, 1969) carefully examine the role of the party leadership. Randall B. Ripley's *Power in the Senate* (New York: St. Martin's Press, 1969) offers several models of the distribution of power in the Senate.

Finally, the student who wishes to follow the issues and workings of Congress on virtually a day-by-day basis should consult *Congressional Quarterly Weekly Report,* a biweekly report of all congressional activity.

# chapter 14

# the bureaucracy
# and policy application

When the Constitution of the United States was written, no one thought of the great bureaucracy that might some day be required to run the country. Articles I and II hint at the possible development of an administrative bureaucracy; Article I grants Congress the right to create administrative agencies, and Article II authorizes the President to appoint public officials, including "all other Officers of the United States, whose Appointments are not herein otherwise provided for, and which shall be established by Law." Today the federal government employs about three million people in a national civil work force of approximately sixty-five million. Some call the bureaucracy the "fourth branch of American government" because it applies policy to every citizen and because the three constituted branches must somehow control it.

## administrative bureaucracy and policy application

"Everywhere," wrote the well-known sociologist Max Weber in *Date Koming*, "the modern state is undergoing bureaucratization." Weber saw society as first evolving from a nonspecialized mass of people when a charismatic leader came along to lead it. A stable foundation for exercising authority was needed, so routine and systematic forms of organization gradually developed. The technological revolution and its accompanying demands for specialization finally produced the highly rational, legalistic, and technical organizations that Weber called "bureaucracies."[1] Without an administrative bureaucracy to carry out policy, government could not function.

## what is policy application?

If we think that Congress, under the system of separated powers, enacts policy and the administrative branch implements it, we oversimplify the reality of the policy process. The will of the community is reflected in public policies, which have to be binding, so someone must find a way to insure compliance with them. One way is to get the achieved public acceptance of the legitimacy of legislative decisions and their subsequent implementation by the administrative branch. Also, however, an element of coercion must be there, either potential or actual. In the narrowest sense, policy application consists of activities that enforce compliance.

But bureaucrats go beyond that narrow activity and take part in the broader work of setting community goals forth. They both enforce the legislation and participate in the negotiations leading to its adoption. They help set the goals by advancing the desires of their agencies and of the pressure groups that work on them. The administrative branch is deeply and continuously involved in politics and policymaking.

POLICY APPLICATION AND COMMUNITY GOALS. Much legislation is written in broad language, merely outlining what an administrative agency can and cannot do. The missing detailed legislative direction is filled in by the agency itself. In fact, some administrators distinguish between their agency's *programs* and the *policies* that are given them by the executive and the legislature to apply. To be sure, the former is intended to serve the latter, but the administrators have much room to make choices and use their discretion. Such choices are, in effect, acts of policymaking that directly affect the distribution of advantages and disadvantages among conflicting interests, as two examples will show. Since 1914, the Federal Trade Commission has been responsible for administering and enforcing laws aimed at protecting consumers. Regulations affecting packaging standards, advertising claims, and "truth in lending" are promulgated and enforced by the commission. The original message on packages of cigarettes, "Caution: Cigarette Smoking May Be Dangerous to Your Health" (and later "... is hazardous to your health") was an effort to protect consumers against cancer. The stronger warnings initially proposed were

---

[1] H. H. Gerth and C. Wright Mills, eds., *From Max Weber: Essays in Sociology* (New York: Oxford University Press, 1946), p. 232.

The Federal Trade Commission administers and enforces policies aimed at consumer protection. Research linking cancer to cigarette smoking led to action warning consumers of the danger.

vigorously opposed by tobacco interests, which felt any messages would be economically injurious.

The Environmental Protection Agency was created by order of President Nixon in 1970 and charged with administering a large part of federal legislation on water and air pollution, radiation protection standards, and the control of fungicides and pesticides. With a budget of $1.4 billion in fiscal 1971, the EPA is the largest federal attempt to develop environmental standards. It must deal with interests (especially industries and local governments) which argue that they are technically or economically unable to meet the standards of quality the agency has suggested.

Administrators take part in representing social conflict as well as its resolution. Norton Long writes that in some ways the bureaucracy represents interests better than Congress does.[2] Its varied composition compensates for defective congressional representation (discussed in Chapter Thirteen), which results in large numbers of "unrepresented, underrepresented, or malrepresented" citizens. The head of the bureaucracy, the President, works toward broader public goals than Congressmen do. Because Congress does not accept responsibility for the success of legislation after it takes administrative form, the bureaucracy provides a continuing structure and constitutional media through which a changing political and social environment can be reflected in new policies to meet new needs and new group demands.

[2] Norton E. Long, *The Polity* (Chicago: Rand McNally, 1962), chap. 5.

459

## who are the bureaucrats?

Long's emphasis on the democratic socioeconomic backgrounds of public employees is accurate only insofar as it relates to the rank and file in public service. Top administrative executives are similar to Congressmen in socioeconomic status. A study of 1,041 federal administrative executives appointed by five Presidents between 1933 and 1965, found that these men were not a cross-section of the American population nor did they resemble the rank-and-file federal employee.[3] The survey included high-ranking appointive officials in ten of the twelve cabinet departments, administrative and deputy administrators of other major agencies such as the Bureau of the Budget, and members of seven regulatory commissions. Compared to the general population in 1950, these federal executives were disproportionately Democratic (Democrats controlled the presidency for all but eight years of the period), highly educated, Protestant, lawyers and businessmen, and from very large cities. Forty-four percent of those with business backgrounds were drawn from the five hundred largest industrial corporations, and 37 percent of those in defense-related agencies between 1960 and 1965 were formerly employed by major defense contractors. Further, 63 percent of these executives had held other government posts immediately before their appointments.

## the civil service: historical patterns

We have looked only at administrative personnel on the highest levels. What about the middle and lower levels of management in government?

RISE OF THE MERIT SYSTEM. Leonard D. White, writing of administrative history between 1790 and 1830,[4] says that Presidents Washington, Adams, and Jefferson emphasized continuity in government personnel, and that personnel were drawn mostly from the relatively better-off parts of society. As White puts it, "Employment legally at pleasure [of the President] became in practice employment during good behavior," and government employees were an elite group of men of stature and long service.[5] This pattern continued until the election of Andrew Jackson in 1828. Jackson

[3] David T. Stanley, Dean E. Mann, Jameson W. Doig, *Men Who Govern: A Biographical Profile of Federal Political Executives* (Washington, D.C.: Brookings Institution, 1967).

[4] Leonard D. White, *The Jeffersonians* (New York: Macmillan, 1951); and *The Jacksonians* (New York: Macmillan, 1954).

[5] White, *The Jeffersonians*, p. 348.

said in his first annual message to Congress that "the duties of federal employees were so plain and simple that men of intelligence may readily qualify themselves for their performance." He brought the "spoils system" to federal employment, rewarding party faithful with government jobs. Jacksonian democracy was extended to the "common man," using rotation in office as a safeguard against elitism. For most of the nineteenth century, partisan supporters of new Presidents were installed in government posts, from the highest to the lowest levels.

Not until 1883, after President James Garfield was assassinated (in 1881) by a rejected office seeker, was the spoils system reformed. The Pendleton Act of 1883 provided for a federal civil service based on merit, to be established by competitive examination and administered by a bipartisan Civil Service Commission. This system, known as the classified service, has grown steadily — 10.5 percent of federal employees in 1884; 41.5 percent in 1901; 79.6 percent in 1930; and more than 85 percent by the late 1960s. Most executive branch agencies now select their employees through the merit system, but a number have systems separate from the Civil Service Commission — the Federal Bureau of Investigation, the Atomic Energy Commission, the Tennessee Valley Authority, the Central Intelligence Agency — each of which has specialized functions.

POLITICAL NEUTRALITY: THE HATCH ACT. The merit system is meant to reduce political pressure in government employment. It provides job security and fairness by procedures and regulations for dismissals, compensation, promotions, etc. To further remove civil servants from political influence, Congress enacted the Hatch Act of 1939, which prohibited some types of partisan political activity by career employees. It also applies to state employees whose salaries are paid in whole or in part by federal grants or loans. It prohibits activities such as running for public office, soliciting contributions for campaigns, serving as delegates to party conventions, and speaking at political rallies. Administered and enforced by the Civil Service Commission, the regulations have confused public employees about what they may or may not do. A 1968 Commission study found that almost 65 percent of federal employees understood at the most five of the ten restrictions under present Hatch Act rules.[6] In July 1972, the Hatch Act was temporarily suspended pending thorough review of its more controversial provisions. This review may answer questions about the effectiveness of the law and criticism that federal employees are being denied some of the citizen's basic rights and privileges.

[6] Cited in James W. Davis, Jr., *The National Executive Branch* (New York: Free Press, 1970), pp. 69–71.

## a professionalized bureaucracy?

President Jackson's "plain and simple" description of government jobs
no longer applies as the bureaucracy's need for professional and technical
employees grows. In 1966, a study of the activities of the top 5,000 career
employees found that 35 percent were program managers (bureau chiefs,
division directors, office heads), another 35 percent were involved in budget management, personnel management, administration, or management
analysis, and 30 percent were professionals (economists, lawyers, engineers, scientists, accountants).[7] About one in every fourteen civil servants
is engaged in engineering and scientific work, and of the 5,000 executives
about two thirds more held master's degrees than bachelor's degrees.

How do federal executives of the upper and middle rank compare with
their counterparts in business? A major study of the social, economic,
and educational background of both groups revealed that *federal* executives are better educated; they reach the top of the administrative structure more rapidly, and they work at more varied occupations because
federal activities are broader in scope than those of business. The two
groups are, however, *similar* in that most come from families in the higher
occupations, although many also come from lower socioeconomic backgrounds. Also, both business and government leaders are likely to be born
in large cities. The conclusion was that although those born at or near
the top of the socioeconomic ladder are more likely to occupy positions
of leadership, the trend in recent years has been toward reducing this
influence in the selection of both government and business managers.[8]

## democratization of the federal service?

That the federal service is becoming more democratic is confirmed by
the growing numbers of minority group citizens now entering the service.
In 1968, two years after President Johnson ordered an Equal Employment
Opportunity program, the Civil Service Commission reported that 14.9
percent of 2.6 million federal personnel surveyed were blacks, a gain of
1.3 percent over 1966. Mexican-Americans and other ethnic groups also
gained. Since 1967, the federal government has worked at eliminating

[7] John J. Corson and R. Shale Paul, *Men Near the Top* (Baltimore, Md.: Johns Hopkins
Press, 1966), pp. 15–19.

[8] W. Lloyd Warner, Paul P. Van Riper, Norman H. Martin, and Orvis F. Collins, *The
American Federal Executive, A Study of the Social and Personal Characteristics of the
Civilian and Military Leaders of the United States Federal Government* (New Haven: Yale
University Press, 1963), pp. 22–24.

arbitrary restrictions and to actively recruit more women into civil service positions.[9] These gains are not equally reflected in administrative positions at the upper and middle levels where educational and social advantages — the basis for upward mobility — are still heavily biased in favor of white males. But as equality of opportunity is better realized, the entire federal bureaucracy will more broadly reflect the American social structure.

MERIT SELECTION VS. OTHER SOCIAL ENDS? Government employment based on open competition and limited to no social class or political party is consistent with the democratic ideal of equality of opportunity and fairness in government employment. We must consider two reservations about whether the merit system ought to be qualified for other social and political purposes, or whether the system of selection is inherently fair as it affects socially and culturally deprived groups.

The *veteran's preference system* was inaugurated by Congress after World War I and has been modified and expanded several times since. Veterans, and in some cases their wives and widows, are given preference in hiring and additional points on competitive examinations. Such preferential treatment, of course, modifies the concept of merit, but it also formalizes the social and political principle of rewarding soldiers who have served their country. It also shows the political power of veteran's organizations, which insisted on preferential treatment. By 1934, although less than 10 percent of the population, veterans held about a fourth of the civil service positions. Between 1949 and 1958, World War II veterans entering the service raised the total to 50 percent of civil service employees.[10]

The claim that *cultural biases* are built into merit system tests is complex because it implies that fairness is part of social equality in a different way. Gordon Clapp described "equal treatment" in federal employment in the years around World War II as "the cold, objective atmosphere of tests, scores, weighted indices and split-digit ranking," and he adds, "these technical trappings have become the symbols of the merit system."[11] Do merit system tests discriminate against some groups? Studies of differences between ethnic groups have consistently shown that some kinds of tests, especially those measuring verbal skills, are not fair to citizens

[9] Milton C. Cummings, M. Kent Jennings, and Franklin P. Kirkpatrick, "Federal and Nonfederal Employees: A Comparative Social-Occupational Analysis," *Public Administration Review* (Dec. 1967): 393–400.

[10] Figures cited in Felix A. Nigro, *Modern Public Administration,* 2nd ed. (New York: Harper & Row, 1970), pp. 276–277; see also Paul P. Van Riper, "Veterans Preference: Policies at Cross-Purposes," in Robert T. Golembrewski and Michael Cohen, *People in Public Service* (Itasca, Ill.: F. E. Peacock, 1970), pp. 537–540.

[11] Quoted in Golembriewski and Cohen, *People in Public Service,* p. 13.

of some ethnic groups because their cultural, educational, and social experience is often very different from those of the majority. Although more blacks and members of other ethnic groups are entering the federal service, civil rights groups have pressed government agencies to eliminate alleged cultural biases in selection by using special testing procedures.[12] Also on-the-job training and education are proposed to qualify otherwise ineligible persons for employment and thus give the socially and economically disadvantaged a better chance.

Their supporters feel that removing testing biases and introducing special provisions to assist the disadvantaged will make the merit concept more realistic. The proposals also reflect the response of the political system to the demands of previously denied minorities for equality of opportunity. These proposals give greater weight to desirable *social* ends over the more traditional and formal emphasis on merit without considering the realistic problems of American political life.

## how representative is the bureaucracy?

Now that we have examined the types of people recruited for government service, we can see that: (1) executives at the highest and middle levels are an elite by educational and socioeconomic standards, but they also have the legal, managerial, and analytic skills needed in modern government; (2) the need to make the civil service accessible to all population groups has brought more members of ethnic minorities into the federal service; (3) the idea of merit in competitive selection procedures has been modified to achieve political and social ends as desirable or more so.

Of the three branches of government, the federal bureaucracy comes closest to reflecting the social, economic, educational, and cultural differences in American society. Although top-level administrators are not a cross-section of the population, it is wrong to conclude that the bureaucracy is therefore responsible only to the demands of elite groups. Policy application is affected by much the same forces that fragment and decentralize power in other parts of the American system. As we shall see, negotiation, persuasion, and compromise are the marks of a pluralistic policymaking process.

## the environment of policy application

The executive branch has activities and responsibilities almost beyond counting. They include every activity of government. Legally and technically they cover two broad functions: *application* of policy decisions

[12] Ollie A. Jensen, "Cultural Bias in Selection," in Golembriewski and Cohen, pp. 287–295.

made by Congress, courts, and the President and *adjudication* of disputes between individuals, groups, and organizations by authority granted by Congress. Laws of Congress and court decisions on taxes, narcotics, welfare, corporations, or civil rights are defined and interpreted by the administrator responsible for their application. Hundreds of rules and regulations come from administrative — not purely legislative — action.

Choice and discretion are inherent in all these activities: when and if to prosecute a violator of law; whether to spend money appropriated and for which purposes; whether to initiate proposals for new or modified laws or to use present authority; whether to centralize or decentralize the administration of a program, etc.

An administrator's environment profoundly affects his choices. Administrators both formulate and adjudicate policy. When they develop rules or guidelines for carrying out the broad intent of Congress as expressed in statutes, they are formulating policy. When a regulatory agency such as the Federal Trade Commission or the Interstate Commerce Commission issues an order to a broadcaster or a trucking company to "cease and desist" from an activity, it is adjudicating policy. It is participating in the resolution of conflict and is therefore subject to many of the same pressures as a legislator or a judge. This environment of conflict will become more easily visible if we briefly study one administrative agency, the Office of Economic Opportunity.

## war on poverty and the oeo

The war on poverty promised by Presidents Kennedy and Johnson began when Congress passed the 1964 Economic Opportunity Act. With its programs to lift citizens out of poverty, unlike the traditional attempts to relieve the effects of poverty, the Act emphasized education and training. It included three major types of assistance: the Job Corps, VISTA (Volunteers in Service to America), and Community Action Programs. It was to be administered by the newly established Office of Economic Opportunity (OEO), and the agency was placed directly in the Executive Office of the President to dramatize its importance and to provide more innovative programs by removing it from the presumably less imaginative established agencies.

The Job Corps, somewhat like the Civilian Conservation Corps (CCC) of the 1930s, was to provide the disadvantaged young with employment training and remedial education. In its first four years, it was given appropriations of almost $1 billion. Costs of training (about $7,500 per trainee per year) were relatively high: many trainees dropped out after a short time and many rural communities gave Job Corps Training Centers a cool reception.

OEO's Community Action Programs such as this shoe store cooperative have been designed to incorporate "maximum feasible participation" of the poor, recognizing that poverty is a national problem.

VISTA, the domestic equivalent of the Peace Corps, is composed of volunteers who work with and bring self-help assistance to slums, rural poverty areas, Indian reservations, and other depressed areas. VISTA has never received strong financial support from Congress and consequently has not been prominent in the war on poverty.

The most controversial OEO activity is the Community Action Programs. The act provided that local antipoverty programs were to be administered as much as possible at the local level and were to encourage "maximum feasible participation" by the citizens they helped. OEO interpreted this broad mandate as requiring that local residents participate in almost all parts of the program, including its design and operation. It also called for election by poor people, whenever feasible, of about a third of the membership in local Community Action Agencies. To enforce these administrative rules, the OEO sometimes threatened to withhold funds for local programs; but often the CAAs have included only a small percentage of the poor, getting most of its members from the professional and middle-class community.

The CAA programs have included day care centers for children, job counseling, vocational education, birth control information centers, legal aid services, and health care centers. The OEO directives on participation by the poor were resisted from the beginning by local political forces, which saw the CAAs as potential political rivals to established political interests in the community. Mayor Richard Daley of Chicago supported

466

federal efforts in funding local programs; but he insisted that local government officials, that is, the Daley political organization, should decide how to spend the money. Other mayors accepted Daley's leadership and these local political interests got strong support from Congressmen, who added their influence to the efforts to force OEO to recognize CAA programs endorsed by local government. OEO also was strongly criticized for activities of some CAA groups. One group in Newark was blamed for contributing to the 1967 riots there, and a group in Syracuse was accused of handing out manuals that called on blacks to use force to achieve their goals. These charges gave added ammunition to conservative Congressmen already suspicious of or hostile to the entire war on poverty program.

Congress responded to these pressures and criticisms by cutting OEO funds and transferring some of its functions to other established agencies. In 1967, it removed OEOs power to approve CAA proposals, and gave it to state and local government units. This action followed an OEO decision to put 60 percent of OEO funds into projects specified by OEO, enraging local poverty group leaders as well as local governments. Congress also exercised its power to earmark funds for specific programs and took measures aimed at denying funds to those taking part in local disorders.

Local interests also applied pressure elsewhere. Community Action Programs have increasingly come under the influence of local political forces or professional groups. Local health programs are designed and mostly controlled by hospitals and local medical societies. Job Corps training programs often are operated under contract by private businesses on a cost-plus basis, which is criticized as a profitable enterprise for private interests in managing government antipoverty programs.

The Nixon administration shifted the OEO's mission from operating antipoverty programs to developing new approaches to social problems. They apparently intend to develop programs that, if successful, would be transferred to permanent agencies. The Job Corps has been transferred to the Labor Department and other OEO programs to Health, Education and Welfare and the Small Business Administration. Despite charges by liberal Democrats in Congress that Nixon had "retreated" from the war on poverty, it appeared that OEO programs and the agency's mission would be modified still more.

The history of OEO clearly reveals how political interests clash and so determine how administrative organization and policy will develop. Dissatisfied local political interests, differences over the desirability of programs, struggling over appropriations, and a change in the presidency brought on changes and a retreat from the original objectives. As a new agency, the OEO was not able to get support either from private interests or from powerful Congressmen that established agencies enjoy. There is little similarity in the power and influence of established political and economic interests and that of the large, but generally weak and unorganized poor. Although the attack on poverty has been supported by all recent Presidents, Congress, and many private groups, no consensus has been found on the best *means* for attacking the problem or on the level of priority that antipoverty measures should have. Administrative agencies like the OEO that are responsible for formulating new programs and administering established ones labor under many political forces that cannot agree on anything beyond admitting that poverty is a national problem and must be dealt with. The national War on Poverty probably will be fought within changing patterns of administrative organization and policy, not on the battlefield of poverty itself.

## bargaining and policy by increment

Policy application is generally characterized by two basic features of the American political community. The formal organization of a bureaucracy suggests that it is directed by formal hierarchical controls, but both the Constitution and extraconstitutional procedures make it highly decentralized. Consequently, it works by *bargaining, not command* — particularly when agency leaders get their own political support from legislators and pressure groups.

The tradition of *policy incrementalism* (see Chapter Eleven), buttressed by the need to bargain and compromise, obstructs the efforts of the administration to secure consistent programs and to pursue long-range goals. Most often, the administrator tries for piecemeal but workable solutions to immediate problems regardless of their future effectiveness. The price support and subsidy program for selected agricultural crops is considered economically unsound by many, but the powerful political interests attached to it have kept it going. Annual tinkering with the amount of support is likely to put off a frontal assault on the policy itself until the program becomes intensely and widely discredited.

## the bureaucracy's growth and organization

### pattern of growth

Legislation is made in response to demands by interests that have sought government help in reaching their goals. Before this century, federal activity in community life was limited because people thought they should be as free of government as possible. An expanding frontier, where land was easy to get and towns were isolated and sparsely populated, encouraged the self-reliance that made Americans suspicious of government interference. This spirit was reinforced by rising laissez-faire social and economic theories. Government was mostly a policing operation. Politics and economics were considered to be separate spheres, and government did not become involved in economic and social legislation until late in the nineteenth century.

Government intervened in the economy first at the state level when agricultural groups like the Granges in the Midwest began to agitate for the regulation of railroads and other economic reforms. As the nation experienced the industrial revolution and the accompanying social and economic adjustments, the demand for federal regulatory action increased. The new federal agencies created by Congress after the turn of the century were justified by reform groups as necessary to control "private interests" whose activities interfered with the "national interest." But the groups that fought the creation of these agencies saw the government's new regulatory role as interference with free enterprise.

By creating administrative agencies, Congress established public policy, but the policies were broad. The tasks assigned to the new agencies were too technical to allow detailed direction by either Congress or the Courts. As a result, congressional directives on administering public policy stipulated that agencies in fulfilling their responsibilities act in a "just" and "reasonable" fashion and in the "public interest." The main burden of reconciling group conflict was shifted from Congress to the administrative bureaucracy, which became the new target for pressure groups seeking to influence the administrators' policy choices. Administrative agencies became focal points for disputes and decisions on policy, as well as for policy application.

## politics of organization

A chart showing the organization of any large federal agency — not to mention the entire federal government (see Chapter Eleven) — reveals how massive and complex federal administration is. Generally speaking, the administrative branch is organized by departments for specialized areas. The pattern is hierarchical: authority and responsibility — the chain of command — are based on superior-subordinate relationships. At the top of this hierarchy, and in formal command of the entire administrative structure (except as discussed below), is the President. Immediately below are the executive departments headed by secretaries who are also members of the Cabinet. These include the Departments of State, the

Treasury, Defense, Justice, the Post Office, the Interior, Agriculture, Commerce, Labor, Health, Education, and Welfare, Housing and Urban Development, and Transportation. Each department is formally divided into bureaus, divisions, sections, and even desks.

Many of these departments have semiautonomous subagencies, and some do a minimum of coordinating administration. The Federal Bureau of Investigation in the Department of Justice, or the Office of Education in the Department of Health, Education, and Welfare are only nominally administered by the Attorney General or the Secretary of Health, Education, and Welfare. Those who try to coordinate the activities of these subagencies often end up with corporate conflict between semiautonomous agencies and their administrative superiors. The same kind of conflict has hindered unification of the Army, Air Force, and Navy under the Department of Defense.

THE INDEPENDENT AGENCIES. Alongside the executive departments are about forty-five independent executive agencies, so termed because they are not within a departmental organization, although many are still under presidential control. The Veterans Administration is formally responsible to the President, but its chief does not carry Cabinet rank. Other independent executive agencies are the Selective Service System, the Atomic Energy Commission, the Tariff Commission, and the National Aeronautics and Space Administration.

Independent *regulatory* agencies are free of direct presidential control. They are "quasi-legislative" or "quasi-judicial" and their authority is not purely executive. The Federal Communications Commission can issue or deny licenses to radio and television stations, mixing legislative and judicial powers. The President appoints the members of each commission, but they can be removed only for causes specified by Congress. The Supreme Court held in 1935 that these agencies perform legislative and judicial functions and that their members may not be removed by the president, thus upholding their independence. The Interstate Commerce Commission, the National Labor Relations Board, the Federal Trade Commission, the Federal Power Commission, the Securities and Exchange Commission, and the Civil Aeronautics Board are independent of presidential control.

OVERSIGHT OR SERVICE AGENCIES. This type of administrative agency serves other government agencies. The General Services Administration is the purchasing agent, storage agency, documents clerk, and builder of federal offices. The Office of Management and Budget aids the President in fiscal control and policy coordination. The General Accounting Office is the congressional auditing watchdog over executive expenditures. The Civil Service Commission recruits employees and manages public personnel policies.

GOVERNMENT CORPORATIONS. Organized much like private businesses, government corporations like the Federal Deposit Insurance Corporation or the Tennessee Valley Authority were created to carry out primarily economic operations not provided by private enterprise. Some of these corporations extend credit to farmers, produce electric power, insure bank deposits, provide loans for home buyers, and operate terminal and port facilities.

## agencies and their clienteles

The administrative agencies created by Congress provide a voice for particular sets of community interests and are called clientele agencies. The Department of Agriculture was created in 1862 to give special assistance to and promote the welfare of farm groups. The Department of Commerce and the Department of Labor were created in 1903 and 1913. The Veterans Administration dispenses about $5 billion per year in benefits to veterans. Government corporations, also meant to provide a voice for particular interests, may be considered clientele agencies. Some functional agencies such as the Department of the Treasury or the Department of State have a specific task instead of serving a particular clientele. Others serve a locality or section, like the Tennessee Valley Authority.

All administrative agencies are like clientele agencies in that they serve and draw support from specific groups. For that support they must pay a price. Vested interests inhibit or prevent change, reducing the agency's flexibility in responding to changes in environment or demands of new interests. The following two examples illustrate the point.

THE TENNESSEE VALLEY AUTHORITY (TVA). The TVA, a government corporation, was established by Congress in 1933 to develop the water, electric power, and agricultural resources of a vast multistate region. The grassroots approach was chosen as a more efficient and democratic model than imposing an administrative hierarchy on top of structures already there. Local and state governments and private interests would carry out the tasks of the Authority. Although this approach did much that it was intended to, some unintended effects were detrimental to other TVA goals. Philip Selznick wrote that TVA, by "a process of informal cooptation," absorbed spokesmen for interest groups in its area into its policymaking structure "as a means of averting threats to its stability or existence."[13] The land-grant colleges in the area integrated the TVA's Agricultural Relations Department's improvement operations into their own extension services. The TVA, in turn, protected the colleges from attempts to remove their special status. The Agricultural Relations Department became the sole contact between the TVA and the colleges, thus transforming the interests of the colleges and such agricultural organizations as the Farm Bureau Federation informally into the structure and personnel of the TVA.

The Agricultural Relations Department forced the Authority to change its initial goal of achieving soil conservation by public ownership of land.[14] The TVA has more recently come into conflict with environmental interest groups over its use of strip-mined coal, on which it depends heavily for producing power. Strip-mining devastates thousands of acres of land and is a major source of water pollution. Environmentalists have attacked a TVA proposal to build a new dam (Tellico), primarily for recreation on the Little Tennessee river. A court suit was brought by environmental interests to halt construction of the dam because it would needlessly flood thousands of acres of land and would destroy the natural beauty of one of the few remaining natural streams in the region. Once supported as a strong friend by naturalists and environmentalists, TVA now finds itself charged with contributing to the deterioration and destruction of our environment.

THE REGULATORY COMMISSIONS: CAPTIVES OF THOSE THEY REGULATE? One of Ralph Nader's investigations in the late 1960s was aimed at the close association of regulatory agencies with clientele groups. Nader specifically questioned how effectively the Federal Trade Commission protects the public against vested economic interests, charging that the FTC, in fact, promoted the interests of groups it was meant to regulate. "Fair competition" was not only not maintained, Nader charged, but Commission members who favored the industries they were supposed to regulate were given high-paying positions by the industries after leaving government employment.[15] Nader's findings reinforced other prior evidence on regulatory agencies. For many years, the Interstate Commerce Commission favored the railroads over other forms of transportation (e.g., the trucking industry) and thus defended the status quo against new developments and changes in transportation media.

[13] Philip Selznick, *TVA and the Grass Roots* (Berkeley, Calif.: University of California Press, 1953), p. 13.

[14] *Ibid.*, pp. 111–116, 190–213.

[15] *The Progressive* (May 1970), pp. 13–22.

Groups are clearly at a disadvantage if they lack access to administrative agencies. Although the Department of Agriculture services agricultural interests, agricultural groups do not get equal representation. The powerful Farm Bureau Federation usually reflects the interests of larger and more prosperous farmers. Although other agricultural interest groups (e.g., Farmers Union) show more interest in preserving the "family farm," the small and economically marginal farmer loses more and more in the conflict over farm policies. Migrant farm laborers are even worse off; they have virtually no access to the Agriculture Department. Both the marginal farmer and the migrant farm laborer are "orphaned," with no government agency representing their interests.

The conditions under which an administrative agency is created determine how well it can fulfill its purposes. The Office of Economic Opportunity has not been able to harmonize the interests of local political forces with its declared policy of getting the poor directly involved in local poverty programs. The intent Congress declared in the 1964 act, requiring "maximum feasible participation" of poor people, was not clear. Some Congressmen and local public officials claimed that the vague provision was not intended to mean that the poor should participate as much as the Office of Economic Opportunity guidelines required. In the ensuing conflict between local political interests and the OEO, Congress intervened on the side of the local interests. David Truman points out that if the terms of a law are ambiguous it is likely that organized interests, not the administrator, will control policy application.[16] The administrator — in this case the OEO — inherits conflicts postponed but not resolved by legislation. Thus the bureaucrats' performance is partly conditioned by the policies they must implement and enforce. Competing interests must be adjusted within the agency's goals and responsibilities as well as the requirements and expectations of Congress and the President.

CONTROLLING AND REORGANIZING THE BUREAUCRACY. Sheer size keeps the executive from dominating even the part of the bureaucracy over which the President has direct legal control. Controlling a constantly expanding "fourth branch" is so difficult that the administrative branch has undergone three major reviews in forty years: Franklin D. Roosevelt's Committee on Administrative Management (Brownlow Committee) in 1937; the Truman-appointed Hoover Commission, headed by former President Herbert Hoover, which reported in 1949; and a second Hoover Commission, which reported in 1955. All emphasized the "integrative principle" of organization by suggesting a hierarchical arrangement with a central

[16] David B. Truman, *The Governmental Process* (New York: Alfred A. Knopf, 1953), pp. 443–444.

superior, a relatively small number of subordinates, usually between three and fifteen, and clear lines of authority and responsibility. No matter how rational and wise an attempt at administrative reorganization may seem, however, it is bound to cause conflict among interests, because the interests and even the agencies may support or oppose change depending upon whether they stand to gain or lose by it.

To be sure, an organization's formal structure is important because "the formal allocation of power, of rights and responsibilities, of authorizations and limitations is affected. . . ."[17] Proposals for reorganization are likely to be made when a new administration takes office and views change as necessary to achieve its programs; when an existing program or structure is subjected to strong criticism (OEO, Selective Service System in 1968); or when an administrator feels that reorganization would help in achieving his goals or preparing him for new demands. Power and access are affected by change; so despite conventional symbols that are brought up to justify change (among them "efficiency" and "economy"), interests will support or oppose reorganization to the extent that they expect to lose or gain by it. Status, influence, and power are at stake; and in view of the decentralized and pluralistic political system, this ensures that the interests fighting over reorganization will be many and varied. Congressmen (and the interests they support) will resist and are unlikely to favor changes that would reduce their access and influence. Conversely, a President may seek such change to enhance his own control and to cut down on the influence that competing interests have over agency policies. It seems inconsistent and illusory to ask for centralized control over administration in a political system characterized by decentralized and fragmented power in spite of the efficiency and economy claimed for it. Further, the improved representation and control usually associated with decentralized structure and local control works against centralized patterns of bureaucratic organization.

## bureaucratic behavior and the politics of administration

An administrator is part of the political system; but he also belongs to an organization formally tied together by a hierarchy of management, rules of procedure, standards of conduct, and the technical and professional tasks of administration. These make the bureaucrat something more than the automaton buried in a forest of red tape that caricaturists portray.

---

[17] James W. Davis, *The Executive Branch*, p. 196. This paragraph is in part based on pp. 194–209 of this book.

J. Edgar Hoover's almost impregnable position as FBI chief resulted largely from his strong support by Congress and the public. Mandatory retirement rules were suspended so that he could serve until his death.

## formal relationships

A stable and predictable environment is a natural goal for any highly formal, continuing organization. Bureaucratic organization is at least partly achieved by a structural arrangement of the various units within the agency into a hierarchy of command and responsibility. Details of organization vary from agency to agency. One may strive for unity of command, making one official ultimately responsible for all policy decisions; another may have a plural executive or a set of officials who share responsibility.

Routine procedures are established for handling appeals by interests, office communications, personnel matters, and the release of information. Ambiguity in the relations of the agency as well as in superior-subordinate relationships within the organization is reduced as much as possible.

Administration is policymaking, and the structure and relationships surrounding those who make decisions are anything but static. We have seen the politics that surround proposals for administrative reorganization; other features of organization also define the role and importance of the bureaucrat.

### procedures and conduct

The bureaucratic organization's massiveness makes relations impersonal and intimidates many individuals making a plea before an agency.

The Federal Power Commission has tried to standardize policy activities. *The Rules of Practice and Procedure* comprises more than sixty pages of small print describing precisely what is expected of the personnel under all circumstances. This handbook discusses who may file petitions before the commission, prehearing conferences and hearings before the commission, procedures for issuing subpoenas, and methods for taking depositions. Even the official seal of the commission is here: "A shield upon the breast of the eagle displaying a belt of lightning sinister-wise complemented by two gas flames representing the Commission's regulatory authority in the fields of electric energy and gas."[18]

The impersonality and the hierarchic structure of a large organization set the individual administrator's status. Each person is superior to some and subordinate to others, and each position has specified rights and duties. The administrator's perspective, of course, is modeled by his understanding of the prerogatives that command or require obedience. Victor A. Thompson mentions a few of the features that distinguish the "boss" from his underlings: he has final say on policy measures, which is subject to no appeal; he may have absolute discretion in decisions affecting employee goals, such as raises and promotions; he has coercive tools that define his decisions as commands; and he can monopolize organizational communications both internally and with the public.[19]

The subordinate's status can be threatened by his chief and by the continuing possibility of congressional investigation or cutbacks of personnel. Robert Presthus, studying the way in which organizational activity has affected American life, calls this characteristic "status anxiety"; the underling is never really secure in his position. His actions will be influenced by the desire to equate his personal interests with his organizational surroundings.[20] He may prefer caution and anonymity rather than risk his status by innovative or unorthodox behavior.

### limits of hierarchic control

Administrative subordinates want to enhance their status and protect their positions from adverse action by superiors, which may lead them

---

[18] Federal Power Commission, *Rules of Practice and Procedure* (Washington, D.C.: U.S. Government Printing Office, 1958), p. 2.

[19] Victor A. Thompson, *Modern Organization* (New York: Alfred A. Knopf, 1963), pp. 60–66.

[20] Robert Presthus, *The Organizational Society* (New York: Alfred A. Knopf, 1962).

to try to modify the superior-subordinate relationship. Special skills, strong public support, alliances with influential Congressmen, or long career service may insulate bureau chiefs from control by superiors. Control of the agency may rest on administrators officially subordinated but actually autonomous. For example, widespread public and congressional support has given the chief of the Forest Service in the Department of Agriculture and the head of the Army Corps of Engineers special status.

The President controls the bureaucracy mostly by his power of appointment and removal of the major department heads. These political executives are his "first team" and share his political responsibility for policies. To succeed, a political executive must work within the bureaucratic structure he heads. It is impossible to draw a clear line between the job of the political executive and career bureaucrats in bureaucratic policymaking. Each depends on the other, though. The bureaucrats depend on the department head to represent them at the highest administrative level, and the department head depends on his subordinates for information and technical knowledge to reach policy goals and formulate new programs. The career bureaucrat will be a part of the structure long after the department head has departed and is needed to administer and help develop the policies of a new administration. Increasing administrative specialization helps the bureaucrat protect his status against threats from the political executives at the top of the hierarchy.

Organization too is specialized. Specific duties are made routine so anyone can carry them out. Standard operating procedures keep the constant movement of trained personnel from disturbing the organization's goals. This division of labor conditions the administrative perspective.

The bureaucrat's idea of his place in the organization influences his outlook on policy application. Performing his duties by routine rather than reflection affects his view of personal discretion in policy affairs, organizational goals, and ultimately community interest. An administrator who feels his discretionary authority is narrow will be less accessible to interests who want to change his point of view than an administrator who believes he has broad discretionary powers. He may choose to "play it safe" instead of risking loss of status (or his job) by new approaches or techniques advocated by interests outside the organization.

Not only are tasks specialized within bureaucratic organizations but individuals also become specialists. Task specialization is illustrated by an individual employed by the Federal Home Loan Bank Board who builds highly specialized competence in handling a particular type of loan application. Subject-matter specialization also characterizes large-scale organizational life. A chemical engineer may specialize in environmental quality controls and become expert in the broad field of ecology. Power and influence can be gained by long experience on the job, making the agency dependent on the individual for information and administrative know-how, creating semiautonomous pockets of power within the organization.

But government administrators are also specialized in that they are government employees. Except for partisan appointees, most come through the ranks of the civil service. A professional outlook colors their conceptions; as career civil servants, they are on the inside of policymaking and their tenure transcends that of partisan appointees, pressure-group leaders, and a community that becomes aware of their existence sporadically. Professional specialization sets bureaucratic administrators apart from superiors who may be less well informed about the agency's jurisdiction or who may be short-term political appointees.

Professionalism is part of modern administration, but it carries risks as well as advantages for the public. The risks are described by Emmette S. Redford as "inertness, separation, and specialization."[21] Inert bureaucrats are "sluggish, self-satisfied, and interested in the survival of their existing habits and thought patterns." They adapt slowly to changing times and circumstances and have little initiative.

A second danger — separation — arises when a bureaucrat becomes so self-centered that he loses contact with public opinion or gets suspicious of outside forces. Specialization, which Redford sees as the "most persistent cause of separateness and the greatest danger of bureaucracy," occurs when administrators see only their own or their clientele's position as valid in a controversy over policy.

Coordinating highly specialized personnel and agencies into a unified, coherent organization is a formidable job. To protect its status within the administrative structure, "each functional organization," says Redford, "develops its own self-centered attitudes," as well as close ties with private groups and key committees and individuals in Congress. A bureau in the Department of Agriculture would have little sympathy for consumer interests that opposed agricultural price-support programs. The military establishment does not appreciate domestic and foreign policy needs that compete with military needs for congressional support. Both the agricultural interests and the military interests have supporters in key congressional positions who help them resist pressures for changes in policy.

Administrative perspective differs from the executive and the legislative perspectives examined earlier. Administrators depend on each other's skills and cooperation in striving to achieve administrative goals, but conflict arises over how much they must rely on one another.[22] One

[21] Emmette S. Redford, *Ideal and Practice in Public Administration* (Birmingham, Ala.: University of Alabama Press, 1958), pp. 63–67.
[22] Thompson, *Modern Organization,* pp. 108–110.

source of disagreement is the refusal to accept new administrative specialties, such as computer specialists, as legitimate participants in policy application. It took some time for the computer specialist to be admitted to the ranks of public administration; but despite continuing resistance, he now occupies positions of high status in the Internal Revenue Service, the Census Bureau, and the Social Security Administration.

Most bureaucratic conflict is caused by the difference in point of view on policy application between the specialist and the individual whose administrative skills lie in the managing of general goals. The specialist is more likely to emphasize innovation in procedures and new approaches to problems. The nonspecialist will consider consolidation of current tasks and adjustment of interests as more important. A highly trained specialist in disposing of industrial waste might find his proposals 'for regulating disposal vetoed or modified by a nonspecialist superior who is sensitive to the political effects of promoting a new policy. Efforts to resolve such conflicts might include formal reorganization of authority; but simply reorganizing lines of command, changing staff and line functions, and modifying organization charts do not get to the source of the disputes. Hence, administrators look outside the organization for support. They form informal policy alliances with partisan appointees, members of Congress, and pressure group leaders; and they supplement internal conflict resolution with external bargaining.

**The USDA has protected farm interests in its application of the pesticide, DDT. Interagency conflict developed when concerns for the environment prompted the Environmental Protection Agency to challenge this practice.**

## congress and the bureaucracy

The view from the bureaucrat's desk is shaped by these personal and organizational factors, but also by the pressures that the legislative branch imposes on him.

Article I of the Constitution empowers Congress to exercise control over the administrative branch by its authority to create administrative agencies, to advise and consent to presidential appointments, or withhold consent, and to exercise the power of the purse. Implicit in such delegations are other powers. Congress derives its right to investigate the operations of the executive from its authority to make laws and to reorganize the bureaucracy and from its power to authorize new programs and departments. From its beginnings, Congress has prescribed how the executive branch will be organized, shaped the government's functions by appropriations, investigated practices and policies, and regulated federal employees.

## congress and the civil service

Students of public administration agree that personnel policies of the civil service covering retirement, salary schedules, organization, public employee organizations, and employee participation in party activities are the province of Congress but that detailed rules and regulations should be left to the President and the Civil Service Commission. Congress has done so, although it has also remained responsive to veteran's organizations that have sought considerations (e.g., veteran's preference) for their members. Also, during and after World War II legislation was enacted that sought presidential "Loyalty Orders" requiring that federal civilian employees be investigated.

## congress and the budget

"The budget is the life-blood of government, the financial reflection of what the government does or intends to do," writes Aaron Wildavsky. "The crucial aspect of budgeting is whose preferences are to prevail in disputes about which activities are to be carried on and to what degree, in the light of limited resources."[23] For the administrator, the appro-

---

[23] Aaron Wildavsky, "Political Implications of Budgetary Reform," *Public Administration Review* 21 (Autumn 1961): 185.

priations process involves several stages of review during which the programs and proposals of his agency are at stake. The first is review by the Office of Management and Budget, which seeks to protect the President's interests in achieving his overall directives on the national budget.

Once the agency's requests have been incorporated into the President's budget, it is considered by Congress. Specifically, an agency's appropriations request will be considered first by one of the subcommittees of the House Appropriations Committee. These subcommittees will usually approach their function of review with the idea that appropriations should be cut. At times, however, an agency may have to accept unwanted programs especially important to the constituency of a powerful Congressman. A bureau chief called to testify before a subcommittee is subjected to close questioning about the general goals and purposes for which the money is to be used to minor but embarrassing matters, such as a complaint about the agency that a subcommittee member may have had from one of his constituents.

Above all, an agency must prevent the appropriations subcommittee from developing a hostile or unsympathetic attitude. It will, therefore, try to build support for its programs among interests outside Congress by associating its own goals with those of its clientele and by maintaining close communications with appropriations committees. Cultivating good relations with subcommittees enhances the power of individual members (especially the subcommittee chairman) and may also produce special protective alliances with congressional interests that oppose presidential policies.

The House Appropriations Committee usually accepts the recommendations of its subcommittees, which normally propose cuts in agency requests. The Senate Appropriations Committee is a kind of appeals court for the agencies, and it frequently restores some or all of the cuts made by the House. Aaron Wildavsky has characterized a member of the Senate Appropriations Committee as seeing his role as the "responsible legislator" who rectifies the wrongs done by "the irrepressible lower House." Conversely, however, the House Appropriations Committee member sees his duty as balancing the action of Senate "dilettantes who swap favors and do not care what happens to the public purse."[24] The bureaucrat must calculate as best he can the reactions of committees in the two chambers, which means assessing what can be obtained in the political environment of committee attitudes, administrative constituency support, and his ability to convince congressmen of the rightness of his agency's request for support.

[24] Aaron Wildavsky, *The Politics of the Budgetary Process* (Boston: Little, Brown, 1964), p. 51.

The Office of Management and Budget (see Chapter Twelve) is less effective in controlling appropriations of agencies with special access to Congress, but politically weaker agencies are more at its mercy in the budget review. The other stages in the appropriations process also reveal the politics of the budgetary process. An agency is involved then in the bargaining, persuasion, and compromise that mark the other policy processes.

## informal congressional supervision

Congress gets informal control over agencies from relationships between executive officials and individual legislators. In committee hearings, legislators can ask questions and make statements from which administrators can gather important clues in the attitudes they reveal. Major decisions are made in standing committees and rarely are rejected by the whole Congress, both administrators and interest groups are aware that the statements legislators make at committee hearings are important. Hearings also can be used by skillful administrators to resist pressure from the President, private groups, and other administrative agencies.

Congressional-administrative relationships are an important informal means of control because Congressmen act as administrative "lobbyists" for their constituents. Inquiries that a Representative or Senator addresses to an agency on behalf of a constituent or interest group usually get special attention, especially if the legislator is in a position to assist or block an agency's program. An administrator will try to avoid antagonizing a legislator; he may not comply with legislators' demands, but he will often try hard to conciliate them.

Pressure groups and administrators, recognizing the powers of congressional committees, often attempt to work out clearance for significant policies in advance. Relationships between agencies and the influential members of a committee, especially its chairman, often are very close. During World War II, Representative Carl Vinson of Georgia, Chairman of the House Naval Affairs Committee, and the Navy Department were intimate because of Vinson's extensive knowledge of naval affairs. Because of more than twenty years of service on the committee and because he was chairman, the Navy Department frequently consulted with him about policy. After the war, when unification of the armed services had been achieved, Vinson became Chairman of the House Armed Services Committee, from which position he was to develop much the same relationship with the Army and Air Force as he had held with the Navy.[25]

[25] Truman, *The Governmental Process*, pp. 423–424.

## limits on congressional control

The power to investigate, to legislate, to reorganize, and to control appropriations are powerful weapons in limiting the bureaucracy's influence in policymaking. Yet these controls are only nominally exercised by Congress.

The most important control is appropriations. Congressional control over spending is marked by restraint, as Richard Fenno found in studying the budget requests of thirty-nine agencies handling domestic policy from 1947 to 1962, twenty-seven received congressional appropriations within an average of 5 percent of what the President had requested and thirty-five were within 10 percent of these requests. Fenno also found that at the administrative budget-review level (OMB), twenty-four of the thirty-six agencies had requested increases over the previous year of at least 10 percent; eleven had requested 20 percent; and two had requested at least 75 percent.[26] Congress does not indulge in dramatic cutbacks in funds, at least in the domestic area. Once the budget process has been completed by the President, Congress makes only small changes. This process of "incremental budgeting" means that "the budgets of most agencies inch upward over the years. Nothing short of a major social or economic crisis seems able to cause a major alteration."[27]

These trends in congressional response to requests for appropriations are explained mostly by the congressional environment. A Congressman has neither the time nor the information to thoroughly review such requests. He must divide his attention among many legislative matters, and he must also service the many requests of his constituents. It is just about impossible for him to learn enough to thoroughly review the operations and programs of all units in the executive branch. Some are able to learn a great deal about parts of the budget. Representative Otto Passman, as chairman of the Foreign Operations Appropriations Subcommittee of the House, has become a highly knowledgeable major opponent of foreign aid appropriations. Generally, however, Congress must rely on the presidential budget and on the knowledge of the vast staff available to him.

The fragmented congressional organization, the bicameral system, and the difficulties of coordinated leadership also reduce congressional control of the bureaucracy to nominal size. Because congressional leadership has no focus in either of the two houses, bureaucratic interests (and the

[26] Richard F. Fenno, Jr., *The Power of the Purse: Appropriations Politics in Congress* (Boston: Little, Brown, 1966).

[27] Ira Sharkansky, *The Routines of Politics* (New York: Van Nostrand Reinhold, 1970), p. 51.

private interests that support them) can get to many veto points in the legislative process. The policy of incrementalism that generally characterizes the legislative process protects and insulates the bureaucracy from more than nominal control by Congress. Reorganization of the executive branch, major changes in policy direction, or dramatic budget cuts are inconsistent with incremental change. Congress can review the administration, but it cannot effectively regulate it. Its influence over the bureaucracy consists of broad policy choices that, once made, are administered with limited legislative controls by the bureaucrats.

## the president and the bureaucracy

Although the President is looked to more and more for policy leadership and initiative, this control over his administration is far from complete. Agencies with quasi-legislative and quasi-judicial functions are largely independent of direct presidential control because their governing executives are not subject to the President's removal powers and they were deliberately established to operate outside the President's chain of command. For most of the administrative structure — over which the President *does* have adequate formal authority — he customarily lacks the time and resources to supervise and direct. Instead, he deals essentially with matters that he considers of greatest importance and leaves much of the bureaucracy free to operate at the discretion of career administrators. The ability of pressure groups to influence policy is enhanced by administrative discretion, especially if the clientele interests of an agency can turn readily to Congress. Even a department head or bureau chief who is loyal to the President may be put in a position in which his support of his chief may arouse the wrath of clientele groups and allied legislators.

When a President does choose to intervene in a dispute within the executive branch, he may not get his way. The classic example (others are less publicized) is the friction between the President and the Army Corps of Engineers. By statute, the corps is in the Department of Defense under the commander in chief, but in fact it sees itself as responsible to Congress.[28] Originally designed to handle federal flood control and harbor projects, in the 1930s the Corps began to expand its activities to include land reclamation, power production, land irrigation, and other matters. The resulting conflict with the Bureau of Reclamation in the Department of Interior caused President Roosevelt, and later President Truman, to intervene on behalf of the bureau. The corps used its close association

[28] Arthur A. Maass, "Congress and Water Resources," *The American Political Science Review* 19 (Sept. 1950), pp. 576–593.

As both enforcer and formulator of public policy, the Selective Service System touched every male citizen.

with Congress to resist presidential directives and policy statements submitted to congressional committees handling water projects. Because corps projects are of special interest to Congressmen and their constituencies, the President has been unable to develop a coordinated water-resources and flood-control policy.

All administrative agencies are interested in their own survival and expansion, which requires that their functions and activities have political support. Each must keep the support of the groups most directly affected by its functions. The agency runs the risk of becoming a captive of these interests. By comparison, the President represents a larger public interest, and his policies and decisions must accommodate a more diversified clientele. The compromises he negotiates in pursuing his goals are likely to differ from those shaped by administrative agencies. The President is only one source of bureaucratic vitality; other sources become, in effect, his rivals for control over the administrative branch.

The President's control, however, is always great. His position as chief administrator and as initiator of policy keeps it great. Congress takes its budgetary cues from the President; and although he cannot prevent some agency requests from winning congressional approval without his support, the budget remains a significant weapon of control.

## popular control and policy application

Liberal democracy requires that policymakers be responsible to the governed. But how can the bureaucracy be kept responsible to the citizens in a democratic system?

Until about the time of the New Deal, Americans were generally more interested in increasing professionalism in the public service than in controlling the power of bureaucracy. The reforms of the later nineteenth century emphasized merit and knowledge as the basis for government employment and paved the way for eliminating the spoils system in the federal service. Since the 1930s, the public administrator's part in policymaking and his relationship to the whole political system have received greater attention.

The bureaucracy is deeply involved in formulating public policy and has great power. Control over it results from direct intervention by the President and Congress and from the limits its own environment imposes on it. Limits on bureaucratic action flow from the system itself, especially from the two basic features of a pluralist community and the fragmentation of policymaking authority.

Separation of powers and checks and balances prevents any branch of government and any combination of interests from controlling the whole of the policymaking process. Federalism also divides governing authority and contributes to the fragmentation of power. Fragmented policymaking is more likely to produce an inefficient administrative organization than a system that is tyrannical or uncontrollable. Multiple sources of power and multiple veto points are more the marks of incremental change and limited central authority than dramatic departures in policy or a unified source of policy. If our system has a problem, it is moving the system rapidly enough to accommodate the demands arising from a rapidly changing environment and traditional and deep-seated pluralistic distribution of power.

Does fragmentated policymaking in a pluralist community encourage development of an autonomous bureaucracy? On the whole, the pattern of decisionmaking reveals that it does not. It is true that great independence of agencies within the bureaucratic structure is promoted by close associations between agencies and congressional committees, the support of agency programs by clientele groups, the ability of an agency to mobilize clientele and employee support in achieving its goals, the possession of technical and specialized knowledge by agency personnel, and the lobbying of Congress by the bureaucracy on behalf of the latter's program objectives.

Two counterforces are important, however. One is the power of the

President, Congress, and the courts to mold policy. The President can and does demand action from the agencies under his control. The courts can and do rule against administrative action. Congress can and does legislate changes and impose restrictions. Further, competition within and between agencies fosters pluralist administrative decisionmaking, a further barrier against bureaucratic autonomy.

Second, pressure flows in several directions. Interests are opposed by competing interests. Access to one committee or one house of Congress is balanced by the opposition's access to other points in the legislative branch. Executive agencies trying to block presidential policy are opposed by other agencies that support him. Moreover, the setting or implementation of policy may be blocked by interests within an agency. Facing the pressures exerted by competing forces, an administrator may choose not to act, or his choice may represent the point of least resistance.

The danger of an arbitrary, manipulative, and irresponsible bureaucracy is probably less real than a bureaucracy immobilized by fragmentation. How can a large bureaucracy, subject to the pulls and pressures of competing forces both from within and without, be effectively mobilized and coordinated to meet the challenges of a rapidly changing social, economic, and political environment? Because of the plural character of American policy initiation, formulation, and application, the answer to this challenge lies in compromise and persuasion. New interests must operate within this policymaking framework, but they are not incapable of effecting change. The very size and complexity of the present bureaucratic structure itself results from new programs that arose in the 1930s, a strong argument that change is both real and possible.

*bibliographical note*

The study of public administration during the past two decades has increasingly concentrated on the bureaucracy as an instrument in policymaking. There are many good introductory texts available: Leonard D. White, *Introduction to the Study of Public Administration* (New York: Macmillan, 1955) is an influential, traditional approach to public administration; Herbert A. Simon, Donald W. Smithburg, and Victor A. Thompson, *Public Administration* (New York: Alfred A. Knopf, 1950) is the first text to introduce behavioral concepts into the study of public administration. For a shorter introductory treatment in paperback form, see Dwight Waldo, *The Study of Public Administration* (Garden City, N.Y.: Doubleday, 1955). An excellent anthology on the role of the federal bureaucracy is Alan A. Altshuler, *The Politics of the Federal Bureaucracy* (New York: Dodd, Mead, 1968).

An outstanding history of the growth and role of American bureaucracy from

1789 to 1901 is found in the following volumes written by Leonard D. White: *The Federalists* (1958); *The Jeffersonians* (1951); *The Jacksonians* (1954); and *The Republican Era* (1958), all published by Macmillan, New York. Paul Van Riper, *History of the United States Civil Service* (New York: Harper & Row, 1958) is an excellent study of federal personnel policies from an historical perspective. Students interested in sampling the most recent literature in personnel administration may consult Robert T. Golembriewski and Michael Cohen, eds., *People in Public Service* (Itasca, Ill.: F. E. Peacock, 1970).

Those interested in examining various approaches to the study of public administration will benefit from Dwight Waldo, *The Administrative State: A Study of the Political Theory of American Public Administration* (New York: Ronald Press, 1948). For a comparative study of bureaucracy, see Robert K. Merton, et al., eds., *Reader in Bureaucracy* (New York: Free Press, 1960).

Students who seek to gain an overview of the role of bureaucracy in policymaking have a wide range of books from which to choose. The following are all available in paperback editions: Peter M. Blau, *The Dynamics of Bureaucracy* (Chicago: University of Chicago Press, 1956) explores the nature of bureaucracy in a democratic society; Robert Presthus, *The Organizational Society* (New York: Alfred A. Knopf, 1962) is a highly readable and scholarly exploration of bureaucracy at all levels of modern American society; Ludwig von Mises, *Bureaucracy* (New Haven, Conn.: Yale University Press, 1962) presents a view of the bureaucratic phenomenon from the perspective of a widely known conservative; Anthony Downs, *Inside Bureaucracy* (Boston: Little, Brown, 1967) develops a theory of bureaucratic decisionmaking and explores its relevance to democracy. Francis E. Rourke, *Bureaucratic Power in National Politics,* 2nd ed. (Boston: Little, Brown, 1972) is an excellent source of readings on various aspects of the politics of bureaucratic relationships. Joseph P. Harris, *Congressional Control of Administration* (Washington, D.C.: Brookings Institution, 1964) explores the efforts of Congress to control the bureaucracy.

Close examination of specific areas of bureaucratic behavior and policymaking are necessary in developing a more sophisticated approach to the administrative role in American politics. Philip Selznick, *Leadership in Administration* (New York: Harper & Row, 1957) presents a sociologist's view of the role of bureaucracy; Victor Thompson, *Modern Organization* (New York: Alfred A. Knopf, 1963) describes bureaucracy as a system of human behavior; a paperback edition, Samuel Krislov and Lloyd D. Musalf, *The Politics of Regulation: A Reader* (Boston: Houghton Mifflin, 1964) explores the growth and importance of the independent regulatory commissions; J. Leiper Freeman, *The Political Process: Executive Bureau-Legislative Committee Relations* (New York: Random House, 1955) covers a vitally important area in the initiation and formulation of public policy, in paperback edition. Aaron Wildavsky's *The Politics of the Budgetary Process* (Boston: Little, Brown, 1964) is almost essential reading in gaining an appreciation of the relation of the budget process to public policy; for a highly respected private interest group's recommendation on how to improve the budgetary process within the context of the formulation and coordination of national goals, see Committee for Economic Development, *Budgeting for National Objectives*

(New York, 1966); Chapter Ten of Harmon Ziegler's *Interest Groups in American Society* (Englewood Cliffs, N.J.: Prentice-Hall, 1964) explores the agency-clientele relationship and overall patterns of conflict representation and resolution within the administrative structure. A very good case study which illustrates the institutional pluralism of the policymaking process is Clyde E. Jacobs and John F. Gallagher, *The Selective Service Act: A Case Study of the Governmental Process* (New York: Dodd Mead, 1967).

The problems, implicit and explicit, of bureaucracy's relationship to democratic and constitutional values are treated in a large body of literature. Paul Appleby, *Big Democracy* (New York: Alfred A. Knopf, 1945) presents the views of a former public official who argues the importance and responsibilities of the public executive. Roscoe C. Martin, ed., *Public Administration and Democracy: Essays in Honor of Paul H. Appleby* (Syracuse, N.Y.: Syracuse University Press, 1965) contains essays by leading scholars in the field of administration. Finally, the debate over bureaucratic social and economic planning and its relation to democratic values is illustrated in two commentaries, both available in paperback edition: Frederick A. Hayek, *The Road to Serfdom* (Chicago: University of Chicago Press, 1944) sees social planning as destructive of political and economic freedom; Herman Finer, *Road to Reaction* (Boston: Little, Brown, 1945) replies to Hayek's argument.

# chapter 15

# the courts
# and policy adjudication

In the fall of 1962, advertisements mailed from Middlesex, New Jersey, announced a new quarterly, *Eros,* "devoted to the subjects of Love and Sex." At about the same time, two other publications, *Housewife's Handbook on Selective Promiscuity* and *Liaison Newsletter,* were also advertised through the mails. All three were distributed by corporations headed by Ralph Ginzburg, a New York publisher.

Within its first year of publication, *Eros* counted over 150,000 subscribers, and large sales of the other two publications were recorded. An investigation by the United States Post Office Department culminated in the indictment of Ginzburg by a federal grand jury in March 1963. Ginzburg was charged with violating a United States law prohibiting use of the mails to send or advertise "obscene, lewd, lascivious, indecent, filthy or vile article, matter, thing, device, or substance." Federal laws dealing with the question of obscene material date back to the 1840s, although such legislation (including state legislation on the same subject) met no strong challenge until the 1950s. "Obscenity" has never enjoyed constitutional protection, but the Supreme Court in *Roth* v. *United States* (1957) attempted to define a standard that government might follow in prohibiting materials it deemed obscene. This test held material to be obscene if "to the average person, applying contemporary community standards, the dominant theme of the material taken as a whole appeals to prurient interests." In two subsequent decisions, the Court added two more tests — the material had to be "patently offensive" and it had to be shown to be "utterly without redeeming social importance."[1] Despite the Court's efforts, the justices themselves could find no standard for agreement and the Court remained divided over the kinds of material that are and are not protected under the Constitution. It appeared, however, to have tightened the standards under which state or federal governments could prohibit the publication of material because it was obscene. Ginzburg may have had the liberalized standards in mind when he launched publication of the periodicals at issue.

Ginzburg argued that the federal statute under which he was being prosecuted violated the First Amendment guarantee of free expression and also the Fifth and Sixth Amendments, because the statute was vague in defining a standard of obscenity. Relying on the three tests for obscenity we have cited, the Federal District Court found Ginzburg guilty. He was fined $28,000 and sentenced to five years in prison. One year later, the decision was upheld by the Federal Court of Appeals; and in 1965, the Supreme Court agreed to hear the case on appeal.

Supplying his own defense, Ginzburg was supported by the American Civil Liberties Union, the Author's League of America, and more than a hundred editors, writers, artists, clergymen, psychiatrists, and literary scholars. The government's case was supported by a nationwide group, the Citizens for Decent Literature, which, along with the groups mentioned above, filed *amicus curiae* briefs. Such a brief (literally "friend of the court") is an argument offered by an interested group not directly party to the suit but interested in its outcome. Thus the issue was extended beyond Ralph Ginzburg; it now involved a broad question of public policy over how much access the public should have to publications deemed objectionable, or legally, "obscene."

In a five-to-four decision, the Supreme Court upheld the conviction. Speaking for the Court majority, Justice Brennan held that although all the material in the publication was not obscene under prior Court tests, the manner in which they were advertised and the purpose for which they were distributed constituted the "sordid business of pandering"; that is, the material "was created, represented and sold solely as a claimed instrument of the sexual stimulation it would bring." The Court thus added a new test — "pandering" — to the three standards for determining obscenity.

In vigorous separate dissents, four Justices warned that the decision of the majority endangered the protections of the First Amendment to the Constitution. Justice Black called the decision "exceedingly dangerous,"

---

[1] See *Manual Enterprises, Inc.* v. *Day*, 370 U.S. 478 (1902), *Jacobellis* v. *Ohio*, 378 U.S. 184 (1964).

The Supreme Court sits at the helm of our hierarchic judicial system
and symbolizes the rule of law in the American system.

for it pushed the country "far along the way to a censorship of the subjects
about which the people can talk or write." Justice Douglas argued that
the First Amendment permits "all ideas to be expressed — whether ortho-
dox, popular, offbeat, or repulsive," and the line between "good" and
"bad" cannot constitutionally be drawn by any form of censorship. Justice
Harlan decried the new and confusing test of "pandering" and argued
that only "hard-core pornography" should be constitutionally restricted.
Finally, Justice Stewart wrote that although he supported the right of
government to constitutionally suppress "hard-core pornography" under

492

previously prescribed court tests, the test of "pandering" and "titillation" laid down in the Ginzburg decision is so vague and elusive that it denies the constitutional guarantee of due process.

Considering the Court's difficulty in finding an acceptable way of balancing the right to free speech with the generally accepted view that obscenity per se is not constitutionally protected, the conflict remains alive. In 1968, the Supreme Court upheld the conviction of a person charged with violating a New York statute that prohibits selling to juveniles under seventeen years of age any material that "predominantly appeals to the prurient, shameful or morbid interest of minors." A sixteen-year-old boy had been sold a "girlie" magazine. Thus the Court upheld a statute that distinguished between literature the state defined as unsuitable for minors but acceptable for adults.[2]

The controversy over legislation against obscenity was heightened by the very controversial *Report of the Commission on Obscenity and Pornography.* After studying the legal, social, and psychological facts about so-called obscene materials, a divided federal commission concluded that standards devised by the judiciary for determining what is obscene are ambiguous, difficult to apply, and subjective. The commission admitted that empirical data show that adults differ significantly on what they consider to be "offensive" and "arousing," and that no "sufficient social justification exists" for prohibiting the dissemination of sexual materials to adults who wish to have them; and they concluded that "it is exceedingly unwise for government to attempt to legislate individual moral values and standards independent of behavior, especially by restrictions upon consensual communication."[3] That the controversial report was received but conspicuously not endorsed by the White House or most Congressmen clearly indicates that the President and Congress did not wish to enter into the public controversy. It will, however, continue to occupy the attention of the courts.

The social conflicts involved in government legislation against obscene materials have grown into a legal controversy. But the Constitution does not categorically state how much, if at all, government may prohibit the dissemination of material deemed obscene. Consequently, the Supreme Court must make its decisions amid uncertainty, and its discretion is broad. In most judicial controversies, however, courts have less discretion. Criminal statutes and the law governing contractual relationships

---

[2] *Ginzberg* v. *New York,* 390 U.S. 629 (1968). See also, *Stanley* v. *Georgia,* 394 U.S. 814 (1969) and *United States* v. *Thirty-Seven Photographs,* 402 U.S. 363 (1971).

[3] *The Report of the Commission on Obscenity and Pornography* (New York: Bantam Books, 1970), pp. 47–50, 60–61. The Commission did, however, recommend that young persons should be protected against such materials and that laws should also protect persons from receiving sexual materials through the mail without their consent.

generally are very specific. Whatever the controversy, however, judges do exercise some discretion in deciding the law; when they have broad discretion, they can make public policy. The resolution of disputes by the judiciary is clearly distinguished from executive or legislative conflict resolution. Yet judicial policymaking is affected by the same features that affect executive and legislative policymaking: federalism, separation of powers, and checks and balances. It differs from the other branches by its constitutional authority, its organization and procedures, and by the selection of judges.

## policy adjudication

Federalism imposes on Americans a dual system of courts: state and national. The Constitution speaks only of federal jurisdiction and assigns the authority to federal courts to hear only specific kinds of cases. The jurisdiction of state courts is fixed primarily by the constitution and laws of each state, subject to the supremacy of the national Constitution. Many areas, however, are covered by both federal and state laws, so that one act may be an offense against federal law and also against state law. It is possible to be tried twice for the same offense; the double jeopardy provision of the Constitution protects only against trial twice for the same offense by one level of government.[4]

## constitutional authority

The extent of judicial power of the federal government is spelled out by Article III, section 2 of the Constitution. This power extends "to all Cases in Law and Equity, arising under this Constitution, the Laws of the United States and Treaties made, or which shall be made, under their Authority." Specifically, Article III extends federal jurisdiction to cases involving specific kinds of *subject matter* and those involving specific parties.

Subject matter cases involve admiralty and maritime laws, federal law, treaties, or the Constitution. The second kind of cases includes suits to which the United States is a party, suits between citizens of different states, suits in which one state sues another, and suits involving foreign ambassadors or other official foreign representatives. State courts are not barred from hearing cases involving these matters because Article III also grants Congress authority to assign jurisdiction to state courts to hear some cases concurrently or even exclusively. Congress has provided that

[4] *Bartkus v. Illinois,* 359 U.S. 121 (1959); *Abbate v. United States,* 359 U.S. 187 (1959).

suits between citizens of different states involving more than $10,000 may be heard in either state or federal courts but those for lesser amounts must be heard in state courts only.

All cases not authorized by the Constitution to federal courts fall within the exclusive jurisdiction of state courts; most cases originate and are finally disposed of at the state level. A violator of state law may under specified conditions appeal to a federal court, but his case must first be heard in a state court. A person convicted of a crime in a state court may appeal to a federal court if he feels that the procedures in this trial violated his constitutional rights.

## limiting demands: legal rules and judicial gatekeeping

A legal controversy represents demands made upon the political system. These may be limited to a controversy between two private parties or a small number of people, or they may represent broad social conflicts involving large numbers of people and interests. Not all demands can be decided by a court; they are subject to control by rules developed and applied by courts or statutes that define the types of issues or controversies that may be taken to a court.

The Supreme Court of the United States has developed some rules of its own in regard to the cases it will consider. They enable the Court to control the issues it will decide and thus serve the function of "gatekeeping," because some issues are not admissible. The Court has refused to render *advisory opinions* on constitutional questions; a law must be tested before the court will rule on its constitutionality. In 1793, the Supreme Court declined to advise President Washington concerning how far his authority went on the policy of neutrality in foreign conflicts.

"STANDING" TO SUE. The party bringing suit must have "standing" to sue — the litigant must be personally involved in a genuine case in controversy. In *Poe* v. *Ullman* (1961) the plaintiffs, a doctor and his patient, wished to challenge an 1889 Connecticut statute that banned the use of contraceptives and giving medical advice about their use. Although Connecticut had not attempted to enforce the statute, the plaintiffs sought a court order declaring that the statute violated the Fourteenth Amendment because it deprived them of liberty without due process of law. The Supreme Court refused to rule on the issue because the state had not engaged in prosecution for a violation of the law.

The Supreme Court can alter its application of this rule. In a 1923 case, it ruled that an "ordinary taxpayer" could not challenge as unconstitutional the expenditure of federal funds because his interest in the matter was small and remote compared to the interests of millions of other tax-payers.[5] In *Flast* v. *Cohen,* however, the Court redefined its limitations upon "standing to sue" by permitting seven taxpayers to file a suit con-tending that the First Amendment's free exercise and establishment of religion clauses were violated by the congressional authorization of aid to parochial schools. In 1963, the Governor of Alabama was unsuccessful in seeking to prevent the President from employing federal troops in Birmingham to maintain order during civil rights marches. The Supreme Court held that the President was only using authority conferred by con-gressional statute and no damage to the plaintiff could be claimed as the result of the action.[6] In *Sierra Club* v. *Morton* (1972), the Court refused to permit a California-based "environmentalist" group, the Sierra Club, to challenge a proposed recreation resort to be constructed by Walt Disney Enterprises. The Sierra Club objected to a twenty-mile highway through Sequoia National Park because it would impose a destructive cost on the park and the national forest. Justice Potter Stewart said the Sierra Club had no standing to sue because none of the members used the planned resort area and none could show any injury from the Disney development.

In 1970, the State of Massachusetts enacted legislation that authorized its attorney general to file suit in federal court asking that the Vietnam War be declared unconstitutional because Congress had not authorized it.[7] Although three Justices dissented, the Court refused to hear the case, partly on grounds that the state lacked standing to sue and partly on grounds that the issue was a "political question" to be resolved by the other two branches of government.

In *Mora* v. *McNamara* (1967) the Supreme Court, by a seven-to-two vote, upheld the dismissal by lower federal courts of a suit brought by draftees who sought to prevent their being sent to Vietnam. The court was asked to declare the war illegal because since Congress had not offi-cially declared war, the President lacked constitutional power to engage in it.

In these cases, the Court officially refused to rule on the "merits" of the question about whether the war was constitutional or not. But by refusing to hear the challenges it prevented opponents of that conflict from using the courts to attack the war. The standing-to-sue doctrine may be related to issues the Court *wants* to hear and decide. The difference between suits based on establishment of religion and those challenging a war may lie more in what the court deems it *politically* feasible to decide than upon any clearly defined criteria as to what constitutes a

[5] *Frothingham* v. *Mellon,* 262 U.S. 447 (1923).
[6] *Alabama* v. *United States,* 373 U.S. 545 (1963).
[7] *Massachusetts* v. *Laird,* 400 U.S. 886 (1970).

Fearful of provoking a constitutional crisis, the Supreme Court has refused to rule on the legality of the Vietnam War.

properly brought action. What effect would a decision holding a military action such as Vietnam unconstitutional have? The Court might be unable to get either the President or Congress to accept its decision which might provoke a constitutional crisis and might also weaken or imperil the Supreme Court's authority to decide other controversial cases.

THE DOCTRINE OF "POLITICAL QUESTIONS." Clearly, the Court accepts cases on appeal at its discretion. Another limit it may apply is the doctrine of a "political question," refusing to decide on a controversy if the issue is one that the Court feels it cannot resolve. This doctrine was employed as early as 1849 when the Supreme Court refused to decide which of two governments claiming legitimacy was the lawful government of Rhode Island. The question, said the Court, was "political" and must be decided by Congress and the executive. The Court has refused to decide when a constitutional Amendment has been legally ratified, what constitutes a "republican form of government" under the guarantee clause of the Constitution, the dates of the duration of a war, questions about the conduct of foreign relations, and the status of Indian tribes.[8]

In a broad sense, all questions decided by the Court are "political." John P. Roche has said the word "can be expanded or contracted in accordion-line fashion to meet the exigencies of the times . . . for at root the logic that supports it is circular: political questions are matters not soluble by the judicial process; matters not soluble by the judicial process are political questions. As an early dictionary explained, violins are small cellos, and cellos are large violins."[9] Conflicts that no one is willing to resolve are sometimes passed from branch to branch.

## federal judicial organization

Unable to resolve the dispute over creating a separate system of federal courts or allowing state courts to decide federal cases subject to a review by a Supreme Court, the Framers provided in Article III for a Supreme Court and granted to Congress the authority to establish lower federal courts (Figure 15-1). The Judiciary Act of 1789 established a Supreme Court with one Chief Justice and five Associate Justices, and provided for thirteen federal district courts. It also created three circuit courts, each consisting of any two justices of the Supreme Court and a judge from the district in which a case was heard. In 1891, Congress substituted a separate system of ten circuit courts of appeals. The number of Justices on the Supreme Court has varied from five in 1801 to as many as ten in 1863; it has remained at nine since 1869. Congress established three other courts — the Court of Customs and Patent Appeals, the Customs Court, and the Court of Claims — to complete the courts required by Article III. The national court system reflects the federal pattern. Judicial districts generally follow state boundaries, and the circuit court system divides the nation into ten geographical units or circuits. Each state has its own system and hierarchy beneath the national system. The Supreme Court supervises state courts through the supremacy clause of the Constitution, which empowers the Court to declare void any state actions that conflict with the "supreme law of the land": the Constitution, valid acts of Congress, and treaties of the United States.

All the courts established under Article III are called *constitutional* courts to distinguish them from the *legislative* courts created by Congress

---

[8] *Coleman v. Miller,* 307 U.S. 433 (1939); *Pacific States Telephone and Telegraph Co.* v. *Oregon,* 223 U.S. 118 (1939); *Ludecke v. Watkins,* 335 U.S. 160 (1948); *The Cherokee Nation* v. *Georgia,* 5 Pet. 1 (1831).

[9] John P. Roche, "Judicial Self-Restraint," *The American Political Science Review* 49 (Sept. 1955).

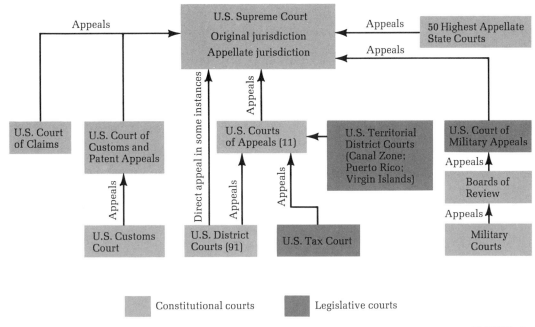

under authority drawn from other clauses in the Constitution. The United States Tax Court is a legislative court established in accordance with congressional authority to levy and collect taxes. The Court of Military Appeals and the system of territorial courts are derived from the congressional authority to regulate the land and naval forces and acquire and govern territories. Legislative courts are not created under Article III, so Congress does not have to adhere to the requirement that judges be given life terms or to restrictions on salary or the removal of federal judges.

Federal courts exercise either *original* or *appellate* jurisdiction, or both. A court exercising original jurisdiction is the first to hear and decide a case; appellate jurisdiction means a court hears appeals on cases already decided at a lower level. Article III requires the Supreme Court to exercise original jurisdiction "in all Cases affecting Ambassadors, other public Ministers and Consuls, and those in which a State shall be a Party." Except for this requirement, Congress may assign original or appellate jurisdiction to district courts and courts of appeals as it sees fit.

Most federal cases are decided by district courts: each year about one hundred thousand cases are initiated in them. These lowest federal courts exercise only original jurisdiction, handling matters ranging from criminal trials to the review and enforcement of orders issued by federal administrative agencies. The ninety-three district courts are distributed so that at least one is located in each of the fifty states, the District of Columbia, Puerto Rico, the Canal Zone, and the Virgin Islands. Almost half the cases heard at this level are filed in the twelve district courts in the larger metropolitan areas. Each district has at least one judge but many have several; there are about three hundred and fifty district judges. Normally one district judge presides over a case, although the law requires a panel of three judges to hear some types of disputes, the most important of which involve the constitutionality of federal or state statutes.

Most civil and criminal cases begun in federal district courts are not terminated by trial. In 1967, 88.5 percent of civil suits were settled out of court and only 14.2 percent of criminal cases were resolved by trial. The remaining criminal cases were dismissed before trial or the accused pleaded guilty or did not contest the charge.[10]

These figures suggest that the judicial process involves participants outside the courtroom. Lawyers often negotiate out-of-court settlements of civil suits for their clients, a bargaining relationship with the opposing party. In criminal cases, defendants engage in "plea bargaining" with law enforcement officials or prosecuting attorneys; in return for a plea of guilty to a lesser charge or promise of a light sentence or both, a defendant agrees to plead guilty without going to trial. Such "bargain justice" reduces the workload of courts, but it also means that "the norms of production may conflict with the norms of law," that these arrangements may be inconsistent with protection of the right to trial by jury.[11]

United States courts of appeals consist of ten circuit courts and one District of Columbia circuit court. Each court has from three to nine members. About 80 percent of 8,887 circuit court cases in 1968 involved appeals from district courts, the remainder consisting of appeals from administrative regulatory agencies and original proceedings. The original jurisdiction cases were less than 2 percent of the total. Only about half the cases were disposed of by formal court decisions after a hearing. The remainder were dismissed without a hearing or consolidated with other cases. Of the cases appealed and decided by formal decision, about 20 percent reversed federal district court or administrative agency decisions.[12]

The Supreme Court exercises both original and appellate jurisdiction,

[10] Data cited is drawn from tables in Sheldon Goldman and Thomas P. Johige, *The Federal Courts As a Political System* (New York: Harper & Row, 1971), pp. 105–106.

[11] James R. Klonaski and Robert I. Mendelsohn, *The Politics of Local Justice* (Boston: Little, Brown, 1970), p. 76.

[12] Goldman and Jahige, *The Federal Courts,* pp. 105–107.

but original jurisdiction covers only a fraction of the Court's work; between 1789 and 1970, it rendered only 123 decisions under its original jurisdiction. Article III gives Congress the power to regulate the appellate jurisdiction of the Supreme Court. The Court gets its workload as well as its influence in policymaking from its authority to review the decisions of lower federal courts and to hear appeals from state courts in matters that involve a "federal question."

Appeals reach the Court on the basis of a *writ of certiorari,* a *writ of appeal,* or by *certification.* Certification, which is very rarely used, is a method by which lower federal courts request instruction on questions of law from the Supreme Court. A writ of certiorari — meaning "made more certain" — is an order issued by the Court directing a lower court to send the records of a case to the Supreme Court for review. The Court usually denies petitions for writs, which means that it will not hear oral arguments or accept written arguments by the petitioning party. At least four justices must vote to grant a writ, a decision limited to cases on legal issues that go beyond the immediate interests of the litigants.

The writ of appeal is granted by statute. Congress has directed that a case may be appealed by the losing party to the Supreme Court under any of these circumstances: (1) if a state court declares a federal statute or treaty is unconstitutional; (2) if a state court upholds a state statute in opposition to a challenge that the statute conflicts with the federal Constitution, federal law, or a federal treaty; (3) if a district court declares a federal statute unconstitutional in a suit to which the United States is a party; (4) if a district court issues an injunction against the enforcement of a state statute; and (5) if a court of appeals declares that a state statute is void because it is contrary to federal law or treaty.

In practice, the Supreme Court may refuse to hear an appeal on the grounds that a "substantial federal question" is lacking or because it has no jurisdiction over the legal issue involved. In a typical annual term — from October to the end of June — more than 50 percent of the appeals based on statutory rights are dismissed. The Court does not explain why it accepts some appeals and rejects others. It has full discretion on whether to issue a writ and therefore, within the bounds of the cases on appeal coming its way, the Court controls the selection of issues it is willing to decide upon.

## constitutional authority and federal organization

The court that has jurisdiction in a case is very significant for the parties involved in litigation as well as for the public affected by judicial decisions. Differences between decisions on civil rights and liberties by some of the state supreme courts and the United States Supreme Court are extensive. District courts in some parts of the nation show similar differences.

District and circuit courts encompass different geographical areas. District courts may include only parts of one state, whereas circuit courts are regional. They reflect different constituency influences based on social and cultural differences. "Policies are formulated by [district] judges with strong local connections, are administered by a locally appointed and sanctioned court staff, and serve a clientele usually drawn from the district."[13]

Courts of appeals have a larger geographical constituency and are therefore more free of the localism that restricts district courts, yet the effects of regional associations are also evident. The pull of regional ties was revealed by the findings of Richardson and Vines, who studied the frequency with which lower court decisions were reversed by higher courts in civil liberties cases from 1956 to 1961. Courts of appeals tended to agree with district court decisions more than the Supreme Court agreed with courts of appeals decisions. Richardson and Vines concluded that "the remnants of parochialism which are maintained in the judicial system by the courts of appeals — the fact that judges are appointed from the circuit, often with district court experience and values, and adjudicating in circuit boundaries along state lines — make the courts of appeals responsive to the district courts."[14]

Localism is lessened, however, by a number of factors: the life tenure of federal judges insulates them against the pressures and demands of local interests; judges are united by experience and values drawn from generally similar legal education; the federal courts are subject to common rules of procedure and legal concepts, and their actions are subject to review and veto by established patterns of appeal. Even so, the localism of federal court organization, reflecting the American federal system, reduces the centralizing tendencies of hierarchic organization, headed by the Supreme Court, which responds to a national constituency.

The hierarchical judicial system, coupled with the Supreme Court's authority to hear appeals from both state and federal courts, emphasizes the Court's influence in policymaking. The Court is the final judicial voice in resolving conflicts over such matters as school segregation, legislative reapportionment, and freedom of expression; all have great political and social consequences. Although final decisions in the vast majority of cases are reached in state and lower federal courts, the Supreme Court is the ultimate arbiter of disputes.

[13] Richard J. Richardson and Kenneth N. Vines, *The Politics of Federal Courts* (Boston: Little, Brown, 1970), p. 46.
[14] Richard J. Richardson and Kenneth N. Vines, "Review, Dissent and the Appellate Process: A Political Interpretation," *Journal of Politics* 29 (Aug. 1967): 605.

selection of judges

DISTRICT AND COURTS OF APPEALS APPOINTMENTS. A "core model" developed by Richardson and Vines shows how lower federal court appointments are made and reveals that a few individuals have most influence over such appointments.

> Senator(s) of the presidential party, and/or [the] local presidential party and the president and his advisers interact to produce a nominee who is then affirmed by the acquiescence of the Senate Judiciary Committee and a majority of the Senate.[15]

Although the Constitution gives the President appointment power and leaves the power to "advise and consent" to the Senate, in practice the roles have been reversed. Senators of the President's party and state party organizations have most influence over these appointments. In selecting judges for district and appeals courts, the President must adhere to the custom of senatorial courtesy. This custom, which the Senate is willing to sustain should the President violate it, permits a Senator of the President's party to block confirmation of appointees to lower court positions in his home state whom he opposes strongly. The President also finds that Senators must be consulted on prospective nominations and are not bashful in sponsoring candidates for judicial appointment. That these appointments are partisan is revealed by the fact that 86 percent of the 1,920 persons appointed to the federal district bench from 1908 to 1960 were of the same party as the President.[16] And of 872 district and circuit court appointments from 1933 through 1970 (Franklin D. Roosevelt to Richard Nixon), 94 percent went to members of the President's party.

The prestige, relatively high salaries, and life tenure of these appointments guarantee that Senators and state party organizations will be deeply interested in influencing the choice of appointees. This influence is obviously enhanced by the localized nature of the federal judicial organization. The federal pattern has required that district and appeals judges be drawn from the state or circuit in which the vacancy opens. Richardson and Vines found that of the district and appeals judges on the bench in 1963 most were born and educated in the law school in the state of the district or circuit. Those not born or educated there were residents at the time of appointment. Although local recruitment does not necessarily mean that judges will reflect local values and behaviors,

[15] Richardson and Vines, *The Politics of Federal Courts*, p. 60. The following description of the process in these appointments draws heavily upon Chapter IV of this book.
[16] *Ibid.*, p. 71.

Supreme Court decisions in the 1960s strengthened the rights of the individual from the time of arrest onward. The Burger Court has already modified some Warren Court doctrines. Here a suspect is interrogated.

there is a popular assumption that the relationship exists and that this belief influences recruitment patterns.[17]

SUPREME COURT APPOINTMENTS. Judges' behavior is influenced by their backgrounds and by the reason for their selection. Most of the ninety-eight justices who have sat on the Supreme Court were selected by Presidents more interested in their "ideological partisanship" — that is, their positions on the socioeconomic issues of the day — than in their scholarly knowledge or prior experience on the bench. Only thirteen candidates not of the President's party have been appointed to the Supreme Court, and Presidents have chosen those whose views were similar to their own. John R. Schmidhauser has studied the social backgrounds of the ninety-two Supreme Court Justices who served between 1789 and 1959. Measured by their educations, family backgrounds, and their political and professional careers, these men form an elite group. One-third came from families with a tradition of judicial service; all but nine of the ninety-two were from socially and economically advantaged families; almost nine out of ten were of British ethnic origin; 88 percent were Protestant; almost all came from politically active families and were themselves politically active; and eight out of ten had been educated in prestigious law schools or had studied law under a prominent lawyer or judge.[18]

[17] The statistics were compiled from Hearings before Subcommittee 5 of the House Judiciary Committee on Bills to Provide for the Appointment of Additional Circuit and District Judges, 87th Congress (March 1 and 2, 1961), pp. 402–403.
[18] John R. Schmidhauser, The Supreme Court (New York: Holt, Rinehart and Winston, 1960), chap. 3.

If the Supreme Court is the guardian of the American conscience, says Schmidhauser, "it is essentially the conscience of the American upper-middle class sharpened by the imperative of individual social responsibility and political activism, and conditioned by the conservative impact of legal training and professional legal attitudes and associations."[19]

The Supreme Court frequently decides major issues of public policy, so the attitudes of the Justices are crucial, and interest groups are deeply interested in the choice of a nominee to the Supreme Court. The Senate refused to confirm President Johnson's nomination of Justice Abe Fortas as Chief Justice in 1968 — he was ultimately forced to withdraw it after a successful Senate filibuster — at least partly because of dissatisfaction and resentment over Supreme Court rulings in criminal law and obscenity. For many Senators as well as the public, Fortas symbolized the "excessively liberal" politics of the Warren Court.

The Senate rejected two of President Nixon's nominations to the Court, dramatizing the clash of interests over the Supreme Court. Following Justice Fortas's resignation from the Court in 1969, Nixon nominated Clement Haynsworth of South Carolina, Chief Justice of the Fourth Circuit Court of Appeals. The Senate Judiciary Committee approved the nomination, but Haynsworth was strongly opposed by labor and civil rights leaders who attacked his voting record on the lower federal court bench. Haynsworth was also accused of ethical impropriety and poor judgment in participating before the Fourth Circuit Court of Appeals in cases in which he was said to have a financial involvement. Despite strong pressure from the White House, the Senate rejected Haynsworth's nomination.

In early 1970, President Nixon nominated another southerner, also an Appeals Court judge, G. Harrold Carswell of Florida. Carswell's nomination was opposed on grounds that he had given a "white supremacy" speech while campaigning for state office in 1948, his voting record as a federal judge revealed "racist" tones, and his mediocre ability. Again, labor and civil rights interests fought the nomination, and despite the President's strong efforts to win approval the nomination was rejected by the Senate. President Nixon charged that no southerner could win confirmation of the Senate. Nixon's intent to replace liberal justices with conservatives — which he made clear in the presidential campaign of 1968 — was thought by many legal scholars to be a major reason for the Senate's rejection of the two nominations. Nominating Harry A. Blackmun of Minnesota, another Court of Appeals judge, the President finally won by unanimous vote Senate confirmation of a conservative justice.

The American Bar Association endorsed the nominations of both Haynsworth and Carswell; it has long sought, with some success, to serve

---

[19] *Ibid.*, 59.

as a consultant to the President in the appointment of judges. President Eisenhower asked the opinion of the ABA's Committee on the Federal Judiciary before submitting the nomination of William J. Brennan, Jr., to the Senate. But President Kennedy appointed Arthur Goldberg without seeking the committee's opinion. Early in his administration, President Nixon indicated that any candidate for a lower federal court appointment rated "not qualified" by the ABA Committee would not be nominated. After the Haynsworth and Carswell nominations were rejected, the President took the unprecedented action of announcing that prospective Supreme Court nominees would be submitted to the ABA Committee for consideration. The implication was that any such nominee who failed to receive a rating of "exceptionally well qualified," "well qualified," or "qualified" would not be nominated.[20]

The ABA has consistently urged Presidents to select judges who demonstrate diligence, legal scholarship, and honesty rather than appointing them for "political" reasons. Beyond these qualifications, the Association has never offered more explicit criteria on the qualities of a good judge; and despite its support for nonpolitical appointments, its stands on socioeconomic policies over the years have had a strong conservative bias. In this respect, it is no different from other groups that seek to influence judicial policymaking by urging that justices with views similar to their own be appointed. But because it is the major representative of the legal profession, the ABA's views have prestige that other interests do not.

Although the background and political orientation of judges must affect judicial policymaking, becoming a judge probably counters class or personal bias. Justice Felix Frankfurter argued that "on the whole judges do lay aside private views in discharging their judicial functions."[21] It is hard to distinguish between private views and judicial objectivity, however. Judicial decisions cannot be ascribed definitely to political and social background, but ignoring their influence is equally dubious.[22] Presidents have been upset by Justices they have appointed. Oliver Wendell Holmes, Jr., infuriated Theodore Roosevelt by voting against him in antitrust cases. Surely President Eisenhower never anticipated that his appointee as Chief Justice, Earl Warren, would help move the Court into an expansion of civil liberties. Most appointees considered politically liberal or conservative when nominated usually reflected that ideology as members of the Court. President Nixon was clearly satisfied with the performance of the four Justices confirmed during his first term of office. In accepting re-

---

[20] *The New York Times* (July 28, 1970), p. 1.

[21] *Public Utilities Commission v. Pollak*, 343 U.S. 451 (1952).

[22] For a discussion of the uses and limits of social background studies see Joel B. Grossman, "Social Backgrounds and Judicial Decision-Making," *Harvard Law Review* 79 (1966): 1551–1564.

nomination as President he pledged that he would continue to make appointments "to strengthen the peace forces in the United States," a reference to the Burger court's modification of the Warren court decisions in cases involving defendants' rights.

## limitations on implementing decisions

FEDERAL COURT LIMITATIONS. The federal system often impedes easy or immediate compliance by lower federal or state courts with Supreme Court holdings. With fifty separate state systems involved, some may ignore the mandates of the Court or interpret them so as to avoid compliance. Of 175 cases reversed by the Supreme Court and returned to state courts for litigation between 1941 and 1951, forty-six were reheard at the state level. In almost half of these, according to one survey, "the winner at the Supreme Court level lost his victory in the state court."[23]

Compliance by lower federal courts with Supreme Court decisions is also by no means assured. In *Brown* v. *Board of Education* in 1954, a unanimous Supreme Court found that racial segregation in public schools violated the equal protection clause of the Fourteenth Amendment. Because of the decision's great influence, the difference in local conditions, and, perhaps, to provide a cooling-off period, the Court postponed considering how its decision should be implemented. It invited all who were interested to submit their views. One year later the Court ordered "full compliance . . . with all deliberate speed." The task of implementing these orders fell to the federal district court and circuit court judges in whose jurisdictions public schools were segregated.

Professor J. W. Peltason has written the story of the forty-eight district judges and ten circuit judges in the South whose courts became the focal point for litigation following the 1954 decision.[24] Peltason stressed the social environment in which the judges had to operate. A district judge usually has long been a resident of the area he serves and reflects the prejudices, social values, and background of his community. He is exposed to local pressures even though he is responsible for applying laws that reflect national values. District judges will sometimes bow to local pressures by choosing an alternative that escapes the spirit, if not the letter, of the law. Many district judges who ordered school boards to desegregate only vaguely stipulated the time and manner of implementation.

[23] See "Evasion of Supreme Court Mandates in Cases Remanded to State Courts since 1941," Harvard Law Review 67 (1954).

[24] J. W. Peltason, *Fifty-eight Lonely Men* (New York: Harcourt, Brace, 1961).

A Supreme Court decision is complied with by local officials and private citizens depending on the type of issue decided by the Court and the resources available to groups who wish to comply or oppose enforcement. In *Brown* v. *Board of Education,* the full legal resources and the political and social power of many southern states fought enforcement of the decision, despite the public support the decision got in all other parts of the nation. The legislative reapportionment decisions of the 1960s were vigorously supported by urban-based interests who had suffered under previous schemes of apportionment. Compliance came relatively quickly and change was extensive.

Supreme Court decisions during the 1960s against the reading of the Bible and recitation of religious prayers in public schools faced strong and widespread opposition among the public. In Tennessee, for example, a "Bible-belt" state, it was found that in 1965 only one of 152 public school districts had ceased all such devotional exercises.[25] Public or official pressures to comply were not pushed, encouraging and condoning noncompliance with Court decisions.

PRESIDENTIAL AND CONGRESSIONAL LIMITATIONS. Separation of powers and checks and balances provide other limitations on implementing Supreme Court decisions. Executive and legislative prerogatives can limit the courts. As Alexander Hamilton wrote in *Federalist* No. 78, "In a government in which [departments] are separated from each other, the judiciary, from the nature of its functions, will always be the least dangerous." It has "neither force nor will, but merely judgment, and must ultimately depend upon the aid of the executive arm even for the efficacy of its judgments." Presidents have sometimes heeded the aprocryphal remark of President Andrew Jackson: "[Chief Justice] John Marshall has made his decision, now let him enforce it." Lincoln bitterly criticized the Court for its decision in *Dred Scott* v. *Sanford;* Franklin D. Roosevelt reportedly was prepared to disobey a prospective Court ruling invalidating his decision to go off the gold standard; President Truman might have kept control of the steel mills in 1952 despite the Court's decision in *Youngstown Sheet and Tube* v. *Sawyer* that declared his seizure of the mills was unconstitutional; and President Eisenhower supported district courts belatedly in the Little Rock desegregation crisis of 1957. The possibility of presidential resistance or constitutional crises are therefore potential restraints on judicial decisions.

Congress also maintains control over the judiciary. Its formal controls are extensive and include the authority to alter or abolish the jurisdiction

---

[25] Robert H. Birkby, "The Supreme Court and the Bible Belt: Tennessee Reaction to the 'Schempp' Decision," *Midwest Journal of Political Science* 10 (1966): 304–319.

of federal courts, except for the Supreme Court's original jurisdiction; to control the purse strings by controlling judges' salaries and providing funds for operating the federal court system; to increase or decrease the number of judges; to remove judges by impeachment, and to determine when the Supreme Court will sit. The Senate has the authority to confirm judicial appointments. Along with these formal controls, Congress may nullify Supreme Court decisions by initiating constitutional amendments or by passing legislation to negate a court interpretation of a congressional statute. In only one instance, the Sixteenth Amendment following the Court's declaring income taxes unconstitutional, has a decision been overturned by amendment.

Most decisions of the Court, however, are based not on constitutional interpretation but on *statutory* interpretation. Congress may nullify a verdict based upon statutory interpretation by changing the law or passing new legislation, but it rarely does this when congressional sentiment on the issue created by a Supreme Court decision is mixed. Professor C. Herman Pritchett's analysis of twenty-one instances of congressional reversal between 1947 and 1957 revealed that most Court decisions provoke mixed congressional reaction and are successfully reversed only under special circumstances, such as an intense, nationwide lobbying campaign.[26]

Prior to the antibusing legislation of 1972, no action removing the Court's jurisdiction because of congressional dissatisfaction with Court decisions had been approved. Acting in response to a proposal by President Nixon, as well as considerable public pressure, Congress added a rider to a higher education bill that placed restrictions on court-ordered school busing for racial balance until January 1, 1974. Court orders requiring busing cannot become effective until January 1, 1974. This controversial legislation raised questions about the constitutionality of such action, because the Supreme Court's school desegregation decisions have rested squarely on the belief that racial segregation violates the Fourteenth Amendment. District courts had ordered busing presumably to comply with the constitutional requirement; and civil rights leaders charged that Congress could not, therefore, override busing orders without violating the principle of separation of powers.

The constitutional issue posed by the antibusing legislation might have arisen earlier had other deliberate attempts to limit the Court's jurisdiction succeeded. An attempt in 1958 to withdraw the Court's appellate jurisdiction in some national security matters was overwhelmingly approved in the House but failed by one vote in the Senate. In 1964, the

[26] C. Herman Pritchett, *Congress Versus the Supreme Court* (Minneapolis, Minn.: University of Minnesota Press, 1961).

House approved a measure to strip the federal jurisdiction in state reapportionment cases. The bill did not pass the Senate, but a substitute motion was jointly sponsored by Democratic Majority Leader Mike Mansfield and Republican Minority Leader Everett Dirksen. This motion would have deferred the execution of court-ordered reapportionments of state legislatures until Congress could submit a constitutional Amendment prohibiting the judiciary from applying the "one man, one vote" principle to the upper houses of state legislatures. A filibuster that followed was ended when Congress resolved that the Supreme Court should not disrupt forthcoming state elections by requiring prior reapportionment.

These efforts came out of widespread congressional and public dissatisfaction with the Supreme Court's decisions under Chief Justice Earl Warren. Southerners, police chiefs, the American Bar Association, church organizations, and even the chief justices of state supreme courts were among the many interests that charged the Court with having gone "too far" in civil rights and liberties (invalidating school segregation, limiting federal loyalty and security programs, protecting personal rights under due process, protecting against self-incrimination); legislative apportionment (decision that the principle of "one man, one vote" must prevail in both houses of state legislatures); and religious freedom (invalidating prayers in state-supported public schools).[27]

The Court has suffered comparatively little direct interference or retribution from these branches during this century. Yet the antibusing legislation shows the judiciary may not be immune to direct intervention.

The four Nixon appointments to the Court (including a new Chief Justice) were clearly intended to provide "conservative" replacements for "liberal" Warren Court justices. Finally, the ideological orientations of the Supreme Court change, thus keeping controversies with Congress short. An active Court in one generation may give way to a more restrained judiciary in the next. It did so in economic matters after 1935 and has been the Burger Court's pattern in civil rights and liberties.

---

[27] See *Brown* v. *Board of Education*, 347 U.S. 483 (1954); *Watkins* v. *United States*, 354 U.S. 178 (1957), in which the Court ruled that questions asked by congressional investigating committees not pertinent to the purpose of the investigation did not have to be answered by a witness; *Cole* v. *Young*, 351 U.S. 536 (1956); and *Service* v. *Dulles*, 354 U.S. 363 (1957), in which the Court limited the scope of certain provisions of the federal loyalty-security program. A 1956 decision, *Pennsylvania* v. *Nelson*, 350 U.S. 497 (1956), invalidated Pennsylvania's antisubversive activities statute on grounds that the federal government had preempted this area of national security by the Smith Act of 1940 and other statutes. In another 1956 decision, *Slochower* v. *Board of Bar Examiners of New Mexico*, 353 U.S. 232 (1957), the Court ruled that New Mexico could not withhold admission to the bar on grounds that Schware was not of "good moral character" because he was an admitted member of the Communist party from 1932 to 1940. A unanimous Court pointed out that the Communist party during this period was a "lawful political party with candidates on the ballot in most states." Further, the state could not properly infer that membership during this time established the participation of Schware in illegal conduct.

## politics of judicial choice

Courts are one instrument used by a political community to regulate conflict. As arbiter of disputes between interests, courts condition the political process by giving interests another way of trying to reach their goals. Judicial decisions are, therefore, a way of getting social change. Courts define rules or norms of permissible behavior and apply sanctions when these rules are violated. By negating laws or formulating new law, courts legitimize changes that have already taken place in society.

Supreme Court decisions liberalizing the rules defining obscenity may have begun to legitimize changed attitudes toward sex in American society. The line between "legal" decisions and "political" decisions is unclear because "law" cannot be separated from "policy." Few court cases involve issues that interest the wide public, but the legal rules and norms applied by courts reflect the tone and temper of the political community.

Issues formally enter the judicial arena in the form of a lawsuit, defining conflict by naming specific facts and specific legal issues. Judicial authority is more structured, less ambiguous, and more limited than legislative or executive authority. Legal arguments in the form of briefs, procedural and jurisdictional rules, and the formal atmosphere of the courtroom distinguish policy adjudication from other forms of policy-making. These features, together with the myth that judges are impartial

Stores like this one in New York's Times Square have benefited from Supreme Court decisions liberalizing regulations controlling obscenity. The right of government to limit or prohibit sale and distribution of such material remains a major constitutional issue.

in their judgments, obscure the judiciary's real place in conflict resolution. The public usually views a judge as a decisionmaker who applies a more or less fixed set of rules to cases, permitting him little discretion and insulating him from external pressures. That popular view is a misreading of policy adjudication.

The parties involved in a judicial controversy, including the judges themselves, seek a favorable resolution of the dispute by utilizing whatever resources they can command within the framework of the judicial arena. The immediate parties to a suit and other interested parties who may become involved, the strategies employed by both sides, the legal precedents that apply to the issues at hand, public opinion, changing social patterns, and the personal values and biases of the judge — all affect decisions. Bargaining takes place within the judicial realm, as it does within the legislative and executive realms, since conflict resolution often depends upon the accommodation of several interests. In this section, we concentrate on the Supreme Court's role in the resolution of social conflict with respect to the environment from which its decisions emerge.

## the supreme court and judicial policymaking

The judicial branch was designed as the instrument for realizing the rule of law. Granting federal judges life terms and protecting their salaries from reduction by Congress helped to insulate them from the demands of popular majorities and others as well. Judges embody the rule of law. Marshall's decision in *Marbury* v. *Madison* emphasized their responsibility to uphold the Constitution against legislative actions. In the event of conflict between a law and the Constitution, said Marshall, "the court must determine which of these conflicting rules governs the case: this is the very essence of judicial duty." Marshall's assertion of the power of judicial review and its exercise by subsequent Supreme Courts contrasts sharply with the role of courts in Great Britain. Although the English system of law was the most significant influence on the development of American law, English courts have never held the power to declare unconstitutional acts of the legislative branch. They may *interpret* legislation, but Parliament is supreme and its will always prevails. Parliamentary power is checked by the party system, the executive branch (Prime Minister), and the great weight of English consensus on protecting individual rights and liberties.

If the American judiciary was designed to ultimately determine the powers of Congress and the executive because of its power of judicial review and to arbitrate relations between the states and the national government, the Constitution does not provide the absolute proof. Its acceptance and enforcement has depended on the cooperation by the other two branches of government and on the public itself. Public acceptance of its actions rests on the notion that judges are not as interested in political conflict as are Congress or the President. Commitment to insulating the administration of justice from popular pressure is profound.

Some of the Supreme Court's decisions have provoked much criticism, but Americans still support the institution. Table 15-1 shows the findings of one study. Specific support was measured by the amount of praise or criticism people gave decisions and individual justices. Diffuse support meant people believed that the Supreme Court was impartial and competent. These data reveal that diffuse support is significantly higher than specific support; 37 percent gave positive responses about the court (diffuse) but only 12.5 percent offered positive responses to specific support. Murphy and Tannenhaus also found that 53.8 percent ("don't know, no response") of the respondents could not identify any specific likes or dislikes about the Court, and 70.6 percent offered general opinions about the Court as an institution. The data suggest that the Supreme Court retains its image as an institution that legitimizes changes in the political system, even though its specific decisions often are criticized by large numbers of the public.

**TABLE 15-1**
**Specific and Diffuse Support**
**of Supreme Court by the American Public, 1966**

| Support level | Specific | Diffuse |
|---|---|---|
| Strong positive[a] | 2.5% | 19.9% |
| Moderate positive | 7.0 | 17.1 |
| Pro/con[b] | 5.0 | 11.9 |
| Moderate negative | 19.2 | 11.4 |
| Strong negative[c] | 12.5 | 10.3 |
| Don't know, no response | 53.8 | |
| Unclassified | | 29.4 |
| Total | 100.0% | 100.0% |
| N = 1,291 | | |

Source: From Walter F. Murphy and Joseph Tannenhaus, "Public Opinion and the United States Supreme Court," *Law and Society Review* 2 (May 1968): 370, 372.
[a] Very strong and strong positive categories combined for specific support data.
[b] Pro/con category refers to responses in which positive and negative comments were about evenly balanced.
[c] Very strong and strong negative categories combined for specific support data.

| | By Congress? | By President? | By Supreme Court? |
|---|---|---|---|
| | **TABLE 15-2** | | |
| | **Confidence in Actions Taken** | | |
| | **by Institutions of the National Government**[a] | | |
| Yes | 50% | 35% | 28% |
| Depends | 20 | 17 | 13 |
| No | 16 | 33 | 39 |
| Don't Know | 14 | 15 | 20 |
| | 100% | 100% | 100% |

N = 627

Source: Kenneth M. Dolbeare, "The Public Views the Supreme Court," in Herbert Jacob, ed., *Law, Politics and the Federal Courts* (Boston: Little, Brown, 1967), p. 197.

[a] Would you be likely to think the right things had been done in Washington if the action had been taken by the Supreme Court (President, Congress)?"

Other survey data suggest that the public's confidence in the Supreme Court during the 1960s was lower than it was in regard to either Congress or the President. Table 15-2 reports the findings of a 1966 survey of Wisconsin adults who were asked to indicate which of the three branches of government would be most likely to do the "right thing." Half the respondents expressed confidence in Congress and 35 percent were favorable toward the President; only 28 percent responded positively to the Supreme Court's actions.

The findings certainly show dissatisfaction with the Warren Court's activities in criminal procedures, civil rights, and religion during the 1960s. Lack of public support for a specific court or specific decisions is not synonymous, however, with lack of support for the Supreme Court as an institution. The failure of President Franklin Roosevelt to win approval for his plan to "pack" the Court in the 1930s shows danger of confusing support for the institution with opinions about its specific decisions.

## legal rules and court response to social conflict

How do legal rules and norms limit the judiciary in choosing among alternatives and responding to new demands? Judicial choice is limited by a fundamental principle of English and American jurisprudence: decisions on law by a higher court having jurisdiction must be followed in similar cases in the future. This rule of *stare decisis* — "stand by the things decided" — lays the stable and predictable foundation of the law. The rule is much more limiting in the lower state and federal courts, and these courts will usually base their decisions on precedents created by higher courts. Although appellate judges are also expected to exhibit consistency and certainty in policy choices, the Justices are sometimes unable or unwilling to follow precedent because changing conditions may demand changing law. Often a new case will differ enough from previous cases to enable the Supreme Court to depart from precedent without specifically contradicting it. Then, too, when precedents conflict, the judge's opportunity to follow one precedent (and neglect the other) leaves him much discretion. The validity of federal aid to parochial schools might be determined by several precedents — some supporting such aid, others not. Precedents impose a limiting but not unalterable restraint on a Justice: "He has free choice, but only among limited alternatives and only after he has satisfied himself that he has met the obligations of consistency and respect for settled principles which his responsibility to the Court imposes upon him."[28]

The Court must also be sensitive to policy goals expressed by the other two branches of the government and by the public. The need for such understanding and restraint is visible in the Supreme Court's activity in economic matters before the 1930s and its reaction to the New Deal.

From 1870 until the 1930s, the Supreme Court dealt with government regulation of property and the rights of individuals in matters of social and economic maladjustment. Before the New Deal, the Court regularly held state and national regulatory statutes unconstitutional on many grounds. By the mid-1930s, it was clear, as Robert G. McCloskey wrote, that the Court looked upon itself as the "protector" of "all the 'common callings' (the grocer, the dairyman, the butcher) from the peril of public rate control."[29] McCloskey was referring to the Court's use of the contract and due process clauses of the Constitution to strike down the efforts of government to regulate economic affairs.

Economic individualism was the symbolic basis on which the great economic interests were built during the 1870s and 1880s. But the small entrepreneur in need of protection from the government was quite unrealistic beside the power and wealth of big business. In 1905, the Court struck down a New York statute that limited the hours of bakers to sixty per week to protect their health. The Court ruled that such legislation

[28] C. Herman Pritchett and Alan F. Westin, *The Third Branch of Government* (New York: Harcourt, Brace, 1963), p. 17.

[29] Robert G. McCloskey, *The American Supreme Court* (Chicago: University of Chicago Press, 1968), p. 166.

interfered with the liberty of *workers* to contract to work *more* hours if they wished to do so. It ignored the economic fact that the bargaining power between employer and individual employee so favored the employer that the freedom of contract was a mockery.[30]

In *Adair* v. *U.S.* (1908), the Court invalidated labor legislation to protect union activity of employees against interference by employers. Such legislation by Congress, the Court said, by its very content violated the liberty of employees to quit their employment and the employer's right to fire workers. The Adair decision illustrates the doctrine of substantive due process which held that in addition to procedural violations of individual liberties, property and liberty could be denied by government regulation itself. The doctrine was devised and used to grant immunity to powerful economic interests from government regulation in working conditions, minimum wages, and standards of health. In short, the right of government to intervene in social and economic problems was subordinated to the rights of property by the Supreme Court. The Court also narrowly construed the power of Congress to regulate business by the commerce clause of the Constitution. A federal law outlawing shipment in interstate commerce of goods produced by child labor was struck down because the manufacturing of goods was not commerce; commerce began only after the goods were produced, and Congress had no authority to regulate production. This interpretation of the commerce clause blunted the efforts of Congress to end the employment and exploitation of children.[31]

Thus, the Supreme Court as "protector" of the "small businessman" was used by dominant economic interests to block governmental response to social and economic needs. The great depression of the 1930s altered American attitudes toward government, a shift symbolized by Franklin D. Roosevelt's New Deal. Acting under its commerce and taxing powers, Congress enacted laws establishing economic controls and social welfare programs; but between 1933 and 1937, the Supreme Court negated some of these and threatened to invalidate the entire New Deal program.[32]

The landslide reelection of Franklin Roosevelt in 1936 and large Democratic majorities in Congress showed that the public approved of the New Deal. To change the negative attitude of the Supreme Court, Roosevelt proposed that one additional Justice be appointed to the Court for every Justice who had served at least ten years and had failed to retire at the

---

[30] *Lochner* v. *New York*, 198 U.S. 45 (1905).

[31] *Hammer* v. *Dagenhart*, 247 U.S. 251 (1918).

[32] See *Panama Refining Company* v. *Ryan*, 293 U.S. 388 (1935); *United States* v. *Butler*, 297 U.S. 1 (1936); *Carter* v. *Carter Coal Company*, 298 U.S. 238 (1936); *Railroad Retirement Board* v. *Alton R.R.*, 295 U.S. 330 (1935); *Schechter Poultry Corp.* v. *United States*, 295 U.S. 495 (1935); and *Morehead* v. *Tipaldo*, 298 U.S. 587 (1936).

age of seventy. These conditions were met, not coincidentally, by six of the nine members of the Court. Roosevelt called it "reorganization," but his opponents dubbed it "court packing." The Senate rejected the proposal as "political tampering" and thus "saved" a Supreme Court that a few months before had been labeled "reactionary." "No issue so great or so deep," wrote Walter Lippmann, "has been raised in America since secession."[33]

Roosevelt lost the battle, but in the end he won the war. Justice Owen Roberts subsequently switched sides on the constitutionality of the New Deal laws and turned a five-to-four majority against these measures into a favorable majority. Robert H. Jackson, then Attorney General and later a Supreme Court Justice, commented that "this paradoxical outcome is accounted for by the recognition on the part of some Justices — belated but vigorous — of the validity of the complaints against their course of decision. They subdued the rebellion against their constitutional dogma by joining it."[34] By the late 1930s, President Roosevelt had been able to make seven new Court appointments, and the "threat" posed by the pre-New Deal Court was ended.

## access to policy application

Litigation represents a campaign. Cases that reach the Supreme Court reflect the carefully planned efforts of interested parties to achieve their goals by legal victory. Groups have many legitimate ways of gaining access to the judiciary. The legal brief is the most important instrument used by lawyers. The amicus curiae ("friend of the court") brief enables groups not directly involved in a case but with a vested interest in it to present their position before the Court. Under Supreme Court rules, amicus briefs require the Court's consent. Generally, it permits such briefs to be filed if a group shows a vital interest in the case and if it offers arguments that may not otherwise be presented. About forty of these briefs are filed each year. In 1962, six were filed for *Engel* v. *Vitale,* a case that involved state-sponsored, nondenominational public school prayer. The American Ethical Union, the American Jewish Committee, and the Synagogue Council of America presented briefs opposing the use of such a prayer. The New York State Board of Regents, a group of parents whose children attended New York public schools, and the attorneys

---

[33] Quoted in Alpheus T. Mason, "Harlan Fiske Stone and FDR's Court Plan," *Yale Law Review* 61 (1952): 706.

[34] Robert H. Jackson, *The Struggle for Judicial Supremacy* (New York: Alfred A. Knopf, 1941), p. vi.

general of twenty-two states that authorized or supported practices similar to those in New York submitted briefs supporting the use of prayer.

Another method of gaining judicial access is the *test case* enabling an interest group to link broad social problems to a specific case.[35] This is a prearranged controversy between two parties who are in "conflict" for the purpose of bringing a legal question to court. The most widely known organization that has used test cases to achieve its ends is the National Association for the Advancement of Colored People. Because the cause of racial equality before the 1940s received little support from the executive and legislative branches of the national government, the NAACP turned to litigation. Many racial cases decided by the Supreme Court in this century in housing, transportation, voting, and education have resulted from primarily test cases initiated by the NAACP. The organization has supplied the financial resources and the legal talent needed for victory in the courts.

The procedural device called *class action* is also important in gaining judicial access. As defined in the *Federal Rules of Civil Procedure,* it permits a group of people to bring suit in the names of persons "constituting a class" so as to ensure "the adequate representation of all" before the courts. The class action is especially appropriate for civil rights cases because it permits large numbers of people in a jurisdiction to appeal against practices without requiring them to seek redress of grievances individually. Cases challenging so-called de facto segregation in public schools have been filed in behalf of both the parties bringing the suit and all others similarly affected.[36] De facto segregation results from such practices as adhering to a neighborhood school policy in cities where Negroes are heavily concentrated, or manipulating school transfer policies to achieve racially segregated schools. The class action suit may also be used by environmental and consumer groups to bring suit on behalf of large numbers of persons.

Influence on judicial decisions may also result from the writings of legal scholars, political scientists, judges, and others whose commentaries on legal issues and court decisions frequently are cited by justices. Just how literature of this type influences judicial choice is very difficult to assess. It is, however, one way of influencing judicial choice. Chester A. Newland writes that "Although objections to judicial reliance on legal periodicals and related sources have erupted in Congress and the press . . . such writing has generally been accepted now for several years as a central part of the judicial process."[37]

[35] Clement E. Vose, "Litigation as a Form of Pressure Group Activity," *The Annals of the American Academy of Political and Social Science* 319 (Sept. 1958): 20–31.

[36] *Bell v. School City of Gary, Indiana,* 324 F. 2D 209 (1963); *Taylor v. Board of Education of New Rochelle,* 82 Sup. Ct. 382 (1961).

[37] Chester A. Newland, "The Supreme Court and Legal Writing: Learned Journals as Vehicles of an Anti-Antitrust Lobby?" *Georgetown Law Journal* 48 (Fall 1959): 105–143.

Judicial activism in civil rights has compelled the integration of public schools. This action obviously illustrates the Court's role in making and shaping public policy.

Though these are ways in which private interest groups seek to influence judicial decisions, the government itself — federal, state, and local — is an interest group. The United States Department of Justice is involved, either as a party or by filing an amicus brief, in about half the cases heard each year by the Supreme Court.[38] Also, states attorneys general, either as a group or individually, often file amicus briefs on behalf of their states. Many states have been able to represent their interests in this manner in cases dealing with such issues as legislative reapportionment and prayer reading in public schools.

Through the Attorney General and the Solicitor General of the United States, the federal government retains control over cases that will be appealed by the government as well as decisions over which arguments and issues will be stressed in arguing a case. The Solicitor General, a subcabinet-level position in the Justice Department, is the "government's lawyer." He clears cases for appeal and assesses the government's chances to win an appeal, the consequences of defeat, and the policy significance of a case. Such decisions clearly affect the degree of access of interest groups to the courts, because government itself goes for or against judicial policy alternatives. Early in 1972, a group of young lawyers in the Civil Rights division of the Department of Justice resigned in angry protest over what they considered to be the Department's policy not to vigorously investigate and prosecute violations of the civil rights law.

[38] Samuel Krislov, *The Supreme Court in the Political Process* (New York: Macmillan, 1965), p. 48.

The devices we have considered expand conflict representation in the courts. They also make possible the judicial reconciliation of potentially explosive conflict by formally presenting to judges the views of widely varied groups. These devices may alter the judiciary's traditional insulation from the political arena.

## decisionmaking within the court

The public sessions of the Supreme Court are conducted in a formal atmosphere with procedural rules, protocol, and dignity. The bargaining, compromises, and negotiations so characteristic of the legislative and executive branches are not so visible in the Supreme Court, yet these styles of decisionmaking are nevertheless present.

The Court determines the cases it will rule on by utilizing its power to hear or not to hear an appeal. Only about one hundred twenty cases a year reach the formal decision stage. Although each decision determines a "winner" and a "loser" among parties to the dispute, the Justices' division of opinion and their reasoning have broader implications. Unanimous opinions are handed down in only about one in four cases. *Concurring* opinions — agreeing with the opinion of the majority of the Court but on different grounds — and *dissenting* opinions — presenting the views of the minority — are more frequently expressed.[39] Any Justice may write or join his fellow Justices in writing a concurring or a dissenting opinion.

Traditional approaches to the Court have closely examined opinions for what they reveal about development of the law, philosophy of the Court, views of individual Justices, and the Court's position compared with the other branches of the government. This approach is both fruitful and necessary. More sophisticated tools of analysis explain more fully the behavior of the Justices.

Glendon Schubert and others have used a technique called "cumulative scaling," which attempts to measure a hypothetical relationship between the values and attitudes of judges and their votes on judicial issues. Studies based on scaling methods have consistently shown two attitudes closely connected to votes on civil liberties and economic matters. The first orientation, the C scale, as defined by Schubert includes cases in which individual rights and liberties conflict with government authorities; the E scale includes cases in which the economically privileged conflict with the economically underprivileged.[40] Schubert used the C and E scales in

---

[39] Decisions are sometimes made on the basis of a tie vote, which can occur when all nine Justices do not participate in a case. The effect of a tie is to uphold the lower court decision, but no formal opinion is written.

[40] Glendon Schubert, *The Judicial Mind* (Evanston, Ill.: Northwestern University Press, 1965), pp. 98–128.

studying the 1968 term of the Supreme Court and found that in forty-seven C scale cases five Justices — Douglas, Fortas, Marshall, Warren, and Brennan — formed a group in opposition to the four other Justices — White, Stewart, Harlan, and Black.[41] The E scale issues in fourteen cases during the 1968 term also divided the Court, but only two Justices — Harlan and Stewart — responded favorably to the economically affluent instead of the underprivileged. Schubert's findings revealed a clear and consistent division of attitudes among the Justices and also indicated that the division was more visible in the civil liberties cases.[42]

As we have said, no one can enter the mind of a Justice, and our analytic tools are not good enough to specify cause and effect relationships in explaining judicial behavior. The Court as an institution is also more private and, therefore, less accessible than other parts of government. Court norms prohibit Justices from publicly criticizing decisions with which they have formally disagreed. Personal antagonisms between Justices are usually not aired in public, although they may be known. Only members of the Court can sit in on the *conference,* a meeting held at least once a week during the Court's term (October to June), in which the business of the Court takes place. Conferences are formal in both procedure and protocol; justices are seated around the table in order of seniority, and the Chief Justice always speaks first. The Court discusses cases, considers and passes upon appeals, takes formal votes, and assigns justices the task of writing opinions.

INNER-COURT RELATIONSHIPS: BARGAINING AND PERSUASION. Decision making on a multiple-member court is a group process. Individual justices with different personalities, goals, and backgrounds must work together to fashion court decisions. If his position on an issue is to prevail, a Justice must get at least four fellow Justices to support him in order to gain a majority of votes. Persuasion, bargaining, and personal relationships mold decisionmaking and behavior of the Supreme Court.

A fascinating glimpse of persuasion is given by J. Woodford Howard's account (based on notes taken in conference by Justice Murphy) of the way in which a major issue on separation of church and state was decided in 1947.[43] The case was *Everson v. Board of Education,* and the issue was a New Jersey statute that authorized payment of subsidies to parents of parochial school children for transporting them to school. Justices Rutledge and Frankfurter argued for a strong decision against the statute on

---

[41] The voting behavior of Justice Black on civil liberties issues in this term was, however, quite different from his liberal voting record on these issues during his thirty-six years on the Court.

[42] Glendon Schubert, *The Judicial Mind,* pp. 101–109.

[43] J. Woodford Howard, Jr., "On the Fluidity of Judicial Choice," *American Political Science Review* 62 (1968).

grounds that the Court should put an end to subsidies of parochial education. Justice Black agreed that there should be absolute separation of
church and state, but argued that the New Jersey subsidy did not violate
that principle. In the end, Black succeeded in persuading four other Justices to his side and the decision reflected his position.

The Court's history reveals that some Justices have been better able
to persuade and influence their fellows. Although some Justices failed to
convince a majority, their positions became majority policy in subsequent
Courts. The lone dissenting opinion of Justice Harlan against the Court's
"separate but equal" doctrine in *Plessy* v. *Ferguson* in 1897 became the
unanimous opinion in *Brown* v. *Board of Education* in 1954. In addition,
the language and arguments used in Court opinions often reflect the bargaining that took place inside the Court. If the Justice writing the opinion
of the Court ignores the suggestions of other Justices in the majority he
risks losing his majority. A note to Justice Frankfurter from Chief Justice
Stone about a proposed opinion said: "If you wish to write, placing the
case on the ground which I think tenable and desirable, I shall cheerfully
join you. If not, I will add a few observations for myself."[44]

When the Court is divided on an issue, the losing interests outside the
Court will have an incentive to exploit this division with further litigation,
and the Court may lose public support for its decisions. Severe public
criticism is more likely when the Court is divided or uncertain. The
unanimous opinion in *Brown* v. *Topeka* and the subsequent unanimity
in segregation cases have given strong authority to Court policy in these
matters. But frequent five-to-four decisions in cases on the procedural
rights ("due process") of accused persons under the Fifth and Fourteenth
Amendments have brought down on it severe criticism and great uncertainty among public prosecutors about the standards the Court requires.[45]

THE CHIEF JUSTICE. The Chief Justice is in on every part of the Court's
work. He presides over sessions of the Court and the conference. When
in the majority, he assigns the writing of the opinion of the Court to one
of the Justices in the majority, or he may even write the opinion himself.
(The minority opinion is assigned by the senior Justice in the minority.)
The Chief Justice is also responsible for administering the Court's docket
of cases and he controls the timetable of the conference.

---

[44] Quoted in Walter F. Murphy, *Elements of Judicial Strategy* (Chicago: University of
Chicago Press, 1964), p. 59.

[45] See, for example, *Escobedo* v. *Illinois*, 378 U.S. 476 (1964) (right to counsel); *Gideon* v.
*Wainwright*, 372 U.S. 335 (1963) (right to counsel); *Townsend* v. *Sain*, 372 U.S. 293 (1963)
(forced confession by use of "truth serum"); *Malloy* v. *Hogan*, 378 U.S. 1 (1964) (applying
Fifth Amendment ban on compulsory self-incrimination against the states via the "due
process" clause of the Fourteenth Amendment).

David Danelski has devised a concept of dual leadership — task leadership and social leadership — to evaluate leadership within the Court.[46] The task leader is highly esteemed by his colleagues but reserved in his personal relations. He presents his views forcefully in conference, leads the discussion, and provides guidance on difficult questions. The social leader has a warm and responsive personality and concentrates on the "emotional needs of his associates by affirming their value as individuals and as Court members." His primary aim is unity and cohesion within the Court. Frequently the Chief Justice will exercise either task or social leadership, but not both; he will share leadership with one of his associates. In Danelski's opinion, Chief Justice Charles Evans Hughes exercised both roles; his successor, Harlan F. Stone, neither.

The Chief Justice's leadership abilities depend upon many factors, including his personality, his view of his role, and the personalities of other members of the Court. Strong Chief Justices, such as Marshall, Taft, and Hughes, have maintained unity and cohesion in spite of drastic inner-court differences over policy and strong personality conflicts. Others have failed. "The chief justiceship supplies numerous opportunities to exert influence," wrote Walter F. Murphy, "it offers no guaranty that the incumbent can utilize these opportunities to achieve his policy goals."[47]

## activism or self-restraint: which role for the court?

Debate over what the Supreme Court's job *ought* to be has gone on since the Marshall Court. In recent years, the controversy has intensified because Court decisions have profoundly affected broad areas of social and economic policy. The definitions of judicial activism and judicial self-restraint differ. They are sometimes defined within the context of the checks and balances principle: each branch has powers to check the other but each must exercise restraint to avoid going beyond constitutional boundaries. The activist position is that the Supreme Court has not overstepped its boundaries because, along with the formal checks that Congress and the President may exercise, public opinion is a major restraining force.

Another view of activism and self-restraint holds that judicial activists are "reform minded" and pay little attention to restraining court activity in order not to endanger or destroy the Court's role as primarily the

[46] David Danelski, "The Influence of the Chief Justice in the Decisional Process of the Supreme Court," in Walter F. Murphy and C. Herman Pritchett, eds., *Courts, Judges, and Politics* (New York: Random House, 1961), pp. 497–508.

[47] Walter F. Murphy, *Elements of Judicial Strategy* (Chicago: University of Chicago Press, 1964), p. 89.

*interpreter,* not molder, of legislative policy. Thus Justice John M. Harlan warned of what he considered to be the dangers of Court interpretations that extended civil rights and liberties into areas not intended by the Constitution, and reflected the misguided assumption that federal institutions can rectify all wrongs. For Justice Harlan, "there is no such thing in our constitutional jurisprudence as a doctrine of civil rights at large, standing independent of other constitutional limitations or giving rise to rights born only out of the personal predilections of judges as to what is good."[48]

Definitions differ, but the underlying denominator of judicial activism is to give the Court the job of being a major architect of policy to promote social and political goals. The judicial activist may or may not be in accord with legislative or public opinion and policy choices, but from his point of view such accord is subordinate to other values required by the Constitution's broad directives. Thus the activist Courts of the late nineteenth and early twentieth centuries read economic rights as predominant values over competing social and political claims. The Warren Court of the 1950s and 1960s emphasized other rights and liberties and extended protection of the individual against government to states as well as the national government. Justice Hugo Black, one of the staunchest supporters of judicial activism in First Amendment controversies, argued that the Bill of Rights contains "absolutes" in that government "was denied all power to do some things *under any and all* circumstances."[49]

Those who advocate judicial self-restraint, on the other hand, emphasize the Court's duty not to intervene in policy matters unless such intervention is clearly necessary to correct violations of the Constitution. Like Justice Harlan, they consider maintaining a constitutional balance between governing branches to be more important than achieving social or personal values of judges or courts. Judicial policymaking is unavoidable, but advocates of self-restraint would keep it to a minimum. The Supreme Court of the late 1930s and 1940s can be considered a self-restraining Court in that it accepted the broad congressional interpretations of the commerce and tax clauses of the Constitution that were used to enact major social and economic legislation. The Warren Court was self-restrained in economic matters, yet it was also the most active in history in civil rights and liberties.

The foremost advocate of judicial self-restraint was Justice Felix Frankfurter, who died in 1965. Frankfurter's view was clearly expressed

[48] John Marshall Harlan, "The Bill of Rights and the Constitution," in David F. Forte, ed., *The Supreme Court in American Politics* (Lexington, Mass.: D. C. Heath, 1972), pp. 51–52.
[49] Hugo L. Black, "The Bill of Rights and the Federal Government," in Edmond Cahn, ed., *The Great Rights* (New York: Macmillan, 1963), p. 45.

in his dissenting opinion in *Baker* v. *Carr,* the 1962 decision that held for the first time that federal courts could hear and decide cases challenging state legislative apportionment. Arguing that the Court should not get itself involved in this "political thicket," the Justice stressed that courts are "ill-adapted" to handle such matters. Courts, he added, should not be "arbiters of the broad issues of political organization historically committed to other institutions and for whose adjustment the judicial process is ill-adapted."

Arguments over self-restraint and activism are heavily influenced by the extent to which the protagonists agree or disagree with decisions or policy directions of the Court. Those who criticized the Warren Court for "going too far" will support the more restrained position of the Burger Court in its view of the rights of the defendant. Whether it follows the pattern of self-restraint or activism, no Court can avoid being a major policymaker in the American system. And whichever policy alternative is chosen in specific areas of law, some interests will benefit and others will be hurt.

## the supreme court and public policy

When Congress was considering a proposal by Senator William E. Jenner in 1958 to strip the Supreme Court of jurisdiction in cases dealing with contempt of Congress and the federal loyalty and security program, Senator Thomas Hennings labeled it a "kill the umpire" proposal. The Court is an enforcer of the rules and it is also the object of abuse when it meets its responsibilities. It is also to be expected that an institution able to veto the actions of other branches of government, to act contrary to public opinion, and to formulate new policies on its own will be controversial. It seems paradoxical that the Court — especially over the last two decades — has been the object of bitter and frequently widespread criticism, and yet has weathered almost all efforts to alter its jurisdiction or formally reverse its decisions by legislative action or constitutional amendment. How can this strength be explained?

Part of the answer may lie in one's feelings about court power and its relationship to other policymaking levels. Is the Court a "democratic" institution? If democratic is defined as "chosen by election by the governed," the Court obviously does not qualify. Justices are appointed for life and their social, educational, and economic backgrounds make them probably the most elite group of governors in the American system. Nine men who cannot be deposed and who are intentionally insulated from public pressure, control the destiny of millions — that is scarcely democratic.

Public outrage and occasional noncompliance occur when the judiciary veers far from the limits of popular acceptance. This sign obstructs the busdriver's vision.

If, however, we define democracy as the rights of the individual against arbitrary government power, or the principle of equality (political and social), then it may seem that the Supreme Court during the past three decades has been more democratic than other branches of government. Protecting and advancing the rights to dissent, a fair trial, social and educational equality, and political equality in casting a ballot as well as having it count equally ("one man, one vote") — all these are the products of Supreme Court decisions. They have also produced the greatest criticisms against the exercise of judicial power ("usurpation," "irresponsible," "coddling the criminal," etc.).

Historically, of course, the Supreme Court has supported different interests and has fostered different causes at different periods. The philosophy of laissez-faire economics dominated Court decisions from the 1890s to the mid-1930s, and finally gave way to a Court that endorsed the social and political reforms of the New Deal. The Warren Court of the 1950s emphasized both individual rights and the goals of equality, the first Court in American history to foster *both* of these attributes of democracy.[50] The

[50] Glendon Schubert, *The Constitutional Polity* (Boston, Mass.: Boston University Press, 1970), p. 52.

Court has enjoyed majority support among the public for only part of these periods, yet it has consistently survived criticism and efforts to "curb" its activities. We suggest that because the Court has assisted in realizing and protecting fundamental democratic norms, even though its membership and organization are overtly undemocratic, its position as "guardian of the Constitution" protects it against its worst critics. In short, the Supreme Court symbolizes the values built into the Constitution itself, and efforts to alter its jurisdiction or its structure are viewed with suspicion.

Yet we have not fully answered the original question: How does the Court survive under the stress of severe criticism? The answer may lie in the nature of the majorities in pluralist America.

Majorities are coalitions of interests that elect Presidents, articulate opinion, and translate demands into public policy. Americans normally look to the party system and elections as the instruments through which majorities act. The activity of the Supreme Court has followed the effectiveness or lack of effectiveness of such majorities.

Wallace Mendelson has argued that courts have been unsuccessful in determining national policy in times when cohesion within dominant partisan alliances was great.[51] According to Mendelson's data, between 1790 and 1864 the Supreme Court declared only two congressional measures unconstitutional, in *Marbury v. Madison* and *Dred Scott v. Sanford*. From 1865 to 1937, the Court vetoed congressional legislation in seventy-six instances. According to Mendelson, the use of judicial review of legislation grew substantially because of disagreement between the interests forming the dominant Republican coalition — businessmen, grain farmers, and laborers — which left the Court free to exercise a veto without united opposition. Business interests in the coalition were victorious, not because of legislative victories but because the Supreme Court exercised its judicial veto over legislative economic policy. The pro-business, laissez-faire leaning of the Court lasted until the New Deal made the Democrats dominant. Since 1937, the Court has exercised restraint in cases dealing with economic legislation. Mendelson concludes that "judicial 'legislation' apparently feeds on defects in the political structure."

Whether the Mendelson thesis can explain the success of the activistic Warren Court is difficult to assess. That Court spent far less time blocking the actions of Congress than in extending the scope of constitutional provisions to areas that legislative majorities were unable to accept. The 1972 moratorium on busing followed federal district court interpretations of Supreme Court mandates in school desegregation that neither Congress

[51] Wallace Mendelson, "Judicial Review and Party Politics," *Vanderbilt Law Review* 12 (March 1959): 447–457.

nor the public could support. And of course many Warren Court decisions were applied against *state* government practices in racial equality and individual rights.

The activism of the 1960s may, however, be giving way to an era of Court restraint in balancing the rights of the individual and the rights of society as defined by legislatures. Four new Justices appointed by President Nixon have swung the balance of the Court toward such restraint in interpreting defendants' rights. Thus the Nixon administration, avowedly on the side of Court restraint in this area of law, has, by the power of appointment, moved the Court toward moderation.

Robert Dahl holds that the common assumption that the Supreme Court protects minorities against majorities cannot be supported. The Court can delay, but not permanently block, a majority in Congress. In fact the Court has often served to legitimize the policy of the dominant party. Yet, says Dahl, the Court is more than simply an "agent" of a party; it is an essential part of political leadership and possesses "bases of power of its own, the most important of which is the unique legitimacy attributed to its interpretation of the Constitution." Thus, "the Court operates to confer legitimacy, not simply on the particular and parochial policies of the dominant political alliance, but upon the basic patterns of behavior required for the operation of a democracy."[52]

The judiciary legitimizes policy formulated by administrators, Congressmen, and pressure-group leaders; moreover, it protects the political and individual rights and freedoms that make democracy operable. At the same time, it mirrors the ambivalence in liberal ideology — the emphasis upon both individual rights and majority rule. The judiciary's ability to make policy rests upon its official role as umpire of the system, but it is limited and conditioned by the realities of pluralistic power in the American political system. History shows that the Court cannot stray too far from the limits of public acceptance of new doctrines. It is hard to describe precisely how the Court manages to adjust the demands of majority rule to its position as guardian of the law. The difficulty may lie, Glendon Schubert suggests, in "the tension between constant institutional structures and the inconstant humans who operate them."[53]

*bibliographical note*

Until recent years, literature on the judiciary was largely confined to judicial history and case law, the examination of substantive issues. Current research and writing, however, heavily emphasizes factors that place the courts, especially

[52] Robert A. Dahl, "Decision-making in a Democracy: The Supreme Court as a National Policy-maker," *The Journal of Public Law* 6 (Fall 1957): 279–295.
[53] Schubert, *The Constitutional Polity,* p. 5.

the Supreme Court, in a political setting. Essential to an appreciation of this approach, however, is an understanding of the historical background and a knowledge of case law in substantive areas. The standard history of the Supreme Court is Charles Warren, *The Supreme Court in United States History*, 3 vols. (Boston: Little, Brown, 1922–1923). The following paperbacks combine historical outlines of the development of constitutional law with analyses of major areas of controversy: Carl Brent Swisher, *The Growth of Constitutional Power in the United States* (Chicago: University of Chicago Press, 1946) treats the Court from Marshall onward; Alpheus T. Mason, *The Supreme Court from Taft to Warren* (New York: W. W. Norton, 1958) examines major substantive issues within the context of the debate over the proper function of the courts in the American system; R. G. McCloskey, ed., *Essays in Constitutional Law* (New York: Vintage Books, 1957) contains commentary on broad substantive questions such as federalism, economic rights, and the separation of church and state by leading authorities in the field.

The procedures and structures of the judiciary are treated in a number of books. Paperback works at the undergraduate level include Henry J. Abraham, *The Judicial Process*, 2nd ed. (New York: Oxford University Press, 1968), which also discusses the nature of law and provides some comparison of the American and other judicial systems; and Herbert Jacob, *Justice in America* (Boston: Little, Brown, 1968) effectively integrates description of structure and procedure with a view of the courts as political instruments.

Behavioral and systems approaches to the judiciary have been incorporated in many recent works. Among the foremost representatives of the behavioral frame of reference is Glendon Schubert. His *Constitutional Politics* (New York: Holt, Rinehart & Winston, 1960) is a sophisticated undergraduate text that focuses upon how and why the Supreme Court makes certain decisions. He has also edited *Judicial Behavior: A Reader in Theory and Research* (Chicago: Rand McNally, 1964), a comprehensive cross-cultural approach that discusses the relationship between the study of judicial behavior and other disciplines such as traditional public law and history. Paperback editions at the introductory level that represent contemporary behavioral approaches to the study of the judicial process are: Samuel Krislov, *The Supreme Court in the Political Process* (New York: Macmillan, 1965), especially useful in understanding internal relationship and processes of the Supreme Court; Sheldon Goldman and Thomas P. Jahnige, *The Federal Courts as a Political System* (New York: Harper & Row, 1971), a highly readable application of the systems approach; and Jack Peltason, *Federal Courts in the Political Process* (New York: Random House, 1956), which analyzes the federal judicial system from the point of view of interest group theory. Walter F. Murphy, *Elements of Judicial Strategy* (Chicago: University of Chicago Press, 1964) views the role and functions of judicial policymaking within the context of the policy-oriented judge. Lower federal courts are analyzed in an excellent work, Richard J. Richardson and Kenneth N. Vines, *The Politics of Federal Courts* (Boston: Little, Brown, 1970). Elements of the impact of court decisions are well-covered in Stephen Wasby, *The Impact of the United States Supreme Court: Some Perspectives* (Homewood, Ill.: Dorsey Press, 1970).

The politics of judicial selection and the social background of Supreme Court Justices are discussed in John R. Schmidhauser, *The Supreme Court: Its Politics,*

*Personalities, and Procedures* (New York: Holt, Rinehart and Winston, 1961). Also available in paperback. David J. Danelski, *A Supreme Court Justice is Appointed* (New York: Random House, 1964) is an engaging account of the nomination of a Supreme Court Justice and provides valuable insight into the nominating process in general.

The empirical measurement of judicial behavior has become progressively more sophisticated. A seminal work in the measurement of judicial attitudes is C. Herman Pritchett's *The Roosevelt Court* (New York: Macmillan, 1948), which studies the 1937–1947 period on the basis of the voting records of individual justices. Pritchett's *Civil Liberties and the Vinson Court* (Chicago: University of Chicago Press, 1954) also applies bloc voting analysis. Quantitative measurement of judicial decisionmaking is the subject of Glendon Schubert's *Quantitative Analysis of Judicial Behavior* (Glencoe, Ill.: Free Press, 1959), especially chap. 4.

Debate over judicial activism versus self-restraint has been widespread. It is inextricably involved with the larger question of the relationship of judicial review to the democratic system. A classic study in this area is Edward S. Corwin's *The Doctrine of Judicial Review* (Princeton, N.J.: Princeton University Press, 1914). The following are available in paperback editions: Alexander M. Bickel, *The Least Dangerous Branch* (Indianapolis: Bobbs-Merrill, 1962) argues that the role and function of the Supreme Court is consistent with the theory and practice of democracy; Robert H. Jackson, *The Supreme Court in the American System of Government* (New York: Harper & Row, 1955) is a brief, but penetrating view of the Court and its relationship to democratic government by a former Justice; Alan F. Westin, ed., *The Supreme Court: Views from Inside* (New York: W. W. Norton, 1961) presents the views of some of the Justices on this important matter.

Judicial biography is an excellent source of insight into the workings of the Court. Among the many outstanding biographies of Justices are the following: Charles Fairman, *Mr. Justice Miller and the Supreme Court 1862–1890* (Cambridge, Mass.: Harvard University Press, 1939); Merlo J. Pusey, *Charles Evans Hughes,* 2 vols. (New York: Macmillan, 1951); and Alpheus T. Mason, *Harlan Fiske Stone: Pillar of the Law* (New York: Viking Press, 1956).

# concluding note: aspiration, achievement, and problems in a pluralist democracy

As America left the 1960s the pluralist approach to conflict regulation that had been accepted since the republic was born was being widely criticized and condemned, in both word and deed. "Hypocritical," "exploitative," "facist," "corrupt," "irresponsible," "imperialistic," and "irrelevant" were the words thrown up by disillusioned and disaffected social interests. Scholarly and journalistic critics alike found pluralist politics wanting because it could not meet the test of the times and it was accused of being a front for rule by an insensitive, unresponsive affluent elite. As the decade ended, urban riots, disruptions on college campuses, antiwar demonstrations, and violent outbursts against authority shouted of deep cleavages within America that seemed beyond mending within the derided "pluralist system." Yet, in the 1970s the cry, perhaps the hope, for revolutionary political change became less strident. Striking displays of protest continued, as when students protested in the spring of 1972 against the renewed American bombing of North Vietnam. But student disillusionment seemed different. A nationwide survey of students in fifty colleges and universities revealed in 1971 that two-thirds believed campus radicalism was no longer on the rise and three-fourths felt that to change the society it is best to "work within the system."[1] And many did work within the system, as for George McGovern's bid for the Democratic presidential nomination in 1972.

Lest we complacently think the "return to normalcy" means that tradi-

[1] Daniel Yankelovich, *The Changing Values on Campus: Political and Personal Attitudes of Today's College Students* (New York: Pocket Books, 1972).

tional pluralist politics is again beyond reproach and we need expect no more protests against it, we will conclude by taking a final look at pluralist democracy to see what can be said of its aspirations, recent achievements, and future prospects.

There are a variety of alternatives to pluralist government; direct rule by popular majorities (popular democracy), the rule of one man in his own interest (a dictatorship), and the rule of one group in its own interest (oligarchy) are among them. The pluralist method of regulating social conflict is different from others because it tries to bring all diverse social interests into government, to give them legal recognition and security enough so they can and will speak freely, and to listen to them and conciliate them as far as possible. *It is the pluralist aspiration to draw all social interests into each other so that individually and collectively they can make a positive contribution to the community.*

We have seen that the pluralist method characterizes American government, although it is questionable that all its goals are achieved. We know that it is not tied to any ideology, that American government strives not for universal consensus on the fundamental tenets of democracy but for workable solutions to the perpetual and shifty problem of conciliating diverse interests. Many well-organized interests and a decentralized, fragmented constitutional structure provide basic pluralist patterns for representing and resolving conflict. By their many ways of participating in politics — holding and expressing opinions, exercising leadership, voting, taking part in party politics, and organizing demands — Americans represent a multitude of diverse interests. And social and political pluralism facilitate and sustain a bargaining and incrementalist approach to policymaking within the Presidency, the Congress, the administrative bureaucracy, and the courts.

This framework of pluralist democracy has great strengths and weaknesses. It is strong because interests do have a voice in government. Over the years they have been able to publicize and promote their demands. From time to time they have succeeded in changing government action and public policy as new circumstances dictated new demands. Government has dramatically increased its activity in economic and social affairs since the 1930s; in civil rights and liberties in the last three decades; and it has steadily expanded its programs to meet the problems of urban life, education, poverty, aging, consumer protection, and environmental control since the early 1960s. All attest to the influence newly organized interests have had on policymaking.

But if pluralist aspiration has been approached, it still has weaknesses and it most certainly has not been fulfilled. Although great improvements have come about in recent years in getting opportunities, resources, and motivations for political participation distributed, the representation of social conflict remains distorted. Perhaps no method of rule can guarantee equality in these distributions, but certainly equity must be great enough so that no interest is deprived of its voice in conflict representation. Nor is conflict resolved in the best possible ways. To be sure, the emphasis is on conciliating conflicting interests. But under the pluralist, bargaining, incrementalist approach to formulating policy, demands by special interests are too often served and larger and rationally derived community goals get lost in the compromises imposed by bargaining. Working agreements among coalitions of public and private leaders make it difficult, and often impossible, to place the responsibility for making specific public policies. Interest leaders, trying to conserve their bargaining resources for more important matters, often avoid issues outside their own bargaining arena, so that significant social tensions are ignored until they have reached the critical stage. Moreover, pluralist rule, as practiced in bargaining and incrementalist policymaking, limits the rate and extent of policy change. Widely diffused centers of power offer many chances for demands to be represented, but they also make it possible to shunt aside, veto, or simply overlook policy proposals. The consequence is that sudden and dramatic reversals of policy or great changes in institutional arrangements are unlikely, and necessary adaptations to changing times and conditions are often thwarted. Instead, the continuing adjustment of interest demands reinforces the status quo and discourages innovative response to new demands.

Any governing arrangement, including pluralist democracy, distributes advantages and disadvantages unevenly among social interests. Policies that benefit one group of interests may damage others. We do not suggest that American government must or can be blindly impartial in regulating social disputes. Nor do we indict American democracy as being so far from realizing the pluralist aspiration that everything must be scrapped and we must start anew. With all its faults, our pluralist democracy has survived its severest critics and has recruited many of its staunchest opponents to its support. But, to survive it must undergo periodic political reform to accommodate it to the changing relationships among interests. It will do no good to label those who speak for specific reforms as "dangerous radicals" or "disloyal dissenters;" nor will anything be accomplished by calling those opposed to those reforms "rabid reactionaries," "irrelevant," or "self-serving." If Americans are to realize the individual dignity inherent in liberal democracy without sacrificing the equally important viability of the community, new and hitherto unrepresented interests must always be admitted to a free and open governing system. On the other hand, though, the twin ideals of individual perfectibility and collective stability cannot be attained unless all interests forego absolutist, uncompromising demands and accept the contingencies that surround the give-and-take of social conflicts in a democratic setting. This is how pluralism works in the politics of a liberal democracy.

# appendix: the constitution of the united states

We the People of the United States, in Order to form a more perfect Union, establish Justice, insure domestic Tranquility, provide for the common defence, promote the general Welfare, and secure the Blessings of Liberty to ourselves and our Posterity, do ordain and establish this Constitution for the United States of America.

## article I

SECTION 1. All legislative Powers herein granted shall be vested in a Congress of the United States, which shall consist of a Senate and House of Representatives.

SECTION 2. (1) The House of Representatives shall be composed of Members chosen every second Year by the People of the several States, and the Electors in each State shall have the Qualifications requisite for Electors of the most numerous Branch of the State Legislature.

(2) No Person shall be a Representative who shall not have attained to the Age of twenty-five Years, and been seven Years a Citizen of the United States, and who shall not, when elected, be an Inhabitant of that State in which he shall be chosen.

(3) [Representatives and direct Taxes[1] shall be apportioned among the several States which may be included within this Union, according to their respective Numbers, which shall be determined by adding to the whole Number of free Persons, including those bound to Service for a Term of Years, and excluding Indians not taxed, three fifths of all other Persons.][2] The actual Enumeration shall

[1] The Sixteenth Amendment replaced this with respect to income taxes.

be made within three Years after the first Meeting of the Congress of the United States, and within every subsequent Term of ten Years, in such Manner as they shall by Law direct. The Number of Representatives shall not exceed one for every thirty Thousand, but each State shall have at Least one Representative; and until such enumeration shall be made, the State of New Hampshire shall be entitled to choose three, Massachusetts eight, Rhode-Island and Providence Plantations one, Connecticut five, New-York six, New Jersey four, Pennsylvania eight, Delaware one, Maryland six, Virginia ten, North Carolina five, South Carolina five, and Georgia three.

(4) When vacancies happen in the Representation from any State, the Executive Authority thereof shall issue Writs of Election to fill such Vacancies.

(5) The House of Representatives shall choose their Speaker and other Officers; and shall have the sole Power of Impeachment.

SECTION 3. (1) The Senate of the United States shall be composed of two Senators from each State, [chosen by the Legislature][3] thereof, for six Years; and each Senator shall have one Vote.

(2) Immediately after they shall be assembled in Consequence of the first Election, they shall be divided as equally as may be into three Classes. The Seats of the Senators of the first Class shall be vacated at the Expiration of the second Year, of the second Class at the Expiration of the fourth Year, and of the third Class at the Expiration of the sixth Year, so that one-third may be chosen every second Year; [and if Vacancies happen by Resignation, or otherwise, during the Recess of the Legislature of any State, the Executive thereof may make temporary Appointments until the next Meeting of the Legislature, which shall then fill such Vacancies.][4]

(3) No person shall be a Senator who shall not have attained to the Age of thirty Years, and been nine Years a Citizen of the United States, and who shall not, when elected, be an Inhabitant of that State for which he shall be chosen.

(4) The Vice President of the United States shall be President of the Senate, but shall have no Vote, unless they be equally divided.

(5) The Senate shall choose their other Officers, and also a President pro tempore, in the absence of the Vice President, or when he shall exercise the Office of President of the United States.

(6) The Senate shall have the sole Power to try all Impeachments. When sitting for that Purpose, they shall be on Oath or Affirmation. When the President of the United States is tried, the Chief Justice shall preside: And no Person shall be convicted without the Concurrence of two thirds of the Members present.

(7) Judgment in Cases of Impeachment shall not extend further than to removal from Office, and disqualification to hold and enjoy any Office of honor, Trust or Profit under the United States: but the Party convicted shall nevertheless be liable and subject to Indictment, Trial, Judgment and Punishment according to Law.

[2] Repealed by the Fourteenth Amendment.
[3] Repealed by the Seventeenth Amendment, Section 1.
[4] Changed by the Seventeenth Amendment.

SECTION 4. (1) The Times, Places and Manner of holding Elections for Senators and Representatives, shall be prescribed in each State by the Legislature thereof; but the Congress may at any time by Law make or alter such Regulations, except as to the Places of Choosing Senators.

(2) The Congress shall assemble at least once in every Year, and such Meeting shall [be on the first Monday in December,][5] unless they shall by Law appoint a different Day.

SECTION 5. (1) Each House shall be the Judge of the Elections, Returns and Qualifications of its own Members, and a Majority of each shall constitute a Quorum to do Business; but a smaller number may adjourn from day to day, and may be authorized to compel the Attendance of absent Members, in such Manner, and under such Penalties as each House may provide.

(2) Each House may determine the Rules of its Proceedings, punish its Members for disorderly Behavior, and, with the Concurrence of two thirds, expel a Member.

(3) Each House shall keep a Journal of its Proceedings, and from time to time publish the same, excepting such Parts as may in their Judgment require Secrecy; and the Yeas and Nays of the Members of either House on any question shall, at the Desire of one fifth of those Present, be entered on the Journal.

(4) Neither House, during the Session of Congress, shall, without the Consent of the other, adjourn for more than three days, nor to any other Place than that in which the two Houses shall be sitting.

SECTION 6. (1) The Senators and Representatives shall receive a Compensation for their Services, to be ascertained by Law, and paid out of the Treasury of the United States. They shall in all Cases, except Treason, Felony and Breach of the Peace, be privileged from Arrest during their Attendance at the Session of their respective Houses, and in going to and returning from the same; and for any Speech or Debate in either House, they shall not be questioned in any other Place.

(2) No Senator or Representative shall, during the Time for which he was elected, be appointed to any civil Office under the Authority of the United States, which shall have been created, or the Emoluments whereof shall have been increased during such time; and no Person holding any Office under the United States, shall be a Member of either House during his Continuance in Office.

SECTION 7. (1) All Bills for raising Revenue shall originate in the House of Representatives; but the Senate may propose or concur with Amendments as on other Bills.

(2) Every Bill which shall have passed the House of Representatives and the Senate, shall, before it become a Law, be presented to the President of the United States; If he approve he shall sign it, but if not he shall return it, with his Objections to that House in which it shall have originated, who shall enter the Objections at large on their Journal, and proceed to reconsider it. If after such Reconsideration two thirds of that House shall agree to pass the Bill, it shall be sent, together with the Objections, to the other House, by which it shall likewise be

---

[5] Changed by the Twentieth Amendment, Section 2.

reconsidered, and if approved by two thirds of that House, it shall become a Law. But in all such Cases the Votes of both Houses shall be determined by Yeas and Nays, and the Names of the Persons voting for and against the Bill shall be entered on the Journal of each House respectively. If any Bill shall not be returned by the President within ten Days (Sundays excepted) after it shall have been presented to him, the Same shall be a Law, in like Manner as if he had signed it, unless the Congress by their Adjournment prevent its Return, in which Case it shall not be a Law.

(3) Every Order, Resolution, or Vote to which the Concurrence of the Senate and House of Representatives may be necessary (except on a question of Adjournment) shall be presented to the President of the United States; and before the Same shall take Effect, shall be approved by him, or being disapproved by him, shall be repassed by two thirds of the Senate and House of Representatives, according to the Rules and Limitations prescribed in the Case of a Bill.

SECTION 8. (1) The Congress shall have Power To lay and collect Taxes, Duties, Imposts and Excises, to pay the Debts and provide for the common Defence and general Welfare of the United States; but all Duties, Imposts and Excises shall be uniform throughout the United States;

(2) To borrow money on the credit of the United States;

(3) To regulate Commerce with foreign Nations, and among the several States, and with the Indian Tribes;

(4) To establish an uniform Rule of Naturalization, and uniform Laws on the subject of Bankruptcies throughout the United States;

(5) To coin Money, regulate the Value thereof, and of foreign Coin, and fix the Standard of Weights and Measures;

(6) To provide for the Punishment of counterfeiting the Securities and current Coin of the United States;

(7) To establish Post Office and post Roads;

(8) To promote the Progress of Science and useful Arts, by securing for limited Times to Authors and Inventors the exclusive Right to their respective Writings and Discoveries;

(9) To constitute Tribunals inferior to the supreme Court;

(10) To define and punish Piracies and Felonies committed on the high Seas, and Offenses against the Law of Nations;

(11) To declare War, grant Letters of Marque and Reprisal, and make Rules concerning Captures on Land and Water;

(12) To raise and support Armies, but no Appropriation of Money to that Use shall be for a longer Term than two Years;

(13) To provide and maintain a Navy;

(14) To make Rules for the Government and Regulation of the land and naval Forces;

(15) To provide for calling forth the Militia to execute the Laws of the Union, suppress Insurrections and repel Invasions;

(16) To provide for organizing, arming, and disciplining the Militia, and for governing such Part of them as may be employed in the Service of the United States, reserving to the States respectively, the Appointment of the Officers, and

the Authority of training the Militia according to the discipline prescribed by Congress;

(17) To exercise exclusive Legislation in all Cases whatsoever, over such District (not exceeding ten Miles square) as may, by Cession of particular States, and the acceptance of Congress, become the Seat of the Government of the United States, and to exercise like Authority over all Places purchased by the Consent of the Legislature of the State in which the Same shall be, for the Erection of Forts, Magazines, Arsenals, dock-Yards, and other needful Buildings; — And

(18) To make all Laws which shall be necessary and proper for carrying into Execution the foregoing Powers, and all other Powers vested by this Constitution in the Government of the United States, or in any Department or Officer thereof.

SECTION 9. (1) The Migration or Importation of such Persons as any of the States now existing shall think proper to admit, shall not be prohibited by the Congress prior to the Year one thousand eight hundred and eight, but a tax or duty may be imposed on such Importation, not exceeding ten dollars for each Person.

(2) The privilege of the Writ of Habeas Corpus shall not be suspended, unless when in Cases of Rebellion or Invasion the public Safety may require it.

(3) No Bill of Attainder or ex post facto Law shall be passed.

(4) No capitation, or other direct, Tax shall be laid, unless in Proportion to the Census or Enumeration herein before directed to be taken.[6]

(5) No Tax or Duty shall be laid on Articles exported from any State.

(6) No Preference shall be given by any Regulation of Commerce or Revenue to the Ports of one State over those of another: nor shall Vessels bound to, or from, one State, be obliged to enter, clear, or pay Duties in another.

(7) No Money shall be drawn from the Treasury, but in Consequence of Appropriations made by Law; and a regular Statement and Account of the Receipts and Expenditures of all public Money shall be published from time to time.

(8) No Title of Nobility shall be granted by the United States: And no Person holding any Office of Profit or Trust under them, shall, without the Consent of the Congress, accept of any present, Emolument, Office, or Title, of any kind whatever, from any King, Prince, or foreign State.

SECTION 10. (1) No State shall enter into any Treaty, Alliance, or Confederation; grant Letters of Marque and Reprisal; coin Money; emit Bills of Credit; make any Thing but gold and silver Coin a Tender in Payment of Debts; pass any Bill of Attainder, ex post facto Law, or Law impairing the Obligation of Contracts, or grant any Title of Nobility.

(2) No State shall, without the Consent of the Congress, lay any Imposts or Duties on Imports or Exports, except what may be absolutely necessary for executing its inspection Laws: and the net Produce of all Duties and Imposts, laid by any State on Imports or Exports, shall be for the Use of the Treasury of the United States; and all such Laws shall be subject to the Revision and Control of the Congress.

(3) No State shall, without the Consent of Congress, lay any duty of Tonnage, keep Troops, or Ships of War in time of Peace, enter into any Agreement or

[6] Changed by the Sixteenth Amendment.

Compact with another State, or with a foreign Power, or engage in War, unless actually invaded, or in such imminent Danger as will not admit of delay.

**article II**

SECTION 1. (1) The executive Power shall be vested in a President of the United States of America. He shall hold his Office during the Term of four Years, and, together with the Vice-President, chosen for the same Term, be elected, as follows

(2) Each State shall appoint, in such Manner as the Legislature thereof may direct, a Number of Electors, equal to the whole Number of Senators and Representatives to which the State may be entitled in the Congress: but no Senator or Representative, or Person holding an Office of Trust or Profit under the United States, shall be appointed an Elector.

[The Electors shall meet in their respective States, and vote by Ballot for two persons, of whom one at least shall not be an Inhabitant of the same State with themselves. And they shall make a List of all the Persons voted for, and of the Number of Votes for each; which List they shall sign and certify, and transmit sealed to the Seat of the Government of the United States, directed to the President of the Senate. The President of the Senate shall, in the Presence of the Senate and House of Representatives, open all the Certificates, and the Votes shall then be counted. The Person having the greatest Number of Votes shall be the President, if such Number be a Majority of the whole Number of Electors appointed; and if there be more than one who have such Majority, and have an equal Number of Votes, then the House of Representatives shall immediately choose by Ballot one of them for President; and if no Person have a Majority, then from the five highest on the List the said House shall in like Manner choose the President. But in choosing the President, the Votes shall be taken by States, the Representation from each State having one Vote; A quorum for this Purpose shall consist of a Member or Members from two-thirds of the States, and a Majority of all the States shall be necessary to a Choice. In every Case, after the Choice of the President, the Person having the greatest Number of Votes of the Electors shall be the Vice President. But if there should remain two or more who have equal Votes, the Senate shall choose from them by Ballot the Vice-President.]

(3) The Congress may determine the Time of choosing the Electors, and the Day on which they shall give their Votes; which Day shall be the same throughout the United States.

(4) No person except a natural born Citizen, or a Citizen of the United States, at the time of the Adoption of this Constitution, shall be eligible to the Office of President; neither shall any Person be eligible to that Office who shall not have attained to the Age of thirty-five Years, and been fourteen Years a Resident within the United States.

[7] This paragraph was superseded in 1804 by the Twelfth Amendment.

(5) In case of the Removal of the President from Office, or of his Death, Resignation, or Inability to discharge the Powers and Duties of the said Office, the same shall devolve on the Vice President, and the Congress may by Law provide for the Case of Removal, Death, Resignation or Inability, both of the President and Vice President, declaring what Officer shall then act as President, and such Officer shall act accordingly, until the Disability be removed, or a President shall be elected.

(6) The President shall, at stated Times, receive for his Services, a Compensation, which shall neither be increased nor diminished during the Period for which he shall have been elected, and he shall not receive within that Period any other Emolument from the United States, or any of them.

(7) Before he enter on the Execution of his Office, he shall take the following Oath or Affirmation: — "I do solemnly swear (or affirm) that I will faithfully execute the Office of President of the United States, and will to the best of my Ability, preserve, protect and defend the Constitution of the United States."

SECTION 2. (1) The President shall be Commander in Chief of the Army and Navy of the United States, and of the Militia of the several States, when called into the actual Service of the United States; he may require the Opinion in writing, of the principal Officer in each of the executive Departments, upon any subject relating to the Duties of their respective Offices, and he shall have Power to Grant Reprieves and Pardons for Offenses against the United States, except in Cases of Impeachment.

(2) He shall have Power, by and with the Advice and Consent of the Senate, to make Treaties, provided two-thirds of the Senators present concur; and he shall nominate, and by and with the Advice and Consent of the Senate, shall appoint Ambassadors, other public Ministers and Consuls, Judges of the supreme Court, and all other Officers of the United States, whose Appointments are not herein otherwise provided for, and which shall be established by Law: but the Congress may by Law vest the Appointment of such inferior Officers, as they think proper, in the President alone, in the Courts of Law, or in the Heads of Departments.

(3) The President shall have Power to fill up all Vacancies that may happen during the Recess of the Senate, by granting Commissions which shall expire at the End of their next Session.

SECTION 3. He shall from time to time give to the Congress Information of the State of the Union, and recommend to their Consideration such Measures as he shall judge necessary and expedient; he may, on extraordinary Occasions, convene both Houses, or either of them, and in Case of Disagreement between them, with Respect to the Time of Adjournment, he may adjourn them to such Time as he shall think proper; he shall receive Ambassadors and other public Ministers; he shall take Care that the Laws be faithfully executed, and shall Commission all the Officers of the United States.

SECTION 4. The President, Vice President and all civil Officers of the United States, shall be removed from Office on Impeachment for, and Conviction of, Treason, Bribery, or other high Crimes and Misdemeanors.

**article III**

SECTION 1. The judicial Power of the United States, shall be vested in one supreme Court, and in such inferior Courts as the Congress may from time to time ordain and establish. The Judges, both of the supreme and inferior Courts, shall hold their Offices during good Behavior, and shall, at stated Times, receive for their Services a Compensation which shall not be diminished during their Continuance in Office.

SECTION 2. (1) The judicial Power shall extend to all Cases, in Law and Equity, arising under this Constitution, the Laws of the United States, and Treaties made, or which shall be made, under their Authority; — to all Cases affecting Ambassadors, other public Ministers and Consuls; — to all Cases of admiralty and maritime Jurisdiction; — to Controversies to which the United States shall be a Party; — to Controversies between two or more States; — [between a State and Citizens of another State];[8] — between Citizens of different States; — between Citizens of the same State claiming Lands under Grants of different States, and [between a State, or the Citizens thereof, and foreign States, Citizens or Subjects.][9]

(2) In all Cases affecting Ambassadors, other public Ministers and Consuls, and those in which a State shall be Party, the supreme Court shall have original Jurisdiction. In all other Cases before mentioned, the supreme Court shall have appellate Jurisdiction, both as to Law and Fact, with such Exceptions, and under such Regulations as the Congress shall make.

(3) The trial of all Crimes, except in Cases of Impeachment, shall be by Jury; and such Trial shall be held in the State where the said Crimes shall have been committed; but when not committed within any State, the Trial shall be at such Place or Places as the Congress may by Law have directed.

SECTION 3. (1) Treason against the United States, shall consist only in levying War against them, or in adhering to their Enemies, giving them Aid and Comfort. No Person shall be convicted of Treason unless on the Testimony of two Witnesses to the same overt Act, or on Confession in open Court.

(2) The Congress shall have power to declare the Punishment of Treason, but no Attainder of Treason shall work Corruption of Blood, or Forfeiture except during the Life of the Person attained.

**article IV**

SECTION 1. Full Faith and Credit shall be given in each State to the public Acts, Records, and judicial Proceedings of every other State. And the Congress may by general Laws prescribe the Manner in which such Acts, Records and Proceedings shall be proved, and the Effect thereof.

SECTION 2. (1) The Citizens of each State shall be entitled to all Privileges and Immunities of Citizens in the several States.

[8] Restricted by the Eleventh Amendment.
[9] Restricted by the Eleventh Amendment.

(2) A Person charged in any State with Treason, Felony, or other Crime, who shall flee from Justice, and be found in another State, shall on demand of the executive Authority of the State from which he fled, be delivered up, to be removed to the State having Jurisdiction of the Crime.

(3) [No Person held to Service or Labor in one State, under the Laws thereof, escaping into another, shall, in Consequence of any Law or Regulation therein, be discharged from such Service or Labor, but shall be delivered up on Claim of the Party to whom such Service or Labor may be due.][10]

SECTION 3. (1) New States may be admitted by the Congress into this Union; but no new State shall be formed or erected within the Jurisdiction of any other State; nor any State be formed by the Junction of two or more States, or parts of States, without the Consent of the Legislatures of the States concerned as well as of the Congress.

(2) The Congress shall have Power to dispose of and make all needful Rules and Regulations respecting the Territory or other Property belonging to the United States; and nothing in this Constitution shall be so construed as to Prejudice any Claims of the United States, or of any particular State.

SECTION 4. The United States shall guarantee to every State in this Union a Republican Form of Government, and shall protect each of them against Invasion; and on Application of the Legislature, or of the Executive (when the Legislature cannot be convened) against domestic Violence.

## article V

The Congress, whenever two-thirds of both Houses shall deem it necessary, shall propose Amendments to this Constitution, or, on the Application of the Legislatures of two-thirds of the several States, shall call a Convention for proposing Amendments, which, in either Case, shall be valid to all Intents and Purposes, as part of this Constitution, when ratified by the Legislatures of three-fourths of the several States, or by Conventions in three-fourths thereof, as the one or the other Mode of Ratification may be proposed by the Congress; Provided that no Amendment which may be made prior to the Year One thousand eight hundred and eight shall in any Manner affect the first and fourth Clauses in the Ninth Section of the first Article; and that no State, without its Consent, shall be deprived of its equal Suffrage in the Senate.

## article VI

(1) All Debts contracted and Engagements entered into, before the Adoption of this Constitution, shall be as valid against the United States under this Constitution, as under the Confederation.

---

[10] This paragraph has been superseded by the Thirteenth Amendment.

(2) This Constitution, and the Laws of the United States which shall be made in Pursuance thereof; and all Treaties made, or which shall be made, under the Authority of the United States, shall be the supreme Law of the Land; and the Judges in every State shall be bound thereby, any Thing in the Constitution or Laws of any State to the Contrary notwithstanding.

(3) The Senators and Representatives before mentioned, and the Members of the several State Legislatures, and all executive and judicial Officers, both of the United States and of the several States, shall be bound by Oath or Affirmation, to support this Constitution; but no religious Test shall ever be required as a Qualification to any Office or public Trust under the United States.

### article VII

The Ratification of the Conventions of nine States, shall be sufficient for the Establishment of this Constitution between the States so ratifying the Same.

Done in Convention by the Unanimous Consent of the States present the Seventeenth Day of September in the Year of our Lord one thousand seven hundred and Eighty seven and of the Independence of the United States of America the Twelfth. In Witness whereof We have hereunto subscribed our Names.

Go WASHINGTON
*Presidt and deputy from Virginia*

ARTICLES IN ADDITION TO, AND AMENDMENT OF, THE CONSTITUTION OF THE UNITED STATES OF AMERICA, PROPOSED BY CONGRESS, AND RATIFIED BY THE LEGISLATURES OF THE SEVERAL STATES, PURSUANT TO THE FIFTH ARTICLE OF THE ORIGINAL CONSTITUTION.

### amendment I[11]

Congress shall make no law respecting an establishment of religion, or prohibiting the free exercise thereof; or abridging the freedom of speech, or of the press; or the right of the people peaceably to assemble, and to petition the Government for a redress of grievances.

### amendment II

A well regulated Militia, being necessary to the security of a free State, the right of the people to keep and bear Arms, shall not be infringed.

[11] The first ten Amendments were adopted in 1791.

### amendment III

No Soldier shall, in time of peace be quartered in any house, without the consent of the Owner, nor in time of war, but in a manner to be prescribed by law.

### amendment IV

The right of the people to be secure in their persons, houses, papers, and effects, against unreasonable searches and seizures, shall not be violated, and no Warrants shall issue, but upon probable cause, supported by Oath or affirmation, and particularly describing the place to be searched, and the persons or things to be seized.

### amendment V

No person shall be held to answer for a capital, or otherwise infamous crime, unless on a presentment or indictment of a Grand Jury, except in cases arising in the land or naval forces, or in the Militia, when in actual service in time of War or public danger; nor shall any person be subject for the same offence to be twice put in jeopardy of life or limb; nor shall be compelled in any criminal case to be a witness against himself, nor be deprived of life, liberty, or property, without due process of law; nor shall private property be taken for public use, without just compensation.

### amendment VI

In all criminal prosecutions, the accused shall enjoy the right to a speedy and public trial, by an impartial jury of the State and district wherein the crime shall have been committed, which district shall have been previously ascertained by law, and to be informed of the nature and cause of the accusation; to be confronted with the witnesses against him; to have compulsory process for obtaining witnesses in his favor, and to have the Assistance of Counsel for his defence.

### amendment VII

In suits at common law, where the value in controversy shall exceed twenty dollars, the right of trial by jury shall be preserved, and no fact tried by a jury, shall be otherwise reexamined in any Court of the United States, than according to the rules of the common law.

### amendment VIII

Excessive bail shall not be required, nor excessive fines imposed, nor cruel and unusual punishments inflicted.

### amendment IX

The enumeration in the Constitution, of certain rights, shall not be construed to deny or disparage others retained by the people.

### amendment X

The powers not delegated to the United States by the Constitution, nor prohibited by it to the States, are reserved to the States respectively, or to the people.

### amendment XI[12]

The Judicial power of the United States shall not be construed to extend to any suit in law or equity, commenced or prosecuted against one of the United States by Citizens of another State, or by Citizens or Subjects of any Foreign State.

### amendment XII[13]

The Electors shall meet in their respective states and vote by ballot for President and Vice-President, one of whom, at least, shall not be an inhabitant of the same state with themselves; they shall name in their ballots the person voted for as President, and in distinct ballots the person voted for as Vice-President, and they shall make distinct lists of all persons voted for as President, and of all persons voted for as Vice-President, and of the number of votes for each, which lists they shall sign and certify, and transmit sealed to the seat of the government of the United States, directed to the President of the Senate; — The President of the Senate shall, in presence of the Senate and House of Representatives, open all the certificates and the votes shall then be counted; — The person having the greatest number of votes for President, shall be the President, if such number be a majority of the whole number of Electors appointed; and if no person have such majority, then from the persons having the highest numbers not exceeding three on the list of those voted for as President, the House of Representatives

---

[12] Adopted in 1798.
[13] Adopted in 1804.

shall choose immediately, by ballot, the President. But in choosing the President, the votes shall be taken by states, the representation from each state having one vote; a quorum for this purpose shall consist of a member or members from two-thirds of the states, and a majority of all the states shall be necessary to a choice. [And if the House of Representatives shall not choose a President whenever the right of choice shall devolve upon them, before the fourth day of March next following, then the Vice-President shall act as President, as in the case of the death or other constitutional disability of the President.][14] — The person having the greatest number of votes as Vice-President, shall be the Vice-President, if such number be a majority of the whole number of Electors appointed, and if no person have a majority, then from the two highest numbers on the list, the Senate shall choose the Vice-President; a quorum for the purpose shall consist of two-thirds of the whole number of Senators, and a majority of the whole number shall be necessary to a choice. But no person constitutionally ineligible to the office of President shall be eligible to that of Vice-President of the United States.

### amendment XIII[15]

SECTION 1. Neither slavery nor involuntary servitude, except as a punishment for crime whereof the party shall have been duly convicted, shall exist within the United States, or any place subject to their jurisdiction.

SECTION 2. Congress shall have power to enforce this article by appropriate legislation.

### amendment XIV[16]

SECTION 1. All persons born or naturalized in the United States, and subject to the jurisdiction thereof, are citizens of the United States and of the State wherein they reside. No state shall make or enforce any law which shall abridge the privileges or immunities of citizens of the United States; nor shall any State deprive any person of life, liberty, or property, without due process of law; nor deny to any person within its jurisdiction the equal protection of the laws.

SECTION 2. Representatives shall be apportioned among the several States according to their respective numbers, counting the whole number of persons in each State, excluding Indians not taxed. But when the right to vote at any election for the choice of electors for President and Vice-President of the United States, Representatives in Congress, the Executive and Judicial officers of a State, or the members of the Legislature thereof, is denied to any of the male inhabitants of such State, being twenty-one years of age, and citizens of the United States, or

[14] Superseded by the Twentieth Amendment, Section 3.
[15] Adopted in 1865.
[16] Adopted in 1868.

in any way abridged, except for participation in rebellion, or other crime, the basis of representation therein shall be reduced in the proportion which the number of such male citizens shall bear to the whole number of male citizens twenty-one years of age in such State.

SECTION 3. No person shall be a Senator or Representative in Congress, or elector of President and Vice-President, or hold any office, civil or military, under the United States, or under any State, who, having previously taken an oath, as a member of Congress, or as an officer of the United States, or as a member of any State legislature, or as an executive or judicial officer of any State, to support the Constitution of the United States, shall have engaged in insurrection or rebellion against the same, or given aid or comfort to the enemies thereof. But Congress may by a vote of two-thirds of each House, remove such disability.

SECTION 4. The validity of the public debt of the United States, authorized by law, including debts incurred for payment of pensions and bounties for services in suppressing insurrection or rebellion, shall not be questioned. But neither the United States nor any State shall assume or pay any debt or obligation incurred in aid of insurrection or rebellion against the United States, or any claim for the loss or emancipation of any slave; but all such debts, obligations and claims shall be held illegal and void.

SECTION 5. The Congress shall have power to enforce, by appropriate legislation, the provisions of this article.

### amendment XV[17]

SECTION 1. The right of citizens of the United States to vote shall not be denied or abridged by the United States or by any State on account of race, color, or previous condition of servitude —

SECTION 2. The Congress shall have power to enforce this article by appropriate legislation.

### amendment XVI[18]

The Congress shall have power to lay and collect taxes on incomes, from whatever source derived, without appointment among the several States, and without regard to any census or enumeration.

### amendment XVII[19]

The Senate of the United States shall be composed of two Senators from each State, elected by the people thereof, for six years; and each Senator shall have

[17] Adopted in 1870.
[18] Adopted in 1913.
[19] Adopted in 1913.

one vote. The electors in each State shall have the qualifications requisite for electors of the most numerous branch of the State legislatures.

When vacancies happen in the representation of any State in the Senate, the executive authority of such State shall issue writs of election to fill such vacancies: *Provided,* That the legislature of any State may empower the executive thereof to make temporary appointments until the people fill the vacancies by election as the legislature may direct.

This amendment shall not be so construed as to affect the election or term of any Senator chosen before it becomes valid as part of the Constitution.

## amendment XVIII[20]

SECTION 1. After one year from the ratification of this article the manufacture, sale, or transportation of intoxicating liquors within, the importation thereof into, or the exportation thereof from the United States and all territory subject to the jurisdiction thereof for beverage purposes is hereby prohibited.

SECTION 2. The Congress and the several States shall have concurrent power to enforce this article by appropriate legislation.

SECTION 3. This article shall be inoperative unless it shall have been ratified as an amendment to the Constitution by the legislatures of the several States, as provided in the Constitution, within seven years from the date of the submission hereof to the States by the Congress.

## amendment XIX[21]

The right of citizens of the United States to vote shall not be denied or abridged by the United States or by any State on account of sex.

Congress shall have power to enforce this article by appropriate legislation.

## amendment XX[22]

SECTION 1. The terms of the President and Vice President shall end at noon on the 20th day of January, and the terms of Senators and Representatives at noon on the 3d day of January, of the years in which such terms would have ended if this article had not been ratified; and the terms of their successors shall then begin.

SECTION 2. The Congress shall assemble at least once in every year, and such meeting shall begin at noon on the 3d day of January, unless they shall by law appoint a different day.

SECTION 3. If, at the time fixed for the beginning of the term of the President,

[20] Adopted in 1919. Repealed by Section 1 of the Twenty-first Amendment.
[21] Adopted in 1920.
[22] Adopted in 1933.

the President elect shall have died, the Vice President elect shall become President. If a President shall not have been chosen before the time fixed for the beginning of his term, or if the President elect shall have failed to qualify, then the Vice President elect shall act as President until a President shall have qualified; and the Congress may by law provide for the case wherein neither a President elect nor a Vice President elect shall have qualified, declaring who shall then act as President, or the manner in which one who is to act shall be selected, and such person shall act accordingly until a President or Vice President shall have qualified.

SECTION 4. The Congress may by law provide for the case of the death of any of the persons from whom the House of Representatives may choose a President whenever the right of choice shall have devolved upon them, and for the case of the death of any of the persons from whom the Senate may choose a Vice President whenever the right of choice shall have devolved upon them.

SECTION 5. Sections 1 and 2 shall take effect on the 15th day of October following the ratification of this article.

SECTION 6. This article shall be inoperative unless it shall have been ratified as an amendment to the Constitution by the legislatures of three-fourths of the several states within seven years from the date of its submission.

### amendment XXI[23]

SECTION 1. The eighteenth article of amendment to the Constitution of the United States is hereby repealed.

SECTION 2. The transportation or importation into any State, Territory, or possession of the United States for delivery or use therein of intoxicating liquors, in violation of the laws thereof, is hereby prohibited.

SECTION 3. This article shall be inoperative unless it shall have been ratified as an amendment to the Constitution by conventions in the several States, as provided in the Constitution, within seven years from the date of the submission hereof to the States by the Congress.

### amendment XXII[24]

SECTION 1. No person shall be elected to the office of the President more than twice, and no person who has held the office of President, or acted as President, for more than two years of a term to which some other person was elected President shall be elected to the office of the President more than once. But this Article shall not apply to any person holding the office of President when this Article was proposed by the Congress, and shall not prevent any person who may be holding the office of President, or acting as President, during the term

[23] Adopted in 1933.
[24] Adopted in 1951.

within which this Article becomes operative from holding the office of President or acting as President during the remainder of such term.

SECTION 2. This article shall be inoperative unless it shall have been ratified as an amendment to the Constitution by the legislatures of three-fourths of the several States within seven years from the date of its submission to the States by the Congress.

## amendment XXIII[25]

SECTION 1. The District constituting the seat of Government of the United States shall appoint in such manner as the Congress may direct:

A number of electors of President and Vice President equal to the whole number of Senators and Representatives in Congress to which the District would be entitled if it were a State, but in no event more than the least populous State; they shall be in addition to those appointed by the States, but they shall be considered, for the purposes of the election of President and Vice President, to be electors appointed by a State; and they shall meet in the District and perform such duties as provided by the twelfth article of amendment.

SECTION 2. The Congress shall have power to enforce this article by appropriate legislation.

## amendment XXIV[26]

SECTION 1. The right of citizens of the United States to vote in any primary or other election for President or Vice President, for electors for President or Vice President, or for Senator or Representative in Congress, shall not be denied or abridged by the United States or any state by reasons of failure to pay any poll tax or other tax.

SECTION 2. The Congress shall have power to enforce this article by appropriate legislation.

## amendment XXV[27]

SECTION 1. In case of the removal of the President from office or of his death or resignation, the Vice President shall become President.

SECTION 2. Whenever there is a vacancy in the office of the Vice President, the President shall nominate a Vice President who shall take office upon confirmation by a majority vote of both Houses of Congress.

[25] Adopted in 1961.
[26] Adopted in 1964.
[27] Adopted in 1967.

SECTION 3. Whenever the President transmits to the President pro tempore of the Senate and the Speaker of the House of Representatives his written declaration that he is unable to discharge the powers and duties of his office, and until he transmits to them a written declaration to the contrary, such powers and duties shall be discharged by the Vice President as Acting President.

SECTION 4. Whenever the Vice President and a majority of either the principal officers of the executive departments or of such other body as Congress may by law provide, transmit to the President pro tempore of the Senate and the Speaker of the House of Representatives their written declaration that the President is unable to discharge the powers and duties of his office, the Vice President shall immediately assume the powers and duties of the office as Acting President.

Thereafter, when the President transmits to the President pro tempore of the Senate and the Speaker of the House of Representatives his written declaration that no inability exists, he shall resume the powers and duties of his office unless the Vice President and a majority of either the principal officers of the executive departments or of such other body as Congress may by law provide, transmit within four days to the President pro tempore of the Senate and the Speaker of the House of Representatives their written declaration that the President is unable to discharge the powers and duties of his office. Thereupon Congress shall decide the issue, assembling within forty-eight hours for that purpose if not in session. If the Congress, within twenty-one days after receipt of the latter written declaration, or, if Congress is not in session, within twenty-one days after Congress is required to assemble, determines by two-thirds vote of both Houses that the President is unable to discharge the same as Acting President; otherwise, the President shall resume the powers and duties of his office.

## amendment XXVI[28]

SECTION 1. The right of citizens of the United States, who are eighteen years of age or older, to vote shall not be denied or abridged by the United States or any state on account of age.

SECTION 2. The Congress shall have the power to enforce this article by appropriate legislation.

---

[28] Adopted in 1971.

# index

# photograph credits

### part I

pp. xiv–1: Left, Editorial Photocolor Archives Newsphoto; Top, Copyright © Burk Uzzle, Magnum; Right, Bernie Boston, *The Washington Star-News*. p. 4: Dan McCoy, Black Star. p. 6: Copyright © Burk Uzzle, Magnum. p. 8: Bernie Boston, *The Washington Star-News*. p. 13: Francis Miller, Copyright *Life Magazine*. p. 18: Pictorial Parade, Editorial Photocolor Archives. p. 19: United Press International. p. 27: Editorial Photocolor Archives. p. 29: United Press International. p. 32: Jeff Albertson, Stock, Boston. p. 38: Y. R. Okamoto, courtesy of the Lyndon Baines Johnson Library. p. 43: Top, Editorial Photocolor Archives Newsphoto; Bottom, Hap Stewart, Black Star.

### part II

pp. 50–51: Left, Flip Schulke, Black Star; Top, Jeff Albertson, Stock, Boston; Right, Roger Malloch, © 1970 Magnum. p. 55: Eve Arnold, Magnum. p. 58: Declan Haun, Black Star. p. 68: Wide World Photos. p. 71: Charles Harbutt, © 1968 Magnum. p. 73: Bruce Davidson, © 1965 Magnum. p. 81: Roger Malloch, © 1970 Magnum. p. 95: Bruce Davidson, © Magnum. p. 102: Fred Ward, Black Star. p. 106: Dan McCoy, Black Star. p. 108: De Wys, Inc. p. 113: Fred Ward, Black Star. p. 115: Jeff Albertson, Stock, Boston.

### part III

pp. 118–19: Left and top, Wide World Photos; Bottom, Burt Glinn, © 1970 Magnum. p. 126: Patricia Gross, Stock, Boston. p. 135: Jon Lewis, Photofind, S.F. p. 141: Bruce Davidson, © 1968 Magnum. p. 143: T. A. Rothschild, Stock, Boston. p. 158: Wide World Photos. p. 159: C. Wolinsky, Stock, Boston. pp. 164–65: Wide World Photos. p. 172: © Charles Gatewood, Magnum. p. 176: Hap Stewart, Black Star. p. 185: Mary Ellen Mark, Magnum. p. 190: © Leonard Freed, Magnum. p. 197: Burt Glinn, © 1970 Magnum. p. 199: Editorial Photocolor Archives Newsphoto. p. 200: Dennis Brack, Black Star. p. 207: Jon Lewis, Photofind, S.F. p. 208: Daniel S. Brody, Editorial Photocolor Archives. p. 211: Wide World Photos. p. 218: © Lionel Martinez. p. 223: Burt Glinn, © 1969 Magnum. p. 230: Brown Brothers. p. 233: United Press International. p. 250: Stern, Black Star. p. 251: Fred Ward, Black Star. pp. 258, 263: Wide World Photos. p. 266: NBC News. p. 270: Bob Fitch, Black Star. p. 282: Nicholas Sapieha, Rapho Guillumette. p. 283: Paul Thomas, Black Star. p. 289: Wide World Photos. p. 293: Dennis Brack, Black Star. p. 297: Charles Harbutt, © 1968 Magnum. p. 300: Y. R. Okamoto, courtesy of the Lyndon Baines Johnson Library. p. 309: Editorial Photocolor Archives Newsphoto. p. 315: Franklin Wing, Stock, Boston. p. 320: Copyright © 1970 Norman Hurst, Stock, Boston. p. 323: Ken Heinen, *The Washington Star-News*. p. 326: Helen Nestor, Photofind, S.F. p. 331: United Press International. p. 335: Editorial Photocolor Archives Newsphoto.

### part IV

pp. 342–43: Left, Copyright Fred J. Maroon from *Courage and Hesitation*, Doubleday, 1971 – from Louis Mercier. Top, U.S. Army photograph, Authenticated News International; Right, Burt Glinn, © 1969 Magnum. p. 348: United Press International. p. 355: Wide World Photos. p. 364: U.S. Army photograph, Authenticated News International. p. 368: Ronald Kennedy. p. 371: Y. R. Okamoto, courtesy of the Lyndon Baines Johnson Library. p. 375: Authenticated News International. p. 381: Copyright Fred J. Maroon from *Courage and Hesitation*, Doubleday, 1971 – from Louis Mercier. p. 384: Ollie Atkins. p. 390: Wide World Photos. p. 395: United Press International. p. 406. Wide World Photos. p. 409: Burt Glinn, © 1969 Magnum. p. 414: Copyright Fred J. Maroon from *Courage and Hesitation*, Doubleday, 1971 – from Louis Mercier. p. 421: Copyright Fred J. Maroon from *Washington Magnificent Capitol*, Doubleday, 1965 – from Louis Mercier. p. 426: United Press International. p. 431: Editorial Photocolor Archives Newsphoto. pp. 437, 442: Wide World Photos, p. 445: Copyright Fred J. Maroon from *Washington Magnificent Capitol*, Doubleday, 1965 – from Louis Mercier. p. 451: Wide World Photos. p. 459: Editorial Photocolor Archives. p. 466: Marcia Keegan, Office of Economic Opportunity. p. 475: Y. R. Okamoto, Rapho Guillumette. p. 479: U.S. Department of Agriculture. p. 485: Authenticated News International. p. 492: Fred Ward, Black Star. p. 497: Robert Ellison, Black Star. p. 504: Donald McCullin, © 1968 Magnum. p. 511: Richard L. Stack, Black Star, p. 519: Dennis Brack, Black Star. p. 526: George L. Walker III, Black Star.